THE
UNFINISHED
NATION

THE UNFINISHED NATION

A Concise History of the
American People
Volume 1: To 1877

Seventh Edition

Alan Brinkley
Columbia University

McGraw Hill

*Connect
Learn
Succeed*™

THE UNFINISHED NATION: A CONCISE HISTORY OF THE AMERICAN PEOPLE, VOLUME 1,
SEVENTH EDITION

Published by McGraw-Hill, a business unit of The McGraw-Hill Companies, Inc., 1221 Avenue of the Americas,
New York, NY 10020. Copyright © 2014 by The McGraw-Hill Companies, Inc. All rights reserved. Printed
in the United States of America. Previous editions © 2010, 2008, and 2004. No part of this publication may
be reproduced or distributed in any form or by any means, or stored in a database or retrieval system, without
the prior written consent of The McGraw-Hill Companies, Inc., including, but not limited to, in any network
or other electronic storage or transmission, or broadcast for distance learning.

Some ancillaries, including electronic and print components, may not be available to customers outside the
United States.

This book is printed on acid-free paper.

1 2 3 4 5 6 7 8 9 0 DOC/DOC 1 0 9 8 7 6 5 4 3

ISBN 978-0-07-741229-6
MHID 0-07-741229-X

Senior Vice President, Products & Markets: *Kurt L. Strand*	Content Project Manager: *April R. Southwood*
	Buyer: *Nicole Baumgartner*
Vice President, General Manager, Products & Markets: *Michael Ryan*	Senior Designer: *David W. Hash*
	Cover/Interior Designer: *John Joran*
Vice President, Content Production & Technology Services: *Kimberly Meriwether David*	Cover Image: *Lincoln Memorial,* © *Ron Chapple/ CORBIS; Worker assembling Lincoln by Daniel*
Managing Director: *Gina Boedeker*	*Chester French in the Lincoln Memorial,* © *CORBIS*
Director: *Matthew Busbridge*	Lead Content Licensing Specialist: *Carrie K. Burger*
Brand Coordinator: *Kaelyn Schulz*	Photo Research: *PhotoSearch*
Director of Development: *Rhona Robbin*	Compositor: *Aptara®, Inc.*
Managing Development Editor: *Nancy Crochiere*	Typeface: *10/12 Adobe Caslon Pro Regular*
Development Editor: *Briana Porco*	Printer: *R. R. Donnelley*
Marketing Manager: *Stacy Best*	

All credits appearing on page or at the end of the book are considered to be an extension of the copyright page.

Page ix (T): The Granger Collection, NYC; (B): Rare Book Division, New York Public Library, Astor, Lenox and Tilden Foundations; xi (T): Library of Congress; xi (B): MPI/Archive Photos/Getty Images; xii: New York Public Library, Astor, Lenox and Tilden Foundations; xii: Image copyright © The Metropolitan Museum of Art / Art Resource, NY; xiv: Courtesy of The Saint Louis Art Museum, Gift of Bank of America; xvi (T): Bridgeman-Giraudon/Art Resource, NY; (B): Joseph Mustering the Nauvoo Legion by C.C.A. Christensen. Courtesy of Brigham Young University Museum of Art. All rights reserved.; xviii (T): © Bettmann/Corbis; xviii (B): The Museum of the Confederacy, Richmond, Virginia

Library of Congress Cataloging-in-Publication Data for the Main Title

Brinkley, Alan.
  The unfinished nation : a concise history of the American people / Alan Brinkley, Columbia University. —
Seventh edition.
    pages cm
  Includes bibliographical references and index.
  ISBN 978–0–07–340698–5 — ISBN 0–07–340698–8 (hard copy : acid-free paper) 1. United States–History.
I. Title.
  E178.1.B827 2014
  973–dc23

                                                                                                                2012043288

www.mhhe.com

BRIEF CONTENTS

ABOUT THE AUTHOR

ALAN BRINKLEY is the Allan Nevins Professor of History at Columbia University. He served as University Provost at Columbia from 2003 to 2009. He is the author of *Voices of Protest: Huey Long, Father Coughlin, and the Great Depression*, which won the 1983 National Book Award; *American History: Connecting with the Past*; *The End of Reform: New Deal Liberalism in Recession and War*; *Liberalism and Its Discontents*; *Franklin D. Roosevelt*; and *The Publisher: Henry Luce and His American Century*. He is the chair of the board of the national Humanities Center, the chair of the board of the Century Foundation, and a trustee of Oxford University Press. He is a member of the Academy of Arts and Sciences. In 1998–1999, he was the Harmsworth Professor of History at Oxford University, and in 2011–2012, the Pitt Professor at the University of Cambridge. He won the Joseph R. Levenson Memorial Teaching Award at Harvard and the Great Teacher Award at Columbia. He was educated at Princeton and Harvard.

CONTENTS

3 SOCIETY AND CULTURE IN PROVINCIAL AMERICA 53

4 THE EMPIRE IN TRANSITION 82

5 THE AMERICAN REVOLUTION 105

6 THE CONSTITUTION AND THE NEW REPUBLIC 131

9   JACKSONIAN AMERICA 197

THE title *The Unfinished Nation* is meant to suggest several things. It is a reminder of America's exceptional diversity—of the degree to which, despite all the many efforts to build a single, uniform definition of the meaning of the American nationhood, that meaning remains contested. It is a reference to the centrality of change in American history—to the ways in which the nation has continually transformed itself and to how it continues to do so in our own time. And it is also a description of the writing of American history itself—of the ways in which historians are engaged in a continuing, ever unfinished, process of asking new questions.

Like any history, *The Unfinished Nation* is a product of its time and reflects the views of the past that historians of recent generations have developed. The writing of our nation's history—like our nation itself—changes constantly. It is not, of course, the past that changes; rather, there are shifts in the way historians, and the publics they serve, ask and answer questions about the past. There are now, as there have always been, critics of changes in historical understanding who argue that history is a collection of facts and should not be subject to "interpretation" or "revision." But historians insist that history is not and cannot be simply a collection of facts. Names and dates and a record of events are only the beginning of historical understanding. It is up to the writers and readers of history to try to interpret the evidence before them; and in doing so, they will inevitably bring to the task their own questions, concerns, and experiences.

Our history requires us to examine the many different peoples and ideas that have shaped American society. But it also requires us to understand that the United States is a nation whose people share many things: a common political system, a connection to an integrated national (and now international) economy, and a familiarity with a shared and enormously powerful mass culture. To understand the American past, it is necessary to understand both the forces that divide Americans and the forces that draw them together.

It is a daunting task to attempt to convey the remarkable history of the United States in a single book, and the seventh edition of *The Unfinished Nation* has, as have all previous editions, been carefully written and edited to keep the book as concise and readable as possible. In this edition, I have added significant additions throughout the book on the history of conservatism, which has become an important part of American life. I have also added new material on the U.S. Constitution; coverage of the early Africans in America before slavery; revised sections on the middle colonies; a description of the changing way Americans voted in the nineteenth century; and additional material on the emergence of "containment" as a core of American foreign policy and the conservative opposition to it. And I have provided new material on the recent past, including the 2012 election.

In addition to these changes, the seventh edition of *The Unfinished Nation* now contains a new set of primary source features titled "Consider the Source." My hope is that these features will prompt students to not only consider the way that historians read historical documents but also to think carefully about the many sources of information they encounter daily. All content is now reinforced and supplemented by a rich set of online practice and assessment resources, housed within the Connect platform. It is not only the writing of history that changes with time—the tools and technologies through which information is delivered change as well.

As always, I want to thank the students, teachers, and other readers of this book who have offered comments, criticism, and corrections. Suggestions can be sent to me at Department of History, Columbia University, New York, NY 10027; or by email to ab65@columbia.edu.

ALAN BRINKLEY

ACKNOWLEDGMENTS

WE are grateful to the many advisers and reviewers who generously offered comments, suggestions, and ideas at various stages in the development of this project. Our thanks go to:

Academic Reviewers

Tramaine Anderson, *Tarrant County College, Northeast*

Darlene Antezana, *Prince George's Community College*

Maj. Paul Belmont, *U.S. Military Academy, West Point*

Peter Belser, *Ivy Tech Community College*

Robert Bender, *Eastern New Mexico University, Roswell*

Devan Bissonette, *Excelsior College*

Blanche Brick, *Blinn College*

Brian Cervantez, *Tarrant County College Northwest*

Keith D. Dickson, *Old Dominion University*

Angela S. Edwards, *Florence-Darlington Technical College*

Ron Enders, *Ashland Community College*

Amy Essington, *California State University, Long Beach*

Glen Findley, *Odessa College*

Brandon Franke, *Blinn College*

Mary E. Frederickson, *Miami University of Ohio*

Joy Giguere, *Ivy Tech Community College*

Donn Hall, *Ivy Tech Community College*

Andrew Hollinger, *Tarrant Community College Northeast*

Brian Johnson, *Tarrant County College South*

Philbert Martin, *San Jacinto College South*

Linda McCabe, *Tarrant County College, Northeast*

Maureen A. McCormick, *Florida State College at Jacksonville*

Wesley Moody, *Florida State College*

Rebekkah Morrow, *Western Oklahoma State College*

Matt Schaffer, *Florence Darlington Technical College*

Rebecca Seaman, *Elizabeth City State University*

Eddie Weller, *San Jacinto College, South*

Ann K. Wentworth, *Excelsior College*

Geoffrey Willbanks, *Tyler Junior College*

Cary Wintz, *Texas Southern University*

Connect Board of Advisors

Michael Downs, *University of Texas— Arlington*

Jim Halverson, *Judson University*

Reid Holland, *Midlands Technical College*

Stephen Katz, *Rider University*

David Komito, *Eastern Oregon University*

Wendy Sarti, *Oakton Community College*

Linda Scherr, *Mercer County Community College*

Eloy Zarate, *Pasadena City College*

Symposium and Digiposium Attendees

Gisela Ables, *Houston Community College*

Sal Anselmo, *Delgado Community College*

Mario A. J. Bennekin, *Georgia Perimeter College*

C. J. Bibus, *Wharton County Junior College*

Olwyn M. Blouet, *Virginia State University*

Michael Botson, *Houston Community College*

Cathy Briggs, *Northwest Vista College*

Brad Cartwright, *University of Texas—El Paso*

Roger Chan, *Washington State University*

June Cheatham, *Richland College*

Karl Clark, *Coastal Bend College*

Bernard Comeau, *Tacoma Community College*

Kevin Davis, *North Central Texas College*

Michael Downs, *Tarrant County College*

Laura Dunn, *Brevard Community College*

Arthur Durand, *Metropolitan Community College*

Amy Forss, *Metropolitan Community College*

Jim Good, *Lone Star College*

R. David Goodman, *Pratt Institute*

Wendy Gunderson, *Colin County Community College*

Debbie Hargis, *Odessa College*

John Hosler, *Morgan State University*

James Jones, *Prairie View A&M University*

Philip Kaplan, *University of North Florida*

Carol A. Keller, *San Antonio College*

Greg Kelm, *Dallas Baptist University*

Michael Kinney, *Calhoun Community College*

Meredith R. Martin, *Collin College*

Linda McCabe, *North Lake College*

Sandy Norman, *Florida Atlantic University*

Michelle Novak, *Houston Community College*
Jessica Patton, *Tarrant County College*
Robert Risko, *Trinity Valley Community College*
Esther Robinson, *Lone Star College*
Geri Ryder, *Ocean County College*
Linda Scherr, *Mercer County Community College*
Jeffrey Smith, *Lindenwood University*
Rachel Standish, *San Joaquin Delta College*
Roger Ward, *Colin County Community College*
Don Whatley, *Blinn College*
Geoffrey Willbanks, *Tyler Junior College*
Scott M. Williams, *Weatherford College*
Carlton Wilson, *North Carolina*
Chad Wooley, *Tarrant County College*

Focus Group Participants

Simon Baatz, *John Jay College*
Manu Bhagavan, *Hunter College*
David Dzurec, *University of Scranton*

Mark Jones, *Central Connecticut State University*
Stephen Katz, *Philadelphia University*
Jessica Kovler, *John Jay College*
David Lansing, *Ocean County College*
Benjamin Lapp, *Montclair State University*
Julian Madison, *Southern Connecticut State University*
David Marshall, *Suffolk Community College*
George Monahan, *Suffolk Community College*
Tracy Musacchio, *John Jay College*
Mikal Nash, *Essex County College*
Veena Oldenburg, *Baruch College*
Edward Paulino, *John Jay College*
Craig Pilant, *County College of Morris*
Susan Schmidt Horning, *Saint John's University*
Donna Scimeca, *College of Staten Island*
Matthew Vaz, *City College of New York*
Christian Warren, *Brooklyn College*

Special thanks to Volker Janssen for his contributions to the "Consider the Source" feature, and Major Adrienne Harrison for her detailed review of the history of the middle colonies.

EXPERIENCE SUCCESS IN HISTORY

The Unfinished Nation makes history relevant to students through a series of engaging features:

New > *CONSIDER THE SOURCE* FEATURES

These features guide students through careful analysis of historical documents, and prompt them to closely examine the ideas expressed, as well as the historical circumstances. Among the classic sources included are Benjamin Franklin's testimony against the Stamp Act, the Gettysburg Address, a radio address from FDR, and Eisenhower's farewell speech on the Military Industrial Complex.

New > CRITICAL THINKING QUESTIONS

"Looking Ahead" and "Recall and Reflect" prompts bookend each chapter, encouraging students to move beyond memorization of facts and names to explore the importance and significance of the chapter themes. In addition, "Understand, Analyze, and Evaluate" questions at the end of each essay cue students to think critically about the featured content.

CONSIDER THE SOURCE

BARTOLOME DE LAS CASAS, "OF THE ISLAND OF HISPANIOLA" (1542)

LOOKING AHEAD

1. How did the English colonies in ...
2. How "English" were the colonies ...
3. What did the English want from settlement in North America?

UNDERSTAND, ANALYZE, & EVALUATE

1. What do historians say is the relationship between racism and slavery?
2. What are the economic forward by historians t system of slave labor America? Do these arg fully for the developme

RECALL AND REFLECT

1. How did patterns of family life and attitudes toward women differ in the northern and southern colonies?
2. How did the lives of African slaves change over the course of the first century of slavery?
3. Who emigrated to North America in the seventeenth century, and why did they come?
4. What was the intellectual culture of colonial America, as expressed in literature, philosophy, science, education, and law?
5. How and why did life in the English colonies diverge from life in England?

DEBATING THE PAST FEATURES

Twenty-two essays introduce students to the contested quality of much of the American past, and they provide a sense of the evolving nature of historical scholarship. From examining specific differences in historical understandings of the Constitution, to exploring the character of slavery and the causes of the Great Depression, these essays familiarize students with the interpretive character of historical understanding.

DEBATING THE PAST

THE ORIGINS OF SLAVERY

AMERICA IN THE WORLD FEATURES

THE ATLANTIC CONTEXT OF EARLY AMERICAN HISTORY

MOST Americans understand that our nation has recently become intimately bound up with the rest of the world—that we live in what some call the "age of globalization." Until recently, however, most historians have examined the nation's part in relative isolation. Among the first areas of American history to be reexamined in an international perspective is the earliest period of European settlement of the Americas. Many scholars of early American history now examine what happened in the "New World" in the context of what has become known as the "Atlantic World."

The idea of an Atlantic World rests in part on the obvious connections between western Europe and the Spanish, British, French, and Dutch colonies in North and South America. All the early European civilizations of the Americas were part of a great imperial project launched by the major powers of Europe. The massive European and African immigrations to the Americas beginning in the sixteenth century, the defeat and devastation of native populations, the creation of European agricultural and urban settlements, and the imposition of imperial regulations on trade, commerce, landowning, and political life—all of these forces reveal the influence of Old World imperialism on the history of the New World.

But the expansion of empires is only one part of the creation of the Atlantic World. At least equally important—and closely related—is the expansion of commerce from Europe and Africa to the Americas. Although some Europeans traveled to the New World in search of religious freedom, or to escape oppression, or to search for adventure, the great majority of European immigrants were in search of economic opportunity. Not surprisingly, therefore, the European settlements in the Americas were almost from the start intimately connected to Europe through the growth of commerce between them—commerce that grew more extensive and more complex with every passing year. The commercial relationship between America and Europe was responsible not just for the growth of trade, but also for the increases in migration over time—as the demand for labor in the New World drew more and more settlers from the Old World. Commerce was also the principal reason for the rise of slavery in the Americas, and for the growth of the slave trade between European America and Africa. The Atlantic World, in other words, included not just Europe and the Americas, but Africa as well.

Religion was another force binding together the Atlantic World. The vast majority of people of European descent were Christians, and most of them maintained important religious ties to part of a hierarchical church based in Rome with close ties with the Vatican. But the Protestant faiths that predominated in North America were intimately linked to their European counterparts as well. New religious ideas and movements spread back and forth across the Atlantic with astonishing speed. Great revivals that began in Europe moved quickly to America. The "Great Awakening" of the mid-eighteenth century, for example, began in Britain and traveled to America in large part through the efforts of the English evangelist George Whitefield. American evangelists later carried religious ideas from the New World back to the Old.

The early history of European America was also closely bound up with the intellectual life of Europe. The Enlightenment—the cluster of ideas that emerged in Europe in the seventeenth and eighteenth centuries emphasizing the power of human reason—moved quickly to the Americas, producing intellectual ferment throughout the New World, but particularly in the British colonies in North America and the Caribbean. The ideas of the British philosopher John Locke, for example, helped shape the founding of Georgia. The English Constitution, and the idea of the "rights of Englishmen," shaped the way North Americans developed their own concepts of politics. Many of the ideas that underlaid the American Revolution were products of British and continental philosophy that had traveled across the Atlantic. The reinterpretation of those ideas by Americans to help justify their drive to independence—by, among others, Thomas Paine—moved back to Europe and helped, among other things, to inspire the French Revolution. Scientific and technological knowledge—another product of the

(The I. N. Phelps Stokes Collection of American Historical Prints, Prints Division, The New York Public Library, Astor, Lenox and Tilden Foundations)

Enlightenment—traveled constantly across the Atlantic and back. Americans borrowed much of its early knowledge of electricity from experiments done in America. But the Enlightenment was only one part of the continuing intellectual connections within the Atlantic World, connections that spread artistic, scholarly, and political ideas widely through the lands bordering the ocean.

Instead of thinking of the early history of what became the United States simply as the story of the growth of thirteen small colonies along the Atlantic seaboard of North America, the idea of the "Atlantic World" encourages us to think of early American history as a vast pattern of exchanges and interactions—trade, migration, religious and intellectual exchange, and many other relationships—among all the societies bordering the Atlantic: western Europe, western Africa, the Caribbean, and North and South America. •

UNDERSTAND, ANALYZE, & EVALUATE

1. What is the Atlantic World?
2. What has led historians to begin studying the idea of an Atlantic World?

These fifteen essays focus on specific parallels between American history and those of other nations, and demonstrate the importance of the many global influences on the American story. Topics such as the global industrial revolution, the abolition of slavery, and the origins of the Cold War provide concrete examples of the connections between the history of the United States and the history of other nations.

PATTERNS OF POPULAR CULTURE FEATURES

TAVERNS IN REVOLUTIONARY MASSACHUSETTS

IN colonial Massachusetts, as in many other American colonies in the 1760s and 1770s, taverns (or "public houses," as they were often known) were crucial to the development of popular resistance to British rule. The Puritan culture of New England created some resistance to taverns, and reformers tried to regulate or close them to reduce the problems caused by "public drunkenness," "lewd behavior," and "anarchy." But as the commercial life of the colonies expanded and more people began living in towns and cities, taverns became a central institution in American social life—and eventually in its political life as well.

Taverns were appealing, of course, because they provided alcoholic drinks in a culture where the craving for alcohol—and the extent of drunkenness—was very high. But taverns had other attractions as well. They were one of the few places where people could meet and talk openly in public; indeed, many colonists considered the life of the tavern as the only vaguely democratic experience available to them. The tavern was a mostly male institution, just as politics was considered a mostly male concern. And so the fusion of male camaraderie and political discourse emerged naturally out of the tavern culture.

As the Revolutionary crisis deepened, taverns and pubs became the central meeting places for airing the ideas that fueled resistance to British policies. Educated and uneducated men alike joined in animated discussions of events. Those who could not read—and there were many—could learn about the contents of Revolutionary pamphlets from listening to tavern conversations. They could join in the discussion of the new republican ideas emerging in America by participating in tavern celebrations of, for example, the anniversaries of resistance to the Stamp Act. Those anniversaries inspired elaborate toasts in public houses throughout the colonies.

In an age before any wide distribution of newspapers, taverns and tavernkeepers were important sources of information about the political and social turmoil of the time. Taverns were also the settings for political events. In 1770, for example, a report circulated through the taverns of Danvers, Massachusetts, about a local man who was continuing to sell tea despite the colonial boycott. The Sons of Liberty brought the seller to the Bell Tavern and persuaded him to sign a confession and apology before a crowd of defiant men in the public room.

Almost all politicians who wanted any real contact with the public found it necessary to visit taverns in colonial Massachusetts. Samuel Adams spent considerable time in the public houses of Boston, where he sought to encourage resistance to British rule while taking care to drink moderately so as not to erode his stature as a leader. His cousin John

TAVERN BILLIARDS Gentlemen in Hanover Town, Virginia, gather for a game of billiards in a local tavern in this 1797 drawing by Benjamin Henry Latrobe. (Maryland Historical Society, Baltimore)

Adams, although somewhat more skeptical of taverns and more sensitive to the vices they encouraged, also recognized their political value. In taverns, he once said, "bastards and legislatures are frequently begotten." •

UNDERSTAND, ANALYZE, & EVALUATE

1. Why were taverns so important in educating colonists about the relationship with Britain?
2. What gathering places today serve the same purposes as taverns did in colonial America?

These nine essays bring fads, crazes, hang-outs, hobbies, and entertainment into the story of American history, encouraging students to expand their definition of what constitutes history, and to think about how we can best understand the living experience of past lives.

The book's **Online Learning Center** at www.mhhe.com/unfinishednation7e includes an instructor's manual, computerized test bank, and PowerPoint presentations.

Design your ideal course materials with **McGraw-Hill Create™,** www.mcgrawhillcreate.com! Rearrange or omit chapters, combine material from other sources, and upload your syllabus or any other content you have written to make the perfect resource for your students. Register today at **www.mcgrawhillcreate.com,** and get a complimentary review copy in print or electronically.

McGraw-Hill Campus® is a new one-stop teaching and learning experience available to users of any learning management system. This institutional service allows faculty and students to enjoy **single sign-on (SSO) access to all McGraw-Hill Higher Education materials,** including the award-winning McGraw-Hill Connect platform, from directly within the institution's web site. With this program enabled, faculty and students will never need to create another account to access McGraw-Hill products and services.

McGraw-Hill Tegrity® is a service that makes class time available all the time by automatically capturing every lecture in a searchable format for students to review. With a simple one-click start-and-stop process, you capture all computer screens and corresponding audio. Students can replay any part of any class with easy-to-use, browser-based viewing on a PC or Mac. Help turn all of your students' study time into learning moments immediately supported by your lecture. To learn more about Tegrity, watch a 2-minute demo at http://tegritycampus.mhhe.com.

CourseSmart offers thousands of the most commonly adopted textbooks across hundreds of courses from a wide variety of higher education publishers. It is the only place for faculty to review and compare the full text of a textbook online, providing immediate access without the environmental impact of requesting a printed exam copy. At CourseSmart, students can save up to 50 percent off the cost of a printed book, reduce their impact on the environment, and gain access to powerful web tools for learning, including full text search, notes and highlighting, and e-mail tools for sharing notes among classmates. Learn more at www.coursesmart.com.

THE
UNFINISHED
NATION

1 THE COLLISION OF CULTURES

AMERICA BEFORE COLUMBUS
EUROPE LOOKS WESTWARD
THE ARRIVAL OF THE ENGLISH

LOOKING AHEAD

1. How did the societies of native people in the South differ from those in the North in the precontact period (before the arrival of the Europeans)?
2. What effects did the arrival of Europeans have on the native peoples of the Americas?
3. How did patterns of settlement differ among the Spanish, English, French, and Dutch immigrants to the Americas?

THE DISCOVERY OF THE AMERICAS did not begin with Christopher Columbus. It began many thousands of years earlier, when human beings first crossed into the new continents and began to people them. By the end of the fifteenth century A.D., when the first important contact with Europeans occurred, the Americas were the home of millions of men and women.

These ancient civilizations had experienced many changes and many catastrophes during their long history. But it is likely that none of these experiences was as tragically transforming as the arrival of Europeans. In the first violent years of Spanish and Portuguese exploration and conquest, the impact of the new arrivals was profound. Europeans brought with them diseases (most notably smallpox) to which natives, unlike the invaders, had no immunity. The result was a great demographic catastrophe that killed millions of people, weakened existing societies, and greatly aided the Spanish and Portuguese in their rapid and devastating conquest of the existing American empires.

But the European immigrants were never able to eliminate the influence of the indigenous peoples (whom they came to call "Indians"). In their many interactions, whether beneficial or catastrophic, these very different civilizations shaped one another, learned from one another, and changed one another permanently and profoundly.

TIME LINE

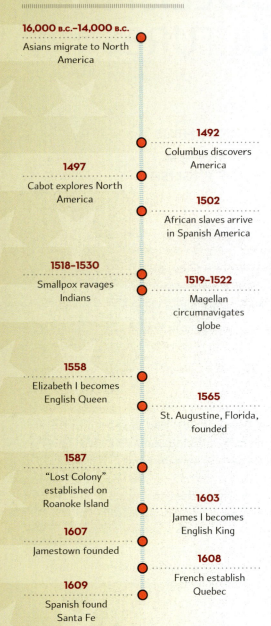

16,000 B.C.–14,000 B.C.

Asians migrate to North America

1492

Columbus discovers America

1497

Cabot explores North America

1502

African slaves arrive in Spanish America

1518–1530

Smallpox ravages Indians

1519–1522

Magellan circumnavigates globe

1558

Elizabeth I becomes English Queen

1565

St. Augustine, Florida, founded

1587

"Lost Colony" established on Roanoke Island

1603

James I becomes English King

1607

Jamestown founded

1608

French establish Quebec

1609

Spanish found Santa Fe

AMERICA BEFORE COLUMBUS

We know relatively little about the first peoples in the Americas, but archaeologists have uncovered new evidence from artifacts that have survived over many millennia. We continue to learn more about the earliest Americans.

THE PEOPLES OF THE PRECONTACT AMERICAS

For many decades, scholars believed that all early migrations into the Americas came from humans crossing an ancient land bridge over the Bering Strait into what is now Alaska, approximately 11,000 years ago. The migrations were probably a result of the development of new stone tools—spears and other hunting implements—used to pursue the large animals that crossed between Asia and North America. All of these land-based migrants are thought to have come from a Mongolian stock related to that of modern-day Siberia. Scholars refer to these migrants as the "Clovis" people, so named for a town in New Mexico where archaeologists first discovered evidence of their tools and weapons in the 1930s.

More recent archaeological evidence suggests that not all the early migrants to the Americas came across the Bering Strait. Some migrants from Asia appear to have settled as far south as Chile and Peru even before people began moving into North America by land. These first South Americans may have come not by land but by sea, using boats.

This new evidence suggests that the early population of the Americas was more diverse and more scattered than scholars used to believe. Recent DNA evidence has identified a possible early population group that does not seem to have Asian characteristics. This suggests that thousands of years before Columbus, there may have been some migration from Europe.

Que figur anzaigt vns das volck vnd insel die gefunden ist durch den christenlichen kunig zu Portugal oder von seinen vnterthonen. Die leut sind also nacket hübsch, braun wolgestalt von leib, ir heubter hals, arm, schäm, füß, frawen vnd mann ain wenig mit federn bedeckt. Auch haben die mann in iren angesichten vnd brust vil edel gestain. Es hat auch nyemantz nichts sunder sind alle ding gemain. Vnnd die mann habendt weyber welche in gefallen, es sy müter, schwester oder freündt, darinn haben sy kain vnterschayd. Sy streyten auch mit anander. Sy essen auch anander selbs die erschlagen werden, vnd henckt das selbig fleisch in den rauch. Sy werden alt hundert vnd funfzig ... Vnd haben kain regimentt.

FIRST ENCOUNTERS WITH NATIVE AMERICANS This 1505 engraving is one of the earliest European images of the way Native Americans lived in the Americas. It also represents some of the ways in which white Europeans would view the people they called Indians for many generations. Native Americans here are portrayed as exotic savages, whose sexuality was not contained within stable families and whose savagery was evidenced in their practice of eating the flesh of their slain enemies. In the background are the ships that have brought the European visitors who recorded these images. (The Granger Collection, NYC)

The "Archaic" period is a scholarly term for the early history of humans in America, beginning around 8000 B.C. In the first part of this period, most humans supported themselves through hunting and gathering, using the same stone tools that earlier Americans had brought with them from Asia.

Later in the Archaic period, population groups began to expand their activities and to develop new tools, such as nets and hooks for fishing, traps for smaller animals, and baskets for gathering berries, nuts, seeds, and other plants. Still later, some groups began to farm. Farming, of course, requires people to stay in one place. In agricultural areas, the first sedentary settlements slowly began to form, creating the basis for larger civilizations.

THE GROWTH OF CIVILIZATIONS: THE SOUTH

The most elaborate early civilizations emerged in South and Central America and in Mexico. In Peru, the Incas created the largest empire in the Americas, stretching almost 2,000 miles along western South America. The Incas developed a complex administrative system and a large network of paved roads that welded together the populations of many tribes under a single government.

Organized societies of Mesoamericans emerged around 10,000 B.C. They created a civilization in what is now Mexico and much of Central America. They were known as the Olmec people. The first truly complex society in the region began in approximately 1000 B.C. A more sophisticated culture grew up around A.D. 800 in parts of Central

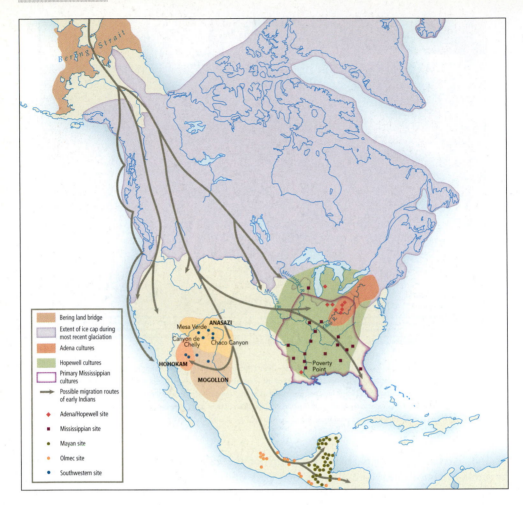

NORTH AMERICAN MIGRATIONS   This map tracks some of the very early migrations into, and within, North America in the centuries preceding contact with Europe. The map shows the now-vanished land bridge between Siberia and Alaska over which thousands, perhaps millions, of migrating people passed into the Americas. It also shows the locations of some of the earliest settlements in North America. • *What role did the extended glacial field in what is now Canada play in residential patterns in the ancient American world?*

America and in the Yucatán peninsula of Mexico, in an area known as Maya. Mayan civilization developed a written language, a numerical system similar to the Arabic, an accurate calendar, an advanced agricultural system, and important trade routes into other areas of the continents.

Gradually, the societies of the Maya region were superseded by other Mesoamerican tribes, who have become known collectively (and somewhat inaccurately) as the Aztec. They called themselves Mexica. In about A.D. 1300, the Mexica built the city of Tenochtitlán on a large island in a lake in central Mexico, the site of present-day Mexico City. With a population as high as 100,000 by 1500, Tenochtitlán featured large and impressive public buildings, schools that all male children attended, an organized military, a medical system, and a slave workforce drawn from conquered tribes. A warlike people, the Mexica gradually established their dominance over almost all of central Mexico.

Like other Mesoamerican societies, the Mexica developed a religion based on the belief that the gods could be satisfied only by being fed the living hearts of humans. The Mexica sacrificed people—largely prisoners captured in combat—on a scale unknown in other American civilizations. The Mesoamerican civilizations were for many centuries the center of civilized life in North and Central America—the hub of culture and trade.

The Civilizations of the North

The peoples north of Mexico developed less elaborate but still substantial civilizations. Inhabitants of the northern regions of the continent subsisted on combinations of hunting, gathering, and fishing. They included the Eskimo (or Inuit) of the Arctic Circle, who fished and hunted seals; big-game hunters of the northern forests, who led nomadic lives based on the pursuit of moose and caribou; tribes of the Pacific Northwest, whose principal occupation was salmon fishing and who created substantial permanent settlements

THE INDIAN VILLAGE OF SECOTON (ca. 1585), BY JOHN WHITE John White created this illustration of life among the Eastern Woodland Indians in coastal North Carolina. It shows the diversified agriculture practiced by the natives: squash, tobacco, and three varieties of corn. The hunters shown in nearby woods suggest another element of the native economy. At bottom right, Indians perform a religious ritual, which White described as "strange gestures and songs." (The Granger Collection, NYC)

HOW THE EARLY NORTH AMERICANS LIVED This map shows the various ways in which the native tribes of North America supported themselves before the arrival of European civilization. Like most precommercial peoples, the Native Americans survived largely on the resources available in their immediate surroundings. Note, for example, the reliance on the products of the sea of the tribes along the northern coastlines of the continent, and the way in which tribes in relatively inhospitable climates in the North—where agriculture was difficult—relied on hunting large game. Most Native Americans were farmers. • *What different kinds of farming would have emerged in the very different climates of the agricultural regions shown on this map?*

along the coast; and a group of tribes spread through relatively arid regions of the Far West, who developed successful communities based on fishing, hunting small game, and gathering edible plants.

Other societies in North America were agricultural. Among the most developed were those in the Southwest. The people of that arid region built large irrigation systems, and they constructed towns of stone and adobe. In the Great Plains region, too, most tribes were engaged in sedentary farming (corn and other grains). They lived in large permanent settlements.

The eastern third of what is now the United States—much of it covered with forests and inhabited by the Woodland Indians—had the greatest food resources of any area of the continent. Most of the many tribes of the region engaged in farming, hunting, gathering, and fishing simultaneously. In the South there were permanent settlements and large trading networks based on the corn and other grains grown in the rich lands of the Mississippi River valley. Cahokia, a trading center located near present-day St. Louis, had a population of 40,000 at its peak in A.D. 1200.

The agricultural societies of the Northeast were more mobile. Farming techniques there were designed to exploit the land quickly rather than to develop permanent settlements. Many of the tribes living east of the Mississippi River were linked together loosely by common linguistic roots. The largest of these language groups consisted of the Algonquian tribes, who lived along the Atlantic seaboard from Canada to Virginia; the Iroquois Confederacy, which was centered in what is now upstate New York; and the Muskogean tribes, which consisted of the tribes in the southernmost regions of the eastern seaboard.

Religion was usually closely linked with the natural world on which the tribes depended. Native Americans worshiped many gods, whom they associated variously with crops, game, forests, rivers, and other elements of nature.

All tribes assigned women the jobs of caring for children, preparing meals, and gathering certain foods. But the allocation of other tasks varied from one society to another. Some tribal groups reserved farming tasks almost entirely for men. Among other groups, women tended the fields, while men engaged in hunting, warfare, or clearing land. Because women and children were often left alone for extended periods while men were away hunting or fighting, women in some tribes controlled the social and economic organization of the settlements.

EUROPE LOOKS WESTWARD

Europeans were almost entirely unaware of the existence of the Americas before the fifteenth century. A few early wanderers—Leif Eriksson, an eleventh-century Norse seaman, and others—had glimpsed parts of the New World on their voyages. But even if their discoveries had become common knowledge (and they did not), there would have been little incentive for others to follow. Europe in the Middle Ages (roughly A.D. 500–1500) was too weak, divided, and decentralized to inspire many great ventures. By the end of the fifteenth century, however, conditions in Europe had changed, and the incentive for overseas exploration had grown.

COMMERCE AND NATIONALISM

Two important changes encouraged Europeans to look toward new lands. One was the significant growth in Europe's population in the fifteenth century. The Black Death, a catastrophic epidemic of the bubonic plague that began in Constantinople in 1347, had killed more than a third of the people of the Continent (according to some estimates). But a century and a half later, the population had rebounded. With that growth came a reawakening of commerce. A new merchant class was emerging to meet the rising demand for goods from abroad. As trade increased, and as advances in navigation made long-distance sea travel more feasible, interest in expanding trade grew even more quickly.

The second change was the emergence of new governments that were more united and powerful than the feeble political entities of the feudal past. In the western areas of Europe in particular, strong new monarchs were eager to enhance the commercial development of their nations.

In the early fourteenth century, Marco Polo and other adventurers had returned from Asia bearing exotic spices, cloths, and dyes and even more exotic tales. Europeans who craved commercial glory had dreamed above all of trade with the East. For two centuries, that trade had been limited by the difficulties of the long overland journey to the Asian courts. But in the fourteenth century, talk of finding a faster, safer sea route to East Asia began.

The Portuguese were the preeminent maritime power in the fifteenth century, largely because of Prince Henry the Navigator, who devoted much of his life to the promotion of exploration. In 1486, after Henry's death, the Portuguese explorer Bartholomeu Dias rounded the southern tip of Africa (the Cape of Good Hope). In 1497–1498, Vasco da Gama proceeded all the way around the cape to India. But the Spanish, not the Portuguese, were the first to encounter the "New World."

CHRISTOPHER COLUMBUS

Christopher Columbus was born and reared in Genoa, Italy. He spent his early seafaring years in the service of the Portuguese. By the time he was a young man, he had developed great ambitions. He believed he could reach East Asia by sailing west, across the Atlantic, rather than east, around Africa. Columbus thought the world was far smaller than it actually is. He also believed that the Asian continent extended farther eastward than it actually does. Most important, he did not realize that anything lay to the west between Europe and the lands of Asia.

Columbus failed to enlist the leaders of Portugal to back his plan, so he turned instead to Spain. The marriage of Spain's two most powerful regional rulers, Ferdinand of Aragon and Isabella of Castile, had produced the strongest and most ambitious monarchy in Europe. Columbus appealed to Queen Isabella for support for his proposed westward voyage, and in 1492, she agreed. Commanding ninety men and three ships—the *Niña*, the *Pinta*, and the *Santa María*—Columbus left Spain in August 1492 and sailed west into the Atlantic. Ten weeks later, he sighted land and assumed he had reached an island off Asia. In fact, he had landed in the Bahamas. When he pushed on and encountered Cuba, he assumed he had reached China. He returned to Spain, bringing with him several captured natives as evidence of his achievement. (He called the natives "Indians" because he believed they were from the East Indies in the Pacific.)

But Columbus did not, of course, bring back news of the great khan's court in China or any samples of the fabled wealth of the Indies. And so a year later, he tried again, this time with a much larger expedition. As before, he headed into the Caribbean, discovering several other islands and leaving a small and short-lived colony on Hispaniola. On a third voyage, in 1498, he finally reached the mainland and cruised along the northern coast of South America. He then realized, for the first time, that he had encountered not a part of Asia but a separate continent.

Columbus ended his life in obscurity. Ultimately, he was even unable to give his name to the land he had revealed to the Europeans. That distinction went instead to a Florentine merchant, Amerigo Vespucci, who wrote a series of vivid descriptions of the lands he visited on a later expedition to the New World and helped popularize the idea that the Americas were new continents.

Partly as a result of Columbus's initiative, Spain began to devote greater resources and energy to maritime exploration. In 1513, the Spaniard Vasco de Balboa crossed the Isthmus of Panama and became the first known European to gaze westward upon the great ocean that separated America from China. Seeking access to that ocean, Ferdinand Magellan, a Portuguese in Spanish employ, found the strait that now bears his name at the southern

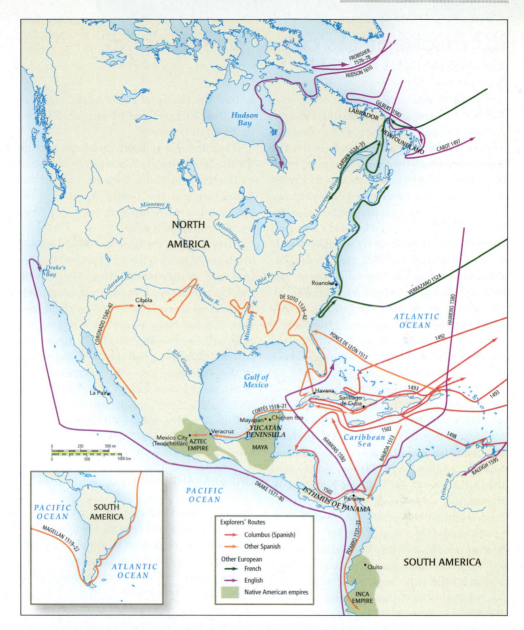

EUROPEAN EXPLORATION AND CONQUEST, 1492–1583 This map shows the many voyages of exploration to and conquest of North America launched by Europeans in the late fifteenth and sixteenth centuries. Note how Columbus and the Spanish explorers who followed him tended to move quickly into the lands of Mexico, the Caribbean, and Central and South America, while the English and French explored the northern territories of North America. • *What factors might have led these various nations to explore and colonize different areas of the New World?*

end of South America, struggled through the stormy narrows and into the ocean (so calm by contrast that he christened it the *Pacific*), and then proceeded to the Philippines. There Magellan died in a conflict with natives, but his expedition went on to complete the first known circumnavigation of the globe (1519–1522). By 1550, Spaniards had explored the coasts of North America as far north as Oregon in the west and Labrador in the east.

CONSIDER THE SOURCE

BARTOLOME DE LAS CASAS, "OF THE ISLAND OF HISPANIOLA" (1542)

GOD has created all these numberless people to be quite the simplest, without malice or duplicity, most obedient, most faithful to their natural Lords, and to the Christians, whom they serve; the most humble, most patient, most peaceful and calm, without strife nor tumults; not wrangling, nor querulous, as free from uproar, hate and desire of revenge as any in the world . . . Among these gentle sheep, gifted by their Maker with the above qualities, the Spaniards entered as soon as they knew them, like wolves, tigers and lions which had been starving for many days, and since forty years they have done nothing else; nor do they afflict, torment, and destroy them with strange and new, and divers kinds of cruelty, never before seen, nor heard of, nor read of . . .

The Christians, with their horses and swords and lances, began to slaughter and practice strange cruelty among them. They penetrated into the country and spared neither children nor the aged, nor pregnant women, nor those in child labour, all of whom they ran through the body and lacerated, as though they were assaulting so many lambs herded in their sheepfold. They made bets as to who would slit a man in two, or cut off his head at one blow: or they opened up his bowels. They tore the babes from their mothers' breast by the feet, and dashed their heads against the rocks. Others they seized by the shoulders and threw into the rivers, laughing and joking, and when they fell into the water they exclaimed: "boil body of so and so!" They spitted the bodies of other babes, together with their mothers and all who were before them, on their swords.

They made a gallows just high enough for the feet to nearly touch the ground, and by thirteens, in honor and reverence of our Redeemer and the twelve Apostles, they put wood underneath and, with fire, they burned the Indians alive.

They wrapped the bodies of others entirely in dry straw, binding them in it and setting fire to it; and so they burned them. They cut off the hands of all they wished to take alive, made them carry them fastened on to them, and said: "Go and carry letters": that is; take the news to those who have fled to the mountains.

They generally killed the lords and nobles in the following way. They made wooden gridirons of stakes, bound them upon them, and made a slow fire beneath; thus the victims gave up the spirit by degrees, emitting cries of despair in their torture. . . .

UNDERSTAND, ANALYZE, & EVALUATE

1. How did Bartolome de Las Casas characterize the natives? How do you think they would have responded to this description?
2. What metaphor did Las Casas use to describe the natives and where does this metaphor come from?
3. What role did Las Casas expect the Spaniards to play on Hispaniola? What did they do instead?

Source: Francis Augustus MacNutt, *Bartholomew de Las Casas: His Life, His Apostolate, and His Writings* (New York: G.P. Putnam's Sons, 1909), p. 14.

THE SPANISH EMPIRE

In time, Spanish explorers in the New World stopped thinking of America simply as an obstacle to their search for a route to Asia and began instead to consider it a possible source of wealth in itself. The Spanish claimed for themselves the whole of the New

World, except for a large part of the east coast of South America (today's Brazil) that was reserved by a papal decree for the Portuguese.

In 1518, Hernando Cortés, who had been an unsuccessful Spanish government official in Cuba for fourteen years, led a small military expedition (about 600 men) against the Aztecs in Mexico and their powerful emperor, Montezuma, after hearing stories of great treasures there. His first assault on Tenochtitlán, the Aztec capital, failed. But Cortés and his army had unwittingly exposed the natives to smallpox, to which the natives, unlike the Europeans, had developed no immunity. The epidemic decimated the Aztec population and made it possible for the Spanish to triumph in their second attempt at conquest. Through his ruthless suppression of the surviving natives, Cortés established himself as one of the most brutal of the Spanish "conquistadores" (conquerors). Twenty years later, Francisco Pizarro conquered the Incas in Peru and opened the way for other Spanish advances into South America.

The first Spanish settlers in America were interested only in exploiting the American stores of gold and silver, and they were fabulously successful. For 300 years, beginning in the sixteenth century, the mines of Spanish America yielded more than ten times as much gold and silver as all the rest of the world's mines combined. Before long, however, most Spanish settlers in America traveled to the New World for other reasons. Many went in hopes of profiting from agriculture. They helped establish elements of European civilization permanently in America. Other Spaniards—priests, friars, and missionaries—went to America to spread the Christian religion; through their efforts, the influence of the Catholic Church ultimately extended throughout South and Central America and Mexico.

By the end of the sixteenth century, the Spanish Empire included the Caribbean islands, Mexico, and southern North America. It also spread into South America and included what is now Chile, Argentina, and Peru. In 1580, when the Spanish and Portuguese monarchies temporarily united, Brazil came under Spanish jurisdiction as well.

THE MEXICANS STRIKE BACK In this vivid scene from the Durán Codex, Mexican artists illustrate a rare moment in which Mexican warriors gained the upper hand over the Spanish invaders. Driven back by native fighters, the Spanish have taken refuge in a room in the royal palace in Tenochtitlán while brightly attired Mexican warriors besiege them. Although the Mexicans gained a temporary advantage in this battle, the drawing illustrates one of the reasons for their inability to withstand the Spanish in the longer term. The Spanish soldiers are armed with rifles and crossbows, while the Indians carry only spears and shields. (Biblioteca Nacional, Madrid, Spain/Bridgeman Art Library)

NORTHERN OUTPOSTS

In 1565, the Spanish established the fort of St. Augustine in Florida, their first permanent settlement in what is now the United States. But it was little more than a small military outpost. A more substantial colonizing venture began in the Southwest in 1598, when Don Juan de Oñate traveled north from Mexico with a party of 500, claimed for Spain some of the lands of the Pueblo Indians in what is now New Mexico, and began to establish a colony. Oñate granted *encomiendas* (the right to exact tribute and labor from the natives on large tracts of land) to favored Spaniards. In 1609, Spanish colonists founded Santa Fe. By 1680, there were over 2,000 Spanish colonists living among about 30,000 Pueblos. The economic heart of the colony was cattle and sheep, raised on the *ranchos* that stretched out around the small towns Spanish settlers established.

Despite widespread conversions to Catholicism, most natives (including the converts) continued to practice their own religious rituals. In 1680, Spanish priests and the colonial government tried to suppress these rituals. In response, Pope, an Indian religious leader, led an uprising that killed hundreds of European settlers, captured Santa Fe, and drove the Spanish from the region. Twelve years later, the Spanish returned and crushed a last revolt in 1696.

After the revolts, many Spanish colonists realized that they could not hope to prosper in New Mexico in constant conflict with a native population that greatly outnumbered them. Although the Spanish intensified their efforts to assimilate the Indians, they also now permitted the Pueblos to own land. They stopped commandeering Indian labor, and they tolerated the survival of tribal religious rituals. There was significant intermarriage between Europeans and Indians. By 1750, the Spanish population had grown to about 4,000. The Pueblo population had declined (through disease, war, and migration) to about 13,000—less than half what it had been in 1680. New Mexico had by then become a reasonably stable but still weak and isolated outpost of the Spanish Empire.

BIOLOGICAL AND CULTURAL EXCHANGES

European and native cultures never entirely merged in the Spanish Empire. Nevertheless, the arrival of whites launched a process of interaction between different peoples that left no one unchanged.

That Europeans were exploring the Americas at all was a result of early contacts with the natives, from whom they had learned of the rich deposits of gold and silver. From then on, the history of the Americas became one of increasing levels of exchanges— some beneficial, others catastrophic—among different peoples and cultures. The first and perhaps most profound result of this exchange was the importation of European diseases to the New World. It would be difficult to exaggerate the consequences of the exposure of Native Americans to such illnesses as influenza, measles, typhus, and above all smallpox. Millions died. In some areas, native populations were virtually wiped out within a few decades of their first contact with whites. On Hispaniola, where Columbus had landed in the 1490s, the native population quickly declined from approximately 1 million to about 500. In the Maya area of Mexico, as much as 95 percent of the population perished within a few years of the natives' first contact with the Spanish. Many (although not all) of the tribes north of Mexico were spared the worst of the epidemics. But for

SPANISH AMERICA From the time of Columbus's initial voyage in 1492 until the mid-nineteenth century, Spain was the dominant colonial power in the New World. From the southern regions of South America to the northern regions of the Pacific Northwest, Spain controlled one of the world's vastest empires. Note how much of the Spanish Empire was simply grafted upon the earlier empires of native peoples—the Incas in what is today Chile and Peru and the Aztecs across much of the rest of South America, Mexico, and the Southwest of what is now the United States. • *What characteristics of Spanish colonization would account for their preference for already settled regions?*

other areas of the New World, this was a catastrophe at least as grave as, and in some places far worse than, the Black Death that had killed over one-third of the population of Europe two centuries before. Some Europeans, watching this biological catastrophe, saw it as evidence of God's will that they should dominate the New World—and its native population.

THE AMERICAN POPULATION BEFORE COLUMBUS

NO one knows how many people lived in the Americas in the centuries before Columbus. But scholars, and others, have spent more than a century debating the question. Interest in this question survives because the debate over the pre-Columbian population is closely connected to the much larger debate over the consequences of European settlement of the Western Hemisphere.

Throughout the nineteenth century, Native Americans spoke often of the great days before Columbus when there were many more people in their tribes. The painter and ethnographer George Catlin, who spent much time among the tribes in the 1830s, listened to these oral legends and estimated that there had been 16 million Indians in North America before the Europeans came. Other white Americans dismissed such claims as preposterous, insisting that Indian civilization was far too primitive ever to have sustained a population even as large as a million.

In 1928, James Mooney, an ethnologist at the Smithsonian Institution, drawing from early accounts of soldiers and missionaries in the sixteenth century, came up with the implausibly precise figure of 1.15 million natives who lived north of Mexico in the early sixteenth century. That was a larger figure than nineteenth-century writers had suggested, but still much smaller than the Indians themselves claimed. A few years later, the anthropologist Alfred Kroeber used some of Mooney's methods to come up with an estimate considerably larger than Mooney's but much lower than Catlin's. He concluded in 1934 that there were 8.4 million people in the Americas in 1492, half in North America and half in the Caribbean and South America.

These low early estimates reflected an assumption that the arrival of the Europeans did not greatly reduce the native population. But in the 1960s and 1970s, scholars discovered that the early tribes had been catastrophically decimated by European

The decimation of native populations in the southern regions of the Americas was not only a result of exposure to infection. It was also a result of the conquistadores's deliberate policy of subjugation and extermination. Their brutality was in part a reflection of the ruthlessness with which Europeans waged war in all parts of the world. It was also a result of their conviction that the natives were "savages"—uncivilized peoples who could be treated as somehow not fully human. By the 1540s, the combined effects of European diseases and European military brutality had all but destroyed the empires of Mexico and South America.

Not all aspects of the exchange were disastrous to the Indians. The Europeans introduced to the natives important new crops (among them sugar and bananas), domestic livestock (cattle, pigs, and sheep), and, perhaps most significant, the horse, which gradually became central to the lives of many natives and transformed their societies.

plagues not long after the arrival of Columbus—that the numbers Europeans observed even in the late 1500s were already dramatically smaller than the numbers in 1492. Historians such as William McNeill in 1976 and Alfred Crosby a decade later produced powerful accounts of the near extinction of some tribes and the dramatic depopulation of others in a pestilential holocaust with few parallels in history.

(© Wil Meinderts/FotoNatura/Minden Pictures/Corbis)

The belief that the native population was much larger in 1492 than it was a few decades later has helped spur much larger estimates of how many people were in America before Columbus. Henry Dobyns, an anthropologist, claimed in 1966 that there were between 10 and 12 million people north of Mexico in 1492 and between 90 and 112 million in all of the Americas. No subsequent scholar has made so high a claim, but most subsequent estimates have been much closer to Dobyns's than to Kroeber's. The geographer William M. Denevan, for example, argued in 1976 that the American population in 1492 was around 55 million and that the population north of Mexico was under 4 million. These are among the lowest of modern estimates, but still dramatically higher than the nineteenth-century numbers.

The vehemence with which scholars, and at times the larger public, have debated these figures does not stem solely from the inherent difficulty of determining population size. It is also because the debate over the population is part of the debate over whether the arrival of Columbus—and the millions of Europeans who followed him—was a great advance in the history of civilization or an unparalleled catastrophe that virtually exterminated a large and flourishing native population. How to balance the many achievements of European civilization in the New World after 1492 against the terrible destruction of native peoples that accompanied it is, in the end, less a historical question, perhaps, than a moral one. •

UNDERSTAND, ANALYZE, & EVALUATE

1. What are some of the difficulties in trying to determine the size of the pre-Columbian population?
2. What are the advantages and disadvantages of using oral history as a source of information about the past?

The exchange was at least as important (and more beneficial) to the Europeans. In both North and South America, the arriving white peoples learned from the natives new agricultural techniques appropriate to the demands of the new land. They discovered new crops—above all maize (corn), which Columbus took back to Europe from his first trip to America. Such foods as squash, pumpkins, beans, sweet potatoes, tomatoes, peppers, and potatoes all found their way into European diets.

In South America, Central America, and Mexico, Europeans and natives lived in intimate, if unequal, contact with one another. Many natives gradually came to speak Spanish or Portuguese, but they created a range of dialects fusing the European languages with elements of their own. European men outnumbered European women by at least ten to one. Intermarriage—often forcible—became frequent between Spanish immigrants and native women. Before long, the population of the colonies came to be dominated (numerically, at least) by people of mixed race, or *mestizos*.

THE ATLANTIC CONTEXT OF EARLY AMERICAN HISTORY

MOST Americans understand that our nation has recently become intimately bound up with the rest of the world—that we live in what some call the "age of globalization." Until recently, however, most historians have examined the nation's past in relative isolation. Among the first areas of American history to be reexamined in an international perspective is the earliest period of European settlement of the Americas. Many scholars of early American history now examine what happened in the "New World" in the context of what has become known as the "Atlantic World."

The idea of an Atlantic World rests in part on the obvious connections between western Europe and the Spanish, British, French, and Dutch colonies in North and South America. All the early European civilizations of the Americas were part of a great imperial project launched by the major powers of Europe. The massive European and African immigrations to the Americas beginning in the sixteenth century, the defeat and devastation of native populations, the creation of European agricultural and urban settlements, and the imposition of imperial regulations on trade, commerce, landowning, and political life—all of these forces reveal the influence of Old World imperialism on the history of the New World.

But the expansion of empires is only one part of the creation of the Atlantic World. At least equally important—and closely related—is the expansion of commerce from Europe and Africa to the Americas. Although some Europeans traveled to the New World in search of religious freedom, or to escape oppression, or to search for adventure, the great majority of European immigrants were in search of economic opportunity. Not surprisingly, therefore, the European settlements in the Americas were almost from the start intimately connected to Europe through the growth of commerce between them—commerce that grew more extensive and more complex with every passing year. The commercial relationship between America and Europe was responsible not just for the growth of trade, but also for the increases in migration over time—as the demand for labor in the New World drew more and more settlers from the Old World. Commerce was also the principal reason for the rise of slavery in the Americas, and for the growth of the slave trade between European America and Africa. The Atlantic World, in other words, included not just Europe and the Americas, but Africa as well.

Religion was another force binding together the Atlantic World. The vast majority of people of European descent were

Virtually all the enterprises of the Spanish and Portuguese colonists depended on Indian workforces. In some places, Indians were sold into slavery. More often, colonists used a coercive (or "indentured") wage system, under which Indians worked in the mines and on the plantations under duress for fixed periods. That was not, in the end, enough to meet the labor needs of the colonists. As early as 1502, European settlers began importing slaves from Africa.

Christians, and most of them maintained important religious ties to part of a hierarchical church based in Rome with close ties with the Vatican. But the Protestant faiths that predominated in North America were intimately linked to their European counterparts as well. New religious ideas and movements spread back and forth across the Atlantic with astonishing speed. Great revivals that began in Europe moved quickly to America. The "Great Awakening" of the mid-eighteenth century, for example, began in Britain and traveled to America in large part through the efforts of the English evangelist George Whitefield. American evangelists later carried religious ideas from the New World back to the Old.

The early history of European America was also closely bound up with the intellectual life of Europe. The Enlightenment—the cluster of ideas that emerged in Europe in the seventeenth and eighteenth centuries emphasizing the power of human reason—moved quickly to the Americas, producing intellectual ferment throughout the New World, but particularly in the British colonies in North America and the Caribbean. The ideas of the British philosopher John Locke, for example, helped shape the founding of Georgia. The English Constitution, and the idea of the "rights of Englishmen," shaped the way North Americans developed their own concepts of politics. Many of the ideas that underlaid the American Revolution were products of British and continental philosophy that had traveled across the Atlantic. The reinterpretation of those ideas by Americans to help justify their drive to independence—by, among others, Thomas Paine—moved back to Europe and helped, among other things, to inspire the French Revolution. Scientific and technological knowledge—another product of the

(The I. N. Phelps Stokes Collection of American Historical Prints, Prints Division, The New York Public Library, Astor, Lenox and Tilden Foundations)

Enlightenment—traveled constantly across the Atlantic and back. Americans borrowed industrial technology from Britain. Europe acquired much of its early knowledge of electricity from experiments done in America. But the Enlightenment was only one part of the continuing intellectual connections within the Atlantic World, connections that spread artistic, scholarly, and political ideas widely through the lands bordering the ocean.

Instead of thinking of the early history of what became the United States simply as the story of the growth of thirteen small colonies along the Atlantic seaboard of North America, the idea of the "Atlantic World" encourages us to think of early American history as a vast pattern of exchanges and interactions—trade, migration, religious and intellectual exchange, and many other relationships—among all the societies bordering the Atlantic: western Europe, western Africa, the Caribbean, and North and South America. •

UNDERSTAND, ANALYZE, & EVALUATE

1. What is the Atlantic World?
2. What has led historians to begin studying the idea of an Atlantic World?

AFRICA AND AMERICA

Over one-half of all the immigrants to the New World between 1500 and 1800 were Africans, virtually all of them sent to the Americas against their will. Most came from a large region below the Sahara Desert, known as Guinea.

Europeans and white Americans came to portray African society as primitive and uncivilized. But most Africans were, in fact, highly civilized peoples with well-developed economies and political systems. The residents of upper Guinea had substantial commercial contact with the Mediterranean world—trading ivory, gold, and slaves for finished goods—and, largely as a result, became early converts to Islam. After the collapse of the ancient kingdom of Ghana around A.D. 1100, they created the even larger empire of Mali, whose trading center at Timbuktu became fabled as a center of education and a meeting place of the peoples of many lands.

Farther south, Africans were more isolated from Europe and the Mediterranean and were more politically fragmented. The central social unit was the village, which usually consisted of members of an extended family group. Some groups of villages united in small kingdoms. But no large empires emerged in the south. Nevertheless, these southern societies developed extensive trade, both among themselves and, to a lesser degree, with the outside world.

African civilizations developed economies that reflected the climates and resources of their lands. In upper Guinea, fishing and rice cultivation, supplemented by the extensive trade with Mediterranean lands, were the foundation of the economy. Farther south, Africans grew wheat and other food crops, raised livestock, and fished. There were some more nomadic tribes in the interior, who subsisted largely on hunting and gathering. But most Africans were sedentary, farming people.

As in many Indian societies in America, African families tended to be matrilineal: they traced their heredity through and inherited property from their mothers. Women played a major role, often the dominant role, in trade. In many areas, they were the principal farmers (while the men hunted, fished, and raised livestock), and everywhere, they managed child care and food preparation. Most tribes also divided political power by gender, with men choosing leaders to manage male affairs and women choosing parallel leaders to handle female matters.

Small elites of priests and nobles stood at the top of many African societies. Most people belonged to a large middle group of farmers, traders, crafts workers, and others. At the bottom of society were slaves—men and women, not all of them African, who were put into bondage after being captured in wars, because of criminal behavior, or as a result of unpaid debts. Slaves in Africa were generally in bondage for a fixed term, and in the meantime they retained certain legal protections (including the right to marry). Children did not inherit their parents' condition of bondage.

The African slave trade long preceded European settlement in the New World. As early as the eighth century, west Africans began selling small numbers of slaves to traders from the Mediterranean and later to the Portuguese. In the sixteenth century, however, the market for slaves increased dramatically as a result of the growing European demand for sugarcane. The small areas of sugar cultivation in the Mediterranean could not meet the demand, and production soon spread to new areas: to the island of Madeira off the African coast, which became a Portuguese colony, and not long thereafter (still in the sixteenth century) to the Caribbean islands and Brazil. Sugar was a labor-intensive crop, and the demand for African workers in these new areas of cultivation was high. At first the slave traders were overwhelmingly Portuguese. By the seventeenth century, the Dutch had won control of most of the market. In the eighteenth century, the English dominated it. (Despite some recent claims, Jews were never significantly involved in the slave trade.) By 1700, slavery had spread well beyond its original locations in the Caribbean and South America and into the English colonies to the north.

THE ARRIVAL OF THE ENGLISH

England's first documented contact with the New World came only five years after Spain's. In 1497, John Cabot (like Columbus, a native of Genoa) sailed to the northeastern coast of North America on an expedition sponsored by King Henry VII, in an unsuccessful search for a northwest passage through the New World to the Orient. But nearly a century passed before the English made any serious efforts to establish colonies in America.

INCENTIVES FOR COLONIZATION

Interest in colonization grew in part as a response to social and economic problems in sixteenth-century England. The English people suffered from frequent and costly European wars, and they suffered from almost constant religious strife within their own land. Many suffered, too, from harsh economic changes in their countryside. Because the worldwide demand for wool was growing rapidly, landowners were converting their land from fields for crops to pastures for sheep. The result was a reduction in the amount of land available for growing food. England's food supply declined at the same time that the English population was growing—from 3 million in 1485 to 4 million in 1603. To some of the English, the New World began to seem attractive because it offered something that was growing scarce in England: land.

At the same time, new merchant capitalists were prospering by selling the products of England's growing wool-cloth industry abroad. At first, most exporters did business almost entirely as individuals. In time, however, merchants formed companies, whose charters from the king gave them monopolies for trading in particular regions. Investors in these companies often made fantastic profits, and they were eager to expand their trade.

Central to this trading drive was the emergence of a new concept of economic life known as mercantilism. Mercantilism rested on the belief that one person or nation could grow rich only at the expense of another, and that a nation's economic health depended, therefore, on selling as much as possible to foreign lands and buying as little as possible from them. The principles of mercantilism spread throughout Europe in the sixteenth and seventeenth centuries. One result was the increased attractiveness of acquiring colonies, which became the source of raw materials and a market for the colonizing power's goods.

In England, the mercantilistic program thrived at first on the basis of the flourishing wool trade with the European continent, and particularly with the great cloth market in Antwerp. In the 1550s, however, that glutted market began to collapse, and English merchants had to look elsewhere for overseas trade. Some English believed colonies would solve their problems.

There were also religious motives for colonization—a result of the Protestant Reformation. Protestantism began in Germany in 1517, when Martin Luther challenged some of the basic practices and beliefs of the Roman Catholic Church. Luther quickly won a wide following among ordinary men and women in northern Europe. When the pope excommunicated him in 1520, Luther began leading his followers out of the Catholic Church entirely.

The Swiss theologian John Calvin went even further in rejecting the Catholic belief that human behavior could affect an individual's prospects for salvation. Calvin introduced

MERCANTILISM AND COLONIAL COMMERCE

FOR more than two centuries, the theory known as mercantilism shaped Europe's economic life and that of its growing colonial possessions. The actual application of mercantilism differed from country to country and empire to empire, but virtually all versions of mercantilism shared a belief in the importance of colonies to the economy of the colonizing nations. As a result, mercantilism helped spur the growth of European empires around the world.

In one sense, mercantilism was a highly nationalist theory. It rested on the conviction that the nation (not the individual) was at the center of economic life and that each nation should work to maximize its own share of the finite wealth for which all nations were competing. A gain for France, mercantilism taught, was in effect a loss for Britain or Spain. Thus, mercantilism encouraged each nation to work for itself and to attempt to weaken its rivals. But mercantilism was also a global force. What made it so was the belief that each nation must search for its own sources of trade and raw materials around the world. Every European state was trying to find markets for its exports, which would bring wealth into the nation, while trying at the same time to limit imports, which would transfer wealth to others. (Most of these central mercantilist tenets would eventually be overturned in Adam Smith's 1776 tract *The Wealth of Nations,* which instead advocated free trade among nations and individual self-interest over national largesse as the best route to increasing global—and thus national—wealth.)

In a mercantilist economy, colonies were critical to a nation's economic well-being. They served both as providers of raw materials and markets for finished goods. A colony, mercantilism taught, should trade only with its home nation, and wealth should flow only in one direction, toward the center of the empire. Naval power became an integral part of the mercantilist idea. Only by controlling the sea-lanes between the colonies and the homeland could a nation preserve its favorable balance of trade.

Despite the common assumptions underlying all forms of mercantilism, the system took many different forms, often depending on whether colonial merchants or state bureaucrats drove the economic

the doctrine of predestination. God "elected" some people to be saved and condemned others to damnation; each person's destiny was determined before birth, and no one could change that predetermined fate. But those who accepted Calvin's teachings came to believe that the way they led their lives might reveal to them their chances of salvation. A wicked or useless existence would be a sign of damnation; saintliness, diligence, and success could be signs of grace. The new creed spread rapidly throughout northern Europe.

In 1529, King Henry VIII of England, angered by the refusal of the pope to grant him a divorce from his Spanish wife, broke England's ties with the Catholic Church and discussion. In England, Spain, and the Netherlands, mercantilism was closely identified with the emerging middle class, which stood to profit personally from the increased trade (hence the term "mercantilism," from merchant). In France and Germany, on the other hand, state officials—rather than private citizens—laid more of the groundwork for mercantilist principles. In France, mercantilism was often known as "Colbertism," after its primary proponent, Jean-Baptiste Colbert, foreign minister under Louis XIV. In Germany, the theory was known as "cameralism," for the *Kammer*, or royal treasury.

In its early years, mercantilism was closely associated with "bullionism," which is the theory that only gold and silver defined a nation's wealth. As such, the early Spanish colonies of the New World emphasized the procurement of gold, silver, and other precious metals for the home nation. (English colonies such as Jamestown were founded in part with the same intention, but they were much less successful at finding precious metals.) Even when gold and silver were scarce, however, colonies could provide other important resources for the imperial capitals—for example, fur, timber, sugar, tobacco, and slaves.

Because mercantilism taught that any wealth a nation acquired was, in effect, taken away from some other nation, mercantilists believed that nations should heavily regulate the economic affairs of their colonies. To this end, England in the 1760s passed the Navigation Acts—laws that sharply restricted colonial trade with anyone but England. England was not alone in imposing such restrictions. Spain also took control over its colonial economies, passing similarly intensive regulations and, until 1720, insisting that all colonial trade must pass through the port of Seville.

Still, naval vessels could not be everywhere at once. And despite the many laws restricting colonial economies to their home nations, many colonial merchants struck up unregulated trade with their non-affiliated neighbors when possible. The French, Spanish, and Dutch West Indies in particular became the site of a thriving intercolonial trade that was, according to mercantilist doctrine, illegal. Indeed, so many traders from so many countries violated mercantile laws in the eighteenth century—and so many of them amassed great profits in the process—that the mercantilist system gradually began to unravel. By the time of the American Revolution, which resulted in part from the colonists' resistance to mercantilist policies, the patterns of global trade were already moving toward the freer, less regulated trading patterns of the modern capitalist world. •

UNDERSTAND, ANALYZE, & EVALUATE

1. What effect did mercantilism have on colonial economies? Did the effects differ according to which European nation owned the colony?
2. How did mercantilism contribute to power rivalries among the European nations?

established himself as the head of the Christian faith in his country. This was known as the English Reformation. After Henry's death, his Catholic daughter, Queen Mary, restored England's allegiance to Rome and persecuted Protestants. But when Mary died in 1558, her half sister, Elizabeth I, became England's sovereign and once again severed the nation's connection with the Catholic Church, this time for good.

To many English people, however, the new Church of England was not reformed enough. They clamored for reforms that would "purify" the church. As a result, they became known as Puritans.

The most radical Puritans, known as Separatists, were determined to worship in their own independent congregations, despite English laws that required all subjects to attend regular Anglican services. Most Puritans did not wish to leave the Church of England. They wanted, rather, to simplify Anglican forms of worship and reform the leadership of the church. Like the Separatists, they grew increasingly frustrated by the refusal of political and ecclesiastical authorities to respond to their demands.

Puritan discontent grew rapidly after the death of Elizabeth, the last of the Tudors, and the accession of James I, the first of the Stuarts, in 1603. Convinced that kings ruled by divine right, James quickly antagonized the Puritans by resorting to illegal and arbitrary taxation, by favoring English Catholics in the granting of charters and other favors, and by supporting "high-church" forms of ceremony. By the early seventeenth century, some religious nonconformists were beginning to look for places of refuge outside the kingdom.

England's first experience with colonization came not in the New World but in neighboring Ireland. The English had long laid claim to the island, but only in the late sixteenth century did serious efforts at colonization begin. The long, brutal process by which the English attempted to subdue the Irish created an important assumption about colonization: the belief that settlements in foreign lands must retain a rigid separation from the native populations. Unlike the Spanish in America, the English in Ireland tried to build a separate society of their own, peopled with emigrants from England itself. They would take that concept with them to the New World.

THE FRENCH AND THE DUTCH IN AMERICA

English settlers in North America encountered not only natives but also other Europeans who were, like them, driven by mercantilist ideas. There were scattered North American outposts of the Spanish Empire and, more important, there were French and Dutch settlers who were also vying for a stake in the New World.

France founded its first permanent settlement in North America at Quebec in 1608, less than a year after the English started their first at Jamestown. The colony's population grew slowly. Unlike the early English settlers, the French forged close ties with Native Americans deep inside the continent. French Jesuit missionaries established some of the first contacts between the two peoples. More important were the *coureurs de bois*—adventurous fur traders and trappers—who also penetrated far into the wilderness and developed an extensive trade that became one of the underpinnings of the French colonial economy. The French traders formed partnerships with the Indians. They often lived among the natives and married Indian women. The fur trade helped open the way for French agricultural estates (or *seigneuries*) along the St. Lawrence River and for the development of trade and military centers at Quebec and Montreal.

The Dutch, too, established a presence in North America. Holland in the early seventeenth century was one of the leading nations of the world, and its commerce moved to America in the seventeenth century. In 1609, an English explorer in the employ of the Dutch sailed up the river that was to be named for him in what was then New Netherlands. His explorations led to a Dutch claim on the territory. The Dutch built a town on Manhattan Island. From it, Dutch trappers moved into the interior toward the Appalachian Mountains and built a profitable trade in furs.

In 1624, not long after the first two permanent English colonies took root in Jamestown and Plymouth, the Dutch created a wedge between them when the Dutch

West India Company established a series of permanent trading posts on the Hudson, Delaware, and Connecticut rivers that soon became the colony of New Netherland. Its principal town, New Amsterdam, was on Manhattan Island.

THE FIRST ENGLISH SETTLEMENTS

The first permanent English settlement in the New World was established at Jamestown, in Virginia, in 1607. But for nearly thirty years before that, English merchants and adventurers had been engaged in a series of failed efforts to create colonies in America.

Through much of the sixteenth century, the English had harbored mixed feelings about the New World. They were intrigued by its possibilities, but they were also leery of Spain, which remained the dominant force in America. In 1588, however, King Philip II of Spain sent one of the largest military fleets in the history of warfare—the Spanish Armada—across the English Channel to attack England itself. The smaller English fleet, taking advantage of its greater maneuverability, defeated the armada and, in a single stroke, ended Spain's domination of the Atlantic. This great shift in naval power caused English interest in colonizing the New World to grow quickly.

The pioneers of English colonization were Sir Humphrey Gilbert and his half brother Sir Walter Raleigh—both veterans of earlier colonial efforts in Ireland. In 1578, Gilbert obtained from Queen Elizabeth a six-year patent granting him the exclusive right "to inhabit and possess any remote and heathen lands not already in the possession of any Christian prince." Five years later, after several setbacks, he led an expedition to Newfoundland, looking for a good place to build a profitable colony. But a storm sank his ship, and he was lost at sea. The next year, Sir Walter Raleigh secured his own six-year grant from the queen and sent a small group of men on an expedition to explore the North American coast. When they returned, Raleigh named the region they had explored Virginia, in honor of Elizabeth, who was known as the "Virgin Queen."

In 1585, Raleigh recruited his cousin, Sir Richard Grenville, to lead a group of men to the island of Roanoke, off the coast of what is now North Carolina, to establish a colony. Grenville deposited the settlers on the island, destroyed an Indian village as retaliation for a minor theft, and returned to England. The following spring, with long-overdue supplies and reinforcements from England, Sir Francis Drake unexpectedly arrived in Roanoke. The dispirited colonists boarded his ships and left.

Raleigh tried again in 1587, sending an expedition to Roanoke carrying ninety-one men, seventeen women, and nine children. The settlers attempted to take up where the first group of colonists had left off. John White, the commander of the expedition, returned to England after several weeks, in search of supplies and additional settlers. Because of a war with Spain, he was unable to return to Roanoke for three years. When he did, in 1590, he found the island deserted, with no clue to the fate of the settlers other than the cryptic inscription "Croatoan" carved on a post.

The Roanoke disaster marked the end of Sir Walter Raleigh's involvement in English colonization of the New World. No later colonizers would receive grants of land in America as vast or undefined as those Raleigh and Gilbert had acquired. Yet the colonizing impulse remained very much alive. In the early years of the seventeenth century, a group of London merchants decided to renew the attempt at colonization in Virginia. A rival group of merchants, from the area around Plymouth, was also interested in American ventures and was sponsoring voyages of exploration farther north. In 1606, James I issued a new charter, which divided North America between the two groups. The London group got the exclusive right to colonize the south, and the Plymouth merchants received the same right in the north. Through the efforts of these and other companies, the first enduring English colonies would soon be established in North America.

CONCLUSION

The lands that Europeans eventually named the Americas were the home of many millions of people before the arrival of Columbus. Having migrated from Asia thousands of years earlier, the pre-Columbian Americans spread throughout the Western Hemisphere and eventually created great civilizations. Among the most notable of them were the Incas in Peru and the Mayas and Aztecs in Mexico. In the regions north of what was later named the Rio Grande, the human population was smaller and the civilizations were less advanced than they were farther south. Even so, North American natives created a cluster of civilizations that thrived and expanded.

In the century after European contact, these native populations suffered a series of catastrophes that all but destroyed the civilizations they had built: brutal invasions by Spanish and Portuguese conquistadores and a series of plagues inadvertently imported by Europeans. By the middle of the sixteenth century, the Spanish and Portuguese—no longer faced with effective resistance from the native populations—had established colonial control over all of South America and much of North America.

In the parts of North America that would eventually become the United States, the European presence was for a time much less powerful. The Spanish established an important northern outpost in what is now New Mexico, a society in which Europeans and Indians lived together intimately, if unequally. On the whole, however, the North American Indians remained largely undisturbed by Europeans until English, French, and Dutch migrations began in the early seventeenth century.

RECALL AND REFLECT

1. How did contact between the European arrivals and the native peoples of the Americas affect both groups?
2. How did Spanish settlement in America differ from that of the English, Dutch, and French?
3. What were the effects of the importation of African slaves into the Americas?
4. What is mercantilism, and what did it have to do with the European colonization of North America?
5. How did the English experience at colonization in Ireland affect English colonization in America?

2 TRANSPLANTATIONS AND BORDERLANDS

THE EARLY CHESAPEAKE

THE GROWTH OF NEW ENGLAND

THE RESTORATION COLONIES

BORDERLANDS AND MIDDLE GROUNDS

THE DEVELOPMENT OF EMPIRE

LOOKING AHEAD

1. How did the English colonies in the Chesapeake, New England, and mid-Atlantic differ from one another in purpose and administration?
2. How "English" were the colonies in the decades after the British settlements?
3. What did the English want from the colonies in the first century of English settlement in North America?

THE FIRST PERMANENT ENGLISH SETTLEMENTS were mostly business enterprises—small, fragile communities, generally unprepared for the hardships they were to face. As in Ireland, there were few efforts to blend English society with the society of the natives. The Europeans attempted, as best they could, to isolate themselves from the Indians and create enclosed societies that were wholly their own—"transplantations" of the English world they had left behind. This proved an impossible task. The English immigrants in America found a world populated by Native American tribes; by colonists, explorers, and traders from Spain, France, and the Netherlands; and by immigrants from other parts of Europe and, soon, Africa. American society was from the beginning a fusion of many cultures—what historians have come to call a "middle ground," in which disparate people and cultures coexist.

All of British North America was, in effect, a borderland, or middle ground, during the early years of colonization. Through much of the seventeenth century, European colonies both relied on and did battle with the Indian tribes and struggled with challenges from other Europeans in their midst. Eventually, however, some areas of English settlement—most notably the growing communities along the eastern seaboard—managed to dominate their own regions, marginalizing or expelling Indians and other challengers. In these eastern

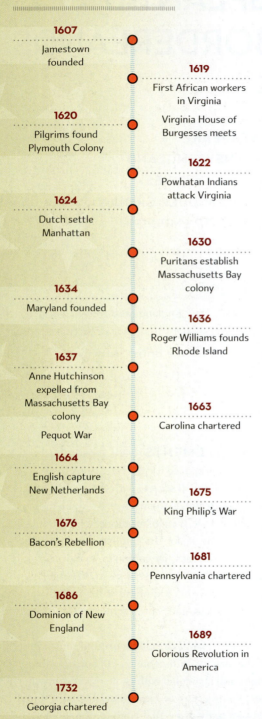

1607
Jamestown founded

1619
First African workers in Virginia

Virginia House of Burgesses meets

1620
Pilgrims found Plymouth Colony

1622
Powhatan Indians attack Virginia

1624
Dutch settle Manhattan

1630
Puritans establish Massachusetts Bay colony

1634
Maryland founded

1636
Roger Williams founds Rhode Island

1637
Anne Hutchinson expelled from Massachusetts Bay colony

Pequot War

1663
Carolina chartered

1664
English capture New Netherlands

1675
King Philip's War

1676
Bacon's Rebellion

1681
Pennsylvania chartered

1686
Dominion of New England

1689
Glorious Revolution in America

1732
Georgia chartered

colonies, the English created significant towns and cities; built political, religious, and educational institutions; and created agricultural systems of great productivity. They also developed substantial differences from one another—perhaps most notably in the growth of a slave-driven agricultural economy in the South, which had few counterparts in the North.

Middle grounds survived well into the nineteenth century in much of North America, but increasingly in the borderland in the interior of the continent. These were communities in which Europeans had not yet established full control, in which both Indians and Europeans exercised influence and power and lived intimately, if often uneasily, with one another.

THE EARLY CHESAPEAKE

Once James I had issued his 1606 charters, the London Company moved quickly and decisively to launch a colonizing expedition headed for Virginia—a party of 144 men aboard three ships, the *Godspeed*, the *Discovery*, and the *Susan Constant*, which set sail for America in 1607.

COLONISTS AND NATIVES

Only 104 men survived the journey. They reached the American coast in the spring of 1607, sailed into the Chesapeake and up a river they named the James. They established their colony on a peninsula on the river. They called it Jamestown. They chose an inland setting because they believed it would provide security from the natives. But they chose poorly. The site was low and swampy. It was surrounded by thick woods. The result could have hardly been more disastrous. A few months later, in January 1608, other ships appeared with additional men and supplies.

Their difficulties were to a large degree of their own making. The English colonists were vulnerable to local diseases, particularly malaria, which was especially virulent along the marshy rivers. They focused less on growing food and building a community than on searching futilely for gold and other exports. Those efforts made it harder for them to raise enough food. And they could create no real community without women, who had not come to Jamestown. The settlers had no real households and thus no real stakes in the communities.

That the colonies survived at all was a result of the neighboring powerful Indians. They slowly learned from the natives how to manage living in the new land. The Jamestown settlers expressed hostility toward their Indian neighbors, convinced that they were savages. The English civilization was greatly superior to that of the natives, they believed. The English, after all, had oceangoing vessels, muskets, and other advanced weaponry. But the survival of Jamestown was, in the end, largely a result of agricultural technologies developed by the Indians and borrowed by the struggling English. Native agriculture was far better adapted to the soil and climate of Virginia than the agricultural traditions the English settlers brought with them. The local natives were settled farmers whose villages were surrounded by neatly ordered fields. They grew a variety of crops—beans, pumpkins, vegetables, and above all maize (corn). Some of the Indian farmlands stretched over hundreds of acres and supported substantial populations.

The tiny English populations had no choice but to learn from the Indians. They recognized the value of corn, which was easy to cultivate and produced large yields. The English also learned the advantages of growing beans alongside corn to enrich the soil. Like the natives, the English quickly learned to combine the foods they grew and foods they hunted and fished, just as the local Indians did. And like the natives, they learned to borrow and, eventually, to build canoes, which were good at navigating the local streams. They learned from the Indians how to build canoes by hollowing out a single log (dugouts) or sewing birchbark around a simple frame, sealing it with resin. Without what they learned from the natives, the early settlers would not have survived.

A few months after the first colonists arrived in Virginia, additional ships appeared with more men and supplies. By then, of the 144 men who had sailed to America only 38 were still alive, the rest killed by diseases and famine. Jamestown survived largely because of two important events. One was what they learned from the local Indians. The other was the leadership of Captain John Smith, who at age twenty-seven was already a famous world traveler. He imposed work and order on the community, created a shaky relationship with the natives (sometimes negotiating with the Indians, and at other times stealing food and kidnapping natives).

Jamestown was a tiny colony for more than a decade. The natives were far more powerful than the English for years. Coastal Virginia had numerous tribes: the Algonquians, the Sioux, and the Iroquois. They had drawn together as part of the Powhatan Confederacy, named after the great chief who controlled a large area near the coasts. What the English called Virginia, the natives called Tsenacommacah.

REORGANIZATION AND EXPANSION

As Jamestown struggled to survive, the London Company (now renamed the Virginia Company) was already dreaming of bigger things. In 1609, it obtained a new charter from the king, which increased its power and enlarged its territory. It offered stock in the company to planters who were willing to migrate at their own expense. And it provided free passage to Virginia for poorer people who would agree to serve the company for seven

TOBACCO PLANT This 1622 woodcut, later hand-colored, represents the tobacco plant cultivated by English settlers in Virginia in the early seventeenth century after John Rolfe introduced it to the colonists. On the right is an image of a man smoking the plant through a very large pipe. (MPI/Getty Images)

years. In the spring of 1609, two years after the first arrival of the English, a fleet of nine vessels was dispatched to Jamestown with approximately 600 people, including some women and children.

Nevertheless, disaster followed. One of the Virginia-bound ships was lost at sea in a hurricane. Another ran aground in the Bermuda islands and was unable to sail for months. Many of the new settlers succumbed to fevers before winter came. And the winter of 1609–1610 was especially severe, a period known as "starving time." By then, the natives realized that the colonists were a threat to their civilization, and they stopped the English from moving inland into the Indian lands. Barricaded in the small palisade, unable to hunt or cultivate food, they lived on what they could find: "dogs, cats, rats, snakes, toadstools, horsehides," and even "the corpses of dead men," as one survivor recalled. When the migrants who had run aground in Bermuda finally arrived in Jamestown the following May, they found only about 60 emaciated people still alive. The new arrivals took the survivors onto their ship and sailed for England. But as the refugees proceeded down the James, they met an English ship coming up the river—part of a fleet bringing supplies and the colony's first governor, Lord De La Warr. The departing settlers agreed to return to Jamestown. New relief expeditions soon began to arrive, and the effort to turn a profit in Jamestown resumed.

New settlements began lining the river above and below Jamestown. There they discovered a newly found crop—tobacco, which was already popular among the Spanish colonies to the south. It was already being imported to Europe. In 1612, the Jamestown planter John Rolfe began trying to cultivate the crop in Virginia. Other planters began planting tobacco up and down the James River. Tobacco was the first profitable crop in the new colony, and it encouraged tobacco planters to move farther and farther into the inland, intruding more and more into the native farmlands.

The tobacco economy also created a heavy demand for labor. To entice new workers to the colony, the Virginia Company established what it called the "headright system." Headrights were fifty-acre grants of land. Those who already lived in the colony received two headrights (100 acres) apiece. Each new settler received a single headright for himself or herself. This system encouraged family groups to migrate together, since the more family members who traveled to America, the more land the family would receive. In addition, anyone who paid for the passage of immigrants to Virginia would receive an extra headright for each arrival. As a result, some colonists were able to assemble large plantations.

The company also transported ironworkers and other skilled craftsmen to Virginia to diversify the economy. In 1619, it sent 100 Englishwomen to the colony to become the wives of male colonists. It promised the male colonists the full rights of Englishmen, an end to strict and arbitrary rule, and even a share in self-government. On July 30, 1619, delegates from the various communities met as the House of Burgesses, the first elected legislature within what was to become the United States.

A month later in 1619, Virginia established another important precedent. As John Rolfe recorded, "about the latter end of August" a Dutch ship brought in "20 and odd Negroes." At first, their status was not clear. There is some reason to believe that the colonists thought of these first Africans as servants, to be held for a term of years and then freed. For a time, the use of African labor was limited. But not many years later, the African servants became more numerous and were slaves, without any possibility of freedom. It marked the first step toward the enslavement of Africans within what was to become the American republic.

At the same time, Europeans began to arrive as indentured servants—mostly English immigrants who were also held for a time and then released. For a while, indentured servants were by far the most populous workers in Virginia and other colonies.

The European settlers in Virginia built their society also on the effective suppression of the local Indians. For two years in the 1610s, Sir Thomas Dale, De La Warr's successor as governor, led unrelenting assaults against the Powhatan Indians, led by (and named for) their formidable chief, Powhatan. In the process, Dale kidnapped Powhatan's young daughter Pocahontas. Several years earlier, Pocahontas had played a role in mediating differences between her people and the Europeans. But now, Powhatan refused to ransom her. Living among the English, Pocahontas gradually adapted to many of their ways. She converted to Christianity and in 1614 married John Rolfe and visited England with him. There she stirred interest among many English in projects to "civilize" the Indians. She died shortly before her planned return to Virginia.

By the time of Pocahontas's marriage, Powhatan had ceased his attacks on the English in the face of overwhelming odds. But after his death several years later, his brother, Opechancanough, began secretly to plan the elimination of the English intruders. On a March morning in 1622, tribesmen called on the white settlements as if to offer goods for sale; then they suddenly attacked. Not until 347 whites of both sexes and all ages (including John Rolfe) lay dead were the Indian warriors finally forced to retreat. And not until over twenty years later were the Powhatans finally defeated.

By then, the Virginia Company in London was defunct. In 1624, James I revoked the company's charter, and the colony came under the control of the crown, where it would remain until 1776. The colony, if not the company, had survived—but at a terrible cost. In Virginia's first seventeen years, more than 8,500 white settlers had arrived in the colony, and nearly 80 percent of them had died.

MARYLAND AND THE CALVERTS

The Maryland colony ultimately came to look much like Virginia, but its origins were very different. George Calvert, the first Lord Baltimore, envisioned establishing a colony in America both as a great speculative venture in real estate and as a refuge for English Catholics like himself. Calvert died while he was still negotiating with the king in London for a charter to establish a colony in the Chesapeake region. But in 1632, his son Cecilius, the second Lord Baltimore, finally received the charter.

Lord Baltimore remained in England, but he named his brother, Leonard Calvert, governor of the colony. In March 1634, two ships—the *Ark* and the *Dove*—bearing Calvert along with 200 or 300 other colonists entered the Potomac River, turned into one of its eastern tributaries, and established the village of St. Mary's on a high, dry bluff. Neighboring Indians befriended the settlers and provided them with temporary shelter and with stocks of corn.

The Calverts needed to attract thousands of settlers to Maryland if their expensive colonial venture was to pay. As a result, they had to encourage the immigration of Protestants as well as their fellow English Catholics. The Calverts soon realized that Catholics would always be a minority in the colony, and so they adopted a policy of religious toleration: the 1649 "Act Concerning Religion." Nevertheless, politics in Maryland remained plagued for years by tensions, and at times violence, between the Catholic minority and the Protestant majority.

At the insistence of the first settlers, the Calverts agreed in 1635 to the calling of a representative assembly—the House of Delegates. But the proprietor retained absolute authority to distribute land as he wished; and since Lord Baltimore granted large estates to his relatives and to other English aristocrats, a distinct upper class soon established itself. By 1640, a severe labor shortage forced a modification of the land-grant procedure; and Maryland, like Virginia, adopted a headright system—a grant of 100 acres to each male settler, another 100 for his wife and each servant, and 50 for each of his children. But the great landlords of the colony's earliest years remained powerful. Like Virginia, Maryland became a center of tobacco cultivation; planters worked their land with the aid, first, of indentured servants imported from England and then, beginning late in the seventeenth century, of slaves imported from Africa.

BACON'S REBELLION

For more than thirty years, one man—Sir William Berkeley, the royal governor of Virginia—dominated the politics of the colony. He took office in 1642 at the age of thirty-six and with but one brief interruption remained in control of the government until 1677. In his first years as governor, he helped open up the interior of Virginia by sending explorers across the Blue Ridge Mountains and crushing a 1644 Indian uprising. The defeated Indians agreed to a treaty ceding to England most of the territory east of the mountains and establishing a boundary, west of which white settlement would be

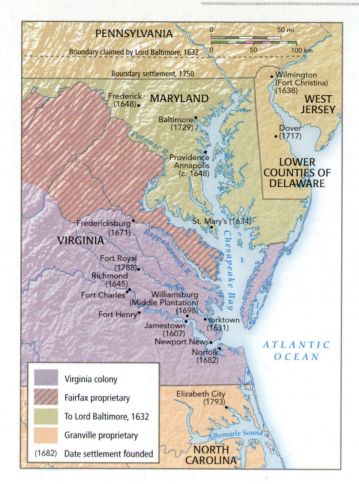

THE GROWTH OF THE CHESAPEAKE, 1607–1750 This map shows the political forms of European settlement in the region of the Chesapeake Bay in the seventeenth and early eighteenth centuries. Note the several different kinds of colonial enterprises: the royal colony of Virginia, controlled directly by the English crown after the failure of the early commercial enterprises there; and the proprietary regions of Maryland, northern Virginia, and North Carolina, which were under the control of powerful English aristocrats. • *Did these political differences have any significant effect on the economic activities of the various Chesapeake colonies?*

prohibited. But the rapid growth of the Virginia population made this agreement difficult to sustain. Between 1640 and 1660, Virginia's population rose from 8,000 to over 40,000. By 1652, English settlers had established three counties in the territory set aside by the treaty for the Indians.

In the meantime, Berkeley was expanding his own powers. By 1670, the vote for delegates to the House of Burgesses, once open to all white men, was restricted to landowners. Elections were rare, and the same burgesses, representing the established planters of the eastern (or tidewater) region of the colony, remained in office year after year. The more recent settlers on the frontier were underrepresented.

Resentment of the power of the governor and the tidewater aristocrats grew steadily in the newly settled lands of the west (often known as the "backcountry"). In 1676, this resentment helped create a major conflict, led by Nathaniel Bacon. Bacon had a good farm in the West and a seat on the governor's council. But like other members of the new backcountry gentry, he resented the governor's attempts to hold the line. Bacon's hostility toward Berkeley was a result of the governor's refusal to allow white settlers to move farther west. Berkeley forbid further settlement for fear of antagonizing Indians. Adding to the resentment was that Berkeley controlled the lucrative fur trade. Bacon wanted a piece of that trade.

The turbulence in Virginia was not just the tension between Berkeley and Bacon, both of them frontier aristocrats. It was also a result of the consequences of the indentured servant system. By the 1670s, many young men had finished their term as indentures and had found themselves without a home or any money. Many of them began moving around the colony, sometimes working, sometimes begging, sometimes stealing. They would soon become a factor in what became Bacon's rebellion.

In 1675, a major conflict erupted in the west between English settlers and natives. As the fighting escalated, Bacon and other concerned landholders demanded that the governor send the militia. When Berkeley refused, Bacon responded by offering to organize a volunteer army of backcountry men who would do their own fighting. Berkeley rejected that offer too. Bacon ignored him and launched a series of vicious but unsuccessful pursuits of the Indian challengers. When Berkeley heard of the unauthorized military effort, he proclaimed Bacon and his men to be rebels. Bacon now turned his army against the governor and, in what became known as Bacon's Rebellion, twice led his troops east to Jamestown. The first time he won a temporary pardon from the governor; the second time, after the governor repudiated the agreement, Bacon burned much of the city and drove the governor into exile. But then Bacon died suddenly of dysentery, and Berkeley soon regained control. In 1677, the Indians reluctantly signed a new treaty that opened new lands to white settlement.

Bacon's Rebellion was part of a continuing struggle to define the Indian and white spheres of influence in Virginia. It also revealed the bitterness of the competition among rival white elites, and it demonstrated the potential for instability in the colony's large population of free, landless men. One result was that landed elites in both eastern and western Virginia began to recognize a common interest in quelling social unrest from below. That was among the reasons that they turned increasingly to the African slave trade to fulfill their need for labor. African slaves, unlike white indentured servants, did not need to be released after a fixed term and hence did not threaten to become an unstable, landless class.

THE GROWTH OF NEW ENGLAND

The northern regions of British North America were slower to attract settlers than those in the south. That was in part because the Plymouth Company was never able to mount a successful colonizing expedition after receiving its charter in 1606. It did, however, sponsor other explorations. Captain John Smith, after his departure from Jamestown, made an exploratory journey for the Plymouth merchants, wrote an enthusiastic pamphlet about the lands he had seen, and called them New England.

PLYMOUTH PLANTATION

A discontented congregation of Puritan Separatists in England (unconnected to the Plymouth Company) established the first enduring European settlement in New England. In 1608, a congregation of Separatists from the English hamlet of Scrooby began emigrating quietly (and illegally), a few at a time, to Leyden, Holland, where they believed they could enjoy freedom of worship. But as foreigners in Holland, they had to work at unskilled and poorly paid jobs. They also watched with alarm as their children began to adapt to Dutch society and drift away from their church. Finally, some of the Separatists decided to move again, across the Atlantic, where they hoped to create a stable, protected community where they could spread "the gospel of the Kingdom of Christ in those remote parts of the world."

In 1620, leaders of the Scrooby group obtained permission from the Virginia Company to settle in Virginia. The "Pilgrims," as they saw themselves, sailed from Plymouth, England, in September 1620 on the *Mayflower*; thirty-five "saints" (Puritan Separatists) and sixty-seven "strangers" (people who were not part of the congregation) were aboard. In November, after a long and difficult voyage, they sighted land—the shore of what is now Cape Cod. That had not been their destination, but it was too late in the year to sail farther south. So the Pilgrims chose a site for their settlement in the area just north of the cape, a place John Smith had labeled "Plymouth" on a map he had drawn during his earlier exploration of New England. Because Plymouth lay outside the London Company's territory, the settlers were not bound by the company's rules. While still aboard ship, the saints in the group drew up an agreement, the Mayflower Compact, to establish a government for themselves. Then, on December 21, 1620, they stepped ashore at Plymouth Rock.

The Pilgrims' first winter was a difficult one. Half the colonists perished from malnutrition, disease, and exposure. But the colony survived, in large part because of crucial assistance from local Indians. Trade and other exchanges with the Indians were critical to the settlers and attractive to the natives. The tribes provided the colonists with furs. They also showed the settlers how to cultivate corn and how to hunt wild animals for meat. After the first autumn harvest, the settlers invited the natives to join them in a festival, the original Thanksgiving. But the relationship between the settlers and the local Indians was not a happy one for long. Thirteen years after the Pilgrims arrived, a devastating smallpox epidemic—a result of natives' exposure to Europeans carrying the disease—wiped out much of the Indian population around Plymouth.

The Pilgrims could not create rich farms on the sandy and marshy soil around Plymouth, but they developed a profitable trade in fish and furs. New colonists arrived from England, and in a decade the population reached 300. The people of Plymouth Plantation chose as their governor William Bradford, who governed successfully for many years. The Pilgrims were always poor. As late as the 1640s, they had only one plow among them. But they were, on the whole, content to be left alone to live their lives in what they considered godly ways.

THE MASSACHUSETTS BAY EXPERIMENT

Events in England encouraged other Puritans to migrate to the New World. King James I had repressed Puritans for years. When he died in 1625, his son and successor, Charles I, was even more hostile to Puritans and imprisoned many of them for their beliefs. The king dissolved Parliament in 1629 (it was not recalled until 1640), ensuring that there would be no one in a position to oppose him.

In the midst of this turmoil, a group of Puritan merchants began organizing a new colonial venture in America. They obtained a grant of land in New England for most of the area now comprising Massachusetts and New Hampshire. They acquired a charter from the king allowing them to create the Massachusetts Bay Company and to establish a colony in the New World. Some members of the Massachusetts Bay Company wanted to create a refuge in New England for Puritans. They bought out the interests of company members who preferred to stay in England, and the new owners elected a governor, John Winthrop. They then sailed for New England in 1630. With 17 ships and 1,000 people, it was the largest single migration of its kind in the seventeenth century. Winthrop carried with him the charter of the Massachusetts Bay Company, which meant that the colonists would be responsible to no company officials in England.

The Massachusetts migration quickly produced several settlements. The port of Boston became the capital, but in the course of the next decade colonists established several other towns in eastern Massachusetts: Charlestown, Newtown (later renamed Cambridge), Roxbury, Dorchester, Watertown, Ipswich, Concord, Sudbury, and others.

The Massachusetts Puritans were not grim or joyless, as many critics would later come to believe. But they were serious and pious. They strove to lead useful, conscientious lives of thrift and hard work, and they honored material success as evidence of God's favor. Winthrop and the other founders of Massachusetts believed they were founding a holy commonwealth, a model—a "city upon a hill"—for the corrupt world to see and emulate. Colonial Massachusetts was a "theocracy," a society in which the church was almost indistinguishable from the state. Residents had no more freedom of worship than the Puritans themselves had had in England.

Like other new settlements, the Massachusetts Bay colony had early difficulties. During the first winter (1629–1630), nearly 200 people died and many others decided to leave. But the colony soon grew and prospered. The nearby Pilgrims and neighboring Indians helped with food and advice. Incoming settlers brought needed tools and other goods. The dominance of families in the colony helped ensure a feeling of commitment to the community and a sense of order among the settlers, and it also ensured that the population would reproduce itself.

THE EXPANSION OF NEW ENGLAND

It did not take long for English settlement to begin moving outward from Massachusetts Bay. Some people migrated in search of soil more productive than the stony land around Boston. Others left because of the oppressiveness of the church-dominated government of Massachusetts.

The Connecticut River valley, about 100 miles west of Boston, began attracting English families as early as the 1630s because of its fertile lands and its isolation from Massachusetts Bay. In 1635, Thomas Hooker, a minister of Newtown (Cambridge), defied the Massachusetts government, led his congregation west, and established the town of Hartford. Four years later, the people of Hartford and of two other newly founded towns nearby adopted a constitution known as the Fundamental Orders of Connecticut, which created an independent colony with a government similar to that of Massachusetts Bay but gave a larger proportion of the men the right to vote and hold office. (Women were barred from voting virtually everywhere.)

Another Connecticut colony grew up around New Haven on the Connecticut coast. Unlike Hartford, the Fundamental Articles of New Haven (1639) established a Bible-based government even stricter than that of Massachusetts Bay. New Haven remained independent until 1662, when a royal charter officially gave the Hartford colony jurisdiction over the New Haven settlements.

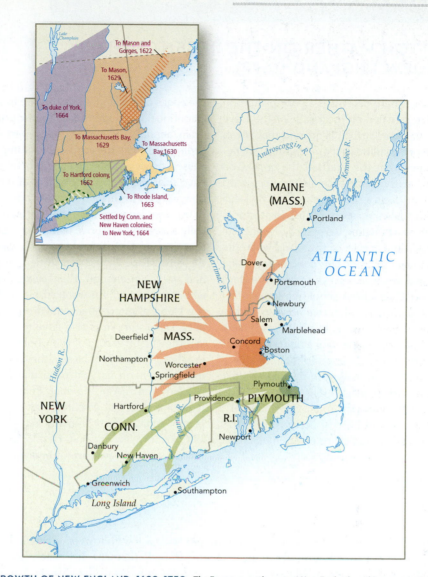

THE GROWTH OF NEW ENGLAND, 1620–1750 The European settlement of New England, as this map reveals, traces its origins primarily to two small settlements on the Atlantic Coast. The first was the Pilgrim settlement at Plymouth, which began in 1620 and spread out through Cape Cod, southern Massachusetts, and the islands of Martha's Vineyard and Nantucket. The second, much larger settlement began in Boston in 1630 and spread rapidly through western Massachusetts, north into New Hampshire and Maine, and south into Connecticut. • *Why would the settlers of Massachusetts Bay have expanded so much more rapidly and expansively than those of Plymouth?*

European settlement in what is now Rhode Island was a result of the religious and political dissent of Roger Williams, a controversial young minister who lived for a time in Salem, Massachusetts. Williams was a confirmed Separatist who argued that the Massachusetts church should abandon all allegiance to the Church of England. He also proclaimed that the land the colonists were occupying belonged to the natives. The colonial government voted to deport him, but he escaped before they could do so. During the winter of 1635–1636, he took refuge with Narragansett tribesmen; the following

COTTON MATHER ON THE RECENT HISTORY OF NEW ENGLAND (1692)

I believe there never was a poor plantation more pursued by the wrath of the Devil than our poor New England; and that which makes our condition very much the more deplorable is that the wrath of the great God himself at the same time also presses hard upon us. It was a rousing alarm to the Devil when a great company of English Protestants and Puritans came to erect evangelical churches in a corner of the world where he had reigned without any control for many ages; and it is a vexing eye-sore to the Devil that our Lord Christ should be known and owned and preached in this howling wilderness. Wherefore he has left no stone unturned, that so he might undermine this plantation and force us out of our country.

First, the Indian Powwows used all their sorceries to molest the first planters here; but God said unto them, "Touch them not!" Then, seducing spirits came to root in this vineyard, but God so rated them off that they have not prevailed much farther than the edges of our land. After this, we have had a continual blast upon some of our principal grain, annually diminishing a vast part of our ordinary food. Herewithal, wasting sicknesses, especially burning and mortal agues, have shot the arrows of death in at our windows. Next, we have had many adversaries of our own language, who have been perpetually assaying to deprive us of those English liberties in the encouragement whereof these territories have been settled. As if this had not been enough, the Tawnies among whom we came have watered our soil with the blood of many hundreds of our inhabitants. Desolating fires also have many times laid the chief treasure of the whole province in ashes. As for losses by sea, they have been multiplied upon us; and particularly in the present French War, the whole English nation have observed that no part of the nation has proportionately had so many vessels taken as our poor New England. Besides all which, now at last the devils are (if I may so speak)

spring he bought a tract of land from them, and with a few followers, created the town of Providence. In 1644, after obtaining a charter from Parliament, he established a government similar to that of Massachusetts but without any ties to the church. For a time, Rhode Island was the only colony in which all faiths (including Judaism) could worship without interference.

Another challenge to the established religious order in Massachusetts Bay came from Anne Hutchinson, an intelligent and charismatic woman from a substantial Boston family. She argued that many clergy were not among the "elect" and were, therefore, entitled to no spiritual authority. Such teachings (known as the Antinomian heresy) were a serious threat to the spiritual authority of the established clergy. Hutchinson also challenged prevailing assumptions about the proper role of women in Puritan society. As her influence grew, and as she began to deliver open attacks on members of the clergy, the Massachusetts hierarchy mobilized to stop her. In 1637, she was convicted of heresy and sedition and was banished. With her family and some of her followers, she moved to a point on Narragansett Bay not far from Providence. Later she moved south into New York, where in 1643 she and her family died during an Indian uprising.

in person come down upon us, with such a wrath as is justly much and will quickly be more the astonishment of the world. Alas, I may sigh over this wilderness, as Moses did over his, in Psalm 90.7, 9: "We are consumed by thine anger, and by thy wrath we are troubled: All our days are passed away in thy wrath." And I may add this unto it: the wrath of the Devil too has been troubling and spending of us all our days. . . .

Let us now make a good and a right use of the prodigious descent which the Devil in great wrath is at this day making upon our land. Upon the death of a great man once, an orator called the town together, crying out, "Concurrite cives, dilapsa cunt vestra moenia!" That is, "Come together neighbors, your town walls are fallen down!" But such is the descent of the Devil at this day upon our selves that I may truly tell you, the walls of the whole world are broken down! The usual walls of defense about mankind have such a gap made in them that the very devils are broke in upon us to seduce the souls, torment the bodies, sully the credits, and consume the estates of our neighbors, with impressions both as real and as furious as if the invisible world were becoming incarnate on purpose for the vexing of us. . . .

In as much as the devil is come down in great wrath, we had need labor, with all the care and speed we can, to divert the great wrath of Heaven from coming at the same time upon us. The God of Heaven has with long and loud admonitions been calling us to a reformation of our provoking evils as the only way to avoid that wrath of his which does not only threaten but consume us. It is because we have been deaf to those calls that we are now by a provoked God laid open to the wrath of the Devil himself.

UNDERSTAND, ANALYZE, & EVALUATE

1. According to Cotton Mather, what particular hardships did the colonists suffer?
2. What did Mather mean when he wrote that "now at last the devils [have descended] in person"?
3. What deeper explanation did Cotton Mather offer for New England's crisis? What response did he suggest?

Source: Cotton Mather, *The Wonders of the Invisible Word* (Boston, 1692), 41–43, 48; cited in Richard Godbeer, *The Salem Witch Hunt: A Brief History with Documents* (Boston: Bedford St. Martin's), pp. 48–49.

New Hampshire and Maine were established in 1629 by two English proprietors. But few settlers moved into these northern regions until the religious disruptions in Massachusetts Bay. In 1639, John Wheelwright, a disciple of Anne Hutchinson, led some of his fellow dissenters to Exeter, New Hampshire. Others soon followed. New Hampshire became a separate colony in 1679. Maine remained a part of Massachusetts until 1820.

SETTLERS AND NATIVES

The first white settlers in New England had generally friendly relations with the natives. Indians taught whites how to grow vital food crops such as corn, beans, pumpkins, and potatoes. European farmers also benefited from the extensive lands Indians had already cleared (and had either abandoned or sold). White traders used Indians as partners in some of their most important trading activities. Indeed, commerce with the Indians was responsible for the creation of some of the first great fortunes in British North America. Other white settlers attempted to educate the Indians in European religion and culture. Protestant missionaries converted some natives to Christianity, and a few Indians became at least partially assimilated into white society.

But as in other areas of white settlement, tensions soon developed—primarily as a result of the white colonists' insatiable appetite for land. The religious leaders of New England came to consider the tribes a threat to their hopes of creating a godly community in the New World. Gradually, the image of Indians as helpful neighbors came to be replaced by the image of Indians as "heathens" and barbarians.

KING PHILIP'S WAR AND THE TECHNOLOGY OF BATTLE

In 1637, hostilities broke out between English settlers in the Connecticut Valley and the Pequot Indians of the region, a conflict (known as the Pequot War) in which the natives were almost wiped out. But the bloodiest and most prolonged encounter between whites and Indians in the seventeenth century began in 1675, a conflict that whites called King Philip's War. The Wampanoag tribe, under the leadership of a chieftain known to the white settlers as King Philip and among his own people as Metacomet, rose up to resist the English. For three years, the natives inflicted terror on a string of Massachusetts towns, killing over a thousand people. But beginning in 1676, the white settlers gradually prevailed, with the help of a group of Mohawk allies who ambushed Metacomet and killed him. Without Metacomet, the fragile alliance among the tribes collapsed, and the white settlers were soon able to crush the uprising.

A PEQUOT VILLAGE DESTROYED An English artist drew this view of a fortified Pequot village in Connecticut surrounded by English soldiers and their allies from other tribes during the Pequot War in 1637. The invaders massacred more than 600 residents of the settlement. (Rare Books Division, New York Public Library, Astor, Lenox and Tilden Foundations)

The conflicts between natives and settlers were crucially affected by earlier exchanges of technology between the English and the tribes. In particular, the Indians made effective use of a relatively new European weapon that they acquired from the English: the flintlock rifle. It replaced the earlier staple of colonial musketry, the matchlock rifle, which proved too heavy, cumbersome, and inaccurate to be effective. The matchlock had to be steadied on a fixed object and ignited with a match before firing. The flintlock could be held up without support and fired without a match.

Many English settlers were slow to give up their matchlocks, but the Indians recognized the advantages of the newer rifles right away and began purchasing them in large quantities. Despite rules forbidding colonists to instruct natives on how to use and repair the weapons, the natives learned to handle the rifles, and even to repair them very effectively on their own. In King Philip's War, the very high casualties on both sides were a result of the use of these more advanced rifles.

Indians also used more traditional military technologies—especially the construction of forts. The Narragansett, allies of the Wampanoag in King Philip's War, built an enormous fort in the Great Swamp of Rhode Island in 1675, which became the site of one of the bloodiest battles of the war before English attackers burned it down. After that, a band of Narragansett set out to build a large stone fort, with the help of a member of the tribe who had learned masonry while working with the English. When English soldiers discovered the stone fort in 1676, after the end of King Philip's War, they killed most of its occupants and destroyed it. In the end, the technological skills of the Indians were no match for the overwhelming advantages of the English settlers in both numbers and firepower.

THE RESTORATION COLONIES

For nearly thirty years after Lord Baltimore received the charter for Maryland in 1632, no new English colonies were established in America. England was dealing with troubles of its own at home.

THE ENGLISH CIVIL WAR

After Charles I dissolved Parliament in 1629 and began ruling as an absolute monarch, he alienated a growing number of his subjects. Finally, desperately in need of money, Charles called Parliament back into session in 1640 and asked it to levy new taxes. But he antagonized the members by dismissing them twice in two years; and in 1642, members of Parliament organized a military force, thus beginning the English Civil War.

The conflict between the Cavaliers (the supporters of the king) and the Roundheads (the forces of Parliament, who were largely Puritans) lasted seven years. In 1649, the Roundheads defeated the king's forces and shocked all of Europe by beheading the monarch. The stern Roundhead leader Oliver Cromwell assumed the position of "protector." But when Cromwell died in 1658, his son and heir proved unable to maintain his authority. Two years later, Charles II, son of the executed king, returned from exile and seized the throne, in what became known as the Restoration.

Among the results of the Restoration was the resumption of colonization in America. Charles II rewarded faithful courtiers with grants of land in the New World, and in the twenty-five years of his reign he issued charters for four additional colonies: Carolina, New York, New Jersey, and Pennsylvania.

Charles II faced some of the same problems that his father had confronted, mostly because of the belief that he was secretly a Roman Catholic. The king supported religious toleration—which would allow Catholicism again in England, to the dismay of many Protestants. The Parliament refused to agree. Charles was prudent enough not to fight for the right of Catholics to worship openly. But he himself made a private agreement with Louis XIV of France that he would become a Catholic—which he did only on his deathbed. His son, James II, faced many of the same problems.

THE CAROLINAS

In charters issued in 1663 and 1665, Charles II awarded joint title to eight proprietors. They received a vast territory stretching south from Virginia to the Florida peninsula and west to the Pacific Ocean. Like Lord Baltimore, they received almost kingly powers over their grant, which they prudently called Carolina (a name derived from the Latin word for "Charles"). They reserved tremendous estates for themselves and distributed the rest through a headright system similar to those in Virginia and Maryland. Although committed Anglicans themselves, the proprietors guaranteed religious freedom to all Christian faiths. They also created a representative assembly. They hoped to attract settlers from the existing American colonies and to avoid the expense of financing expeditions from England.

But their initial efforts to profit from settlement in Carolina failed dismally. Anthony Ashley Cooper, however, persisted. He convinced the other proprietors to finance expeditions to Carolina from England, the first of which set sail with 300 people in the spring of 1670. The 100 people who survived the difficult voyage established a settlement at Port Royal on the Carolina coast. Ten years later, they founded a city at the junction of the Ashley and Cooper rivers, which in 1690 became the colonial capital. They called it Charles Town (it was later renamed Charleston).

With the aid of the English philosopher John Locke, Cooper (now the earl of Shaftesbury) drew up the Fundamental Constitution for Carolina in 1669. It divided the colony into counties of equal size and divided each county into equal parcels. It also established a social hierarchy with the proprietors themselves (who were to be known as "seigneurs") at the top, a local aristocracy (consisting of lesser nobles known as "landgraves" or "caciques") below them, and then ordinary settlers ("leet-men"). At the bottom of this stratified society would be poor whites, who would have few political rights, and African slaves. Proprietors, nobles, and other landholders would have a voice in the colonial parliament in proportion to the size of their landholdings.

In reality, Carolina developed along lines quite different from the carefully ordered vision of Shaftesbury and Locke. For one thing, the northern and southern regions of settlement were widely separated and socially and economically distinct from each other. The northern settlers were mainly backwoods farmers. In the South, fertile lands and the good harbor at Charles Town promoted a more prosperous economy and a more stratified, aristocratic society. Settlements grew up rapidly along the Ashley and Cooper rivers, and colonists established a flourishing trade, particularly (beginning in the 1660s) in rice.

Southern Carolina very early developed commercial ties to the large (and overpopulated) European colony on the Caribbean island of Barbados. During the first ten years of settlement, in fact, most of the new residents in Carolina were Barbadians, some of whom established themselves as substantial landlords. African slavery had taken root on Barbados earlier than in any of the mainland colonies, and the white Caribbean migrants—tough, uncompromising profit seekers—established a similar slave-based plantation society in Carolina.

Carolina was one of the most divided English colonies in America. There were tensions between the small farmers of the Albemarle region in the north and the wealthy planters in the south. And there were conflicts between the rich Barbadians in southern Carolina and the smaller landowners around them. After Lord Shaftesbury's death, the proprietors proved unable to establish order. In 1719, the colonists seized control of the colony from them. Ten years later, the king divided the region into two royal colonies, North Carolina and South Carolina.

New Netherland, New York, and New Jersey

In 1664, Charles II granted his brother James, the duke of York, all the territory lying between the Connecticut and Delaware rivers. But the grant faced a major challenge from the Dutch, who also claimed the area.

In 1664, vessels of the English navy, under the command of Richard Nicolls, put in at New Amsterdam, the capital of the Dutch colony of New Netherland, and extracted a surrender from the governor, Peter Stuyvesant. Several years later, in 1673, the Dutch reconquered and briefly held their old provincial capital. But they lost it again, this time for good, in 1674.

The duke of York renamed his territory New York. It contained not only Dutch and English but also Scandinavians, Germans, French, and a large number of Africans (imported as slaves by the Dutch West India Company), as well as members of several different Indian tribes. James wisely made no effort to impose his own Roman Catholicism on the colony. He delegated powers to a governor and a council but made no provision for representative assemblies.

Property holding and political power remained highly divided and highly unequal in New York. In addition to confirming the great Dutch "patroonships" already in existence, James granted large estates to some of his own political supporters. Power in the colony thus remained widely dispersed among wealthy English landlords, Dutch patroons, wealthy fur traders, and the duke's political appointees. By 1685, when the duke of York ascended the English throne as James II, New York contained about four times as many people (around 30,000) as it had twenty years before.

Shortly after James received his charter, he gave a large part of the land south of New York to a pair of political allies, both Carolina proprietors, Sir John Berkeley and Sir George Carteret. Carteret named the territory New Jersey. But the venture in New Jersey generated few profits, and in 1674, Berkeley sold his half interest. The colony was divided into two jurisdictions, East Jersey and West Jersey, which squabbled with each other until 1702, when the two halves of the colony were again joined. New Jersey, like New York, was a colony of enormous ethnic and religious diversity, and the weak colonial government made few efforts to impose strict control over the fragmented society. But unlike New York, New Jersey developed no important class of large landowners.

The Quaker Colonies

Pennsylvania was born out of the efforts of a dissenting English Protestant sect, the Society of Friends. They wished to find a home for their own distinctive social order. The Society began in the mid-seventeenth century under the leadership of George Fox, a Nottingham shoemaker, and Margaret Fell. Their followers came to be known as Quakers (from Fox's instruction to them to "tremble at the name of the Lord"). Unlike the Puritans, Quakers rejected the concept of predestination and original sin. All people, they believed, had divinity within themselves and needed only learn to cultivate it; all could attain salvation.

The Quakers had no formal church government and no paid clergy; in their worship they spoke up one by one as the spirit moved them. Disregarding distinctions of gender and class, they addressed one another with the terms "thee" and "thou," words commonly used in other parts of English society only in speaking to servants and social inferiors. As confirmed pacifists, they would not take part in wars. Unpopular in England, the Quakers began looking to America for asylum. A few migrated to New England or Carolina, but most Quakers wanted a colony of their own. As members of a despised sect, however, they could not get the necessary royal grant without the aid of someone influential at the court.

Fortunately for the Quaker cause, a number of wealthy and prominent men had converted to the faith. One of them was William Penn, who, over his aristocratic father's objections, converted to Quakerism, took up evangelism, and had been in prison several times. He soon began working with George Fox to create a Quaker colony in America. When his father died in 1681, Charles II settled a large debt he had owed to the older Penn by making an enormous grant to the son of territory between New York and Maryland. At the king's insistence, the territory was to be named Pennsylvania, after Penn's late father.

Through his informative and honest advertising, Penn soon made Pennsylvania the best-known and most cosmopolitan of all the English colonies in America. More than any other English colony, Pennsylvania prospered from the outset because of Penn's successful recruiting, his careful planning, and the region's mild climate and fertile soil. Penn sailed to Pennsylvania in 1682 to oversee the laying out of the city he named Philadelphia ("Brotherly Love") between the Delaware and Schuylkill rivers.

Penn's relatively good relations with the Indians were a result in large part of his religious beliefs. Quakerism was a faith that included a refusal to participate in war or any violence and that believed that all people, whatever their background, were capable of becoming Christian. Penn worked to respect the natives and their culture. He recognized Indians' claim to the land in the province, and he was usually scrupulous in reimbursing the natives for their land. In later years, the relationships between the English residents of Pennsylvania and the natives were not always so peaceful.

By the late 1690s, some residents of Pennsylvania were beginning to resist the nearly absolute power of the proprietor. Pressure from these groups grew to the point that in 1701, shortly before he departed for England for the last time, Penn agreed to a Charter of Liberties for the colony. The charter established a representative assembly (consisting, alone among the English colonies, of only one house) that greatly limited the authority of the proprietor. The charter also permitted "the lower counties" of the colony to establish their own representative assembly. The three counties did so in 1703 and as a result became, in effect, a separate colony—Delaware—although until the American Revolution it continued to have the same governor as Pennsylvania.

BORDERLANDS AND MIDDLE GROUNDS

The English colonies clustered along the Atlantic seaboard of North America eventually united, expanded, and became the beginnings of a great nation. But in the seventeenth and early eighteenth centuries, their future was not at all clear. In those years, they were small, frail settlements surrounded by other, competing societies and settlements. The British Empire in North America was, in fact, a much smaller and weaker one than the great Spanish Empire to the south, and in many ways weaker than the enormous French Empire to the north.

The continuing contests for control of North America were most clearly visible in areas around the borders of English settlement—the Caribbean and along the northern, southern, and western borders of the coastal colonies. In the regions of the borderlands emerged societies very different from those in the English seaboard colonies—areas described as middle grounds, in which diverse civilizations encountered one another and, for a time at least, shaped one another.

THE CARIBBEAN ISLANDS

The Chesapeake was the site of the first permanent English settlements in the North American continent. Throughout the first half of the seventeenth century, however, the most important destinations for English immigrants were the islands of the Caribbean and the northern way station of Bermuda. More than half of the English migrants to the New World in the early seventeenth century settled on these islands.

Before the arrival of Europeans, most of the Caribbean islands had substantial native populations. But beginning with Christopher Columbus's first visit in 1492, and accelerating after 1496, the native populations were all but wiped out by European epidemics.

The Spanish Empire claimed title to all the islands in the Caribbean, but Spain created substantial settlements only on the largest of them: Cuba, Hispaniola, and Puerto Rico. English, French, and Dutch traders began settling on some of the smaller islands early in the sixteenth century, despite the Spanish claim to them. After Spain and the Netherlands went to war in 1621 (distracting the Spanish navy and leaving the English in the Caribbean relatively unmolested), the pace of English colonization increased. By midcentury, there were several substantial English settlements on the islands, the most important of them on Antigua, St. Kitts, Jamaica, and Barbados.

In their first years in the Caribbean, English settlers experimented unsuccessfully with tobacco and cotton. But they soon discovered that the most lucrative crop was sugar, for which there was a substantial and growing market in Europe. Sugarcane could also be distilled into rum, for which there was also a booming market abroad. Planters devoted almost all of their land to sugarcane.

Because sugar was a labor-intensive crop, English planters quickly found it necessary to import laborers. As in the Chesapeake, they began by bringing indentured servants from England. But the arduous work discouraged white laborers. By midcentury, therefore, the English planters in the Caribbean (like the Spanish colonists) were relying more and more heavily on an enslaved African workforce, which soon substantially outnumbered them.

On Barbados and other islands where a flourishing sugar economy developed, the English planters were a tough, aggressive, and ambitious people. Since their livelihoods depended on their workforces, they expanded and solidified the system of African slavery there remarkably quickly. By the late seventeenth century, there were four times as many African slaves as there were white settlers.

MASTERS AND SLAVES IN THE CARIBBEAN

Fearful of slave revolts, whites in the Caribbean monitored their labor forces closely and often harshly. Planters paid little attention to the welfare of their workers. Many concluded that it was cheaper to buy new slaves periodically than to protect the well-being of those they already owned, and it was not uncommon for masters literally to work their slaves to death. Few African workers survived more than a decade in the brutal Caribbean working environment—they were either sold to planters in North America or died. Even whites, who worked far less hard than did the slaves, often succumbed to the harsh climate; most died before the age of forty.

Establishing a stable society and culture was extremely difficult for people living in such harsh and even deadly conditions. White landowners in the Caribbean islands returned to England with their fortunes when they could and left their estates in the hands of overseers. Europeans in the Caribbean lacked many of the institutions that gave stability to the North American settlements: church, family, community.

Africans in the Caribbean faced much greater difficulties than did whites, but because they had no chance of leaving, they created what was in many ways a more elaborate culture than did the white settlers. They started families (although many of them were broken up by death or the slave trade); they sustained African religious and social traditions (and resisted Christianity); and within the rigidly controlled world of the sugar plantations, they established patterns of resistance.

The Caribbean settlements were an important part of the Atlantic trading world in which many Americans became involved—a source of sugar and rum and a market for goods made in the mainland colonies and in England. They were the first principal source of African slaves for the mainland colonies.

THE SOUTHWEST BORDERLANDS

By the end of the seventeenth century, the Spanish had established a sophisticated and impressive empire. Their capital, Mexico City, was the most dazzling metropolis in the Americas. The Spanish residents, well over a million, enjoyed much greater prosperity than all but a few English settlers in North America.

But the principal Spanish colonies north of Mexico—Florida, Texas, New Mexico, Arizona, and California—were relatively unimportant economically to the empire. They attracted religious minorities, Catholic missionaries, and independent ranchers fleeing the heavy hand of imperial authority. Spanish troops defended the northern flank of the empire. But they remained weak and peripheral parts of the great empire to their south.

New Mexico was the most prosperous and populous of these Spanish outposts. By the end of the eighteenth century, New Mexico had a non-Indian population of over 10,000—the largest European settlement west of the Mississippi and north of Mexico—and it was steadily expanding through the region.

The Spanish began to colonize California once they realized that other Europeans—among them English merchants and French and Russian trappers—were beginning to establish a presence in the region. Formal Spanish settlement of California began in the 1760s, when the governor of Baja California was ordered to create outposts of the empire farther north. Soon a string of missions, forts (or *presidios*), and trading communities were springing up along the Pacific Coast: beginning with San Diego and Monterey in 1769 and eventually San Francisco (1776), Los Angeles (1781), and Santa Barbara (1786). The arrival of the Spanish in California had a devastating effect on the native population, who died in great numbers from the diseases the colonists imported. As the new settlements spread, the Spanish insisted that the remaining natives convert to Catholicism. That explains the centrality of missions in almost all the major Spanish outposts in California. But the Spanish colonists were also intent on creating a prosperous agricultural economy, and they enlisted Indian laborers to help them do so. California's Indians had no choice but to accede to the demands of the Spanish, although there were frequent revolts by natives against the harsh conditions imposed on them.

The Spanish considered the greatest threat to the northern borders of their empire to be the growing ambitions of the French. In the 1680s, French explorers traveled down the Mississippi Valley to the mouth of the river and claimed those lands for France in 1682. They called the territory Louisiana. Fearful of French incursions farther west, the Spanish began to fortify their claim to Texas by establishing new forts, missions, and settlements there, including San Fernando (later San Antonio) in 1731. Much of the region that is now Arizona was also becoming increasingly tied to the Spanish Empire and was governed from Santa Fe.

The Spanish colonies in the Southwest were the sparsely populated edges of the great Spanish Empire to the south—created less to increase the wealth of the empire than to defend it from threats by other European powers in the North. Nevertheless, these Spanish outposts helped create enduring societies that were very unlike those being established by the English along the Atlantic seaboard. The Spanish colonies did not displace the native populations. Rather they enlisted them. They sought to convert them to Catholicism, to recruit them (sometimes forcibly) as agricultural workers, and to cultivate them as trading partners.

THE SOUTHEAST BORDERLANDS

The southeastern areas of what is now the United States posed a direct challenge to English ambitions in North America. After Spain claimed Florida in the 1560s, missionaries and traders began moving northward into Georgia and westward into what is now known as the Florida panhandle. Some ambitious Spaniards began to dream of expanding their empire still farther north, into what became the Carolinas and beyond. The founding of Jamestown in 1607 dampened those hopes and replaced them with fears. The English colonies, the Spaniards feared, could threaten their existing settlements in Florida and Georgia. As a result, the Spanish built forts in both regions to defend themselves against the increasing English presence there. Throughout the eighteenth century, the area between the Carolinas and Florida was the site of continuing tension and frequent conflict, between the Spanish and the English—and, to a lesser degree, between the Spanish and the French, who were threatening their northwestern borders with settlements in Louisiana and in what is now Alabama.

There was no formal war between England and Spain in these years, but that did not dampen the hostilities in the Southeast. English pirates continually harassed the Spanish settlements and, in 1668, actually sacked St. Augustine. The English encouraged Indians in Florida to rise up against the Spanish missions. The Spanish offered freedom to African slaves owned by English settlers in the Carolinas if they agreed to convert to Catholicism. About 100 Africans accepted the offer, and the Spanish later organized some of them into a military regiment to defend the northern border of New Spain. By the early eighteenth century, the constant fighting in the region had driven almost all the Spanish out of Florida except for settlers in St. Augustine on the Atlantic Coast and Pensacola on the Gulf Coast.

Eventually, after more than a century of conflict in the southeastern borderlands, the English prevailed—acquiring Florida in the aftermath of the Seven Years' War (known in America as the French and Indian War) and rapidly populating it with settlers from their colonies to the North. Before that point, however, protecting the southern boundary of the British Empire in North America was a continual concern to the English and contributed in crucial ways to the founding of the colony of Georgia.

THE FOUNDING OF GEORGIA

Georgia—the last English colony to be established in what would become the United States—was founded to create a military barrier against Spanish lands on the southern border of English America. It was also designed to provide a refuge for the impoverished, a place where English men and women without prospects at home could begin anew. Its founders, led by General James Oglethorpe, served as unpaid trustees of a society created to serve the needs of the British Empire.

Oglethorpe, himself a veteran of the most recent Spanish wars with England, was keenly aware of the military advantages of an English colony south of the Carolinas. Yet his interest in settlement rested even more on his philanthropic commitments. As head of a parliamentary committee investigating English prisons, he had been appalled by the plight of honest debtors rotting in confinement. Such prisoners, and other poor people in danger of succumbing to a similar fate, could, he believed, become the farmer-soldiers of the new colony in America.

In 1732, King George II granted Oglethorpe and his fellow trustees control of the land between the Savannah and Altamaha rivers. Their colonization policies reflected the vital military purposes of the colony. They limited the size of landholdings to make the settlement compact and easier to defend against Spanish and Indian attacks. They excluded Africans, free or slave; Oglethorpe feared that slave labor would produce internal revolts and that disaffected slaves might turn to the Spanish as allies. The trustees strictly regulated trade with the Indians, again to limit the possibility of wartime insurrection. They also excluded Catholics for fear they might collude with their coreligionists in the Spanish colonies to the south.

Oglethorpe himself led the first colonial expedition to Georgia, which built a fortified town at the mouth of the Savannah River in 1733 and later constructed additional forts south of the Altamaha. In the end, only a few debtors were released from jail and sent to Georgia. Instead, the trustees brought hundreds of impoverished tradesmen and artisans from England and Scotland and many religious refugees from Switzerland and Germany. Among the immigrants was a small group of Jews. English settlers made up a lower proportion of the European population of Georgia than of any other English colony.

Oglethorpe (whom some residents of Georgia began calling "our perpetual dictator") created almost constant dissensions and conflict through his heavy-handed regulation of the colony. He also suffered military disappointments, such as a 1740 assault on the Spanish outpost at St. Augustine, Florida, which ended in failure. Gradually, as the threats from Spain receded, he lost his grip on the colony, which over time became more like the rest of British North America, with an elected legislature that loosened the restrictions on settlers. Georgia continued to grow more slowly than the other southern colonies, but in other ways it now developed along lines roughly similar to those of South Carolina.

MIDDLE GROUNDS

The struggle for the North American continent was not just one among competing European empires. It was also a series of contests among the many different peoples who shared the continent—the Spanish, English, French, Dutch, and other colonists, on one hand, and the many Indian tribes with whom they shared the continent, on the other.

In some parts of the British Empire—Virginia and New England, for example—English settlers fairly quickly established their dominance, subjugating and displacing most natives until they had established societies that were dominated almost entirely by Europeans. But in other regions, the balance of power was for many years far more precarious. Along the western borders of English settlement, in particular, Europeans and Indians lived together in regions in which neither side was able to establish clear dominance. In these middle grounds, the two populations—despite frequent conflicts—carved out ways of living together, with each side making concessions to the other.

These were the peripheries of empires, in which the influence of formal colonial governments was at times almost invisible. European settlers, and the soldiers scattered in forts throughout these regions to protect them, were unable to displace the Indians. So they had to carve out their own relationships with the tribes. In those relationships, the Europeans found themselves obligated to adapt to tribal expectations at least as much as the Indians had to adapt to European ones.

To the Indians, the European migrants were both menacing and appealing. They feared the power of these strange European people: their guns, their rifles, their forts. But they also wanted the French and British settlers to behave like "fathers"—to help them mediate their own internal disputes, to offer them gifts, to moderate their conflicts. Europeans came from a world in which the formal institutional and military power of a nation or empire governed relationships between societies. But the natives had no understanding of the modern notion of a "nation" and thought much more in terms of ceremony and kinship. Gradually, Europeans learned to fulfill at least some of their expectations—to settle disputes among tribes, to moderate conflicts within tribes, to participate solemnly in Indian ceremonies, and to offer gifts as signs of respect.

In the seventeenth century, before many English settlers had entered the interior, the French were particularly adept at creating successful relationships with the tribes. French migrants in the interior regions of the continent were often solitary fur traders, and some of them welcomed the chance to attach themselves to—even to marry within—tribes. They also recognized the importance of treating tribal chiefs with respect and channeling gifts and tributes through them. But by the mid-eighteenth century, French influence in the interior was in decline, and British settlers gradually became the dominant European group in the middle grounds. Eventually, the British learned the lessons that the French had long ago absorbed—that simple commands and raw force were ineffective in creating a workable relationship with the tribes; that they too had to learn to deal with Indian leaders through gifts and ceremonies and mediation. In large western regions—especially those around the Great Lakes—they established a precarious peace with the tribes that lasted for several decades.

But as the British (and after 1776) American presence in the region grew, the balance of power between Europeans and natives shifted. Newer settlers had difficulty adapting to the complex rituals that the earlier migrants had developed. The stability of the relationship between the Indians and whites deteriorated. By the early nineteenth century, the middle ground had collapsed, replaced by a European world in which Indians were ruthlessly subjugated and eventually removed. Nevertheless, for a considerable period of early American history, the story of the relationship between whites and Indians was not simply a story of conquest and subjugation, but also—in some regions—a story of difficult but stable accommodation and tolerance.

NATIVE AMERICANS AND THE MIDDLE GROUND

FOR many generations, historians chronicling the westward movement of European settlement in North America portrayed Native Americans largely as weak and inconvenient obstacles swept aside by the inevitable progress of "civilization." Indians were presented either as murderous savages or as relatively docile allies of white people, but rarely as important actors of their own. Francis Parkman, the great nineteenth-century American historian, described Indians as a civilization "crushed" and "scorned" by the march of European powers in the New World. Many subsequent historians departed little from his assessment.

In more recent years, historians have challenged this traditional view by examining how white civilization victimized the tribes. Gary Nash's *Red, White, and Black* (1974) was one of the important modern presentations of this approach, and Ramon Guttierez's *When Jesus Came, the Corn Mothers Went* (1991) was a more recent contribution. They, and other scholars, rejected the optimistic, progressive view of white triumph over adversity and presented, instead, a picture of white brutality and futile Indian resistance, ending in defeat.

More recently, however, a new view of the relationship between the peoples of the Old and New Worlds has emerged. It sees Native Americans and Euro-Americans as uneasy partners in the shaping of a new society in which, for a time at least, both were a vital part. Richard White's influential 1991 book, *The Middle Ground,* was among the first important statements of this view. White examined the culture of the Great Lakes region in the eighteenth century, in which Algonquian Indians created a series of complex trading and political relationships with French, English, and American settlers and travelers. In this "borderland" between the growing European settlements in the east and the still largely intact Indian civilizations farther west, a new kind of hybrid society emerged in which many cultures intermingled. James Merrell's *Into the American Woods* (1999) contributed further to this new view of collaboration by examining the world of negotiators and go-betweens along the western Pennsylvania frontier in the seventeenth and eighteenth centuries. Like White, he emphasized the complicated blend of European and Native American diplomatic rituals that allowed both groups to conduct business, make treaties, and keep the peace.

Daniel Richter extended the idea of a middle ground further in two important books: *The Ordeal of the Long-house* (1992) and *Facing East from Indian Country* (2001). Richter demonstrates that the Iroquois Confederacy was an active participant in the power relationships in the Hudson River basin; and in his later book, he tells the story of European colonization from the Native American perspective, revealing how Western myths of "first contact" such as the story of John Smith and Pocahontas look entirely different when seen through the eyes of Native Americans, who remained in many ways the more powerful of the two societies in the seventeenth century.

How did these important collaborations collapse? What happened to the middle ground? Over time, the delicate partnerships along the frontiers of white settlement gave

(Historical Society of Pennsylvania [AM 1702 CAM])

way to the sheer numbers of Europeans (and in some places Africans) who moved westward. Joyce Chaplin's *Subject Matter* (2001) argues as well that Old World Americans at first admired the natives as a kind of natural nobility until European diseases ravaged the tribes. Their vulnerability to disease strengthened the sense of superiority among Europeans that had been a part of their view of Indians from the beginning. Jill Lepore's *The Name of War* (1998) describes how the violence of King Philip's War in seventeenth-century New England helped transform English views of the tribes. That was because of the white victory over the Indians and because of their success in turning this victory into a rationale for the moral superiority of Europeans. In fact, Europeans had used at least as much "savagery" against the natives as the natives had used against them. As the pressures of white settlement grew, as the Indian populations weakened as a result of disease and war, and as the relationship between the tribes and the European settlers grew more and more unequal, the cultural middle ground that for many decades characterized much of the contact between the Old and New Worlds gradually disappeared. By the time historians began seriously chronicling this story in the late nineteenth century, the Indian tribes had indeed become the defeated, helpless "obstacles" that they portrayed. But for generations before, the relationship between white Americans and Native Americans was much more equal than it later became.   •

UNDERSTAND, ANALYZE, & EVALUATE

1. How have historians' views of Native Americans and their role in the European colonization of North America changed over time?
2. Why did the "middle ground" between Native Americans and European settlers disappear?

THE DEVELOPMENT OF EMPIRE

The English colonies in America had begun as separate projects, and for the most part they grew up independent of one another and subject to only nominal control from London. But by the mid-seventeenth century, the growing commercial success of the colonial ventures was producing pressure in England for a more uniform structure to the empire.

The English government began trying to regulate colonial trade in the 1650s, when Parliament passed laws to keep Dutch ships out of the English colonies. Later, Parliament passed three important Navigation Acts. The first of them, in 1660, closed the colonies to all trade except that carried by English ships. The British also required that tobacco and other items be exported from the colonies only to England or to English possessions. The second act, in 1663, required that all goods sent from Europe to the colonies pass through England on the way, where they would be subject to English taxation. The third act, in 1673, imposed duties on the coastal trade among the English colonies, and it provided for the appointment of customs officials to enforce the Navigation Acts. These acts formed the legal basis of England's regulation of the colonies for a century.

THE DOMINION OF NEW ENGLAND

Before the creation of Navigation Acts, all the colonial governments except that of Virginia had operated largely independently of the crown, with governors chosen by the proprietors or by the colonists themselves and with powerful representative assemblies. Officials in London recognized that to increase their control over the colonies, they would have to increase British authority in order to enforce the new laws.

In 1675, the king created a new body, the Lords of Trade, to make recommendations for imperial reform. In 1679, the king moved to increase his control over Massachusetts. He stripped it of its authority over New Hampshire and chartered a separate, royal colony there whose governor he would himself appoint. And in 1684, citing the colonial assembly's defiance of the Navigation Acts, he revoked the Massachusetts charter.

Charles II's brother, James II, who succeeded him to the throne in 1685, went further. He created a single Dominion of New England, which combined the government of Massachusetts with the governments of the rest of the New England colonies and later with those of New York and New Jersey as well. He appointed a single governor, Sir Edmund Andros, to supervise the entire region from Boston. Andros's rigid enforcement of the Navigation Acts and his brusque dismissal of the colonists' claims to the "rights of Englishmen" made him highly unpopular.

THE "GLORIOUS REVOLUTION"

James II, unlike his father, was openly Catholic. In addition, he made powerful enemies as he appointed his fellow Catholics to high offices. The restoration of Catholicism led to fears that the Vatican and the pope would soon overtake England, and that the king would support him. At the same time, he tried to control Parliament and the courts, making himself an absolute monarch. By 1688, the opposition to the king was so great that Parliament voted to force out James II, who showed no resistance to giving up the crown, aware of his grandfather's execution. He eventually left the country and spent the rest of his life in France. His daughter, Mary II, and her husband, William of Orange, of the Netherlands—both Protestants—replaced James II to reign jointly. No

Catholic monarch has reigned since. This bloodless coup came to be known as the "Glorious Revolution."

When Bostonians heard of the overthrow of James II, they arrested and imprisoned the unpopular Andros. The new sovereigns in England abolished the Dominion of New England and restored separate colonial governments. In 1691, however, they combined Massachusetts with Plymouth and made it a single, royal colony. The new charter restored the colonial assembly, but it gave the crown the right to appoint the governor. It also replaced church membership with property ownership as the basis for voting and officeholding.

Andros had been governing New York through a lieutenant governor, Captain Francis Nicholson, who enjoyed the support of the wealthy merchants and fur traders of the province. Other, less-favored colonists had a long accumulation of grievances against Nicholson and his allies. The leader of the New York dissidents was Jacob Leisler, a German merchant. In May 1689, when news of the Glorious Revolution and the fall of Andros reached New York, Leisler raised a militia, captured the city fort, drove Nicholson into exile, and proclaimed himself the new head of government in New York. For two years, he tried in vain to stabilize his power in the colony amid fierce factional rivalry. In 1691, when William and Mary appointed a new governor, Leisler briefly resisted. He was convicted of treason and executed. Fierce rivalry between what became known as the "Leislerians" and the "anti-Leislerians" dominated the politics of the colony for years thereafter.

In Maryland, many people wrongly assumed that their proprietor, the Catholic Lord Baltimore, who was living in England, had sided with the Catholic James II and opposed William and Mary. So in 1689, an old opponent of the proprietor's government, the Protestant John Coode, led a revolt that drove out Lord Baltimore's officials and led to Maryland's establishment as a royal colony in 1691. The colonial assembly then established the Church of England as the colony's official religion and excluded Catholics from public office. Maryland became a proprietary colony again in 1715, after the fifth Lord Baltimore joined the Anglican Church.

The Glorious Revolution of 1688 in England touched off revolutions, mostly bloodless ones, in several colonies. Under the new king and queen, the representative assemblies that had been abolished were revived, and the scheme for colonial unification from above was abandoned. But the Glorious Revolution in America did not stop the reorganization of the empire. The new governments that emerged in America actually increased the crown's potential authority. As the first century of English settlement in America came to its end, the colonists were becoming more a part of the imperial system than ever before.

CONCLUSION

The English colonization of North America was part of a larger effort by several European nations to expand the reach of their increasingly commercial societies. Indeed, for many years, the British Empire in America was among the smallest and weakest of the imperial ventures there, overshadowed by the French to the north and the Spanish to the south.

In the British colonies along the Atlantic seaboard, new agricultural and commercial societies gradually emerged—those in the South centered on the cultivation of tobacco and cotton and were reliant on slave labor; those in the northern colonies centered on more traditional food crops and were based mostly on free labor. Substantial trading centers emerged in such cities as Boston, New York, Philadelphia, and Charleston, and a growing proportion of the population became prosperous and settled in these increasingly complex communities. By the early eighteenth century, English settlement had spread from northern New England (in what is now Maine) south into Georgia.

But this growing British Empire coexisted with, and often found itself in conflict with, the presence of other Europeans—most notably the Spanish and the French—in other areas of North America. In these borderlands, societies did not assume the settled, prosperous form they were taking in the Tidewater and New England. They were raw, sparsely populated settlements in which Europeans, including over time increasing numbers of English, had to learn to accommodate not only one another but also the still-substantial Indian tribes with whom they shared these interior lands. By the middle of the eighteenth century, there was a significant European presence across a broad swath of North America—from Florida to Maine, and from Texas to Mexico to California—only a relatively small part of it controlled by the British. But changes were under way within the British Empire that would soon lead to its dominance through a much larger area of North America.

RECALL AND REFLECT

1. Compare patterns of settlement and expansion in the Chesapeake with those in New England. What were the major differences? Were there any similarities?
2. What were the reasons for the revolts and rebellions that occurred in the colonies of Virginia, Maryland, Massachusetts, and New York between 1660 and 1700? How were these rebellions resolved?
3. How did the institution of slavery in England's Atlantic seaboard colonies differ from slavery in the Caribbean? What accounted for these differences?
4. What were the middle grounds, and how did conditions there differ from conditions in the colonies along the Atlantic seaboard?
5. How did the Glorious Revolution in England affect England's North American colonies?

3 SOCIETY AND CULTURE IN PROVINCIAL AMERICA

THE COLONIAL POPULATION
THE COLONIAL ECONOMIES
PATTERNS OF SOCIETY
AWAKENINGS AND ENLIGHTENMENTS

LOOKING AHEAD

1. What accounted for the rapid increase in the colonial population in the seventeenth century?
2. Why did African slavery expand so rapidly in the late seventeenth century?
3. How did religion shape and influence colonial society?

MOST PEOPLE IN BOTH ENGLAND and America believed that the British colonies were outposts of the British world. And it is true that as the colonies grew and became more prosperous, they also became more English. Some of the early settlers had come to America to escape what they considered English tyranny. But by the early eighteenth century, many, perhaps most, colonists considered themselves English just as much as the men and women in England itself did.

At the same time, however, life in the colonies was diverging in many ways from England simply by the nature of the New World. The physical environment was very different—vaster and less tamed. The population was more diverse as well. The area that would become the United States was a magnet for immigrants from many lands other than England: Scotland, Ireland, the European continent, eastern Russia, and the Spanish and French empires already established in America. English North America became as well the destination for thousands of forcibly transplanted Africans.

To the degree that the colonists emulated English society, they were becoming more and more like one another. To the degree that they were shaped by the character of their own regions, they were becoming more and more different.

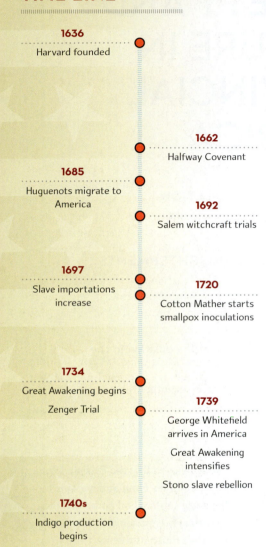

1636
Harvard founded

1662
Halfway Covenant

1685
Huguenots migrate to America

1692
Salem witchcraft trials

1697
Slave importations increase

1720
Cotton Mather starts smallpox inoculations

1734
Great Awakening begins

Zenger Trial

1739
George Whitefield arrives in America

Great Awakening intensifies

Stono slave rebellion

1740s
Indigo production begins

THE COLONIAL POPULATION

After uncertain beginnings, the non-Indian population of English North America grew rapidly and substantially, through continued immigration and through natural increase. By the late seventeenth century, European and African immigrants outnumbered the natives along the Atlantic Coast.

A few of the early settlers were members of the English upper classes, but the dominant group was English laborers. Some came independently, such as the religious dissenters in early New England. But in the Chesapeake, at least three-fourths of the immigrants in the seventeenth century arrived as indentured servants.

INDENTURED SERVITUDE

The system of temporary (or "indentured") servitude developed out of practices in England. Young men and women bound themselves to masters for fixed terms of servitude (usually four to five years) in exchange for passage to America, food, and shelter. Male indentures were supposed to receive clothing, tools, and occasionally land upon completion of their service. In reality, however, many left service with nothing. Most women indentures—who constituted roughly one-fourth of the total in the Chesapeake—worked as domestic servants and were expected to marry when their terms of servitude expired.

By the late seventeenth century, the indentured servant population had become one of the largest elements of the colonial population and was creating serious social problems. Some former indentures managed to establish themselves successfully as farmers, tradespeople, or artisans, and some of the women married propertied men. Others (mostly males) found themselves without land, without employment, without families, and without prospects. As a result, there grew up in some areas, particularly in the Chesapeake, a large floating population of young single men who were a source of social unrest.

Beginning in the 1670s, a decrease in the birth rate in England and an improvement in economic conditions there reduced the pressures on laboring men and women to emigrate, and the flow of indentured servants into America declined. Those who did travel to America as indentures now generally avoided the southern colonies, where prospects for advancement were slim. In the Chesapeake, therefore, landowners began to rely much more heavily on African slavery as their principal source of labor.

BIRTH AND DEATH

Immigration remained for a time the greatest source of population growth in the colonies. But the most important long-range factor in the increase of the colonial population was its ability to reproduce itself. Improvement in the reproduction rate began in New England and the mid-Atlantic colonies in the second half of the seventeenth century. After the 1650s, natural increase became the most important source of population growth in those areas. The New England population more than quadrupled through reproduction alone in the second half of the seventeenth century. This rise was a result not only of families having large numbers of children. It was also because life expectancy in New England was unusually high.

Conditions improved much more slowly in the South. The high death rates in the Chesapeake region did not begin to decline to levels found elsewhere until the mid-eighteenth century. Throughout the seventeenth century, the average life expectancy for European men in the region was just over forty years, and for women slightly less. One in four white children died in infancy, and half died before the age of twenty. Children who survived infancy often lost one or both of their parents before reaching maturity. Widows, widowers, and orphans thus formed a substantial proportion of the white Chesapeake population. Only after settlers developed immunity to local diseases (particularly malaria) did life expectancy increase significantly. Population growth was substantial in the region, but it was largely a result of immigration.

The natural increases in the population in the seventeenth century were in large part a result of steady improvement in the balance between men and women in the colonies. In the early years of settlement, more than three-quarters of the white population of the Chesapeake consisted of men. And even in New England, which from the beginning had attracted more families (and thus more women) than the southern colonies, 60 percent of the inhabitants were male in 1650. Gradually, however, more women began to arrive in the colonies; and increasing birth rates contributed to shifting the sex ratio (the balance between men and women) as well. Throughout the colonial period, the population almost doubled every twenty-five years. By 1775, the non-Indian population of the colonies was over 2 million.

MEDICINE IN THE COLONIES

There were very high death rates of women who bore children in the colonial era. Physicians had little or no understanding of infection and sterilization. As a result, many women and babies died from infections contracted during childbirth or surgery. Unaware of bacteria, many communities were plagued with infectious diseases transmitted by garbage or unclean water.

Because of the limited extent of medical knowledge, it was relatively easy for people to practice medicine, even without any professional training. The biggest beneficiaries of this were women, who established themselves in considerable numbers as midwives. Midwives

DR. WILLIAM GLEASON The American artist Winthrop Chandler painted this image of a doctor examining a female patient in 1780. The doctor obviously considers it inappropriate to view a woman lying in bed, so he takes her pulse as she slips her hand through the curtain obscuring her. (Ohio Historical Society)

assisted women in childbirth, but they also dispensed other medical advice. They were popular because they were usually friends and neighbors of the people they treated, unlike physicians, who were few and therefore not often well known to their patients. Male doctors felt threatened by the midwives and struggled continually to drive them from the field, although they did not make substantial progress in doing so until the nineteenth century.

Midwives and doctors alike practiced medicine on the basis of the prevailing assumptions of their time, most of them derived from the theory of "humoralism" popularized by the famous second-century Roman physician Galen. Galen argued that the human body was governed by four "humors" that were lodged in four bodily fluids: yellow bile (or "choler"), black bile ("melancholy"), blood, and phlegm. In a healthy body, the four humors existed in balance. Illness represented an imbalance and suggested the need for removing from the body the excesses of whatever fluid was causing the imbalance. That was the rationale that lay behind the principal medical techniques of the seventeenth century: purging, expulsion, and bleeding. Bleeding was practiced mostly by male physicians. Midwives favored "pukes" and laxatives. The great majority of early Americans, however, had little contact with physicians, or even midwives, and sought instead to deal with illness on their own. The assumption that treating illness was the exclusive province of trained professionals, so much a part of the twentieth century and beyond, lay far in the distance in the colonial era.

That seventeenth-century medicine rested so much on ideas produced 1,400 years before is evidence of how little support there was for the scientific method in England and America at the time. Bleeding, for example, had been in use for hundreds of years, during which time there had been no evidence at all that it helped people recover from illness; indeed, there was considerable evidence that bleeding could do great harm. But what would seem in later eras to be the simple process of testing scientific assumptions was not yet a common part of Western thought. That was one reason that the birth of the Enlightenment in the late seventeenth century—with its faith in human reason and its belief in the capacity of individuals and societies to create better lives—was important not just to politics but also to science.

WOMEN AND FAMILIES IN THE COLONIES

Because there were many more men than women in seventeenth-century America, few women remained unmarried for long. The average European woman in America married for the first time at twenty or twenty-one years of age. Because of the large numbers of indentured servants who were forbidden to marry until their terms of service expired, premarital sexual relationships were common. Children born out of wedlock to indentured women were often taken from their mothers at a young age and were themselves bound as indentured servants.

Women in the Chesapeake could anticipate a life consumed with childbearing. The average wife experienced pregnancies every two years. Those who lived long enough bore an average of eight children apiece (up to five of whom typically died in infancy or early childhood). Since childbirth was one of the most frequent causes of female death, many women did not survive to see their children grow to maturity. Those who did, however, were often widowed, since they were usually much younger than their husbands.

In New England, where many more immigrants arrived with family members and where death rates declined more quickly, family structure was much more stable than in the Chesapeake. The sex ratio was more balanced than in the Chesapeake, so most men could expect to marry. As in the Chesapeake, women married young, began producing children early, and continued to do so well into their thirties. In contrast to their southern counterparts, however, northern children were more likely to survive, and their families were more likely to remain intact. Fewer New England women became widows, and those who did generally lost their husbands later in life.

The longer life span in New England meant that parents continued to control their children longer than did parents in the South. Few sons and daughters could choose a spouse entirely independently of their parents' wishes. Men tended to rely on their fathers for land to cultivate. Women needed dowries from their parents if they were to attract desirable husbands. Stricter parental supervision of children meant, too, that fewer women became pregnant before marriage than was the case in the South.

Puritanism placed a high value on the family, and the position of wife and mother was highly valued in Puritan culture. At the same time, however, Puritanism served to reinforce the idea of nearly absolute male authority. A wife was expected to devote herself almost entirely to serving the needs of her husband and the family economy.

THE BEGINNINGS OF SLAVERY IN ENGLISH AMERICA

The demand for African servants to supplement the scarce southern labor force existed almost from the first moments of settlement. For a time, however, black workers were hard to find. Not until the mid-seventeenth century, when a substantial commerce in slaves grew up between the Caribbean islands and the southern colonies, did black workers become generally available in North America.

The demand for slaves in North America helped expand the transatlantic slave trade. And as slave trading grew more extensive and more sophisticated, it also grew more horrible. Before it ended in the nineteenth century, it was responsible for the forced immigration of as many as 11 million Africans to North and South America and the Caribbean. In the flourishing slave marts on the African coast, native chieftains brought captured members of rival tribes to the ports. The terrified victims were then packed into the dark, filthy holds of ships for the horrors of the "middle passage"—the long journey to the Americas, during which the prisoners were usually kept chained in the bowels of the slave ships and supplied with only minimal food and water. Many slave traders tried to cram as many Africans as possible into their ships to ensure that enough would survive to yield a profit at journey's end. Those who died en route, and many did, were simply thrown overboard. Upon arrival in the New World, slaves were auctioned off to white landowners and transported, frightened and bewildered, to their new homes.

North America was a less important direct destination for African slaves than were such other parts of the New World as the Caribbean islands and Brazil; fewer than 5 percent of the Africans imported to the Americas arrived first in the English colonies. Through most of the seventeenth century, those blacks who were transported to what became the United States came not directly from Africa but from the West Indies. Not until the 1670s did traders start importing blacks directly from Africa to North America. Even then, the flow remained small for a time, mainly because a single group, the Royal African Company of England, monopolized the trade and kept prices high and supplies low.

A turning point in the history of the black population in North America was 1697, the year rival traders broke the Royal African Company's monopoly. With the trade now open

AFRICANS BOUND FOR AMERICA   Shown here are the below-deck slave quarters of a Spanish vessel en route to the West Indies. A British warship captured the slaver, and a young English naval officer (Lt. Francis Meynell) made this watercolor sketch on the spot. The Africans seen in this picture appear somewhat more comfortable than prisoners on some other slave ships, who were often chained and packed together so tightly that they had no room to stand or even sit. (National Maritime Museum, Greenwich, London)

to competition, prices fell and the number of Africans greatly increased. In 1700, about 25,000 African slaves lived in English North America. Because African Americans were so heavily concentrated in a few southern colonies, they were already beginning to out-number whites in some areas. There were perhaps twice as many black men as black women in most areas, but in some places the African American population grew by natural increase nevertheless. By 1760, the number of Africans in the English mainland colonies had increased to approximately a quarter of a million, the vast majority of whom lived in the South. By then blacks had almost wholly replaced white indentured servants as the basis of the southern workforce.

For a time, the legal and social status of the African laborers remained somewhat fluid. In some areas, white and black laborers worked together on terms of relative equality. Some blacks were treated much like white hired servants, and some were freed after a fixed term of servitude. By the late seventeenth century, however, a rigid dis-tinction emerged between blacks and whites. Gradually, the assumption spread that blacks would remain in service permanently and that black children would inherit their parents' bondage. White beliefs about the inferiority of Africans reinforced the growing rigidity of the system, but so did the economic advantages of the system to white slaveowners.

The system of permanent servitude—American slavery—became legal in the early eigh-teenth century when colonial assemblies began to pass "slave codes" granting white mas-ters almost absolute authority over their slaves. Only one factor determined whether a person was subject to the slave codes: color. In the colonial societies of Spanish America, people of mixed race were granted a different (and higher) status than pure Africans. English America recognized no such distinctions.

Changing Sources of European Immigration

The most distinctive and enduring feature of the American population was that it brought together peoples of many different races, ethnic groups, and nationalities. North America was home to a highly diverse population. The British colonies were the home to Native Americans, English immigrants, forcibly imported Africans, and a wide range of other European groups. Among the earliest European immigrants were about 300,000 French Calvinists (known as Huguenots). The Edict of Nantes of 1598 had assured them freedom of religion in France. But in 1685, the Edict was revoked, driv-ing many Huguenots to North America. Germany had similar laws banning Protestantism, driving many Germans to America where they settled in Pennsylvania. They came to be known as the "Pennsylvania Dutch," a corruption of the German term for their nationality, *Deutsch*. Frequent wars in Europe drove many other immigrants to the American colonies.

The most numerous of the newcomers were the so-called Scotch-Irish—Scotch Presbyterians who had settled in northern Ireland (in the province of Ulster) in the early seventeenth century. Most of the Scotch-Irish in America pushed out to the western edges of European settlement and occupied land without much regard for who actually claimed to own it.

There were also immigrants from Scotland itself and from southern Ireland. The Irish migrated steadily over a long period. Many of them abandoned their Roman Catholic religion and much of their ethnic identity after they arrived in America.

THE ORIGINS OF SLAVERY

THE debate among historians over how and why white Americans created a system of slave labor in the seventeenth century—and how and why only African Americans should be slaves—has been an unusually lively one. At its center is a debate over whether slavery was a result of white racism, or whether racism was a result of slavery.

In 1950, Oscar and Mary Handlin published an influential article comparing slavery to other systems of "unfreedom" in the colonies. What separated slavery from other conditions of servitude, they argued, was that it was restricted to people of African descent, that it was permanent, and that it passed from one generation to the next. The unique characteristics of slavery, the Handlins argued, were part of an effort by colonial legislatures to increase the available labor force. White laborers needed an incentive to come to America; black laborers, forcibly imported from Africa, did not. The distinction between the conditions of white workers and the conditions of black workers was, therefore, based on legal and economic motives, not on racism.

Winthrop Jordan was one of a number of historians who later challenged the Handlins' thesis and argued that white racism, more than economic interests, produced African slavery. In *White Over Black* (1968) and other works, Jordan argued that Europeans had long viewed people of color as inferior beings. Those attitudes migrated with white Europeans to the New World, and white racism shaped the treatment of Africans in America from the beginning. Even without the economic incentives the Handlins described, in other words, whites would have been likely to oppress blacks in the New World.

Peter Wood's *Black Majority* (1974), a study of seventeenth-century South Carolina, was one of a number of works that moved the debate back toward social and economic conditions. Wood demonstrated that blacks and whites often worked together on relatively equal terms in the early years of settlement. But as rice cultivation expanded, it became more difficult to find white laborers willing to do the arduous work. The increase in the forcible importation of African slaves was a response to this growing demand for labor. It was also a response to fears among whites that without slavery it would be difficult to control a labor force brought to America against its will. Edmund Morgan's *American Slavery, American Freedom* (1975) argued similarly that the southern labor system was at first relatively flexible and later grew more rigid. In colonial Virginia, he claimed, white settlers did not at first intend to create a system of permanent bondage. But as the tobacco economy grew and created a high demand for cheap labor, white landowners began to feel uneasy about their reliance on a large group of dependent white workers. Such workers were difficult to recruit and control. Slavery, therefore, was less a result of racism than of the desire for whites to find a reliable and stable labor force.

Robin Blackburn's *The Making of New World Slavery* (1996) argues particularly strenuously that while race was a factor in making the enslavement of Africans easier

LONDON'S VIRGINIA.

(The Granger Collection, NYC)

for whites to justify to themselves, the real reasons for the emergence of slavery were hardheaded economic decisions by ambitious entrepreneurs who realized very early that a slave-labor system in the labor-intensive agricultural world of the American South and the Caribbean was more profitable than a free-labor system. Slavery served the interests of a powerful combination of groups: planters, merchants, industrialists, and consumers. The most important reason for the creation and continuation of the system, therefore, was not racism but the pursuit of profit. Slavery was not, Blackburn concludes, an antiquated remnant of an older world. It was a recognizably modern labor system that served the needs of an emerging market economy. •

UNDERSTAND, ANALYZE, & EVALUATE

1. What do historians say is the relationship between racism and slavery?
2. What are the economic arguments put forward by historians to explain the system of slave labor that developed in America? Do these arguments account fully for the development of slavery?

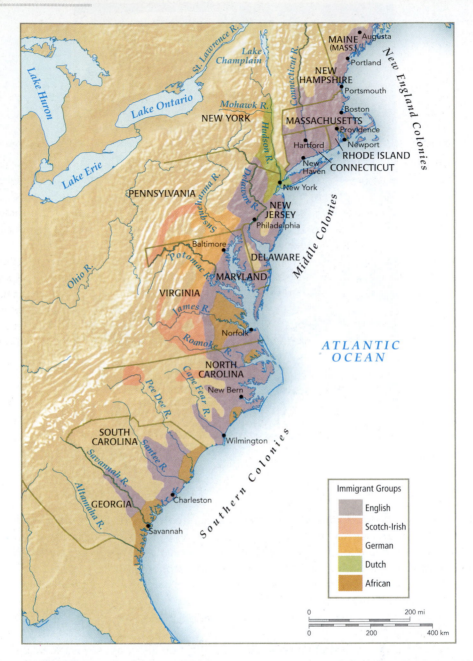

IMMIGRANT GROUPS IN COLONIAL AMERICA, 1760 Even though the entire Atlantic seaboard of what is now the United States had become a series of British colonies by 1760, the population consisted of people from many nations. As this map reveals, English settlers dominated most of the regions of North America. But note the large areas of German settlement in the western Chesapeake and Pennsylvania; the swath of Dutch settlement in New York and New Jersey; the Scotch-Irish regions in the western regions of the South; and the large areas in which Africans were becoming the majority of the population, even if subjugated by the white minority. • *What aspects of the history of these colonies help explain their ethnic composition?*

THE COLONIAL ECONOMIES

Farming, hunting, and fishing dominated almost all areas of European and African settlement in North America throughout the seventeenth and eighteenth centuries. Even so, the economies of the different regions varied markedly.

THE SOUTHERN ECONOMY

A strong European demand for tobacco enabled some planters in the Chesapeake (Maryland and Virginia) to become enormously wealthy and at times allowed the region as a whole to prosper. But throughout the seventeenth and eighteenth centuries, production of tobacco frequently exceeded demand, and as a result the price of the crop sometimes suffered severe declines. The result was a boom-and-bust cycle in the Chesapeake economy, with the first major bust occurring in 1640.

South Carolina and Georgia relied on rice production, since the low-lying coastline with its many tidal rivers made it possible to create rice paddies that could be flooded and drained. Rice cultivation was so difficult and unhealthy that white laborers generally refused to perform it. Hence planters in South Carolina and Georgia were much more dependent on slaves than were their northern counterparts. African workers were adept at rice cultivation, in part because some of them had come from rice-producing regions

PREPARING TOBACCO   This 1790 engraving is designed to illustrate the African origins of the enslaved workers who processed tobacco in Virginia. Their "primitive" costumes seemed to the artist, a French visitor to America, to be in keeping with the crude processes they had created for drying, rolling, and sorting tobacco. (The Stapleton Collection/Bridgeman Art Library)

of west Africa and in part because they were generally more accustomed to the hot, humid climate than were Europeans. They also had a greater natural immunity to malaria. But the work was arduous and debilitating for them nevertheless.

Because of their dependence on large-scale cash crops, the southern colonies developed less of a commercial or industrial economy than the colonies of the North. The trading in tobacco and rice was handled largely by merchants based in London and, later, in the northern colonies.

NORTHERN ECONOMIC AND TECHNOLOGICAL LIFE

In the North, as in the South, agriculture continued to dominate, but it was agriculture of a more diverse kind. In northern New England, colder weather and hard, rocky soil made it difficult for colonists to develop the kind of large-scale commercial farming system that southerners were creating. Conditions for agriculture were better in southern New England and the middle colonies, where the soil was fertile and the weather more temperate. New York, Pennsylvania, and the Connecticut River valley were the chief suppliers of wheat to much of New England and to parts of the South. Even there, however, a substantial commercial economy emerged alongside the agricultural one.

Almost every colonist engaged in a certain amount of industry at home. Occasionally these home industries provided families with surplus goods they could trade or sell. Beyond these domestic efforts, craftsmen and artisans established themselves in colonial towns as cobblers, blacksmiths, riflemakers, cabinetmakers, silversmiths, and printers. In some areas, entrepreneurs harnessed water power to run small mills for grinding grain, processing cloth, or milling lumber. And in several places, large-scale shipbuilding operations began to flourish.

The first effort to establish a significant metals industry in the colonies was an ironworks established in Saugus, Massachusetts, in the 1640s. The Saugus works used water power to drive a bellows, which controlled the heat in a charcoal furnace. The carbon from the burning charcoal helped remove the oxygen from the ore and thus reduced its melting temperature. As the ore melted, it trickled down into molds or was taken in the form of simple "sow bars" to a nearby forge to be shaped into iron objects such as pots and anvils. There was also a mill suitable for turning the sow bars into narrow rods that blacksmiths could cut into nails. The Saugus works was a technological success but a financial failure. It began operations in 1646; in 1668, its financial problems forced it to close its doors.

Metalworks, however, gradually became an important part of the colonial economy. The largest industrial enterprise anywhere in English North America was the ironworks of the German ironmaster Peter Hasenclever in northern New Jersey. Founded in 1764 with British capital, it employed several hundred laborers. There were other, smaller iron-making enterprises in every northern colony, and there were ironworks as well in several of the southern colonies. Even so, these and other growing industries did not become the basis for the kind of explosive industrial growth that Great Britain experienced in the late eighteenth century—in part because English parliamentary regulations such as the Iron Act of 1750 restricted metal processing in the colonies. Similar prohibitions limited the manufacture of woolens, hats, and other goods. But the biggest obstacles to industrialization in America were an inadequate labor supply, a small domestic market, and inadequate transportation facilities and energy supplies.

More important than manufacturing were industries that exploited the natural resources of the continent. By the mid-seventeenth century, the flourishing fur trade of earlier years was in decline. Taking its place were lumbering, mining, and fishing. These industries provided commodities that could be exported to England in exchange for manufactured goods. And they helped produce the most distinctive feature of the northern economy: a thriving commercial class.

THE EXTENT AND LIMITS OF TECHNOLOGY

Despite the technological progress that was occurring in the seventeenth and eighteenth centuries, much of colonial society was conspicuously lacking in even very basic technological capacities. Up to half the farmers in the colonies were so primitively equipped that they did not even own a plow. Substantial numbers of households owned no pots or kettles for cooking. And only about half the households in the colonies owned guns or rifles. The relatively low levels of ownership of these and other elementary tools was not because such things were difficult to make but because most Americans remained too poor or too isolated to be able to afford them. Many households had few if any candles because they were unable to afford candle molds or tallow (wax) or because they had no access to commercially produced candles. In the early eighteenth century, very few farmers owned wagons. Most made do with two-wheeled carts, which were inefficient for transporting crops to market. The most commonly owned tool on American farms was the axe.

Few colonists were self-sufficient in the late seventeenth and early eighteenth centuries. A popular image of early American households is of people who grew their own food, made their own clothes, and bought little from anyone else. In fact, relatively few colonial families owned spinning wheels or looms, which suggests that most people purchased whatever yarn and cloth they needed. Most farmers who grew grain took it to centralized facilities for processing. In general, people who lived in isolated or poor areas owned fewer tools and had less access to advanced technologies than did those in more populous or affluent areas.

THE RISE OF COLONIAL COMMERCE

Perhaps the most remarkable feature of colonial commerce was that it was able to survive at all. American merchants faced such bewildering obstacles, and lacked so many of the basic institutions of trade, that they managed to stay afloat only with great difficulty and through considerable ingenuity. The colonies had almost no gold or silver, and their paper currency was not acceptable as payment for goods from abroad. For many years, colonial merchants had to rely on barter or on money substitutes such as beaver skins.

A second obstacle was lack of information about supply and demand. Traders had no way of knowing what they would find in foreign ports; vessels sometimes stayed at sea for years, journeying from one port to another, trading one commodity for another, attempting to find some way to turn a profit. There was also an enormous number of small, fiercely competitive companies, which made the problem of rationalizing the system even more acute.

Nevertheless, commerce in the colonies survived and grew. There was elaborate trade among the colonies themselves and with the West Indies. The mainland colonies offered their Caribbean trading partners rum, agricultural products, meat, and fish. The islands offered sugar, molasses, and at times slaves in return. There was also trade with England, continental Europe, and the west coast of Africa. This commerce has often been described, somewhat inaccurately, as the "triangular trade," suggesting a neat process by which

GOTTLIEB MITTELBERGER, THE PASSAGE OF INDENTURED SERVANTS (1750)

BOTH in Rotterdam and in Amsterdam the people are packed densely, like herrings so to say, in the large sea-vessels. One person receives a place of scarcely 2 feet width and 6 feet length in the bedstead, while many a ship carries four to six hundred souls; not to mention the innumerable implements, tools, provisions, water-barrels and other things which likewise occupy such space.

On account of contrary winds it takes the ships sometimes 2, 3, and 4 weeks to make the trip from Holland to . . . England. But when the wind is good, they get there in 8 days or even sooner. Everything is examined there and the custom-duties paid, whence it comes that the ships ride-there 8, 10 or 14 days and even longer at anchor, till they have taken in their full cargoes. During that time every one is compelled to spend his last remaining money and to consume his little stock of provisions which had been reserved for the sea; so that most passengers, finding themselves on the ocean where they would be in greater need of them, must greatly suffer from hunger and want. Many suffer want already on the water between Holland and Old England.

When the ships have for the last time weighed their anchors near the city of Kaupp [Cowes] in Old England, the real misery begins with the long voyage. For from there the ships, unless they have good wind, must often sail 8, 9, 10 to 12 weeks before they reach Philadelphia. But even with the best wind the voyage lasts 7 weeks.

But during the voyage there is on board these ships terrible misery, stench, fumes, horror, vomiting, many kinds of seasickness, fever, dysentery, headache, heat, constipation, boils, scurvy, cancer, mouth rot, and the like, all of which come from old and sharply salted food and meat, also from very bad and foul water, so that many die miserably.

Add to this want of provisions, hunger, thirst, frost, heat, dampness, anxiety, want, afflictions and lamentations, together with other trouble, as . . . the lice abound so frightfully, especially on sick people, that they can be scraped off the body. The misery reaches the climax when a gale rages for 2 or 3 nights and days, so that every one believes that the ship will go to the bottom with all human beings on board. In such a visitation the people cry and pray most piteously.

Children from 1 to 7 years rarely survive the voyage. I witnessed . . . misery in no less than 32 children in our ship, all of whom were thrown into the sea. The parents grieve all the more since their children find no resting-place in the earth, but are devoured by the monsters of the sea.

That most of the people get sick is not surprising, because, in addition to all other trials and hardships, warm food is served only three times a week, the rations being very poor and very little. Such meals can hardly be eaten, on account of being so unclean. The water which is served out of the ships is often very black, thick and full of worms, so that one cannot drink it without loathing, even with the greatest thirst. Toward the end we were compelled to eat the ship's biscuit which had been spoiled long ago; though in a whole biscuit there was scarcely a piece the size of a dollar that had not been full of red worms and spiders' nests. . . .

At length, when, after a long and tedious voyage, the ships come in sight of land, so that the promontories can be seen, which the people were so eager and anxious to see, all creep from below on deck to see the land from afar and they weep for joy, and pray and sing, thanking and praising God. The sight of the land makes the people on board the ship, especially the sick and the half dead, alive again, so that their hearts leap within them; they shout and rejoice, and are content to bear their misery in patience, in the hope that they may soon reach the land in safety. But alas!

When the ships have landed at Philadelphia after their long voyage, no one is permitted to leave them except those who pay for their passage or can give good security; the others, who cannot pay, must remain on board the ships till they are purchased, and are released from the ships by their purchasers. The sick always fare the worst, for the healthy are naturally preferred and purchased first; and so the sick and wretched must often remain on board in front of the city for 2 or 3 weeks, and frequently die, whereas many a one, if he could pay his debt and were permitted to leave the ship immediately, might recover and remain alive.

The sale of human beings in the market on board the ship is carried out thus: Every day Englishmen, Dutchmen and High-German people come from the city of Philadelphia and other places, in part from a great distance, say 20, 30, or 40 hours away, and go on board the newly arrived ship that has brought and offers for sale passengers from Europe, and select among the healthy persons such as they deem suitable for their business, and bargain with them how long they will serve for their passage money, which most of them are still in debt for. When they have come to an agreement, it happens that adult persons bind themselves in writing to serve 3, 4, 5 or 6 years for the amount due by them, according to their age and strength. But very young people, from 10 to 15 years, must serve till they are 21 years old.

Many parents must sell and trade away their children like so many head of cattle; for if their children take the debt upon themselves, the parents can leave the ship free and unrestrained; but as the parents often do not know where and to what people their children are going, it often happens that such parents and children, after leaving the ship, do not see each other again for many years, perhaps no more in all their lives. . . . It often happens that whole families, husband, wife and children, are separated by being sold to different purchasers, especially when they have not paid any part of their passage money.

When a husband or wife has died at sea, when the ship has made more than half of her trip, the survivor must pay or serve not only for himself or herself but also for the deceased.

When both parents have died over halfway at sea, their children, especially when they are young and have nothing to pawn or pay, must stand for their own and their parents' passage, and serve till they are 21 years old. When one has served his or her term, he or she is entitled to a new suit of clothes at parting; and if it has been so stipulated, a man gets in addition a horse, a woman, a cow. When a serf has an opportunity to marry in this country, he or she must pay for each year which he or she would have yet to serve, 5 or 6 pounds.

UNDERSTAND, ANALYZE, & EVALUATE

1. What hardships did passengers suffer at sea? What relief could they hope for upon reaching Philadelphia?
2. Explain the different purchase agreements between passengers and masters. How did the death of a family member affect a passenger's indenture contracts?
3. What do the ordeals of indentured servants tell us about prospects in Europe? What does it tell us about the concept of liberty in the colonies?

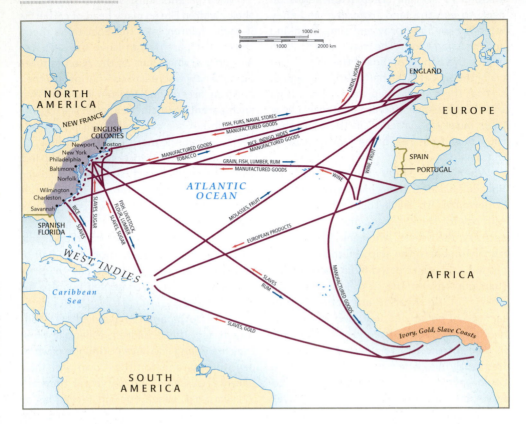

THE "TRIANGULAR TRADE"   This map illustrates the complex pattern of trade that fueled the colonial American economy in the seventeenth and eighteenth centuries. A simple explanation of this trade is that the American colonies exported raw materials (agricultural products, furs, and others) to Britain and Europe and imported manufactured goods in return. But while that explanation is accurate, it is not complete, largely because the Atlantic trade was not a simple exchange between America and Europe, but a complex network of exchanges involving the Caribbean, Africa, and the Mediterranean. Note the important exchanges between the North American mainland and the Caribbean islands; the important trade between the American colonies and Africa; and the wide range of European and Mediterranean markets in which Americans were active. Not shown on this map, but also very important to colonial commerce, was a large coastal trade among the various regions of British North America. • *Why did the major ports of trade emerge almost entirely in the northern colonies?*

merchants carried rum and other goods from New England to Africa, exchanged their merchandise for slaves, whom they then transported to the West Indies (hence the term "middle passage" for the dreaded journey—it was the second of the three legs of the voyage), and then exchanged the slaves for sugar and molasses, which they shipped back to New England to be distilled into rum. In reality, the so-called triangular trade in rum, slaves, and sugar was a complicated maze of highly diverse trade routes. Out of this risky trade emerged a group of adventurous entrepreneurs who by the mid-eighteenth century were beginning to constitute a distinct merchant class. The British Navigation Acts protected them from foreign competition in the colonies. They had ready access to the market in England for such colonial products as furs, timber, and American-built ships. But they also developed markets illegally outside the British Empire—in the French, Spanish, and Dutch West Indies—where they could often get higher prices for their goods than in the British colonies.

THE RISE OF CONSUMERISM

As affluent residents of the colonies grew in number, the growing prosperity and commercialism of British America created both new appetites and new opportunities to satisfy them. The result was a growing preoccupation with the consumption of material goods.

The growth of eighteenth-century consumerism increased the class divisions in the American colonies. As the difference between the upper and lower classes became more glaring, people of means became more intent on demonstrating their own membership in the upper ranks of society. The ability to purchase and display consumer goods was an important way of doing so, particularly for wealthy people in cities and towns, who did not have large estates to boast their success. But the growth of consumerism was also a product of the early stages of the industrial revolution. Although there was relatively little industry in America in the eighteenth century, England and Europe were making rapid advances and producing more and more affordable goods for affluent Americans to buy.

To facilitate the new consumer appetites, merchants and traders began advertising their goods in journals and newspapers. Agents of urban merchants—the ancestors of the traveling salesman—fanned out through the countryside, attempting to interest wealthy landowners and planters in the luxury goods now available to them. George and Martha Washington, for example, spent considerable time and money ordering elegant furnishings for their home at Mount Vernon, goods that were shipped to them mostly from England and Europe.

One feature of a consumer society is that things that once were considered luxuries quickly come to be seen as necessities once they are readily available. In the colonies, items that became commonplace after having once been expensive luxuries included tea, household linens, glassware, manufactured cutlery, crockery, furniture, and many other things. Another result of consumerism is the association of material goods—of the quality of a person's home and possessions and clothing, for example—with virtue and "refinement." The ideal of the cultivated "gentleman" and the gracious "lady" became increasingly powerful throughout the colonies in the eighteenth century. In part that meant striving to become educated and "refined" in speech and behavior. Americans read books on manners and fashion. They bought magazines about London society. And they strove to develop themselves as witty and educated conversationalists. They also commissioned portraits of themselves and their families, devoted large portions of their homes to entertainment, built shelves and cases in which they could display fashionable possessions, constructed formal gardens, and lavished attention on their wardrobes and hairstyles.

PATTERNS OF SOCIETY

Although there were sharp social distinctions in the colonies, the well-defined and deeply entrenched class system of England failed to reproduce itself in America. Aristocracies emerged, to be sure, but they tended to rely less on landownership than on control of a substantial workforce, and they were generally less secure and less powerful than their English counterparts. More than in England, white people in America faced opportunities for social mobility—both up and down. There were also new forms of community in America, and they varied greatly from one region to another.

MASTERS AND SLAVES ON THE PLANTATION

The plantation system of the American South produced one form of community. The first plantations emerged in the tobacco-growing areas of Virginia and Maryland. Some of the early planters became established aristocrats with vast estates. On the whole, however, seventeenth-century colonial plantations were rough and relatively small. In the early days in Virginia, they were little more than crude clearings where landowners and indentured servants worked side by side in conditions so harsh that death was an everyday occurrence. Most landowners lived in rough cabins or houses, with their servants or slaves nearby. The economy of the plantation was precarious. Planters could not control their markets, so even the largest plantations were constantly at risk. When prices fell, planters faced the prospect of ruin. The plantation economy created many new wealthy landowners, but it also destroyed many.

The enslaved African Americans, of course, lived very differently. On the smaller farms with only a handful of slaves, it was not always possible for a rigid separation to develop between whites and blacks. But by the early eighteenth century, over three-fourths of all slaves lived on plantations of at least ten slaves, and nearly one-half lived in communities of fifty slaves or more. In those settings, they were able to develop a society and culture of their own. Although whites seldom encouraged formal marriages among slaves, many blacks themselves developed strong and elaborate family structures. There was also a distinctive slave religion, which blended Christianity with African folklore and which became a central element in the emergence of an independent black culture.

Nevertheless, black society was subject to constant intrusions from and interaction with white society. Black house servants, for example, were isolated from their own community. Black women were often subject to unwanted sexual advances from owners and overseers and hence to bearing mulatto children, who were rarely recognized by their white fathers. On some plantations, black workers were treated with kindness and responded to their owners with genuine devotion. On others, they encountered physical brutality and occasionally even sadism, against which they were virtually powerless.

Slaves often resisted their masters, in large ways and small. The most serious example in the colonial period was the Stono Rebellion in South Carolina in 1739, during which about 100 slaves rose up, seized weapons, killed several whites, and attempted to escape south to Florida. The uprising was quickly crushed, and most participants were executed. A more frequent form of resistance was simply running away, but that provided no real solution either. For most, there was nowhere to go. Resistance more often took the form of subtle, and often undetected, defiance or evasion of their masters' wishes.

Most slaves, male and female, worked as field hands. But on the larger plantations that aspired to genuine self-sufficiency, some slaves learned trades and crafts: blacksmithing, carpentry, shoemaking, spinning, weaving, sewing, midwifery, and others. These skilled craftspeople were at times hired out to other planters. Some set up their own establishments in towns or cities and shared their profits with their owners. A few were able to buy their freedom.

THE PURITAN COMMUNITY

The characteristic social unit in New England was not the isolated farm or the large plantation but the town. In the early years of colonization, each new settlement drew up a "covenant" binding all residents tightly together both religiously and socially. Colonists laid out a village, with houses and a meetinghouse arranged around a central pasture, or "common." Thus families generally lived with their neighbors close by. They divided up

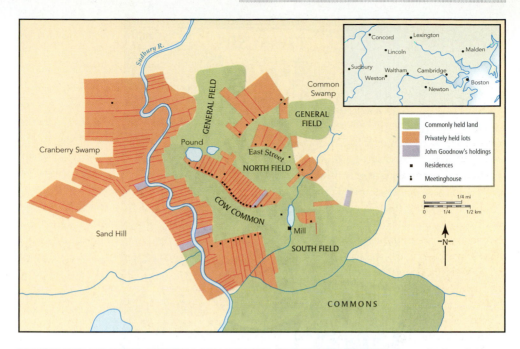

THE NEW ENGLAND TOWN: SUDBURY, MASSACHUSETTS, SEVENTEENTH CENTURY Just as the plantation was a characteristic social form in the southern colonies, the town was the most common social unit in New England. This map shows the organization of Sudbury, Massachusetts, a town just west of Boston, in its early years in the seventeenth century. Note the location of the houses, which are grouped mostly together around a shared pasture (or "commons") and near the church. Note, too, the outlying fields, which were divided among residents of the town, even though they were often not connected to the land on which the owners lived. The map illustrates the holdings of a single resident of Sudbury, John Goodnow, whose house was on the common, but whose lands were scattered over a number of areas of Sudbury. • *What aspects of New England life might help explain the clustering of residences at the center of the town?* (From Sumner Chilton Powell, *Puritan Village: The Formation of a New England Town*. Copyright © 1963 by Wesleyan University. Reprinted by permission from Wesleyan University Press.)

the outlying fields and woodlands among the residents; the size and location of a family's field depended on the family's numbers, wealth, and social station.

Once a town was established, residents held a yearly "town meeting" to decide important questions and to choose a group of "selectmen," who ran the town's affairs. Participation in the meeting was generally restricted to adult males who were members of the church. Only those who could give evidence of being among the elect assured of salvation (the "visible saints") were admitted to full church membership, although other residents of the town were required to attend church services.

New Englanders did not adopt the English system of primogeniture—the passing of all property to the firstborn son. Instead, a father divided up his land among all his sons. His control of this inheritance gave him great power over the family. Often a son would reach his late twenties before his father would allow him to move into his own household and work his own land. Even then, sons would usually continue to live in close proximity to their fathers.

The early Puritan community was a tightly knit organism. But as the years passed and the communities grew, strains and tensions began to affect this communal structure. This was partly due to the increasing commercialization of New England society. It was also partly due to population growth. In the first generations, fathers generally controlled

SINNERS IN HELL, 1744   This mid-eighteenth-century religious image illustrates both the fears and prejudices of many colonial Christians. The idyllic city of Sion, in the center of the drawing, is threatened on all sides by forces of evil, which include images not just of Satan and sin, but also of some of the perceived enemies of Protestants—the Catholic Church (symbolized by the image of the pope) and Islam (symbolized by Turks). (The Granger Collection, NYC)

enough land to satisfy the needs of all their sons. After several generations, however, there was often too little to go around, particularly in communities surrounded by other towns, with no room to expand outward. The result was that in many communities, groups of younger residents broke off and moved elsewhere to form towns of their own.

The tensions building in Puritan communities could produce bizarre and disastrous events. One example was the widespread hysteria in the 1680s and 1690s over accusations of witchcraft (the human exercise of satanic powers) in New England. The most famous outbreak was in Salem, Massachusetts, where adolescent girls leveled charges of witchcraft against several West Indian servants steeped in voodoo lore. Hysteria spread throughout the town, and hundreds of people (most of them women) were accused of witchcraft. Nineteen residents of Salem were put to death before the trials finally ended in 1692; the girls who had been the original accusers later recanted and admitted that their story had been fabricated.

The Salem experience was not unique. Accusations of witchcraft spread through many New England towns in the early 1690s and centered mostly on women. Research into the background of accused witches reveals that most were middle-aged women, often widowed, with few or no children. Many accused witches were of low social position, were often involved in domestic conflicts, had frequently been accused of other crimes, and were considered abrasive by their neighbors. Others were women who, through inheritance or hard work, had come into possession of substantial property of their own and thus challenged the gender norms of the community.

The witchcraft controversies were a reflection of the highly religious character of New England societies. New Englanders believed in the power of Satan. Belief in witchcraft was not a marginal superstition rejected by the mainstream. It was a common feature of Puritan religious conviction.

CITIES

In the 1770s, the two largest colonial ports—Philadelphia and New York—had populations of 28,000 and 25,000, respectively, which made them larger than most English urban centers of their time. Boston (16,000), Charles Town (later Charleston), South Carolina (12,000), and Newport, Rhode Island (11,000), were also substantial communities by the standards of the day.

Colonial cities served as trading centers for the farmers of their regions and as marts for international commerce. Cities were the centers of what industry existed in the colonies. They were the locations of the most advanced schools and sophisticated cultural activities and of shops where imported goods could be bought. In addition, they were communities with urban social problems: crime, vice, pollution, traffic. Unlike smaller towns, cities needed to set up constables' offices and fire departments and develop systems for supporting the urban poor, whose numbers became especially large in times of economic crisis.

Finally, cities were places where new ideas could circulate and be discussed. There were newspapers, books, and other publications from abroad, and hence new intellectual influences. The taverns and coffeehouses of cities provided forums in which people could gather and debate the issues of the day. That is one reason why the Revolutionary crisis, when it began to build in the 1760s and 1770s, originated in the cities.

INEQUALITY

New England, for all its belief in community and liberty, was far from an egalitarian society. "Some must be rich and some poor," John Winthrop wrote in the early seventeenth century, and his prediction perhaps exceeded his expectations. Wealthy families and socially distinguished ones (who were usually the same people) had privileges and rights that were not available to poorer citizens. Elites were called "ladies" and "gentlemen," while people in the lower levels of society were known as "goodman" or "goodwife." The elite were given the best seats in their churches and had the greatest influence over the parish. Men had more power than women. Servants had few rights. The church itself taught that inequality reflected God's intention.

In cities, such economic stratification was significant—although, unlike in later eras, the rich were the largest sector of the population, and in Boston in the eighteenth century, the majority. That was so partly because wealthy people were most likely to move to cities and participate in commerce. In the agricultural countryside, differences in wealth were less extreme.

THE WITCHCRAFT TRIALS

THE witchcraft trials of the 1690s— which began in Salem, Massachusetts, and spread to other areas of New England—have been the stuff of popular legend for centuries. They have also engaged the interest of generations of historians, who have tried to explain why these seventeenth-century Americans became so committed to the belief that some of their own neighbors were agents of Satan. Although there have been many explanations of the witchcraft phenomenon, some of the most important in recent decades have focused on the central place of women in the story.

Through the first half of the twentieth century, most historians dismissed the witchcraft trials as "hysteria," prompted by the intolerance and rigidity of Puritan society. This interpretation informed the most prominent popular portrayal of witchcraft in the twentieth century: Arthur Miller's play *The Crucible,* first produced in 1953,

which was clearly an effort to use the Salem trials as a comment on the great anticommunist frenzy of his own era. But at almost the same time, Perry Miller, the renowned scholar of Puritanism, argued in a series of important studies that belief in witchcraft was not a product of hysteria or intolerance but a widely shared part of the religious worldview of the seventeenth century. To the Puritans, witchcraft seemed not only plausible but scientifically rational.

A new wave of interpretation of witchcraft began in the 1970s, with the publication of *Salem Possessed* (1976), by Paul Boyer and Stephen Nissenbaum. Their examination of the town records of Salem in the 1690s led them to conclude that the witchcraft controversy was a product of class tensions between the poorer, more marginal residents of one part of Salem and the wealthier, more privileged residents of another. These social tensions,

AWAKENINGS AND ENLIGHTENMENTS

Intellectual life in colonial America revolved around the conflict between the traditional emphasis on a personal God deeply involved in individual lives, and the new spirit of the Enlightenment, which stressed the importance of science and human reason. The old views placed a high value on a stern moral code in which intellect was less important than faith. The Enlightenment suggested that people had substantial control over their own lives and societies.

THE PATTERN OF RELIGIONS

Religious toleration flourished in America to a degree unmatched in any European nation. Settlers in America brought with them so many different religious practices that it proved impossible to impose a single religious code on any large area.

The Church of England was established as the official faith in Virginia, Maryland, New York, the Carolinas, and Georgia. Except in Virginia and Maryland, however, the laws which could not find easy expression on their own terms, led some poorer Salemites to lash out at their richer neighbors by charging them, or their servants, with witchcraft. A few years later, John Demos, in *Entertaining Satan* (1983), examined witchcraft accusations in a larger area of New England and similarly portrayed them as products of displaced anger about social and economic grievances that could not be expressed otherwise. Demos provided a far more complex picture of the nature of these grievances than had Boyer and Nissenbaum, but like them, he saw witchcraft as a symptom of a persistent set of social and pyschological tensions.

At about the same time, however, a number of scholars were beginning to look at witchcraft through the scholarly lens of gender. Carol Karlsen's *The Devil in the Shape of a Woman* (1987) demonstrated through intensive scrutiny of records across New England that a disproportionate number of those accused of witchcraft were property-owning widows or unmarried women—in other words, women who did not fit comfortably into the normal pattern of male-dominated families. Karlsen concluded that such women were vulnerable to these accusations because they seemed threatening to people (including many women) who were accustomed to women as subordinate members of the community.

More recently, Mary Beth Norton's *In the Devil's Snare* (2002) placed the witchcraft trials in the context of other events of their time—and in particular the terrifying upheavals and dislocations that the Indian Wars of the late seventeenth century created in Puritan communities. In the face of this crisis, in which refugees from King William's War were fleeing towns destroyed by the Indians and flooding Salem and other eastern towns, fear and social instability grew. The witchcraft trials helped create a greater-than-normal readiness to connect aberrant behavior (such as the actions of unusually independent or eccentric women) to supernatural causes. The result was a wave of witchcraft accusations that ultimately led to the execution of at least twenty people.   •

UNDERSTAND, ANALYZE, & EVALUATE

1. How did the Salem witchcraft trials reflect attitudes toward women and the status of women in colonial New England?
2. Why were colonial New Englanders willing to believe accusations of witchcraft about their fellow colonists?

establishing the Church of England as the official colonial religion were largely ignored. Even in New England, where the Puritans had originally believed that they were all part of a single faith, there was a growing tendency in the eighteenth century for different congregations to affiliate with different denominations. In parts of New York and New Jersey, Dutch settlers had established their own Calvinist denomination, Dutch Reformed. American Baptists developed a great variety of sects and shared the belief that rebaptism, usually by total immersion, was necessary when believers reached maturity. But while some Baptists remained Calvinists (believers in predestination), others came to believe in salvation by free will.

Protestants extended toleration to one another more readily than they did to Roman Catholics. New Englanders, in particular, viewed their Catholic neighbors in New France (Canada) not only as commercial and military rivals but also as dangerous agents of Rome. In most of the English colonies, however, Roman Catholics were too few to cause serious conflict. They were most numerous in Maryland, where they numbered 3,000. Perhaps for that reason they suffered the most persecution in that colony. After the overthrow of the original proprietors in 1691, Catholics in Maryland not only lost their political rights but also were forbidden to hold religious services except in private houses.

Jews in provincial America totaled no more than about 2,000 at any time. The largest community lived in New York City. Smaller groups settled in Newport and Charleston, and there were scattered Jewish families in all the colonies. Nowhere could they vote or hold office. Only in Rhode Island could they practice their religion openly.

By the beginning of the eighteenth century, some Americans were growing troubled by the apparent decline in religious piety in their society. The movement of the population westward and the wide scattering of settlements had caused many communities to lose touch with organized religion. The rise of commercial prosperity created a more secular outlook in urban areas. The progress of science and free thought caused at least some colonists to doubt traditional religious beliefs.

Concerns about weakening piety surfaced as early as the 1660s in New England, where the Puritan oligarchy warned of a decline in the power of the church. Ministers preached sermons of despair (known as "jeremiads"), deploring the signs of waning piety. By the standards of other societies or other eras, the Puritan faith remained remarkably strong. But to New Englanders, the "declension" of religious piety seemed a serious problem.

THE GREAT AWAKENING

By the early eighteenth century, similar concerns about declining piety were emerging in other regions and among members of other faiths. The result was the first great American revival: the Great Awakening.

The Great Awakening began in earnest in the 1730s and reached its climax in the 1740s. The revival had particular appeal to women (the majority of converts) and to younger sons of the third or fourth generation of settlers—those who stood to inherit the least land and who faced the most uncertain futures. The rhetoric of the revival emphasized the potential for every person to break away from the constraints of the past and start anew in his or her relationship with God. Such beliefs reflected in part the desires of many people to break away from their families or communities and start a new life.

Powerful evangelists from England helped spread the revival. John and Charles Wesley, the founders of Methodism, visited Georgia and other colonies in the 1730s. George Whitefield, a powerful open-air preacher from England, made several evangelizing tours through the colonies and drew tremendous crowds. But the outstanding preacher of the Great Awakening was the New England Congregationalist Jonathan Edwards. From his pulpit in Northampton, Massachusetts, Edwards attacked the new doctrines of easy salvation for all. He preached anew the traditional Puritan ideas of the absolute sovereignty of God, predestination, and salvation by God's grace alone. His vivid descriptions of hell could terrify his listeners.

The Great Awakening led to the division of existing congregations (between "New Light" revivalists and "Old Light" traditionalists) and to the founding of new ones. It also affected areas of society outside the churches. Some of the revivalists denounced book learning as a hindrance to salvation. But other evangelists saw education as a means of furthering religion, and they founded or led schools for the training of New Light ministers.

THE ENLIGHTENMENT

The Great Awakening caused one great cultural upheaval in the colonies. The Enlightenment caused another, very different one. The Enlightenment was the product of scientific and intellectual discoveries in Europe in the seventeenth century—discoveries that revealed the "natural laws" that regulated the workings of nature. The new scientific knowledge encouraged many thinkers to begin celebrating the power of human reason and to argue that rational thought, not just religious faith, could create progress and advance knowledge in the world.

In celebrating reason, the Enlightenment encouraged men and women to look to themselves and their own intellect—not just to God—for guidance as to how to live their lives and shape their societies. It helped produce a growing interest in education and a heightened concern with politics and government.

In the early seventeenth century, Enlightenment ideas in America were largely borrowed from Europe—from such thinkers as Francis Bacon and John Locke of England, Baruch Spinoza of Amsterdam, and René Descartes of France. Later, however, such Americans as Benjamin Franklin, Thomas Paine, Thomas Jefferson, and James Madison made their own important contributions to Enlightenment thought.

LITERACY AND TECHNOLOGY

White male Americans achieved a high degree of literacy in the eighteenth century. By the time of the Revolution, well over one-half of all white men could read and write. The literacy rate for women lagged behind the rate for men until the nineteenth century. While opportunities for education beyond the primary level were scarce for men, they were almost nonexistent for women.

The large number of colonists who could read created a market for the first widely circulated publications in America other than the Bible: almanacs. By 1700, there were dozens, perhaps hundreds, of almanacs circulating throughout the colonies and even in the sparsely settled lands to the west. Most families had at least one. Almanacs provided medical advice, navigational and agricultural information, practical wisdom, humor, and predictions about the future—most famously, predictions about weather patterns for the coming year, which many farmers used as the basis for decisions about crops, even though the predictions were notoriously unreliable. The most famous almanac in eighteenth-century America was *Poor Richard's Almanac*, published by Benjamin Franklin in Philadelphia.

The wide availability of reading material in colonial America by the eighteenth century was a result of the spread of printing technology. The first printing press began operating in the colonies in 1639, and by 1695 there were more towns in America with printers than there were in England. At first, many of these presses did not get very much use. Over time, however, the rising literacy of the society created a demand for books, pamphlets, and almanacs that the presses rushed to fill.

The first newspaper in the colonies, *Publick Occurrences*, was published in Boston in 1690 using a relatively advanced printing facility. It was the first step toward what would eventually become a large newspaper industry. One reason the Stamp Act of 1765, which imposed a tax on printed materials, created such a furor was because printing technology had by then become central to colonial life.

EDUCATION

Even before Enlightenment ideas penetrated America, colonists placed a high value on formal education. Some families tried to teach their children to read and write at home, although the heavy burden of work in most agricultural households limited the time available for schooling. In Massachusetts, a 1647 law required that every town support a school; and a modest network of public schools emerged as a result. The Quakers and other sects operated church schools, and in some communities widows or unmarried women conducted "dame schools" in their homes. In cities, some master craftsmen set up evening schools for their apprentices.

African Americans had virtually no access to education. Occasionally a master or mistress would teach slave children to read and write; but as the slave system became more firmly entrenched, strong social (and ultimately legal) sanctions developed to discourage such efforts. Indians, too, remained largely outside the white educational system—to a large degree by choice. Some white missionaries and philanthropists established schools for Native Americans and helped create a small population of Indians literate in spoken and written English.

Harvard, the first American college, was established in 1636 by Puritan theologians who wanted to create a training center for ministers. (The college was named for a Charlestown minister, John Harvard, who had left it his library and one-half of his estate.) In 1693, William and Mary College (named for the English king and queen) was established in Williamsburg, Virginia, by Anglicans. And in 1701, conservative Congregationalists,

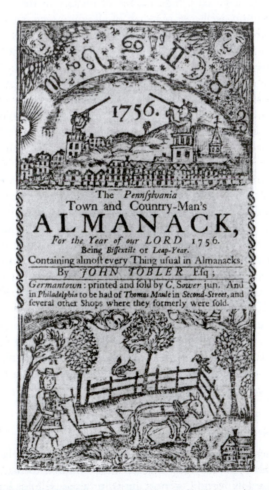

TOWN AND COUNTRY-MAN'S ALMANACK As the population of colonial cities and towns grew, almanacs—originally targeted mainly at farmers—began to appeal to townspeople as well. (Sinclair Hamilton Collection, Graphic Arts Division, Department of Rare Books and Special Collections, Princeton University Library)

dissatisfied with the growing religious liberalism of Harvard, founded Yale (named for one of its first benefactors, Elihu Yale) in New Haven, Connecticut. Out of the Great Awakening emerged the College of New Jersey, founded in 1746 and known later as Princeton (after the town in which it was located); one of its first presidents was Jonathan Edwards. Despite the religious basis of these colleges, most of them offered curricula that included not only theology but logic, ethics, physics, geometry, astronomy, rhetoric, Latin, Hebrew, and Greek. King's College, founded in New York City in 1754 and later renamed Columbia, was specifically devoted to the spread of secular knowledge. The Academy and College of Philadelphia, founded in 1755 and later renamed the University of Pennsylvania, was also a secular institution, established by a group of laymen under the inspiration of Benjamin Franklin.

After 1700, most colonial leaders received their entire educations in America (rather than attending university in England, as had once been the case). But higher education remained available only to a few relatively affluent white men.

The Spread of Science

The clearest indication of the spreading influence of the Enlightenment in America was an increasing interest in scientific knowledge. Most of the early colleges established chairs in the natural sciences and introduced some of the advanced scientific theories of Europe, including Copernican astronomy and Newtonian physics, to their students. But the most vigorous promotion of science in these years occurred through the private efforts of amateurs and the activities of scientific societies. Leading merchants, planters, and even theologians became corresponding members of the Royal Society of London, the leading English scientific organization. Benjamin Franklin won international fame through his experiments with electricity. Particularly notable was his 1747 theory—and his 1752 demonstration, using a kite—that lightning and electricity were the same. (Previously, most scientists had believed that there were several distinct types of electricity.) His research on the way in which electricity could be "grounded" led to the development of the lightning rod, which greatly reduced fires and other damage to buildings during thunderstorms.

The high value that influential Americans were beginning to place on scientific knowledge was clearly demonstrated by the most daring and controversial scientific experiment of the eighteenth century: inoculation against smallpox. The Puritan theologian Cotton Mather had learned of experiments in England by which people had been deliberately infected with mild cases of smallpox in order to immunize them against the deadly disease. Despite strong opposition, he urged inoculation on his fellow Bostonians during an epidemic in the 1720s. The results confirmed the effectiveness of the technique. Other theologians took up the cause, along with many physicians. By the mid-eighteenth century, inoculation had become a common medical procedure in America.

Concepts of Law and Politics

In law and politics, as in other parts of their lives, Americans in the seventeenth and eighteenth centuries believed that they were re-creating in the New World the practices and institutions of the Old World. But as in other areas, they created something very different. Although the American legal system adopted most of the essential elements of the English system, including such ancient rights as trial by jury, significant differences

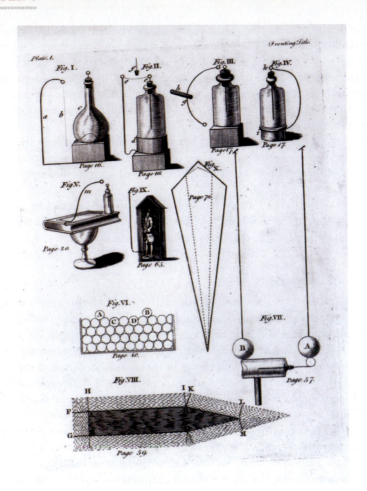

BENJAMIN FRANKLIN ON ELECTRICITY The discovery of electricity was one of the great scientific events of the eighteenth century, even though large-scale practical use of electrical energy emerged much later. Benjamin Franklin was one of the first Americans, and certainly the most famous American, to experiment with electricity. This is the frontispiece for a book, originally published in 1750 in Philadelphia, that describes his "experiments and observations." The pages shown here are from the London edition, which appeared in 1774. (Getty Images)

developed in court procedures, punishments, and the definition of crimes. In England, for example, a printed attack on a public official, whether true or false, was considered libelous. At the 1734–1735 trial of the New York publisher John Peter Zenger, the courts ruled that criticisms of the government were not libelous if factually true—a verdict that removed some colonial restrictions on the freedom of the press.

More significant for the future relationship between the colonies and England were differences emerging between the American and British political systems. Because the royal government was so far away, Americans created a group of institutions of their own that gave them a large measure of self-government. In most colonies, local communities grew accustomed to running their own affairs with minimal interference from higher authorities. The colonial assemblies came to exercise many of the powers that Parliament exercised in England. Provincial governors (appointed by the king after the 1690s) had broad powers on paper, but their actual influence was limited.

The result of all this was that the provincial governments became accustomed to acting more or less independently of Parliament, and a set of assumptions and expectations about the rights of the colonists took hold in America that was not shared by policymakers in England. These differences caused few problems before the 1760s, because the British did little to exert the authority they believed they possessed. But when, beginning in 1763, the English government began attempting to tighten its control over the American colonies, a great imperial crisis resulted.

CONCLUSION

Between the 1650s and the 1750s, the English colonies in America grew steadily in population, in the size of their economies, and in the sophistication—and diversity—of their cultures. Although most white Americans in the 1750s still believed that they were fully a part of the British Empire, they were in fact living in a world that had become very different from that of England.

Many distinct societies developed in the colonies, but the greatest distinction was between the colonies of the North and those of the South. In the North, society was dominated by relatively small family farms and by towns and cities of growing size. A thriving commercial class was developing, and with it an increasingly elaborate urban culture. In the South, there were many family farms as well. But there were also large plantations cultivating tobacco, rice, indigo, and cotton for export. By the late seventeenth century, these plantations were relying heavily on African workers who had been brought to the colonies forcibly as slaves. There were few significant towns and cities in the South, and little commerce other than the marketing of crops.

The colonies did, however, have much in common. Most white Americans accepted common assumptions about racial inequality. That enabled them to tolerate the enslavement of African men and women and to justify a campaign of displacement and often violence against Native Americans. Most white Americans (and, in different ways, most nonwhite Americans as well) were deeply religious. The Great Awakening, therefore, had a powerful impact throughout the colonies. And most white colonists shared a belief in certain basic principles of law and politics, which they considered embedded in the English constitution. Their interpretation of that constitution, however, was becoming increasingly different from that of the Parliament in England and was laying the groundwork for future conflict.

RECALL AND REFLECT

1. How did patterns of family life and attitudes toward women differ in the northern and southern colonies?
2. How did the lives of African slaves change over the course of the first century of slavery?
3. Who emigrated to North America in the seventeenth century, and why did they come?
4. What was the intellectual culture of colonial America, as expressed in literature, philosophy, science, education, and law?
5. How and why did life in the English colonies diverge from life in England?

4 THE EMPIRE IN TRANSITION

LOOSENING TIES
THE STRUGGLE FOR THE CONTINENT
THE NEW IMPERIALISM
STIRRINGS OF REVOLT
COOPERATION AND WAR

LOOKING AHEAD

1. How did the Seven Years' War change the balance of power in North America and throughout the world?
2. What policies did Parliament implement with regard to the colonies in the 1760s and 1770s, and why did Britain adopt these policies?
3. How did the colonists respond to Parliament's actions?

AS LATE AS THE 1750s, few Americans objected to their membership in the British Empire. The imperial system provided many benefits to the Americans, and for the most part the English government left the colonies alone. By the mid-1770s, however, the relationship between the American colonies and their British rulers had become so strained that the empire was on the verge of unraveling. And in the spring of 1775, the first shots were fired in a war that would ultimately win America its independence. How had it happened? And why so quickly?

LOOSENING TIES

In one sense, it had not happened quickly at all. Ever since the first days of English settlement, the ideas and institutions of the colonies had been diverging from those in Britain. In another sense, however, the Revolutionary crisis emerged in response to relatively sudden changes in the administration of the empire. In 1763, the English government began to enforce a series of colonial policies that brought the differences between the two societies into sharp focus.

A DECENTRALIZED EMPIRE

In the fifty years after the Glorious Revolution, the English Parliament established a growing supremacy over the king. Under Kings George I (1714–1727) and George II (1727–1760), the prime minister and his cabinet became the nation's real executives. Because they depended politically on the great merchants and landholders of England, they were less inclined than the seventeenth-century monarchs had been to try to tighten control over the empire, which many merchants feared would disrupt the profitable commerce with the colonies. As a result, administration of the colonies remained loose, decentralized, and inefficient.

The character of royal officials in America contributed further to the looseness of the imperial system. Few governors were able men. Many, perhaps most, had used bribery to obtain their offices and continued to accept bribes once in office. Some appointees remained in England and hired substitutes to take their places in America.

The colonial assemblies, taking advantage of the weak imperial administration, had asserted their own authority to levy taxes, make appropriations, approve appointments, and pass laws. The assemblies came to look upon themselves as little parliaments, each practically as sovereign within its colony as Parliament itself was in England.

THE COLONIES DIVIDED

Even so, the colonists continued to think of themselves as loyal English subjects. Many felt stronger ties to England than they did to the other American colonies. Although the colonies had slowly learned to cooperate with one another on such practical matters as intercolonial trade, road construction, and a colonial postal service, they remained reluctant to cooperate in larger ways, even when, in 1754, they faced a common threat from their old rivals, the French, and France's Indian allies. Delegates from Pennsylvania,

TIME LINE

1754
Beginning of French and Indian War

1756
Seven Years' War begins

1760
George III becomes king

1763
Peace of Paris
Proclamation of 1763

1764
Sugar Act

1765
Stamp Act

1766
Stamp Act repealed
Declaratory Act

1767
Townshend Duties

1770
Boston Massacre
Most Townshend Duties repealed

1771
Regulator movement in North Carolina

1772
Committees of correspondence in Boston
Gaspée incident

1773
Tea Act;
Boston Tea Party

1774
Intolerable Acts
First Continental Congress in Philadelphia

1775
Battles of Lexington and Concord
American Revolution begins

Maryland, New York, and New England met in Albany in that year to negotiate a treaty with the Iroquois. They tentatively approved a proposal by Benjamin Franklin to set up a "general government" to manage relations with the Indians. War with the French and Indians was already beginning when the Albany Plan was presented to the colonial assemblies. None approved it.

THE STRUGGLE FOR THE CONTINENT

The war that raged in North America through the late 1750s and early 1760s was part of a larger struggle between England and France. The British victory in that struggle, known in Europe as the Seven Years' War, confirmed England's commercial supremacy and cemented its control of the settled regions of North America. In America, the conflict, which colonists called the French and Indian War, was also the final stage in a long struggle among the three principal powers in northeastern North America: the English, the French, and the Iroquois.

New France and the Iroquois Nation

By the end of the seventeenth century, the French Empire in America was vast: the whole length of the Mississippi River and its delta (named Louisiana, after their king) and the continental interior as far west as the Rocky Mountains and as far south as the Rio Grande. France claimed, in effect, the entire interior of the continent.

To secure their hold on these enormous claims, they founded a string of widely separated communities, fortresses, missions, and trading posts. Would-be feudal lords established large estates *(seigneuries)* along the banks of the St. Lawrence River. On a high bluff above the river stood the fortified city of Quebec. Montreal to the south and Sault Sainte Marie and Detroit to the west marked the northern boundaries of French settlement. On the lower Mississippi there were plantations much like those in the southern colonies of English America, worked by African slaves and owned by "Creoles" (white immigrants of French descent). New Orleans, founded in 1718 to service the French plantation economy, was soon as big as some of the larger cities of the Atlantic seaboard; Biloxi and Mobile to the east completed the string of French settlement.

Both the French and the English were aware that the battle for control of North America would be determined in part by who could best win the allegiance of native tribes. The English—with their more advanced commercial economy—could usually offer the Indians better and more plentiful goods. But the French offered tolerance. Unlike the English, the French settlers in the interior generally adjusted their own behavior to Indian patterns. French fur traders frequently married Indian women and adopted tribal ways; Jesuit missionaries interacted comfortably with the natives and converted them to Catholicism by the thousands without challenging most of their social customs. By the mid-eighteenth century, therefore, the French had better and closer relations with most of the Indians of the interior than did the English.

The most powerful native group, however, had remained aloof from both sides. The Iroquois Confederacy—five Indian nations (Mohawk, Seneca, Cayuga, Onondaga, and Oneida) that had formed a defensive alliance in the fifteenth century—had been the most powerful native presence in the Ohio Valley since the 1640s. The Iroquois maintained their autonomy by trading successfully with both the French and the English and astutely played them against each other.

ANGLO-FRENCH CONFLICTS

As long as peace and stability in the North American interior survived, English and French colonists coexisted without serious difficulty. But after the Glorious Revolution in England, a complicated series of Anglo-French wars erupted in Europe and continued intermittently for nearly eighty years, creating important repercussions in America.

King William's War (1689–1697) produced only a few, indecisive clashes between the English and the French in northern New England. Queen Anne's War, which began in 1701 and continued for nearly twelve years, generated more substantial conflicts. The Treaty of Utrecht, which brought the conflict to a close in 1713, transferred substantial territory from the French to the English in North America, including Acadia (Nova Scotia) and Newfoundland. Two decades later, disputes over British trading rights in the Spanish colonies produced a conflict between England and Spain that soon grew into a much larger European war. The English colonists in America were drawn into the struggle, which they called King George's War (1744–1748). New Englanders captured the French bastion at Louisbourg on Cape Breton Island, but the peace treaty that finally ended the conflict forced them to abandon it.

In the aftermath of King George's War, relations among the English, French, and Iroquois in North America quickly deteriorated. The Iroquois (in what appears to have been a major blunder) granted trading concessions in the interior to English merchants for the first time. The French feared (probably correctly) that the English were using the concessions as a first step toward expansion into French lands. They began in 1749 to construct new fortresses in the Ohio Valley. The English responded by increasing their military forces and building fortresses of their own. The balance of power that the Iroquois had carefully maintained for so long rapidly disintegrated.

For the next five years, tensions between the English and the French increased. In the summer of 1754, the governor of Virginia sent a militia force (under the command of an inexperienced young colonel, George Washington) into the Ohio Valley to challenge French expansion. Washington built a crude stockade (Fort Necessity) not far from France's Fort Duquesne, on the site of what is now Pittsburgh. After the Virginians staged an unsuccessful attack on a French detachment, the French countered with an assault on Fort Necessity, trapping Washington and his soldiers inside. After one-third of them died in the fighting, Washington surrendered. The clash marked the beginning of the French and Indian War.

THE GREAT WAR FOR THE EMPIRE

The French and Indian War lasted nearly nine years, and it moved through three distinct phases. The first phases—from the Fort Necessity debacle in 1754 until the expansion of the war to Europe in 1756—was primarily a local, North American conflict. The Iroquois remained largely passive in the conflict. But virtually all the other tribes were allied with the French. They launched a series of raids on western English settlements. The English colonists fought to defend themselves against those raids. By late 1755, many English settlers along the frontier had withdrawn to the east of the Allegheny Mountains to escape the hostilities.

The second phase of the struggle began in 1756, when the Seven Years' War began in Europe and beyond. The fighting now spread to the West Indies, India, and Europe itself. But the principal struggle remained the war in North America, where so far England had suffered nothing but frustration and defeat. Beginning in 1757, William Pitt, the English

A LL thofe who prefer the Glory of bearing Arms to any fervile mean Employ, and have Spirit to ftand forth in **Defence** of their **King** and **Country,** againft the treacherous Defigns of *France* and *Spain*, in the

Suffex Light Dragoons,

Commanded by

Lt. Col. John Baker Holroyd,

Let them repair to

Where they fhall be handfomely Cloathed, moft compleatly Accoutred, mounted on noble Hunters, and treated with Kindnefs and Generofity.

RECRUITING FOR THE FRENCH AND INDIAN WAR The extravagant promises in this recruiting poster, distributed to colonists during the French and Indian War, suggest how difficult it sometimes was to persuade Americans to fight in the British army. (© Bettmann/Corbis)

secretary of state (and future prime minister), brought the war fully under British control. He planned military strategy, appointed commanders, and issued orders to the colonists. British commanders began forcibly enlisting colonists into the army (a practice known as "impressment"). Officers also seized supplies from local farmers and tradesmen and compelled colonists to offer shelter to British troops—all generally without compensation. The Americans resented these new impositions and firmly resisted them. By early 1758, the friction between the British authorities and the colonists was threatening to bring the war effort to a halt.

Beginning in 1758, Pitt initiated the third and final phase of the war by relaxing many of the policies that Americans had found obnoxious. He agreed to reimburse the colonists for all supplies requisitioned by the army. He returned control over recruitment to the colonial assemblies. And he dispatched large numbers of additional British troops to America. Finally, the tide of battle began to turn in England's favor. The French had always been outnumbered by the British colonists. After 1756, moreover, the French suffered from a series of poor harvests and were unable to sustain their early military successes. By mid-1758, British regulars and colonial militias were seizing one French stronghold after another. Two brilliant English generals, Jeffrey Amherst and James Wolfe, captured the fortress at Louisbourg in July 1758; a few months later Fort Duquesne fell without a fight. The next year, at the end of a siege of Quebec, the army of General Wolfe struggled up a hidden ravine under cover of darkness, surprised the larger forces of the Marquis de Montcalm, and defeated them in a battle in which both commanders were killed. The dramatic fall of Quebec on September 13, 1759, marked the beginning of the end of the American phase of the war. A year later, in September 1760, the French army formally surrendered to Amherst in Montreal. Peace finally came in 1763, with the Peace of Paris, by which the French ceded to Great Britain some of their West Indian islands, most of their colonies in India and Canada, and all other French territory in North America east of the Mississippi. The French then ceded New Orleans and their claims west of the Mississippi to Spain, surrendering all title to the mainland of North America.

The French and Indian War greatly expanded England's territorial claims in the New World. At the same time, the cost of the war greatly enlarged Britain's debt and substantially increased British resentment of the Americans. English leaders were contemptuous of the colonists for what they considered American military ineptitude during the war; they were angry that the colonists had made so few financial contributions to a struggle waged, they believed, largely for American benefit; they were particularly bitter that colonial merchants had been selling food and other goods to the French in the West Indies throughout the conflict. All these factors combined to persuade many English leaders that a major reorganization of the empire would be necessary. Part of that reorganization was increased authority of London over the colonies.

The war had an equally profound effect on the American colonists. It was an experience that forced them, for the first time, to act in concert against a common foe. The 1758 return of authority to the colonial assemblies seemed to many Americans to confirm the illegitimacy of English interference in local affairs.

For the Indians of the Ohio Valley, the British victory was disastrous. Those tribes that had allied themselves with the French had earned the enmity of the victorious English. The Iroquois Confederacy, which had not allied with the French, fared only slightly better. English officials saw the passivity of the Iroquois during the war as evidence of duplicity. In the aftermath of the peace settlement, the fragile Iroquois alliance with the British quickly unraveled. The tribes would continue to contest the English for control of the Ohio Valley for another fifty years, but increasingly divided and increasingly outnumbered. They would seldom again be in a position to deal with their European rivals on terms of military or political equality.

THE NEW IMPERIALISM

With the treaty of 1763, England found itself truly at peace for the first time in more than fifty years. As a result, the British government could now turn its attention to the organization of its empire. Saddled with enormous debts from the many years of war, England was desperately in need of new revenues. Responsible for vast new lands in the New World, the imperial government believed it must increase its administrative capacities in America. The result was a dramatic and, for England, disastrous redefinition of the colonial relationship.

BURDENS OF EMPIRE

The experience of the French and Indian War should have suggested that increasing imperial control over the colonies would not be easy. Not only had the resistance of the colonists forced Pitt to relax his policies in 1758, but the colonial assemblies continued to defy imperial trade regulations and other British demands. But the most immediate problem for London was its staggering war debt. Landlords and merchants in England were objecting strenuously to any further tax increases, and the colonial assemblies had repeatedly demonstrated their unwillingness to pay for the war effort. Many officials in England believed that only by taxing the Americans directly could the empire effectively meet its financial needs.

THE FIRST GLOBAL WAR

THE French and Indian War in North America was only a small part of a much larger conflict. Known in Europe as the Seven Years' War, it was one of the longest, most widespread, and most important wars in modern history. The war thrust Great Britain into conflicts across Europe and North America. Winston Churchill once wrote of it as the first "world war."

In North America, the war was a result of tensions along the frontiers of the British Empire. But it was much more a result of larger conflicts among the great powers in Europe. It began in the 1750s with what historians have called a "diplomatic revolution." Well-established alliances between Britain and the Austro-Hungarian Empire and between France and Prussia collapsed, replaced by a new set of alliances setting Britain and Prussia against France and Austria. The instability that these changing alliances produced helped speed the European nations toward war.

The Austrian-British alliance collapsed because Austria suffered a series of significant defeats at the hands of the Prussians. To the British government, these failures suggested that the Austro-Hungarian Empire was now too weak to help Britain balance French power. As a result, England launched a search for new partnerships with the rising powers of northern Germany, Austria's enemies. In response, the Austrians sought an alliance with France to help protect them from the power of their former British allies. (One later result of this new alliance was the 1770 marriage of the future French king Louis XVI to the Austrian princess Marie Antoinette.) In the aftermath of these realignments, Austria sought again to defeat the Prussian-Hanover forces in Germany. In the process, Russia became concerned about the Austro-Hungarian Empire's possible dominance in central Europe and allied itself with the British and the Prussians. These complicated realignments eventually led to the Seven Years' War, which soon spread across much of the world. The war engaged not only most of the great powers in Europe, from England to Russia, but also the emerging colonial worlds—India, West Africa, the Caribbean, and the Philippines—as the powerful British navy worked to strip France, and eventually Spain, of its valuable colonial holdings.

Like most modern conflicts, the Seven Years' War was at heart a struggle for economic power. Colonial possessions, many European nations believed, were critical to their future wealth and well worth fighting for. The war's outcome affected not only the future of America but also the distribution of power throughout much of the world. It destroyed the French navy and much of the French Empire, and it elevated Great Britain to undisputed preeminence among the colonizing powers—especially when, at the conclusion of the war, India and all of eastern North America fell firmly under English control. The war also reorganized the balance of power in Europe, with Britain now preeminent among the great powers and Prussia (later to become the core of modern Germany) rapidly rising in wealth and military power.

(The Granger Collection, NYC)

The Seven Years' War was not only one of the first great colonial wars but also one of the last great wars of religion, and it extended the dominance of Protestantism in Europe. In what is now Canada, the war replaced French with British rule and thus replaced Catholic with Protestant dominance. The Vatican, no longer a military power itself, had relied on the great Catholic empires—Spain, France, and Austria-Hungary—as bulwarks of its power and influence. The shift of power toward Protestant governments in Europe and North America weakened the Catholic Church and reduced its geopolitical influence.

The conclusion of the Seven Years' War strengthened Britain and Germany and weakened France. But it did not provide any lasting solution to the rivalries among the great colonial powers. In North America, a dozen years after the end of the conflict, the American Revolution—the origins of which were in many ways a direct result of the Seven Years' War—stripped the British Empire of one of its most important and valuable colonial appendages. By the time the American Revolution came to an end, the French Revolution had sparked another lengthy period of war, culminating in the Napoleonic Wars of the early nineteenth century, which once again redrew the map of Europe and, for a while, the world. •

UNDERSTAND, ANALYZE, & EVALUATE

1. How did the Seven Years' War change the balance of power among the nations of Europe? Who gained and who lost in the war?
2. Why is the Seven Years' War described as one of the "most important wars in modern history"?

THE THIRTEEN COLONIES IN 1763 This map is a close-up of the thirteen colonies at the end of the Seven Years' War. It shows the line of settlement established by the Proclamation of 1763 (the red line), as well as the extent of actual settlement in that year (the blue line). Note that in the middle colonies (North Carolina, Virginia, Maryland, and southern Pennsylvania), settlement had already reached the red line—and in one small area of western Pennsylvania moved beyond it—by the time of the Proclamation of 1763. Note also the string of forts established beyond the Proclamation line. • *How do the forts help to explain the efforts of the British to restrict settlement? And how does the extent of actual settlement help explain why it was so difficult for the British to enforce their restrictions?*

At this crucial moment in Anglo-American relations, the government of England was thrown into turmoil by the 1760 accession to the throne of George III. He brought two particularly unfortunate qualities to the office. First, he was determined to reassert the authority of the monarchy. He removed from power the relatively stable coalition of Whigs that had governed for much of the century and replaced it with a new and very unstable coalition of his own. The weak new ministries that emerged as a result each lasted in office an average of only about two years.

Second, the king had serious intellectual and psychological limitations. He suffered, apparently, from a rare mental disease that produced intermittent bouts of insanity. (Indeed, in the last years of his long reign he was, according to most accounts, unable to perform any official functions.) Yet even when George III was lucid, which was most of the time in the 1760s and 1770s, he was painfully immature and insecure. The king's personality, therefore, contributed both to the instability and to the rigidity of the British government during these critical years.

More directly responsible for the problems that soon emerged with the colonies, however, was George Grenville, whom the king made prime minister in 1763. Grenville shared the prevailing opinion within Britain that the colonists should be compelled to pay a part of the cost of defending and administering the empire.

THE BRITISH AND THE TRIBES

With the defeat of the French, frontiersmen from the English colonies began immediately to move over the mountains and into tribal lands in the upper Ohio Valley. An alliance of Indian tribes, under the Ottawa chieftain Pontiac, struck back. Fearing that an escalation of the fighting might threaten western trade, the British government—in the Proclamation of 1763—forbade settlers to advance beyond the Appalachian Mountains.

Many Indian groups supported the Proclamation as the best bargain available to them. The Cherokee, in particular, worked actively to hasten the drawing of the boundary, hoping finally to put an end to white movements into their lands. Relations between the western tribes and the British improved for a time, partly as a result of the work of the sympathetic Indian superintendents the British appointed.

In the end, however, the Proclamation of 1763 was ineffective. White settlers continued to swarm across the boundary and to claim lands farther and farther into the Ohio Valley. The British authorities failed to enforce limits to the expansion. In 1768, new agreements with the western tribes pushed the permanent boundary farther west. But these treaties and subsequent ones also failed to stop the white advance.

BATTLES OVER TRADE AND TAXES

The Grenville ministry tried to increase its authority in the colonies in other ways as well. Regular British troops were stationed permanently in America, and under the Mutiny Act of 1765 the colonists were required to help provision and maintain the army. Ships of the British navy patrolled American waters to search for smugglers. The customs service was reorganized and enlarged. Royal officials were required to take up their colonial posts in person instead of sending substitutes. Colonial manufacturing was restricted so that it would not compete with rapidly expanding industries in Great Britain.

The Sugar Act of 1764 raised the duty on sugar while lowering the duty on molasses. It also established new vice-admiralty courts in America to try accused smugglers—thus cutting them off from sympathetic local juries. The Currency Act of 1764 required that the colonial assemblies stop issuing paper money.

At first, it was difficult for the colonists to resist these unpopular new laws. That was partly because Americans continued to harbor as many grievances against one another as they did against the authorities in London. In 1763, for example, a band of Pennsylvania frontiersmen known as the Paxton Boys descended on Philadelphia to demand tax relief and financial support for their defense against Indians. Bloodshed was averted only by concessions from the colonial assembly. In 1771, a small-scale civil war broke out in North Carolina when the "Regulators," farmers of the interior, organized and armed themselves to resist high taxes. The colonial governor appointed sheriffs to enforce the levies. An army of militiamen, most of them from the eastern counties, crushed the Regulator revolt.

The unpopularity of the Grenville program helped the colonists overcome their internal conflicts and see that the policies from London were a threat to all Americans. Northern merchants would suffer from restraints on their commerce. The closing of the West to land speculation and fur trading enraged many colonists. Others were angered by the restriction of opportunities for manufacturing. Southern planters, in debt to English merchants, would be unable to ease their debts by speculating in western land. Small farmers would suffer from the abolition of paper money, which had been the source of most of their loans. Workers in towns faced the prospect of narrowing opportunities, particularly because of the restraints on manufacturing and currency. Everyone stood to suffer from increased taxes.

Most Americans soon found ways to live with the new British laws without terrible economic hardship. But their political grievances remained. Americans were accustomed to wide latitude in self-government. They believed that colonial assemblies had the sole right to control appropriations for the costs of government within the colonies. By attempting to raise extensive revenues directly from the public, the British government was challenging the basis of colonial political power.

STIRRINGS OF REVOLT

By the mid-1760s, a hardening of positions had begun in both England and America. The result was a progression of events that, more rapidly than imagined, destroyed the British Empire in America.

THE STAMP ACT CRISIS

Grenville could not have devised a better method for antagonizing and unifying the colonies than the Stamp Act of 1765. Unlike the Sugar Act of a year earlier, which affected only a few New England merchants, the tax on printed documents fell on everyone. It required taxes on every printed document in the colonies: newspapers, almanacs, pamphlets, deeds, wills, licenses. British officials were soon collecting more than ten times as much revenue in America as they had been before 1763. More alarming than these taxes, however, was the precedent they seemed to create. In the past, taxes and duties on colonial trade had always been designed to regulate commerce. The Stamp Act, however, was clearly an attempt by England to raise revenue from the colonies without the consent of the colonial assemblies.

Few colonists believed that they could do anything more than grumble until the Virginia House of Burgesses aroused Americans to action. Patrick Henry made a dramatic speech to the House in May 1765, concluding with a vague prediction that if present policies were not revised, George III, like earlier tyrants, might lose his head. Amid shocked cries of "Treason!" Henry introduced a set of resolutions (only some of which the assembly passed) declaring that Americans possessed the same rights as the English, especially the right to be taxed only by their own representatives; that Virginians should pay no taxes except those voted by the Virginia assembly; and that anyone advocating the right of Parliament to tax Virginians should be deemed an enemy of the colony. Henry's resolutions were printed and circulated as the "Virginia Resolves."

In Massachusetts at about the same time, James Otis persuaded his fellow members of the colonial assembly to call an intercolonial congress to take action against the new tax. And in October 1765, the Stamp Act Congress, as it was called, met in New York with delegates from nine colonies. In a petition to the British government, the congress denied that the colonies could rightfully be taxed except through their own provincial assemblies.

In the summer of 1765, meanwhile, mobs were rising up in several colonial cities against the Stamp Act. The largest was in Boston, where men belonging to the newly organized Sons of Liberty terrorized stamp agents and burned stamps. The mob also attacked such supposedly pro-British aristocrats as the lieutenant governor, Thomas Hutchinson (who had privately opposed passage of the Stamp Act but who felt obliged to support it once it became law). Hutchinson's elegant house was pillaged and virtually destroyed.

The crisis finally subsided largely because England backed down. The authorities in London were less affected by the political protests than by economic pressure. Many New Englanders had stopped buying English goods to protest the Sugar Act of 1764, and the Stamp Act caused the boycott to spread. With pressure from English merchants, Parliament—under a new prime minister, the Marquis of Rockingham—repealed the unpopular law on March 18, 1766. To satisfy his strong and vociferous opponents, Rockingham also pushed through the Declaratory Act, which confirmed parliamentary authority over the colonies "in all cases whatsoever." But in their rejoicing over the Stamp Act repeal, most Americans paid little attention to this sweeping declaration of power.

INTERNAL REBELLIONS

The conflicts with Britain were not the only uprisings emerging in the turbulent years of the 1760s. In addition to the Stamp Act crisis and other challenges to London, there were internal rebellions that had their roots in the class system in New York and New England. In the Hudson Valley in New York, great estates had grown up, in which owners had rented out their land to small farmers. The Revolutionary fervor of the time led many of these tenants to demand ownership of the land they worked. To emphasize their determination, they stopped paying rents. The rebellion soon failed, but other challenges continued. In Vermont, which still was governed by New York, insurgent farmers challenged landowners (many of them the same owners whom tenants had challenged on the Hudson) by taking up arms and demanding ownership of the land they worked. Ethan Allen (later a hero of the Revolutionary War and himself a land speculator) took up the cause of the Green Mountain farmers and accused the landowners of trying to "enslave a free people." Allen eventually succeeded in making Vermont into a separate state, which broke up some of the large estates.

THE TOWNSHEND PROGRAM

When the Rockingham government's policy of appeasement met substantial opposition in England, the king dismissed the ministry and replaced it with a new government led by the aging but still powerful William Pitt, who was now Lord Chatham. Chatham had in the past been sympathetic toward American interests. Once in office, however, he was at times so incapacitated by mental illness that leadership of his administration fell to the chancellor of the exchequer, Charles Townshend.

CONSIDER THE SOURCE

BENJAMIN FRANKLIN, TESTIMONY AGAINST THE STAMP ACT (1766)

IN 1765 Parliament passed the first internal tax on the colonists, known as the Stamp Act. Benjamin Franklin was a colonial agent in London at the time, and as colonial opposition to the act grew, he found himself representing these views to the British government. In his testimony from Parliament he describes the role of taxes in Pennsylvania and the economic relationship between the colonies and the mother country.

Q. What is your name, and place of abode?

A. Franklin, of Philadelphia.

Q. Do the Americans pay any considerable taxes among themselves?

A. Certainly many, and very heavy taxes.

Q. What are the present taxes in Pennsylvania, laid by the laws of the colony?

A. There are taxes on all estates, real and personal; a poll tax; a tax on all offices, professions, trades, and businesses, according to their profits; an excise on all wine, rum, and other spirit; and a duty of ten pounds per head on all Negroes imported, with some other duties.

Q. For what purposes are those taxes laid?

A. For the support of the civil and military establishments of the country, and to discharge the heavy debt contracted in the last [Seven Years'] war. . . .

Q. Are not all the people very able to pay those taxes?

A. No. The frontier counties, all along the continent, have been frequently ravaged by the enemy and greatly impoverished, are able to pay very little tax. . . .

Q. Are not the colonies, from their circumstances, very able to pay the stamp duty?

A. In my opinion there is not gold and silver enough in the colonies to pay the stamp duty for one year.

Q. Don't you know that the money arising from the stamps was all to be laid out in America?

A. I know it is appropriated by the act to the American service; but it will be spent in the conquered colonies, where the soldiers are, not in the colonies that pay it.

Q. Do you think it right that America should be protected by this country and pay no part of the expense?

A. That is not the case. The colonies raised, clothed, and paid, during the last war, near 25,000 men, and spent many millions.

Q. Where you not reimbursed by Parliament?

A. We were only reimbursed what, in your opinion, we had advanced beyond our proportion, or beyond what might reasonably be expected from us; and it was a very small part of what we spent. Pennsylvania, in particular, disbursed about 500,000 pounds, and the reimbursements, in the whole, did not exceed 60,000 pounds. . . .

Q. Do you think the people of America would submit to pay the stamp duty, if it was moderated?

A. No, never, unless compelled by force of arms. . . .

Q. What was the temper of America towards Great Britain before the year 1763?

A. The best in the world. They submitted willingly to the government of the Crown, and paid, in all their courts, obedience to acts of Parliament. . . .

Q. What is your opinion of a future tax, imposed on the same principle with that of the Stamp Act? How would the Americans receive it?

A. Just as they do this. They would not pay it.

Q. Have not you heard of the resolutions of this House, and of the House of Lords, asserting the right of Parliament relating to

America, including a power to tax the people there?

A. Yes, I have heard of such resolutions.

Q. What will be the opinion of the Americans on those resolutions?

A. They will think them unconstitutional and unjust.

Q. Was it an opinion in America before 1763 that the Parliament had no right to lay taxes and duties there?

A. I never heard any objection to the right of laying duties to regulate commerce; but a right to lay internal taxes was never supposed to be in Parliament, as we are not represented there.

Q. Did the Americans ever dispute the controlling power of Parliament to regulate the commerce?

A. No.

Q. Can anything less than a military force carry the Stamp Act into execution?

A. I do not see how a military force can be applied to that purpose.

Q. Why may it not?

A. Suppose a military force sent into America; they will find nobody in arms; what are they then to do? They cannot force a man to take stamps who chooses to do without them. They will not find a rebellion; they may indeed make one.

Q. If the act is not repealed, what do you think will be the consequences?

A. A total loss of the respect and affection the people of America bear to this country, and of all the commerce that depends on that respect and affection.

Q. How can the commerce be affected?

A. You will find that, if the act is not repealed, they will take very little of your manufactures in a short time.

Q. Is it in their power to do without them?

A. I think they may very well do without them.

Q. Is it their interest not to take them?

A. The goods they take from Britain are either necessaries, mere conveniences, or superfluities. The first, as cloth, etc., with a little industry they can make at home; the second they can do without till they are able to provide them among themselves; and the last, which are mere articles of fashion, purchased and consumed because of the fashion in a respected country; but will now be detested and rejected. The people have already struck off, by general agreement, the use of all goods fashionable in mourning.

Q. If the Stamp Act should be repealed, would it induce the assemblies of America to acknowledge the right of Parliament to tax them, and would they erase their resolutions [against the Stamp Act]?

A. No, never.

Q. Is there no means of obliging them to erase those resolutions?

A. None that I know of; they will never do it, unless compelled by force of arms.

Q. Is there a power on earth that can force them to erase them?

A. No power, how great so ever, can force men to change their opinions. . . .

Q. What used to be the pride of the Americans?

A. To indulge in the fashions and manufactures of Great Britain.

Q. What is now their pride?

A. To wear their old clothes over again, till they can make new ones.

UNDERSTAND, ANALYZE, & EVALUATE

1. What kind of taxes did colonists pay according to Franklin? What did the interviewer seem to think of the colonists' tax burden? What disagreements existed between Franklin and his interviewer on the purpose, legality, and feasibility of the stamp tax?

2. How did Franklin characterize the British-colonial relationship prior to 1763?

3. What colonial response to the Stamp Act and other "internal taxes" did Franklin predict? What, if anything, could Parliament do to enforce the colonists' compliance?

Source: *The Parliamentary History of England* (London, 1813), XVI, 138–159; in Charles Morris, *The Great Republic by the Master Historians* Vol. II (R.S. Belcher Co., 1902).

With the Stamp Act repealed, the greatest remaining American grievance involved the Mutiny (or Quartering) Act of 1765, which required colonists to shelter and supply British troops. The colonists objected not so much to the actual burden as to being required by London to do so. The Massachusetts and New York assemblies went so far as to refuse to vote the mandated supplies to the troops.

Townshend responded in 1767 by disbanding the New York Assembly until the colonists agreed to obey the Mutiny Act. By singling out New York, he believed, he would avoid antagonizing all the colonies at once. He also imposed new taxes (known as the Townshend Duties) on various goods imported to the colonies from England—lead, paint, paper, and tea. Townshend assumed that since these were taxes purely on "external" transactions (imports from overseas), as opposed to the internal transactions the Stamp Act had taxed, the colonists would not object. But all the colonies resented the suspension of the New York Assembly, believing it to be a threat to every colonial government. And all the colonies rejected Townshend's careful distinction between external and internal taxation.

Townshend also established a board of customs commissioners in America. The new commissioners established their headquarters in Boston. They virtually ended smuggling in Boston (although smugglers continued to carry on a busy trade in other colonial seaports). The Boston merchants—angry that the new commission was diverting the lucrative smuggling trade elsewhere—helped organize a boycott of British goods that were subject to the Townshend Duties. Merchants in Philadelphia and New York joined them in a nonimportation agreement in 1768, and later some southern merchants and planters also agreed to cooperate. Throughout the colonies, American homespun and other domestic products became suddenly fashionable.

Late in 1767, Charles Townshend died. In March 1770, the new prime minister, Lord North, hoping to end the American boycott, repealed all the Townshend Duties except the tea tax.

THE BOSTON MASSACRE

Before news of the repeal reached America, an event in Massachusetts electrified colonial opinion. The harassment of the new customs commissioners in Boston had grown so intense that the British government had placed four regiments of regular troops in the city. Many of the poorly paid British soldiers looked for jobs in their off-duty hours and thus competed with local workers. Clashes between the two groups were frequent.

On the night of March 5, 1770, a mob of dockworkers, "liberty boys," and others began pelting the sentries at the customs house with rocks and snowballs. Hastily, Captain Thomas Preston of the British regiment lined up several of his men in front of the building to protect it. There was some scuffling; one of the soldiers was knocked down; and in the midst of it all, apparently, several British soldiers fired into the crowd, killing five people.

This murky incident, almost certainly the result of panic and confusion, was quickly transformed by local resistance leaders into the "Boston Massacre." It became the subject of such lurid (and inaccurate) accounts as the widely circulated pamphlet *Innocent Blood Crying to God from the Streets of Boston*. A famous engraving by Paul Revere portrayed the massacre as a calculated assault on a peaceful crowd. The British soldiers, tried before a jury of Bostonians, were found guilty only of manslaughter and given token punishment. But colonial pamphlets and newspapers convinced many Americans that the soldiers were guilty of official murder.

THE BOSTON MASSACRE (1770), BY PAUL REVERE This sensationalized engraving of the conflict between British troops and Boston laborers is one of many important propaganda documents, by Revere and others, for the Patriot cause in the 1770s. Among the victims of the massacre listed by Revere was Crispus Attucks, probably the first black man to die in the struggle for American independence. (Library of Congress)

The leading figure in fomenting public outrage over the Boston Massacre was Samuel Adams. England, he argued, had become a morass of sin and corruption; only in America did public virtue survive. In 1772, he proposed the creation of a "committee of correspondence" in Boston to publicize the grievances against England. Other colonies followed Massachusetts's lead, and a loose intercolonial network of political organizations was soon established that kept the spirit of dissent alive through the 1770s.

THE PHILOSOPHY OF REVOLT

Although a superficial calm settled on the colonies after the Boston Massacre, the crises of the 1760s had helped arouse enduring ideological challenges to English authority and had produced powerful instruments for publicizing colonial grievances. Gradually a political outlook gained a following in America that would ultimately serve to justify revolt.

The ideas that would support the Revolution emerged from many sources. Some were drawn from religious (particularly Puritan) sources or from the political experiences of the colonies. Others came from abroad. Most important, perhaps, were the "radical" ideas of the political opposition in Great Britain. Some were Scots, who considered the English

TAVERNS IN REVOLUTIONARY MASSACHUSETTS

IN colonial Massachusetts, as in many other American colonies in the 1760s and 1770s, taverns (or "public houses," as they were often known) were crucial to the development of popular resistance to British rule. The Puritan culture of New England created some resistance to taverns, and reformers tried to regulate or close them to reduce the problems caused by "public drunkenness," "lewd behavior," and "anarchy." But as the commercial life of the colonies expanded and more people began living in towns and cities, taverns became a central institution in American social life—and eventually in its political life as well.

Taverns were appealing, of course, because they provided alcoholic drinks in a culture where the craving for alcohol—and the extent of drunkenness—was very high. But taverns had other attractions as well. They were one of the few places where people could meet and talk openly in public; indeed, many colonists considered the life of the tavern as the only vaguely democratic experience available to them. The tavern was a mostly male institution, just as politics was considered a mostly male concern. And so the fusion of male camaraderie and political discourse emerged naturally out of the tavern culture.

As the Revolutionary crisis deepened, taverns and pubs became the central meeting places for airing the ideas that fueled resistance to British policies. Educated and uneducated men alike joined in animated discussions of events. Those who could not read—and there were many—could learn about the

state tyrannical. Others were embittered "country Whigs," who felt excluded from power and considered the existing system corrupt and oppressive. Drawing from some of the great philosophical minds of earlier generations—most notably John Locke—these English dissidents framed a powerful argument against their government.

Central to this emerging ideology was a new concept of what government should be. Because humans were inherently corrupt and selfish, government was necessary to protect individuals from the evil in one another. But because any government was run by corruptible people, the people needed safeguards against its possible abuses of power. Most people in both England and America considered the English constitution the best system ever devised to meet these necessities. By distributing power among the three elements of society—the monarchy, the aristocracy, and the common people—the English political system had ensured that no individual or group could exercise unchecked authority. Yet by the mid-seventeenth century, dissidents in both England and America had become convinced that the constitution was in danger. A single center of power—the king and his ministers—was becoming so powerful that it could not be effectively checked.

Such arguments found little sympathy in most of England. The English constitution was not a written document or a fixed set of unchangeable rules. It was a general sense contents of Revolutionary pamphlets from listening to tavern conversations. They could join in the discussion of the new republican ideas emerging in America by participating in tavern celebrations of, for example, the anniversaries of resistance to the Stamp Act. Those anniversaries inspired elaborate toasts in public houses throughout the colonies.

In an age before any wide distribution of newspapers, taverns and tavernkeepers were important sources of information about the political and social turmoil of the time. Taverns were also the settings for political events. In 1770, for example, a report circulated through the taverns of Danvers, Massachusetts, about a local man who was continuing to sell tea despite the colonial boycott. The Sons of Liberty brought the seller to the Bell Tavern and persuaded him to sign a confession and apology before a crowd of defiant men in the public room.

Almost all politicians who wanted any real contact with the public found it necessary to visit taverns in colonial Massachusetts. Samuel Adams spent considerable time in the public houses of Boston, where he sought to encourage resistance to British rule while taking care to drink moderately so as not to erode his stature as a leader. His cousin John

TAVERN BILLIARDS Gentlemen in Hanover Town, Virginia, gather for a game of billiards in a local tavern in this 1797 drawing by Benjamin Henry Latrobe. (Maryland Historical Society, Baltimore (1960.108.1.3.11))

Adams, although somewhat more skeptical of taverns and more sensitive to the vices they encouraged, also recognized their political value. In taverns, he once said, "bastards and legislatores are frequently begotten."   •

UNDERSTAND, ANALYZE, & EVALUATE

1. Why were taverns so important in educating colonists about the relationship with Britain?
2. What gathering places today serve the same purposes as taverns did in colonial America?

of the "way things are done," and most people in England were willing to accept changes in it. Americans, by contrast, drew from their experience with colonial charters, in which the shape and powers of government were permanently inscribed on paper. They resisted the idea of a flexible, changing set of basic principles.

One basic principle, Americans believed, was the right of people to be taxed only with their own consent—a belief that gradually took shape in the popular slogan "No taxation without representation." Whatever the nature of a tax, it could not be levied without the consent of the colonists themselves.

This clamor about "representation" made little sense to the English. According to English constitutional theory, members of Parliament did not represent individuals or particular geographical areas. Instead, each member represented the interests of the whole nation and indeed the whole empire. The many boroughs of England that had no representative in Parliament, the whole of Ireland, and the colonies thousands of miles away—all were thus represented in the Parliament at London, even though they elected no representatives of their own. This was the theory of "virtual" representation. But Americans, drawing from their experiences with their town meetings and their colonial assemblies, believed in "actual" representation. Every community was entitled to its own representative, elected by the people of that community. Since the colonists had none of their own representatives in Parliament, it followed that they were not represented there. Americans believed that the colonial assemblies played the same role within the colonies as Parliament did within England. The empire, the Americans argued, was a sort of federation of commonwealths, each with its own legislative body, all tied together by loyalty to the king.

Such ideas illustrated a fundamental difference of opinion between England and America over the question of where ultimate power lay. By arguing that Parliament had the right to legislate for the empire as a whole but that only the provincial assemblies could legislate for the individual colonies, Americans were in effect arguing for a division of sovereignty. Parliament would be sovereign in some matters, the assemblies in others. To the British, such an argument was absurd. In any system of government there must be a single, ultimate authority. And since the empire was, in their view, a single, undivided unit, there could be only one authority within it: the English government of king and Parliament.

SITES OF RESISTANCE

Colonists kept the growing spirit of resistance alive in many ways, but most of all through writing and talking. Dissenting leaflets, pamphlets, and books circulated widely through the colonies. In towns and cities, men gathered in churches, schools, town squares, and, above all, taverns to discuss politics.

Taverns were also places where resistance pamphlets and leaflets could be distributed and where meetings for the planning of protests and demonstrations could be held. Massachusetts had the most elaborately developed tavern culture, which was perhaps one reason why the spirit of resistance grew more quickly there than anywhere else.

The apparent calm in America in the 1770s hid a growing sense of resentment about the continued enforcement of the Navigation Acts. Popular anger was visible in occasional acts of rebellion. At one point, colonists seized a British revenue ship on the lower Delaware River. In 1772, angry residents of Rhode Island boarded the British schooner *Gaspée,* set it afire, and sank it.

THE TEA EXCITEMENT

The Revolutionary fervor of the 1760s intensified as a result of a new act of Parliament—one that involved the business of selling tea. In 1773, Britain's East India Company (on the verge of bankruptcy) was sitting on large stocks of tea that it could not sell in England. In an effort to save it, the government passed the Tea Act of 1773, which gave the company the right to export its merchandise directly to the colonies without paying any of the regular taxes that were imposed on colonial merchants, who had traditionally served as the middlemen in such transactions. With these privileges, the company could under-sell American merchants and monopolize the colonial tea trade.

The act angered influential colonial merchants and, more important, revived American passions about the issue of taxation without representation. The law provided no new tax on tea. But the original Townshend duty on the commodity survived; and the East India Company was now exempt from paying it. Lord North had assumed that most colonists would welcome the new law because it would reduce the price of tea to consumers by removing the middlemen. But resistance leaders in America argued that the law, in effect, represented an unconstitutional tax on American merchants. The colonists responded by boycotting tea.

Unlike earlier protests, most of which had involved relatively small numbers of people, the tea boycott mobilized large segments of the population. It also helped link the colonies together in a common experience of mass popular protest. Particularly important to the movement were the activities of colonial women, who led the boycott. The Daughters of Liberty—a recently formed women's patriotic organization—proclaimed, "rather than Freedom, we'll part with our Tea."

In the last weeks of 1773, with strong popular support, some colonial leaders made plans to prevent the East India Company from landing its cargoes. In Philadelphia and New York, determined colonists kept the tea from leaving the company's ships, and in Charleston, they stored it away in a public warehouse. In Boston, local patriots staged a spectacular drama. On the evening of December 16, 1773, three companies of fifty men each, masquerading as Mohawk Indians, went aboard three ships, broke open the tea chests, and heaved them into the harbor. As the electrifying news of the Boston "tea party" spread, colonists in other seaports staged similar acts of resistance.

Parliament retaliated in four acts of 1774: closing the port of Boston, drastically reducing the powers of self-government in Massachusetts, permitting royal officers in America to be tried for crimes in other colonies or in England, and providing for the quartering of troops by the colonists. These Coercive Acts were more widely known in America as the "Intolerable Acts."

The Coercive Acts backfired. Far from isolating Massachusetts, they made it a martyr in the eyes of residents of other colonies and sparked new resistance up and down the coast. Colonial legislatures passed a series of resolves supporting Massachusetts. Women's groups mobilized to extend the boycotts of British goods and to create substitutes for the tea, textiles, and other commodities they were shunning. In Edenton, North Carolina, fifty-one women signed an agreement in October 1774 declaring their "sincere adherence" to the anti-British resolutions of their provincial assembly and proclaiming their duty to do "every thing as far as lies in our power" to support the "publick good."

COOPERATION AND WAR

Beginning in 1765, colonial leaders developed a variety of organizations for converting popular discontent into action—organizations that in time formed the basis for an independent government.

New Sources of Authority

The passage of authority from the royal government to the colonists themselves began on the local level. In colony after colony, local institutions responded to the resistance movement by simply seizing authority. At times, entirely new institutions emerged.

The most effective of these new groups were the committees of correspondence. Virginia established the first intercolonial committees of correspondence, which helped make possible continuous cooperation among the colonies. After the royal governor dissolved the assembly in 1774, a rump session met in the Raleigh Tavern at Williamsburg, declared that the Intolerable Acts menaced the liberties of every colony, and issued a call for a Continental Congress.

Delegates from all the colonies except Georgia were present when, in September 1774, the First Continental Congress convened in Philadelphia. They made five major decisions.

First, they rejected a plan for a colonial union under British authority. Second, they endorsed a relatively moderate statement of grievances, which addressed the king as "Most Gracious Sovereign," but which also included a demand for the repeal of all oppressive legislation passed since 1763. Third, they approved a series of resolutions recommending that military preparations be made for defense against possible attack by the British troops in Boston. Fourth, they agreed to a series of boycotts that they hoped would stop all trade with Great Britain, and they formed a "Continental Association" to see that these agreements were enforced. Fifth, the delegates agreed to meet again the following spring.

During the winter, the Parliament in London debated proposals for conciliating the colonists, and early in 1775 Lord North finally won approval for a series of measures known as the Conciliatory Propositions. Parliament proposed that the colonies would tax themselves at Parliament's demand. With this offer, Lord North hoped to separate the American moderates, whom he believed represented the views of the majority, from the extremist minority. But his offer was too little and too late. It did not reach America until after the first shots of war had been fired.

LEXINGTON AND CONCORD

For months, the farmers and townspeople of Massachusetts had been gathering arms and ammunition and preparing "minutemen" to fight on a minute's notice. The Continental Congress had approved preparations for a defensive war, and the citizen-soldiers waited only for an aggressive move by the British regulars in Boston.

In Boston, General Thomas Gage, commanding the British garrison, considered his army too small to do anything without reinforcements. He resisted the advice of less cautious officers, who assured him that the Americans would back down quickly before any show of British force. When General Gage received orders to arrest the rebel leaders Sam Adams and John Hancock, known to be in the vicinity of Lexington, he still hesitated. But when he heard that the minutemen had stored a large supply of gunpowder in Concord (eighteen miles from Boston), he decided to act. On the night of April 18, 1775, he sent a detachment of about 1,000 men out toward Lexington, hoping to surprise the colonials and seize the illegal supplies without bloodshed.

But Patriots in Boston were watching the British movements closely, and during the night two horsemen, William Dawes and Paul Revere, rode out to warn the villages and farms. When the redcoats arrived in Lexington the next day, several dozen minutemen awaited them on the town common. Shots were fired and minutemen fell; eight were killed and ten wounded. Advancing to Concord, the British discovered that the Americans had hastily removed most of the powder supply. All along the road back to Boston, the British were harassed by the gunfire of farmers hiding behind trees, rocks, and stone walls. By the end of the day, the British had lost almost three times as many men as the Americans.

The first shots—the "shots heard 'round the world," as Americans later called them—had been fired. But who had fired them first? According to one of the minutemen at Lexington, the British commander, Major Thomas Pitcairn, had shouted to the colonists on his arrival, "Disperse, ye rebels!" When they ignored him, he ordered his troops to fire. British officers and soldiers claimed that the minutemen had fired first. Whatever the truth, the rebels succeeded in circulating their account well ahead of the British version, adorning it with tales of British atrocities. The effect was to rally thousands of colonists to the rebel cause.

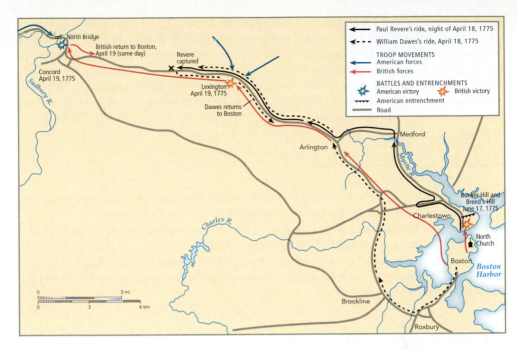

THE BATTLES OF LEXINGTON AND CONCORD, 1775 This map shows the fabled series of events that led to the first battle of the American Revolution. On the night of April 18, 1775, Paul Revere and William Dawes rode out from Boston to warn the outlying towns of the approach of British troops. Revere was captured just west of Lexington, but Dawes escaped and returned to Boston. The next morning, British forces moved out of Boston toward Lexington, where they met armed American minutemen on the Lexington common and exchanged fire. The British dispersed the Americans in Lexington. But they next moved on to Concord, where they encountered more armed minutemen, clashed again, and were driven back toward Boston. All along their line of march, they were harassed by riflemen. • *What impact did the Battles of Lexington and Concord (and the later Battle of Bunker Hill, also shown on this map) have on colonial sentiment toward the British?*

It was not immediately clear at the time that the skirmishes at Lexington and Concord were the first battles of a war. But whether people recognized it at the time or not, the War for Independence had begun.

CONCLUSION

When the French and Indian War ended in 1763, it might have seemed reasonable to expect that relations between the English colonists in America and Great Britain itself would have been cemented more firmly than ever. But in fact, the end of the French and Indian War altered the imperial relationship forever, in ways that ultimately drove Americans to rebel against English rule and begin a war for independence. To the British, the lesson of the French and Indian War was that the colonies in America needed firmer control from London. The empire was now much bigger, and it needed better administration. The war had produced great debts, and the Americans—among the principal beneficiaries of the war—should help pay them. And so for more than a decade after the end of the fighting, the British tried one strategy after another to tighten control over and extract money from the colonies.

To the colonists, this effort to tighten imperial rule appeared to be both a betrayal of the sacrifices they had made in the war and a challenge to their long-developing assumptions about the rights of English people to rule themselves. Gradually, white Americans came to see in the British policies evidence of a conspiracy to establish tyranny in the New World. And so throughout the 1760s and 1770s, the colonists developed an ideology of resistance and defiance. By the time the first shots were fired in the American Revolution in 1775, Britain and America had come to view each other as two very different societies. Their differences, which came to seem irreconcilable, propelled them into a war that would change the course of both countries' history.

RECALL AND REFLECT

1. What Native Americans fought in the French and Indian War, and how did the war's outcome affect them? What about Native Americans who did not participate in the war?
2. How and why did the colonists' attitude toward Britain change from the time of the Seven Years' War to the beginning of the American Revolution?
3. What were the philosophical underpinnings of the colonists' revolt against Britain?
4. What did the slogan "No taxation without representation" mean, and why was it a rallying cry for the colonists?

5 THE AMERICAN REVOLUTION

THE STATES UNITED

THE WAR FOR INDEPENDENCE

WAR AND SOCIETY

THE CREATION OF STATE GOVERNMENTS

THE SEARCH FOR A NATIONAL GOVERNMENT

LOOKING AHEAD

1. What were the military strategies (both British and American) of each of the three phases of the American Revolution? How successful were these strategies during each phase?

2. How did the American Revolution become an international conflict, not just a colonial war against the British?

3. How did the new national government of the United States reflect the assumptions of republicanism?

TWO STRUGGLES OCCURRED SIMULTANEOUSLY DURING the seven years of war that began in April 1775. The first was the military conflict with Great Britain. The second was a political conflict within America.

The military conflict was, by the standards of later wars, a relatively modest one. By the standards of its own day, however, it was an unusually savage conflict, pitting not only army against army but the civilian population against a powerful external force. The shift of the war from a traditional, conventional struggle to a new kind of conflict—a revolutionary war for liberation—is what made it possible for the United States to defeat the more powerful British.

At the same time, Americans were wrestling with the great political questions that the conflict necessarily produced: first, whether to demand independence from Britain; second, how to structure the new nation they had proclaimed; and third, how to deal with questions that the Revolution had raised about slavery, the rights of Indians, the role of women, and the limits of religious tolerance in the new American society.

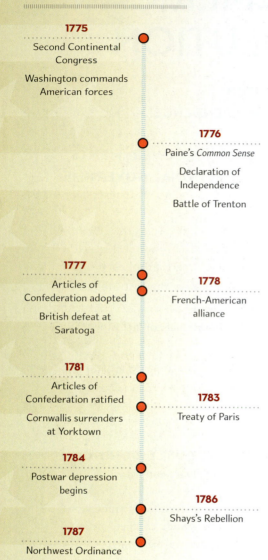

1775

Second Continental
Congress

Washington commands
American forces

1776

Paine's *Common Sense*

Declaration of
Independence

Battle of Trenton

1777

Articles of
Confederation adopted

British defeat at
Saratoga

1778

French-American
alliance

1781

Articles of
Confederation ratified

Cornwallis surrenders
at Yorktown

1783

Treaty of Paris

1784

Postwar depression
begins

1786

Shays's Rebellion

1787

Northwest Ordinance

THE STATES UNITED

Although some Americans had long been expecting a military conflict with Britain, the actual beginning of hostilities in 1775 found the colonies generally unprepared for war against the world's greatest armed power.

DEFINING AMERICAN WAR AIMS

Three weeks after the Battles of Lexington and Concord, when the Second Continental Congress met in Philadelphia, delegates from every colony (except Georgia, which had not yet sent a representative) agreed to support the war. But they disagreed about its purpose. At one extreme was a group led by the Adams cousins (John and Samuel), Richard Henry Lee of Virginia, and others, who already favored independence; at the other extreme was a group led by such moderates as John Dickinson of Pennsylvania, who hoped for a quick reconciliation with Great Britain.

Most Americans believed at first that they were fighting not for independence but for a remedy of grievances within the British Empire. During the first year of fighting, however, many colonists began to change their minds. The costs of the war were so high that the original war aims began to seem too modest to justify them. Many colonists were enraged when the British began trying to recruit Indians, African slaves, and German mercenaries (the hated "Hessians") against them. When the British government blockaded colonial ports and rejected all efforts at conciliation, many colonists concluded that independence was the only remaining option.

Thomas Paine's impassioned pamphlet *Common Sense* crystallized these feelings in January 1776. Paine, who had emigrated from England less than two years before, wanted to turn the anger of Americans away from particular parliamentary measures and toward what he considered the root of the problem—the English constitution itself.

It was simple common sense, he wrote, for Americans to break completely with a political system that could inflict such brutality on its own people. *Common Sense* sold more than 100,000 copies in only a few months and helped build support for the idea of independence in the early months of 1776.

THE DECLARATION OF INDEPENDENCE

In the meantime, the Continental Congress in Philadelphia was moving toward a complete break with England. At the beginning of the summer, it appointed a committee to draft a formal declaration of independence; and on July 2, 1776, it adopted a resolution: "That these United Colonies are, and, of right, ought to be, free and independent states; that they are absolved from all allegiance to the British crown, and that all political connexion between them and the state of Great Britain is, and ought to be, totally dissolved." Two days later, on July 4, Congress approved the Declaration of Independence itself, which provided formal justifications for this resolution.

The Declaration launched a period of energetic political innovation, as one colony after another reconstituted itself as a "state." By 1781, most states had produced written constitutions for themselves. At the national level, however, the process was more uncertain. In November 1777, finally, Congress adopted a plan for union, the Articles of Confederation. The document confirmed the existing weak, decentralized system.

Thomas Jefferson, a thirty-three-year-old Virginian, wrote most of the Declaration, with help from Benjamin Franklin and John Adams. The Declaration expressed concepts that had been circulating throughout the colonies over the previous few months in the form of at least ninety other, local "declarations of independence"—declarations drafted up and down the coast by town meetings, artisan and militia organizations, county officials, grand juries, Sons of Liberty, and colonial assemblies. Jefferson borrowed heavily from these texts.

The final document was in two parts. In the first, the Declaration restated the familiar contract theory of John Locke: the theory that governments were formed to protect what Jefferson called "life, liberty and the pursuit of happiness." In the second part, it listed the alleged crimes of the king, who, with the backing of Parliament, had violated his contract with the colonists and thus had forfeited all claim to their loyalty.

MOBILIZING FOR WAR

Financing the war was difficult. Congress had no authority to levy taxes on its own, and when it requisitioned money from the state governments, none contributed more than a small part of its expected share. Congress had little success borrowing from the public, since few Americans could afford to buy bonds. Instead, Congress issued paper money. Printing presses turned out enormous amounts of "Continental currency," and the states printed currencies of their own. The result, predictably, was soaring inflation, and Congress soon found that the Continental currency was virtually worthless. Ultimately, Congress financed the war mostly by borrowing from other nations.

After a first surge of patriotism in 1775, volunteer soldiers became scarce. States had to pay bounties or use a draft to recruit the needed men. At first, the militiamen remained under the control of their respective states. But Congress recognized the need for a centralized military command, and it created a Continental army with a single commander in chief: George Washington. Washington, an early advocate of independence with considerable military experience, was admired, respected, and trusted by nearly all Patriots. He took

THE AMERICAN REVOLUTION

THE long-standing debate over the origins of the American Revolution has tended to reflect two broad schools of interpretation. One sees the Revolution largely as a political and intellectual event; the other, as a social and economic phenomenon.

The Revolutionary generation itself portrayed the conflict as a struggle over ideals, and this interpretation prevailed through most of the nineteenth century. But in the early twentieth century, historians influenced by the reform currents of the progressive era began to identify social and economic forces that they believed had contributed to the rebellion. Carl Becker, for example, wrote in a 1909 study of New York that two questions had shaped the Revolution: "The first was the question of home rule; the second was the question . . . of who should rule at home." The colonists were not only fighting the British, but also were engaged in a kind of civil war, a contest between radicals and conservatives.

Other "progressive" historians elaborated on Becker's thesis. J. Franklin Jameson, writing in 1926, argued, "Many economic desires, many social aspirations, were set free by the political struggle, many aspects of society profoundly altered by the forces thus let loose." Arthur M. Schlesinger maintained in a 1917 book that colonial merchants, motivated by their own interest in escaping the restrictive policies of British mercantilism, aroused American resistance in the 1760s and 1770s.

Beginning in the 1950s, a new generation of scholars began to reemphasize the role of ideology and de-emphasize the role of economic interests. Robert E. Brown (in 1955) and Edmund S. Morgan (in 1956) both argued that most eighteenth-century Americans shared common political principles and that the social and economic conflicts the progressives had identified were not severe. The rhetoric of the Revolution, they suggested, was not propaganda but a real reflection of the ideas of the colonists. Bernard Bailyn, in *The Ideological Origins of the American Revolution* (1967), demonstrated the complex roots of the ideas behind the Revolution and argued that this carefully constructed political stance was not a disguise for economic interests but a genuine ideology, rooted in deeply held convictions about rights and power. The Revolution, he exclaimed, "was above all an ideological, constitutional, political struggle and not primarily a controversy between social groups undertaken to force changes in the organization of the society or the economy."

By the late 1960s, a new generation of historians—many influenced by the New Left—were reviving economic interpretations of the Revolution by exploring the social and economic tensions that they claimed shaped the Revolutionary struggle. Historians cited the actions of mobs in colonial cities, the economic pressures on colonial merchants, the growing climate of economic distress in colonial cities, and other changes in the character of American culture and society as critical prerequisites for the growth of the Revolutionary movement. Gary Nash, attempting to reconcile the emphasis on economic interests with the role of ideology, argued that the two things were not incompatible. "Everyone has economic interests," he claimed, "and everyone . . . has

THE BRITISH SURRENDER   This contemporary drawing depicts the formal surrender of British troops at Yorktown on October 19, 1781. Columns of American troops and a large French fleet flank the surrender ceremony, suggesting part of the reason for the British defeat. General Cornwallis, the commander of British forces in Virginia, did not himself attend the surrender. He sent a deputy in his place. (MPI/Archive Photos/Getty Images)

an ideology." Exploring the relationship between the two, he argued, is critical to historians' ability to understand either. Also, as Linda Kerber and others have argued, the newer social interpretations have raised increasing interest in the experience of workers, slaves, women, Native Americans, and other groups previously considered marginal to public life as part of the explanation of the Revolutionary struggle.

Finally, Gordon Wood, in *The Radicalism of the American Revolution* (1992), revived an idea once popular and recently unfashionable: that the Revolution was a genuinely radical event that led to the breakdown of such long-standing characteristics of society as deference, patriarchy, and traditional gender relations. Class conflict may not have caused the Revolution, he argued, but the Revolution had a profound, even radical, effect on society nevertheless.   •

UNDERSTAND, ANALYZE, & EVALUATE

1. In what way was the American Revolution an ideological struggle?
2. In what way was the American Revolution a social and economic conflict?

REVOLUTIONARY SOLDIERS   Jean Baptist de Verger, a French officer serving in America during the Revolution, kept an illustrated journal of his experiences. Here he portrays four American soldiers carrying different kinds of arms: a black infantryman with a light rifle, a musketman, a rifleman, and an artilleryman. (Anne S. K. Brown Military Collection, Brown University Library)

command of the new army in June 1775. With the aid of foreign military experts such as the Marquis de Lafayette from France and the Baron von Steuben from Prussia, he built a force that prevailed against the mightiest power in the world. Even more important, perhaps, Washington's steadiness, courage, and dedication to his cause provided the army—and the people—with a symbol of stability around which they could rally.

THE WAR FOR INDEPENDENCE

As the War for Independence began, the British seemed to have overwhelming advantages: the greatest navy and the best-equipped army in the world, the resources of an empire, a coherent structure of command. Yet the United States had advantages, too. Americans were fighting on their own ground. They were more committed to the conflict than were the British. And, beginning in 1777, they received substantial aid from abroad.

But the American victory was also a result of a series of early blunders and miscalculations by the British. And it was, finally, a result of the transformation of the war—through three distinct phases—into a new kind of conflict that the British military, for all its strength, was unable to win.

THE FIRST PHASE: NEW ENGLAND

For the first year of the conflict—from the spring of 1775 to the spring of 1776—many English authorities thought that British forces were not fighting a real war, but simply quelling pockets of rebellion in the contentious area around Boston. After the redcoats withdrew from Lexington and Concord in April, American forces besieged them in Boston. In the Battle of Bunker Hill (actually fought on Breed's Hill) on June 17, 1775, the Patriots suffered severe casualties and withdrew. But they inflicted even greater losses on the enemy. The siege continued. Early in 1776, finally, the British decided that Boston was a poor place from which to fight. It was in the center of the most anti-British part of America and tactically difficult to defend because it was easily isolated and surrounded. And so, on March 17, 1776, the redcoats evacuated Boston for Halifax, Nova Scotia, with hundreds of Loyalist refugees (Americans still loyal to England and the king).

In the meantime, a band of southern Patriots, at Moore's Creek Bridge in North Carolina, crushed an uprising of Loyalists on February 27, 1776. And to the north, the Americans began an invasion of Canada. Generals Benedict Arnold and Richard Montgomery unsuccessfully threatened Quebec in late 1775 and early 1776 in a battle in which Montgomery was killed and Arnold was wounded.

By the spring of 1776, it had become clear to the British that the conflict was not just a local phenomenon. The American campaigns in Canada, the agitation in the South, and the growing evidence of colonial unity all suggested that England must prepare to fight a much larger conflict.

THE SECOND PHASE: THE MID-ATLANTIC REGION

During the next phase of the war, which lasted from 1776 until early 1778, the British were in a good position to win. Indeed, had it not been for a series of blunders and misfortunes, they probably would have crushed the rebellion.

The British regrouped quickly after their retreat from Boston. During the summer of 1776, hundreds of British ships and 32,000 British soldiers arrived in New York, under the command of General William Howe. He offered Congress a choice: surrender with royal pardon or face a battle against apparently overwhelming odds. To oppose Howe's great force, Washington could muster only about 19,000 soldiers; he had no navy at all. Even so, the Americans rejected Howe's offer. The British then pushed the Patriot forces out of Manhattan and off Long Island and drove them in slow retreat over the plains of New Jersey, across the Delaware River, and into Pennsylvania.

The British settled down for the winter in northern and central New Jersey, with an outpost of Hessians at Trenton, on the Delaware River. But Washington did not sit still. On Christmas night 1776, he daringly recrossed the icy Delaware River, surprised and scattered the Hessians, and occupied Trenton. Then he advanced to Princeton and drove a force of redcoats from their base in the college there. But Washington was unable to hold either Princeton or Trenton and finally took refuge in the hills around Morristown. Still, the campaign of 1776 came to an end with the Americans having triumphed in two minor battles and with their main army still intact.

For the campaigns of 1777, the British devised a strategy to divide the United States in two. Howe would move from New York up the Hudson to Albany, while another force would come down from Canada to meet him. John Burgoyne, commander of the northern force, began a two-pronged attack to the south along both the Mohawk and the upper Hudson approaches to Albany. But having set the plan in motion, Howe strangely abandoned his part of it. Instead of moving north to meet Burgoyne, he went south and captured Philadelphia, hoping that his seizure of the rebel capital would bring the war to a speedy conclusion. Philadelphia fell with little resistance—and the Continental Congress moved into exile in York, Pennsylvania. After launching an unsuccessful Patriot attack against the British on October 4 at Germantown (just outside Philadelphia), Washington went into winter quarters at Valley Forge.

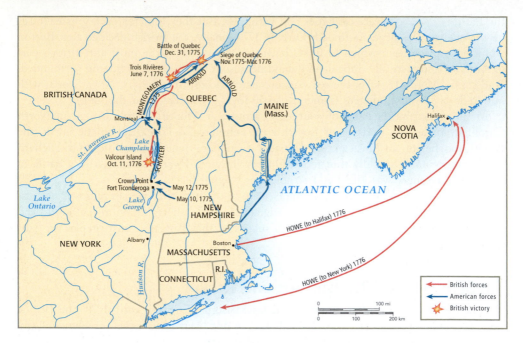

THE REVOLUTION IN THE NORTH, 1775–1776 After initial battles in and around Boston, the British forces left Massachusetts and (after a brief stay in Halifax, Canada) moved south to New York. In the meantime, American forces moved north in an effort to capture British strongholds in Montreal and Quebec, with little success. • *Why would the British have considered New York a better base than Boston?*

Howe's move to Philadelphia left Burgoyne to carry out the campaign in the north alone. He sent Colonel Barry St. Leger up the St. Lawrence River toward Lake Ontario. Burgoyne himself advanced directly down the upper Hudson Valley and easily seized Fort Ticonderoga. But Burgoyne soon experienced two staggering defeats. In one of them—at Oriskany, New York, on August 6—Patriots held off St. Leger's force of Indians and Loyalists. That allowed Benedict Arnold to close off the Mohawk Valley to St. Leger's advance. In the other battle—at Bennington, Vermont, on August 16—New England militiamen mauled a detachment that Burgoyne had sent to seek supplies. Short of materials, with all help cut off, Burgoyne fought several costly engagements and then withdrew to Saratoga, where General Horatio Gates surrounded him. On October 17, 1777, Burgoyne surrendered.

The campaign in upstate New York was not just a British defeat. It was a setback for the ambitious efforts of several Iroquois leaders. Although the Iroquois Confederacy had declared its neutrality in the Revolutionary War in 1776, some of its members allied themselves with the British, among them a Mohawk brother and sister, Joseph and Mary Brant. This ill-fated alliance further divided the already weakened Iroquois Confederacy, because only three of the Iroquois nations (the Mohawk, the Seneca, and the Cayuga) followed the Brants in support of the British. A year after the defeat at Oriskany, Iroquois forces joined British troops in a series of raids on white settlements in upstate New York. Patriot forces under the command of General John Sullivan harshly retaliated, wreaking such destruction on Indian settlements that large groups of Iroquois fled north into Canada to seek refuge. Many never returned.

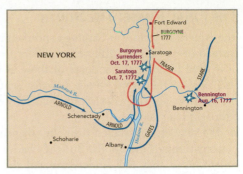

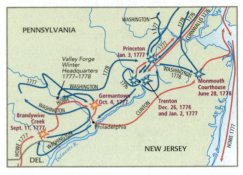

THE REVOLUTION IN THE MIDDLE COLONIES, 1776–1778 These maps illustrate the major campaigns of the Revolution in the middle colonies—New York, New Jersey, and Pennsylvania—between 1776 and 1778. The large map on the left shows the two prongs of the British strategy: first, a movement of British forces south from Canada into the Hudson Valley and, second, a movement of other British forces, under General William Howe, out from New York. The strategy was designed to trap the American army between the two British movements. • *What movements of Howe helped thwart that plan?* The two smaller maps on the right show a detailed picture of some of the major battles. The upper one reveals the surprising American victory at Saratoga. The lower one shows a series of inconclusive battles between New York and Philadelphia in 1777 and 1778.

SECURING AID FROM ABROAD

The leaders of the American effort knew that victory would not be likely without aid from abroad. Their most promising allies, they realized, were the French, who stood to gain from seeing Britain lose a crucial part of its empire. At first, France provided the United States with badly needed supplies. But they remained reluctant to grant formal diplomatic recognition to the new nation, despite the efforts of Benjamin Franklin in Paris to lobby for aid and diplomatic recognition. France's foreign minister, the Count de Vergennes, wanted evidence that the Americans had a real chance of winning. The British defeat at Saratoga, he believed, offered that evidence.

When the news from Saratoga arrived in London and Paris in early December 1777, a shaken Lord North made a new peace offer: complete home rule within the empire for Americans if they would quit the war. Vergennes feared the Americans might accept the offer and thus destroy France's opportunity to weaken Britain. Encouraged by Franklin, he agreed on February 6, 1778, to give formal recognition to the United States and to provide it with greatly expanded military assistance.

France's decision made the war an international conflict, which over the years pitted France, Spain, and the Netherlands against Great Britain. That helped reduce the resources available for the English effort in America. But France remained America's most important ally.

THE FINAL PHASE: THE SOUTH

The American victory at Saratoga and the intervention of the French transformed the war. Instead of mounting a full-scale military struggle against the American army, the British now tried to enlist the support of those elements of the American population who were still loyal to the crown. Since Loyalist sentiment was strongest in the South, and since the English also hoped slaves would rally to their cause, the main focus of the British effort shifted there.

The new strategy failed dismally. British forces spent three years (from 1778 to 1781) moving through the South. But they had badly overestimated the extent of Loyalist sentiment. And they had underestimated the logistical problems they would face. Patriot forces could move at will throughout the region, blending in with the civilian population and leaving the British unable to distinguish friend from foe. The British, by contrast, suffered all the disadvantages of an army in hostile territory.

It was this phase of the conflict that made the war "revolutionary"—not only because it introduced a new kind of warfare, but because it had the effect of mobilizing and politicizing large groups of the population. With the war expanding into previously isolated communities, with many civilians forced to involve themselves whether they liked it or not, the political climate of the United States grew more heated than ever. And support for independence, far from being crushed, greatly increased.

In the North, the fighting settled into a stalemate. Sir Henry Clinton replaced the unsuccessful William Howe in May 1778 and moved what had been Howe's army from Philadelphia back to New York. The British troops stayed there for more than a year. In the meantime, George Rogers Clark led a Patriot expedition over the Appalachian Mountains and captured settlements in the Illinois country from the British and their Indian allies. On the whole, however, there was relatively little military activity in the North after 1778. There was, however, considerable intrigue. In the fall of 1780, American forces were shocked by the exposure of treason on the part of General Benedict Arnold. Convinced that the American cause was hopeless, Arnold conspired with British agents to betray the Patriot stronghold at West Point on the Hudson River. When the scheme was exposed and foiled, Arnold fled to the safety of the British camp, where he spent the rest of the war.

The British did have some significant military successes during this period. On December 29, 1778, they captured Savannah, Georgia. On May 12, 1780, they took the port of Charleston, South Carolina, and advanced into the interior. But although the British were able to win conventional battles, they were constantly harassed by Patriot guerrillas led by such resourceful fighters as Thomas Sumter, Andrew Pickens, and Francis Marion, the "Swamp Fox." Penetrating to Camden, South Carolina, Lord Cornwallis (whom Clinton named British commander in the South) met and crushed a Patriot force under Horatio Gates on August 16, 1780. Congress recalled Gates, and Washington replaced him with Nathanael Greene, one of the ablest American generals of his time.

Even before Greene arrived in the South, the tide of battle had begun to turn against Cornwallis. At King's Mountain (near the North Carolina–South Carolina border) on October 7, 1780, a band of Patriot riflemen from the backwoods killed, wounded, or captured every man in a force of 1,100 New York and South Carolina Loyalists upon whom Cornwallis had depended. Once Greene arrived, he confused and exasperated Cornwallis by dividing the American forces into fast-moving contingents while avoiding

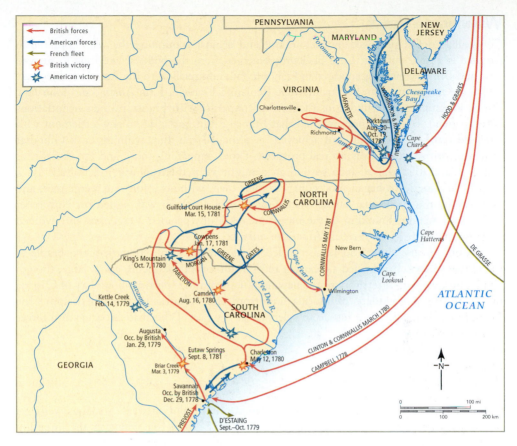

THE REVOLUTION IN THE SOUTH, 1778–1781 The final phase of the American Revolution occurred largely in the South, which the British thought would be a more receptive region for their troops. • *Why did they believe that?* This map reveals the many scattered military efforts of the British and the Americans in those years, none of them conclusive. It also shows the final chapter of the Revolution around the Chesapeake Bay and the James River. • *What errors led the British to their surrender at Yorktown?*

open, conventional battles. One of the contingents inflicted what Cornwallis admitted was "a very unexpected and severe blow" at Cowpens on January 17, 1781. Finally, after receiving reinforcements, Greene combined all his forces and maneuvered to meet the British at Guilford Court House, North Carolina. After a hard-fought battle there on March 15, 1781, Greene was driven from the field; but Cornwallis had lost so many men that he decided to abandon the Carolina campaign. Instead, he moved north, hoping to conduct raids in the interior of Virginia. But Clinton, fearful that the southern army might be destroyed, ordered him to take up a defensive position at Yorktown.

American and French forces quickly descended on Yorktown. Washington and the Count de Rochambeau marched a French-American army from New York to join the Marquis de Lafayette in Virginia, while Admiral de Grasse took a French fleet with additional troops up Chesapeake Bay to the York River. These joint operations caught Cornwallis between land and sea. After a few shows of resistance, he surrendered on October 17, 1781. Two days later, as a military band played "The World Turned Upside Down," he surrendered his whole army of more than 7,000.

WINNING THE PEACE

Cornwallis's defeat provoked outcries in England against continuing the war. Lord North resigned as prime minister; Lord Shelburne emerged from the political wreckage to succeed him; and British emissaries appeared in France to talk informally with the American diplomats there. The three American negotiators were Benjamin Franklin, John Adams, and John Jay.

The Americans were under instructions to cooperate with France in their negotiations with England. But Vergennes insisted that France could not agree to any settlement with England until its ally Spain had achieved its principal war aim: winning back Gibraltar from the British. There was no real prospect of that happening soon, and the Americans began to fear that the alliance with France might keep them at war indefinitely. As a result, the Americans began proceeding on their own, without informing Vergennes, and soon drew up a preliminary treaty with Great Britain, which was signed on November 30, 1782. Benjamin Franklin, in the meantime, skillfully pacified Vergennes and avoided an immediate rift in the French-American alliance.

The final treaty, signed September 3, 1783, was, on the whole, remarkably favorable to the United States. It provided a clear-cut recognition of independence and a large, though ambiguous, cession of territory to the new nation—from the southern boundary of Canada to the northern boundary of Florida and from the Atlantic to the Mississippi. The American people had good reason to celebrate as the last of the British occupation forces embarked from New York.

WAR AND SOCIETY

Historians have long debated whether the American Revolution was a social as well as a political revolution. (See "Debating the Past," pp. 108–109.) But whatever the intention of those who launched and fought the war, the conflict transformed American society.

LOYALISTS AND MINORITIES

Estimates differ as to how many Americans remained loyal to England during the Revolution, but it is clear that there were many—at least one-fifth (and some estimate as much as one-third) of the white population. Some were officeholders in the imperial government. Others were merchants whose trade was closely tied to the imperial system. Still others were people who lived in relative isolation and had simply retained their traditional loyalties. And there were those who, expecting the British to win the war, were currying favor with the anticipated victors.

Many of these Loyalists were hounded by Patriots in their communities and harassed by legislative and judicial actions. Up to 100,000 fled the country. Those who could afford it moved to England. Others moved to Canada, establishing the first English-speaking community in the French-speaking province of Quebec. Some returned to America after the war and gradually reentered the life of the nation.

The war weakened other groups as well. The Anglican Church, many of whose members were Loyalists, lost its status as the official religion of Virginia and Maryland. By the time the fighting ended, many Anglican parishes could no longer even afford clergymen. Also weakened were the Quakers, whose pacifism won them widespread unpopularity.

Other Protestant denominations, however, grew stronger. Presbyterian, Congregational, and Baptist churches successfully tied themselves to the Patriot cause. And most American

Catholics also supported the Patriots and won increased popularity as a result. Shortly after the peace treaty was signed, the Vatican provided the United States with its own hierarchy and, in 1789, its first bishop.

THE WAR AND SLAVERY

For some African Americans, the war meant freedom, because the British enabled many escaped slaves to leave the country as a way of disrupting the American war effort. In South Carolina, for example, nearly one-third of all slaves defected during the war.

For other African Americans, the Revolution meant an increased exposure to the concept, although seldom to the reality, of liberty. Most African Americans could not read, but few could avoid exposure to the new and exciting ideas circulating through the towns and cities, and even at times on the plantations, where they lived. In several communities, slaves exposed to Revolutionary ideas engaged in open resistance to white control. In Charleston, South Carolina, for example, Thomas Jeremiah, a free black man, was executed after white authorities learned of elaborate plans for a slave uprising.

Slaveowners opposed the British efforts to emancipate their slaves, but they also feared that the Revolution itself would foment slave rebellions. Although the ideals of the Revolution produced occasional challenges to slavery by white southerners (including laws in Virginia and Maryland permitting slaveowners to free—"manumit"—their slaves if they wished), white support for slavery survived. Southern churches, some of which flirted briefly with voicing objections to the system, quickly rejected the antislavery ideas of the North and worked instead to reinforce white superiority.

In much of the North, by contrast, the combination of Revolutionary sentiment and evangelical Christian fervor helped spread antislavery sentiments widely through society. The first target was the slave trade, which was prohibited by several states (Pennsylvania, Rhode Island, and Connecticut among them). The next target of the antislavery movement was state laws forbidding owners from freeing their slaves. Quakers and other antislavery activists succeeded in pressuring legislatures to allow legal emancipation in all the northern states, and even in Kentucky and Tennessee, before the end of the Revolution. The final step was emancipation of all slaves in a state. Pennsylvania was the first state to declare slavery illegal within its borders—again in part because of the influence of the fiercely antislavery Quakers—in 1780. One by one, all the northern states except New York and New Jersey abolished slavery before the end of the Revolution. New York followed in 1799 and New Jersey in 1804. But northern emancipation was a gradual process in most states, despite changes in the law. A significant, although steadily dwindling, number of slaves remained in the North for several decades.

The Revolution exposed the continuing tension between the nation's commitment to liberty and its simultaneous commitment to slavery. To people in our time, and even to some people in Revolutionary times, it seems obvious that liberty and slavery are incompatible with each other. But to many white Americans in the eighteenth century, especially in the South, that did not seem obvious. Many white southerners believed, in fact, that enslaving Africans—whom they considered inferior and unfit for citizenship—was the best way to ensure liberty for white people. They feared that without slaves, it would be necessary to recruit a servile white workforce in the South, and that the resulting inequalities would jeopardize the survival of liberty. One of the ironies of the American Revolution was that many white Americans were fighting both to secure freedom for themselves and to preserve slavery for others.

THE AGE OF REVOLUTIONS

THE American Revolution was a result of tensions and conflicts between imperial Britain and its North American colonies. But it was also both a part, and a cause, of what historians have come to call an "age of revolutions," which spread through much of the Western world in the last decades of the eighteenth century and the first decades of the nineteenth.

The modern idea of revolution—the over-turning of old systems and regimes and the creation of new ones—was to a large degree a product of the ideas of the Enlightenment. Among those ideas was the notion of popular sovereignty, articulated by, among others, the English philosopher John Locke. Locke argued that political authority did not derive from the divine right of kings or the inherited authority of aristocracies, but from the consent of the governed. A related Enlightenment idea was the concept of individual freedom, which challenged the traditional belief that governments had the right to prescribe the way people act, speak, and even think. Champions of individual freedom in the eighteenth century—among them the French philosopher Voltaire—advocated religious toleration and freedom of thought and expression. The Enlightenment also helped spread the idea of political and legal equality for all people—the end of special privileges for aristocrats and elites and the right of all citizens to participate in the formation of policies and laws. Jean-Jacques Rousseau, a Swiss-French theorist, helped define these new ideas of equality. Together, Enlightenment ideas formed the basis for challenges to existing social orders in many parts of the Western world, and eventually beyond it.

The American Revolution was the first and in many ways most influential of the Enlightenment-derived uprisings against established orders. It served as an inspiration to people in other lands who were trying to find a way to oppose unpopular regimes. In 1789, a little over a decade after the beginning of the American Revolution, revolution began in France—at first through a revolt by the national legislature against the king, and then through a series of increasingly radical challenges to established authority. The monarchy was abolished (and the king and queen publicly executed in 1793), the authority of the Catholic Church was challenged and greatly weakened, and at the peak of revolutionary chaos during the Jacobin period (1793–1794), over 40,000 suspected enemies of the revolution were executed and hundreds of thousands of others imprisoned. The radical phase of the revolution came to an end in 1799, when Napoleon Bonaparte, a young general, seized power and began to build a new French empire. But France's *ancien regime* of king and aristocracy never wholly revived.

Together, the French and American revolutions helped inspire uprisings in many other parts of the Atlantic World. In 1791, a major slave revolt began in Haiti and soon attracted over 100,000 rebels. The slave army defeated both the white settlers of the island and the French colonial armies sent to quell their rebellion. Under the leadership of Toussaint-Louverture, they began to agitate for independence, which they obtained on January 1, 1804, a few months after Toussaint's death.

The ideas of these revolutions spread next into Spanish and Portuguese colonies in the Americas, particularly among the so-called Creoles, people of European ancestry born in America. In the late eighteenth century, they began to resist the continuing authority of colonial officials from Spain and Portugal and to demand a greater say in governing their own

STORMING THE BASTILLE This painting portrays the storming of the great Parisian fortress and prison, the Bastille, on July 14, 1789. The Bastille was a despised symbol of royal tyranny to many of the French, because of the arbitrarily arrested and imprisoned people who were sent there. The July assault was designed to release the prisoners, but in fact the revolutionaries found only seven people in the vast fortress. Even so, the capture of the Bastille—which marked one of the first moments in which ordinary Frenchmen joined the Revolution—became one of the great moments in modern French history. The anniversary of the event, "Bastille Day," remains the French national holiday. (Bridgeman–Giraudon/Art Resource, NY)

lands. When Napoleon's French armies invaded Spain and Portugal in 1807, they weakened the ability of the European regimes to sustain authority over their American colonies. In the years that followed, revolutions swept through much of Latin America. Mexico became an independent nation in 1821, and provinces of Central America that had once been part of Mexico (Guatemala, El Salvador, Honduras, Nicaragua, and Costa Rica) established their independence three years later. Simón Bolívar, modeling his efforts on those of George Washington, led a great revolutionary movement that won independence for Brazil in 1822 and also helped lead revolutionary campaigns in Venezuela, Ecuador, and Peru—all of which won their independence in the 1820s. At about the same time, Greek patriots—drawing from the examples of other revolutionary nations—launched a movement to win their independence from the Ottoman Empire, which finally succeeded in 1830.

The age of revolutions left many new, independent nations in its wake. It did not,

however, succeed in establishing the ideals of popular sovereignty, individual freedom, and political equality in all the nations it affected. Slavery survived in the United States and in many areas of Latin America. New forms of aristocracy and even monarchy emerged in France, Mexico, Brazil, and elsewhere. Women—many of whom had hoped the revolutionary age would win new rights for them—made few legal or political gains in this era. But the ideals that the revolutionary era introduced to the Western world continued to shape the histories of nations throughout the nineteenth century and beyond. •

UNDERSTAND, ANALYZE, & EVALUATE

1. How did the American Revolution influence the French Revolution, and how were other nations affected by it?
2. What was the significance of the revolution in Haiti, and how much attention did it get in other nations?

NATIVE AMERICANS AND THE REVOLUTION

Indians also viewed the American Revolution with considerable uncertainty. Most tribes ultimately chose to stay out of the war. But many Indians feared that the Revolution would replace a somewhat trustworthy ruling group (the British, who had tried to limit the expansion of white settlement into tribal land) with one they considered generally hostile to them (the Patriots, who had spearheaded the expansion). Thus some Indians chose to join the English cause. Still others took advantage of the conflict to launch attacks of their own.

In the western Carolinas and Virginia, Cherokee led by Chief Dragging Canoe launched a series of attacks on outlying white settlements in the summer of 1776. Patriot militias responded in great force, ravaging Cherokee lands and forcing the chief and many of his followers to flee west across the Tennessee River. Those Cherokee who remained behind agreed to a new treaty by which they gave up still more land. Some Iroquois, despite the setbacks at Oriskany, continued to wage war against Americans in the West and caused widespread destruction in agricultural areas of New York and Pennsylvania. The retaliating American armies inflicted heavy losses on the Indians, but the attacks continued.

In the end, the Revolution generally weakened the position of Native Americans in several ways. The Patriot victory increased white demand for western lands. Many whites resented the assistance such nations as the Mohawk had given the British and insisted on treating them as conquered people. Others drew from the Revolution a paternalistic view of the tribes. Thomas Jefferson, for example, came to view the Indians as "noble savages," uncivilized in their present state but redeemable if they were willing to adapt to the norms of white society.

The triumph of the American Patriots in the Revolution contributed to the ultimate defeat of the Indian tribes. To white Americans, independence meant, among other things, their right to move aggressively into the western lands, despite the opposition of the Indians. To the Indians, American independence was "the greatest blow that could have been dealt us," one tribal leader warned.

WOMEN'S RIGHTS AND WOMEN'S ROLES

The long Revolutionary War had a profound effect on American women. The departure of so many men to fight in the Patriot armies left women in charge of farms and businesses. Often, women handled these tasks with great success. But in other cases, inexperience, inflation, the unavailability of male labor, or the threat of enemy troops led to failure. Some women whose husbands or fathers were called away to war did not have even a farm or shop to fall back on. Cities and towns had significant populations of impoverished women, who on occasion led protests against price increases, rioted, or looted food. At other times, women launched attacks on occupying British troops, whom they were required to house and feed at considerable expense.

Not all women stayed behind when the men went off to war. Some joined their male relatives in the camps of the Patriot armies. These female "camp followers" increased army morale and provided a ready source of volunteers to cook, launder, nurse, and do other necessary tasks. In the rough environment of the camps, traditional gender distinctions proved difficult to maintain. Considerable numbers of women became involved, at least intermittently, in combat. A few women even disguised themselves as men so as to be able to fight.

The emphasis on liberty and the "rights of man" led some women to begin to question their own position in society. Abigail Adams wrote to her husband, John Adams, in 1776, "In the new code of laws which I suppose it will be necessary for you to make, I desire you would remember the ladies and be more generous and favorable to them than your ancestors." Adams was calling simply for new protections against abusive and tyrannical men. A few women, however, went further. Judith Sargent Murray, one of the leading essayists of the late eighteenth century, wrote in 1779 that women's minds were as good as those of men and that girls as well as boys therefore deserved access to education.

But little changed as a result. Under English common law, an unmarried woman had some legal rights, but a married woman had virtually no rights at all. Everything she owned and everything she earned belonged to her husband. Because she had no property rights, she could not engage in any legal transactions on her own. She could not vote. She had no legal authority over her children. Nor could she initiate a divorce; that, too, was a right reserved almost exclusively for men. After the Revolution, it did become easier for women to obtain divorces in a few states. Otherwise, there were few advances and some setbacks—including the loss of widows' rights to regain their dowries from their husbands' estates. The Revolution, in other words, did not really challenge, but actually confirmed and strengthened, the patriarchal legal system.

Still, the Revolution did encourage people of both sexes to reevaluate the contribution of women to the family and society. As the new republic searched for a cultural identity for itself, it attributed a higher value to the role of women as mothers. The new nation was, many Americans liked to believe, producing a new kind of citizen, steeped in the principles of liberty. Mothers had a particularly important task, therefore, in instructing their children in the virtues that the republican citizenry now was expected to possess.

THE WAR ECONOMY

The Revolution also produced important changes in the structure of the American economy. After more than a century of dependence on the British imperial system, American commerce suddenly found itself on its own. English ships no longer protected American vessels. In fact, they tried to drive them from the seas. British imperial ports were closed to American trade. But this disruption in traditional economic patterns strengthened the American economy in the long run. Enterprising merchants in New England and elsewhere began to develop new commercial networks in the Caribbean and South America. By the mid-1780s, American merchants were also developing an important trade with Asia.

When English imports to America were cut off, states desperately tried to stimulate domestic manufacturing. No great industrial expansion resulted, but there was a modest increase in production and an even greater increase in expectations. Trade also increased substantially among the American states.

THE CREATION OF STATE GOVERNMENTS

At the same time as Americans were struggling to win their independence on the battlefield, they were also struggling to create new institutions of government to replace the British system they had repudiated.

ABIGAIL ADAMS DISCUSSES WOMEN'S RIGHTS IN REVOLUTIONARY AMERICA WITH JOHN ADAMS AND MERCY OTIS WARREN (1776)

ABIGAIL Adams to John Adams, March 31, 1776:

I long to hear that you have declared an independancy [sic] and by the way in the new Code of Laws which I suppose it will be necessary for you to make I would desire you would Remember the Ladies, and be more generous and favourable to them than your ancestors. Do not put such unlimited power into the hands of the Husbands. Remember all men would be tyrants if they could. If particuliar care and attention is not paid to the Ladies we are determined to foment a Rebelion, and will not hold ourselves bound by any Laws in which we have no voice, or Representation.

That your Sex are Naturally Tyrannical is a Truth so thoroughly established as to admit of no dispute, but such of you as wish to be happy willingly give up the harsh title of Master for the more tender and endearing one of Friend. Why then, not put it out of the power of the vicious and the Lawless to use us with cruelty and indignity with impunity. Men of Sense in all Ages abhor those customs which treat us only as the vassals of your Sex. Regard us then as Beings placed by providence under your protection and in immitation of the Supreme Being make use of that power only for our happiness.

John Adams to Abigail Adams, April 14, 1776:
As to Declarations of Independency, be patient. Read our Privateering Laws, and our Commercial Laws. What signifies a Word.

As to your extraordinary Code of Laws, I cannot but laugh. We have been told that our Struggle has loosened the bands of Government every where. That Children and Apprentices were disobedient—that schools and Colleges were grown turbulent— that Indians slighted their Guardians and Negroes grew insolent to their Masters. But your Letter was the first Intimation that another Tribe more numerous and powerful than all the rest were grown discontented. This is rather too coarse a Compliment but you are so saucy, I wont blot it out.

Depend upon it, We know better than to repeal our Masculine systems. Altho they are in full Force, you know they are little more than Theory. We dare not exert our Power in its full Latitude. We are obliged to go fair, and softly, and in Practice you know We are the subjects. We have only the Name of Masters, and rather than give up this, which would completely subject Us to the Despotism of the Peticoat, I hope General Washington, and all our brave Heroes would fight. . . .

Abigail Adams to Mercy Otis Warren, Braintree April 27, 1776:
He is very saucy to me in return for a List of Female Grievances which I transmitted to him I think I will get you to join me in a petition to Congress. I thought it was very probable our wise Statesmen would erect a

THE ASSUMPTIONS OF REPUBLICANISM

If Americans agreed on nothing else, they agreed that their new governments would be republican. To them, that meant a political system in which all power came from the people, rather than from some supreme authority (such as a king). The success of such a

New Government and form a new code of Laws. I ventured to speak a word on behalf of our Sex, who are rather hardly dealt with by the Laws of England which gives such unlimited power to the Husband to use his wife.

I requested that our Legislators would consider our case and as all Men of Delicacy and Sentiment are adverse to Exercising the power they possess, yet as there is a natural propensity in Human Nature to domination, I thought the most generous plan was to put it out of the power of the Arbitrary and tyranick to injure us with impunity by Establishing some Laws in favour upon just and Liberal principals. I believe I even threatened fomenting a Rebellion in case we were not considered and assured him we would not hold ourselves bound by any Laws in which we had neither a voice nor representation.

In return he tells me he cannot but Laugh at my extraordinary Code of Laws. That he had heard their Struggle had loosened the bands of Government, that children and apprentices were disobedient, that Schools and Colleges had grown turbulent, that Indians slighted their Guardians, and Negroes grew insolent to their Masters. But my Letter was the first intimation that another Tribe more numerous and powerful than all the rest were grown discontented. This is rather too coarse a complement, he adds, but that I am so saucy he wont blot it out.

So I have helped the Sex abundantly, but I will tell him I have only been making trial of the Disinterestedness of his Virtue, and when weigh'd in the balance have found it

wanting. It would be bad policy to grant us greater power say they since under all the disadvantages we Labour we have the ascendency over their Hearts. And charm by accepting, by submitting sway.

Abigail Adams to John Adams, May 7, 1776: I can not say that I think you very generous to the Ladies, for whilst you are proclaiming peace and good will to men, Emancipating all Nations, you insist upon retaining an absolute power over Wives. But you must remember that Arbitrary power is like most other things which are very hard, very liable to be broken and notwithstanding all your wise Laws and Maxims we have it in our power not only to free our selves but to subdue our Masters, and without violence throw both your natural and legal authority at our feet.

"Charm by accepting, by submitting sway
Yet have our Humour most when we obey."

UNDERSTAND, ANALYZE, & EVALUATE

1. What was Abigail Adams' opinion of men in power and what did she request of John Adams as they declared independence?

2. To what other social developments did John Adams compare his wife's request? What did he mean by the "Despotism of the Peticoat" (a women's undergarment)?

3. What did Abigail Adams predict in her second letter to John Adams? What do you think of her assessment of "Arbitrary power"?

Source: *The Adams Family Correspondence*, eds. L. H. Butterfield et al. (Cambridge, Massachusetts: Belknap Press of Harvard University Press, 1963), vol. I, 29–31.

government depended on the character of its citizenry. If the population consisted of sturdy, independent property owners imbued with civic virtue, then the republic could survive. If it consisted of a few powerful aristocrats and a great mass of dependent workers, then it would be in danger. From the beginning, therefore, the ideal of the small freeholder (the independent landowner) was basic to American political ideology. Jefferson, the great champion of the independent yeoman farmer, once wrote: "Dependence begets subservience and venality, suffocates the germ of virtue, and prepares fit tools for the designs of ambition."

Another crucial part of that ideology was the concept of equality. The Declaration of Independence had given voice to the idea in its most ringing phrase: "All men are created equal." The innate talents and energies of individuals, not their positions at birth, would determine their roles in society. Some people would inevitably be wealthier and more powerful than others. But all people would have to earn their success. There might be no equality of condition, but there would be equality of opportunity.

In reality, of course, the United States was never a nation in which all citizens were independent property holders. From the beginning, there was a sizable dependent labor force, white and black. American women remained both politically and economically subordinate. Native Americans were systematically exploited and displaced. Nor was there ever full equality of opportunity. American society was more open and more fluid than that of most European nations, but the condition of a person's birth was almost always a crucial determinant of success.

Nevertheless, in embracing the assumptions of republicanism, Americans were adopting a powerful—even revolutionary—ideology, and their experiment in statecraft became a model for many other countries.

THE FIRST STATE CONSTITUTIONS

Two states—Connecticut and Rhode Island—already had governments that were republican in all but name. They simply deleted references to England and the king from their charters and adopted them as constitutions. The other eleven states, however, produced new documents.

The first and perhaps most basic decision was that the constitutions were to be written down, because Americans believed the vagueness of England's unwritten constitution had produced corruption. The second decision was that the power of the executive, which Americans believed had grown too great in England, must be limited. Pennsylvania eliminated the executive altogether. Most other states inserted provisions limiting the power of governors over appointments, reducing or eliminating their right to veto bills, and preventing them from dismissing the legislature. Most important, every state forbade the governor or any other executive officer from holding a seat in the legislature, thus ensuring that, unlike in England, the executive and legislative branches of government would remain separate.

Even so, most new constitutions did not embrace direct popular rule. In Georgia and Pennsylvania, the legislature consisted of one popularly elected house. But in every other state, there were an upper and a lower chamber, and in most cases, the upper chamber was designed to represent the "higher orders" of society. There were property requirements for voters—some modest, others substantial—in all states.

REVISING STATE GOVERNMENTS

By the late 1770s, Americans were growing concerned about the apparent instability of their new state governments. Many believed the problem was one of too much democracy. As a result, most of the states began to revise their constitutions to limit popular power. By waiting until 1780 to ratify its first constitution, Massachusetts became the first state to act on the new concerns.

Two changes in particular differentiated the Massachusetts and later constitutions from the earlier ones. The first was a change in the process of constitution writing itself. Most of the first documents had been written by state legislatures and thus could easily be amended (or violated) by them. Massachusetts created the constitutional convention: a special assembly of the people that would meet only for the purpose of writing the constitution.

The second change was a significant strengthening of the executive. The 1780 Massachusetts constitution made the governor one of the strongest in any state. He was to be elected directly by the people; he was to have a fixed salary (in other words, he would not be dependent on the legislature each year for his wages); he would have significant appointment powers and a veto over legislation. Other states followed. Those with weak or nonexistent upper houses strengthened or created them. Most increased the powers of the governor. Pennsylvania, which had no executive at all at first, now produced a strong one. By the late 1780s, almost every state had either revised its constitution or drawn up an entirely new one in an effort to produce greater stability in government.

TOLERATION AND SLAVERY

Most Americans continued to believe that religion should play some role in government, but they did not wish to give special privileges to any particular denomination. The privileges that churches had once enjoyed were now largely stripped away. In 1786, Virginia enacted the Statute of Religious Liberty, written by Thomas Jefferson, which called for the complete separation of church and state.

More difficult to resolve was the question of slavery. In areas where slavery was already weak—New England and Pennsylvania—it was gradually abolished. Even in the South, there were some pressures to amend or even eliminate the institution; every state but South Carolina and Georgia prohibited further importation of slaves from abroad, and South Carolina banned the slave trade during the war. Virginia passed a law encouraging the voluntary freeing of slaves.

Nevertheless, slavery survived in all the southern and border states. There were several reasons: racist assumptions among whites about the inferiority of blacks; the enormous economic investments many white southerners had in their slaves; and the inability of even such men as Washington and Jefferson, who had moral misgivings about slavery, to envision any alternative to it. If slavery were abolished, what would happen to the black people in America? Few whites believed that black men and women could be integrated into American society as equals.

THE SEARCH FOR A NATIONAL GOVERNMENT

Americans were much quicker to agree on state institutions than they were on the structure of their national government. At first, most believed that the central government should remain relatively weak and that each state would be virtually a sovereign nation. It was in response to such ideas that the Articles of Confederation emerged.

THE CONFEDERATION

The Articles of Confederation, which the Continental Congress had adopted in 1777, provided for a national government much like the one already in place before independence. Congress remained the central—indeed the only—institution of national authority.

Its powers expanded to give it authority to conduct wars and foreign relations and to appropriate, borrow, and issue money. But it did not have power to regulate trade, draft troops, or levy taxes directly on the people. For troops and taxes, it had to make formal requests to the state legislatures, which could—and often did—refuse them. There was no separate executive; the "president of the United States" was merely the presiding officer at the sessions of Congress. Each state had a single vote in Congress, and at least nine of the states had to approve any important measure. All thirteen state legislatures had to approve any amendment of the Articles.

During the process of ratifying the Articles of Confederation (which required approval by all thirteen states), broad disagreements over the plan became evident. The small states had insisted on equal state representation, but the larger states wanted representation to be based on population. The smaller states prevailed on that issue. More important, the states claiming western lands wished to keep them, but the rest of the states demanded that all such territory be turned over to the national government. New York and Virginia had to give up their western claims before the Articles were finally approved. They went into effect in 1781.

The Confederation, which existed from 1781 until 1789, was not a complete failure, but it was far from a success. It lacked adequate powers to deal with interstate issues or to enforce its will on the states.

Diplomatic Failures

In the peace treaty of 1783, the British had promised to evacuate American territory; but British forces continued to occupy a string of frontier posts along the Great Lakes within the United States. Nor did the British honor their agreement to make restitution to slaveowners whose slaves the British army had confiscated. Disputes also erupted over the northeastern boundary of the new nation and over the border between the United States and Florida. Most American trade remained within the British Empire, and Americans wanted full access to British markets; England, however, placed sharp restrictions on that access.

In 1784, Congress sent John Adams as minister to London to resolve these differences, but Adams made no headway with the English, who were never sure whether he represented a single nation or thirteen different ones. Throughout the 1780s, the British government refused even to send a diplomatic minister to the American capital.

Confederation diplomats agreed to a treaty with Spain in 1786. The Spanish accepted the American interpretation of the Florida boundary. In return, the Americans recognized the Spanish possessions in North America and accepted limits on the right of United States vessels to navigate the Mississippi for twenty years. But southern states, incensed at the idea of giving up their access to the Mississippi, blocked ratification.

The Confederation and the Northwest

The Confederation's most important accomplishment was its resolution of controversies involving the western lands. The Confederation had to find a way to include these areas in the political structure of the new nation.

The Ordinance of 1784, based on a proposal by Thomas Jefferson, divided the western territory into ten self-governing districts, each of which could petition Congress for statehood when its population equaled the number of free inhabitants of the smallest existing

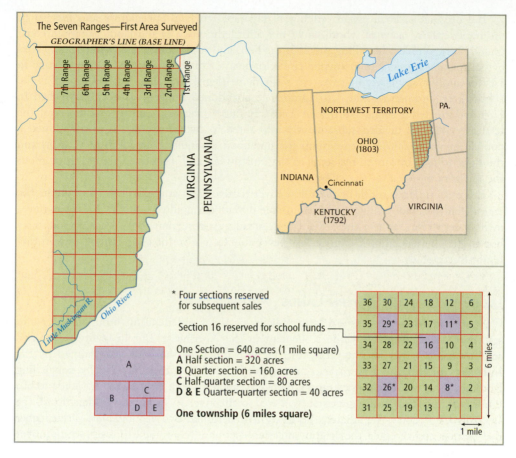

LAND SURVEY: ORDINANCE OF 1785 In the Ordinance of 1785, the Congress established a new system for surveying and selling western lands. These maps illustrate the way in which the lands were divided in an area of Ohio. Note the highly geometrical grid pattern that the ordinance imposed on these lands. Each of the squares in the map on the left was subdivided into 36 sections, as illustrated in the map at the lower right. • *Why was this grid pattern so appealing to the planners of the western lands?*

state. Then, in the Ordinance of 1785, Congress created a system for surveying and selling the western lands. The territory north of the Ohio River was to be surveyed and marked off into neat rectangular townships, each divided into thirty-six identical sections. In every township, four sections were to be reserved by the federal government for future use or sale (a policy that helped establish the idea of "public land"). The revenue from the sale of one of these federally reserved sections was to support creation of a public school.

The precise rectangular pattern imposed on the Northwest Territory—the grid—became a model for all subsequent land policies of the federal government and for many other planning decisions in states and localities. The grid also became characteristic of the layout of many American cities. It had many advantages. It eliminated the uncertainty about property borders that earlier, more informal land systems had produced. It sped the development of western lands by making land ownership simple and understandable. But it also encouraged a dispersed form of settlement—with each farm family separated from its neighbors—that made the formation of community more difficult. Whatever its consequences, however, the 1785 Ordinance made a dramatic and indelible mark on the American landscape.

The original ordinances proved highly favorable to land speculators and less so to ordinary settlers, many of whom could not afford the price of the land. Congress compounded the problem by selling much of the best land to the Ohio and Scioto Companies before making it available to anyone else. Criticism of these policies led to the passage in 1787 of another law governing western settlement—legislation that became known as the "Northwest Ordinance." The 1787 Ordinance abandoned the ten districts established in 1784 and created a single Northwest Territory out of the lands north of the Ohio; the territory could be divided subsequently into three to five territories. It also specified a population of 60,000 as a minimum for statehood, guaranteed freedom of religion and the right to trial by jury to residents of the Northwest, and prohibited slavery throughout the territory.

The western lands south of the Ohio River received less attention from Congress. The region that became Kentucky and Tennessee developed rapidly in the late 1770s as slave-owning territories, and in the 1780s began setting up governments and asking for statehood. The Confederation Congress was never able to resolve the conflicting claims in that region successfully.

Indians and the Western Lands

On paper at least, the western land policies of the Confederation brought order and stability to the process of white settlement in the Northwest. But in reality, order and stability came slowly and at great cost, because much of the land was claimed by the Indians. Congress tried to resolve that problem in 1784, 1785, and 1786 by persuading Iroquois, Choctaw, Chickasaw, and Cherokee leaders to sign treaties ceding lands to the United States. But those agreements proved ineffective. In 1786, the leadership of the Iroquois Confederacy repudiated the treaty it had signed two years earlier. Other tribes had never really accepted the treaties affecting them and continued to resist white movement into their lands.

Violence between whites and Indians on the Northwest frontier reached a crescendo in the early 1790s. In 1790 and again in 1791, the Miami, led by the famed warrior Little Turtle, defeated United States forces in two major battles. Efforts to negotiate a settlement failed because of the Miami's insistence that no treaty was possible unless it forbade white settlement west of the Ohio River. Negotiations did not resume until after General Anthony Wayne led 4,000 soldiers into the Ohio Valley in 1794 and defeated the Indians in the Battle of Fallen Timbers.

A year later, the Miami signed the Treaty of Greenville, ceding substantial new lands to the United States in exchange for a formal acknowledgment of their claim to the territory they had managed to retain. This was the first time the new federal government recognized the sovereignty of Indian nations; in doing so, it affirmed that Indian lands could be ceded only by the tribes themselves. That hard-won assurance, however, proved a frail protection against the pressure of white expansion.

Debts, Taxes, and Daniel Shays

The postwar depression, which lasted from 1784 to 1787, increased the perennial American problem of an inadequate money supply, a problem that weighed particularly heavily on debtors. The Confederation itself had an enormous outstanding debt, accumulated during the Revolutionary War, and few means with which to pay it. It had sold war bonds that were now due to be repaid; it owed money to its soldiers; it had substantial debts abroad. But with no power to tax, it could only request money from the states, and it received only about one-sixth of the money it asked for. The fragile new nation was faced with the grim prospect of defaulting on its obligations.

This alarming possibility brought to prominence a group of leaders who would play a crucial role in the shaping of the republic for several decades. Robert Morris, the head of the Confederation's treasury; Alexander Hamilton, his young protégé; James Madison of Virginia; and others—all called for a "continental impost," a 5 percent duty on imported goods to be levied by Congress and used to fund the debt. Many Americans, however, feared that the impost plan would concentrate too much financial power in the hands of Morris and his allies in Philadelphia. Congress failed to approve the impost in 1781 and again in 1783.

The states had war debts, too, and they generally relied on increased taxation to pay them. But poor farmers, already burdened by debt, considered such policies unfair. They demanded that the state governments issue paper currency to increase the money supply and make it easier for them to meet their obligations. Resentment was especially high among farmers in New England, who felt that the states were squeezing them to enrich already wealthy bondholders in Boston and other towns.

Throughout the late 1780s, therefore, mobs of distressed farmers rioted periodically in various parts of New England. Dissidents in the Connecticut Valley and the Berkshire Hills of Massachusetts rallied behind Daniel Shays, a former captain in the Continental army. Shays issued a set of demands that included paper money, tax relief, a moratorium on debts, and the abolition of imprisonment for debt. During the summer of 1786, the Shaysites prevented the collection of debts, private or public, and used force to keep courts from sitting and sheriffs from selling confiscated property. When winter came, the rebels

DANIEL SHAYS AND JOB SHATTUCK Shays and Shattuck were the principal leaders of the 1786 uprising of poor Massachusetts farmers demanding relief from their indebtedness. Shattuck led an insurrection in the east, which collapsed when he was captured on November 30. Shays organized the rebellion in the west, which continued until it was finally dispersed by state militia in late February 1787. The following year, state authorities pardoned Shays; even before that, the legislature responded to the rebellion by providing some relief to the impoverished farmers. This drawing is part of a hostile account of the rebellion published in 1787 in a Boston almanac. (The National Portrait Gallery, Smithsonian Institution/Art Resource, NY)

advanced on Springfield, hoping to seize weapons from the arsenal there. In January 1787, an army of state militiamen set out from Boston, met Shays's band, and dispersed his ragged troops.

As a military enterprise, Shays's Rebellion was a failure, although it did produce some concessions to the aggrieved farmers. Shays and his lieutenants, at first sentenced to death, were later pardoned, and Massachusetts offered the protesters some tax relief and a postponement of debt payments. But the rebellion had important consequences for the future of the United States, for it added urgency to the movement to produce a new, national constitution.

CONCLUSION

Between a small, inconclusive battle on a village green in New England in 1775 and a momentous surrender at Yorktown in 1781, the American people fought a great and terrible war against the mightiest military nation in the world. Few would have predicted in 1775 that the makeshift armies of the colonies could withstand the armies and navies of the British Empire. But a combination of luck, brilliance, determination, costly errors by the British, and timely aid from abroad allowed the Patriots, as they began to call themselves, to make full use of the advantages of fighting on their home soil and to frustrate British designs.

The war was not just a historic military event. It was also a great political one, for it propelled the colonies to unite, to organize, and to declare their independence. Having done so, they fought with even greater determination, defending now not just a set of principles, but an actual, fledgling nation. By the end of the war, they had created new governments at both the state and national level and had begun experimenting with new political forms.

The war was also important for its effects on American society—for the way it shook the existing social order; for the way it caused women to question their place in society; and for the way it spread notions of liberty and freedom throughout a society that in the past had mostly been rigidly hierarchical. Even African American slaves absorbed some of the ideas of the Revolution, although it would be many years before they would be in any position to make much use of them.

Victory in the American Revolution solved many of the problems of the new nation, but it also produced others. What should the United States do about its relations with the Indians and with its neighbors to the north and south? What should it do about the distribution of western lands? What should it do about slavery? How should it balance its commitment to liberty with its need for order? These questions bedeviled the new national government in its first years of existence.

RECALL AND REFLECT

1. What questions did the Second Continental Congress debate, and how did it answer them?
2. What was the impact of Thomas Paine's *Common Sense* on Americans' view of the war with Britain?
3. What were the ideological ideals of the new state and national governments, and how did those ideals compare with the realities of American society?
4. What was the purpose of the Articles of Confederation?
5. How did the Revolution affect the role of religion and the position of churches in American society?

6

THE CONSTITUTION AND THE NEW REPUBLIC

FRAMING A NEW GOVERNMENT
ADOPTION AND ADAPTATION
FEDERALISTS AND REPUBLICANS
ESTABLISHING NATIONAL SOVEREIGNTY
THE DOWNFALL OF THE FEDERALISTS

LOOKING AHEAD

1. What were the most important questions debated at the Constitutional Convention of 1787, and how were they resolved?
2. What were the main tenets of the Federalist and Antifederalist arguments on ratification of the Constitution?
3. What were the origins of America's "first party system"?

BY THE LATE 1780s, MANY Americans had grown dissatisfied with the Confederation. It was, they believed, ridden with factions, unable to deal effectively with economic problems, and frighteningly powerless in the face of Shays's Rebellion. A decade earlier, Americans had deliberately avoided creating a strong national government. Now they reconsidered. In 1787, the nation produced a new constitution and a much more powerful government with three independent branches. But the adoption of the Constitution did not complete the creation of the republic, for although most Americans came to agree that the Constitution was a nearly perfect document, they often disagreed on what that document meant.

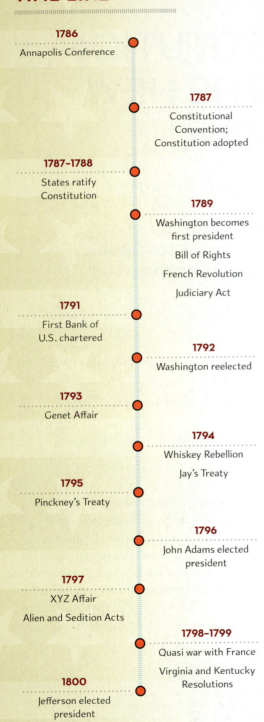

1786
Annapolis Conference

1787
Constitutional
Convention;
Constitution adopted

1787–1788
States ratify
Constitution

1789
Washington becomes
first president

Bill of Rights

French Revolution

Judiciary Act

1791
First Bank of
U.S. chartered

1792
Washington reelected

1793
Genet Affair

1794
Whiskey Rebellion

Jay's Treaty

1795
Pinckney's Treaty

1796
John Adams elected
president

1797
XYZ Affair

Alien and Sedition Acts

1798–1799
Quasi war with France

Virginia and Kentucky
Resolutions

1800
Jefferson elected
president

FRAMING A NEW GOVERNMENT

The Confederation Congress had become so unpopular and ineffectual by the mid-1780s that it began to lead an almost waiflike existence. In 1783, its members timidly withdrew from Philadelphia to escape army veterans demanding their back pay. They took refuge for a while in Princeton, New Jersey, then moved on to Annapolis, and in 1785 settled in New York. Delegates were often scarce. Only with great difficulty could Congress produce a quorum to ratify the treaty with Great Britain, ending the Revolutionary War.

ADVOCATES OF REFORM

In the 1780s, some of the wealthiest and most powerful groups in the population began to clamor for a stronger national government. By 1786, such demands had grown so intense that even defenders of the existing system reluctantly agreed that the government needed strengthening at its weakest point—its lack of power to tax.

The most effective advocate of a stronger national government was Alexander Hamilton, the illegitimate son of a Scottish merchant in the West Indies, who had become a successful New York lawyer. Hamilton now called for a national convention to overhaul the Articles of Confederation. He found an important ally in James Madison of Virginia, who persuaded the Virginia legislature to convene an interstate conference on commercial questions. Only five states sent delegates to the meeting, which took place at Annapolis, Maryland, in 1786; but the conference approved a proposal by Hamilton for a convention of special delegates from all the states to meet in Philadelphia the next year.

At first there seemed little reason to believe the Philadelphia convention would attract any more delegates than had the Annapolis meeting. Then, early in 1787, the news of Shays's Rebellion spread throughout the nation, alarming many previously apathetic leaders, including George Washington, who promptly made plans to travel to Philadelphia for the Constitutional Convention. Washington's support gave the meeting wide credibility.

A DIVIDED CONVENTION

Fifty-five men, representing all the states except Rhode Island, attended one or more sessions of the convention that sat in the Philadelphia State House from May to September 1787. These "Founding Fathers," as they became known much later, were relatively young (the average age was forty-four) and well educated by the standards of their time. Most were wealthy property owners, and many feared what one of them called the "turbulence and follies" of democracy. Yet all retained the Revolutionary suspicion of concentrated power.

The convention unanimously chose Washington to preside over its sessions and then closed it to the public and the press. It then ruled that each state delegation would have a single vote and that major decisions would require not unanimity, as they did in Congress, but a simple majority. Almost all the delegates agreed that the United States needed a stronger central government. But there agreement ended.

Virginia, the most populous state, sent a well-prepared delegation to Philadelphia led by James Madison (thirty-six years old), who had devised in some detail a plan for a new "national" government. The Virginia Plan shaped the agenda of the convention from the moment Edmund Randolph of Virginia opened the debate by proposing that "a national government ought to be established, consisting of a supreme Legislative, Executive, and

GEORGE WASHINGTON AT MOUNT VERNON Washington was in his first term as president in 1790 when an anonymous folk artist painted this view of his home at Mount Vernon, Virginia. Washington appears in uniform, along with members of his family, on the lawn. After he retired from office in 1797, Washington returned happily to his plantation and spent the two years before his death in 1799 "amusing myself in agricultural and rural pursuits." He also played host to an endless stream of visitors from throughout the country and Europe. (Gift of Edgar William and Bernice Chrysler Garbisch, © 1998 Board of Trustees, National Gallery of Art, Washington)

Judiciary." Even that brief description outlined a government very different from the Confederation. But the delegates were so committed to fundamental reform that they approved the resolution after only brief debate.

There was less agreement about the details of Madison's Virginia Plan. It called for a national legislature of two houses. In the lower house, states would be represented in proportion to their population. Members of the upper house were to be elected by the lower house under no rigid system of representation; thus some of the smaller states might at times have no members at all in the upper house.

The proposal aroused immediate opposition among delegates from the smaller states. William Paterson of New Jersey offered an alternative (the New Jersey Plan) that would retain the essence of the Confederacy with its one-house legislature in which all states had equal representation. It would, however, give Congress expanded powers to tax and to regulate commerce. The convention rejected Paterson's proposal, but supporters of the Virginia Plan now realized they would have to make concessions to the smaller states. They agreed to permit members of the upper house (what became the Senate) to be elected by the state legislatures.

Many questions remained unresolved. Among the most important was the question of slavery. There was no serious discussion of abolishing slavery during the convention. But other issues were debated heatedly. Would slaves be counted as part of the population in determining representation in Congress? Or would they be considered property, not entitled to representation? Delegates from the states with large slave populations wanted to have it both ways. They argued that slaves should be considered persons in determining representation but as property if the new government levied taxes on the states on the basis of population. Representatives from states where slavery had disappeared or was expected soon to disappear argued that slaves should be included in calculating taxation but not representation.

COMPROMISE

The delegates bickered for weeks. By the end of June, as both temperature and tempers rose to uncomfortable heights, the convention seemed in danger of collapsing. But the delegates refused to give up. Finally, on July 2, the convention created a "grand committee," chaired by Franklin and with one delegate from each state, which produced a proposal that became the basis of the "Great Compromise." It called for a two-house legislature. In the lower house, the states would be represented on the basis of population; each slave would be counted as three-fifths of a free person in determining the basis for both representation and direct taxation. In the upper house, the states would be represented equally with two members apiece. On July 16, 1787, the convention voted to accept the compromise.

In the next few weeks, the convention agreed to another important compromise. To placate southern delegates, who feared the new government would interfere with slavery, the convention agreed to bar the new government from stopping the slave trade for twenty years.

Some significant issues remained unaddressed. The Constitution provided no definition of citizenship. Nor did it resolve the status of the Indian tribes. Most important to many Americans was the absence of a list of individual rights, which would restrain the powers of the national government. Madison opposed the idea, arguing that specifying rights that were reserved to the people would, in effect, limit those rights. Others, however, feared that without such protections the national government might abuse its new authority.

THE CONSTITUTION OF 1787

Many people contributed to the creation of the American Constitution, but the most important person in the process was James Madison. Madison had devised the Virginia Plan, and he did most of the drafting of the Constitution itself. Madison's most important achievement, however, was in helping resolve two important philosophical questions: the question of sovereignty and the question of limiting power.

How could a national government exercise sovereignty concurrently with state governments? Where did ultimate sovereignty lie? The answer, Madison and his contemporaries decided, was that all power, at all levels of government, flowed ultimately from the people. Thus neither the federal government nor the state governments were truly sovereign. All of them derived their authority from below. The resolution of the problem of sovereignty made possible one of the distinctive features of the Constitution—its "federalism," or division of powers between the national and state governments. The Constitution and the government it created were to be the "supreme law" of the land. At the same time, however, the Constitution left important powers in the hands of the states.

In addition to solving the question of sovereignty, the Constitution produced a distinctive solution to the problem of concentrated authority. Drawing from the ideas of the French philosopher Baron de Montesquieu, most Americans had long believed that the best way to avoid tyranny was to keep government close to the people. A large nation would breed corruption and despotism because distant rulers could not be controlled by the people.

Madison, however, helped break the grip of these assumptions by arguing that a large republic would be less likely to produce tyranny because no single group would ever be able to dominate it. The idea of many centers of power "checking one another" and preventing any single, despotic authority from emerging also helped shape the internal structure of the federal government. The Constitution's most distinctive feature was its "separation of powers" within the government, its creation of "checks and balances" among the legislative, executive, and judicial branches. The forces within the government would constantly compete with one another. Congress would have two chambers, each checking the other, since both would have to agree before any law could be passed. The president would have the power to veto acts of Congress. The federal courts would be protected from both the executive and the legislature, because judges would serve for life.

The "federal" structure of the government was designed to protect the United States from the kind of despotism that Americans believed had emerged in England. But it was also designed to protect the nation from another kind of despotism: the tyranny of the people. Shays's Rebellion, most of the founders believed, had been only one example of what could happen if a nation did not defend itself against the unchecked exercise of popular will. Thus in the new government, only the members of the House of Representatives would be elected directly by the people. Senators would be chosen by state legislators. The president would be chosen by an electoral college. Federal judges would be appointed by the president and confirmed by the Senate. On September 17, 1787, thirty-nine delegates signed the Constitution.

The Constitution of 1789 was a document that established a democratic republic for white people, mostly white men. Indians and African Americans, the two largest population groups sharing the lands of the United States with Anglo-Americans, enjoyed virtually none of the rights and privileges provided to the white population. Native Americans had at least the semblance of a legal status within the nation, through treaties that assured them lands that would be theirs forever. But most of these treaties did not survive for

THE BACKGROUND OF THE CONSTITUTION

THE Constitution of the United States has inspired debate from the moment it was drafted. Some argue that the Constitution is a flexible document intended to evolve in response to society's evolution. Others argue that it has a fixed meaning, rooted in the "original intent" of the framers, and that to move beyond that is to deny its value.

Historians, too, disagree about why the Constitution was written and what it meant. To some scholars, the creation of the federal system was an effort to preserve the ideals of the Revolution and to create a strong national government capable of exercising real authority. To others, the Constitution was an effort to protect the economic interests of existing elites, even at the cost of betraying the principles of the Revolution. And to still others, the Constitution was designed to protect individual freedom and to limit the power of the federal government.

The first influential exponent of the heroic view of the Constitution as the culmination of the Revolution was John Fiske, whose book *The Critical Period of American History* (1888) painted a grim picture of political life under the Articles of Confederation. Many problems, including economic difficulties, the weakness and ineptitude of the national government, threats from abroad, interstate jealousies, and widespread lawlessness, beset the new nation. Fiske argued that only the timely adoption of the Constitution saved the young republic from disaster.

In *An Economic Interpretation of the Constitution of the United States* (1913), Charles A. Beard presented a powerful challenge to Fiske's view. According to Beard, the 1780s had been a "critical period" primarily for conservative business interests who feared that the decentralized political structure of the republic imperiled their financial position. Such men, he claimed, wanted a government able to promote industry and trade, protect private property, and perhaps, most of all, make good the public debt—much of which was owed to them. The Constitution was, Beard claimed, "an economic document drawn with superb skill by men whose property interests were immediately at stake" and who won its ratification over the opposition of a majority of the people.

A series of powerful challenges to Beard's thesis emerged in the 1950s. The Constitution, many scholars now began to argue, was not an effort to preserve property but an enlightened effort to ensure stability and order. Robert E. Brown, for example, argued in 1956 that "absolutely no correlation" could be shown between the wealth of the delegates to the Constitutional Convention and their position on the Constitution. Examining the debate between the Federalists and the Antifederalists, Forrest McDonald, in *We the People* (1958), also concluded that there was no consistent relationship between wealth and property and support for the Constitution. Instead, opinion on the new system was far more likely to reflect local and regional interests. These challenges greatly weakened Beard's argument; few historians any longer accept his thesis without reservation.

In the 1960s, scholars began again to revive an economic interpretation of the Constitution—but one that differed from Beard's and nevertheless emphasized social and economic factors as motives for supporting the federal system. Jackson Turner Main argued in *The Anti-federalists* (1961) that supporters of the Constitution were

We the People

(National Archives)

"cosmopolitan commercialists," eager to advance the economic development of the nation; the Antifederalists, by contrast, were "agrarian localists," fearful of centralization. Gordon Wood, in *The Creation of the American Republic* (1969), suggested that the debate over the state constitutions in the 1770s and 1780s reflected profound social divisions and that those same divisions helped shape the argument over the federal Constitution. The Federalists, Wood suggested, were largely traditional aristocrats who had become deeply concerned by the instability of life under the Articles of Confederation and were particularly alarmed by the decline in popular deference toward social elites. The creation of the Constitution was part of a larger search to create a legitimate political leadership based on the existing social hierarchy; it reflected the efforts of elites to contain what they considered the excesses of democracy.

In recent years, historians have continued to examine the question of "intent." Did the framers intend a strong, centralized political system; or did they intend to create a decentralized system with a heavy emphasis on individual rights? The answer, according to Jack Rakove's *Original Meanings* (1996), is both—and many other things as well. The Constitution, he argues, was the result of a long and vigorous debate through which the views of many different groups found their way into the document. James Madison, generally known as the father of the Constitution, was a strong nationalist, as was Alexander Hamilton. They believed that only a powerful central government could preserve stability in a large nation, and they saw the Constitution as a way to protect order and property and defend the nation against the dangers of too much liberty. But if Madison and Hamilton feared too much liberty, they also feared too little. And that made them receptive to the demands of the Antifederalists for protections of individual rights, which culminated in the Bill of Rights.

The framers differed as well in their views of the proper relationship between the federal government and the state governments. Madison favored unquestioned federal supremacy, while many others, who wanted to preserve the rights of the states, saw in the federal system—and in its division of sovereignty among different levels and branches of government—a guarantee against too much national power. The Constitution is not, Rakove argues, "infinitely malleable." But neither does it have a fixed meaning that can be an inflexible guide to how we interpret it today. •

UNDERSTAND, ANALYZE, & EVALUATE

1. Is the Constitution a conservative, liberal, or radical document? Did the framers consider the Constitution something "finished" (with the exception of constitutional amendments), or did they consider it a document that would evolve in response to changes in society over time?

2. Which parts of the Constitution suggest that the framers' intent was to create a strong, centralized political system? Which parts suggest that the framers' intent was to create a decentralized system with heavy emphasis on individual rights?

long, and the Indians found themselves driven farther and farther west without very much of the protection that the government had promised them.

Among the white leaders of the United States, there were eminent figures who believed Indians could in fact join the republic as citizens. Jefferson was among them, believing that they could be taught the ways of "civilization." Jefferson, and other Americans with good intentions, sought to teach the Indians to live as white Americans did. Efforts to teach them Anglo farming methods were based on sedentary farms that relied on men doing the farming and women caring for the home. Indians had no interest in such ways and preferred to retain their own traditional cultures. Their repudiation of white civilization contributed to the erosion of support among white Americans. They were not granted citizenship of the United States until the 1920s.

Far more removed from the guarantees of the Constitution were African American slaves, who were given virtually none of the rights and protections that the new government provided to white people. They were not, one southern official noted, "constituent members of our society." The French-Canadian writer Hector St. John de Crevecoeur, who after the Revolution settled in the United States, wrote a famous book titled, *Letters from an American Farmer,* in 1782. In it, he posed what became a famous question: What then is the American, this new man? Crevecoeur answered his own question by noting that "individuals of all nations" would become "melted" into a common citizenry. But he saw no room for African Americans in the community of the "new man." Indeed, among the first laws passed by the new United States under the Constitution was the Naturalization Act of 1790, which helped legalize the stream of immigrants coming into the country and allowed them to become citizens. But it defined citizenry as a status available only to white people. Even free black people were barred from inclusion.

Jefferson, who had briefly tried without result to give Indians a legal status within the new nation, had no such aspirations for African Americans. He was an uneasy defender of slavery, worrying about excluding "a whole race of men" from the natural rights that Jefferson himself had done much to promote. But he could never accept the idea that black men and women could attain the level of knowledge and intelligence of white people. Jefferson's long romantic relationship with a black woman, Sally Hemmings, did nothing to change his mind. Hemmings was a light-skinned woman who was a slave on Jefferson's plantation in Virginia. He lived with her after the death of his wife and fathered several of her children. But his intimate relationship with the Hemmings family did not ultimately change his position on slavery. Unlike George Washington, who freed his slaves after his death, Jefferson (deeply in debt) required his heirs to sell his slaves after he died (after liberating the Hemmings family). Not until the end of the Civil War were black men and women eligible to live as citizens in the United States, and even then with only partial rights until a century later. For almost a century, the United States Constitution was a document that governed and protected white people only.

ADOPTION AND ADAPTATION

The delegates at Philadelphia had greatly exceeded their instructions from Congress and the states. Instead of making simple revisions in the Articles of Confederation, they had produced a plan for a completely different form of government. They feared that the Constitution would not be ratified under the rules of the Articles of Confederation, which required unanimous approval by the state legislatures. So the convention changed the rules, proposing that the new government would come into being when nine of the thirteen states ratified the Constitution and recommending that state conventions, not state legislatures, be called to ratify it.

FEDERALISTS AND ANTIFEDERALISTS

The Congress in New York accepted the convention's work and submitted it to the states for approval. All the state legislatures except Rhode Island elected delegates to ratifying conventions, most of which began meeting in early 1788. Even before the ratifying conventions convened, however, a great national debate on the new Constitution had begun.

Supporters of the Constitution had a number of advantages. Better organized than their opponents, they seized an appealing label for themselves: "Federalists"—a term that opponents of centralization had once used to describe themselves—thus implying that they were less committed to a "nationalist" government than in fact they were. In addition, the Federalists had the support of not only the two most eminent men in America, Franklin and Washington, but also the ablest political philosophers of their time: Alexander Hamilton, James Madison, and John Jay. Under the joint pseudonym "Publius," these three men wrote a series of essays, widely published in newspapers throughout the nation, explaining the meaning and virtues of the Constitution. The essays were later gathered together and published as a book. They are known today as *The Federalist Papers*.

The Federalists called their critics "Antifederalists," suggesting that their rivals had nothing to offer except opposition. But the Antifederalists, too, led by such distinguished Revolutionary leaders as Patrick Henry and Samuel Adams, had serious and intelligent arguments. They were, they believed, the defenders of the true principles of the Revolution. They believed that the Constitution would increase taxes, weaken the states, wield dictatorial powers, favor the "well-born" over the common people, and abolish individual liberty. But their biggest complaint was that the Constitution lacked a bill of rights. Only by enumerating the natural rights of the people, they argued, could there be any certainty that those rights would be protected.

Despite the efforts of the Antifederalists, ratification proceeded quickly during the winter of 1787–1788. The Delaware convention, the first to act, ratified the Constitution unanimously, as did the New Jersey and Georgia conventions. And in June 1788, New Hampshire, the critical ninth state, ratified the document. It was now theoretically possible for the Constitution to go into effect. But a new government could not hope to succeed without Virginia and New York, the largest states, whose conventions remained closely divided. But by the end of June, first Virginia and then New York consented to the Constitution by narrow margins—on the assumption that a bill of rights would be added in the form of amendments to the Constitution. North Carolina's convention adjourned without taking action, waiting to see what happened to the amendments. Rhode Island did not even consider ratification.

COMPLETING THE STRUCTURE

The first elections under the Constitution were held in the early months of 1789. There was never any doubt about who would be the first president. George Washington had presided at the Constitutional Convention, and many who had favored ratification did so only because they expected him to preside over the new government as well. Washington received the votes of all the presidential electors. (John Adams, a leading Federalist, became vice president.) After a journey from his estate at Mount Vernon, Virginia, marked by elaborate celebrations along the way, Washington was inaugurated in New York on April 30, 1789.

The first Congress served in many ways as a continuation of the Constitutional Convention. Its most important task was drafting a bill of rights. By early 1789, even Madison had come to agree that some sort of bill of rights would be essential to legitimize the new government. On September 25, 1789, Congress approved twelve amendments, ten of which were ratified by the states by the end of 1791. These first ten amendments to the Constitution comprise what we know as the Bill of Rights. Nine of them placed limitations on the new government by forbidding it to infringe on certain fundamental rights: freedom of religion, speech, and the press; immunity from arbitrary arrest; trial by jury; and others.

The Bill of Rights had very specific terms. The Federal Courts had no such details. The Constitution said only: "The judicial power of the United States shall be vested in one Supreme Court, and in such inferior courts as the Congress may from time to time ordain and establish." It was left to Congress to determine the number of Supreme Court judges to be appointed and the kinds of lower courts to be organized. In the Judiciary Act of 1789, Congress provided for a Supreme Court of six members and a system of lower district courts and courts of appeal. It also gave the Supreme Court the power to make the final decision in cases involving the constitutionality of state laws.

The Constitution also said little about the organization of the executive branch. It referred indirectly to executive departments but did not specify which ones or how many there should be. The first Congress created three such departments—state, treasury, and war—and also established the offices of the attorney general and postmaster general. To the office of secretary of the treasury, Washington appointed Alexander Hamilton of New York. For secretary of war, he chose a Massachusetts Federalist, General Henry Knox. He named Edmund Randolph of Virginia as attorney general and chose another Virginian, Thomas Jefferson, for secretary of state.

FEDERALISTS AND REPUBLICANS

The framers of the Constitution had dealt with many controversies by papering them over with a series of vague compromises; as a result, the disagreements survived to plague the new government.

At the heart of the controversies of the 1790s was the same basic difference in philosophy that had fueled the debate over the Constitution. On one side stood a powerful group who envisioned America as a genuine nation-state, with centralized authority and a complex commercial economy. On the other side stood another group whose members envisioned a more modest national government. Rather than aspire to be a highly commercial or urban nation, it should remain predominantly rural and agrarian. The centralizers became known as the Federalists and gravitated to the leadership of Alexander Hamilton. Their opponents acquired the name Republicans and gathered under Thomas Jefferson and James Madison.

HAMILTON AND THE FEDERALISTS

For twelve years, the Federalists retained firm control of the new government. That was in part because George Washington had always envisioned a strong national government. But the president, Washington believed, should stand above political controversies, and so he avoided personal involvement in the deliberations of Congress. As a result, the dominant figure in his administration became Alexander Hamilton. Of all the national leaders of his time, Hamilton was one of the most aristocratic in his political philosophy; he believed that a stable and effective government required an elite ruling class. Thus the new government needed the support of the wealthy and powerful; and to get that, it needed to give elites a stake in its success. Hamilton proposed, therefore, that the existing public debt be "funded": that the various certificates of indebtedness that the old Congress had issued during and after the Revolution—many of them now in the possession of wealthy speculators—be called in and exchanged for interest-bearing bonds. He also recommended that the states' Revolutionary debts be "assumed" (taken over) to cause state bondholders also to look to the central government for eventual payment. Hamilton wanted to create a permanent national debt, with new bonds being issued as old ones were paid off. The result, he believed, would be that the wealthy classes, who were the most likely to lend money to the government, would always have a reason to want the government to survive.

Hamilton also wanted to create a national bank. It would provide loans and currency to businesses, give the government a safe place for the deposit of federal funds, facilitate the collection of taxes and the disbursement of the government's expenditures, and provide a stable center to the nation's small and feeble banking system. The bank would be chartered by the federal government, but much of its capital would come from private investors.

The funding and assumption of debts would require new sources of revenue. Hamilton recommended two kinds of taxes to complement the receipts anticipated from the sales of public land. One was an excise tax on alcoholic beverages, a tax that would be most burdensome to the whiskey distillers of the backcountry, small farmers who converted part of their corn and rye crops into whiskey. The other was a tariff on imports, which Hamilton saw not only as a way to raise money but as a way to protect domestic industries from foreign competition. In his famous "Report on Manufactures" of 1791, he outlined a plan for stimulating the growth of industry and spoke glowingly of the advantages to society of a healthy manufacturing sector.

The Federalists, in short, offered more than a vision of a stable new government. They offered a vision of the sort of nation America should become—a nation with a wealthy, enlightened ruling class, a vigorous, independent commercial economy, and a thriving manufacturing sector.

ENACTING THE FEDERALIST PROGRAM

Few members of Congress objected to Hamilton's plan for funding the national debt, but many did oppose his proposal to exchange new bonds for old certificates of indebtedness on a dollar-for-dollar basis. Many of the original holders had been forced to sell during the hard times of the 1780s to speculators, who had bought them at a fraction of their face value. James Madison, now a representative from Virginia, argued for a plan by which the new bonds would be divided between the original purchasers and the speculators. But Hamilton's allies insisted that the honor of the government required a literal fulfillment of its earlier promises to pay whoever held the bonds. Congress finally passed the funding bill Hamilton wanted.

Hamilton's proposal that the federal government assume the state debts encountered greater difficulty. Its opponents argued that if the federal government took over the state debts, the states with small debts would have to pay taxes to service the states with large

WASHINGTON'S FAREWELL ADDRESS, *PHILADELPHIA'S AMERICAN DAILY ADVERTISER*, SEPTEMBER 19, 1796

OBSERVE good faith and justice toward all nations. Cultivate peace and harmony with all. Religion and morality enjoin this conduct. And can it be that good policy does not equally enjoin it? It will be worthy of a free, enlightened, and, at no distant period, a great nation to give to mankind the magnanimous and too novel example of a people always guided by an exalted justice and benevolence. . . .

In the execution of such a plan nothing is more essential than that permanent, inveterate antipathies against particular nations and passionate attachments for others should be excluded, and that, in place of them just and amicable feelings toward all should be cultivated. The nation which indulges toward another an habitual hatred or an habitual fondness is in some degree a slave. It is a slave to its animosity or to its affection either of which is sufficient to lead it astray from its duty and its interest. The nation prompted by ill will and resentment sometimes impels to war the government, contrary to the best calculations of policy. The government sometimes participates in the national propensity, and adopts through passion what reason would reject. . . .

So, likewise, a passionate attachment of one nation for another produces a variety of evils. Sympathy for the favorite nation, facilitating the illusion of an imaginary common interest in cases where no real common interest exists, and infusing into one the enmities of the other, betrays the former into a participation in the quarrels and wars of the latter without adequate inducement or justification. . . .

As avenues to foreign influence in innumerable ways, such attachments are particularly alarming to the truly enlightened and independent patriot. How many opportunities do they afford to tamper with domestic factions to practice the arts of seduction, to mislead public opinion, to influence or awe the public councils! Such an attachment of a small or weak toward a great and powerful nation dooms the former to be the satellite of the latter.

Against the insidious wiles of foreign influence (I conjure you to believe me, fellow citizens) the jealousy of a free people ought to be constantly awake, since history and experience prove that foreign influence is one of the most baneful foes of republican government. . . .

The great rule of conduct for us in regard to foreign nations is, in extending our commercial relation to have with them as little political connection as possible. So far as we have already formed engagements, let them be fulfilled with perfect good faith. Here let us stop.

Europe has a set of primary interests which to us have no, or a very remote, relation.

ones. Massachusetts, for example, owed much more money than did Virginia. Only by striking a bargain with the Virginians were Hamilton and his supporters able to win passage of the assumption bill.

The deal involved the location of the national capital, which the Virginians wanted near them in the South. Hamilton and Jefferson met and agreed to exchange northern

Hence she must be engaged in frequent controversies, the causes of which are essentially foreign to our concerns. Hence, therefore, it must be unwise in us to implicate ourselves by artificial ties in the ordinary vicissitudes of her politics, or the ordinary combinations and collisions of her friendships or enmities.

Our detached and distant situation invites and enables us to pursue a different course. If we remain one people, under an efficient government, the period is not far off when we may defy material injury from external annoyance; when we may take such an attitude as will cause the neutrality we may at any time resolve upon to be scrupulously respected; when belligerent nations, under the impossibility of making acquisitions upon us, will not lightly hazard giving us provocation; when we may choose peace or war, as our interest, guided by justice, shall counsel.

Why forego the advantages of so peculiar a situation? Why quit our own to stand upon foreign ground? Why, by interweaving our destiny with that of any part of Europe, entangle our peace and prosperity in the toils of European ambition, rivalship, interest, humor, or caprice?

It is our true policy to steer clear of permanent alliances with any portion of the foreign world, so far, I mean, as we are now at liberty to do it. For let me not be understood as capable of patronizing infidelity to existing engagements. I hold the maxim of less applicable to public than to private affairs that honesty is always the best policy. I repeat therefore, let those engagements be observed in their genuine sense. But in my opinion it is unnecessary and would be unwise to extend them.

Taking care always to keep ourselves by suitable establishments on a respectable defensive posture, we may safely trust to temporary alliances for extraordinary emergencies.

Harmony, liberal intercourse with all nations, are recommended by policy, humanity, and interest. But even our commercial policy should hold an equal and impartial hand, neither seeking nor granting exclusive favors or preferences; . . . constantly keeping in view that it is folly in one nation to look for disinterested favors from another; that it must pay with a portion of its independence for whatever it may accept under that character; that by such acceptance it may place itself in the condition of having given equivalents for nominal favors, and yet of being reproached with ingratitude for not giving more. There can be no greater error than to expect or calculate upon real favors from nation to nation. It is an illusion which experience must cure, which a just pride ought to discard.

UNDERSTAND, ANALYZE, & EVALUATE

1. What advice did George Washington offer on foreign policy?
2. Did Washington advocate the complete isolation of the United States from Europe? Explain.
3. How did Washington characterize Europe? What circumstances of the 1790s may have inspired this assessment?

Source: http://www.senate.gov/artandhistory/history/minute/Washingtons_Farewell_Address.htm.

support for placing the capital in the South for Virginia's votes for the assumption bill. The bargain called for the construction of a new capital city on the banks of the Potomac River, which divided Maryland and Virginia, on land to be selected by George Washington.

Hamilton's bank bill produced the most heated debates. Madison, Jefferson, Randolph, and others argued that because the Constitution made no provision for a national bank,

Congress had no authority to create one. But Congress agreed to Hamilton's bill despite these objections, and Washington signed it. The Bank of the United States began operations in 1791.

Hamilton also had his way with the excise tax, although protests from farmers later forced revisions to reduce the burden on the smaller distillers. He failed to win passage of a tariff as highly protective as he had hoped for, but the tariff law of 1792 did raise the rates somewhat.

Once enacted, Hamilton's program won the support of manufacturers, creditors, and other influential segments of the population. But others found Hamilton's program less appealing. Small farmers complained that they were being taxed excessively. They and others began to argue that the Federalist program served the interests of a small number of wealthy elites rather than the people at large. From these sentiments, an organized political opposition arose.

THE REPUBLICAN OPPOSITION

The Constitution made no reference to political parties. Most of the framers believed that organized parties were dangerous "factions" to be avoided. Disagreement was inevitable on particular issues, but they believed that such disagreements need not and should not lead to the formation of these permanent factions.

Yet not many years had passed after the ratification of the Constitution before Madison and others became convinced that Hamilton and his followers had become a dangerous, self-interested faction. The Federalists had used the powers of their offices to reward their supporters and win additional allies. They were doing many of the same things, their opponents believed, that the corrupt British governments of the early eighteenth century had done.

Because the Federalists appeared to their critics to be creating such a menacing and tyrannical structure of power, there was no alternative but to organize a vigorous opposition. The result was the emergence of an alternative political organization, whose members called themselves "Republicans." (These first Republicans are not institutionally related to the modern Republican Party, which was created in the 1850s.) By the late 1790s, the Republicans were going to even greater lengths than the Federalists to create vehicles of partisan influence. In every state they formed committees, societies, and caucuses; Republican groups banded together to influence state and local elections. Neither side was willing to admit that it was acting as a party, nor would either concede the right of the other to exist. This institutionalized factionalism is known to historians as the "first party system."

From the beginning, the preeminent figures among the Republicans were Thomas Jefferson and James Madison. The most prominent spokesman for the cause, Jefferson promoted a vision of an agrarian republic, in which most citizens would farm their own land. Jefferson did not scorn commercial or industrial activity. But he believed that the nation should be wary of too much urbanization and industrialization.

Although both parties had supporters across the country and among all classes, there were regional and economic differences. The Federalists were most numerous in the commercial centers of the Northeast and in such southern seaports as Charleston; the Republicans were stronger in the rural areas of the South and the West. The difference in their philosophies was visible in, among other things, their reactions to the progress of the French Revolution. As that revolution grew increasingly radical in the 1790s, the Federalists expressed horror. But the Republicans applauded the democratic, antiaristocratic spirit they believed the French Revolution displayed.

When the time came for the nation's second presidential election, in 1792, both Jefferson and Hamilton urged Washington to run for a second term. The president reluctantly agreed. But while Washington had the respect of both factions, he was, in reality, more in sympathy with the Federalists than with the Republicans.

ESTABLISHING NATIONAL SOVEREIGNTY

The Federalists consolidated their position by acting effectively in managing the western territories and diplomacy.

SECURING THE WEST

Despite the Northwest Ordinance, the old Congress had largely failed to tie the outlying western areas of the country firmly to the national government. Farmers in western Massachusetts had rebelled; settlers in Vermont, Kentucky, and Tennessee had flirted with seceding from the Union. And at first, the new government under the Constitution faced similar problems.

In 1794, farmers in western Pennsylvania raised a major challenge to federal authority when they refused to pay the new whiskey excise tax and began terrorizing tax collectors in the region. But the federal government did not leave settlement of the so-called Whiskey Rebellion to the authorities of Pennsylvania. At Hamilton's urging, Washington called out the militias of three states and assembled an army of nearly 15,000—and he personally led the troops into Pennsylvania. At the approach of the militiamen, the rebellion quickly collapsed.

A COMMENT ON THE WHISKEY REBELLION   Although Thomas Jefferson and other Republicans claimed to welcome occasional popular uprisings, the Federalists were horrified by such insurgencies as Shays's Rebellion in Massachusetts and later the Whiskey Rebellion in Pennsylvania. This Federalist cartoon portrays the rebels as demons who pursue and eventually hang an unfortunate "exciseman" (tax collector), who has confiscated two kegs of rum. (© Philadelphia History Museum at the Atwater Kent/Bridgeman Art Library)

The federal government won the allegiance of the whiskey rebels through intimidation. It won the loyalties of other western people by accepting new states as members of the Union. The last two of the original thirteen colonies joined the Union once the Bill of Rights had been appended to the Constitution—North Carolina in 1789 and Rhode Island in 1790. Vermont became the fourteenth state in 1791, after New York and New Hampshire agreed to give up their claims to it. Next came Kentucky, in 1792, when Virginia gave up its claim to that region. After North Carolina ceded its western lands to the Union, Tennessee became a state in 1796.

The new government faced a greater challenge in more distant areas of the Northwest and the Southwest. The ordinances of 1784–1787, establishing the terms of white settlement in the West, had produced a series of border conflicts with Indian tribes. The new government inherited these clashes, which continued with few interruptions for nearly a decade.

These clashes revealed another issue the Constitution had done little to resolve: the place of the Indian nations within the new federal structure. The Constitution gave Congress power to "regulate Commerce . . . with the Indian tribes." And it bound the new government to respect treaties negotiated by the Confederation, most of which had been with the tribes. But none of this did very much to clarify the precise legal standing of Indians or Indian nations within the United States. The tribes received no direct representation in the new government. Above all, the Constitution did not address the major issue of land. Indian nations lived within the boundaries of the United States, yet they claimed (and the white government at times agreed) that they had some measure of sovereignty over their own land. But neither the Constitution nor common law offered any clear guide to the rights of a "nation within a nation" or to the precise nature of tribal sovereignty.

MAINTAINING NEUTRALITY

A crisis in Anglo-American relations emerged in 1793, when the revolutionary French government went to war with Great Britain. Both the president and Congress took steps to establish American neutrality in the conflict, but that neutrality was severely tested.

Early in 1794, the Royal Navy began seizing hundreds of American ships engaged in trade in the French West Indies. Hamilton was deeply concerned. War would mean an end to imports from England, and most of the revenue for maintaining his financial system came from duties on those imports. Hamilton and the Federalists did not trust the State Department, now in the hands of the ardently pro-French Edmund Randolph, to find a solution to the crisis. So they persuaded Washington to name a special commissioner—the chief justice of the Supreme Court, John Jay—to go to England and negotiate a solution. Jay was instructed to secure compensation for the recent British assaults on American shipping, to demand withdrawal of British forces from their posts on the frontier of the United States, and to negotiate a commercial treaty with Britain.

The long and complex treaty Jay negotiated in 1794 failed to achieve these goals. But it settled the conflict with Britain, avoiding a likely war. It provided for undisputed American sovereignty over the entire Northwest and produced a reasonably satisfactory commercial relationship. Nevertheless, when the terms became known in America, criticism was intense. Opponents of the treaty went to great lengths to defeat it, but in the end the Senate ratified what was by then known as Jay's Treaty.

Jay's Treaty paved the way for a settlement of important American disputes with Spain. Under Pinckney's Treaty (negotiated by Thomas Pinckney and signed in 1795), Spain recognized the right of Americans to navigate the Mississippi to its mouth and to deposit goods at New Orleans for reloading on oceangoing ships; agreed to fix the northern boundary of Florida along the 31st parallel; and commanded its authorities to prevent the Indians in Florida from launching raids north across the border.

THE DOWNFALL OF THE FEDERALISTS

Since almost everyone in the 1790s agreed that there was no place in a stable republic for organized parties, the emergence of the Republicans as a powerful and apparently permanent opposition seemed to the Federalists a grave threat to national stability. And so when international perils confronted the government in the 1790s, Hamilton and his followers moved forcefully against this "illegitimate" opposition.

THE ELECTION OF 1796

George Washington refused to run for a third term as president in 1796. Jefferson was the obvious presidential candidate of the Republicans that year, but the Federalists faced a more difficult choice. Hamilton had created too many enemies to be a credible candidate. Vice President John Adams, who was not directly associated with any of the controversial Federalist achievements, received the party's nomination for president at a caucus of the Federalists in Congress.

The Federalists were still clearly the dominant party. But without Washington to mediate, they fell victim to fierce factional rivalries. Adams defeated Jefferson by only three electoral votes and assumed the presidency as head of a divided party facing a powerful opposition. Jefferson became vice president as a result of finishing second. (Not until the adoption of the Twelfth Amendment in 1804 did electors vote separately for president and vice president.)

THE QUASI WAR WITH FRANCE

American relations with Great Britain and Spain improved as a result of Jay's and Pinckney's treaties. But the nation's relations with revolutionary France quickly deteriorated. French vessels captured American ships on the high seas. The French government refused to receive Charles Cotesworth Pinckney when he arrived in Paris as the new American minister. In an effort to stabilize relations, Adams appointed a bipartisan commission to negotiate with France. When the Americans arrived in Paris in 1797, three agents of the French foreign minister, Prince Talleyrand, demanded a loan for France and a bribe for French officials before any negotiations could begin. Pinckney, a member of the commission, responded, "No! No! Not a sixpence!"

When Adams heard of the incident, he sent a message to Congress urging preparations for war. Before giving the commissioners' report to Congress, he deleted the names of the three French agents and designated them only as Messrs. X, Y, and Z. When the report was published, the "XYZ Affair," as it quickly became known, provoked widespread popular outrage at France's actions and strong popular support for the Federalists' response.

For nearly two years, 1798 and 1799, the United States found itself engaged in an unde-clared war with France.

Adams persuaded Congress to cut off all trade with France, to abrogate the treaties of 1778, and to authorize American vessels to capture French armed ships on the high seas. In 1798, Congress created the Department of the Navy. The navy soon won a number of battles and captured a total of eighty-five French ships. The United States also began cooperating closely with the British. At last, the French began trying to conciliate the United States. Adams sent another commission to Paris in 1800, and the new French government (headed now by "First Consul" Napoleon Bonaparte) agreed to a treaty with the United States that canceled the old agreements of 1778 and established new com-mercial arrangements. As a result, the "quasi war" came to a reasonably peaceful end.

REPRESSION AND PROTEST

The conflict with France helped the Federalists increase their majorities in Congress in 1798. They now began to consider ways to silence the Republican opposition. The result was some of the most controversial legislation in American history: the Alien and Sedition acts.

The Alien Act placed new obstacles in the way of foreigners who wished to become American citizens. The Sedition Act allowed the government to prosecute those who engaged in "sedition" against the government. In theory, only libelous or treasonous activ-ities were subject to prosecution; but since such activities had no clear definition, the law, in effect, gave the government authority to stifle virtually any opposition. The Republicans interpreted the new laws as part of a Federalist campaign to destroy them.

President Adams signed the new laws but was cautious in implementing them. He did not deport any aliens, and he prevented the government from launching a broad crusade against the Republicans. But the Alien Act discouraged immigration and encouraged some foreigners already in the country to leave. And the administration used the Sedition Act to arrest and convict ten men, most of them Republican newspaper editors whose only crime had been criticism of the Federalists in government.

Republican leaders began to look for ways to reverse the Alien and Sedition acts. Some looked to the state legislatures for help. They developed a theory to justify action by the states against the federal government in two sets of resolutions of 1798–1799, one written (anonymously) by Jefferson and adopted by the Kentucky legislature and the other drafted by Madison and approved by the Virginia legislature. The Virginia and Kentucky resolu-tions, as they were known, used the ideas of John Locke and the Tenth Amendment to the Constitution to argue that the federal government had been formed by a "compact," or contract, among the states and possessed only certain delegated powers. Whenever a state decided that the central government had exceeded those powers, it had the right to "nullify" the appropriate laws.

The Republicans did not win wide support for the nullification idea; they did, however, succeed in elevating their dispute with the Federalists to the level of a national crisis. By the late 1790s, the entire nation was deeply and bitterly politicized. State legislatures at times resembled battlegrounds. Even the United States Congress was plagued with violent disagree-ments. In one celebrated incident in the chamber of the House of Representatives, Matthew Lyon, a Republican from Vermont, responded to an insult from Roger Griswold, a Federalist from Connecticut, by spitting in Griswold's eye. Griswold attacked Lyon with his cane, Lyon fought back with a pair of fire tongs, and soon the two men were wrestling on the floor.

CONGRESSIONAL BRAWLERS, 1798 This savage cartoon was inspired by the celebrated fight on the floor of the House of Representatives between Matthew Lyon, a Republican representative from Vermont, and Roger Griswold, a Federalist from Connecticut. Griswold *(at right)* attacks Lyon with his cane, and Lyon retaliates with fire tongs. Other members of Congress are portrayed enjoying the battle. (New York Public Library, Astor, Lenox and Tilden Foundations)

THE "REVOLUTION" OF 1800

These bitter controversies shaped the presidential election of 1800. The presidential candidates were the same as four years earlier: Adams for the Federalists, Jefferson for the Republicans. But the campaign of 1800 was very different from the one preceding it. Adams and Jefferson themselves displayed reasonable dignity, but their supporters showed no such restraint. The Federalists accused Jefferson of being a dangerous radical whose followers were wild men who, if they should come to power, would bring on a reign of terror comparable to that of the French Revolution. The Republicans portrayed Adams as a tyrant conspiring to become king, and they accused the Federalists of plotting to impose slavery on the people. The election was close, and the crucial contest was in New York. There, Aaron Burr mobilized an organization of Revolutionary War veterans, the Tammany Society, to serve as a Republican political machine. Through Tammany's efforts, the party carried the city by a large majority, and with it the state. Jefferson was, apparently, elected.

But an unexpected complication soon jeopardized the Republican victory. The Constitution called for each elector to "vote by ballot for two persons." The expectation was that an elector would cast one vote for his party's presidential candidate and the other for his party's vice presidential candidate. To avoid a tie, the Republicans had intended that one elector would refrain from voting for the party's vice presidential candidate, Aaron Burr. But when the votes were counted, Jefferson and Burr each had 73. No candidate had a majority, and the House of Representatives had to choose between the two top candidates, Jefferson and Burr. Each state delegation would cast a single vote.

The new Congress, elected in 1800 with a Republican majority, was not to convene until after the inauguration of the president, so it was the Federalist Congress that had to decide the question. After a long deadlock, several leading Federalists concluded, following

Hamilton's advice, that Burr was too unreliable to trust with the presidency. On the thirty-sixth ballot, Jefferson was elected.

After the election of 1800, the only branch of the federal government left in Federalist hands was the judiciary. The Adams administration spent its last months in office taking steps to make the party's hold on the courts secure. With the Judiciary Act of 1801, the Federalists reduced the number of Supreme Court justiceships by one but greatly increased the number of federal judgeships as a whole. Adams quickly appointed Federalists to the newly created positions. He also appointed a leading Federalist, John Marshall, to be chief justice of the Supreme Court, a position Marshall held for 34 years. Indeed, there were charges that he stayed up until midnight on his last day in office to finish signing the new judges' commissions. These officeholders became known as the "midnight appointments."

Even so, the Republicans viewed their victory as almost complete. The nation had, they believed, been saved from tyranny. The exuberance with which the victors viewed the future—and the importance they ascribed to the defeat of the Federalists—was evident in the phrase Jefferson himself later used to describe his election. He called it the "Revolution of 1800."

CONCLUSION

The writing of the Constitution of 1787 was the single most important political event in the history of the United States. In creating a federal system of dispersed authority—authority divided among national and state governments, and among an executive, a legislature, and a judiciary—the young nation sought to balance its need for an effective central government against its fear of concentrated and despotic power. The ability of the delegates to the Constitutional Convention to compromise revealed the deep yearning among them for a stable political system. The same willingness to compromise allowed the greatest challenge to the ideals of the new democracy—slavery—to survive intact.

The writing and ratifying of the Constitution settled some questions about the shape of the new nation. The first twelve years under the government created by the Constitution solved others. And yet by the year 1800, a basic disagreement about the future of the nation remained unresolved and was creating bitter divisions and conflicts within the political world. The election of Thomas Jefferson to the presidency that year opened a new chapter in the nation's public history. It also brought to a close, at least temporarily, savage political conflicts that had seemed to threaten the nation's future.

RECALL AND REFLECT

1. How did the Constitution of 1787 attempt to resolve the weaknesses of the Articles of Confederation?
2. What role did *The Federalist Papers* play in the battle over ratification of the Constitution?
3. What were the main tenets of Alexander Hamilton's financial program?
4. What diplomatic crises did the United States face in the first decade of its existence, and how did the new government respond to these crises?
5. What was the "Revolution of 1800" and in what way was it a revolution?

7 THE JEFFERSONIAN ERA

LOOKING AHEAD

1. How successful was Jefferson's effort to create a "republican" society dominated by sturdy, independent farmers?
2. How did the Napoleonic wars affect the United States?
3. What events and issues led to the War of 1812?

THOMAS JEFFERSON AND HIS FOLLOWERS assumed control of the national government in 1801 as the champions of a distinctive vision of America. They favored a society of sturdy, independent farmers, happily free from the workshops, the industrial towns, and the city mobs of Europe. They celebrated localism and republican simplicity. Above all, they proposed a federal government of sharply limited power.

Almost nothing worked out as they had planned, for during their years in power the young republic was developing in ways that made much of their vision obsolete. The American economy became steadily more diversified and complex, making the ideal of a simple, agrarian society impossible to maintain. American cultural life was dominated by a vigorous and ambitious nationalism. And Jefferson himself contributed to the changes by exercising strong national authority at times and by arranging the greatest single increase in the size of the United States in its history.

1793

Eli Whitney invents cotton gin

1800

U.S. capital moves to Washington

1801

Second Great Awakening begins

Marshall chief justice of Supreme Court

1803

Louisiana Purchase

Marbury v. Madison

1804–1806

Lewis and Clark expedition

1804

Jefferson reelected

1807

Embargo

1808

Madison elected president

1809

Non-Intercourse Act

Tecumseh Confederacy formed

1810

Macon's Bill No. 2

1811

Battle of Tippecanoe

1812

U.S. declares war on Great Britain

Madison reelected

1814

Hartford Convention

Treaty of Ghent

1815

Battle of New Orleans

THE RISE OF CULTURAL NATIONALISM

In many respects, American cultural life in the early nineteenth century reflected the Republican vision of the nation's future. Opportunities for education increased, the nation's literary and artistic life began to free itself from European influences, and American religion began to adjust to the spread of Enlightenment rationalism. In other ways, however, the new culture was posing a serious challenge to Republican ideals.

EDUCATIONAL AND LITERARY NATIONALISM

Central to the Republican vision of America was the concept of a virtuous and enlightened citizenry. Republicans believed, therefore, in the creation of a nationwide system of public schools in which all male citizens would receive free education. Such hopes were not fulfilled. Schooling remained primarily the responsibility of private institutions, most of which were open only to those who could afford to pay for them. In the South and in the mid-Atlantic states, most schools were run by religious groups. In New England, private academies were often more secular, many of them modeled on those founded by the Phillips family at Andover, Massachusetts, in 1778, and at Exeter, New Hampshire, three years later. Many were frankly aristocratic in outlook. Some educational institutions were open to the poor, but not nearly enough to accommodate everyone, and the education they offered was usually clearly inferior to that provided for more prosperous students.

Private secondary schools such as those in New England generally accepted only male students; even many public schools excluded females from the classroom. Yet the late eighteenth and early nineteenth centuries did see some important advances in education for women. As Americans began to place a higher value on the importance of the "Republican mother" who would help train the new generation for citizenship, people began to ask how mothers could raise their children to be enlightened if the mothers themselves were uneducated. Such concerns helped speed the creation of female academies throughout the nation (usually for the daughters of affluent families). In 1789, Massachusetts required that its public schools serve females as well as males. Other states, although not all, soon followed.

Some women aspired to more. In 1784, Judith Sargent Murray published an essay defending the right of women to education. Women and men were equal in intellect and potential, Murray argued. Women, therefore, should have precisely the same educational opportunities as men. What was more, they should have opportunities to earn their own livings and to establish roles in society apart from their husbands and families. Murray's ideas attracted relatively little support.

Because Jefferson and his followers liked to think of Native Americans as "noble savages" (uncivilized but not necessarily uncivilizable), they hoped that schooling the Indians in white culture would "uplift" the tribes. Missionaries and mission schools proliferated among the tribes. But there were no comparable efforts to educate enslaved African Americans.

Higher education similarly diverged from Republican ideals. The number of colleges and universities in America grew substantially, from nine at the time of the Revolution to twenty-two in 1800. None of the new schools, however, was truly public. Even universities established by state legislatures relied on private contributions and tuition fees to survive. Scarcely more than one white man in a thousand (and virtually no women, blacks, or Indians) had access to any college education, and those few who did attend universities were, almost without exception, members of prosperous, propertied families.

MEDICINE AND SCIENCE

Medicine and science were not always closely connected to each other in the early nineteenth century, but many physicians were working hard to strengthen the link. The University of Pennsylvania created the first American medical school in 1765. Most doctors, however, studied medicine by working with an established practitioner. Some American physicians believed in applying new scientific methods to medicine, but they had to struggle against age-old prejudices and superstitions. Efforts to teach anatomy, for example, encountered strong public hostility because of the dissection of cadavers that the study required. Municipal authorities had virtually no understanding of medical science and almost no idea of what to do in the face of the severe epidemics that so often swept their populations; only slowly did they respond to warnings that the lack of adequate sanitation programs was to blame for much disease.

Individual patients often had more to fear from their doctors than from their illnesses. Even the leading advocates of scientific medicine often embraced useless and dangerous treatments. George Washington's death in 1799 was probably less a result of the minor throat infection that had afflicted him than of his physicians' efforts to cure him by bleeding and purging.

The medical profession also used its newfound commitment to the "scientific" method to justify expanding its control over kinds of care that had traditionally been outside its domain. Most childbirths, for example, had been attended by female midwives in the eighteenth century. In the early nineteenth century, physicians began to handle deliveries themselves. Among the results of that change were a narrowing of opportunities for women and a restriction of access to childbirth care for poor mothers (who could have afforded midwives, but who could not pay the higher physicians' fees).

Cultural Aspirations of the New Nation

Many Americans dreamed of an American literary and artistic life that would rival the greatest achievements of Europe. The 1772 "Poem on the Rising Glory of America" predicted that America was destined to become the "seat of empire" and the "final stage" of civilization. Noah Webster, the Connecticut schoolmaster, lawyer, and author of widely used American spellers and dictionaries, echoed such sentiments, arguing that the American schoolboy should be educated as a nationalist. "As soon as he opens his lips," Webster wrote, "he should rehearse the history of his own country; he should lisp the praise of liberty, and of those illustrious heroes and statesmen who have wrought a revolution in her favor."

A growing number of writers began working to create a strong American literature. Among the most ambitious was the Philadelphia writer Charles Brockden Brown. But his fascination with horror and deviance kept him from developing a popular audience. More successful was Washington Irving of New York, whose popular folktales, recounting the adventures of such American rustics as Ichabod Crane and Rip Van Winkle, made him the widely acknowledged leader of American literary life in the early eighteenth century.

Religion and Revivalism

By elevating ideas of individual liberty and reason, the American Revolution had weakened traditional forms of religious practice and challenged many ecclesiastical traditions. By the 1790s, only a small proportion of white Americans were members of formal churches, and ministers were complaining about the "decay of vital piety."

Religious traditionalists were particularly alarmed about the emergence of new, "rational" religious doctrines—theologies that reflected modern, scientific attitudes. "Deism," which had originated among Enlightenment philosophers in France, attracted such educated Americans as Jefferson and Franklin and by 1800 was reaching a moderately broad popular audience. Deists accepted the existence of God, but they considered Him a remote "watchmaker" who, after having created the universe, had withdrawn from direct involvement with the human race and its sins. Religious skepticism also produced the philosophies of "universalism" and "unitarianism." Disciples of these new ideas rejected the traditional Calvinist belief in predestination and the idea of the Trinity. Jesus was only a great religious teacher, they claimed, not the son of God. But religious skepticism attracted relatively few people. Most Americans clung to more traditional faiths. Beginning in 1801, traditional religion staged a dramatic comeback in a wave of revivalism known as the Second Great Awakening.

The origins of the Awakening lay in the efforts of conservative theologians to fight the spread of religious rationalism and of church establishments. Presbyterians expanded their efforts on the western fringes of white settlement. Itinerant Methodist preachers traveled throughout the nation to win recruits for their new church, which soon became the fastest-growing denomination in America. Almost as successful were the Baptists, who found an especially fervent following in the South.

By 1800, the revivalist energies of all these denominations were combining to create the greatest surge of evangelical fervor since the first Great Awakening sixty years before. In only a few years, membership in those churches embracing revivalism was mushrooming. At Cane Ridge, Kentucky, in the summer of 1801, a group of evangelical ministers presided over the nation's first "camp meeting"—an extraordinary revival that lasted several days and impressed all who saw it with its size (some estimated that 25,000 people attended) and its fervor. Such events became common in subsequent years.

The basic message of the Second Great Awakening was that individuals must readmit God and Christ into their daily lives. They must embrace a fervent, active piety, and they must

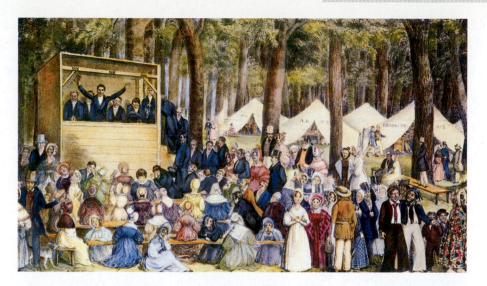

METHODIST CAMP MEETING, 1837 Camp (or revival) meetings were popular among some evangelical Christians in America as early as 1800. By the 1820s, there were approximately 1,000 meetings a year, most of them in the South and the West. After one such meeting in 1806, a participant wrote: "Will I ever see anything more like the day of Judgement on the side of eternity—to see the people running, yes, running from every direction to the stand, weeping, shouting, and shouting for joy.... O! Glorious day they went home singing shouting." This lithograph, dated 1837, suggests the degree to which women predominated at many revivals. (The Granger Collection, NYC)

reject the skeptical rationalism that threatened traditional beliefs. Yet the wave of revivalism did not restore the religion of the past. Few denominations any longer accepted the idea of predestination, and the belief that people could affect their own destinies added intensity to the individual's search for salvation. The Awakening, in short, combined a more active piety with a belief in a God whose grace could be attained through faith and good works.

One of the striking features of the Awakening was the preponderance of women within it. Female converts far outnumbered males. That may have been due in part to the movement of industrial work out of the home and into the factory. That process robbed women of one of their roles as part of a household-based economy and left many feeling isolated. Religious enthusiasm provided, among other things, access to a new range of activities— charitable societies ministering to orphans and the poor, missionary organizations, and others—in which women came to play important parts.

In some areas of the country, revival meetings were open to people of all races. From these revivals emerged a group of black preachers who became important figures within the slave community. Some of them translated the apparently egalitarian religious message of the Awakening—that salvation was available to all—into a similarly liberating message for blacks in the present world. Out of black revival meetings in Virginia, for example, arose an elaborate plan in 1800 (devised by Gabriel Prosser, the brother of a black preacher) for a slave rebellion and an attack on Richmond. The plan was discovered and foiled in advance by whites, but revivalism continued in subsequent years to create occasional racial unrest in the South.

The spirit of revivalism was particularly strong among Native Americans. Presbyterian and Baptist missionaries were active among the southern tribes and sparked a wave of conversions. But the most important revivalist was Handsome Lake, a Seneca whose seemingly miraculous "rebirth" after years of alcoholism helped give him a special stature within his tribe. Handsome Lake called for a revival of traditional Indian ways, a repudiation of the individualism of white society, and a restoration of the communal quality of the Indian world. His message spread through the scattered Iroquois communities that had survived the military and political setbacks of previous decades and inspired many Indians to give up whiskey, gambling, and other destructive customs derived from white society. But Handsome Lake also encouraged Christian missionaries to become active within the tribes, and he urged Iroquois men to abandon their roles as hunters and become sedentary farmers instead. As in much of white society, Iroquois women, who had traditionally done the farming, were to move into more domestic roles.

STIRRINGS OF INDUSTRIALISM

While Americans had been engaged in a revolution to win their independence, an even more important revolution had been in progress in England: the emergence of modern industrialism. Power-driven machines were permitting manufacturing to become more rapid and extensive—with profound social and economic consequences.

TECHNOLOGY IN AMERICA

Nothing comparable to the English industrial revolution occurred in America in the first two decades of the nineteenth century. Yet even while Jeffersonians warned of the dangers of rapid economic change, they witnessed a series of technological advances that would ultimately help ensure that the United States, too, would be transformed. Some of these technological advances were English imports. Despite efforts by the British government to prevent the export of textile machinery or the emigration of skilled mechanics, a number of immigrants with advanced knowledge of English technology arrived in the United States, eager to introduce the new machines to America. Samuel Slater, for example, used the knowledge he had acquired before leaving England to build a spinning mill in Pawtucket, Rhode Island, for the Quaker merchant Moses Brown in 1790.

America also produced notable inventors of its own. In 1793, Eli Whitney invented a machine that performed the arduous task of removing the seeds from short-staple cotton quickly and efficiently. It was dubbed the cotton gin ("gin" was a derivative of "engine"). With the device, a single operator could clean as much cotton in a few hours as it once took a group of workers to do in a day. The results were profound. Soon cotton growing spread throughout the South. (Previously it had been restricted largely to the coast and the Sea Islands, the only places where long-staple cotton—easily cleaned without the cotton gin—could be grown.) Within a decade, the total cotton crop increased eightfold. African American slavery, which with the decline of tobacco production had seemed for a time to be a dwindling institution, expanded and firmly fixed itself upon the South. The large supply of domestically produced fiber also served as a strong incentive to entrepreneurs in New England and elsewhere to develop a native textile industry.

Whitney was an important figure in the history of American technology for another reason as well. He helped introduce the concept of interchangeable parts to the United States. As machines such as the cotton gin began to be widely used, it became increasingly important for owners of such machines to have access to spare parts—and for the parts to be made so that they fit the machines properly. Whitney designed not only the cotton gin, but also machine tools that could manufacture its component parts to exact specifications. The U.S. government later commissioned Whitney to manufacture 1,000 muskets for the army. Each part of the gun had to be interchangeable with the equivalent part in every other gun.

Interchangeability was of great importance in the United States because of the great distances many people had to travel to reach towns or cities and the relatively limited

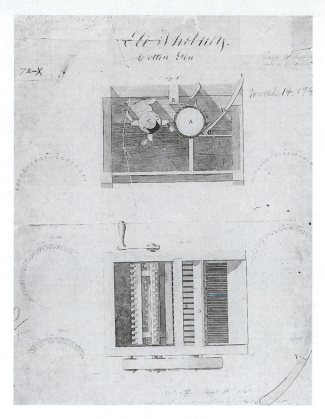

THE COTTON GIN Eli Whitney's cotton gin revolutionized the cotton economy of the South by making the processing of short-staple cotton simple and economical. These 1794 drawings are part of Whitney's application for a federal patent on his device. (National Archives)

transportation systems available to them. Interchangeable parts meant that a farmer could repair a machine himself. But the interchangeability that Whitney championed was not easy to achieve. In theory, many parts were designed to be interchangeable. In reality, the actual manufacturing of such parts was for many years not nearly precise enough. Farmers and others often had to do considerable fitting before the parts would work in their equipment. Not until later in the century would machine tools be developed to the point that they could make truly interchangeable parts.

TRANSPORTATION INNOVATIONS

One of the prerequisites for industrialization is a transportation system that allows the efficient movement of raw materials to factories and of finished goods to markets. The United States had no such system in the early years of the republic, and thus it had no domestic market extensive enough to justify large-scale production. But projects were under way that would ultimately remove the transportation obstacle.

One such project was the development of the steamboat. England had pioneered steam power, and even steam navigation, in the eighteenth century, and there had been experiments in America in the 1780s and 1790s in various forms of steam-powered transportation.

THE GLOBAL INDUSTRIAL REVOLUTION

WHILE Americans were engaged in a revolution to win their independence, they were also taking the first steps toward another great revolution—one that was already in progress in England and Europe. It was the emergence of modern industrialism. Historians differ over precisely when the industrial revolution began, but it is clear that by the end of the eighteenth century it was well under way in many parts of the world. A hundred years later, the global process of industrialization had transformed the societies of Britain, most of continental Europe, Japan, and the United States. Its social and economic consequences were complex and profound and continue to shape the nature of global society.

For Americans, the industrial revolution was largely a result of rapid changes in Great Britain, the nation with which they had the closest relations. Britain was the first nation to develop significant industrial capacity. The factory system took root in England in the late eighteenth century, revolutionizing the manufacture of cotton thread and cloth. One invention followed another in quick succession. Improvements in weaving drove improvements in spinning, and these changes created a demand for new devices for carding (combing and straightening the fibers for the spinner). Water, wind, and animal power continued to be important in the textile industry; but more important was the emergence of steam power—which began to proliferate after the appearance of James Watt's advanced steam engine (patented in 1769). Cumbersome and inefficient by modern standards, Watt's engine was nevertheless a major improvement over earlier "atmospheric" engines. England's textile industry quickly became the most profitable in the world, and it helped encourage comparable advances in other fields of manufacturing as well.

Despite the efforts of the British government to prevent the export of English industrial technology, knowledge of the new machines reached other nations quickly, usually through the emigration of people who had learned the technology in British factories. America benefited the most from English technology, because it received more immigrants from Great Britain than from any other country. But English technology spread quickly to the nations of continental Europe as well. Belgium was the first, developing a significant coal, iron, and armaments industry in the early nineteenth century. France—profiting from the immigration of approximately fifteen thousand British workers with advanced technological skills—had created a substantial industrial capacity in textiles and metals by the end of the 1820s, which in turn contributed to a great boom in railroad construction later in the century. German industrialization progressed rapidly after 1840, beginning with coal and iron production and then, in the 1850s, moving into large-scale railroad construction. By the late nineteenth century, Germany had created some of the world's largest industrial corporations. In Japan, the sudden intrusion of American

A major advance emerged out of the efforts of the inventor Robert Fulton and the promoter Robert R. Livingston, who made possible the launching of a steamboat large enough to carry passengers. Their *Clermont*, equipped with paddle wheels and an English-built engine, sailed up the Hudson in the summer of 1807.

and European traders helped cause the so-called Meiji reforms of the 1880s and 1890s, which launched a period of rapid industrialization there as well.

Industrialization changed not just the world's economies but also its societies. First in England and then in Europe, America, and Japan, social systems underwent wrenching changes. Hundreds of thousands of men and women moved from rural areas into cities to work in factories, where they experienced both the benefits and the costs of industrialization. The standard of living of the new working class, when objectively quantified, was usually significantly higher than that of the rural poor. Most of those who moved from farm to factory, in other words, experienced some improvement in nutrition and other material circumstances, and even in their health. But the psychological costs of being suddenly uprooted from one way of life and thrust into another, fundamentally different one could outweigh the economic gains. There was little in most workers' prior experience to prepare them for the nature of industrial labor. It was disciplined, routinized work with a fixed and rigid schedule, a sharp contrast to the varying, seasonal work pattern of the rural economy. Nor were many factory workers prepared for life in the new industrial towns and expanding cities. Industrial workers experienced, too, a fundamental change in their relationship with their employers. Unlike rural landlords and local aristocrats, factory owners and managers were usually remote and inaccessible figures. But the new class of industrial capitalists, many of them accumulating unprecedented wealth, dealt with their workers impersonally, and the result was a growing schism between the two classes— each lacking access to or understanding of the other. Working men and women throughout the globe began thinking of themselves as a distinct class, with common goals and interests. And their efforts simultaneously to adjust to their new way of life and to resist its most damaging aspects sometimes created great social turbulence. Battles between workers and employers became a characteristic feature of industrial life throughout the world.

Life in industrial nations changed at every level. Populations in industrial nations grew rapidly, and people began to live longer. At the same time, pollution, crime, and— until modern sanitation systems emerged— infectious disease increased greatly in industrialized cities. Around the industrial world, middle classes expanded and came, in varying degrees, to dominate the economy (although not always the culture or the politics) of their nations.

Not since the agrarian revolution thousands of years earlier, when many humans had turned from hunting to farming for sustenance, had there been an economic change of a magnitude comparable to the industrial revolution. Centuries of traditions, of social patterns, of cultural and religious assumptions were challenged and often shattered. The tentative stirrings of industrial activity in the United States in the early nineteenth century, therefore, were part of a vast movement that over the course of the next century was to transform much of the globe. •

UNDERSTAND, ANALYZE, & EVALUATE

1. Why did the British government attempt to prevent the export of Britain's industrial technology?
2. Was the industrial revolution truly a global revolution? Why or why not?

Meanwhile, what was to become known as the "turnpike era" had begun. In 1794, a corporation constructed a toll road running the sixty miles from Philadelphia to Lancaster, Pennsylvania, with a hard-packed surface of crushed stone that provided a good year-round surface with effective drainage (but was very expensive to use). The Pennsylvania

HORSE RACING

INFORMAL horse racing began in North America almost as soon as Europeans settled the English colonies. Formal racing followed quickly. The first racetrack in North America—New Market (named for a popular racecourse in England)—was established in 1665 on Long Island, near present-day Garden City, New York. Tracks quickly developed wide appeal, and soon horse racing had spread up and down the Atlantic Coast. By the time of the American Revolution, it was popular in almost every colony and was moving as well into the newly settled areas of the Southwest. Andrew Jackson was a founder of the first race track in Nashville, Tennessee, in the early nineteenth century. Kentucky—whose native bluegrass was early recognized as ideal for grazing horses—had eight tracks by 1800.

Like almost everything else in the life of early America, the world of horse racing was bounded by lines of class and race. For many years, it was considered the exclusive preserve of "gentlemen," so much so that in 1674, a Virginia court fined James Bullocke, a tailor, for proposing a race, "it being contrary to Law for a Labourer to make a race, being a sport only for Gentlemen." But while white aristocrats retained control of racing, they were not the only people who participated in it. Southern planters often trained young male slaves as jockeys for their horses, just as northern horse owners employed the services of free blacks as riders. In the North and the South, African Americans eventually emerged as some of the most talented and experienced trainers of racing horses. And despite social and legal pressures, free blacks and poor whites often staged their own informal races.

Racing also began early to reflect the growing sectional rivalry between the North and the South. In 1824, the Union Race Course on Long Island established an astounding $24,000 purse for a race between two famous thoroughbreds: American Eclipse (from the North) and Sir Henry (from the South). American Eclipse won two of the three heats. A southern racehorse prevailed in another such celebrated contest in 1836. These intersectional races, which drew enormous crowds and created tremendous publicity, continued into the 1850s, until the North-South rivalry began to take a more deadly form.

Horse racing remained popular after the Civil War, but two developments changed its character considerably. One was the successful effort to drive African Americans

venture proved so successful that similar turnpikes (so named from the kind of tollgate frequently used) were laid out from other cities to neighboring towns.

The process of building the turnpikes was a difficult one. Companies had to survey their routes with many things in mind, particularly elevation. Horse-drawn vehicles had great difficulty traveling along roads with more than a five-degree incline, which required many roads to take very circuitous routes to avoid steep hills. Building roads over mountains was an almost insurmountable task, and no company was successful in doing so until governments began to participate in the financing of the projects.

OAKLAND HOUSE AND RACE COURSE This 1840 painting by Robert Brammer and August A. Von Smith portrays men and women flocking to an early race course in Louisville, Kentucky, which provided entertainment to affluent white southerners. (*Oakland House and Race Course, Louisville, 1840.* By Robert Brammer and August A. Von Smith. Collection of The Speed Art Museum, Louisville, Kentucky. Purchase, Museum Art Fund, 56.19)

out of the sport. At least until the 1890s, black jockeys and trainers remained central to racing. At the first Kentucky Derby, in 1875, fourteen of the fifteen horses had African American riders. One black man, Isaac Murphy, won a remarkable 44 percent of all races in which he rode, including three Kentucky Derbys. Gradually, however, the same social dynamics that enforced racial segregation in so many other areas of American life penetrated racing as well. By the beginning of the twentieth century, white jockeys and organized jockey clubs had driven almost all black riders and many black trainers out of the sport.

The second change was the introduction of formalized betting. In the late nineteenth century, racetracks created betting systems to lure customers to the races. At the same time that the breeding of racehorses was moving into the hands of enormously wealthy families, the audience for racing was becoming increasingly working class and lower middle class. The people who now came to racetracks were mostly white men, and some white women, who were lured not by a love of horses but by the usually futile hope of quick and easy riches through gambling. •

UNDERSTAND, ANALYZE, & EVALUATE

1. Why do you think horse racing was such a popular spectator sport in early America? Why has it continued to be popular?
2. How did changes in the sport of horse racing reflect similar changes in American society at large?

COUNTRY AND CITY

Despite all the changes, America remained an overwhelmingly rural and agrarian nation. Only 3 percent of the population lived in towns of more than 8,000 in 1800. Even the nation's largest cities could not begin to compare with such European capitals as London and Paris (although Philadelphia, with 70,000 residents, New York, with 60,000, and others were becoming centers of commerce, learning, and urban culture comparable to many of the secondary cities of Europe).

People in cities and towns lived differently from the vast majority of Americans who continued to work as farmers. Among other things, urban life produced affluence, and affluent people sought increasing elegance and refinement in their homes, their grounds, and their dress. They also looked for diversions—music, theater, dancing, and, for many people, horse racing. Informal horse racing had begun as early as the 1620s, and the first formal race course opened near New York City in 1665. By the early nineteenth century, it was a popular activity in most areas of the country. The crowds that gathered at horse races were an early sign of the vast appetite for popular, public entertainments that would be an enduring part of American culture.

It was still possible for some to believe that this small, half-formed nation might not become a complex modern society. But the forces already at work would soon lastingly transform the United States. And Thomas Jefferson, for all his commitment to the agrarian ideal, found himself as president obliged to confront and accommodate them.

JEFFERSON THE PRESIDENT

Privately, Thomas Jefferson may well have considered his victory over John Adams in 1800 to be what he later termed it: a revolution "as real . . . as that of 1776." Publicly, however, he was restrained and conciliatory, attempting to minimize the differences between the two parties and calm the passions that the bitter campaign had aroused. There was no public repudiation of Federalist policies, no true "revolution." Indeed, at times Jefferson seemed to outdo the Federalists at their own work.

The Federal City and the "People's President"

The relative unimportance of the federal government during the Jeffersonian era was symbolized by the character of the newly founded national capital, the city of Washington. There were many who envisioned that the raw, uncompleted town, designed by the French architect Pierre L'Enfant, would soon emerge as the Paris of the United States.

In reality, throughout most of the nineteenth century Washington remained little more than a straggling, provincial village. Although the population increased steadily from the 3,200 counted in the 1800 census, it never rivaled that of New York, Philadelphia, or the other major cities of the nation and remained a raw, inhospitable community. Members of Congress viewed Washington not as a home but as a place to visit briefly during sessions of the legislature. Most lived in a cluster of simple boardinghouses in the vicinity of the Capitol. It was not unusual for a member of Congress to resign his seat in the midst of a session to return home if he had an opportunity to accept the more prestigious post of member of his state legislature.

Jefferson was a wealthy planter by background, but as president he conveyed to the public an image of plain, almost crude disdain for pretension. Like an ordinary citizen, he walked to and from his inauguration at the Capitol. In the presidential mansion, which had not yet acquired the name "White House," he disregarded the courtly etiquette of his predecessors. He did not always bother to dress up, prompting the British ambassador to complain of being received by the president in clothes that were "indicative of utter slovenliness and indifference to appearances."

Yet Jefferson managed nevertheless to impress most of those who knew him. He probably had a wider range of interests and accomplishments than any major political figure in American history, with the possible exception of Benjamin Franklin. In addition to politics and diplomacy, he was an active architect, educator, inventor, farmer, and philosopher-scientist.

THOMAS JEFFERSON   This 1805 portrait by the noted American painter Rembrandt Peale shows Jefferson at the beginning of his second term as president. It also conveys (through the simplicity of dress and the slightly unkempt hair) the image of democratic simplicity that Jefferson liked to project as the champion of the "common man." (Collection of the New-York Historical Society)

Jefferson was, above all, a shrewd and practical politician. He worked hard to exert influence as the leader of his party, giving direction to Republicans in Congress by quiet and sometimes even devious means. Although the Republicans had objected strenuously to the efforts of their Federalist predecessors to build a network of influence through patronage, Jefferson used his powers of appointment as an effective political weapon. Like Washington before him, he believed that federal offices should be filled with men loyal to the principles and policies of the administration. By the end of his second term, practically all federal jobs were held by loyal Republicans. Jefferson was a popular president and had little difficulty winning reelection against Federalist Charles C. Pinckney in 1804. Jefferson won by the overwhelming electoral majority of 162 to 14, and Republican membership of both houses of Congress increased.

DOLLARS AND SHIPS

Under Washington and Adams, the Republicans believed, the government had been needlessly extravagant. Yearly federal expenditures had almost tripled between 1793 and 1800, as Hamilton had hoped. The public debt had also risen, and an extensive system of internal taxation had been erected.

The Jefferson administration moved deliberately to reverse these trends. In 1802, the president persuaded Congress to abolish all internal taxes, leaving customs duties and the sale of western lands as the only sources of revenue for the government. Meanwhile, Secretary of the Treasury Albert Gallatin drastically reduced government spending. Although Jefferson was unable entirely to retire the national debt as he had hoped, he did cut it almost in half (from $83 million to $45 million).

Jefferson also scaled down the armed forces. He reduced the already tiny army of 4,000 men to 2,500 and pared down the navy from twenty-five ships in commission to seven. Anything but the smallest of standing armies, he argued, might menace civil liberties and civilian control of government. Yet Jefferson was not a pacifist. At the same time that he was reducing the size of the army and navy, he helped establish the United States Military Academy at West Point, founded in 1802. And when trouble started brewing overseas, he began again to build up the fleet. Such trouble appeared first in the Mediterranean, off the coast of northern Africa.

For years the Barbary states of North Africa—Morocco, Algiers, Tunis, and Tripoli—had been demanding protection money, paid to avoid piracy, from all nations whose ships sailed the Mediterranean. During the 1780s and 1790s the United States, too, had agreed to treaties providing for annual tribute to the Barbary states, but Jefferson showed reluctance to continue this policy of appeasement.

In 1801, the pasha of Tripoli forced Jefferson's hand. Unhappy with American responses to his demands, he ordered the flagpole of the American consulate chopped down—a symbolic declaration of war. Jefferson responded cautiously and built up American naval forces in the area over the next several years. Finally, in 1805, he agreed to terms by which the United States ended the payment of tribute to Tripoli but paid a substantial (and humiliating) ransom for the release of American prisoners.

CONFLICT WITH THE COURTS

Having won control of the executive and legislative branches of government, the Republicans looked with suspicion on the judiciary, which remained largely in the hands of Federalist judges. Soon after Jefferson's first inauguration, his followers in Congress launched an attack on this last preserve of the opposition. Their first step was the repeal of the Judiciary Act of 1801, thus eliminating the judgeships to which Adams had made his "midnight appointments."

The debate over the courts led to one of the most important judicial decisions in the history of the nation. Federalists had long maintained that the Supreme Court had the authority to nullify acts of Congress, and the Court itself had actually exercised the power of judicial review in 1796 when it upheld the validity of a law passed by Congress. But the Court's authority in this area would not be secure, it was clear, until it actually declared a congressional act unconstitutional. In 1803, in the case of *Marbury v. Madison*, it did so. William Marbury, one of Adams's midnight appointments, had been named a justice of the peace in the District of Columbia. But his commission, although signed and sealed, had not been delivered to him before Adams left office. When Jefferson took office, his secretary of state, James Madison, refused to hand over the commission. Marbury asked the Supreme Court to direct Madison to perform his official duty. But the Court ruled that while Marbury had a right to his commission, the Court had no authority to order Madison to deliver it. On the surface, therefore, the decision was a victory for the administration. But of much greater importance than the relatively insignificant matter of Marbury's commission was the Court's reasoning in the decision.

The original Judiciary Act of 1789 had given the Court the power to compel executive officials to act in such matters as the delivery of commissions, and it was on that basis that Marbury had filed his suit. But the Court ruled that Congress had exceeded its authority, that the Constitution defined the powers of the judiciary, and that the legislature had no right to expand them. The relevant section of the 1789 act was, therefore, void. In seeming to deny its own authority, the Court was in fact radically enlarging it. The justices had repudiated a relatively minor power (the power to force the delivery of a commission) by asserting a vastly greater one (the power to nullify an act of Congress).

The chief justice of the United States at the time of the ruling (and until 1835) was John Marshall. A leading Federalist and prominent Virginia lawyer, he had served John Adams as secretary of state. Ironically, it was Marshall who had failed to deliver Marbury's commission. In 1801, just before leaving office, Adams had appointed him chief justice, and almost immediately Marshall established himself as the dominant figure of the Court, shaping virtually all its most important rulings—including, of course, *Marbury v. Madison.* Through a succession of Republican presidents, he battled to give the federal government unity and strength. And in so doing, he established the judiciary as a coequal branch of government with the executive and the legislature.

DOUBLING THE NATIONAL DOMAIN

In the same year Jefferson was elected president of the United States, Napoleon Bonaparte made himself ruler of France with the title of first consul. In the year Jefferson was reelected, Napoleon named himself emperor. The two men had little in common, yet for a time they were of great assistance to each other in international politics.

JEFFERSON AND NAPOLEON

Having failed in a grandiose plan to seize India from the British Empire, Napoleon began to dream of restoring French power in the New World. The territory east of the Mississippi, which France had ceded to Great Britain in 1763, was now part of the United States, but Napoleon hoped to regain the lands west of the Mississippi, which had belonged to Spain since the end of the Seven Years' War. In 1800, under the secret Treaty of San Ildefonso, France regained title to Louisiana, which included almost the whole of the Mississippi Valley to the west of the river. The Louisiana Territory would, Napoleon hoped, become the heart of a great French empire in America.

Jefferson was unaware at first of Napoleon's imperial ambitions in America. For a time he pursued a foreign policy that reflected his well-known admiration for France. But he began to reassess American relations with the French when he heard rumors of the secret transfer of Louisiana. Particularly troubling to Jefferson was French control of New Orleans, the outlet through which the produce of the fast-growing western regions of the United States was shipped to the markets of the world.

Jefferson was even more alarmed when, in the fall of 1802, he learned that the Spanish intendant at New Orleans (who still governed the city, since the French had not yet taken formal possession of the region) had announced a disturbing new regulation. American ships sailing the Mississippi River had for many years been accustomed to depositing their cargoes in New Orleans for transfer to oceangoing vessels. The intendant now forbade the practice, even though Spain had guaranteed Americans that right in the Pinckney Treaty of 1795.

Westerners demanded that the federal government do something to reopen the river, and the president faced a dilemma. If he yielded to the frontier clamor and tried to change the policy by force, he would run the risk of a major war with France. If he ignored the westerners' demands, he would lose political support. But Jefferson envisioned another solution. He instructed Robert Livingston, the American ambassador in Paris, to negotiate for the purchase of New Orleans. Livingston, on his own authority, proposed that the French sell the United States the rest of Louisiana as well.

In the meantime, Jefferson persuaded Congress to appropriate funds for an expansion of the army and the construction of a river fleet, and he hinted that American forces might soon descend on New Orleans and that the United States might form an alliance with Great Britain if the problems with France were not resolved. Perhaps in response, Napoleon suddenly decided to offer the United States the entire Louisiana Territory.

Napoleon had good reasons for the decision. His plans for an empire in America had already gone seriously awry, partly because a yellow fever epidemic had wiped out much of the French army in the New World and partly because the expeditionary force he wished to send to reinforce the troops had been icebound in a Dutch harbor through the winter of 1802–1803. By the time the harbor thawed in the spring of 1803, Napoleon was preparing for a renewed war in Europe. He would not, he realized, have the resources to secure an empire in America.

THE LOUISIANA PURCHASE

Faced with Napoleon's sudden proposal, Livingston and James Monroe, whom Jefferson had sent to Paris to assist in the negotiations, had to decide whether they should accept it even if they had no authorization to do so. But fearful that Napoleon might withdraw the offer, they decided to proceed. After some haggling over the price, Livingston and Monroe signed an agreement with Napoleon on April 30, 1803.

By the terms of the treaty, the United States was to pay a total of 80 million francs ($15 million) to the French government. The United States was also to grant certain exclusive commercial privileges to France in the port of New Orleans and to incorporate the residents of Louisiana into the Union with the same rights and privileges as other citizens. The boundaries of the purchase were not clearly defined.

In Washington, the president was both pleased and embarrassed when he received the treaty. He was pleased with the terms of the bargain; but he was uncertain about his authority to accept it, since the Constitution said nothing about the acquisition of new territory. But Jefferson's advisers persuaded him that his treaty-making power under the Constitution would justify the purchase, and Congress promptly approved the treaty. Finally, late in 1803, General James Wilkinson, a commissioner of the United States, took formal control of the territory. Before long, the Louisiana Territory was organized on the general pattern of the Northwest Territory, with the assumption that it would be divided eventually into states. The first of these was admitted to the Union as the state of Louisiana in 1812.

EXPLORING THE WEST

Meanwhile, a series of explorations revealed the geography of the far-flung new territory to white Americans. In 1803, Jefferson helped plan an expedition that was to cross the continent to the Pacific Ocean, gather geographical facts, and investigate prospects for trade with the Indians. The expedition began in May 1804. He named as its leader the twenty-nine-year-old Meriwether Lewis, a veteran of Indian wars who was skilled in the ways of the wilderness. Lewis chose as a colleague the thirty-four-year-old William Clark,

UNDER MY WINGS EVERY THING PROSPERS

NEW ORLEANS IN 1803   Because of its location near the mouth of the Mississippi River, New Orleans was the principal port of western North America in the early nineteenth century. Through it, western farmers shipped their produce to markets in the East and Europe. This 1803 painting celebrates the American acquisition of the city from France as part of the Louisiana Purchase. (Chicago Historical Society)

an experienced frontiersman and Indian fighter. Lewis and Clark, with a company of four dozen men, started up the Missouri River from St. Louis. With the Shoshone woman Sacajawea as their interpreter, they eventually crossed the Rocky Mountains, descended along the Snake and Columbia rivers, and in the late autumn of 1805 camped on the Pacific Coast. In September 1806, they were back in St. Louis with elaborate records of the geography and the Indian civilizations they had observed along the way.

While Lewis and Clark explored, Jefferson dispatched other groups to other parts of the Louisiana Territory. Lieutenant Zebulon Montgomery Pike, twenty-six years old, led an expedition in the fall of 1805 from St. Louis into the upper Mississippi Valley. In the summer of 1806, he set out again, proceeding up the valley of the Arkansas River and into what later became Colorado. His account of his western travels helped create an enduring (and inaccurate) impression among most Americans that the land between the Missouri River and the Rockies was an uncultivatable desert.

THE BURR CONSPIRACY

Jefferson's triumphant reelection in 1804 suggested that most of the nation approved of the new territorial acquisition. But some New England Federalists raged against it. They realized that the more new states that joined the Union, the less power their region and party would retain. In Massachusetts, a group of the most extreme Federalists, known as the Essex Junto, concluded that the only recourse for New England was to secede from the Union and form a separate "northern confederacy." If a northern

THOMAS JEFFERSON TO MERIWETHER LEWIS, JUNE 20, 1803

TO Meriwether Lewis, esquire, Captain of the 1st regiment of infantry of the United States of America: Your situation as Secretary of the President of the United States has made you acquainted with the objects of my confidential message of Jan. 18, 1803, to the legislature . . . you are appointed to carry them into execution.

Instruments for ascertaining by celestial observations the geography of the country thro' which you will pass, have already been provided. Light articles for barter, & presents among the Indians, arms for your attendants, say for from 10 to 12 men, boats, tents, & other travelling apparatus, with ammunition, medicine, surgical instruments & provisions you will have prepared with such aids as the Secretary at War can yield in his department; & from him also you will receive authority to engage among our troops, by voluntary agreement, the number of attendants above mentioned, over whom you, as their commanding officer are invested with all the powers the laws give in such a case. . . .

Your mission has been communicated to the Ministers here from France, Spain & Great Britain, and through them to their governments: and such assurances given them as to it's objects as we trust will satisfy them. The country of Louisiana having been ceded by Spain to France, the passport you have from the Minister of France, the representative of the present sovereign of the country, will be a protection with all its subjects: And that from the Minister of England will entitle you to the friendly aid of any traders of that allegiance with whom you may happen to meet.

The object of your mission is to explore the Missouri river, & such principal stream of it, as, by it's course & communication with the waters of the Pacific Ocean, may offer the most direct & practicable water communication across this continent, for the purposes of commerce.

Beginning at the mouth of the Missouri, you will take observations of latitude & longitude, at all remarkable points on the river, & especially at the mouths of rivers, at rapids, at islands & other places & objects distinguished by such natural marks & characters of a durable kind, as that they may with certainty be recognized hereafter. . . . The interesting points of the portage between the heads of the Missouri & the water offering the best communication with the Pacific Ocean should also be fixed by observation, & the course of that water to the ocean, in the same manner as that of the Missouri.

Your observations are to be taken with great pains & accuracy, to be entered distinctly, & intelligibly for others as well as yourself, to comprehend all the elements necessary, with the aid of the usual tables, to fix the latitude and longitude of the places at which they were taken, & are to be rendered to the war office, for the purpose of having the calculations made concurrently by proper persons within the U.S. Several copies of these, as well as your other notes, should be made at leisure times & put into the care of the most trustworthy of your attendants, to guard by multiplying them, against the accidental losses to which they will be exposed. A further guard would be that one of these copies be written on the paper of the birch, as less liable to injury from damp than common paper.

The commerce which may be carried on with the people inhabiting the line you will pursue, renders a knowledge of these people important. You will therefore endeavor to make yourself acquainted, as far as a diligent pursuit of your journey shall admit, with the names of the nations & their numbers; the extent & limits of their possessions; their relations with other tribes or nations; their language, traditions, monuments; their ordinary occupations in agriculture, fishing, hunting, war, arts, & the implements for these; their food, clothing, & domestic accomodations; the diseases prevalent among them, & the remedies they use; moral & physical circumstances which distinguish them from the tribes we know; peculiarities in their laws, customs & dispositions; and articles of commerce they may need or furnish, & to what extent.

And considering the interest which every nation has in extending & strengthening the authority of reason & justice among the people around them, it will be useful to acquire what knowledge you can of the state of morality, religion & information among them, as it may better enable those who endeavor to civilize & instruct them, to adapt their measures to the existing notions & practises of those on whom they are to operate.

Other objects worthy of notice will be the soil & face of the country, it's growth & vegetable productions; especially those not of the U.S.; the animals of the country generally, & especially those not known in the U.S., the remains and accounts of any which may be deemed rare or extinct; the mineral productions of every kind; but more particularly metals, limestone, pit coal & saltpetre; salines & mineral waters, noting the temperature of the last, & such circumstances as may indicate their character. Volcanic appearances. Climate as characterized by the thermometer, by the proportion of rainy, cloudy & clear days, by lightening, hail, snow, ice, by the access & recess of frost, by the winds prevailing at different seasons, the dates at which particular plants put forth or lose their flowers, or leaf, times of appearance of particular birds, reptiles or insects.
[. . .]

In all your intercourse with the natives treat them in the most friendly & conciliatory manner which their own conduct will admit; allay all jealousies as to the object of your journey, satisfy them of it's innocence, make them acquainted with the position, extent, character, peaceable & commercial dispositions of the U.S., of our wish to be neighborly, friendly & useful to them, & of our dispositions to a commercial intercourse with them; confer with them on the points most convenient as mutual emporiums, & the articles of most desireable interchange for them & us. If a few of their influential chiefs, within practicable distance, wish to visit us, arrange such a visit with them, and furnish them with authority to call on our officers, on their entering the U.S. to have them conveyed to this place at public expence. If any of them should wish to have some of their young people brought up with us, & taught such arts as may be useful to them, we will receive, instruct & take care of them, such a mission. . . .

UNDERSTAND, ANALYZE, & EVALUATE

1. At the time that Jefferson wrote this letter, who held official possession of Louisiana? What European nations were present in the Louisiana territory?
2. What do the details of this letter reveal about Jefferson's own interest in nature and science?
3. What guidance did Jefferson offer Lewis in regard to natives? What policy toward Native Americans did Jefferson seem to have in mind for the future?

Source: Gunther Barth (ed.), *The Lewis and Clark Expedition; Selections from the Journals, Arranged by Topic* (New York: Bedford St. Martin's, 1998), pp.18–22. Original manuscript in Bureau of Rolls, *Jefferson Papers*, ser. 1, vol. 9, doc. 269, reprinted in Thwaites, *Original Journals of the Lewis and Clark Expedition*, 7:247–252.

confederacy were to have any hope for lasting success as a separate nation, the Federalists believed, it would have to include New York and New Jersey as well as New England. But the leading Federalist in New York, Alexander Hamilton, refused to support the secessionist scheme.

Federalists in New York then turned to Hamilton's greatest political rival, Vice President Aaron Burr. Burr accepted a Federalist proposal that he become their candidate for governor of New York in 1804, and there were rumors that he had also agreed to support the Federalist plans for secession. Hamilton accused Burr of plotting treason and made numerous private remarks, widely reported in the press, about Burr's "despicable" character. When Burr lost the election, he blamed his defeat on Hamilton's malevolence and challenged him to a duel. Hamilton feared that refusing Burr's challenge would brand him a coward. And so, on a July morning in 1804, the two men met at Weehawken, New Jersey. Hamilton was mortally wounded; he died the next day.

Burr now had to flee New York to avoid an indictment for murder. He found new outlets for his ambitions in the West. Even before the duel, he had begun corresponding with General James Wilkinson, now governor of the Louisiana Territory. Burr and

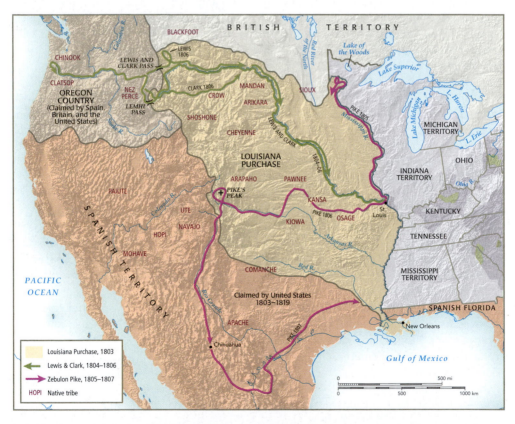

EXPLORING THE LOUISIANA PURCHASE, 1804–1807 When Jefferson purchased the Louisiana Territory from France in 1803, he doubled the size of the nation. But few Americans knew what they had bought. The Lewis and Clark expedition set out in 1804 to investigate the new territory, and this map shows their route, along with that of another inveterate explorer, Zebulon Pike. Note the vast distances the two parties covered (including, in both cases, a great deal of land outside the Louisiana Purchase). Note, too, how much of this enormous territory lay outside the orbit of even these ambitious explorations. • *How did the American public react to the addition of this new territory?*

Wilkinson, it seems clear, hoped to lead an expedition that would capture Mexico from the Spanish. But there were also rumors that they wanted to separate the Southwest from the Union and create a western empire that Burr would rule. (There is little evidence that these rumors were true.)

Whether true or not, many of Burr's opponents chose to believe the rumors—including, ultimately, Jefferson himself. When Burr led a group of armed followers down the Ohio River by boat in 1806, disturbing reports flowed into Washington (the most alarming from Wilkinson, who had suddenly turned against Burr) that an attack on New Orleans was imminent. Jefferson ordered the arrest of Burr and his men as traitors. Burr was brought to Richmond for trial. But to Jefferson's chagrin, Chief Justice Marshall limited the evidence the government could present and defined the charge in such a way that the jury had little choice but to acquit Burr. Burr soon faded from the public eye. But when he learned of the Texas revolution against Mexico years later, he said, "What was treason in me thirty years ago is patriotic now."

The Burr conspiracy was in part the story of a single man's soaring ambitions and flamboyant personality. But it was also a symbol of the larger perils still facing the new nation. With a central government that remained deliberately weak, with ambitious political leaders willing, if necessary, to circumvent normal channels in their search for power, the legitimacy of the federal government—and indeed the existence of the United States as a stable and united nation—remained to be fully established.

EXPANSION AND WAR

Two very different conflicts were taking shape in the last years of Jefferson's presidency. One was the continuing tension in Europe, which in 1803 escalated once again into a full-scale conflict (the Napoleonic Wars). As fighting between the British and the French increased, each side took steps to prevent the United States from trading with the other. The other conflict occurred in North America itself, a result of the ceaseless westward expansion of white settlement, which was colliding with a native population committed to protecting its lands from intruders. In both the North and the South, the threatened tribes mobilized to resist white encroachments. They began as well to forge connections with British forces in Canada and Spanish forces in Florida. The Indian conflict on land, therefore, became intertwined with the European conflict on the seas, and ultimately helped cause the War of 1812.

CONFLICT ON THE SEAS

In 1805, at the Battle of Trafalgar, a British fleet virtually destroyed what was left of the French navy. Because France could no longer challenge the British at sea, Napoleon now chose to pressure England in other ways. The result was what he called the Continental System, designed to close the European continent to British trade. Napoleon issued a series of decrees barring British ships and neutral ships touching at British ports from landing their cargoes at any European port controlled by France or its allies. The British government replied to Napoleon's decrees by establishing a blockade of the European coast. The blockade required that any goods being shipped to Napoleon's Europe be carried either in British vessels or in neutral vessels stopping at British ports—precisely what Napoleon's policies forbade.

In the early nineteenth century, the United States had developed one of the most important merchant marines in the world, one that soon controlled a large proportion of the trade between Europe and the West Indies. But the events in Europe now challenged that control, because American ships were caught between Napoleon's decrees and Britain's blockade. If they sailed directly for the European continent, they risked being captured by the British navy. If they sailed by way of a British port, they ran the risk of seizure by the French. Both of the warring powers were violating America's rights as a neutral nation. But most Americans considered the British, with their greater sea power, the worse offender—especially since British vessels frequently stopped American ships on the high seas and seized sailors off the decks, making them victims of "impressment."

IMPRESSMENT

Many British sailors called their navy—with its floggings, its low pay, and its terrible shipboard conditions—a "floating hell." Few volunteered. Most had had to be "impressed" (forced) into the service, and at every opportunity they deserted. By 1807, many of these deserters had emigrated to the United States and joined the American merchant marine or American navy. To check this loss of manpower, the British claimed the right to stop and search American merchantmen and reimpress deserters. They did not claim the right to take native-born Americans, but they did insist on the right to seize naturalized Americans born on British soil. In practice, the British navy often made no careful distinctions, impressing British deserters and native-born Americans alike.

In the summer of 1807, the British went to more provocative extremes. Sailing from Norfolk, with several alleged deserters from the British navy among the crew, the American naval frigate *Chesapeake* was hailed by the British ship *Leopard*. When the American commander, James Barron, refused to allow the British to search the *Chesapeake*, the *Leopard* opened fire. Barron had no choice but to surrender, and a boarding party from the *Leopard* dragged four men off the American frigate.

When news of the *Chesapeake-Leopard* incident reached the United States, there was a great popular clamor for revenge. Jefferson and Madison tried to maintain the peace. Jefferson expelled all British warships from American waters to lessen the likelihood of future incidents. Then he sent instructions to his minister in England, James Monroe, to demand from the British government an end to impressment. The British government disavowed the actions of the *Leopard*'s commanding officer and recalled him; it offered compensation for those killed and wounded in the incident; and it promised to return three of the captured sailors (one of the original four had been hanged). But the British cabinet refused to renounce impressment and instead reasserted its right to recover deserting seamen.

"PEACEABLE COERCION"

In an effort to prevent future incidents that might bring the nation again to the brink of war, Jefferson persuaded Congress to pass a drastic measure late in 1807. It was known as the Embargo, and it prohibited American ships from leaving the United States for any foreign port anywhere in the world. The law was widely evaded, but it was effective enough to create a serious depression throughout most of the nation. Hardest hit were the merchants and shipowners of the Northeast, most of them Federalists.

The presidential election of 1808 came in the midst of this Embargo-induced depression. James Madison was elected president, but the Federalist candidate, Charles Pinckney again, ran much more strongly than he had in 1804. The Embargo was clearly a growing political liability, and Jefferson decided to back down. A few days before leaving office, he approved a bill ending his experiment with what he called "peaceable coercion."

To replace the Embargo, Congress passed the Non-Intercourse Act just before Madison took office. It reopened trade with all nations but Great Britain and France. A year later, in 1810, the Non-Intercourse Act expired and was replaced by Macon's Bill No. 2, which reopened free commercial relations with Britain and France but authorized the president to prohibit commerce with either belligerent if it should continue violating neutral shipping after the other had stopped. Napoleon, in an effort to induce the United States to reimpose the Embargo against Britain, announced that France would no longer interfere with American shipping. Madison announced that an embargo against Great Britain alone would automatically go into effect early in 1811 unless Britain renounced its restrictions on American shipping.

In time, this new, limited embargo persuaded England to repeal its blockade of Europe. But the repeal came too late to prevent war. In any case, naval policies were only part of the reason for tensions between Britain and the United States.

The "Indian Problem" and the British

Given the ruthlessness with which white settlers in North America had continued to dislodge Indian tribes, it was hardly surprising that Indians continued to look to England for protection. The British in Canada, for their part, had relied on the Indians as partners in the lucrative fur trade. There had been relative peace in the Northwest for over a decade after Jay's Treaty and Anthony Wayne's victory over the tribes at Fallen Timbers in 1794. But the 1807 war crisis following the *Chesapeake-Leopard* incident revived the conflict between Indians and white settlers.

The Virginia-born William Henry Harrison, already a veteran Indian fighter at age twenty-six, went to Washington as the congressional delegate from the Northwest Territory in 1799. An advocate of development in the western lands, he was largely responsible for the passage in 1800 of the so-called Harrison Land Law, which enabled white settlers to acquire farms from the public domain on much easier terms than before.

In 1801, Jefferson appointed Harrison governor of the Indiana Territory to administer the president's proposed solution to the "Indian problem." Jefferson offered the Indians a choice: they could convert themselves into settled farmers and become a part of white society, or they could migrate west of the Mississippi. In either case, they would have to give up their claims to their tribal lands in the Northwest.

Jefferson considered the assimilation policy a benign alternative to the continuing conflict between Indians and white settlers. But to the tribes, the new policy seemed far from benign, especially given the bludgeonlike efficiency with which Harrison set out to implement it. He used threats, bribes, trickery, and whatever other tactics he felt would help him conclude treaties. In the first decade of the nineteenth century, the number of western Americans who had settled west of the Appalachians had grown to more than 500,000—a population far larger than that of the Native Americans. It was becoming almost inevitable, as a result, that the tribes would face ever-growing pressure to move out of the way of the rapidly growing white settlements.

By 1807 the United States had extracted treaty rights to eastern Michigan, southern Indiana, and most of Illinois from reluctant tribal leaders.

Meanwhile, in the Southwest, white Americans were taking millions of acres from other tribes in Georgia, Tennessee, and Mississippi. The Indians wanted desperately to resist, but the separate tribes were helpless by themselves against the power of the United States. They might have accepted their fate passively but for the emergence of two new factors.

One factor was the policy of British authorities in Canada. After the *Chesapeake* incident, they began to expect an American invasion of Canada and took desperate measures for their own defense. Among those measures were efforts to renew friendship with the Indians.

TECUMSEH AND THE PROPHET

A second, and more important, factor intensifying the border conflict was the rise of two remarkable native leaders. One was Tenskwatawa, a charismatic religious leader and orator known as "the Prophet." Like Handsome Lake, he had experienced a mystical awakening in the process of recovering from alcoholism. Having freed himself from what he considered the evil effects of white culture, he began to speak to his people of the superior virtues of Indian civilization and the sinfulness and corruption of the white world. In the process, he inspired a religious revival that spread through numerous tribes and helped unite them. The Prophet's headquarters at the meeting of Tippecanoe Creek and the Wabash River (known as Prophetstown) became a sacred place for people of many tribes. Out of their common religious experiences, they began to consider joint military efforts as well. Tenskwatawa advocated an Indian society entirely separate from that of white Americans and a culture rooted in tribal tradition. The effort to trade with the Anglos and to borrow from their culture would, he argued, lead to the death of Indian ways.

Tecumseh—the chief of the Shawnees, called by his tribe "the Shooting Star"—was in many ways even more militant than his brother. "Where today are the Pequot," he thundered. "Where are . . . the other powerful tribes of our people? They have vanished before the avarice and oppression of the white man." And he warned of his tribe's extermination if they did not take action against the white Americans moving into their lands.

Tecumseh understood, as few other Indian leaders had, that only through united action could the tribes hope to resist the steady advance of white civilization. Beginning in 1809, he set out to unite all the tribes of the Mississippi Valley into what became known as the Tecumseh Confederacy. Together, he promised, they would halt white expansion, recover the whole Northwest, and make the Ohio River the boundary between the United States and Indian country. He maintained that Harrison and others, by negotiating treaties with individual tribes, had obtained no real title to land. The land belonged to all the tribes; none of them could rightfully cede any of it without the consent of the others. In 1811, Tecumseh left Prophetstown and traveled down the Mississippi to visit the tribes of the South and persuade them to join the alliance.

During Tecumseh's absence, Governor Harrison saw a chance to destroy the growing influence of the two Indian leaders. With 1,000 soldiers, he camped near Prophetstown, and on November 7, 1811, he provoked an armed conflict. Although the white forces suffered losses as heavy as those of the natives, Harrison drove off the Indians and burned the town. The Battle of Tippecanoe (named for the creek near which it was fought) disillusioned many of the Prophet's followers, and Tecumseh returned to find the confederacy in disarray. But there were still warriors eager for combat, and by spring of 1812 they were active along the frontier, raiding white settlements and terrifying settlers.

The bloodshed along the western borders was largely a result of the Indians' own initiative, but Britain's agents in Canada had encouraged and helped to supply the uprising.

To Harrison and most white residents of the regions, there seemed only one way to make the West safe for Americans: to drive the British out of Canada and annex that province to the United States.

FLORIDA AND WAR FEVER

While white frontiersmen in the North demanded the conquest of Canada, those in the South looked to the acquisition of Spanish Florida. The territory was a continuing threat to whites in the southern United States. Slaves escaped across the Florida border; Indians in Florida launched frequent raids north. But white southerners also coveted Florida because through it ran rivers that could provide residents of the Southwest with access to valuable ports on the Gulf of Mexico.

In 1810, American settlers in West Florida (the area presently part of Mississippi and Louisiana) seized the Spanish fort at Baton Rouge and asked the federal government to annex the territory to the United States. President Madison happily agreed and then began planning to get the rest of Florida, too. The desire for Florida became yet another motivation for war with Britain. Spain was Britain's ally, and a war with England might provide an excuse for taking Spanish as well as British territory.

By 1812, therefore, war fever was raging on both the northern and southern borders of the United States. The demands of the residents of these areas found substantial support in Washington among a group of determined young congressmen who soon earned the name "War Hawks."

In the congressional elections of 1810, voters elected a large number of representatives of both parties eager for war with Britain. The most influential of them came from the new states in the West or from the backcountry of the old states in the South. Two of their leaders, both recently elected to the House of Representatives, were Henry Clay of Kentucky and John C. Calhoun of South Carolina, men of great intellect, magnetism, and ambition. Both were supporters of war with Great Britain.

Clay was elected Speaker of the House in 1811, and he appointed Calhoun to the crucial Committee on Foreign Affairs. Both men began agitating for the conquest of Canada. Madison still preferred peace but was losing control of Congress. On June 18, 1812, he approved a declaration of war against Britain.

THE WAR OF 1812

The British were not eager for an open conflict with the United States. Even after the Americans declared war, Britain largely ignored them for a time. But in the fall of 1812, Napoleon launched a catastrophic campaign against Russia that left his army in disarray. By late 1813, with the French Empire on its way to final defeat, Britain was able to turn its military attention to America.

BATTLES WITH THE TRIBES

In the summer of 1812, American forces invaded Canada through Detroit. They soon had to retreat back to Detroit and in August surrendered the fort there. Other invasion efforts also failed. In the meantime, Fort Dearborn (later Chicago) fell before an Indian attack.

Things went only slightly better for the United States on the seas. At first, American frigates won some spectacular victories over British warships. But by 1813, the British navy was counterattacking effectively, driving the American frigates to cover and imposing a blockade on the United States.

The United States did, however, achieve significant early military successes on the Great Lakes. First, the Americans took command of Lake Ontario, permitting them to raid and burn York (now Toronto), the capital of Canada. American forces then seized control of Lake Erie, mainly through the work of the young Oliver Hazard Perry, who engaged and dispersed a British fleet at Put-in Bay on September 10, 1813. This made possible, at last, a more successful invasion of Canada by way of Detroit. William Henry Harrison pushed up the Thames River into upper Canada and on October 5, 1813, won a victory notable for the death of Tecumseh, who was serving as a brigadier general in the British army. The Battle of the Thames resulted in no lasting occupation of Canada, but it weakened and disheartened the Indians of the Northwest.

In the meantime, another white military leader was striking an even harder blow at the Indians of the Southwest. The Creek, supplied by the Spaniards in Florida, had been attacking white settlers near the Florida border. Andrew Jackson, a wealthy Tennessee planter and a general in the state militia, set off in pursuit of the Creek. On March 27, 1814, in the Battle of Horseshoe Bend, Jackson's men took terrible revenge on the Indians, slaughtering women and children along with warriors. The tribe agreed to cede most of its lands to the United States and retreated westward. The vicious battle also won Jackson a commission as major general in the United States Army, and in that capacity he led his men farther south into Florida. On November 7, 1814, he seized the Spanish fort at Pensacola.

BATTLES WITH THE BRITISH

But the victories over the tribes were not enough to win the war. After the surrender of Napoleon in 1814, England decided to invade the United States. A British armada sailed up the Patuxent River from Chesapeake Bay and landed an army that marched to nearby Bladensburg, on the outskirts of Washington, where it dispersed a poorly trained force of American militiamen. On August 24, 1814, the British troops entered Washington and put the government to flight. Then they set fire to several public buildings, including the White House, in retaliation for the earlier American burning of the Canadian capital at York.

Leaving Washington in partial ruins, the invading army proceeded up the bay toward Baltimore. But Baltimore, guarded by Fort McHenry, was prepared. To block the approaching fleet, the American garrison had sunk several ships in the Patapsco River (the entry to Baltimore's harbor), thus forcing the British to bombard the fort from a distance. Through the night of September 13, Francis Scott Key (a Washington lawyer on board one of the British ships to negotiate the return of prisoners) watched the bombardment. The next morning, "by the dawn's early light," he could see the flag on the fort still flying; he recorded his pride in the moment by writing a poem—"The Star-Spangled Banner." The British withdrew from Baltimore, and Key's words were soon set to the tune of an old English drinking song. (In 1931 "The Star-Spangled Banner" became the official national anthem.)

Meanwhile, American forces repelled another British invasion in northern New York. At the Battle of Plattsburgh, on September 11, 1814, they turned back a much larger British naval and land force. In the South, a formidable array of battle-hardened British veterans landed below New Orleans and prepared to advance north up the Mississippi. Awaiting the British was Andrew Jackson with a motley collection of Tennesseans, Kentuckians, Creoles, blacks, pirates, and regular army troops drawn up behind earthen breastworks. On January 8, 1815, the redcoats advanced on the American fortifications,

THE BURNING OF WASHINGTON This dramatic engraving somewhat exaggerates the extent of the blazes in Washington when the British occupied the city in August 1814. But the invaders did set fire to the Capitol, the White House, and other public buildings in retaliation for the American burning of the Canadian capital at York. (The Granger Collection, NYC)

but the exposed British forces were no match for Jackson's well-protected men. After the Americans had repulsed several waves of attackers, the British finally retreated, leaving behind 700 dead, 1,400 wounded, and 500 prisoners. Jackson's losses were 8 killed and 13 wounded. Only later did news reach North America that the United States and Britain had signed a peace treaty several weeks before the Battle of New Orleans.

THE REVOLT OF NEW ENGLAND

With a few notable exceptions, the military efforts of the United States between 1812 and 1815 had failed. As a result, the Republican government became increasingly unpopular. In New England, opposition both to the war and to the Republicans was so extreme that some Federalists celebrated British victories. In Congress, in the meantime, the Republicans had continual trouble with the Federalist opposition, led by a young congressman from New Hampshire, Daniel Webster.

By now the Federalists were in the minority in the country, but they were still the majority party in New England. Some of them began to dream once again of creating a separate nation. Talk of secession reached a climax in the winter of 1814–1815.

On December 15, 1814, delegates from the New England states met in Hartford, Connecticut, to discuss their grievances against the Madison administration. The would-be seceders at the Hartford Convention were outnumbered by a comparatively moderate majority. But while the convention's report only hinted at secession, it reasserted the right

THE WAR OF 1812 This map illustrates the military maneuvers of the British and the Americans during the War of 1812. It shows all the theaters of the war, from New Orleans to southern Canada, the extended land and water battle along the Canadian border and in the Great Lakes, and the fighting around Washington and Baltimore. Note how in all these theaters there are about the same number of British and American victories. • *What finally brought this inconclusive war to an end?*

of nullification and proposed seven amendments to the Constitution—amendments designed to protect New England from the growing influence of the South and the West.

Because the war was going so badly, the New Englanders assumed that the Republicans would have to agree to their demands. Soon after the convention adjourned, however, the news of Jackson's victory at New Orleans reached the cities of the Northeast. A day or two later, reports of a peace treaty arrived from abroad. In the changed atmosphere, the aims of the Hartford Convention and the Federalist Party came to seem futile, irrelevant, even treasonable.

THE PEACE SETTLEMENT

Negotiations between the United States and Britain began in August 1814, when American and British diplomats met in Ghent, Belgium. John Quincy Adams, Henry Clay, and Albert Gallatin led the American delegation. Although both sides began with extravagant demands, the final treaty did little except end the fighting itself. The Americans gave up their demand for a British renunciation of impressment and for the cession of Canada to the United States.

The British abandoned their call for the creation of an Indian buffer state in the Northwest and made other, minor territorial concessions. The treaty was signed on Christmas Eve 1814.

Both sides had reason to accept this skimpy agreement. The British, exhausted and in debt from their prolonged conflict with Napoleon, were eager to settle the lesser dispute in North America. The Americans realized that with the defeat of Napoleon in Europe, the British would no longer have much incentive to interfere with American commerce.

Other settlements followed the Treaty of Ghent. A commercial treaty in 1815 gave Americans the right to trade freely with England and much of the British Empire. The Rush-Bagot agreement of 1817 provided for mutual disarmament on the Great Lakes; eventually (although not until 1872) the Canadian-American boundary became the longest "unguarded frontier" in the world.

For the other parties to the War of 1812—the Indian tribes east of the Mississippi—the conflict was another disastrous blow to their ability to resist white expansion. Tecumseh was dead. The British were gone from the Northwest. And the intertribal alliance of Tecumseh and the Prophet had collapsed. As the end of the war spurred a new white movement westward, the Indians were less able than ever to defend their land.

CONCLUSION

Thomas Jefferson called his election to the presidency the "Revolution of 1800," and his supporters believed that his victory would bring a dramatic change in the character of the nation—a retreat from Hamilton's dreams of a powerful, developing nation and a return to an ideal of a simple agrarian republic.

But American society was changing rapidly, making it virtually impossible for the Jeffersonian dream to prevail. The nation's population was expanding and diversifying. Its cities were growing, and its commercial life was becoming ever more important. In 1803, Jefferson himself made one of the most important contributions to the growth of the United States: the Louisiana Purchase, which dramatically expanded the physical boundaries of the nation—and which began extending white settlement deeper into the continent. In the process, it greatly widened the battles between Europeans and Native Americans.

The growing national pride and commercial ambitions of the United States gradually created another serious conflict with Great Britain: the War of 1812, a war that was settled finally in 1814 on terms at least mildly favorable to the United States. By then, the bitter party rivalries that had characterized the first years of the republic had to some degree subsided, and the nation was poised to enter what became known, quite inaccurately, as the "era of good feelings."

RECALL AND REFLECT

1. What was the impact of the Second Great Awakening on women, African Americans, and Native Americans?
2. What was the long-term significance of the *Marbury v. Madison* ruling?
3. How did Americans respond to the Louisiana Purchase?
4. What foreign entanglements and questions of foreign policy did Jefferson have to deal with during his presidency? How did these affect his political philosophy?
5. What were the consequences of the War of 1812?

8 VARIETIES OF AMERICAN NATIONALISM

STABILIZING ECONOMIC GROWTH
EXPANDING WESTWARD
THE "ERA OF GOOD FEELINGS"
SECTIONALISM AND NATIONALISM
THE REVIVAL OF OPPOSITION

LOOKING AHEAD

1. How did the economic developments and territorial expansion of this era affect American nationalism?
2. What was the "era of good feelings," and why was it given that name?
3. How did the Marshall Court seek to establish a strong national government?

LIKE A "FIRE BELL IN the night," as Thomas Jefferson said, the issue of slavery arose after the War of 1812 to threaten the unity of the nation. The debate began when the territory of Missouri applied for admission to the Union, raising the question of whether it would be a free or a slaveholding state. But the larger issue was whether the vast new western regions of the United States would ultimately move into the orbit of the North or the South.

The Missouri crisis was significant because it was a sign of sectional crises to come. But at the time, it was also significant because it stood in such sharp contrast to the rising American nationalism of the years following the war. Whatever forces might have been working to pull the nation apart, stronger ones were acting, at least for a time, to draw it together.

STABILIZING ECONOMIC GROWTH

The end of the War of 1812 allowed the United States to resume its economic growth and territorial expansion. A vigorous postwar boom led to a disastrous bust in 1819. Brief though it was, the collapse was evidence that the United States continued to lack some of the basic institutions necessary to sustain long-term growth.

THE GOVERNMENT AND ECONOMIC GROWTH

The War of 1812 produced chaos in shipping and banking, and it exposed dramatically the inadequacy of the nation's existing transportation and financial systems. The aftermath of the war, therefore, led to new efforts to strengthen national economic development.

The wartime experience underlined the need for another national bank. After the expiration of the first bank's charter, a large number of state banks had issued vast quantities of banknotes, creating a confusing variety of currency of widely differing value. It was difficult to tell what any banknote was really worth, and counterfeiting was easy. In response to these problems, Congress chartered a second Bank of the United States in 1816, much like its predecessor of 1791 but with more capital. The national bank could not forbid state banks from issuing notes, but its size and power enabled it to compel the state banks to issue only sound notes or risk being forced out of business.

Congress also acted to promote manufacturing, which the war (by cutting off imports) had already greatly stimulated. The American textile industry, in particular, had grown dramatically. Between 1807 and 1815, the total number of cotton spindles in the country increased more than fifteenfold, from 8,000 to 130,000. Before the war, the textile factories—most of them in New England—produced only yarn and thread; families operating

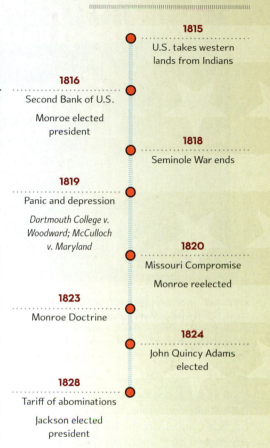

TIME LINE

1815
U.S. takes western lands from Indians

1816
Second Bank of U.S.
Monroe elected president

1818
Seminole War ends

1819
Panic and depression
Dartmouth College v. Woodward; McCulloch v. Maryland

1820
Missouri Compromise
Monroe reelected

1823
Monroe Doctrine

1824
John Quincy Adams elected

1828
Tariff of abominations
Jackson elected president

AN EARLY MILL IN NEW ENGLAND This early folk painting of about 1814 shows the small town of East Chelmsford, Massachusetts—still primarily agrarian, with its rural houses, open fields, and grazing livestock, but with a small textile mill already operating along the stream, at right. A little more than a decade later, the town had been transformed into a major manufacturing center and renamed Lowell, for the family that owned the mills. (Abby Aldrich Rockefeller Folk Art Museum, The Colonial Williamsburg Foundation, Williamsburg, VA)

hand looms at home did the actual weaving of cloth. Then the Boston merchant Francis Cabot Lowell, after examining textile machinery in England, developed a power loom better than its English counterpart. In 1813, in Waltham, Massachusetts, Lowell founded the first mill in America to carry on the processes of spinning and weaving under a single roof.

The end of the war suddenly dimmed the prospects for American industry. British ships swarmed into American ports and unloaded cargoes of manufactured goods, many priced below cost. In response, in 1816, protectionists in Congress passed a tariff law that effectively limited competition from abroad on a wide range of items, including cotton cloth, despite objections from agricultural interests, who stood to pay higher prices for manufactured goods.

TRANSPORTATION

The nation's most pressing economic need was a better transportation system to link the vast territories of the growing United States. An old debate resumed. Should the federal government help to finance roads and other "internal improvements"? The idea of using government funds to finance road building was not a new one. When Ohio entered the Union in 1803, the federal government agreed that part of the proceeds from the sale of public lands there should finance road construction. And in 1807, Congress enacted a law proposed by the Jefferson administration that permitted using revenues from Ohio land sales to finance a National Road from the Potomac River to the Ohio. By 1818, the highway ran as far as Wheeling, Virginia, on the Ohio River; and the Lancaster Pike, financed in part by the state of Pennsylvania, extended westward to Pittsburgh.

DECK LIFE ON THE *PARAGON*, 1811–1812   The North River steamboat *Clermont*, launched in 1806 by the inventor Robert Fulton and propelled by an engine he had developed, traveled from Manhattan to Albany (about 150 miles) in thirty-two hours. That was neither the longest nor the fastest steam voyage to date, but the *Clermont* proved to be the first steam-powered vessel large enough and reliable enough to be commercially valuable. Within a few years, Fulton and his partner Robert R. Livingston had several steamboats operating profitably around New York. The third vessel in their fleet, the *Paragon*, shown here in a painting by the Russian diplomat and artist Pavel Petrovich Svinin, could carry 150 people and contained an elegant dining salon fitted with bronze, mahogany, and mirrors. Svinin called it "a whole floating town," and Fulton told a friend that the *Paragon* "beats everything on the globe, for made as you and I are we cannot tell what is in the moon." (Image copyright © The Metropolitan Museum of Art/Art Resource, NY)

At the same time, steam-powered shipping was expanding rapidly. By 1816, river steamers were sailing up the Mississippi to the Ohio River and up the Ohio as far as Pittsburgh. Steamboats were soon carrying more cargo on the Mississippi than all the earlier forms of river transport—flatboats, barges, and others—combined. They stimulated the agricultural economy of the West and the South by providing cheaper access to markets, and they enabled eastern manufacturers to send their finished goods west much more readily.

Nevertheless, serious gaps in the nation's transportation network remained, as the War of 1812 had shown. Once the British blockade had cut off Atlantic shipping, the coastal roads had become choked by the unaccustomed volume of north-south traffic. Congress passed a bill introduced by Representative John C. Calhoun that would use government funds to finance internal improvements. But Madison, on his last day in office, vetoed it. He believed that Congress lacked authority to fund the improvements without a constitutional amendment. For a time, state governments and private enterprise were left on their own to build the transportation network necessary for the growing American economy.

EXPANDING WESTWARD

Another reason for the growing interest in internal improvements was the dramatic surge in the westward expansion of white Americans. By 1820, white settlers had pushed well beyond the Mississippi River, and the population of western regions was increasing more rapidly than the rest of the nation.

THE GREAT MIGRATION

The westward movement of the white American population was one of the most important developments of the nineteenth century. It occurred for several reasons.

One was population growth, which drove many white Americans out of the crowded East. Between 1800 and 1820, the American population nearly doubled—from 5.3 million to 9.6 million. Most Americans were still farmers, and the agricultural lands of the East were by now largely occupied or exhausted. In the South, the spread of the plantation system limited opportunities for new settlers. Another reason for westward migration was that the West itself was increasingly attractive to white settlers. Land there was much more plentiful than it was in the East. And in the aftermath of the War of 1812, the federal government continued its policy of pushing the Indian tribes farther and farther west. Migrants from throughout the East flocked in increasing numbers to what was then known as the Old Northwest (now part of the Midwest). Most settlers floated downstream on flatboats on the Ohio River, then left the river (often at Cincinnati) and traveled overland with wagons, handcarts, packhorses, cattle, and hogs.

WHITE SETTLERS IN THE OLD NORTHWEST

Having arrived at their new lands, most settlers built lean-tos or cabins, hewed clearings out of the forest, and planted crops of corn to supplement wild game and domestic animals. It was a rough and lonely existence. Men, women, and children worked side by side in the fields—and at times had virtually no contact for weeks or months with anyone outside their own families.

Life in the western territories was not, however, entirely solitary or individualistic. Migrants often journeyed westward in groups and built communities with schools, churches, and stores. The labor shortage in the interior led neighbors to develop systems of mutual aid. They gathered periodically to raise a barn, clear land, or harvest crops.

Another common feature of life in the Old Northwest was mobility. Individuals and families were constantly on the move, settling for a few years in one place and then selling their land (often at a significant profit) and resettling somewhere else. When new areas for settlement opened farther to the west, it was often the people already on the western edges of white settlement—rather than those coming from the East—who flocked to them first.

THE PLANTATION SYSTEM IN THE OLD SOUTHWEST

In the Old Southwest (later known as the Deep South), the new agricultural economy emerged along different lines. The market for cotton continued to grow, and the Old Southwest contained a broad zone where cotton could thrive. That zone became known as the Black Belt, mostly in the vast prairie with a dark, productive soil of Alabama and Mississippi.

The first arrivals in the uncultivated regions of the Old Southwest were usually small farmers who made rough clearings in the forest. But wealthier planters soon followed. They bought up the cleared land, as the original settlers moved farther west. Success in the wilderness was by no means assured, even for the wealthiest settlers. Many planters managed to do little more than subsist in their new environment, and others experienced utter ruin. But some planters soon expanded small clearings into vast cotton fields. They replaced the cabins of the early pioneers with more sumptuous log dwellings and ultimately with imposing mansions. They also built up large slave workforces.

The rapid growth of the Old Northwest and Southwest resulted in the admission of four new states to the Union: Indiana in 1816, Mississippi in 1817, Illinois in 1818, and Alabama in 1819.

TRADE AND TRAPPING IN THE FAR WEST

Not many Anglo-Americans yet knew much about or were much interested in the far western areas of the continent. Nevertheless, a significant trade began to develop between these western regions and the United States early in the nineteenth century, and it grew steadily for decades.

Mexico, which continued to control Texas, California, and much of the rest of the far Southwest, won its independence from Spain in 1821. Almost immediately, it opened its northern territories to trade with the United States. American traders poured into the region and quickly displaced Indian and Mexican traders. In New Mexico, for example, the Missouri merchant William Becknell began in 1821 to offer American manufactured goods for sale, priced considerably below the inferior Mexican goods that had dominated the market in the past. Mexico effectively lost its markets in its own colony as a steady traffic of commercial wagon trains began moving back and forth along the Santa Fe Trail between Missouri and New Mexico.

Fur traders created a wholly new kind of commerce. After the War of 1812, John Jacob Astor's American Fur Company and other firms extended their operations from the Great Lakes area westward to the Rockies. At first, fur traders did most of their business by purchasing pelts from the Indians. But increasingly, white trappers entered the region and joined the Iroquois and other Indians in pursuit of beaver and other furs.

The trappers, or "mountain men," who began trading in the Far West were small in number. But they developed important relationships with the existing residents of the West—Indian and Mexican—and altered the character of society there. White trappers

THE RENDEZVOUS   The annual rendezvous of fur trappers and traders was a major event for the lonely men who made their livelihoods gathering furs. It was also a gathering of representatives of the many cultures that mingled in the Far West, among them Anglo-Americans, French Canadians, Indians, and Hispanics. (Denver Public Library, Western History Collection, Trans. #72)

were mostly young, single men. Perhaps unsurprisingly, many of them entered into sexual relationships with Indian and Mexican women. Most of them married. They also recruited women as helpers in the difficult work of preparing furs and skins for trading.

In 1822, Andrew and William Ashley founded the Rocky Mountain Fur Company and recruited white trappers to move permanently into the Rockies. The Ashleys dispatched supplies annually to their trappers in exchange for furs and skins. The arrival of the supply train became the occasion for a gathering of scores of mountain men, some of whom lived much of the year in considerable isolation. But however isolated their daily lives, these mountain men were closely bound up with the expanding market economy, an economy in which the bulk of the profits from the trade flowed to the merchants, not the trappers.

EASTERN IMAGES OF THE WEST

Americans in the East were only dimly aware of the world of the trappers. They were more aware of the explorers, many of them dispatched by the United States government. In 1819 and 1820, the War Department ordered Stephen H. Long to journey up the Platte and South Platte rivers through what is now Nebraska and eastern Colorado (where he discovered the peak that would be named for him). He then returned eastward along the Arkansas River through what is now Kansas. He failed to find the headwaters of the Red River. But he wrote an influential report on his trip, which echoed the dismissive conclusions of Zebulon Pike fifteen years before. The region "between the Missouri River and the Rocky Mountains," Long wrote, "is almost wholly unfit for cultivation, and of course uninhabitable by a people depending upon agriculture for their subsistence." On the published map of his expedition, he labeled the Great Plains the "Great American Desert."

THE "ERA OF GOOD FEELINGS"

The expansion of the economy, the growth of white settlement and trade in the West, the creation of new states—all reflected the rising spirit of nationalism that was spreading through the United States in the years following the War of 1812. That spirit found reflection for a time as well in the character of national politics.

THE END OF THE FIRST PARTY SYSTEM

Ever since 1800, the presidency seemed to have been the possession of Virginians. After two terms in office, Jefferson chose his secretary of state, James Madison, to succeed him, and after two more terms, Madison secured the presidential nomination for his secretary of state, James Monroe. Many in the North were expressing impatience with the so-called Virginia Dynasty, but the Republicans had no difficulty electing their candidate in 1816. Monroe received 183 ballots in the electoral college; his Federalist opponent, Rufus King of New York, received only 34.

Monroe entered office under what seemed to be remarkably favorable circumstances. With the decline of the Federalists, his party faced no serious opposition. And with the conclusion of the War of 1812, the nation faced no important international threats. Some American politicians had dreamed since the first days of the republic of a time in which partisan divisions and factional disputes might come to an end. In the prosperous postwar years, Monroe attempted to use his office to realize that dream.

He made that clear, above all, in the selection of his cabinet. For secretary of state, he chose former Federalist John Quincy Adams of Massachusetts, son of the second president. Jefferson, Madison, and Monroe had all served as secretary of state before becoming president; Adams, therefore, immediately became the heir apparent, suggesting that the Virginia Dynasty would soon come to an end. Speaker of the House Henry Clay declined an offer to be secretary of war, so Monroe named John C. Calhoun instead.

Soon after his inauguration, Monroe made a goodwill tour through the country. In New England, so recently the scene of rabid Federalist discontent, he was greeted everywhere with enthusiastic demonstrations. The *Columbian Centinel*, a Federalist newspaper in Boston, observed that an "era of good feelings" had arrived. And on the surface, at least, that seemed to be the case. In 1820, Monroe was reelected without opposition. For all practical purposes, the Federalist Party had now ceased to exist.

JOHN QUINCY ADAMS AND FLORIDA

Like his father, the second president of the United States, John Quincy Adams had spent much of his life in diplomatic service. And even before becoming secretary of state, he had been one of the great diplomats in American history. He was also a committed nationalist, and he considered his most important task to be the promotion of American expansion.

SEMINOLE DANCE This 1838 drawing by a U.S. military officer portrays a dance by Seminole Indians near Fort Butler in Florida. It was made in the midst of the prolonged Second Seminole War, which ended in 1842 with the removal of most of the tribe from Florida to reservations west of the Mississippi. (The Huntington Art Collection and Botanical Gardens, San Marino, California/Superstock)

His first challenge was Florida. The United States had already annexed West Florida, but that claim was in dispute. Most Americans, moreover, still believed the nation should gain possession of the entire peninsula. In 1817, Adams began negotiations with the Spanish minister, Luis de Onís, over the territory.

In the meantime, however, events in Florida itself were taking their own course. Andrew Jackson, now in command of American troops along the Florida frontier, had orders from Secretary of War Calhoun to "adopt the necessary measures" to stop continuing raids on American territory by Seminole Indians south of the border. Jackson used those orders as an excuse to invade Florida and seize the Spanish forts at St. Marks and Pensacola. The operation became known as the Seminole War.

Instead of condemning Jackson's raid, Adams urged the government to assume responsibility for it. The United States, he said, had the right under international law to defend itself against threats from across its borders. Jackson's raid demonstrated to the Spanish that the United States could easily take Florida by force. Adams implied that the nation might consider doing so.

Onís realized, therefore, that he had little choice but to negotiate a settlement. Under the provisions of the Adams-Onís Treaty of 1819, Spain ceded all of Florida to the United States and gave up its claim to territory north of the 42nd parallel in the Pacific Northwest. In return, the American government gave up its claims to Texas—for a time.

THE PANIC OF 1819

The Monroe administration had little time to revel in its diplomatic successes, for the nation was facing a serious economic crisis: the Panic of 1819. It followed a period of high foreign demand for American farm goods and thus of exceptionally high prices for American farmers. But the rising prices for farm goods stimulated a land boom in the western United States. Fueled by speculative investments, land prices soared.

The availability of easy credit to settlers and speculators—from the government (under the land acts of 1800 and 1804), from state banks and wildcat banks, even for a time from the rechartered Bank of the United States—fueled the land boom. Beginning in 1819, however, new management at the national bank began tightening credit, calling in loans, and foreclosing mortgages. This precipitated a series of failures by state banks. The result was a financial panic. Six years of depression followed.

Some Americans saw the Panic of 1819 and the widespread distress that followed as a warning that rapid economic growth and territorial expansion would destabilize the nation. But by 1820, most Americans were irrevocably committed to the idea of growth and expansion.

SECTIONALISM AND NATIONALISM

For a brief but alarming moment in 1819–1820, the increasing differences between the North and the South threatened the unity of the United States—until the Missouri Compromise averted a sectional crisis.

THE MISSOURI COMPROMISE

When Missouri applied for admission to the Union as a state in 1819, slavery was already well established there. Even so, Representative James Tallmadge, Jr., of New York

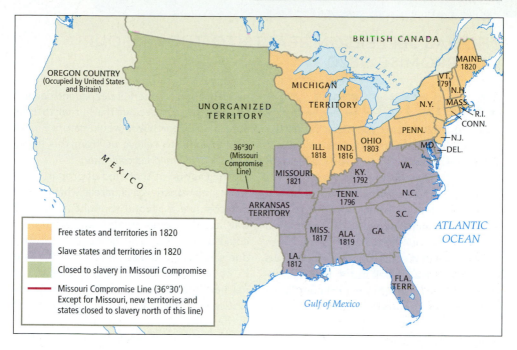

THE MISSOURI COMPROMISE, 1820 This map illustrates the way in which the Missouri Compromise proposed to settle the controversy over slavery in the new western territories of the United States. The compromise rested on the virtually simultaneous admission of Missouri and Maine to the Union, one a slave state and the other a free one. Note the red line extending beyond the southern border of Missouri, which in theory established a permanent boundary between areas in which slavery could be established and areas where it could not be. • *What precipitated the Missouri Compromise?*

proposed an amendment to the Missouri statehood bill that would prohibit the further introduction of slaves into Missouri and provide for the gradual emancipation of those already there. The Tallmadge Amendment provoked a controversy that raged for the next two years.

Since the beginning of the republic, new states had come into the Union mostly in pairs, one from the North, another from the South. In 1819, there were eleven free states and eleven slave states. The admission of Missouri would upset that balance. Hence the controversy over slavery and freedom in Missouri.

Complicating the Missouri question was the admission of Maine as a new (and free) state. Speaker of the House Henry Clay informed northern members that if they blocked Missouri from entering the Union as a slave state, southerners would block the admission of Maine. But ultimately the Senate agreed to combine the Maine and Missouri proposals into a single bill. Maine would be admitted as a free state, Missouri as a slave state. Then Senator Jesse B. Thomas of Illinois proposed an amendment prohibiting slavery in the rest of the Louisiana Purchase territory north of the southern boundary of Missouri (the 36°30' parallel). The Senate adopted the Thomas Amendment, and Speaker Clay, with great difficulty, guided the amended Maine-Missouri bill through the House.

Nationalists in both the North and South hailed this settlement—which became known as the Missouri Compromise—as a happy resolution of a danger to the Union.

THOMAS JEFFERSON REACTS TO THE MISSOURI COMPROMISE, 1820

MONTICELLO, April 22, 1820 I thank you, Dear Sir, for the copy you have been so kind as to send me of the letter to your constituents on the Missouri question. It is a perfect justification to them. I had for a long time ceased to read newspapers, or pay any attention to public affairs, confident they were in good hands, and content to be a passenger in our bark to the shore from which I am not distant. But this momentous question, like a firebell in the night, awakened and filled me with terror. I considered it at once as the knell of the Union. It is hushed, indeed, for the moment. But this is a reprieve only, not a final sentence. A geographical line, coinciding with a marked principle, moral and political, once conceived and held up to the angry passions of men, will never be obliterated; and every new irritation will mark it deeper and deeper. I can say, with conscious truth, that there is not a man on earth who would sacrifice more than I would to relieve us from this heavy reproach, in any *practicable* way.

The cession of that kind of property, for so it is misnamed, is a bagatelle which would not cost me a second thought, if, in that way, a general emancipation and *expatriation* could be effected; and gradually, and with due sacrifices, I think it might be. But as it is, we have the wolf by the ears, and we can neither hold him, nor safely let him go. Justice is in one scale, and self-preservation in the other. Of one thing I am certain, that as the passage of slaves from one state to another would not make a slave of a single human being who would not be so without it, so their diffusion over a greater surface would make them individually happier, and

MARSHALL AND THE COURT

John Marshall served as chief justice of the United States from 1801 to 1835. More than anyone but the framers themselves, he molded the development of the Constitution: strengthening the Supreme Court, increasing the power of the federal government, and advancing the interests of the propertied and commercial classes.

Committed to promoting commerce, the Marshall Court staunchly defended the inviolability of contracts. In *Fletcher v. Peck* (1810), which arose out of a series of notorious land frauds in Georgia, the Court had to decide whether the Georgia legislature of 1796 could repeal the act of the previous legislature granting lands under shady circumstances to the Yazoo Land Companies. In a unanimous decision, Marshall held that a land grant was a valid contract and could not be repealed even if corruption was involved.

Dartmouth College v. Woodward (1819) further expanded the meaning of the contract clause of the Constitution. Having gained control of the New Hampshire state government, Republicans tried to revise Dartmouth College's charter to convert the private college into a state university. Daniel Webster argued the college's case. The Dartmouth charter, he insisted, was a contract, protected by the same doctrine that the Court had already upheld in *Fletcher v. Peck*. The Court ruled for Dartmouth, proclaiming that corporation charters such as the one the colonial legislature had granted the college were contracts and thus inviolable. The decision placed important restrictions on the ability of state governments to control corporations.

proportionally facilitate the accomplishment of their emancipation, by dividing the burden on a greater number of coadjutors. An abstinence too, from this act of power, would remove the jealousy excited by the undertaking of Congress to regulate the condition of the different descriptions of men composing a state. This certainly is the exclusive right of every state, which nothing in the Constitution has taken from them and given to the general government. Could Congress, for example, say that the non-freemen of Connecticut shall be freemen, or that they shall not emigrate into any other state?

I regret that I am now to die in the belief, that the useless sacrifice of themselves by the generation of '76, to acquire self-government and happiness to their country, is to be thrown away by the unwise and unworthy passions of their sons, and that my only consolation is to be, that I live not to weep over it. If they would but dispassionately weigh the blessings they will throw away against an abstract principle more likely to be effected by union than by scission, they would pause before they would perpetrate this act of suicide on themselves, and of treason against the hopes of the world. To yourself, as the faithful advocate of the Union, I tender the offering of my high esteem and respect.

UNDERSTAND, ANALYZE, & EVALUATE

1. What does Jefferson's metaphor of "a firebell in the night" suggest about his own feelings about the Missouri Compromise and its Mason-Dixon line?
2. What was Jefferson referring to when he wrote that Americans had "the wolf by the ears"? How appropriate is this metaphor in your assessment?
3. What seemed to be Jefferson's position on the powers of states and the federal government with respect to slavery?

Source: Library of Congress, *Thomas Jefferson Papers*, Series 1. General Correspondence. 1651–1827, *Thomas Jefferson to John Holmes, April 22, 1820*, http://memory.loc.gov; reproduced in Wayne Franklin (ed.), *The Selected Writings of Thomas Jefferson*, A Norton Critical Edition (New York: W.W. Norton & Company 2010), pp. 361–362.

In overturning the act of the legislature and the decisions of the New Hampshire courts, the justices also implicitly claimed for themselves the right to override the decisions of state courts. But advocates of states' rights, especially in the South, continued to challenge this right. In *Cohens v. Virginia* (1821), Marshall explicitly affirmed the constitutionality of federal review of state court decisions. The states had given up part of their sovereignty in ratifying the Constitution, he explained, and their courts must submit to federal jurisdiction.

Meanwhile, in *McCulloch v. Maryland* (1819), Marshall confirmed the "implied powers" of Congress by upholding the constitutionality of the Bank of the United States. The Bank had become so unpopular in the South and the West that several of the states tried to drive branches out of business. This case presented two constitutional questions to the Supreme Court: Could Congress charter a bank? And if so, could individual states ban it or tax it? Daniel Webster, one of the Bank's attorneys, argued that establishing such an institution came within the "necessary and proper" clause of the Constitution and that the power to tax involved a "power to destroy." If the states could tax the Bank at all, they could tax it to death. Marshall adopted Webster's words in deciding for the Bank.

In the case of *Gibbons v. Ogden* (1824), the Court strengthened Congress's power to regulate interstate commerce. The state of New York had granted the steamboat company of Robert Fulton and Robert Livingston the exclusive right to carry passengers on the

JOHN MARSHALL The imposing figure in this early photograph is John Marshall, the most important chief justice of the Supreme Court in American history. A former secretary of state, Marshall served as chief justice from 1801 until his death in 1835 at the age of eighty. Such was the power of his intellect and personality that he dominated his fellow justices throughout that period, regardless of their previous party affiliations or legal ideologies. Marshall established the independence of the Court, gave it a reputation for nonpartisan integrity, and established its powers, which were only vaguely described by the Constitution. (National Archives)

Hudson River to New York City. Fulton and Livingston then gave Aaron Ogden the business of carrying passengers across the river between New York and New Jersey. But Thomas Gibbons, who had a license granted by Congress, began competing with Ogden for the ferry traffic. Ogden brought suit against him and won in the New York courts. Gibbons appealed to the Supreme Court. The most important question facing the justices was whether Congress's power to give Gibbons a license superseded the state of New York's power to grant Ogden a monopoly. Marshall claimed that the power of Congress to regulate interstate commerce (which, he said, included navigation) was "complete in itself" and might be "exercised to its utmost extent." Ogden's state-granted monopoly, therefore, was void.

The highly nationalist decisions of the Marshall Court established the primacy of the federal government over the states in regulating the economy and opened the way for an increased federal role in promoting economic growth. They protected corporations and other private economic institutions from local government interference.

The Court and the Tribes

The nationalist inclinations of the Marshall Court were visible as well in a series of decisions concerning the legal status of Indian tribes. But these decisions did not simply affirm the supremacy of the United States; they also carved out a distinctive position for Native Americans within the constitutional structure.

The first of the crucial Indian decisions was *Johnson v. McIntosh* (1823). Leaders of the Illinois and Pinakeshaw tribes had sold parcels of their land to a group of white settlers (including Johnson) but had later signed a treaty with the federal government ceding territory that included those same parcels to the United States. The government proceeded to grant homestead rights to new white settlers (among them McIntosh) on the land claimed by Johnson. The Court was asked to decide which claim had precedence. Marshall's ruling, not surprisingly, favored the United States. But in explaining it, he offered a preliminary definition of the place of Indians within the nation. The tribes had a basic right to their tribal lands, he said, that preceded all other American law. Individual American citizens could not buy or take land from the tribes; only the federal government—the supreme authority—could do that.

Even more important was the Court's 1832 decision in *Worcester v. Georgia,* in which the Court invalidated a Georgia law that attempted to regulate access by U.S. citizens to Cherokee country. Only the federal government could do that, Marshall claimed. The tribes, he explained, were sovereign entities in much the same way Georgia was a sovereign entity—"distinct political communities, having territorial boundaries within which their authority is exclusive." In defending the power of the federal government, he was also affirming, indeed expanding, the rights of the tribes to remain free from the authority of state governments.

The Marshall decisions, therefore, did what the Constitution itself had not: they defined a place for Indian tribes within the American political system. The tribes had basic property rights. They were sovereign entities not subject to the authority of state governments. But the federal government, like a "guardian" governing its "ward," had ultimate authority over tribal affairs.

The Latin American Revolution and the Monroe Doctrine

Just as the Supreme Court was asserting American nationalism in shaping the country's economic life, so the Monroe administration was asserting nationalism in formulating foreign policy. American diplomacy had been principally concerned with Europe. But in the 1820s, dealing with Europe forced the United States to develop a policy toward Latin America.

Americans looking southward in the years following the War of 1812 beheld a gigantic spectacle: the Spanish Empire in its death throes and a whole continent in revolt. Already the United States had developed a profitable trade with Latin America. Many believed the success of the anti-Spanish revolutions would further strengthen America's position in the region.

In 1815, the United States proclaimed neutrality in the wars between Spain and its rebellious colonies. But the United States sold ships and supplies to the revolutionaries, a clear indication that it was trying to help the revolutions. Finally, in 1822, President Monroe established diplomatic relations with five new nations—La Plata (later Argentina), Chile, Peru, Colombia, and Mexico—making the United States the first country to recognize them.

In 1823, Monroe went further and announced a policy that would ultimately be known (beginning some thirty years later) as the "Monroe Doctrine," even though it was primarily the work of John Quincy Adams. "The American continents," Monroe declared, ". . . are henceforth not to be considered as subjects for future colonization by any European powers." The United States would consider any foreign challenge to the sovereignty of existing American nations as an unfriendly act. At the same time, he proclaimed, "Our policy in regard to Europe . . . is not to interfere in the internal concerns of any of its powers."

The Monroe Doctrine emerged directly out of America's relations with Europe in the 1820s. Many Americans feared that Spain's European allies (notably France) would help Spain retake its lost empire. Even more troubling was the fear that Great Britain had designs on Cuba. Monroe and Adams wanted to keep Cuba in Spanish hands until it fell to the Americans.

The Monroe Doctrine had few immediate effects, but it was important as an expression of the growing spirit of nationalism in the United States in the 1820s. And it established the idea of the United States as the dominant power in the Western Hemisphere.

THE REVIVAL OF OPPOSITION

After 1816, the Federalist Party ceased to exist. The Republican Party became the only national political organization in America for a short time. In many ways, it now resembled the defunct Federalist Party in its commitment to economic growth and centralized government. But divisions were growing, just as they had in the late eighteenth century. By the 1820s, a two-party system was emerging once again. The mighty Republican Party split apart, and two new parties emerged. One was the Democratic Republican Party (later the Democrats), which leaned toward the old Jeffersonian vision of a decentralized nation. The Democrats opposed the federal government's growing role in the economy. The other party was the National Republican Party (later the Whigs), which leaned toward the old Federalists' belief in a centralized government. The Whigs believed in a strong national bank and a centralized economy. Both parties believed in economic growth and expansion. But they disagreed on whether the national government should oversee the economy or whether the economy should be decentralized without interference.

THE "CORRUPT BARGAIN"

Until 1820, presidential candidates were nominated by party caucuses in Congress. But in 1824, "King Caucus" was overthrown. The Republican caucus nominated William H. Crawford of Georgia, the favorite of the extreme states' rights faction of the party. But other candidates received nominations from state legislatures and won endorsements from irregular mass meetings throughout the country.

One of them was Secretary of State John Quincy Adams. But he was a man of cold and forbidding manners, with little popular appeal. Another contender was Henry Clay, the Speaker of the House. He had a devoted personal following and a definite and coherent program: the "American System," which proposed creating a great home market for factory and farm producers by raising the protective tariff, strengthening the national bank, and financing internal improvements. Andrew Jackson, the fourth major candidate, had no significant political record—even though he was a new member of the United States Senate. But he was a military hero and had the help of shrewd political allies from his home state of Tennessee.

Jackson received more popular and electoral votes than any other candidate, but not a majority. The Twelfth Amendment to the Constitution (passed in the aftermath of the contested 1800 election) required the House of Representatives to choose among the three candidates with the largest numbers of electoral votes. Crawford was seriously ill. Clay was out of the running, but he was in a strong position to influence the result. Jackson was Clay's most dangerous political rival in the West, so Clay supported Adams, in part because Adams was an ardent nationalist and a likely supporter of the American System. With Clay's endorsement, Adams won election in the House.

The Jacksonians believed that their large popular and electoral pluralities entitled their candidate to the presidency, and they were enraged when he lost. But they grew angrier still when Adams named Clay his secretary of state. The State Department was the well-established route to the presidency, and Adams thus appeared to be naming Clay as his own successor. The outrage the Jacksonians expressed at what they called a "corrupt bargain" haunted Adams throughout his presidency.

THE SECOND PRESIDENT ADAMS

Adams proposed an ambitiously nationalist program reminiscent of Clay's American System, but Jacksonians in Congress blocked most of it. Adams also experienced diplomatic frustrations. He appointed delegates to an international conference that the Venezuelan liberator Simón Bolívar had called in Panama in 1826. But Haiti was one of the participating nations, and southerners in Congress opposed the idea of white Americans mingling with the black delegates. Congress delayed approving the Panama mission so long that the American delegation did not arrive until after the conference was over.

Even more damaging to the administration was its support for a new tariff on imported goods in 1828. This measure originated with the demands of New England woolen manufacturers. But to win support from middle and western states, the administration had to accept duties on other items. In the process, it antagonized the original supporters of the bill; the benefits of protecting their manufactured goods from foreign competition now had to be weighed against the prospects of having to pay more for raw materials. Adams signed the bill, earning the animosity of southerners, who cursed it as the "tariff of abominations."

JACKSON TRIUMPHANT

By the time of the 1828 presidential election, the new two-party system was now in place. On one side stood the supporters of John Quincy Adams and the National Republicans. Opposing them were the followers of Andrew Jackson and the Democratic Republicans. Adams attracted the support of most of the remaining Federalists; Jackson appealed to a broad coalition that opposed the "economic aristocracy."

But issues seemed to count for little in the end, as the campaign degenerated into a war of personal invective. The Jacksonians charged that Adams had been guilty of gross waste and extravagance. Adams's supporters hurled even worse accusations at Jackson. They called him a murderer and distributed a "coffin handbill," which listed, within coffin-shaped outlines, the names of militiamen whom Jackson was said to have shot in cold blood during the War of 1812. (The men had been deserters who were legally executed after sentence by a court-martial.) And they called his wife a bigamist. Jackson had married his beloved Rachel at a time when the pair incorrectly believed her first husband had divorced her. (When Jackson's wife read of the accusations against her, she collapsed and, a few weeks later, died.)

Jackson's victory was decisive, but sectional. Adams swept virtually all of New England and showed significant strength in the mid-Atlantic region. Nevertheless, the Jacksonians considered their victory as complete and as important as Jefferson's in 1800. Once again, the forces of privilege had been driven from Washington. Once again, a champion of democracy would occupy the White House. America had entered, some Jacksonians claimed, a new era of democracy, the "era of the common man."

CONCLUSION

In the aftermath of the War of 1812, a vigorous nationalism increasingly came to characterize the political and popular culture of the United States. In all regions of the country, white men and women celebrated the achievements of the early leaders of the republic, the genius of the Constitution, and the success of the nation in withstanding serious challenges from both without and within. Party divisions faded.

But the broad nationalism of the "era of good feelings" disguised some deep divisions. Indeed, the character of American nationalism differed substantially from one region, and one group, to another. Battles continued between those who favored a strong central government committed to advancing the economic development of the nation and those who wanted a decentralization of power to open opportunity to more people. Battles continued as well over the role of slavery in American life—and in particular over the place of slavery in the new western territories. The Missouri Compromise of 1820 postponed the day of reckoning on that issue—but only for a time.

RECALL AND REFLECT

1. How did the War of 1812 stimulate the national economy?
2. What were the reasons for the rise of sectional differences in this era? What attempts were made to resolve these differences? How successful were those attempts?
3. Why was the Monroe Doctrine proclaimed?
4. What was the significance of Andrew Jackson's victory in the election of 1828?

9 JACKSONIAN AMERICA

THE RISE OF MASS POLITICS
"OUR FEDERAL UNION"
THE REMOVAL OF THE INDIANS
JACKSON AND THE BANK WAR
THE CHANGING FACE OF AMERICAN POLITICS
POLITICS AFTER JACKSON

LOOKING AHEAD

1. How did the electorate expand during the Jacksonian era, and what were the limits of that expansion?

2. What events fed the growing tension between nationalism and states' rights, and what were the arguments on both sides of that issue?

3. What was the Second Party System, and how did its emergence and rise change national politics?

MANY AMERICANS IN THE 1830s were growing apprehensive about the future of their expanding republic. Some feared that rapid growth would produce social chaos; they insisted that the country's first priority was to establish order and a clear system of authority. Others argued that the greatest danger facing the nation was the growth of inequality and privilege; they wanted to eliminate the favored status of powerful elites and make opportunity more widely available. Advocates of this latter vision seized control of the federal government in 1829 with the inauguration of Andrew Jackson.

THE RISE OF MASS POLITICS

On March 4, 1829, thousands of Americans from all regions of the country crowded before the United States Capitol to watch the inauguration of Andrew Jackson. After the ceremonies, the crowd poured into a public reception at the White House, where, in their eagerness to shake the new president's hand, they filled the state rooms to overflowing, trampled one another, soiled the carpets, and damaged the upholstery. "It was a proud day for the people," wrote Amos Kendall, one of Jackson's closest political associates. Supreme Court Justice Joseph Story, a friend and colleague of John Marshall, remarked with disgust: "The reign of King 'Mob' seems triumphant."

In fact, the "age of Jackson" was much less a triumph of the common people than Kendall hoped and Story feared. But it did mark a transformation of American politics. Once restricted to a relatively small elite of property owners, politics now became open to virtually all the nation's white male citizens. In a political sense at least, the era had some claim to the title the Jacksonians gave it: the "era of the common man."

THE EXPANDING DEMOCRACY

What some have called the "age of Jackson" did not much advance the cause of economic equality. The distribution of wealth and property in America was little different at the end of the Jacksonian era than it had been at the start. But it did mark a transformation of American politics that widely extended to new groups the right to vote.

Until the 1820s, relatively few Americans had been permitted to vote. Most states restricted the franchise to white male property owners or taxpayers or both. But even before Jackson's election, the franchise began to expand. Change came first in Ohio and other new states of the West, which, on joining the Union, adopted constitutions that guaranteed all adult white males—not just property

THE VERDICT OF THE PEOPLE **(1855), BY GEORGE CALEB BINGHAM**   This scene of an election-day gathering is peopled almost entirely by white men. Women and blacks were barred from voting, but political rights expanded substantially in the 1830s and 1840s among white males. (Courtesy of the Saint Louis Art Museum, Gift of Bank of America)

owners or taxpayers—the right to vote and permitted all voters the right to hold public office. Older states, concerned about the loss of their population to the West, began to drop or reduce their own property ownership or taxpaying requirements.

The wave of state reforms was generally peaceful, but in Rhode Island, democratization efforts created considerable instability. The Rhode Island constitution barred more than half the adult males in the state from voting in the 1830s. In 1840, the lawyer and activist Thomas L. Dorr and a group of his followers formed a "People's party," held a convention, drafted a new constitution, and submitted it to a popular vote. It was overwhelmingly approved, and the Dorrites began to set up a new government, with Dorr as governor. The existing legislature, however, rejected the legitimacy of Dorr's constitution. And so, in 1842, two governments were claiming to be the real power in Rhode Island. The old state government proclaimed that Dorr and his followers were rebels and began to imprison them. The Dorrites, meanwhile, made an ineffectual effort to capture the state arsenal. The Dorr Rebellion, as it was known, quickly failed, but the episode helped spur the old guard to draft a new constitution that greatly expanded the suffrage.

The democratization process was far from complete. In much of the South, of course, no slaves could vote. In addition, southern election laws continued to favor the planters and politicians of the older counties. Free blacks could not vote anywhere in the South and hardly anywhere in the North. In no state could women vote. Nowhere was the ballot secret, and often it was cast as a spoken vote, which meant that voters could be easily bribed or intimidated. Despite the persisting limitations, however, the number of voters increased much more rapidly than did the population as a whole.

One of the most striking political trends of the early nineteenth century was the change in the method of choosing presidential electors. In 1800, the legislatures had chosen the presidential electors in ten states; the electors were chosen by the people in only six states.

ALEXIS DE TOCQUEVILLE, *THE CHOICE OF THE PEOPLE, AND THE INSTINCTIVE PREFERENCES OF THE AMERICAN DEMOCRACY*

MANY people in Europe are apt to believe without saying it, or to say without believing it, that one of the great advantages of universal suffrage is that it entrusts the direction of affairs to men who are worthy of the public confidence. They admit that the people are unable to govern of themselves, but they aver that the people always wish the welfare of the state and instinctively designate those who are animated by the same good will and who are the most fit to wield the supreme authority. I confess that the observations I made in America by no means coincide with these opinions. On my arrival in the United States I was surprised to find so much distinguished talent among the citizens and so little among the heads of the government. It is a constant fact that at the present day the ablest men in the United States are rarely placed at the head of affairs; and it must be acknowledged that such has been the result in proportion as democracy has exceeded all its former limits. The race of American statesmen has evidently dwindled most remarkably in the course of the last fifty years.

Several causes may be assigned for this phenomenon. It is impossible, after the most strenuous exertions, to raise the intelligence of the people above a certain level. Whatever may be the facilities of acquiring information, whatever may be the profusion of easy methods and cheap science, the human mind can never be instructed and developed without devoting considerable time to these objects.

The greater or lesser ease with which people can live without working is a sure index of intellectual progress. This boundary is more remote in some countries and more restricted in others, but it must exist somewhere as long as the people are forced to work in order to procure the means of subsistence; that is to say, as long as they continue to be the people. It is therefore quite as difficult to imagine a state in which all the citizens are very well informed as a state in which they are all wealthy; these two difficulties are correlative. I readily admit that the mass of the citizens sincerely wish to promote the welfare of the country; nay, more, I *even* grant that the lower classes mix fewer considerations of personal interest

By 1828, electors were chosen by popular vote in every state but South Carolina. In the presidential election of 1824, fewer than 27 percent of adult white males had voted. Only four years later, the figure was 58 percent; and in 1840, 80 percent.

TOCQUEVILLE AND *DEMOCRACY IN AMERICA*

The rapid growth of the electorate—and the emergence of political parties—was among the most striking events of the early nineteenth century. As the right to vote spread widely in these years, it came to be the mark of freedom and democracy. One of the most important commentaries on this extraordinary moment in American life was a book by the French aristocrat Alexis de Tocqueville. He spent two years in the United States in the 1830s watching the dramatic political changes in the age of Andrew Jackson. The French government had requested him to make a study of American prisons, which were thought to be more humane and effective institutions than those in Europe. But Tocqueville with their patriotism than the higher orders; but it is always more or less difficult for them to discern the best means of attaining the end which they sincerely desire. Long and patient observation and much acquired knowledge are requisite to form a just estimate of the character of a single individual. Men of the greatest genius often fail to do it, and can it be supposed that the common people will always succeed? The people have neither the time nor the means for an investigation of this kind. Their conclusions are hastily formed from a superficial inspection of the more prominent features of a question. Hence it often happens that mountebanks of all sorts are able to please the people, while their truest friends frequently fail to gain their confidence.

Moreover, democracy not only lacks that soundness of judgment which is necessary to select men really deserving of their confidence, but often have (sic) not the desire or the inclination to find them out. It cannot be denied that democratic institutions strongly tend to promote the feeling of envy in the human heart; not so much because they afford to everyone the means of rising to the same level with others as because those means perpetually disappoint the persons who employ them. Democratic institutions awaken and foster a passion for equality which they can never entirely satisfy. This

complete equality eludes the grasp of the people at the very moment when they think they have grasped it, and "flies," as Pascal says, "with an eternal flight"; the people are excited in the pursuit of an advantage, which is more precious because it is not sufficiently remote to be unknown or sufficiently near to be enjoyed. The lower orders are agitated by the chance of success, they are irritated by its uncertainty; and they pass from the enthusiasm of pursuit to the exhaustion of ill success, and lastly to the acrimony of disappointment. Whatever transcends their own limitations appears to be an obstacle to their desires, and there is no superiority, however legitimate it may be, which is not irksome in their sight.

UNDERSTAND, ANALYZE, & EVALUATE

1. What general assumption about universal suffrage did Alexis de Tocqueville want to counter?
2. What change did Tocqueville observe among American politicians since the Revolution, and how did he explain this change?
3. What relationship between social class and political understanding did Tocqueville see among Americans?

Source: Alexis de Tocqueville, *Democracy in America*, with a new introduction by Daniel J. Boorstin (New York: Vintage Books, 1990 (1945)), pp. 200–201.

quickly went far beyond the study of prisons and wrote a classic study of American life, entitled *Democracy in America*. Tocqueville examined not just the politics of the United States, but also the daily lives of many groups of Americans and their cultures, their associations, and their visions of democracy. In France in the early decades of the nineteenth century, the fruits of democracy were largely restricted to landowners and aristocrats. But Tocqueville recognized that traditional aristocracies were rapidly fading in America and that new elites could rise and fall no matter what their backgrounds.

But Tocqueville also realized that the rising democracy of America had many limits. Democracy was a powerful, visible force in the lives of most white men. Few women could vote, although some shared the democratic ethos through their families. For many other Americans, democracy was a distant hope. Tocqueville wrote of the limits of equality and democracy:

. . . he first who attracts the eye, the first in enlightenment, in power and in happiness, is the white man, the European, man par excellence; below him appear the Negro and the Indian. These two unfortunate races have neither birth, nor face, nor language, nor mores in common; only their misfortunes look alike. Both occupy an equally inferior position in the country that they inhabit; both experience the effects of tyranny; and if their miseries are different, they can accuse the same author for them.

Tocqueville's book helped spread the idea of American democracy into France and other European nations. Only later did it become widely read and studied in the United States as a remarkable portrait of the emerging democracy of the United States.

THE LEGITIMIZATION OF PARTY

The high level of voter participation was only partly the result of an expanded electorate. It was also the result of growing interest in politics and a strengthening of party organization. And it was, and perhaps equally important, party loyalty. Although party competition had been part of American politics almost from the beginning, acceptance of the idea of party had not. For more than thirty years, most Americans who had opinions about the nature of government considered parties as evils to be avoided and thought the nation should seek a broad consensus in which permanent factional lines would not exist. But in the 1820s and 1830s, those assumptions gave way to a new view that permanent, institutionalized parties were a desirable part of the political process, that they were indeed essential to democracy.

PEOPLE'S

Constitutional and State Rights'

TICKET.

[*Election Monday, April 18th, 1842.*]

—

FOR GOVERNOR,

THOMAS W. DORR,

OF PROVIDENCE.

FOR LIEUTENANT GOVERNOR,

AMASA EDDY, JR.

OF GLOCESTER.

WILLIAM H. SMITH, *Secretary of State.*
JOSEPH JOSLIN, *General Treasurer.*
JONAH TITUS, *Attorney General.*

For *Sheriff of the County of Providence,*
BURRINGTON ANTHONY.

THE DORR REBELLION The democratic sentiments that swept much of the nation in the 1830s and 1840s produced, among many other things, the Dorr Rebellion (as its opponents termed it) in Rhode Island. Thomas Dorr was one of many Rhode Islanders who denounced the state's constitution, which limited voting rights to a small group of property owners known as "freeholders." The dissidents crafted a new constitution and submitted it to a vote; a majority of the state's citizens approved it. But the legislature refused to acknowledge its legitimacy, and the result was two separate elections in 1842 for the same state offices. Dorr ran for governor under the new constitution and was elected by a majority of the people. This "ticket" was what his supporters placed in ballot boxes as they cast their votes. Another candidate, Samuel King, ran under the old constitution and was elected by the freeholders. Both men were inaugurated, and not until President Tyler threatened federal intervention on behalf of King did the Dorr movement crumble. A year later, however, the state ratified a new constitution extending the franchise. (Courtesy The Rhode Island Historical Society, RHi X5 304)

Although factional competition was part of American politics from the beginning of the republic, acceptance of the idea of formal political parties emerged slowly. Not until the 1820s and 1830s did most Americans begin to consider permanent, institutionalized parties a desirable part of the political process.

The elevation of party occurred first at the state level, most prominently in New York. There, after the War of 1812, Martin Van Buren led a dissident political faction (known as the "Bucktails"), which challenged the established political elite led by the aristocratic governor, DeWitt Clinton. The Bucktails argued that Clinton's closed elite made genuine democracy impossible. They advocated institutionalized political parties in its place, based on the support of a broad public constituency. A party would need a permanent opposition, they insisted, because competition would force it to remain sensitive to the will of the people. Parties would check and balance one another in much the same way as the different branches of government.

By the late 1820s, this new idea of party had spread beyond New York. The election of Jackson in 1828, the result of a popular movement that stood apart from the usual political elites, seemed further to legitimize it. In the 1830s, finally, a fully formed two-party system began to operate at the national level. The anti-Jackson forces began to call themselves the Whigs. Jackson's followers called themselves Democrats, thus giving a permanent name to what is now the nation's oldest political party.

PRESIDENT OF THE COMMON MAN

Unlike Thomas Jefferson, Jackson was no democratic philosopher. The Democratic Party, much less than the old Jeffersonian Republicans, embraced no clear or uniform ideological position. But Jackson himself did embrace a distinct and simple theory of democracy. Government,

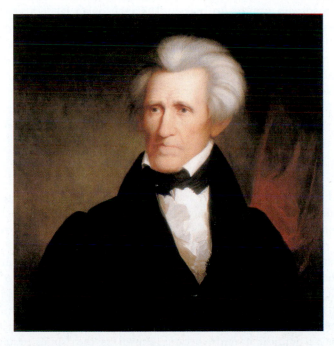

ANDREW JACKSON   This portrait suggests something of the fierce determination that characterized Andrew Jackson's military and political careers. Shattered by the death of his wife a few weeks after his election as president—a death he blamed (not entirely without reason) on the attacks his political opponents had leveled at her—he entered office with a steely determination to live by his own principles and give no quarter to his adversaries. (Collection of the New-York Historical Society)

JACKSONIAN DEMOCRACY

TO many Americans in the 1820s and 1830s, Andrew Jackson was a champion of democracy, a symbol of the spirit of antielitism and egalitarianism that was sweeping American life. Historians, however, have disagreed sharply not only in their assessments of Jackson himself but in their portrayal of American society in his era.

The "progressive" historians of the early twentieth century tended to see Jacksonian politics as a forebear of their own battles against economic privilege and political corruption. Frederick Jackson Turner encouraged scholars to see Jacksonianism as a protest by the frontier against the conservative aristocracy of the East. Jackson represented those who wanted to make government responsive to the will of the people rather than to the power of special interests. The culmination of this progressive interpretation of Jacksonianism was Arthur M. Schlesinger's *The Age of Jackson*

(1945). Less interested in the regional basis of Jacksonianism than the disciples of Turner had been, Schlesinger argued that Jacksonian democracy was an effort "to control the power of the capitalist groups, mainly Eastern, for the benefit of non-capitalist groups, farmers and laboring men, East, West, and South." He portrayed Jacksonianism as an early version of modern reform efforts to "restrain the power of the business community."

Richard Hofstadter, in an influential 1948 essay, sharply disagreed. Jackson, he argued, was the spokesman of rising entrepreneurs—aspiring businessmen who saw the road to opportunity blocked by the monopolistic power of eastern aristocrats. The Jacksonian leaders were less sympathetic to the aspirations of those below them than they were to the destruction of obstacles to their own success. Bray Hammond, writing in 1957, argued similarly that the Jacksonian cause was "one of

he said, should offer "equal protection and equal benefits" to all its white male citizens and favor no one region or class over another. In practice, that meant launching an assault on what Jackson considered the citadels of the eastern aristocracy and extending opportunities to the rising classes of the West and the South.

Jackson's first target was the entrenched officeholders in the federal government, whom he bitterly denounced. Offices, he said, belonged to the people, not to a self-serving bureaucracy. Equally important, a large turnover in the bureaucracy would allow him to reward his own supporters with offices. One of Jackson's allies, William L. Marcy of New York, once explained, "To the victors belong the spoils"; and patronage, the process of giving out jobs as political rewards, became known as the "spoils system." Although Jackson removed no more than one-fifth of existing federal officeholders, his embrace of the spoils system helped cement its place in party politics.

enterpriser against capitalist." Other historians saw Jacksonianism less as a democratic reform movement than as a nostalgic effort to restore a lost past. Marvin Meyers's *The Jacksonian Persuasion* (1957) argued that Jackson and his followers looked with misgivings on the new industrial society emerging around them and yearned instead for a restoration of the agrarian, republican virtues of an earlier time.

In the 1960s, historians began taking less interest in Jackson and his supporters and more in the social and cultural bases of American politics in the time of Jackson. Lee Benson's *The Concept of Jacksonian Democracy* (1961) used quantitative techniques to demonstrate the role of religion and ethnicity in shaping party divisions. Edward Pessen's *Jacksonian America* (1969) portrayed America in the Jacksonian era as an increasingly stratified society. This inclination to look more closely at society than at formal "Jacksonianism" continued into the late twentieth and early twenty-first centuries. Sean Wilentz, in *Chants Democratic* (1984) and in *The Rise of American Democracy* (2005), examined the rise of powerful movements among ordinary citizens who were attracted less to Jackson himself than to the notion of popular democracy.

Gradually, this attention to the nature of society has led to reassessments of Jackson himself and the nature of his regime. In *Fathers and Children* (1975), Michael Rogin portrays Jackson as a leader determined to secure the supremacy of white men in the United States. Alexander Saxton, in *The Rise and Fall of the White Republic* (1990), makes the related argument that "Jacksonian Democracy" was explicitly a white man's democracy that rested on the subjugation of slaves, women, and Native Americans. But the portrayal of Jackson as a champion of the common man has not vanished from scholarship entirely. The most renowned postwar biographer of Jackson, Robert V. Remini, argues that, despite the flaws in his democratic vision, he was a genuine "man of the people." •

UNDERSTAND, ANALYZE, & EVALUATE

1. What was Jacksonian democracy? Was it a reform movement against conservative special interests? Was it a regional movement designed to shift power to the West? Or was it a class-based movement to elevate workers and farmers?
2. Jackson was known as a "man of the people." Which people were attracted to him?

Jackson's supporters also worked to transform the process by which presidential candidates were selected. In 1832, the president's followers staged a national convention to renominate him. Through the convention, its founders believed, power in the party would arise directly from the people rather than from such elite political institutions as the congressional caucus.

"OUR FEDERAL UNION"

Jackson's commitment to extending power beyond entrenched elites led him to want to reduce the functions of the federal government. A concentration of power in Washington would, he believed, restrict opportunity to only people with political connections. But Jackson was also strongly committed to the preservation of the Union. Thus, at the same time as he was promoting an economic program to reduce the power of the national government, he was asserting the supremacy of the Union in the face of a potent challenge. For no sooner had he entered office than his own vice president—John C. Calhoun—began to champion a controversial constitutional theory: nullification.

CALHOUN AND NULLIFICATION

Once an outspoken protectionist, Calhoun had strongly supported the tariff of 1816. But by the late 1820s, he had come to believe that the tariff was responsible for the stagnation of South Carolina's economy—even though the exhaustion of the state's farmland was the real reason for the decline. Some exasperated Carolinians were ready to consider a drastic remedy—secession.

With his future political hopes resting on how he met this challenge in his home state, Calhoun developed the theory of nullification. Drawing from the ideas of Madison and Jefferson and citing the Tenth Amendment to the Constitution, Calhoun argued that since the federal government was a creation of the states, the states—not the courts or Congress— were the final arbiters of the constitutionality of federal laws. If a state concluded that Congress had passed an unconstitutional law, then it could hold a special convention and declare the federal law null and void within the state. The nullification doctrine—and the idea of using it to nullify the 1828 tariff—quickly attracted broad support in South Carolina. But it did nothing to help Calhoun's standing within the new Jackson administration, in part because he had a powerful rival in Martin Van Buren.

THE RISE OF VAN BUREN

Van Buren had served briefly as governor of New York before becoming Jackson's secretary of state in 1829. He soon established himself as a member both of the official cabinet and of the president's unofficial circle of political allies, known as the "Kitchen Cabinet." And Van Buren's influence with the president grew stronger still as a result of a quarrel over etiquette that drove a wedge between Jackson and Calhoun.

Peggy O'Neale was the attractive daughter of a Washington tavern keeper with whom both Andrew Jackson and his friend John H. Eaton had taken lodgings while serving as senators from Tennessee. O'Neale was married, but rumors circulated in Washington in the mid-1820s that she and Senator Eaton were having an affair. O'Neale's husband died in 1828, and she and Eaton were soon married. A few weeks later, Jackson named Eaton secretary of war and thus made the new Mrs. Eaton a cabinet wife. The rest of the administration wives, led by Mrs. Calhoun, refused to receive her. Jackson, who blamed slanderous gossip for the death of his own wife, was furious and demanded that the members of the cabinet accept her into their social world. Calhoun, under pressure from his wife, refused. Van Buren, a widower, befriended the Eatons and thus ingratiated himself with Jackson. By 1831, Jackson had chosen Van Buren to succeed him in the White House, apparently ending Calhoun's dreams of the presidency.

THE WEBSTER-HAYNE DEBATE

In January 1830, in the midst of a routine debate over federal policy toward western lands, a senator from Connecticut suggested that all land sales and surveys be temporarily discontinued. Robert Y. Hayne, a young senator from South Carolina, charged that slowing down the growth of the West was simply a way for the East to retain its political and economic power.

Daniel Webster, now a senator from Massachusetts, attacked Hayne (and through him Calhoun), for what he considered an attack on the integrity of the Union—in effect, challenging Hayne to a debate not on the issues of public lands and the tariff but on the issue of states' rights versus national power. Hayne responded with a defense of nullification. Webster then spent two full afternoons delivering what became known as his "Second Reply to Hayne." He concluded with the ringing appeal: "Liberty and Union, now and for ever, one and inseparable!"

Both sides now waited to hear what President Jackson thought of the argument. That became clear at the annual Democratic Party banquet in honor of Thomas Jefferson. After dinner, guests delivered a series of toasts. The president arrived with a written text in which he had underscored certain words: "Our Federal Union—It must be preserved." While he spoke, he looked directly at Calhoun. The diminutive Van Buren, who stood on his chair to see better, thought he saw Calhoun's hand shake and a trickle of wine run down his glass as he responded to the president's toast with his own: "The Union, next to our liberty most dear."

THE NULLIFICATION CRISIS

In 1832, the controversy over nullification finally produced a crisis when South Carolinians responded angrily to a congressional tariff bill that offered them no relief from the 1828 tariff of abominations. Almost immediately, the legislature summoned a state convention, which voted to nullify the tariffs of 1828 and 1832 and to forbid the collection of duties within the state. At the same time, South Carolina elected Hayne to serve as governor and Calhoun to replace Hayne as senator.

Jackson insisted that nullification was treason. He strengthened the federal forts in South Carolina and ordered a warship to Charleston. When Congress convened early in 1833, Jackson proposed a force bill authorizing the president to use the military to see that acts of Congress were obeyed. Violence seemed a real possibility.

Calhoun faced a predicament as he took his place in the Senate. Not a single state had come to South Carolina's support. But the timely intervention of Henry Clay, also newly elected to the Senate, averted a crisis. Clay devised a compromise by which the tariff would be lowered gradually so that by 1842 it would reach approximately the same level as in 1816. The compromise and the force bill were passed on the same day, March 1, 1833. Jackson signed them both. In South Carolina, the convention reassembled and repealed its nullification of the tariffs. But unwilling to allow Congress to have the last word, the convention nullified the force act—a purely symbolic act, since the tariff had already been repealed. Calhoun and his followers claimed a victory for nullification, which had, they insisted, forced the revision of the tariff. But the episode taught Calhoun and his allies that no state could defy the federal government alone.

THE REMOVAL OF THE INDIANS

There had never been any doubt about Andrew Jackson's attitude toward the Indian tribes who remained in the eastern states and territories of the United States. He wanted them to move west. Since his early military expeditions in Florida, Jackson had harbored a deep hostility toward the Indians. In this he was little different from most white Americans.

WHITE ATTITUDES TOWARD THE TRIBES

In the eighteenth century, many whites had shared Thomas Jefferson's view of the Indians as "noble savages," with an inherent dignity that made civilization possible among them. By the first decades of the nineteenth century, many whites were coming to view Native Americans simply as "savages" who should be removed from all the lands east of the Mississippi. White westerners also favored removal to put an end to violence and conflict in the western areas of white settlement. Most of all, they wanted valuable land that the tribes still possessed.

Events in the Northwest added urgency to the issue of removal. In Illinois, an alliance of Sauk (or Sac) and Fox Indians under Black Hawk fought white settlers in 1831–1832 in an effort to overturn what Black Hawk considered an illegal cession of tribal lands to the United States. The Black Hawk War was notable for its viciousness. White forces attacked the Indians even when they attempted to surrender, pursued them as they retreated, and slaughtered many of them. The brutal war only reinforced the determination of whites to remove all the tribes to the West.

THE "FIVE CIVILIZED TRIBES"

Even more troubling to the government in the 1830s were the remaining Indian tribes of the South. In western Georgia, Alabama, Mississippi, and Florida lived what were known as the "Five Civilized Tribes"—the Cherokee, Creek, Seminole, Chickasaw, and Choctaw. In 1830, both the federal government and several southern states were accelerating efforts to remove the tribes to the West. Most were too weak to resist, but some fought back.

The Cherokee tried to stop Georgia from taking their lands through an appeal in the Supreme Court, and the Court's rulings in *Cherokee Nation v. Georgia* and *Worcester v. Georgia* supported the tribe's contention that the state had no authority to negotiate

BLACK HAWK AND WHIRLING THUNDER   After his defeat by white settlers in Illinois in 1832, the famed Sauk warrior Black Hawk and his son, Whirling Thunder, were captured and sent on a tour by Andrew Jackson, displayed to the public as trophies of war. They showed such dignity through the ordeal that much of the white public quickly began to sympathize with them. This portrait, by John Wesley Jarvis, was painted on the tour's final stop, in New York City. Black Hawk wears the European-style suit, while Whirling Thunder wears native costume to emphasize his commitment to his tribal roots. Soon thereafter, Black Hawk returned to his tribe, wrote a celebrated autobiography, and died in 1838. (© Bettmann/Corbis)

with tribal representatives. But Jackson repudiated the decisions, reportedly responding to news of the rulings with the contemptuous statement: "John Marshall has made his decision. Now let him enforce it." Then, in 1835, the United States government extracted a treaty from a minority faction of the Cherokee that ceded to Georgia the tribe's land in that state in return for $5 million and a reservation west of the Mississippi. The great majority of the 17,000 Cherokee did not recognize the treaty as legitimate. But Jackson sent an army of 7,000 under General Winfield Scott to round them up and drive them westward.

TRAILS OF TEARS

About 1,000 Cherokee fled to North Carolina, where eventually the federal government provided them with a small reservation in the Smoky Mountains that survives today. But most of the rest made a long, forced trek to "Indian Territory," what later became Oklahoma, beginning in the winter of 1838. Thousands, perhaps a quarter or more of the émigrés, perished before reaching their unwanted destination. In the harsh new reservations, the survivors remembered the terrible journey as "The Trail Where They Cried," the Trail of Tears.

Between 1830 and 1838, virtually all the Five Civilized Tribes were forced to travel to Indian Territory. The Choctaw of Mississippi and western Alabama were the first to make the trek, beginning in 1830. The army moved out the Creek of eastern Alabama and

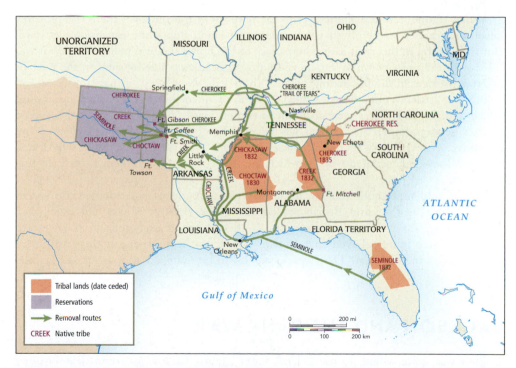

THE EXPULSION OF THE TRIBES, 1830–1835 Well before he became president, Andrew Jackson was famous for his military exploits against the tribes. Once in the White House, he ensured that few Indians would remain in the southern states of the nation, now that white settlement was increasing there. The result was a series of dramatic "removals" of Indian tribes out of their traditional lands and into new territories west of the Mississippi—mostly in Oklahoma. Note the very long distance many of these tribes had to travel. • *Why was the route of the Cherokee, shown in the upper portion of the map, known as the "Trail of Tears"?*

western Georgia in 1836. A year later, the Chickasaw in northern Mississippi began their long march westward and the Cherokee, finally, a year after that.

Only the Seminole in Florida were able to resist the pressures, and even their success was limited. Like other tribes, the Seminole had agreed under pressure to a settlement by which they ceded their lands to the United States and agreed to move to Indian Territory within three years. Most did move west, but a substantial minority, under the leadership of the chieftain Osceola, balked and staged an uprising beginning in 1835 to defend their lands. (Joining the Indians in their struggle was a group of runaway black slaves, who had been living with the tribe.) Jackson sent troops to Florida, but the Seminole and their black allies were masters of guerrilla warfare in the junglelike Everglades. Finally, in 1842, the government abandoned the war. By then, many of the Seminole had been either killed or forced westward.

THE MEANING OF REMOVAL

By the end of the 1830s, virtually all the important Indian societies east of the Mississippi had been removed to the West. The tribes had ceded over 100 million acres to the federal government and had received in return about $68 million and 32 million acres in the far less hospitable lands west of the Mississippi. There they lived, divided by tribe into a series of separate reservations, in a territory surrounded by a string of United States forts and in a region whose climate and topography bore little relation to anything they had known before.

What, if any, were the alternatives to the removal of the Indians? There was probably never any realistic possibility that the government could stop white expansion westward. But there were, in theory at least, alternatives to the brutal removal policy. The West was filled with examples of white settlers and native tribes living side by side. In the pueblos of New Mexico, in the fur trading posts of the Pacific Northwest, in parts of Texas and California, settlers from Mexico, Canada, and the United States had created societies in which Indians and whites were in intimate contact with one another. Sometimes close contact between whites and Indians was beneficial to both sides; often it was cruel and exploitive. But the early multiracial societies of the West did not separate whites and Indians. They demonstrated ways in which the two cultures could interact, each shaping the other.

By the mid-nineteenth century, however, white Americans had adopted a different model. Much as the early British settlers along the Atlantic Coast had established "plantations," from which natives were, in theory, to be excluded, so the western whites of later years believed that Indians could not be partners in the creation of new societies in the West. They were obstacles to be removed and, as far as possible, isolated.

JACKSON AND THE BANK WAR

Jackson was quite willing to use federal power against the Indian tribes. But in other contexts, he was very reluctant to use federal authority, as shown by his 1830 veto of a congressional measure providing a subsidy to the proposed Maysville Road in Kentucky. The bill was unconstitutional, Jackson argued, because the road in question lay entirely within Kentucky and was not, therefore, a part of "interstate commerce." Jackson also thought the bill unwise because it committed the government to what he considered extravagant expenditures. A similar resistance to federal power lay behind Jackson's war against the Bank of the United States.

BIDDLE'S INSTITUTION

The Bank of the United States held a monopoly on federal deposits, provided credit to growing enterprises, issued banknotes that served as a dependable medium of exchange, and exercised a restraining effect on the less well-managed state banks. Nicholas Biddle, who ran the Bank from 1823 on, had done much to put the institution on a sound and prosperous basis. Nevertheless, many Americans—among them Andrew Jackson—were determined to destroy it.

Opposition to the Bank came from two very different groups: the "soft-money" and "hard-money" factions. Advocates of soft money consisted largely of state bankers and their allies. They objected to the Bank because it restrained state banks from issuing notes freely. The hard-money faction believed that coin was the only safe currency, and they condemned *all* banks that issued banknotes, state or federal. The soft-money advocates believed in rapid economic growth and speculation; the hard-money forces embraced older ideas of "public virtue" and looked with suspicion on expansion and speculation. Jackson himself supported the hard-money position, and he made clear that he would not favor renewing the charter of the Bank of the United States, which was due to expire in 1836.

A Philadelphia aristocrat unaccustomed to politics, Biddle nevertheless began granting banking favors to influential men. In particular, he relied on Daniel Webster, whom he named the Bank's legal counsel and director of the Boston branch. Webster helped Biddle enlist the support of Henry Clay as well. Clay, Webster, and other advisers persuaded Biddle to apply to Congress for a recharter bill in 1832, four years ahead of the expiration date. Congress passed the recharter bill; Jackson vetoed it; and the Bank's supporters in Congress failed to override the veto. The Bank question then emerged as the paramount issue of the 1832 election, just as Clay had hoped.

In 1832, Clay ran for president as the unanimous choice of the Whigs. But the "Bank War" failed to provide Clay with the winning issue he had hoped for. Jackson, with Van Buren as his running mate, won an overwhelming victory with 55 percent of the popular vote and 219 electoral votes.

THE "MONSTER" DESTROYED

Jackson was now more determined than ever to destroy the "monster." He could not legally abolish the Bank before the expiration of its charter. But he weakened it by removing the government's deposits from it. When his secretary of the treasury, believing that such an action would destabilize the financial system, refused to give the order, Jackson fired him and appointed a replacement. When the new secretary similarly procrastinated, Jackson fired him, too, and named a third: Roger B. Taney, the attorney general, a close friend and loyal ally of the president.

Taney soon began taking the government's deposits out of the Bank of the United States and putting them in a number of state banks. In response, Biddle called in loans and raised interest rates, explaining that without the government deposits the Bank's resources were stretched too thin. His actions precipitated a short recession.

As financial conditions worsened in the winter of 1833–1834, supporters of the Bank sent petitions to Washington urging its rechartering. But the Jacksonians blamed the recession on Biddle and refused. When the banker finally carried his contraction of credit too far and had to reverse himself to appease the business community, his hopes of winning a recharter of the Bank died in the process. Jackson had won a considerable political victory. But when the Bank of the United States died in 1836, the country was left with a fragmented and chronically unstable banking system that would plague the economy for many years.

THE TANEY COURT

In the aftermath of the Bank War, Jackson moved against the most powerful remaining institution of economic nationalism: the Supreme Court. In 1835, when John Marshall died, the president appointed as the new chief justice his trusted ally Roger B. Taney. Taney did not bring a sharp break in constitutional interpretation, but he did help modify Marshall's vigorous nationalism.

Perhaps the clearest indication of the new judicial climate was the celebrated case of *Charles River Bridge v. Warren Bridge* of 1837. The case involved a dispute between two Massachusetts companies over the right to build a bridge across the Charles River between Boston and Cambridge. One company had a long-standing charter from the state to operate a toll bridge, a charter that the firm claimed guaranteed it a monopoly of the bridge traffic. Another company had applied to the legislature for authorization to construct a second, competing bridge that would—since it would be toll-free—greatly reduce the value of the first company's charter. The first company contended that in granting the second charter, the legislature was engaging in a breach of contract; and it noted that the Marshall Court, in the *Dartmouth College* case and other decisions, had ruled that states had no right to abrogate contracts. But now Taney supported the right of Massachusetts to award the second charter. The object of government, Taney maintained, was to promote the general happiness, an object that took precedence over the rights of property. A state, therefore, had the right to amend or abrogate a contract if such action was necessary to advance the well-being of the community. The decision reflected one of the cornerstones of the Jacksonian idea: that the key to democracy was an expansion of economic opportunity, which would not occur if older corporations could maintain monopolies.

THE CHANGING FACE OF AMERICAN POLITICS

Jackson's forceful—some people claimed tyrannical—tactics in crushing first the nullification movement and then the Bank of the United States helped galvanize a growing opposition coalition. It began as a gathering of national political leaders opposed to Jackson's use of power. Denouncing the president as "King Andrew I," they began to refer to themselves as Whigs, after the party in England that traditionally worked to limit the power of the king. With the emergence of the Whigs, the nation once again had two competing political parties. What scholars now call the "second party system" had begun its relatively brief life.

DEMOCRATS AND WHIGS

The philosophy of the Democratic Party in the 1830s bore the stamp of Andrew Jackson. The federal government, the Democrats believed, should be limited in power, except to the degree that it worked to eliminate social and economic arrangements that entrenched privilege and stifled opportunity. The rights of states should be protected except to the extent that state governments interfered with social and economic mobility. Jacksonian Democrats celebrated "honest workers," "simple farmers," and "forthright businessmen" and contrasted them to the corrupt, monopolistic, aristocratic forces of established wealth. Democrats were more likely than Whigs to support territorial expansion, which would, they believed, widen opportunities for aspiring Americans. Among the most radical members of the party—the so-called Locofocos, mainly workingmen, small businessmen, and professionals in the Northeast—sentiment was strong for a vigorous, perhaps even violent, assault on monopoly and privilege.

In contrast, the political philosophy that became known as Whiggery favored the expansion of federal power and industrial and commercial development. Whigs were cautious about westward expansion, fearful that rapid territorial growth would produce instability. And although Whigs insisted that their vision would result in increasing opportunities for all Americans, they tended to attribute particular value to the entrepreneurs and institutions that most effectively promoted economic growth.

The Whigs were strongest among the more substantial merchants and manufacturers of the Northeast, the wealthier planters of the South, and the ambitious farmers and rising commercial class of the West. The Democrats drew more support from smaller merchants and the workingmen of the Northeast; from southern planters suspicious of industrial growth; and from westerners who favored a predominantly agrarian economy. Whigs tended to be wealthier, to have more aristocratic backgrounds, and to be more commercially ambitious than the Democrats. But Whigs and Democrats alike were more interested in winning elections than in maintaining philosophical purity. And both parties made adjustments from region to region to attract the largest possible number of voters.

In New York, for example, the Whigs developed a popular following through a movement known as Anti-Masonry. The Anti-Mason Party had emerged in the 1820s in response to widespread resentment against the secret and exclusive, hence supposedly undemocratic, Society of Freemasons. Such resentment increased in 1826 when a former Mason, William Morgan, mysteriously disappeared from his home in Batavia, New York, shortly before he was scheduled to publish a book that would allegedly expose the secrets of Freemasonry. With help from a widespread assumption that Morgan had been abducted and murdered by vengeful Masons, Whigs seized on the Anti-Mason frenzy to launch spirited attacks on Jackson and Van Buren (both Freemasons), implying that the Democrats were connected with the antidemocratic conspiracy.

Religious and ethnic divisions also played an important role in determining the constituencies of the two parties. Irish and German Catholics tended to support the Democrats, who appeared to share their own vague aversion to commercial development and who seemed to respect their cultural values. Evangelical Protestants gravitated toward the Whigs because they associated the party with constant development and improvement. They envisioned a society progressing steadily toward unity and order, and they looked on the new immigrant communities as groups that needed to be disciplined and taught "American" ways.

The Whig Party was more successful at defining its positions and attracting a constituency than it was at uniting behind a national leader. No one person was ever able to command the loyalties of the party in the way Jackson commanded those of the Democrats. Instead, Whigs tended to divide their allegiance among the "Great Triumvirate" of Henry Clay, Daniel Webster, and John C. Calhoun.

Clay won support from many who favored internal improvements and economic development with what he called the American System. But Clay's image as a devious political operator and his identification with the West were a liability. He ran for president three times and never won. Daniel Webster won broad support among the Whigs with his passionate speeches in defense of the Constitution and the Union; but his close connection with the Bank of the United States and the protective tariff, his reliance on rich men for financial support, and his excessive fondness for brandy prevented him from developing enough of a national constituency to win him his desired office. John C. Calhoun never considered himself a true Whig, and his identification with the nullification controversy in effect disqualified him from national leadership in any case. Yet he sided with Clay and Webster on the issue of the national bank, and he shared with them a strong animosity toward Andrew Jackson.

The Whigs competed relatively evenly with the Democrats in congressional, state, and local races, but they managed to win only two presidential elections in the more than twenty years of their history. Their problems became particularly clear in 1836. While the Democrats united behind Andrew Jackson's personal choice for president, Martin Van Buren, the Whigs could not even agree on a single candidate. Instead, they ran several candidates in different regions, hoping they might separately draw enough votes from Van Buren to throw the election to the House of Representatives, where the Whigs might be better able to elect one of their candidates. In the end, however, Van Buren won easily, with 170 electoral votes to 124 for all his opponents.

POLITICS AFTER JACKSON

Andrew Jackson retired from public life in 1837, the most beloved political figure of his age. Martin Van Buren was less fortunate. He could not match Jackson's personal magnetism, and his administration suffered from economic difficulties that hurt both him and his party.

VAN BUREN AND THE PANIC OF 1837

Van Buren's success in the 1836 election was a result in part of a nationwide economic boom. Canal and railroad builders were at a peak of activity.

Prices were rising, credit was plentiful, and the land business, in particular, was booming. Between 1835 and 1837, the government sold nearly 40 million acres of public land, nearly three-fourths of it to speculators. These land sales, along with revenues the government received from the tariff of 1833, created a series of substantial federal budget surpluses and made possible a steady reduction of the national debt. From 1835 to 1837, the government for the first and only time in its history was out of debt, with a substantial surplus in the Treasury.

Congress and the administration now faced the question of what to do with the Treasury surplus. Support soon grew for returning the federal surplus to the states. An 1836 "distribution" act required the federal government to pay its surplus funds to the states each year in four quarterly installments as interest-free, unsecured loans. No one expected the "loans" to be repaid. The states spent the money quickly, mainly to promote the construction of highways, railroads, and canals. The distribution of the surplus thus gave further stimulus to the economic boom. At the same time, the withdrawal of federal funds strained the state banks in which they had been deposited by the government; the banks had to call in their own loans to make the transfer of funds to the state governments.

Congress did nothing to check the speculative fever. But Jackson feared that the government was selling land for state banknotes of questionable value. In 1836, he issued an executive order, the "specie circular." It provided that in payment for public lands, the government would accept only gold or silver coins or currency backed by gold or silver. The specie circular produced a financial panic that began in the first months of Van Buren's presidency. Banks and businesses failed; unemployment grew; bread riots occurred in some of the larger cities; and prices fell, especially the price of land. Many railroad and canal projects failed; several of the debt-burdened state governments ceased to pay interest on their bonds, and a few repudiated their debts, at least temporarily. The worst depression in American history to that point, it lasted for five years, and it was a political catastrophe for Van Buren and the Democrats.

The Van Buren administration did little to fight the depression. In fact, some of the steps it took—borrowing money to pay government debts and accepting only specie for payment of taxes—may have made things worse. Other efforts failed in Congress: a "preemption" bill that would have given settlers the right to buy government land near them before it was opened for public sale, and another bill that would have lowered the price of land. Van Buren did succeed in establishing a ten-hour workday on all federal projects via a presidential order, but he had few legislative achievements.

The most important and controversial measure in the president's program was a proposal for a new financial system. Under Van Buren's plan, known as the "independent treasury" or "subtreasury" system, government funds would be placed in an independent treasury in Washington and in subtreasuries in other cities. No private banks would have the government's money or name to use as a basis for speculation. Van Buren called a special session of Congress in 1837 to consider the proposal, but it failed in the House. In 1840, however, the administration finally succeeded in driving the measure through both houses of Congress.

THE LOG CABIN CAMPAIGN

As the campaign of 1840 approached, the Whigs realized that they would have to settle on one candidate for president. In December 1839, they held their first nominating convention. Passing over Henry Clay, they chose William Henry Harrison, a renowned soldier and a popular national figure. The Democrats again nominated Van Buren.

The 1840 campaign was the first in which the new and popular "penny press" carried news of the candidates to large audiences. Such newspapers were deliberately livelier and more sensationalist than the newspapers of the past, which had been almost entirely directed at the upper classes. The *New York Sun,* the first of the new breed, began publishing in 1833 and was from the beginning self-consciously egalitarian. It soon had the largest circulation in New York. Other, similar papers soon began appearing in other cities—reinforcing the increasingly democratic character of political culture and encouraging the inclination of both parties to try to appeal to ordinary voters as they planned their campaigns.

The campaign of 1840 also illustrated how fully the spirit of party competition had established itself in America. The Whigs—who had emerged as a party largely because of their opposition to Andrew Jackson's common-man democracy—presented themselves in

THE PENNY PRESS

ON September 3, 1833, a small newspaper appeared in New York City for the first time: the *New York Sun*, published by a young former apprentice from Massachusetts named Benjamin Day. Four pages long, it contained mostly trivial local news, with particular emphasis on sex, crime, and violence. It sold for a penny, launching a new age in the history of American journalism, the age of the "penny press."

Before the advent of the penny press, newspapers in America were far too expensive for most ordinary citizens to buy. But several important changes in both the business of journalism and the character of American society paved the way for Benjamin Day and others to challenge the established press. New technologies—the steam-powered cylinder printing press, new machines for making paper, railroads and canals for distributing issues to a larger market—made it possible to publish newspapers inexpensively and to sell them widely. A rising popular literacy rate, a result, in part, of the spread of public education, created a bigger reading public.

THE NEW YORK *SUN* This 1834 front page of *The Sun*, which had begun publication a year earlier, contains advertisements, human interest stories, a description of a slave auction in Charleston, S.C., and homespun advice: "Life is short. The poor pittance of several years is not worth being a villain for." (Collection of the New-York Historical Society)

The penny press was also a response to the changing culture of the 1820s and 1830s. The spread of an urban market economy contributed to the growth of the penny press by drawing a large population

1840 as the party of the common people. So, of course, did the Democrats. Both parties used the same techniques of mass voter appeal; what mattered was not the philosophical purity of the party but its ability to win votes. The Whig campaign was particularly effective in portraying William Henry Harrison, a wealthy member of the frontier elite with a considerable estate, as a simple man of the people who loved log cabins and hard cider. The Democrats, already weakened by the depression, had no effective defense against such tactics. Harrison won the election with 234 electoral votes to 60 for Van Buren and with a popular majority of 53 percent.

of workers, artisans, and clerks into large cities, where they became an important market for the new papers. The spirit of democracy—symbolized by the popularity of Andrew Jackson and the rising numbers of white male voters across the country—helped create an appetite for journalism that spoke to and for "the people." The *Sun* and other papers like it were committed to feeding the appetites of the people of modest means, who constituted most of their readership. "Human-interest stories" helped solidify their hold on the working public.

Within six months of its first issue, the *Sun* had the largest circulation in New York—8,000 readers, more than twice the number of its nearest competitors. James Gordon Bennett's *New York Herald*, which began publication in 1835, soon surpassed the *Sun* in popularity, with its lively combination of sensationalism and local gossip and its aggressive pursuit of national and international stories. The *Herald* pioneered a "letters to the editor" column, was the first paper to have regular reviews of books and the arts, and launched the first daily sports section. By 1860, its circulation of more than 77,000 was the largest of any daily newspaper in the world.

Not all the new penny papers were as sensationalistic as the *Sun* and the *Herald*. The *New York Tribune*, founded in 1841 by Horace Greeley, prided itself on serious reporting and commentary. As serious as the *Tribune*, but more sober and self-consciously "objective" in its reportage, was the *New York Times*, which Henry Raymond founded in 1851. "We do not mean to write as if we were in a passion—unless that shall really be the case," the *Times* huffily proclaimed in its first issue, in an obvious reference to Greeley and his impassioned reportage, "and we shall make it a point to get into a passion as rarely as possible."

The newspapers of the penny press initiated the process of turning journalism into a profession. They were the first papers to pay their reporters, and they were also the first to rely heavily on advertisements, often devoting up to half their space to paid advertising. They tended to be sensationalistic and opinionated, but they were also usually aggressive in uncovering serious and important news—in police stations, courts, jails, streets, and private homes as well as in city halls, state capitals, Washington, and the world. •

UNDERSTAND, ANALYZE, & EVALUATE

1. How were the penny press newspapers a product of the Jacksonian era?
2. Before the advent of the penny press, newspapers in America were aimed at a much narrower audience. Some published mainly business news, and others worked to advance the aims of a political party. What nationally circulated newspapers and other media today continue this tradition?

THE FRUSTRATION OF THE WHIGS

Despite their decisive victory, the Whigs found the four years after their resounding victory frustrating and divisive. In large part, that was because their appealing new president died of pneumonia one month after taking office. Vice President John Tyler of Virginia succeeded him.

Tyler was a former Democrat who had left the party in reaction to what he considered Jackson's excessively egalitarian program; Tyler's approach to public policy still showed signs of his Democratic past. The president did agree to bills abolishing Van Buren's

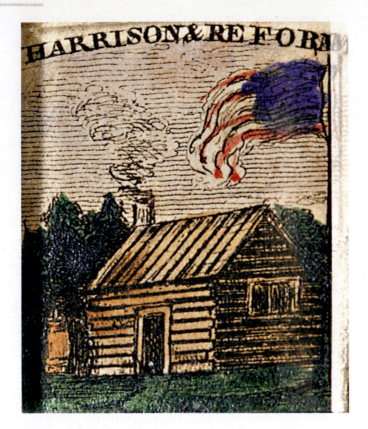

HARRISON AND REFORM This hand-colored engraving was made for a brass brooch during the 1840 presidential campaign and served the same purposes that modern campaign buttons do. It conveys Harrison's presumably humble beginnings in a log cabin. In reality, Harrison was a wealthy, aristocratic man; but the unpopularity of the aristocratic airs of his opponent, President Martin Van Buren, persuaded the Whig Party that it would be good political strategy to portray Harrison as a humble "man of the people." (© David J. & Janice L. Frent Collection/Corbis)

independent-treasury system and raising tariff rates. But he refused to support Clay's attempt to recharter the Bank of the United States, and he vetoed several internal improvement bills sponsored by Clay and other congressional Whigs. Finally, a conference of congressional Whigs read Tyler out of the party. Every cabinet member but Webster, who was serving as secretary of state, resigned; five former Democrats took their places. When Webster, too, left the cabinet, Tyler appointed Calhoun, who had rejoined the Democratic Party, to replace him.

A new political alignment was taking shape. Tyler and a small band of conservative southern Whigs were preparing to rejoin the Democrats. Into the common man's party of Jackson and Van Buren was arriving a faction with decidedly aristocratic political ideas, men who thought that government had an obligation to protect and even expand the institution of slavery and who believed in states' rights with almost fanatical devotion.

WHIG DIPLOMACY

In the midst of these domestic controversies, anti-British factions in Canada launched an unsuccessful rebellion against the colonial government there in 1837. When the insurrection failed, some of the rebels took refuge near the United States border and chartered an American steamship, the *Caroline,* to ship them supplies across the Niagara River from New York. British authorities in Canada seized the *Caroline* and burned it, killing one American in the process. Resentment in the United States grew rapidly. At the same time, tensions flared over the boundary between Canada and Maine, which had been in dispute since the treaty of 1783. In 1838, rival groups of Americans and Canadians, mostly lumberjacks, began moving into the Aroostook River region in the disputed area, precipitating a violent brawl that became known as the "Aroostook War."

Several years later, in 1841, an American ship, the *Creole,* sailed from Virginia for New Orleans with more than 100 slaves aboard. En route the slaves mutinied, seized possession of the ship, and took it to the Bahamas. British officials there declared the slaves free, and the English government refused to overrule them. Many Americans, especially southerners, were furious.

At this critical juncture, a new government eager to reduce tensions with the United States came to power in Great Britain. It sent Lord Ashburton, an admirer of America, to negotiate an agreement on the Maine boundary and other matters. The result was the Webster-Ashburton Treaty of 1842, under which the United States received slightly more than half the disputed area and agreed to a revised northern boundary as far west as the Rocky Mountains. Ashburton also eased the memory of the *Caroline* and *Creole* affairs by expressing regret and promising no future "officious interference" with American ships. Anglo-American relations improved significantly.

During the Tyler administration, the United States established its first diplomatic relations with China. In the 1844 Treaty of Wang Hya, American diplomats secured the same trading privileges as the English. In the next ten years, American trade with China steadily increased.

In their diplomatic efforts, at least, the Whigs were able to secure some important successes. But by the end of the Tyler administration, the party could look back on few other victories. And in the election of 1844, the Whigs lost the White House to James K. Polk, a Democrat with an explicit agenda of westward expansion.

CONCLUSION

The election of Andrew Jackson in 1828 reflected the emergence of a new political world. Throughout the American nation, the laws governing political participation were loosening, and the number of people permitted to vote (which eventually included most white males, but almost no one else) was increasing. Along with this expansion of the electorate was emerging a new spirit of party politics.

Jackson set out as president to entrench his party, the Democrats, in power. A fierce defender of the West and a sharp critic of what he considered the stranglehold of the aristocratic East on the nation's economic life, he sought to limit the role of the federal government in economic affairs and worked to destroy the Bank of the United States, which he considered a corrupt vehicle of aristocratic influence. And he confronted the greatest challenge yet to American unity—the nullification crisis of 1832–1833—with a strong assertion of the power and importance of the Union. These positions won him broad popularity and ensured his reelection in 1832 and the election of his designated successor, Martin Van Buren, in 1836.

But a new coalition of anti-Jacksonians, who called themselves the Whigs, launched a powerful new party that used much of the same anti-elitist rhetoric to win support for their own, much more nationalist program. Their emergence culminated in the campaign of 1840 with the election of the first Whig president.

RECALL AND REFLECT

1. What was Andrew Jackson's political philosophy, and how was it reflected in the policies and actions of his administration?
2. Who benefited under Jacksonian democracy? Who suffered?
3. How did Andrew Jackson change the office of the presidency?
4. Who supported and who opposed the Bank of the United States, and why? Who was right?
5. How and why did white attitudes toward Native Americans change, and how did these changes lead to the Indian Removal Act and the Trail of Tears?

10 | AMERICA'S ECONOMIC REVOLUTION

THE CHANGING AMERICAN POPULATION

TRANSPORTATION AND COMMUNICATIONS REVOLUTIONS

COMMERCE AND INDUSTRY

MEN AND WOMEN AT WORK

PATTERNS OF SOCIETY

THE AGRICULTURAL NORTH

LOOKING AHEAD

1. What were the factors in the U.S. economic revolution of the mid-nineteenth century?
2. How did the U.S. population change between 1820 and 1840, and how did the population change affect the nation's economy, society, and politics?
3. Why did America's industrial revolution affect the northern economy and society differently than it did the southern economy and society?

WHEN THE UNITED STATES ENTERED the War of 1812, it was still an essentially agrarian nation. There were, to be sure, some substantial cities in America and also modest but growing manufacturing, mainly in the Northeast. But the overwhelming majority of Americans were farmers and tradespeople.

By the time the Civil War began in 1861, the United States had transformed itself. Most Americans were still rural people. But even most farmers were now part of a national, and even international, market economy. Equally important, the United States was beginning to challenge the industrial nations of Europe for supremacy in manufacturing. The nation had experienced the beginning of its industrial revolution.

THE CHANGING AMERICAN POPULATION

The American industrial revolution was a result of many factors: advances in transportation and communications, the growth of manufacturing technology, the development of new systems of business organization, and perhaps above all, population growth.

POPULATION TRENDS

Three trends characterized the American population between 1820 and 1840: rapid population increase, movement westward, and the growth of towns and cities where demand for work was expanding.

The American population, 4 million in 1790, had reached 10 million by 1820 and 17 million by 1840. Improvements in public health played a role in this growth. Epidemics declined in both frequency and intensity, and the death rate as a whole declined. But the population increase was also a result of a high birth rate. In 1840, white women bore an average of 6.14 children each.

The African American population increased more slowly than the white population. After 1808, when the importation of slaves became illegal, the proportion of blacks to whites in the nation as a whole steadily declined. The slower increase of the black population was also a result of its comparatively high death rate. Slave mothers had large families, but life was shorter for both slaves and free blacks than for whites—a result of the enforced poverty in which virtually all African Americans lived.

Immigration, choked off by wars in Europe and economic crises in America, contributed little to the American population in the first three decades of the nineteenth century. Of the total 1830 population of nearly 13 million, the foreign-born numbered fewer than 500,000. Soon, however, immigration began to grow once again. Reduced transportation costs and increasing economic opportunities helped stimulate the immigration boom, as did deteriorating economic conditions in some areas of Europe. The migrations introduced new groups to the United States, most notably immigrants from the southern (Catholic) counties of Ireland.

Much of this new European immigration flowed into the rapidly growing cities of the Northeast. But urban growth was a result of substantial internal migration as well. As agriculture in New England and other areas grew less profitable, more and more people picked up stakes and moved—some to promising agricultural regions in the West, but many to eastern cities.

IMMIGRATION AND URBAN GROWTH, 1840–1860

The growth of cities accelerated dramatically between 1840 and 1860. The population of New York, for example, rose from 312,000 to 805,000, making it the nation's largest and most commercially important city. Philadelphia's population grew over the same twenty-year period from 220,000 to 565,000; Boston's, from 93,000 to 177,000. By 1860, 26 percent of the population of the free states was living in towns (places of 2,500 people or more) or cities, up from 14 percent in 1840. The urban population of the South, by contrast, increased from 6 percent in 1840 to only 10 percent in 1860.

The booming agricultural economy of the West produced significant urban growth as well. Between 1820 and 1840, communities that had once been small villages or trading posts became major cities: St. Louis, Pittsburgh, Cincinnati, Louisville. All became centers of the growing carrying trade that connected the farmers of the Midwest with New Orleans and, through it, the cities of the Northeast. After 1830, however, an increasing proportion of this trade moved from the Mississippi River to the Great Lakes, creating such important new port cities as Buffalo, Detroit, Milwaukee, and Chicago, which gradually overtook the river ports.

Immigration from Europe swelled. Between 1840 and 1850, more than 1.5 million Europeans moved to America. In the 1850s, the number rose to 2.5 million. Almost half the residents of New York City in the 1850s were recent immigrants. In St. Louis, Chicago, and Milwaukee, the foreign-born outnumbered those of native birth. Few immigrants settled in the South.

The newcomers came from many different countries, but the overwhelming majority came from Ireland and Germany. By 1860, there were more than 1.5 million Irish-born and approximately 1 million German-born people in the United States. Most of the Irish stayed in the eastern cities where they landed and became part of the unskilled labor force. The largest single group of Irish immigrants comprised young, single women, who worked in factories or in domestic service. Germans, who—unlike the Irish—usually arrived with at least some money and often came in family groups, generally moved on to the Northwest, where they became farmers or small businessmen.

THE RISE OF NATIVISM

Many politicians, particularly Democrats, eagerly courted the support of the new arrivals. Other older citizens, however, viewed the growing foreign population with alarm. Some people argued that the immigrants were racially inferior or that they corrupted politics by selling their votes. Others complained that they were stealing jobs from the native workforce. Protestants worried that the growing Irish population would increase the power of

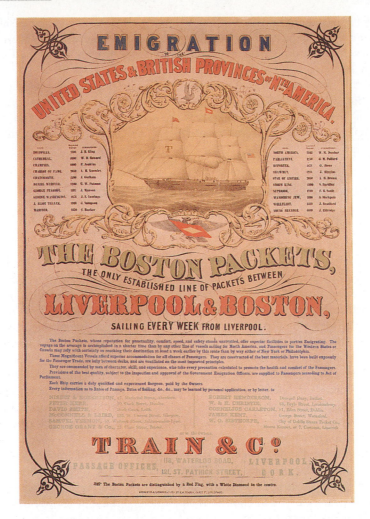

AN APPEAL TO EMIGRANTS   This widely distributed advertising card was one of many appeals to potential English and Irish travelers to America in the 1830s and 1840s. Like many such companies, the Boston Packets tried to attract both affluent passengers (by boasting of "superior accommodations") and working-class people of modest means. (Courtesy of The Bostonian Society/Old State House)

the Catholic Church in America. Older-stock Americans feared that immigrants would become a radical force in politics. Out of these fears and prejudices emerged a number of secret societies to combat the "alien menace."

The first was the Native American Association, founded in 1837, which in 1845 became the Native American Party. In 1850, it joined with other nativist groups to form the Supreme Order of the Star-Spangled Banner, whose demands included banning Catholics or aliens from holding public office, enacting more restrictive naturalization laws, and establishing literacy tests for voting. The order adopted a strict code of secrecy, which included a secret password: "I know nothing." Ultimately, members of the movement came to be known as the "Know-Nothings."

After the 1852 elections, the Know-Nothings created a new political organization that they called the American Party. It scored an immediate and astonishing success in the elections of 1854. The Know-Nothings did well in Pennsylvania and New York and actually won control of the state government in Massachusetts. Outside the Northeast, however, their progress was more modest. After 1854, the strength of the Know-Nothings declined, and the party soon disappeared.

TRANSPORTATION AND COMMUNICATIONS REVOLUTIONS

Just as the industrial revolution required an expanding population, it also required an efficient system of transportation and communications. The first half of the nineteenth century saw dramatic changes in both.

THE CANAL AGE

From 1790 until the 1820s, the so-called turnpike era, the United States had relied largely on roads for internal transportation. But roads alone were not adequate for the nation's expanding needs. And so, in the 1820s and 1830s, Americans began to turn to other means of transportation as well.

The larger rivers became increasingly important as steamboats replaced the slow barges that had previously dominated water traffic. The new riverboats carried the corn and wheat of northwestern farmers and the cotton and tobacco of southwestern planters to New Orleans, where oceangoing ships took the cargoes on to eastern ports or abroad.

But this roundabout river-sea route satisfied neither western farmers nor eastern merchants, who wanted a way to ship goods directly to the urban markets and ports of the Atlantic Coast. New highways across the mountains provided a partial solution to the problem. But the costs of hauling goods overland, although lower than before, were still too high for anything except the most compact and valuable merchandise. And so interest grew in building canals.

The job of financing canals fell largely to the states. New York was the first to act. It had the natural advantage of a good land route between the Hudson River and Lake Erie through the only break in the Appalachian chain. But the engineering tasks were still imposing. The more than 350-mile-long route was interrupted by high ridges and thick woods. After a long public debate, canal advocates prevailed, and digging began on July 4, 1817.

The Erie Canal was the greatest construction project Americans had ever undertaken. The canal itself was basically a simple ditch forty feet wide and four feet deep, with towpaths along the banks for the horses or mules that were to draw the canal boats. But its construction involved hundreds of difficult cuts and fills to enable the canal to pass through hills and over valleys, stone aqueducts to carry it across streams, and eighty-eight locks, of heavy masonry with great wooden gates, to permit ascents and descents. Still, the Erie Canal opened in October 1825, amid elaborate ceremonies and celebrations, and traffic was soon so heavy that within about seven years, tolls had repaid the entire cost of construction. By providing a route to the Great Lakes, the canal gave New York access to Chicago and the growing markets of the West. The Erie Canal also contributed to the decline of agriculture in New England. Now that it was so much cheaper for western farmers to ship their crops east, people farming marginal land in the Northeast found themselves unable to compete.

The system of water transportation extended farther when Ohio and Indiana, inspired by the success of the Erie Canal, provided water connections between Lake Erie and the

CANALS IN THE NORTHEAST, 1823–1860 The great success of the Erie Canal, which opened in 1825, inspired decades of energetic canal building in many areas of the United States, as this map illustrates. But none of the new canals had anything like the impact of the original Erie Canal, and thus none of New York's competitors—among them Baltimore, Philadelphia, and Boston—were able to displace it as the nation's leading commercial center. • *What form of transportation ultimately displaced the canals?*

Ohio River. These canals made it possible to ship goods by inland waterways all the way from New York to New Orleans.

One of the immediate results of these new transportation routes was increased white settlement in the Northwest, because it was now easier for migrants to make the westward journey and to ship their goods back to eastern markets. Much of the western produce continued to go downriver to New Orleans, but an increasing proportion went east to New York. And manufactured goods from throughout the East now moved in growing volume through New York and then to the West via the new water routes.

Rival cities along the Atlantic seaboard took alarm at New York's access to (and control over) so vast a market, largely at their expense. But they had limited success in catching up. Boston, its way to the Hudson River blocked by the Berkshire Mountains, did not even try to connect itself to the West by canal. Philadelphia, Baltimore, Richmond, and Charleston all aspired to build water routes to the Ohio Valley but never completed them. Some cities, however, saw opportunities in a different and newer means of transportation. Even before the canal age had reached its height, the era of the railroad was beginning.

The Early Railroads

Railroads played a relatively small role in the nation's transportation system in the 1820s and 1830s, but railroad pioneers laid the groundwork in those years for the great surge of railroad building in the midcentury. Eventually, railroads became the primary transportation system for the United States, as well as critical sites of development for innovations in technology and corporate organization.

RACING ON THE RAILROAD   Peter Cooper designed and built the first steam-powered locomotives in America in 1830 for the Baltimore and Ohio Railroad. On August 28 of that year, he raced his locomotive (the "Tom Thumb") against a horse-drawn railroad car. This sketch depicts the moment when Cooper's engine overtook the horse-drawn railroad car. *(History of the United States from the Earliest Discovery of American to the Present Day, Volume III* (New York: Charles Scribner's Sons, 1895)III:136.)

Railroads emerged from a combination of technological and entrepreneurial innovations: the invention of tracks, the creation of steam-powered locomotives, and the development of trains as public carriers of passengers and freight. By 1804, both English and American inventors had experimented with steam engines for propelling land vehicles. In 1820, John Stevens ran a locomotive and cars around a circular track on his New Jersey estate. And in 1825, the Stockton and Darlington Railroad in England became the first line to carry general traffic.

American entrepreneurs quickly grew interested in the English experiment. The first company to begin actual operations was the Baltimore and Ohio, which opened a thirteen-mile stretch of track in 1830. In New York, the Mohawk and Hudson began running trains along the sixteen miles between Schenectady and Albany in 1831. By 1836, more than a thousand miles of track had been laid in eleven states.

THE TRIUMPH OF THE RAILS

Railroads gradually supplanted canals and all other forms of transport. In 1840, the total railroad trackage of the country was under 3,000 miles. By 1860, it was over 27,000, miles, mostly in the Northeast. Railroads even crossed the Mississippi at several points by great iron bridges. Chicago eventually became the rail center of the West, securing its place as the dominant city of the West.

The emergence of the great train lines diverted traffic from the main water routes—the Erie Canal and the Mississippi River. By lessening the dependence of the West on the Mississippi, the railroads also helped weaken further the connection between the Northwest and the South.

Railroad construction required massive amounts of capital. Some came from private sources, but much of it came from government funding. State and local governments invested in railroads, but even greater assistance came from the federal government in the form of public land grants. By 1860, Congress had allotted over 30 million acres to eleven states to assist railroad construction.

It would be difficult to exaggerate the impact of the rails on the American economy, on American society, even on American culture. Where railroads went, towns, ranches, and farms grew up rapidly along their routes. Areas once cut off from markets during winter found that the railroad could transport goods to and from them year-round. Most

RAILROAD GROWTH, 1850–1860 These two maps illustrate the dramatic growth of American railroads in the 1850s. Note the particularly extensive increase in mileage in the upper Midwest (known at the time as the Northwest). Note, too, the relatively smaller increase in railroad mileage in the South. Railroads forged a close economic relationship between the upper Midwest and the Northeast and weakened the Midwest's relationship with the South. • *How did this contribute to the South's growing sense of insecurity within the Union?*

of all, the railroads cut the time of shipment and travel. In the 1830s, traveling from New York to Chicago by lake and canal took roughly three weeks. By railroad in the 1850s, the same trip took less than two days.

The railroads were much more than a fast and economically attractive form of transportation. They were also a breeding ground for technological advances, a key to the nation's economic growth, and the birthplace of the modern corporate form of organization. They became a symbol of the nation's technological prowess. To many people, railroads were the most visible sign of American progress and greatness.

THE TELEGRAPH

What the railroad was to transportation, the telegraph was to communication—a dramatic advance over traditional methods and a symbol of national progress and technological expertise.

Before the telegraph, communication over great distances could be achieved only by direct, physical contact. That meant that virtually all long-distance communication relied on the mail, which traveled first on horseback and coach and later by railroad. There were obvious disadvantages to this system, not the least of which was the difficulty in coordinating the railroad schedules. By the 1830s, experiments with many methods of improving long-distance communication had been conducted, among them a procedure for using the sun and reflective devices to send light signals as far as 187 miles.

In 1832, Samuel F. B. Morse—a professor of art with an interest in science—began experimenting with a different system. Fascinated with the possibilities of electricity, Morse set out to find a way to send signals along an electric cable. Technology did not yet permit the use of electric wiring to send reproductions of the human voice or any complex information. But Morse realized that electricity itself could serve as a communication device—that pulses of electricity could themselves become a kind of language. He experimented at first with a numerical code, in which each number would represent a word on a list available to recipients. Gradually, however, he became convinced of the need to find a more universal telegraphic "language," and he developed what became the Morse code, in which alternating long and short bursts of electric current would represent individual letters.

In 1843, Congress appropriated $30,000 for the construction of an experimental telegraph line between Baltimore and Washington; in May 1844 it was complete, and Morse succeeded in transmitting the news of James K. Polk's nomination for the presidency over the wires. By 1860, more than 50,000 miles of wire connected most parts of the country; a year later, the Pacific Telegraph, with 3,595 miles of wire, opened between New York and San Francisco. By then, nearly all the independent lines had joined in one organization, the Western Union Telegraph Company. The telegraph spread rapidly across Europe as well, and in 1866, the first transatlantic cable was laid, allowing telegraphic communication between America and Europe.

One of the first beneficiaries of the telegraph was the growing system of rails. Wires often ran alongside railroad tracks, and telegraph offices were often located in railroad stations. The telegraph allowed railroad operators to communicate directly with stations in cities, small towns, and even rural hamlets—to alert them to schedule changes and warn them about delays and breakdowns. Among other things, this new form of communication helped prevent accidents by alerting stations to problems that engineers in the past had to discover for themselves.

NEW FORMS OF JOURNALISM

Another beneficiary of the telegraph was American journalism. The wires delivered news in a matter of hours—not days, weeks, or months, as in the past—across the country and the world. Where once the exchange of national and international news relied on the cumbersome exchange of newspapers by mail, now it was possible for papers to share their reporting. In 1846, newspaper publishers from around the nation formed the Associated Press to promote cooperative news gathering by wire.

THE *BALTIMORE PATRIOT* SUPPORTS GOVERNMENT REGULATION OF TELEGRAPHY, 1845

THE rapid extension of the magnetic telegraph to all the principal cities of the Union has already given to this means of conveying intelligence an importance that demands the attention of the government. The effect, as we have already seen in the working of the line between this city and Washington, is to annihilate space, so far as the transmission of intelligence is concerned, between all places where the lines extend. Its practical effect must be to supersede, in a general degree, the use of the ordinary mails, and it is scarcely too much to say, that it may ultimately do away with the mails as an agent of commercial intercourse.

In this view we have regretted the neglect of Congress to make the telegraph a government work, to be controlled by its laws, and regulated by its public agents. If it were owned and controlled by the government, it would not be worked for profit, as it of course will be whilst it belongs to private individuals or companies, and as the paying of the expense of operating it would be the only object of the government in making charges for its use, the rate of charge would be so small, that every person might avail of it for sending and receiving communications.

One of the uses to which the telegraph will at once be applied will be the transmission of news for the newspapers. This news is for public use, and not for private advantage, and ought, therefore, as in the case of the exchange papers in the ordinary mail, be sent free. The editor of a paper who receives this news has, and can have, no special advantage in it, and the only use he can make of it is to give the public the benefit of the knowledge of it, as soon as possible after it is received.

These remarks apply as well to Congressional proceedings, as to the general news of the day, and as it fortunately happens, that the telegraphy between Washington and Baltimore is the property of the Government, it has no doubt suggested itself to the Postmaster General, that some provision ought to be made by which the report of the proceedings of Congress could be given, at a cost which would reimburse the Government for the expense it would incur in employing a

---

Other technological advances spurred the development of the American press. In 1846, Richard Hoe invented the steam-powered cylinder rotary press, making it possible to print newspapers much more rapidly and cheaply than had been possible in the past. Among other things, the rotary press spurred the dramatic growth of mass-circulation newspapers. *The New York Sun*, the most widely circulated paper in the nation, had 8,000 readers in 1834. By 1860, its successful rival the *New York Herald*—benefiting from the speed and economies of production the rotary press made possible—had a circulation of 77,000. (See "Patterns of Popular Culture," pp. 216–217.)

COMMERCE AND INDUSTRY

By the mid-nineteenth century, the United States had developed the beginnings of a modern capitalist economy and an advanced industrial capacity. But the economy had developed along highly unequal lines—benefiting some classes and some regions far more than others.

reporter—or, perhaps it would be better, that the Postmaster General should authorize a report of the proceedings, not exceeding a certain length, to be sent free of expense for the telegraph, the business of employing the Congressional reporter being left to the newspapers.

We make this suggestion because it is in accordance with the policy of the Government from its foundation, to carry news for newspapers free of charge, on the obvious ground that all such news is virtually for public information and public benefit—and that the reason of it is stronger in the case of the telegraph than it was in that of the ordinary mail, as the communications of the former are so much more rapidly made, and can therefore be so much more easily used for private speculation.

And because, also the expense to a newspaper in paying for the use of the telegraph for the transmission of news, at anything like the rate of charge now exacted, would be so great as to utterly forbid its use by them for any practical purposes.

We trust the Postmaster General will give this matter his attention, and that the private companies who are constructing telegraphs will also examine the subject, so that a result may be arrived at which will secure the transmission of intelligence, important or interesting to the whole people, free of expense, whilst the cost of the work and whatever profits it may be capable of yielding, will be gathered from those who will use it for *private* benefit or speculation. This will be found, we are sure, to be the true policy of the telegraphs, whether regard be had to their profits or to their use.

UNDERSTAND, ANALYZE, & EVALUATE

1. What future did the author envision for the telegraph? Why did the author believe it was important for government to run telegraph lines? Why, in the author's opinion, was telegraphy so much more likely to become the tool of private exploits than the mail?

2. In the author's view, what significance would government regulation have for the future of news and journalism?

Source: "Magnetic Telegraph," *The Baltimore Patriot*, November 14, 1845, in Regina Lee Blaszczyk and Philip B. Scranton (eds.), *Major Problems in American Business History* (Boston: Houghton Mifflin Company, 2006), pp. 118–119.

THE EXPANSION OF BUSINESS, 1820–1840

American business grew rapidly in the 1820s and 1830s in part because of important innovations in management. Individuals or limited partnerships continued to operate most businesses, and the dominant figures were still the great merchant capitalists, who generally had sole ownership of their enterprises. In some larger businesses, however, the individual merchant capitalist was giving way to the corporation. Corporations, which had the advantage of combining the resources of a large number of shareholders, began to develop particularly rapidly in the 1830s, when some legal obstacles to their formation were removed. Previously, a corporation could obtain a charter only by a special act of a state legislature; by the 1830s, states began passing general incorporation laws, under which a group could secure a charter merely by paying a fee. The laws also permitted a system of limited liability, in which individual stockholders risked losing only the value of their own investment—and not the corporation's larger losses as in the past—if the enterprise failed. These changes made possible much larger manufacturing and business enterprises.

THE EMERGENCE OF THE FACTORY

The most profound economic development in mid-nineteenth-century America was the rise of the factory. Before the War of 1812, most manufacturing took place within households or in small workshops. Later in the nineteenth century, however, New England textile manufacturers began using new water-powered machines that allowed them to bring their operations together under a single roof. This "factory system," as it came to be known, soon penetrated the shoe industry and other industries as well.

Between 1840 and 1860, American industry experienced particularly dramatic growth. For the first time, the value of manufactured goods was roughly equal to that of agricultural products. More than half of the approximately 140,000 manufacturing establishments in the country in 1860, including most of the larger enterprises, were located in the Northeast. The Northeast thus produced more than two-thirds of the manufactured goods and employed nearly three-quarters of the men and women working in manufacturing.

ADVANCES IN TECHNOLOGY

Even the most highly developed industries were still relatively immature. American cotton manufacturers, for example, produced goods of coarse grade; fine items continued to come from England. But by the 1840s, significant advances were occurring.

Among the most important was in the manufacturing of machine tools—the tools used to make machinery parts. The government supported much of the research and development of machine tools, often in connection with supplying the military. For example, a government armory in Springfield, Massachusetts, developed two important tools—the turret lathe (used for cutting screws and other metal parts) and the universal milling machine (which replaced the hand chiseling of complicated parts and dies)—early in the nineteenth century. The precision grinder (which became critical to, among other things, the construction of sewing machines) was designed in the 1850s to help the army produce standardized rifle parts. By the 1840s, the machine tools used in the factories of the Northeast were already better than those in most European factories.

One important result of better machine tools was that the principle of interchangeable parts spread into many industries. Eventually, interchangeability would revolutionize watch and clock making, the manufacturing of locomotives, the creation of steam engines, and the making of many farm tools. It would also help make possible bicycles, sewing machines, typewriters, cash registers, and eventually the automobile.

Industrialization was also profiting from new sources of energy. The production of coal, most of it mined around Pittsburgh in western Pennsylvania, leaped from 50,000 tons in 1820 to 14 million tons in 1860. The new power source, which replaced wood and water power, made it possible to locate mills away from running streams and thus permitted the wider expansion of the industry.

The great industrial advances owed much to American inventors. In 1830, the number of inventions patented was 544; in 1860, it stood at 4,778. Several industries provide particularly vivid examples of how a technological innovation could produce major economic change. In 1839, Charles Goodyear, a New England hardware merchant, discovered a method of vulcanizing rubber (treating it to give it greater strength and elasticity); by 1860, his process had found over 500 uses and had helped create a major American rubber industry. In 1846, Elias Howe of Massachusetts constructed a sewing machine; Isaac Singer made improvements on it, and the Howe-Singer machine was soon being used in the manufacture of ready-to-wear clothing.

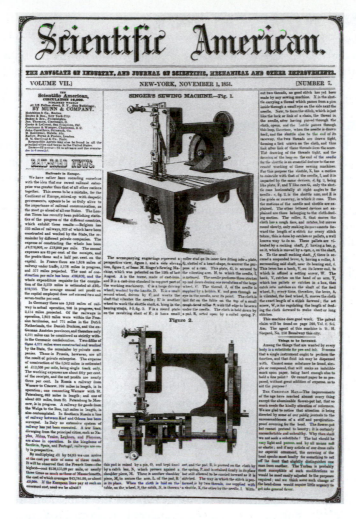

THE EARLY SEWING MACHINE *Scientific American*, which reported American scientific and technological achievements, was a popular journal in the mid-nineteenth century. Here it gives front-page attention to the design and construction of Isaac Singer's sewing machine, alongside articles trumpeting news of the progress of the railroads and urging the invention of a ballpoint pen. (*Scientific American*, 1851)

INNOVATIONS IN CORPORATE ORGANIZATION

The merchant capitalists remained figures of importance in the 1840s. In such cities as New York, Philadelphia, and Boston, influential mercantile groups operated shipping lines to southern ports or dispatched fleets of trading vessels to Europe and Asia. But merchant capitalism was declining by the middle of the century. This was partly because British competitors were stealing much of America's export trade, but mostly because there were greater opportunities for profit in manufacturing than in trade. That was one reason why industries developed first in the Northeast: an affluent merchant class with the money and the will to finance them already existed there. They supported the emerging industrial capitalists and soon became the new aristocrats of the Northeast, with far-reaching economic and political influence.

MEN AND WOMEN AT WORK

In the 1820s and 1830s, factory labor came primarily from the native-born population. After 1840, the growing immigrant population became the most important new source of workers.

RECRUITING A NATIVE WORKFORCE

Recruiting a labor force was not an easy task in the early years of the factory system. Ninety percent of the American people in the 1820s still lived and worked on farms. Many urban residents were skilled artisans who owned and managed their own shops, and the available unskilled workers were not numerous enough to meet industry's needs. But dramatic improvements in agricultural production, particularly in the Midwest, meant that each region no longer had to feed itself; it could import the food it needed. As a result, rural people from relatively unprofitable farming areas of the East began leaving the land to work in the factories.

Two systems of recruitment emerged to bring this new labor supply to the expanding textile mills. One, common in the mid-Atlantic states, brought whole families from the farm to work together in the mill. The second system, common in Massachusetts, enlisted young women, mostly farmers' daughters in their late teens and early twenties. It was known as the Lowell or Waltham system, after the towns in which it first emerged. Many of these women worked for several years, saved their wages, and then returned home to marry and raise children. Others married men they met in the factories or in town. Most eventually stopped working in the mills and took up domestic roles instead.

Labor conditions in these early years of the factory system, hard as they often were, remained significantly better than they would later become. The Lowell workers, for example, were well fed, carefully supervised, and housed in clean boardinghouses and dormitories, which the factory owners maintained. Wages for the Lowell workers were relatively generous by the standards of the time. The women even published a monthly magazine, the *Lowell Offering*.

Yet even these relatively well-treated workers found the transition from farm life to factory work difficult. Forced to live among strangers in a regimented environment, many women had trouble adjusting to the nature of factory work. However uncomfortable women may have found factory work, they had few other options. Work in the mills was in many cases virtually the only alternative to returning to farms that could no longer support them.

The paternalistic factory system of Lowell did not, in any case, survive for long. In the competitive textile market of the 1830s and 1840s, manufacturers found it difficult to maintain the high living standards and reasonably attractive working conditions of before. Wages declined; the hours of work lengthened; the conditions of the boardinghouses deteriorated. In 1834, mill workers in Lowell organized a union—the Factory Girls Association—which staged a strike to protest a 25 percent wage cut. Two years later, the association struck again—against a rent increase in the boardinghouses. Both strikes failed, and a recession in 1837 virtually destroyed the organization. Eight years later, the Lowell women, led by the militant Sarah Bagley, created the Female Labor Reform Association, which agitated for a ten-hour day and for improvements in conditions in the mills. The new association also asked state governments for legislative investigation of conditions in the mills. By then, however, the character of the factory workforce was changing again.

THE LOWELL MILLS   Fifteen years earlier, Lowell, Massachusetts, had been a small farming village known as East Chelmsford. By the 1840s, when Fitzhugh Lane painted *The Middlesex Company Woolen Mills,* the town had become one of the most famous manufacturing centers in America and a magnet for visitors from around the world. Lane's painting shows female workers, who dominated the labor force in Lowell, entering the factory. (American Textile History Museum, Lowell, Massachusetts)

Many mill girls were gradually moving into other occupations: teaching, domestic service, or homemaking. And textile manufacturers were turning to a less demanding labor supply: immigrants.

THE IMMIGRANT WORKFORCE

The increasing supply of immigrant workers after 1840 was a boon to manufacturers and other entrepreneurs. These new workers, because of their growing numbers and their unfamiliarity with their new country, had even less leverage than the women they displaced, and thus they often experienced far worse working conditions. Poorly paid construction gangs, made up increasingly of Irish immigrants, performed the heavy, unskilled work on turnpikes, canals, and railroads. Many of them lived in flimsy shanties, in grim conditions that endangered the health of their families (and reinforced native prejudices toward the "shanty Irish"). Irish workers began to predominate in the New England textile mills as well in the 1840s. Employers began paying piece rates rather than a daily wage and used other devices to speed up production and exploit the labor force more efficiently. The factories themselves were becoming large, noisy, unsanitary, and often dangerous places to work; the average workday was extending to twelve, often fourteen hours; and wages were declining. Women and children, whatever their skills, earned less than most men.

THE FACTORY SYSTEM AND THE ARTISAN TRADITION

Factories were also displacing the trades of skilled artisans. Artisans were as much a part of the older, republican vision of America as sturdy yeoman farmers. Independent craftsmen clung to a vision of economic life that was very different from that promoted by the new capitalist class. The artisans embraced not just the idea of individual, acquisitive success but also a sense of a "moral community." Skilled artisans valued their independence, their stability, and their relative equality within their economic world.

Some artisans made successful transitions into small-scale industry. But others found themselves unable to compete with the new factory-made goods. In the face of this competition, skilled workers in cities such as Philadelphia, Baltimore, Boston, and New York formed societies for mutual aid. During the 1820s and 1830s, these craft societies began to combine on a citywide basis and set up central organizations known as trade unions. In 1834, delegates from six cities founded the National Trades' Union, and in 1836, printers and cordwainers (makers of high-quality shoes and boots) set up their own national craft unions.

THE SHOP AND WAREHOUSE OF DUNCAN PHYFE Duncan Phyfe was a celebrated and (as this watercolor by John Rubens Smith suggests) prosperous furniture maker in New York for many decades, serving the growing population of affluent households in search of refinement and display. The elegant Georgian details on Phyfe's shop on Fulton Street suggest how even places of business were adapting to the new conception of opulence. (Image copyright © The Metropolitan Museum of Art/ Art Resource, NY)

Hostile laws and hostile courts handicapped the unions, as did the Panic of 1837 and the depression that followed. But some artisans managed to retain control over their productive lives.

FIGHTING FOR CONTROL

Industrial workers made continuous efforts to improve their lots. They tried, with little success, to persuade state legislatures to pass laws setting a maximum workday and regulating child labor. Their greatest legal victory came in Massachusetts in 1842, when the state supreme court, in *Commonwealth v. Hunt,* declared that unions were lawful organizations and that the strike was a lawful weapon. Other state courts gradually accepted the principles of the Massachusetts decision, but employers continued to resist.

Virtually all the early craft unions excluded women. As a result, women began establishing their own, new protective unions in the 1850s. Like the male craft unions, the female unions had little power in dealing with employers. They did, however, serve an important role as mutual aid societies for women workers.

Many factors combined to inhibit the growth of better working standards. Among the most important obstacles was the flood into the country of immigrant laborers, who were usually willing to work for lower wages than native workers. Because they were so numerous, manufacturers had little difficulty replacing disgruntled or striking workers with eager immigrants. Ethnic divisions often led workers to channel their resentments into internal bickering among one another rather than into their shared grievances. Another obstacle was the sheer strength of the industrial capitalists, who possessed not only economic but also political and social power.

PATTERNS OF SOCIETY

The industrial revolution was making the United States both dramatically wealthier and increasingly unequal. It was transforming social relationships at almost every level.

THE RICH AND THE POOR

The commercial and industrial growth of the United States greatly elevated the average income of the American people. But this increasing wealth was being distributed highly unequally. Substantial groups of the population—slaves, Indians, landless farmers, and many of the unskilled workers on the fringes of the manufacturing system—shared hardly at all in the economic growth. But even among the rest of the population, disparities of income were growing. Merchants and industrialists were accumulating enormous fortunes; and in the cities, a distinctive culture of wealth began to emerge.

In large cities, people of great wealth gathered together in neighborhoods of astonishing opulence. They founded clubs and developed elaborate social rituals. They looked increasingly for ways to display their wealth—in great mansions, showy carriages, lavish household goods, and the elegant social establishments they patronized. New York developed a particularly elaborate high society. The construction of Central Park, which began in the 1850s, was in part a result of pressure from the members of high society, who wanted an elegant setting for their daily carriage rides.

A significant population of genuinely destitute people also emerged in the growing urban centers. These people were almost entirely without resources, often homeless, and

CENTRAL PARK   The great park attracted people from all over New York, but most of all it was where the affluent New Yorkers came for recreation. Here is a picture of well-dressed skaters on one of the parks lakes. (Bridgeman Art Library International/SuperStock)

dependent on charity or crime, or both, for survival. Substantial numbers of people actually starved to death or died of exposure. Some of these "paupers," as contemporaries called them, were recent immigrants. Some were widows and orphans, stripped of the family structures that allowed most working-class Americans to survive. Some were people suffering from alcoholism or mental illness, unable to work. Others were victims of native prejudice—barred from all but the most menial employment because of race or ethnicity. The Irish were particular victims of such prejudice.

The worst victims in the North were free blacks. Most major urban areas had significant black populations. Some of these African Americans were descendants of families who had lived in the North for generations. Others were former slaves who had escaped or been released by their masters. In material terms, at least, life was not always much better for them in the North than it had been in slavery. Most had access to very menial jobs at best. In most parts of the North, blacks could not vote, attend public schools, or use any of the public services available to white residents. Even so, most African Americans preferred life in the North, however arduous, to life in the South.

SOCIAL MOBILITY

Despite the contrasts between conspicuous wealth and poverty in antebellum America, there was relatively little overt class conflict. For one thing, life, in material terms at least, was better for most factory workers than it had been on the farms or in Europe. A significant amount of mobility within the working class also helped limit discontent. A few workers—a very small number, but enough to support the dreams of others—managed to move from poverty to riches by dint of work, ingenuity, and luck. And a much larger number of workers managed to move at least one notch up the ladder—for example, becoming in the course of a lifetime a skilled, rather than an unskilled, laborer.

More important than social mobility was geographical mobility. Some workers saved money, bought land, and moved west to farm it. But few urban workers, and even fewer poor ones, could afford to make such a move. Much more common was the movement of laborers from one industrial town to another. These migrants, often the victims of layoffs, looked for better opportunities elsewhere. Their search seldom led to marked improvement in their circumstances. The rootlessness of this large and distressed segment of the workforce made effective organization and protest difficult.

MIDDLE-CLASS LIFE

Despite the visibility of the very rich and the very poor in antebellum society, the fastest-growing group in America was the middle class. Economic development opened many more opportunities for people to own or work in shops or businesses, to engage in trade, to enter professions, and to administer organizations. In earlier times, when land owner-ship had been the only real basis of wealth, society had been divided between those with little or no land (people Europeans generally called peasants) and a landed gentry (which in Europe usually became an inherited aristocracy). Once commerce and industry became a source of wealth, these rigid distinctions broke down; many people could become pros-perous without owning land, but by providing valuable services.

Middle-class life in the antebellum years rapidly established itself as the most influen-tial cultural form of urban America. Solid, substantial middle-class houses lined city streets, larger in size and more elaborate in design than the cramped, functional rowhouses in working-class neighborhoods—but also far less lavish than the great houses of the very rich. Middle-class people tended to own their homes, often for the first time. Workers and artisans remained mostly renters.

Middle-class women usually remained in the household, although increasingly they were also able to hire servants—usually young, unmarried immigrant women. In an age when doing the family's laundry could take an entire day, one of the aspirations of middle-class women was to escape from some of the drudgery of housework.

New household inventions altered, and greatly improved, the character of life in middle-class homes. Perhaps the most important was the invention of the cast-iron stove, which began to replace fireplaces as the principal vehicle for cooking in the 1840s. These wood- or coal-burning devices were hot, clumsy, and dirty by later standards, but com-pared to the inconvenience and danger of cooking on an open hearth, they seemed a great luxury. Stoves gave cooks greater control over food preparation and allowed them to cook several things at once.

Middle-class diets were changing rapidly, and not just because of the wider range of cooking that the stove made possible. The expansion and diversification of American agriculture and the ability of distant farmers to ship goods to urban markets by rail greatly increased the variety of food available in cities. Fruits and vegetables were difficult to ship over long distances in an age with little refrigeration, but families had access to a greater variety of meats, grains, and dairy products than in the past. A few households acquired iceboxes, which allowed them to keep meat and dairy products fresh for several days. Most families, however, did not yet have any refrigeration. For them, preserving food meant curing meat with salt and preserving fruits in sugar. Diets were generally much heavier and starchier than they are today, and middle-class people tended to be considerably stouter than would be considered healthy or fashionable now.

Middle-class homes came to differentiate themselves from those of workers and artisans in other ways as well. The spare, simple styles of eighteenth-century homes gave way to the much more elaborate, even baroque household styles of the Victorian era—styles increasingly characterized by crowded, even cluttered rooms, dark colors, lush fabrics, and heavy furniture and draperies. Middle-class homes also became larger. It became less common for children to share beds and for all members of a family to sleep in the same room. Parlors and dining rooms separate from the kitchen—once a luxury—became the norm among the middle class. Some urban middle-class homes had indoor plumbing and indoor toilets by the 1850s—a significant advance over outdoor wells and privies.

THE CHANGING FAMILY

The new industrializing society produced profound changes in the nature of the family. Among them was the movement of families from farms to urban areas. Sons and daughters in urban households were much more likely to leave the family in search of work than they had been in the rural world. This was largely because of the shift of income-earning work out of the home. In the early decades of the nineteenth century, the family itself had been the principal unit of economic activity. Now most income earners left home each day to work in a shop, mill, or factory. A sharp distinction began to emerge between the public world of the workplace and the private world of the family. The world of the family was now dominated not by production but by housekeeping, child rearing, and other primarily domestic concerns.

There was a significant decline in the birth rate, particularly in urban areas and in middle-class families. In 1800, the average American woman could be expected to give birth to approximately seven children. By 1860, the average woman bore five children.

THE "CULT OF DOMESTICITY"

The growing separation between the workplace and the home sharpened distinctions between the social roles of men and women. Those distinctions affected not only factory workers and farmers but also members of the growing middle class.

With fewer legal and political rights than men, most women remained under the virtually absolute authority of their husbands. They were seldom encouraged to pursue education above the primary level. Women students were not accepted in any college or university until 1837. For a considerable time after that, only Oberlin in Ohio offered education to both men and women, and Mount Holyoke in Massachusetts was founded by Mary Lyon as an academy for women.

However unequal the positions of men and women in the preindustrial era, those positions had generally been defined within the context of a household in which all members played important economic roles. In the middle-class family of the new industrial society, by contrast, the husband was assumed to be the principal, usually the only, income producer. The image of women changed from one of contributors to the family economy to one of guardians of the "domestic virtues." Middle-class women learned to place a higher value on keeping a clean, comfortable, and well-appointed home; on entertaining; and on dressing elegantly and stylishly.

Within their own separate sphere, middle-class women began to develop a distinctive female culture. A "lady's" literature began to emerge. Romantic novels written for female readers focused on the private sphere that middle-class women now inhabited, as did women's magazines that focused on fashions, shopping, homemaking, and other purely domestic concerns.

This "cult of domesticity," as some scholars have called it, provided many women greater material comfort than they had enjoyed in the past and placed a higher value on their "female virtues." At the same time, it left women increasingly detached from the public world, with fewer outlets for their interests and energies. Except for teaching and nursing, work by women outside the household gradually came to be seen as a lower-class preserve.

Working-class women continued to work in factories and mills, but under conditions far worse than those that the original, more "respectable" women workers of Lowell and Waltham had experienced. Domestic service became another frequent source of female employment.

LEISURE ACTIVITIES

Leisure time was scarce for all but the wealthiest Americans. Most people worked long hours, and vacations were rare. For most people, Sunday was the only respite from work, and Sundays were generally reserved for religion and rest. For many working-class and middle-class people, therefore, holidays took on a special importance, as suggested by the strikingly elaborate celebrations of the Fourth of July in the nineteenth century. The celebrations were not just expressions of patriotism, but a way of enjoying one of the few nonreligious holidays from work available to most Americans.

Compared to the relentless working schedules of city residents, the erratic pattern of farmwork provided occasional relief to people in rural America. For urban people, however, leisure was something to be seized in what few free moments they had. Men gravitated to taverns for drinking, talking, and game-playing after work. Women gathered in one another's homes for conversation and card games. For educated people, reading became one of the principal leisure activities. Newspapers and magazines proliferated rapidly, and books became staples of affluent homes.

A vigorous culture of public leisure emerged, especially in larger cities. Theaters became increasingly popular and increasingly attracted audiences that crossed class lines. Much of the popular theater of the time consisted of melodrama based on popular novels or American myths. But much of it reflected the great love of Shakespeare that extended through all levels of the theatergoing population.

Minstrel shows—in which white actors wearing blackface mimicked (and ridiculed) African American culture—became increasingly popular. Public sporting events—boxing, horse racing, cockfighting (already becoming controversial), and others—often attracted considerable audiences. Baseball—not yet organized into professional leagues—was beginning to attract large crowds when played in city parks or fields. A particularly exciting event in many communities was the arrival of the circus.

Popular tastes in public spectacle tended toward the bizarre and the fantastic. Relatively few people traveled; and in the absence of film, radio, television, or even much photography, Americans hungered for visions of unusual phenomena. People going to the theater or the circus or the museum wanted to see things that amazed and even frightened them. The most celebrated provider of such experiences was the famous and unscrupulous showman P. T. Barnum, who opened the American Museum in New York in 1842—not a showcase for art or nature, but a great freak show populated by midgets (the most famous named Tom Thumb), Siamese twins, magicians, and ventriloquists. Barnum was a genius in publicizing his ventures with garish posters

SHAKESPEARE IN AMERICA

PERFORMANCES

of Shakespeare began in America as early as 1750, but public interest in his plays reached its peak in the 1830s, 1840s, and 1850s, when theater was at this peak of popularity and Shakespeare was the most powerful playwright. Many, perhaps most, performances of Shakespearean plays were irreverent, inaccurate, and romanticized. Tragedies were rewritten with happy endings. Comedies were interlaced with contemporary, regional humor. Texts were reworked with American dialect, and plays were abbreviated and sandwiched into programs containing other popular works of the time. So familiar were many Shakespearean plots that audiences took delight in seeing them parodied in productions such as *Julius Sneezer, Hamlet and Egglet*, and *Much Ado About a Merchant of Venice*.

People from all walks of life went regularly to the theater. Seating was often divided by class—a tier of boxes for the wealthiest patrons, orchestra seats for the middle class, and balconies for those too poor to sit anywhere else (including virtually all nonwhite members of the audience). But despite these distinctions, going to the theater was a vibrantly democratic experience.

American audiences were often noisy, rambunctious, and—at least in the eyes of many actors—obnoxious. Men and women shouted out reactions to the plays, taunted actors, and occasionally—as in an 1832 performance of *Richard III* in New York—climbed onto the stage and joined the performance, mingling with the actors during a battle scene and charging across the stage as if they were soldiers.

The leading Shakespearean actors of the antebellum era became figures of enormous public interest and at times spurred great popular passion, as evidenced by events in New York City in 1849. The celebrated American actor Edwin Forrest gave a performance of *Macbeth* on the same evening that a renowned English actor, William Macready, was performing the same play elsewhere in the city. Many New Yorkers believed that the aloof, aristocratic Macready—a favorite of the city's wealthy elites—was attempting to humiliate Forrest. Forrest supporters crowded into Macready's performance and hooted him off the stage. Three days later, Macready tried again at the Astor Place Opera House.

and elaborate newspaper announcements. Later, in the 1870s, he launched the famous circus for which he is still best remembered.

Lectures were one of the most popular forms of entertainment in nineteenth-century America. Men and women flocked in enormous numbers to lyceums, churches, schools, and auditoriums to hear lecturers explain the latest advances in science, describe their visits to exotic places, provide vivid historical narratives, or rail against the evils of alcohol or slavery. Messages of social uplift and reform attracted rapt audiences, particularly among women.

THE PARK THEATER This 1821 watercolor by John Searle shows the interior of the Park Theater in New York, which had recently been rebuilt after a fire. The play is a farce by the English playwright William T. Moncrieff. The faces in the audience are all portraits of real New Yorkers at the time. (Collection of the New-York Historical Society)

Shakespeare remained popular throughout the Civil War. In 1864, enthusiastic crowds greeted a performance in New York of *Julius Caesar*, featuring three members of America's most celebrated theatrical family: Junius Brutus Booth, an aging giant who had been the foremost tragic actor of his generation, and his two sons Edwin and John Wilkes. Edwin Booth went on to become America's most revered actor of the last half of the nineteenth century, renowned in particular for his performances of Hamlet and other great Shakespearean roles. His brother, John Wilkes, is best remembered leaping to the stage of Ford's Theater in Washington on April 14, 1865, after having fatally shot Abraham Lincoln. His famous exclamation at the time, "*Sic semper tyrannis*," was the motto of the state of Virginia. But it was better known as the phrase Brutus supposedly uttered after killing Julius Caesar, a quote most familiar to nineteenth-century audiences—and to Booth himself—from performances of Shakespeare's play. •

Ten thousand people, most of them Forrest enthusiasts, gathered outside and tried to force their way into the theater. Militia, called out for the occasion, fired into the crowd, killing at least 22 and wounding more than 150. The "Astor Place Riot," as it was called, was one of the bloodiest civil conflicts of the first half of the nineteenth century.

UNDERSTAND, ANALYZE, & EVALUATE

1. What does the Astor Place riot suggest about the theater in mid-nineteenth-century America?
2. In the late nineteenth century, performances of Shakespeare ceased to be "entertainment for the masses" and became instead part of "high culture." What does this shift suggest about American society in general during this period?

THE AGRICULTURAL NORTH

Even in the rapidly urbanizing and industrializing Northeast, and more so in what nineteenth-century Americans called the Northwest, most people remained tied to the agricultural world. But agriculture, like industry and commerce, was becoming increasingly a part of the new capitalist economy.

NORTHEASTERN AGRICULTURE

The story of agriculture in the Northeast after 1840 is one of decline and transformation. Farmers of this section of the country could no longer compete with the new and richer soil of the Northwest. In 1840, the leading wheat-growing states were New York, Pennsylvania, Ohio, and Virginia. In 1860, they were Illinois, Indiana, Wisconsin, Ohio, and Michigan. Illinois, Ohio, and Missouri also supplanted New York, Pennsylvania, and Virginia as growers of corn. In 1840, the most important cattle-raising areas in the country were New York, Pennsylvania, and New England. By the 1850s, the leading cattle states were Illinois, Indiana, Ohio, and Iowa in the Northwest and Texas in the Southwest.

Some eastern farmers responded to these changes by moving west themselves and establishing new farms. Still others moved to mill towns and became laborers. Some farmers, however, remained on the land and turned to what was known as "truck farming"—supplying food to the growing cities. They raised vegetables or fruit and sold their produce in nearby towns. Supplying milk, butter, and cheese to local urban markets also attracted many farmers in central New York, southeastern Pennsylvania, and various parts of New England.

THE OLD NORTHWEST

Life was different in the states of the Old Northwest (now known as the Midwest). In the two decades before the Civil War, this section of the country experienced steady industrial growth, particularly in and around Cleveland (on Lake Erie) and Cincinnati, the center of meatpacking in the Ohio Valley. Farther west, Chicago was emerging as the national center of the agricultural machinery and meatpacking industries. Most of the major industrial activities of the Old Northwest either served agriculture (as in the case of farm machinery) or relied on agricultural products (as in flour milling, meatpacking, whiskey distilling, and the making of leather goods).

Some areas of the Old Northwest were not yet dominated by whites. Indians remained the most numerous inhabitants of large portions of the upper third of the Great Lakes states until after the Civil War. In those areas, hunting and fishing, along with some sedentary agriculture, remained the principal economic activities.

For the settlers who populated the lands farther south, the Old Northwest was primarily an agricultural region. Its rich lands made farming highly lucrative. Thus the typical citizen of the Old Northwest was not the industrial worker or poor, marginal farmer, but the owner of a reasonably prosperous family farm.

Industrialization, in both the United States and Europe, provided the greatest boost to agriculture. With the growth of factories and cities in the Northeast, the domestic market for farm goods increased dramatically. The growing national and worldwide demand for farm products resulted in steadily rising farm prices. For most farmers, the 1840s and early 1850s were years of increasing prosperity.

The expansion of agricultural markets also had profound effects on sectional alignments in the United States. The Old Northwest sold most of its products to the Northeast and became an important market for the products of eastern industry. A strong economic relationship was emerging between the two sections that was profitable to both—and that was increasing the isolation of the South within the Union.

By 1850, the growing western white population was moving into the prairie regions on both sides of the Mississippi. These farmers cleared forest lands or made use of fields the Indians had cleared many years earlier. And they developed a timber industry to make use of the remaining forests. Although wheat was the staple crop of the region, other crops—corn, potatoes, and oats—and livestock were also important.

The Old Northwest also increased production by adopting new agricultural techniques. Farmers began to cultivate new varieties of seed, notably Mediterranean wheat, which was hardier than the native type; and they imported better breeds of animals, such as hogs and sheep from England and Spain. Most important were improved tools and farm machines. The cast-iron plow remained popular because of its replaceable parts. In 1847, John Deere established at Moline, Illinois, a factory to manufacture steel plows, which were more durable than those made of iron.

Two new machines heralded a coming revolution in grain production. The automatic reaper, the invention of Cyrus H. McCormick of Virginia, took the place of sickle, cradle, and hand labor. Pulled by a team of horses, it had a row of horizontal knives on one side for cutting wheat; the wheels drove a paddle that bent the stalks over the knives, which then fell onto a moving belt and into the back of the vehicle. The reaper enabled a crew of six or seven men to harvest in a day as much wheat as fifteen men could harvest using the older methods. McCormick, who had patented his device in 1834, established a factory at Chicago in 1847. By 1860, more than 100,000 reapers were in use. Almost as important to the grain grower was the thresher—a machine that separated the grain from the wheat stalks—which appeared in large numbers after 1840. (Before that, farmers generally flailed grain by hand or used farm animals to tread it.) The Jerome I. Case factory in Racine, Wisconsin, manufactured most of the threshers. (Modern "harvesters" later combined the functions of the reaper and the thresher.)

The Old Northwest was the most self-consciously democratic section of the country. But its democracy was of a relatively conservative type—capitalistic, property-conscious, middle-class. Abraham Lincoln, an Illinois Whig, voiced the economic opinions of many of the people of his section. "I take it that it is best for all to leave each man free to acquire property as fast as he can," said Lincoln. "When one starts poor, as most do in the race of life, free society is such that he knows he can better his condition; he knows that there is no fixed condition of labor for his whole life."

RURAL LIFE

Life for farming people varied greatly from one region to another. In the more densely populated areas east of the Appalachians and in the easternmost areas of the Old Northwest, farmers made extensive use of the institutions of communities—churches, schools, stores, and taverns. As white settlement moved farther west, farmers became more isolated and had to struggle to find any occasions for contact with people outside their own families.

Religion drew farm communities together more than any other force in remote communities. Town or village churches were popular meeting places, both for services and for social events—most of them dominated by women. Even in areas with no organized churches, farm families—and women in particular—gathered in one another's homes for prayer meetings, Bible readings, and other religious activities. Weddings, baptisms, and funerals also brought communities together.

But religion was only one of many reasons for interaction. Farm people joined together frequently to share tasks such as barn raising. Large numbers of families gathered at harvesttime to help bring in crops, husk corn, or thresh wheat. Women came together to share domestic tasks, holding "bees" in which groups of women made quilts, baked goods, preserves, and other products.

Despite the many social gatherings farm families managed to create, they had much less contact with popular culture and public life than people who lived in towns and cities. Most rural people treasured their links to the outside world—letters from relatives and friends in distant places, newspapers and magazines from cities they had never seen, catalogs advertising merchandise that their local stores never had. Yet many also valued the relative autonomy that a farm life gave them. One reason many rural Americans looked back nostalgically on country life once they moved to the city was that they sensed that in the urban world they had lost some control over the patterns of their daily lives.

CONCLUSION

Between the 1820s and the 1850s, the American economy experienced the beginnings of an industrial revolution—a change that transformed almost every area of life in fundamental ways.

The American industrial revolution was a result of many things: population growth, advances in transportation and communication, new technologies that spurred the development of factories and mass production, the recruiting of a large industrial labor force, and the creation of corporate bodies capable of managing large enterprises. The new economy expanded the ranks of the wealthy, helped create a large new middle class, and introduced high levels of inequality.

Culture in the industrializing areas of the North changed, too, as did the structure and behavior of the family, the role of women, and the way people used their leisure time and encountered popular culture. The changes helped widen the gap in experience and understanding between the generation of the Revolution and the generation of the mid-nineteenth century. They also helped widen the gap between North and South.

RECALL AND REFLECT

1. What were the political responses to immigration in mid-nineteenth-century America? Do you see any parallels to responses to immigration today?
2. Why did the rail system supplant the canal system as the nation's major transportation network?
3. How did the industrial workforce change between the 1820s and the 1840s? What were the effects on American society of changes in the workforce?
4. How did America's industrial revolution and the factory system change family life and women's social and economic roles?
5. How did agriculture in the North change as a result of growing industrialization and urbanization?

11 | COTTON, SLAVERY, AND THE OLD SOUTH

THE COTTON ECONOMY
SOUTHERN WHITE SOCIETY
SLAVERY: THE "PECULIAR INSTITUTION"
THE CULTURE OF SLAVERY

LOOKING AHEAD

1. How did slavery shape the southern economy and society, and how did it make the South different from the North?
2. What was the myth and what was the reality of white society in the South? Why was the myth so pervasive and widely believed?
3. How did slaves resist their enslavement? How successful were their efforts? What was the response of whites?

THE SOUTH, LIKE THE NORTH, experienced significant growth in the middle years of the nineteenth century. Southerners fanned out into the Southwest. The southern agricultural economy grew increasingly productive and prosperous. Trade in such staples as sugar, rice, tobacco, and above all cotton made the South a major force in international commerce. It also tied the South securely to the emerging capitalist world of the United States and its European trading partners.

Yet despite all these changes, the South experienced a much less fundamental transformation in these years than did the North. It had begun the nineteenth century as a primarily agricultural region; it remained overwhelmingly agrarian in 1860. It had begun the century with few important cities and little industry; and so it remained sixty years later. In 1800, a plantation system dependent on slave labor had dominated the southern economy; by 1860, that system had only strengthened its grip on the region. As one historian has written, "The South grew, but it did not develop."

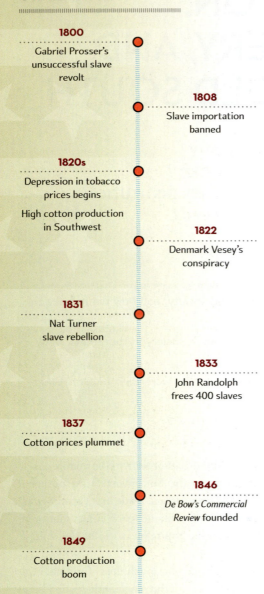

1800

Gabriel Prosser's
unsuccessful slave
revolt

1808

Slave importation
banned

1820s

Depression in tobacco
prices begins

High cotton production
in Southwest

1822

Denmark Vesey's
conspiracy

1831

Nat Turner
slave rebellion

1833

John Randolph
frees 400 slaves

1837

Cotton prices plummet

1846

*De Bow's Commercial
Review* founded

1849

Cotton production
boom

THE COTTON ECONOMY

The most important economic development in the mid-nineteenth-century South was the shift of economic power from the "upper South," the original southern states along the Atlantic Coast, to the "lower South," the expanding agricultural regions in the new states of the Southwest. That shift reflected above all the growing dominance of cotton in the southern economy.

THE RISE OF KING COTTON

Much of the upper South continued to rely on the cultivation of tobacco. But the market for that crop was notoriously unstable, and tobacco rapidly exhausted the land on which it grew. By the 1830s, therefore, many farmers in the old tobacco-growing regions of Virginia, Maryland, and North Carolina were shifting to other crops, while the center of tobacco cultivation was moving westward, into the Piedmont area.

The southern regions of the coastal South—South Carolina, Georgia, and parts of Florida—continued to rely on the cultivation of rice, a more stable and lucrative crop. But rice demanded substantial irrigation and needed an exceptionally long growing season (nine months), so its cultivation remained restricted to a relatively small area. Sugar growers along the Gulf Coast similarly enjoyed a reasonably profitable market for their crop. But sugar cultivation required intensive (and debilitating) labor and a long growing time; only relatively wealthy planters could afford to grow it. In addition, producers faced major competition from the great sugar plantations of the Caribbean. Sugar cultivation, therefore, did not spread much beyond a small area in southern Louisiana and eastern Texas. Long-staple (Sea Island) cotton was another lucrative crop, but like rice and sugar, it could grow only in a limited area—the coastal regions of the Southeast.

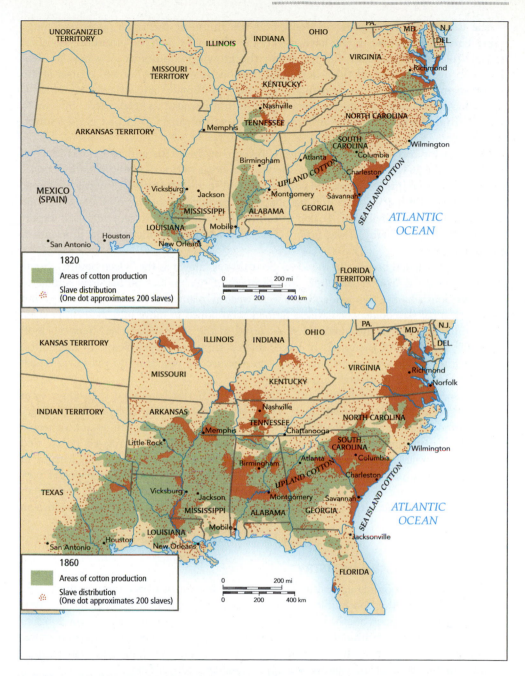

SLAVERY AND COTTON IN THE SOUTH, 1820 AND 1860 These two maps show the remarkable spread of cotton cultivation in the South in the decades before the Civil War. Both maps show the areas of cotton cultivation (the green-colored areas) as well as areas with large slave populations (the brown-dotted areas). Note how in the top map, which represents 1820, cotton production is concentrated largely in the East, with a few areas scattered among Alabama, Mississippi, Louisiana, and Tennessee. Slavery is concentrated along the Georgia and South Carolina coast, areas in which long-staple cotton was grown, with only a few other areas of highly dense slave populations. By 1860, the South had changed dramatically. Cotton production had spread throughout the lower South, from Texas to northern Florida, and slavery had moved with it. Slavery was much denser in the tobacco-growing regions of Virginia and North Carolina, which had also grown. • *How did this economic shift affect the white South's commitment to slavery?*

The decline of the tobacco economy and the limits of the sugar, rice, and long-staple cotton economies might have forced the region to shift its attention to other, nonagricultural pursuits had it not been for the growing importance of a new product that soon overshadowed all else: short-staple cotton. It was a hardier and coarser strain of cotton that could grow successfully in a variety of climates and in a variety of soils. It was harder to process than the long-staple cotton because its seeds were difficult to remove from the fiber. But the invention of the cotton gin in 1793 had largely solved that problem.

Demand for cotton increased rapidly in Britain in the 1820s and 1830s and in New England in the 1840s and 1850s. From the western areas of South Carolina and Georgia, production moved into Alabama and Mississippi and then into northern Louisiana, Texas, and Arkansas. By the 1850s, cotton had become the linchpin of the southern economy. By the time of the Civil War, cotton constituted nearly two-thirds of the total export trade of the United States. It was little wonder that southern politicians now proclaimed, "Cotton is king!"

Cotton production boomed in the lower South (later known as the "Deep South"). Some began to call it the "cotton kingdom." The prospect of tremendous profits drew settlers to the lower South by the thousands. Some were wealthy planters from the older states, but most were small slaveholders or slaveless farmers who hoped to move into the planter class.

A similar shift, if an involuntary one, occurred in the slave population. Between 1840 and 1860, hundreds of thousands of slaves moved from the upper South to the cotton states—either accompanying masters who were themselves migrating to the lower South or (more often) sold to planters already there.

This "second middle passage," as the historian Ira Berlin has called it (using a term usually associated with the transatlantic slave trade), was a traumatic experience for perhaps a million dislocated African Americans. Slave families were broken up and scattered across the expanding cotton kingdom. Marched over hundreds of rugged miles, tied together in "coffles" (as on the earlier slave ships coming from Africa), they arrived in unfamiliar and usually forbidding territory, where they were made to construct new plantations and work in cotton fields. The sale of slaves to the lower South became an important economic activity for whites in the upper South, where agricultural production was declining.

Southern Trade and Industry

In the face of this booming agricultural expansion, other forms of economic activity were slow to develop in the South. Flour milling and textile and iron manufacturing grew, particularly in the upper South, but industry remained a relatively insignificant force in comparison with the agricultural economy. The total value of southern textile manufactures in 1860 was $4.5 million—a threefold increase over the value of those goods twenty years before. But the value of the exports was approximately $200 million.

The limited nonfarm commercial sector that did develop in the South was largely intended to serve the needs of the plantation economy. Particularly important were the brokers, or "factors," who, in the absence of banks, marketed the planters' crops and provided them with credit. Other obstacles to economic development included the South's inadequate transportation system. Canals were almost nonexistent; most roads were crude and unsuitable for heavy transport; and railroads, although they expanded substantially in the 1840s and 1850s, failed to tie the region together effectively. Despite

HAULING THE WHOLE WEEK'S PICKING

HAULING THE WHOLE WEEK'S PICKING   This watercolor by William Henry Brown, painted in approximately 1842, portrays a slave family loading cotton onto a wagon, presumably after a hard day of picking. Even young children participate in the chores. Brown was an artist known for his silhouettes, a form popular in the nineteenth century. (One of his later subjects was Abraham Lincoln.) This picture is part of a five-foot cutout he made as a gift to a family he was visiting. (Historic New Orleans Collection, accession #1975.98.1&2)

the lack of canals, the principal means of transportation was water. Planters generally shipped their crops to market along rivers or by sea; most manufacturing was in or near port towns.

The South, therefore, was becoming more and more dependent on the manufacturers, merchants, and professionals of the North. Concerned by this trend, some southerners began to advocate economic independence for the region, among them James D. B. De Bow of New Orleans, whose magazine, *De Bow's Commercial Review*, called for southern commercial expansion and economic independence from the North. Yet even *De Bow's Commercial Review* was filled with advertisements from northern manufacturing firms; and its circulation was far smaller in the South than such northern magazines as *Harper's Weekly*.

SOURCES OF SOUTHERN DIFFERENCE

An important question about antebellum southern history concerns why the region did so little to develop a larger industrial and commercial economy of its own. Why did it remain so different from the North?

Part of the reason was the great profitability of the region's agricultural system. In the Northeast, many people had turned to manufacturing as the agricultural economy of the region declined. In the South, the agricultural economy was booming, and ambitious capitalists had little incentive to look elsewhere. Another reason was that wealthy southerners had so much capital invested in land and slaves that they had little left for other investments. Some historians have also suggested that the southern climate—with its long, hot, steamy summers—was less suitable for industrial development than the climate of the North.

But this southern failure was also due in part to a set of values distinctive to the South. Many white southerners liked to think of themselves as representatives of a special way of life. Many white southerners argued that grace and refinement were more important than rapid growth and development. But appealing as this image was to southern whites, it conformed to the reality of southern society in very limited ways.

THE NEW ORLEANS COTTON EXCHANGE Edgar Degas, the renowned French painter, painted this scene of cotton traders examining samples in the New Orleans cotton exchange in 1873. By this time the cotton trade was producing less impressive profits than those that had made it the driving force of the booming southern economy of the 1850s. Degas's mother came from a Creole family of cotton brokers in New Orleans, and two of the artist's brothers (depicted here reading a newspaper and leaning against a window) joined the business in America. (Bridgeman-Giraudon/Art Resource, NY)

SOUTHERN WHITE SOCIETY

Only a very small minority of southern whites owned slaves. In 1860, when the white population was just above 8 million, the number of slaveholders was only 383,637. Even with all members of slaveowning families included in the figures, those living in slaveowning households still amounted to perhaps no more than one-quarter of the white population. And only a small proportion of this relatively small number of slaveowners owned slaves in substantial numbers.

THE PLANTER CLASS

How, then, did the South come to be seen as a society dominated by wealthy slaveowning planters? In large part, it was because the planter aristocracy exercised power and influence far in excess of its numbers.

White southerners liked to compare their planter class to the old aristocracies of England and Europe, but the comparison was not a sound one. In some areas of the upper South, the great aristocrats were indeed people whose families had occupied positions of wealth and power for generations. In most of the South, however, many of the great landowners were still first-generation settlers as late as the 1850s, who had only relatively recently started to live in the

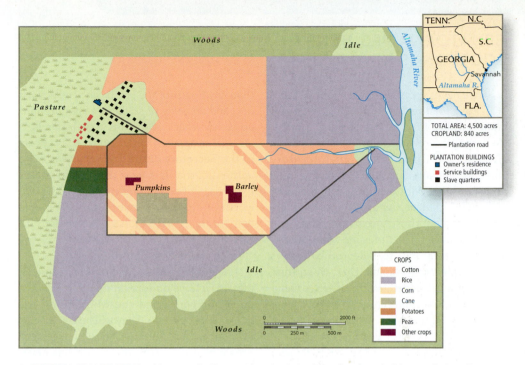

A GEORGIA PLANTATION This map of the Hopeton Plantation in South Carolina shows both how much plantations were connected to the national and world markets and how much they tried to be self-sufficient. Note the large areas of land devoted to the growing of cotton, rice, and sugarcane, all crops for the market. • *Why would a plantation in this part of the South be so much more diversified in the market crops it raised than the cotton plantations in the Mississippi Delta?* Note also the many crops grown for the local market or for consumption by residents of the plantation—potatoes, peas, corn, and others. The top left of the map shows the distribution of living quarters, with slaves' quarters grouped together very near the owner's residence. • *Why would planters want their slaves living nearby? Why might slaves be unhappy about being so close to their owners?*

comfort and luxury for which they became famous. Large areas of the South had been settled and cultivated for less than two decades at the time of the Civil War.

Nor was the world of the planter nearly as leisured and genteel as the aristocratic myth would suggest. Growing staple crops was a tough business. Planters were just as much competitive capitalists as the industrialists of the North. Even many affluent planters lived rather modestly, their wealth so heavily invested in land and slaves that there was often little left for personal comfort. And white planters, including some substantial ones, tended to move frequently as new and presumably more productive areas opened up to cultivation.

Wealthy southern whites sustained their image as aristocrats in many ways. They adopted an elaborate code of "chivalry," which obligated white men to defend their "honor," often through dueling. They avoided such "coarse" occupations as trade and commerce; those who did not become planters often gravitated toward the military. The aristocratic ideal also found reflection in the definition of a special role for southern white women.

THE "SOUTHERN LADY"

In some respects, affluent white women in the South occupied roles very similar to those of middle-class white women in the North. Their lives generally centered in the home, where (according to the South's social ideal) they served as companions to and hostesses for their husbands and as nurturing mothers for their children. "Genteel" southern white women seldom engaged in public activities or found income-producing employment.

CONSIDER THE SOURCE

SENATOR JAMES HENRY HAMMOND DECLARES, "COTTON IS KING," 1858

IF we never acquire another foot of territory for the South, look at her. Eight hundred and fifty thousand square miles. As large as Great Britain, France, Austria, Prussia, and Spain. Is not that territory enough to make an empire that shall rule the world? . . . With the finest soil, the most delightful climate, whose staple productions none of those great countries can grow, we have three thousand miles of continental shore line, so indented with bays and crowded with islands, that, when their shore lines are added, we have twelve thousand miles. Through the heart of our country runs the great Mississippi, the father of waters, into whose bosom are poured thirty-six thousand miles of tributary streams; and beyond we have the desert prairie wastes, to protect us in our rear. Can you hem in such a territory as that? . . .

[. . .] Upon our muster-rolls we have a million of militia. In a defensive war, upon an emergency, every one of them would be available. At any time, the South can raise, equip, and maintain in the field, a larger army than any Power of the earth can send against her, and an army of soldiers—men brought up on horseback, with guns in their hands.

[. . .] It appears, by going to the reports of the Secretary of the Treasury, which are authentic, that last year the United States exported in round numbers $279,000,000 worth of domestic produce, excluding gold and foreign merchandise re-exported. Of this amount $158,000,000 worth is the clear produce of the South; . . .

[. . .] [W]e have nothing to do but to take off restrictions on foreign merchandise and open our ports, and the whole world will come to us to trade. They will be too glad to bring and carry for us, and we never shall dream of a war. Why the South has never yet had a just cause of war. Every time she has drawn her sword it has been on the point of honor, and that point of honor has been mainly loyalty to her sister colonies and sister States, who have ever since plundered and calumniated her.

But if there were no other reason why we should never have war, would any sane

But the life of the "southern lady" was also very different from that of her northern counterpart. For one thing, the cult of honor dictated that southern white men give particular importance to the defense of women. In practice, this generally meant that white men were even more dominant and white women even more subordinate in southern culture than they were in the North. Social theorist George Fitzhugh wrote in the 1850s: "Women, like children, have but one right, and that is the right to protection. The right to protection involves the obligation to obey."

More important in determining the role of southern white women, however, was that the vast majority of them lived on farms, with little access to the "public world" and thus few opportunities to look beyond their roles as wives and mothers. For many white women, living on farms of modest size meant a fuller engagement in the economic life of the family than was typical for middle-class women in the North. These women engaged in spinning, weaving, and other production; they participated in agricultural tasks; they helped supervise the slave workforce. On the larger plantations, however, even nation make war on cotton? Without firing a gun, without drawing a sword, should they make war on us we can bring the whole world to our feet. The South is perfectly competent to go on, one, two, or three years without planting a seed of cotton. I believe that if she was to plant but half her cotton for three years to come, it would be an immense advantage to her. I am not so sure but that after three total years' abstinence she would come out stronger than ever she was before and better prepared to enter afresh upon her great career of enterprise. . . . England would topple headlong and carry the whole civilized world with her, save the South. No, you dare not make war on cotton. No power on earth dares to make war upon it. Cotton *is* king.

In all social systems there must be a class to do the menial duties, to perform the drudgery of life. That is, a class requiring but a low order of intellect and but little skill. Its requisites are vigor, docility, fidelity. . . . Fortunately for the South, she found a race adapted to that purpose to her hand—a race inferior to her own, but eminently qualified in temper, in vigor, in docility, in capacity to stand the climate, to answer all her purposes. We use them for our purpose, and call them slaves. We found them slaves by the "common consent of mankind," which, according to Cicero, *"lex naturae est;"* the highest proof of what is Nature's law. We are old-fashioned at the South yet; it is a word discarded now by "ears polite." I will not characterize that class at the North by that term; but you have it; it is there; it is everywhere; it is eternal.

UNDERSTAND, ANALYZE, & EVALUATE

1. How did Hammond describe the South in comparison to the North? Compare this assessment with the experience of the South in the Civil War. How did Hammond view the South in a global context? What do you think of this assessment?
2. What justifications did Hammond offer for slavery? Describe the comparison Hammond drew between northern wage labor and southern slavery?

Source: James Henry Hammond, Speech on the Kansas-Lecompton Constitution, U.S. Senate, March 4, 1858, in *Congressional Globe*, 35th Cong., 1st Sess., Appendix, pp. 70–71; in Regina Lee Blaszczyk and Philip B. Scranton (eds.), *Major Problems in American Business History*. (Boston: Houghton Mifflin Company, 2006), pp. 149–154.

these limited roles were often considered unsuitable for white women, and the "plantation mistress" became, in some cases, more an ornament for her husband than an active part of the economy or the society. Southern white women also had less access to education than their northern counterparts. The few female "academies" in the South trained women primarily to be suitable wives.

Southern white women had other special burdens as well. The southern white birth rate remained nearly 20 percent higher than that of the nation as a whole, but infant mortality in the region remained higher than elsewhere. The slave labor system also had a mixed impact on white women. It helped spare many of them from certain kinds of arduous labor, but it also damaged their relationships with their husbands. Male slaveowners had frequent sexual relationships with the female slaves on their plantations; the children of those unions served as a constant reminder to white women of their husbands' infidelities. Black women (and men) were obviously the most important victims of such practices, but white women suffered, too.

THE PLAIN FOLK

The typical white southerner was a yeoman farmer. Some of these "plain folk," as they became known, owned a few slaves, with whom they worked and lived more closely than did the larger planters. Some plain folk, most of whom owned their own land, devoted themselves largely to subsistence farming; others grew cotton or other crops for the market but usually could not produce enough to allow them to expand their operations or even get out of debt.

One reason was the southern educational system. For the sons of wealthy planters, the region provided ample opportunities to gain an education. In 1860, there were 260 southern colleges and universities, public and private, with 25,000 students enrolled in them. But as in the rest of the United States, universities were only within the reach of the upper class. The elementary and secondary schools of the South were not only fewer than but also inferior to those of the Northeast. The South had more than 500,000 illiterate whites, over half the nation's total. The subordination of the plain folk to the planter class raises an important question: Why did lower-class whites not oppose the aristocratic social system from which they benefited so little?

Some nonslaveowning whites did oppose the planter elite, but for the most part in limited ways and in isolated areas. These were mainly the "hill people," who lived in the Appalachian ranges east of the Mississippi, in the Ozarks to the west of the river, and in other "hill country" or "backcountry" areas. They practiced a simple form of subsistence agriculture, owned practically no slaves, and were, in most respects, unconnected to the cotton economy. Such whites frequently expressed animosity toward the planter aristocracy. The mountain regions were the only parts of the South to resist the movement toward secession in the early 1860s. Even during the Civil War itself, many refused to support the Confederacy.

Far greater in number, however, were the nonslaveowning whites who lived in the midst of the plantation system. Many, perhaps most of them, accepted that system because they were tied to it in important ways. Small farmers depended on the local plantation aristocracy for access to cotton gins, markets for their modest crops and their livestock, and credit or other financial assistance in time of need. In many areas, moreover, the poorest resident of a county might easily be a cousin of the richest aristocrat. In the 1850s, the cotton boom allowed many small farmers to improve their economic fortunes. Some bought more land, became slaveowners, and moved into at least the fringes of plantation society. Others simply felt more secure in their positions as independent yeomen and hence were more likely to embrace the fierce regional loyalty that was spreading throughout the white South in these years.

There were other white southerners, however, who were known at the time variously as "crackers," "sand hillers," or "poor white trash." Occupying the infertile lands of the pine barrens, the red hills, and the swamps, they lived in genuine squalor. Many owned no land and supported themselves by foraging or hunting. Others worked at times as common laborers for their neighbors. Their degradation resulted partly from dietary deficiencies and disease. Forced to resort at times to eating clay (hence the tendency of more-affluent whites to refer to them disparagingly as "clay eaters"), they suffered from pellagra, hookworm, and malaria. Planters and small farmers alike held them in contempt.

Even among these southerners—the true outcasts of white society—there was no real opposition to the plantation system or slavery. In part, this was because they were so benumbed by poverty that they had little strength to protest. But the single greatest unifying factor among the southern white population was their perception of race. However poor and miserable white southerners might be, they could still look down on the black population of the region and feel a bond with their fellow whites and a sense of racial supremacy.

SLAVERY: THE "PECULIAR INSTITUTION"

White southerners often referred to slavery as the "peculiar institution," meaning that it was distinctive, special. And indeed it was. The South in the mid-nineteenth century was the only area in the Western world—except for Brazil, Cuba, and Puerto Rico—where slavery still existed. Slavery, more than any other single factor, isolated the South from the rest of American society.

Within the South itself, slavery produced paradoxical results. On one hand, it isolated blacks from whites. As a result, African Americans under slavery began to develop a society and culture of their own. On the other hand, slavery created a unique bond between blacks and whites—slaves and masters—in the South. The two groups may have maintained separate spheres, but each sphere was deeply influenced by the other.

VARIETIES OF SLAVERY

Southern slave codes forbade slaves to hold property, to leave their masters' premises without permission, to be out after dark, to congregate with other slaves except at church, to carry firearms, to testify in court against white people, or to strike a white person even in self-defense. The codes prohibited whites from teaching slaves to read or write. The laws contained no provisions to legalize slave marriages or divorces. If an owner killed a slave while punishing him, the act was generally not considered a crime. Slaves, however, faced the death penalty for killing or even resisting a white person and for inciting revolt. The codes also contained extraordinarily rigid provisions for defining a person's race. Anyone with a trace (or, often, even a rumor) of African ancestry was defined as black.

Enforcement of the codes, however, was spotty and uneven. Some slaves did acquire property, did become literate, and did assemble with other slaves. White owners themselves handled most transgressions by their slaves and inflicted widely varying punishments. In other words, despite the rigid provisions of law, there was in reality considerable variety within the slave system. Some slaves lived in almost prisonlike conditions, rigidly and harshly controlled by their masters. Many (probably most) others enjoyed considerable flexibility and autonomy.

The nature of the relationship between masters and slaves depended in part on the size of the plantation. White farmers with few slaves generally supervised their workers directly and often worked closely alongside them. The paternal relationship between such masters and their slaves could be warm and benevolent, or tyrannical and cruel. In general, African Americans themselves preferred to live on larger plantations, where they had a chance for a social world of their own.

Although the majority of slaveowners were small farmers, the majority of slaves lived on plantations of medium or large size, with substantial slave workforces. Thus the relationship between master and slave was much less intimate for the typical slave than for the typical slaveowner. Substantial planters often hired overseers and even assistant

THE CHARACTER OF SLAVERY

NO issue in American history has produced a more spirited debate than the nature of plantation slavery. The debate began well before the Civil War, when abolitionists strove to expose slavery to the world as a brutal, dehumanizing institution, while southern defenders of slavery tried to depict it as a benevolent and paternalistic system. But by the late nineteenth century, with white Americans eager for sectional conciliation, most northern and southern chroniclers of slavery began to accept a romanticized and unthreatening picture of the Old South and its peculiar institution.

The first major scholarly examination of slavery was Ulrich B. Phillips's *American Negro Slavery* (1918), which portrayed slavery as an essentially benign institution in which kindly masters looked after submissive and generally contented African Americans. Phillips's apologia for slavery remained the authoritative work on the subject for nearly thirty years.

In the 1940s, challenges to Phillips began to emerge. Melville J. Herskovits disputed Phillips's contention that black Americans retained little of their African cultural inheritance. Herbert Aptheker published a chronicle of slave revolts as a way of refuting Phillips's claim that blacks were submissive and content.

A somewhat different challenge to Phillips emerged in the 1950s from historians who emphasized the brutality of the institution. Kenneth Stampp's *The Peculiar Institution* (1956) and Stanley Elkins's *Slavery* (1959) described a labor system that did serious physical and psychological damage to its victims. They portrayed slavery as something like a prison, in which men and women had virtually no space to develop their own social and cultural lives. Elkins compared the system to Nazi concentration camps and likened the childlike "Sambo" personality of slavery to tragic distortions of character produced by the Holocaust.

In the early 1970s, an explosion of new scholarship on slavery shifted the emphasis away from the damage the system inflicted on African Americans and toward the striking success of the slaves themselves in building a culture of their own. John Blassingame in 1973 argued that "the most remarkable aspect of the whole process of enslavement is the extent to which the American-born slaves were able to retain their ancestors' culture." Herbert Gutman, in *The Black Family in Slavery and Freedom* (1976), challenged the prevailing belief that slavery had weakened and even destroyed the African American family. On the contrary, Gutman argued, the black family survived slavery with impressive strength, although with some significant differences from the prevailing form of the white family. Eugene Genovese's *Roll, Jordan, Roll* (1974) revealed how African Americans manipulated white paternalist assumptions to build a large cultural space of their own where they could develop their own family life, social traditions, and religious patterns. That same year, Robert Fogel and Stanley Engerman published the controversial *Time on the Cross,* a highly quantitative study that supported some of

(The Granger Collection, NYC)

the claims of Gutman and Genovese about black achievement but that went much further in portraying slavery as a successful and reasonably humane (if ultimately immoral) system. Slave workers, they argued, were better treated and lived in greater comfort than most Northern industrial workers of the same era. Their conclusions produced a storm of criticism.

Other important scholarship includes African American slave women. Elizabeth Fox-Genovese's *Within the Plantation Household* (1988) examined the lives of both white and black women on the plantation. She portrayed slave women as defined by their dual roles as members of the plantation workforce and anchors of the black family. Slave women, she argued, professed loyalty to their mistresses when forced to serve them as domestics; but their real loyalty remained to their own communities and families.

Recent studies by Walter Johnson and Ira Berlin mark an at least partial return to the "damage" approach to slavery of the 1970s. Johnson's *Soul by Soul* (2000) examines the South's largest slave market, New Orleans.

For whites, he argues, purchasing slaves was a way of fulfilling the middle-class male fantasy of success and independence. For the slaves themselves, the trade was dehumanizing and destructive to black families and communities. Berlin's *Many Thousands Gone* (2000) and *Generation of Captivity* (2003)—among the most important studies of slavery in a generation—similarly emphasize the dehumanizing character of the slave market and show that, whatever white slaveowners might say, slavery was less a social system than a commodification of human beings. ●

UNDERSTAND, ANALYZE, & EVALUATE

1. Why might the conclusions drawn by Robert Fogel and Stanley Engerman in *Time on the Cross* have provoked vehement criticism?
2. What might be some reasons for the resurrection of focus on the "damage" thesis of slavery, as in the works by Walter Johnson and Ira Berlin?

overseers to represent them. "Head drivers," trusted and responsible slaves often assisted by several subdrivers, acted under the overseer as foremen.

LIFE UNDER SLAVERY

Most, but not all, slaves received an adequate if rude diet, consisting mainly of cornmeal, salt pork, molasses, and, on rare occasions, fresh meat or poultry. Many slaves cultivated gardens for their own use. Their masters provided them with cheap clothing and shoes. They lived in rough cabins, called slave quarters. The plantation mistress or a doctor retained by the owner provided some medical care, but slave women themselves—as "healers," midwives, or simply as mothers—were the more important source of medical attention.

Slaves worked hard, beginning with light tasks as children. Their workdays were longest at harvesttime. Slave women worked particularly hard. They generally labored in the fields with the men, and they also handled cooking, cleaning, and child rearing. Many slave families were divided. Husbands and fathers often lived on neighboring plantations; at times, one spouse (usually the male) would be sold to a plantation owner far away. As a result, black women often found themselves acting in effect as single parents.

Slaves were, as a group, much less healthy than southern whites. After 1808, when the importation of slaves became illegal, the proportion of blacks to whites in the nation as a whole steadily declined as a result of the comparatively high black death rate. Slave mothers had large families, but the enforced poverty in which virtually all African Americans lived ensured that fewer of their children would survive to adulthood than the

RETURNING FROM THE COTTON FIELD In this photograph, South Carolina field workers return after a day of picking cotton, some of their harvest carried in bundles on their heads. A black slave driver leads the way. (Collection of the New-York Historical Society)

children of white parents. Even those who did survive typically died at a younger age than the average white person.

Household servants had a somewhat easier life—physically at least—than did field hands. On a small plantation, the same slaves might do both field work and housework. But on a large estate, there would generally be a separate domestic staff: nursemaids, housemaids, cooks, butlers, coachmen. These people lived close to the master and his family, eating the leftovers from the family table. Between the blacks and whites of such households, affectionate, almost familial relationships might develop. More often, however, house servants resented their isolation from their fellow slaves and the lack of privacy and increased discipline that came with living in such close proximity to the master's family. When emancipation came after the Civil War, it was often the house servants who were the first to leave the plantations of their former owners.

Female household servants were especially vulnerable to sexual abuse by their masters and white overseers. In addition to being subjected to unwanted sexual attention from white men, female slaves often received vindictive treatment from white women. Plantation mistresses naturally resented the sexual liaisons between their husbands and female slaves. Punishing their husbands was not usually possible, so they often punished the slaves instead—with arbitrary beatings, increased workloads, and various forms of psychological torment.

SLAVERY IN THE CITIES

The conditions of urban slavery differed significantly from those in the countryside. On the relatively isolated plantations, slaves had little contact with free blacks and lower-class whites, and masters maintained a fairly direct and effective control. In the city, however, a master often could not supervise his slaves closely and at the same time use them profitably. Even if they slept at night in carefully watched backyard barracks, they moved about during the day alone, performing errands of various kinds.

There was a considerable market in the South for common laborers, particularly since, unlike in the North, there were few European immigrants to perform menial chores. As a result, masters often hired out slaves for such tasks. Slaves on contract worked in mining and lumbering (often far from cities), but others worked on the docks and on construction sites, drove wagons, and performed other unskilled jobs in cities and towns. Slave women and children worked in the region's few textile mills. Particularly skilled workers such as blacksmiths or carpenters were also often hired out. After regular working hours, many of them fended for themselves; thus urban slaves gained numerous opportunities to mingle with free blacks and with whites. In the cities, the line between slavery and freedom was less distinct than on the plantation.

FREE AFRICAN AMERICANS

Over 250,000 free African Americans lived in the slaveholding states by the start of the Civil War, more than half of them in Virginia and Maryland. In some cases, they were slaves who had somehow earned money to buy their own and their families' freedom. It was most often urban blacks, with their greater freedom of movement and activity, who could take that route. One example was Elizabeth Keckley, a slave woman who bought freedom for herself and her son with proceeds from sewing. She later became a seamstress, personal servant, and companion to Mary Todd Lincoln in the White House. But few masters had any incentive, or inclination, to give up their slaves, so this route was open to relatively few people.

Some slaves were set free by a master who had moral qualms about slavery, or by a master's will after his death—for example, the more than 400 slaves belonging to John Randolph of Roanoke, freed in 1833. From the 1830s on, however, state laws governing slavery became more rigid, in part in response to the fears Nat Turner's revolt (see p. 264) created among white southerners. The new laws made it more difficult, and in some cases practically impossible, for owners to set free (or "manumit") their slaves.

A few free blacks attained wealth and prominence. Some even owned slaves themselves, usually relatives whom they had bought in order to ensure their ultimate emancipation. In a few cities—New Orleans, Natchez, and Charleston—free black communities managed to flourish with relatively little interference from whites and with some economic stability. Most southern free blacks, however, lived in abject poverty. Yet, great as were the hardships of freedom, blacks much preferred it to slavery.

THE SLAVE TRADE

The transfer of slaves from one part of the South to another was one of the most important and terrible consequences of slavery. Sometimes slaves moved to the new cotton lands in the company of their original owners, who were migrating themselves. More often, however, the transfer occurred through the efforts of professional slave traders. The traders took slaves to such central markets as Natchez, New Orleans, Mobile, and Charleston, where purchasers bid for them. A sound young field hand could fetch a price that might vary in the 1840s and 1850s from $500 to $1,700, depending on fluctuations in the market (and the health and age of the slaves).

The domestic slave trade, essential to the growth and prosperity of the system, was one of its most horrible aspects. The trade dehumanized all who were involved in it. It separated children from parents, and parents from each other. Even families kept together by scrupulous owners might be broken up in the division of the estate after the master's death. Planters might deplore the trade, but they eased their consciences by holding the traders in contempt.

The foreign slave trade was bad or worse. Although federal law had prohibited the importation of slaves from 1808 on, some continued to be smuggled into the United States as late as the 1850s when the supply of slaves was inadequate. At the annual southern commercial conventions, planters began to discuss the legal reopening of the trade. "If it is right to buy slaves in Virginia and carry them to New Orleans," William L. Yancey asked his fellow delegates in 1858, "why is it not right to buy them in Cuba, Brazil, or Africa." The convention that year voted to repeal all the laws against slave imports, but the government never acted on their proposal.

The continued smuggling of slaves was not without resistance. In 1839, a group of 53 slaves in Cuba took charge of a ship, the *Amistad*, that was transporting them to another port in Cuba. Their goal was to sail back to their homelands in Africa. The slaves had no experience with sailing, and they tried to compel the crew to steer them across the Atlantic. Instead, the ship sailed up the Atlantic coast until it was captured by a ship of the United States Revenue Service. Many Americans, including President Van Buren, thought the slaves should be returned to Cuba. But at the request of a group of abolitionists, former president John Quincy Adams went before the Supreme Court to argue that they should be freed. Adams argued that the foreign slave trade was illegal and thus the *Amistad* rebels could not be returned to slavery. The Court accepted his argument in 1841, and most of the former slaves were returned to Africa, with funding from American abolitionists.

Two years later, another group of slaves revolted on board a ship and took control of it—this time an American vessel bound from Norfolk, Virginia, to New Orleans, Louisiana—and steered it (and its 135 slaves) to the British Bahamas, where slavery was illegal and the slaves were given sanctuary. Such shipboard revolts were rare, but they were symbols of the continued effort by Africans to resist slavery.

SLAVE RESISTANCE

Slaveowners liked to argue that the slaves were generally content, "happy with their lot." But it is clear that the vast majority of southern blacks yearned for freedom. Evidence for that can be found, if nowhere else, in the reaction of slaves when emancipation finally came. Virtually all reacted to freedom with great joy; few chose to remain in the service of the whites who had owned them before the Civil War.

Rather than contented acceptance, the dominant response of African Americans to slavery was a complex one: a combination of adaptation and resistance. At the extremes,

NURSING THE MASTER'S CHILD   Louisa, a slave on a Missouri plantation owned by the Hayward family in the 1850s, is photographed here holding the master's infant son. Black women typically cared for white children on plantations, sometimes with great affection and sometimes—as this photograph may suggest—dutifully and without enthusiasm. (Missouri History Museum St. Louis)

slavery could produce two very different reactions, each of which served as the basis for a powerful stereotype in white society. One extreme was what became known as the "Sambo"—the shuffling, grinning, head-scratching, deferential slave who acted out what he recognized as the role the white world expected of him. More often than not, the Sambo pattern of behavior was a charade, a facade assumed in the presence of whites. The other extreme was the slave rebel—the African American who resisted either acceptance or accommodation but remained forever rebellious.

Actual slave revolts were extremely rare, but the knowledge that they were possible struck terror into the hearts of white southerners. In 1800, Gabriel Prosser gathered 1,000 rebellious slaves outside Richmond; but two African Americans gave the plot away, and the Virginia militia stymied the uprising before it could begin. Prosser and thirty-five others were executed. In 1822, the Charleston free black Denmark Vesey and his followers—rumored to total 9,000—made preparations for revolt; but again word leaked out, and suppression and retribution followed. On a summer night in 1831, Nat Turner, a slave preacher, led a band of African Americans armed with guns and axes from house to house in Southampton County, Virginia. They killed sixty white men, women, and children before being overpowered by state and federal troops. More than a hundred blacks were executed in the aftermath.

For the most part, however, resistance to slavery took other, less violent forms. Some blacks attempted to resist by running away. A small number managed to escape to the North or to Canada, especially after sympathetic whites and free blacks began organizing secret escape routes, known as the "underground railroad," to assist them in flight. But the odds against a successful escape were very high. The hazards of distance and the slaves' ignorance of geography were serious obstacles, as were the white "slave patrols," which stopped wandering blacks on sight and demanded to see travel permits. Despite all the obstacles to success, however, blacks continued to run away from their masters in large numbers.

Perhaps the most important method of resistance was simply a pattern of everyday behavior by which blacks defied their masters. That whites so often considered blacks to be lazy and shiftless suggests one means of resistance: refusal to work hard. Some slaves stole from their masters or from neighboring whites. Others performed isolated acts of sabotage: losing or breaking tools or performing tasks improperly. In extreme cases, blacks might make themselves useless by cutting off their fingers or even committing suicide. A few turned on their masters and killed them. The extremes, however, were rare. For the most part, blacks resisted by building subtle methods of rebellion into their normal patterns of behavior.

THE CULTURE OF SLAVERY

Resistance was only part of the slave response to slavery. Another was an elaborate process of adaptation. One of the ways blacks adapted was by developing their own, separate culture, one that enabled them to sustain a sense of racial pride and unity.

SLAVE RELIGION

Almost all African Americans were Christians by the early nineteenth century. Some had converted voluntarily and others in response to coercion from their masters and

Protestant missionaries who evangelized among them. Masters expected their slaves to join their denominations and worship under the supervision of white ministers. A separate slave religion was not supposed to exist. Indeed, autonomous black churches were banned by law.

Nevertheless, blacks throughout the South developed their own version of Christianity, at times incorporating into it such practices as voodoo or other polytheistic religious traditions of Africa. Or they simply bent religion to the special circumstances of bondage.

African American religion was often more emotional than its white counterpart and reflected the influence of African customs and practices. Slave prayer meetings routinely involved fervent chanting, spontaneous exclamations from the congregation, and ecstatic conversion experiences. Black religion was also generally more joyful and affirming than that of many white denominations. And above all, African American religion emphasized the dream of freedom and deliverance. In their prayers and songs and sermons, black Christians talked and sang of the day when the Lord would "call us home," "deliver us to freedom," or "take us to the Promised Land." While whites generally chose to interpret such language merely as the expression of hopes for life after death, many blacks used the images of Christian salvation to express their own dreams of freedom in the present world.

LANGUAGE AND MUSIC

In many areas, slaves retained a language of their own. Having arrived in America speaking many different African languages, the first generations of slaves had as much difficulty communicating with one another as they did with white people. To overcome these barriers, they learned a simple, common language (known to linguists as "pidgin"). It retained some African words, but it drew primarily, if selectively, from English. And while slave language grew more sophisticated as blacks spent more time in America, some features of this early pidgin survived in black speech for many generations.

Music was especially important in slave society. Again, the African heritage was an important influence. African music relied heavily on rhythm, and so did black music in America. Slaves often created instruments for themselves out of whatever materials were at hand. The banjo became important to slave music. But more important were voices and song.

Field workers often used songs to pass the time; since they sang them in the presence of the whites, they usually attached relatively innocuous words to them. But African Americans also created more politically challenging music in the relative privacy of their own religious services. It was there that the tradition of the spiritual emerged. Through the spiritual, Africans in America not only expressed their religious faith, but also lamented their bondage and expressed continuing hope for freedom.

Slave songs were rarely written down and often seemed entirely spontaneous; but much slave music was really derived from African and Caribbean traditions passed on through generations. Performers also improvised variations on songs they had heard. When the setting permitted it, African Americans danced to their music—dances very different from and much more spontaneous than the formal steps that nineteenth-century whites generally learned. They also used music to accompany another of their important cultural traditions: storytelling.

THE OLD PLANTATION   This painting, by an unidentified folk artist of the early nineteenth century, suggests the importance of music in the lives of plantation slaves in America. The banjo, which the musician at right is playing, was originally an African instrument. (The Granger Collection, NYC)

THE SLAVE FAMILY

The slave family was the other crucial institution of black culture in the South. Like religion, it suffered from legal restrictions. Nevertheless, what we now call the "nuclear family" consistently emerged as the dominant kinship model among African Americans.

Black women generally began bearing children at younger ages than most whites, often as early as fourteen or fifteen (sometimes as a result of unwanted sexual relations with their masters). Slave communities did not condemn premarital pregnancy in the way white society did, and black couples would often begin living together before marrying. It was customary, however, for couples to marry—in a ceremony involving formal vows—soon after conceiving a child. Husbands and wives on neighboring plantations sometimes visited each other with the permission of their masters, but often such visits had to be in secret, at night. Family ties among slaves were generally no less strong than those of whites.

When marriages did not survive, it was often because of circumstances over which blacks had no control. Up to a third of all black families were broken apart by the slave trade. Extended kinship networks were strong and important and often helped compensate for the breakup of nuclear families. A slave forced suddenly to move to a new area, far from his or her family, might create fictional kinship ties and become "adopted" by a family in the new community. Even so, the impulse to maintain contact with a spouse and children remained strong long after the breakup of a family. One of the most frequent causes of flight from the plantation was a slave's desire to find a husband, wife, or child who had been sent elsewhere.

However much blacks resented their lack of freedom, they often found it difficult to maintain an entirely hostile attitude toward their owners. They depended on whites for the material means of existence—food, clothing, and shelter—and they relied on them as well for security and protection. There was, in short, a paternal relationship between slave and master—sometimes harsh, at other times kindly, but always important. That paternalism, in fact, became a vital instrument of white control. By creating a sense of mutual dependence, whites helped reduce resistance to an institution that served only the interests of the ruling race.

CONCLUSION

While the North was creating a complex and rapidly developing commercial-industrial economy, the South was expanding its agrarian economy without making many fundamental changes in the region's character. Great migrations took many southern whites, and even more African American slaves, into new agricultural areas in the Deep South, where they created a booming "cotton kingdom." The cotton economy created many great fortunes and some modest ones. It also entrenched the planter class as the dominant force within southern society—both as owners of vast numbers of slaves and as patrons, creditors, landlords, and marketers for the large number of poor whites who lived on the edge of the planter world.

The differences between the North and the South were a result of differences in natural resources, social structure, climate, and culture. Above all, they were the result of the existence within the South of an unfree labor system that prevented the kind of social fluidity that an industrializing society usually requires. Within that system, however, slaves created a vital, independent culture and religion in the face of white subjugation.

RECALL AND REFLECT

1. Why did cotton become the leading crop of the South?
2. Why did industry fail to develop in the South to the extent that it did in the North?
3. How did slavery function economically and socially?
4. What was the effect of slavery on white slaveowners? On slaves? On nonslaveowning whites? On free blacks?
5. Through what means did slaves maintain a distinct African American culture?

12 ANTEBELLUM CULTURE AND REFORM

THE ROMANTIC IMPULSE
REMAKING SOCIETY
THE CRUSADE AGAINST SLAVERY

LOOKING AHEAD

1. How did an American national culture of art, literature, philosophy, and communal living develop in the nineteenth century?

2. What were the issues on which social and moral reformers tried to "remake the nation"? How successful were their efforts?

3. Why did the crusade against slavery become the preeminent issue of the reform movement?

THE UNITED STATES IN THE mid-nineteenth century was growing rapidly in size, population, and economic complexity. Most Americans were excited by the new possibilities these changes produced. But many people were also painfully aware of the problems that accompanied them.

One result of these conflicting attitudes was the emergence of movements to "reform" the nation. Some reforms rested on an optimistic faith in human nature, a belief that within every individual resided a spirit that was basically good and that society should attempt to unleash. A second impulse was a desire for order and control. With their traditional values and institutions being challenged and eroded, many Americans yearned above all for stability and discipline. By the end of the 1840s, however, one issue—slavery—had come to overshadow all others. And one group of reformers—the abolitionists—had become the most influential of all.

THE ROMANTIC IMPULSE

"In the four quarters of the globe," wrote the English wit Sydney Smith in 1820, "who reads an American book? or goes to an American play? or looks at an American picture or statue?" The answer, he assumed, was obvious: no one.

American intellectuals were painfully aware of the low regard in which Europeans held their culture, and they tried to create an artistic life that would express their own nation's special virtues. At the same time, many of the nation's cultural leaders were striving for another kind of liberation, which was—ironically—largely an import from Europe: the spirit of romanticism. In literature, in philosophy, in art, even in politics and economics, American intellectuals were committing themselves to the liberation of the human spirit.

NATIONALISM AND ROMANTICISM IN AMERICAN PAINTING

Despite Sydney Smith's contemptuous question, a great many people in the United States were, in fact, looking at American paintings—and they were doing so because they believed Americans were creating important new artistic traditions of their own.

American painters sought to capture the power of nature by portraying some of the nation's most spectacular and undeveloped areas. The first great school of American painters—known as the Hudson River school—emerged in New York. Frederic Church, Thomas Cole, Thomas Doughty, Asher Durand, and others painted the spectacular vistas of the rugged and still largely untamed Hudson Valley. Like Ralph Waldo Emerson and Henry David Thoreau, whom many of the painters read and admired (see p. 272), they considered nature—far more than civilization—the best source of wisdom and fulfillment. In portraying the Hudson Valley, they seemed to announce that in America, unlike in Europe, "wild nature"

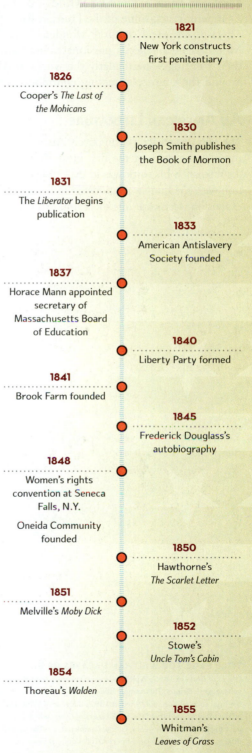

TIME LINE

1821
New York constructs first penitentiary

1826
Cooper's *The Last of the Mohicans*

1830
Joseph Smith publishes the Book of Mormon

1831
The *Liberator* begins publication

1833
American Antislavery Society founded

1837
Horace Mann appointed secretary of Massachusetts Board of Education

1840
Liberty Party formed

1841
Brook Farm founded

1845
Frederick Douglass's autobiography

1848
Women's rights convention at Seneca Falls, N.Y.

Oneida Community founded

1850
Hawthorne's *The Scarlet Letter*

1851
Melville's *Moby Dick*

1852
Stowe's *Uncle Tom's Cabin*

1854
Thoreau's *Walden*

1855
Whitman's *Leaves of Grass*

still existed; and that America, therefore, was a nation of greater promise than the over-developed lands of the Old World.

In later years, some of the Hudson River painters traveled farther west. Their enormous canvases of great natural wonders—the Yosemite Valley, Yellowstone, the Rocky Mountains—touched a passionate chord among the public. Some of the most famous of their paintings—particularly the works of Albert Bierstadt and Thomas Moran—traveled around the country attracting enormous crowds.

AN AMERICAN LITERATURE

The effort to create a distinctively American literature made considerable progress in the 1820s through the work of the first great American novelist: James Fenimore Cooper. What most distinguished his work was its evocation of the American West. Cooper had a lifelong fascination with the human relationship to nature and with the challenges (and dangers) of America's expansion westward. His most important novels—among them *The Last of the Mohicans* (1826)

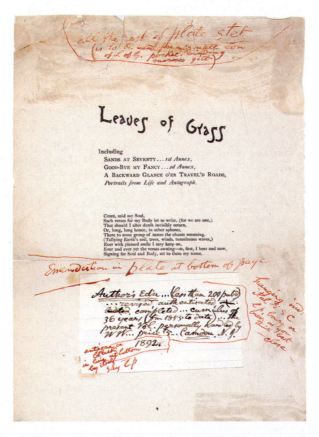

TITLE PAGE FOR WHITMAN'S *LEAVES OF GRASS*   For more than thirty years after the publication of the original *Leaves of Grass* in 1855, Walt Whitman constantly revised and expanded the collection of poems and issued numerous subsequent editions. This sample title page, with notations by Whitman indicating changes and additions he wanted made, is for the final such edition, published in 1892, the year of Whitman's death. In a public announcement he prepared to announce publication, he said that "the book *Leaves of Grass*, which he has been working on at great intervals and partially issued for the past thirty-five or forty years, is now completed. . . . Faulty as it is, he decides it is by far his special and entire self-chosen poetic utterance." (Rare Book and Special Collections Division, Library of Congress)

and *The Deerslayer* (1841)—examined the experience of rugged white frontiersmen with Indians, pioneers, violence, and the law. Cooper evoked the ideal of the independent individual with a natural inner goodness—an ideal that many Americans feared was in jeopardy.

Another, later group of American writers displayed more clearly the influence of romanticism. Walt Whitman's book of poems *Leaves of Grass* (1855) celebrated democracy, the liberation of the individual spirit, and the pleasures of the flesh. In helping to liberate verse from traditional, restrictive conventions, he also expressed a yearning for emotional and physical release and personal fulfillment—a yearning perhaps rooted in part in his own experience as a homosexual living in a society profoundly intolerant of unconventional sexuality.

Less exuberant was Herman Melville, perhaps the greatest American writer of his era. *Moby Dick*, published in 1851, is Melville's most important—although not, in his lifetime, his most popular—novel. It tells the story of Ahab, the powerful, driven captain of a whaling vessel, and his obsessive search for Moby Dick, the great white whale that had once maimed him. It is a story of courage and of the strength of human will. But it is also a tragedy of pride and revenge. In some ways it is an uncomfortable metaphor for the harsh, individualistic, achievement-driven culture of nineteenth-century America.

LITERATURE IN THE ANTEBELLUM SOUTH

The South experienced a literary flowering of its own in the mid-nineteenth century, and it produced writers and artists who were, like their northern counterparts, concerned with defining the nature of America. But white southerners tended to produce very different images of what society was and should be.

The southern writer Edgar Allan Poe produced stories and poems that were primarily sad and macabre. His first book, *Tamerlane and Other Poems* (1827), received little recognition. But later works, including his most famous poem, "The Raven" (1845), established him as a major, if controversial, literary figure. Poe evoked images of individuals rising above the narrow confines of intellect and exploring the deeper—and often painful and horrifying—world of the spirit and emotions.

Other southern novelists of the 1830s (among them Nathaniel Beverley Tucker, William Alexander Caruthers, and John Pendleton Kennedy) produced historical romances and eulogies for the plantation system of the upper South. The most distinguished of the region's men of letters was William Gilmore Simms. For a time, his work expressed a broad nationalism that transcended his regional background; but by the 1840s, he too became a strong defender of southern institutions—especially slavery—against the encroachments of the North. There was, he believed, a unique quality to southern life that it fell to intellectuals to defend.

One group of southern writers, however, produced works that were more broadly American. These writers from the fringes of plantation society—Augustus B. Longstreet, Joseph G. Baldwin, Johnson J. Hooper, and others—depicted the world of the backwoods south and focused on ordinary people and poor whites. Instead of romanticizing their subjects, they were deliberately and sometimes painfully realistic, seasoning their sketches with a robust, vulgar humor that was new to American literature. These southern realists established a tradition of American regional humor that was ultimately to find its most powerful voice in Mark Twain.

THE TRANSCENDENTALISTS

One of the outstanding expressions of the romantic impulse in America came from a group of New England writers and philosophers known as the transcendentalists.

Borrowing heavily from German and English writers and philosophers, the transcendentalists promoted a theory of the individual that rested on a distinction between what they called "reason" and "understanding." Reason, as they defined it, had little to do with rationality. It was, rather, the individual's innate capacity to grasp beauty and truth by giving full expression to the instincts and emotions. Understanding, by contrast, was the use of intellect in the narrow, artificial ways imposed by society; it involved the repression of instinct and the victory of externally imposed learning. Every person's goal, therefore, should be the cultivation of "reason"—and, thus, liberation from "understanding." Each individual should strive to "transcend" the limits of the intellect and allow the emotions, the "soul," to create an "original relation to the Universe."

Transcendentalist philosophy emerged first in America among a small group of intellectuals centered in Concord, Massachusetts, and led by Ralph Waldo Emerson. A Unitarian minister in his youth, Emerson left the clergy in 1832 to devote himself to writing, teaching, and lecturing. In "Nature" (1836), Emerson wrote that in the quest for self-fulfillment, individuals should work for a communion with the natural world: "in the woods, we return to reason and faith. . . . Standing on the bare ground,—my head bathed by the blithe air, and uplifted into infinite space,—all mean egotism vanishes. . . . I am part and particle of God." In other essays, he was even more explicit in advocating a commitment to individuality and the full exploration of inner capacities.

Equally influential was Henry David Thoreau. Thoreau went even further in repudiating the repressive forces of society, which produced, he said, "lives of quiet desperation." Each individual should work for self-realization by resisting pressures to conform to society's expectations and responding instead to his or her own instincts. Thoreau's own effort to free himself—immortalized in *Walden* (1854)—led him to build a small cabin in the Concord woods on the edge of Walden Pond, where he lived alone for two years as simply as he could, attempting to liberate himself from what he considered society's excessive interest in material comforts. In his 1849 essay "Resistance to Civil Government," he extended his critique of artificial constraints in society to government, arguing that when government required an individual to violate his or her own morality, it had no legitimate authority. The proper response was "civil disobedience," or "passive resistance"—a public refusal to obey unjust laws.

THE DEFENSE OF NATURE

As Emerson's and Thoreau's tributes to nature suggest, a small but influential group of Americans in the nineteenth century feared the impact of capitalism on the integrity of the natural world. "The mountains and cataracts, which were to have made poets and painters," wrote the essayist Oliver Wendell Holmes, "have been mined for anthracite and dammed for water power."

To the transcendentalists and others, nature was not just a setting for economic activity, as many farmers, miners, and others believed. It was the source of deep, personal human inspiration—the vehicle through which individuals could best realize the truth within their own souls. Genuine spirituality, they argued, did not come from formal religion but through communion with the natural world.

In making such claims, the transcendentalists were among the first Americans to anticipate the environmental movement of the twentieth century. They had no scientific basis for their defense of the wilderness and little sense of the twentieth-century notion of the interconnectedness of species. But they did believe in, and articulate, an essential unity between humanity and nature—a spiritual unity, they believed, without which civilization would be impoverished. They looked at nature, they said, "with new eyes," and with those eyes they saw that "behind nature, throughout nature, spirit is present."

VISIONS OF UTOPIA

Although transcendentalism was at its heart an individualistic philosophy, it helped spawn one of the most famous nineteenth-century experiments in communal living: Brook Farm. The dream of the Boston transcendentalist George Ripley, Brook Farm was established in 1841 as an experimental community in West Roxbury, Massachusetts. There, according to Ripley, individuals would gather to create a new society that would permit every member to have full opportunity for self-realization. All residents would share equally in the labor of the community so that all could share as well in the leisure, which was essential for cultivation of the self. The tension between the ideal of individual freedom and the demands of a communal society took its toll on Brook Farm. Many residents became disenchanted and left. When a fire destroyed the central building of the community in 1847, the experiment dissolved.

Among the original residents of Brook Farm was the writer Nathaniel Hawthorne, who expressed his disillusionment with the experiment and, to some extent, with transcendentalism in a series of novels. In *The Blithedale Romance* (1852), he wrote scathingly of Brook Farm itself. In other novels—most notably *The Scarlet Letter* (1850) and *The House of the Seven Gables* (1851)—he wrote equally passionately about the price individuals pay for cutting themselves off from society. Egotism, he claimed (in an indirect challenge to the transcendentalist faith in the self), was the "serpent" that lay at the heart of human misery.

Brook Farm was only one of many experimental communities in the years before the Civil War. The Scottish industrialist and philanthropist Robert Owen founded an experimental community in Indiana in 1825, which he named New Harmony. It was to be a "Village of Cooperation," in which every resident worked and lived in total equality. The community was an economic failure, but the vision that had inspired it continued to enchant some Americans. Dozens of other "Owenite" experiments were established in other locations in the ensuing years.

REDEFINING GENDER ROLES

Many of the new utopian communities were centrally concerned with the relationship between men and women. Some experimented with radical redefinitions of gender roles.

One of the most enduring of the utopian colonies of the nineteenth century was the Oneida Community, established in 1848 in upstate New York by John Humphrey Noyes. The Oneida "Perfectionists," as residents of the community called themselves, rejected traditional notions of family and marriage. All residents, Noyes declared, were "married" to all other residents; there were to be no permanent conjugal ties. But Oneida was not, as horrified critics often claimed, an experiment in unrestrained "free love." It was a place where the community carefully monitored sexual behavior, where women were protected from unwanted childbearing, and where children were raised communally, often seeing little of their own parents. The Oneidans took pride in what they considered their liberation of women from the demands of male "lust" and from the traditional bonds of family.

The Shakers, too, redefined traditional gender roles. Founded by "Mother" Ann Lee in the 1770s, the society of the Shakers survived through the twentieth century. (A tiny remnant is left today.) But the Shakers attracted a particularly large following in the mid-nineteenth century and established more than twenty communities throughout the Northeast and Northwest in the 1840s. They derived their name from a unique religious ritual—in which members of a congregation would "shake" themselves free of sin while performing a loud chant and an ecstatic dance.

The most distinctive feature of Shakerism, however, was its commitment to complete celibacy—which meant, of course, that no one could be born into the faith. All Shakers had to choose it voluntarily. Shakerism attracted about 6,000 members in the 1840s, more women than men. They lived in communities where contacts between men and women were strictly limited, and they endorsed the idea of sexual equality, although women exercised the greatest power.

The Shakers were not, however, motivated only by a desire to escape the burdens of traditional gender roles. They were also trying to create a society set apart from the chaos and disorder they believed had come to characterize American life. In that, they were much like other dissenting religious sects and utopian communities of their time.

THE MORMONS

Among the most important efforts to create a new and more ordered society was that of the Church of Jesus Christ of Latter-day Saints—the Mormons. Mormonism began in upstate New York through the efforts of Joseph Smith. In 1830, when he was just twenty-four, he published a remarkable document—the Book of Mormon, named for the ancient prophet who he claimed had written it. It was, he said, a translation of a set of golden tablets he had found in the hills of New York, revealed to him by an angel of God. The Book of Mormon told the story of two ancient civilizations in America, whose people had anticipated the coming of Christ and were rewarded when Jesus actually came to America after his resurrection. Ultimately, both civilizations collapsed because of their rejection of Christian principles. But Smith believed their history as righteous societies could serve as a model for a new holy community in the United States.

In 1831, gathering a small group of believers around him, Smith began searching for a sanctuary for his new community of "saints," an effort that would continue unhappily for more than fifteen years. Time and again, the Latter-day Saints, as they called themselves, attempted to establish peaceful communities. Time and again, they met with persecution from their neighbors, who were suspicious of their radical religious doctrines—their claims of new prophets, new scripture, and divine authority. Opponents were also concerned by their rapid growth and their increasing political strength. Near the end of his life, Joseph Smith introduced the practice of polygamy (giving a man the right to take several wives), which became public knowledge after Smith's death. From then on, polygamy became a central target of anti-Mormon opposition.

Driven from their original settlements in Independence, Missouri, and Kirtland, Ohio, the Mormons founded a new town in Illinois that they named Nauvoo. In the early 1840s, it became an imposing and economically successful community. In 1844, however, bitter enemies of Joseph Smith published an inflammatory attack on him. Smith ordered his followers to destroy the offending press, and he was subsequently arrested and imprisoned in nearby Carthage. There, an angry mob attacked the jail and fatally shot him. The Mormons soon abandoned Nauvoo and, under the leadership of

JOSEPH SMITH REVIEWING HIS TROOPS   After being driven from earlier homes in Missouri, Mormons under the leadership of the religion's founder, Joseph Smith, created a model city in Nauvoo, Illinois—where they also organized an army of over 4,000 men. This painting by the Mormon artist Carl Christensen portrays Smith, aboard the white horse in front, reviewing a vast array of troops—with the pastoral and productive landscape of Nauvoo arrayed in the background. The existence of this large private army aroused great alarm in surrounding non-Mormon communities and contributed to the clashes that led to both the murder of Smith and the expulsion of the Mormons from Illinois. (*Joseph Mustering the Nauvoo Legion* by C.C.A. Christensen. Courtesy Brigham Young University Museum of Art. All Rights Reserved.)

Smith's successor, Brigham Young, traveled—12,000 strong, in one of the largest single group migrations in American history—across the Great Plains and the Rocky Mountains. They established several communities in Utah, including the present Salt Lake City, where, finally, the Mormons were able to create a lasting settlement.

Like other experiments in social organization of the era, Mormonism reflected a belief in human perfectibility. God had once been a man, the church taught, and thus every man or woman could aspire to move continuously closer to God. Within a highly developed and centrally directed ecclesiastical structure, Mormons created a haven for people demoralized by the disorder and uncertainty of the secular world. The original Mormons were white men and women, many of whom felt displaced in their rapidly changing society—economically marginalized by the material growth and social progress of their era. In the new religion, they found a strong and animating faith. In the society it created, they found security and order.

REMAKING SOCIETY

The reform impulse also helped create new movements to remake mainstream society—movements in which, to a striking degree, women formed both the rank and file and the leadership. By the 1830s, such movements had become organized reform societies.

REVIVALISM, MORALITY, AND ORDER

The philosophy of reform arose in part from the optimistic vision of those, such as the transcendentalists, who preached the divinity of the individual. Another source was Protestant revivalism—the movement that had begun with the Second Great Awakening early in the century and had, by the 1820s, evolved into a powerful force for social reform.

The New Light evangelicals embraced the optimistic belief that every individual was capable of salvation through his or her own efforts. Partly as a result, revivalism soon became not only a means of personal salvation but also an effort to reform the larger society. In particular, revivalism produced a crusade against personal immorality.

Evangelical Protestantism greatly strengthened the crusade against drunkenness. No social vice, temperance advocates argued, was more responsible for crime, disorder, and poverty than the excessive use of alcohol. Women complained that men spent money their families needed on alcohol and that drunken husbands often beat and abused their wives. Temperance also appealed to those who were alarmed by immigration; drunkenness, many nativists believed, was responsible for violence and disorder in immigrant communities. By 1840, temperance had become a major national movement, with powerful organizations and more than a million followers who had signed a formal pledge to forgo hard liquor.

HEALTH, SCIENCE, AND PHRENOLOGY

For some Americans, the search for individual and social perfection led to an interest in new theories of health and knowledge. In the nineteenth century, more than half of those who contracted cholera—a severe bacterial infection of the intestines, usually contracted from contaminated food or water—died. Nearly a quarter of the population of New Orleans in 1833 perished from the disease. Many cities established health boards to try to

THE DRUNKARD'S PROGRESS This 1846 lithograph by Nathaniel Currier shows what temperance advocates argued was the inevitable consequence of alcohol consumption. Beginning with an apparently innocent "glass with a friend," the young man rises step by step to the summit of drunken revelry, then declines to desperation and suicide while his abandoned wife and child grieve. (Library of Congress)

find ways to prevent epidemics. But the medical profession of the time, not yet aware of the nature of bacterial infections, had no answers.

Instead, many Americans turned to nonscientific theories for improving health. Affluent men and especially women flocked to health spas for the celebrated "water cure" (known to modern scientists as hydrotherapy), which purported to improve health through immersing people in hot or cold baths or wrapping them in wet sheets. Other people adopted new dietary theories. Sylvester Graham, a Connecticut-born Presbyterian minister and committed reformer, won many followers with his prescriptions for eating fruits, vegetables, and bread made from coarsely ground flour—a prescription not unlike some dietary theories today—and for avoiding meat. (The graham cracker is made from a kind of flour named for him.)

Perhaps strangest of all to modern sensibilities was the widespread belief in the new "science" of phrenology, which appeared first in Germany and became popular in the United States beginning in the 1830s through the efforts of Orson and Lorenzo Fowler, publishers of the *Phrenology Almanac*. Phrenologists argued that the shape of an individual's skull was an important indicator of his or her character and intelligence. They made elaborate measurements of bumps and indentations to calculate the size (and, they claimed, the strength) of different areas of the brain. Phrenology seemed to provide a way of measuring an individual's fitness for various positions in life and to promise an end to the arbitrary process by which people matched their talents to occupations and responsibilities. The theory is now universally believed to have no scientific value at all.

MEDICAL SCIENCE

In an age of rapid technological and scientific advances, medicine sometimes seemed to lag behind. In part, that was because of the character of the medical profession, which—in the absence of any significant regulation—attracted many poorly educated people and many quacks. Efforts to regulate the profession were beaten back in the 1830s and 1840s by those who considered the licensing of physicians to be a form of undemocratic monopoly. The prestige of the profession, therefore, remained low.

The biggest problem facing American medicine, however, was the absence of basic knowledge about disease. The great medical achievement of the eighteenth century—the development of a vaccination against smallpox by Edward Jenner—came from no broad theory of infection but from a brilliant adaptation of folk practices among country people. The development of anesthetics in the nineteenth century came not from medical doctors at first, but from a New England dentist, William Morton, who was looking for ways to help his patients endure the extraction of teeth. Beginning in 1844, Morton began experimenting with sulfuric ether. John Warren, a Boston surgeon, soon began using ether to sedate surgical patients. Even these advances met with stiff resistance from some traditional physicians, who mistrusted innovation and experimentation.

In the absence of any broad acceptance of scientific methods and experimental practice in medicine, it was very difficult for even the most talented doctors to make progress in treating disease. Even so, halting progress toward the discovery of the germ theory did occur in antebellum America. In 1843, the Boston essayist, poet, and physician Oliver Wendell Holmes published a study of large numbers of cases of "puerperal fever" (septicemia in children) and concluded that the disease could be transmitted from one person to another. This discovery of contagion met with a storm of criticism but was later vindicated by the clinical success of the Hungarian physician Ignaz Semmelweis, who noticed that infection seemed to be spread by medical students who had been working with diseased corpses. Once he began requiring students to wash their hands and disinfect their instruments, the infections virtually disappeared.

EDUCATION

One of the most important reform movements of the mid-nineteenth century was the effort to produce a system of universal public education. As of 1830, no state had such a system. Soon after that, however, interest in public education began growing rapidly.

The greatest of the educational reformers was Horace Mann, the first secretary of the Massachusetts Board of Education, which was established in 1837. To Mann and his followers, education was the only way to preserve democracy, for an educated electorate was essential to the workings of a free political system. Mann reorganized the Massachusetts school system, lengthened the academic year (to six months), doubled teachers' salaries, broadened the curriculum, and introduced new methods of professional training for teachers. Other states followed by building new schools, creating teachers' colleges, and offering many children access to education for the first time. By the 1850s, the principle (although not yet the reality) of tax-supported elementary schools was established in every state.

The quality of public education continued to vary widely. In some places—Massachusetts, for example—educators were generally capable men and women, often highly trained. In other areas, however, barely literate teachers and severely limited funding hindered education. Among the highly dispersed population of the West, many children had no access to schools at all. In the South, all African Americans were barred from education, and only about a third of all white children of school age were actually enrolled in schools in 1860. In the North, 72 percent were enrolled, but even there, many students attended classes only briefly and casually.

Among the goals of educational reformers was to teach children the social values of thrift, order, discipline, punctuality, and respect for authority. Horace Mann, for example, spoke of the role of public schools in extending democracy and expanding individual opportunity. But he spoke, too, of their role in creating social order: "Train up a child in the way he should go, and when he is old he will not depart from it."

The interest in education contributed to the growing movement to educate American Indians. Some reformers believed that Indians could be "civilized" if only they could be taught the ways of the white world. Efforts by missionaries and others to educate Indians and encourage them to assimilate were particularly prominent in such areas of the Far West as Oregon, where conflicts with the natives had not yet become acute. Nevertheless, the great majority of Native Americans remained outside the reach of white educational reform.

Despite limitations and inequities, the achievements of the school reformers were impressive. By the beginning of the Civil War, the United States had one of the highest literacy rates of any nation of the world: 94 percent of the population of the North, 83 percent of the white population (and 58 percent of the total population) of the South.

REHABILITATION

The belief in the potential of the individual also sparked the creation of new institutions to help the disabled—institutions that formed part of a great network of charitable activities known as the Benevolent Empire. Among them was the Perkins School for the Blind in Boston. Nothing better exemplified the romantic reform spirit of the era than the belief of those who founded Perkins. They believed that even society's supposedly most disadvantaged members could be helped to discover their own inner strength and wisdom.

Similar impulses produced another powerful movement of reform: the creation of "asylums" for criminals and the mentally ill. In advocating prison and hospital reform, Americans were reacting against one of society's most glaring ills: antiquated jails and mental institutions whose inmates lived in almost inhuman conditions. Beginning in the 1820s, many states built new penitentiaries and mental asylums. New York built the first penitentiary at Auburn in 1821. In Massachusetts, the reformer Dorothea Dix began a national movement for new methods of treating the mentally ill.

New forms of prison discipline were designed to reform and rehabilitate criminals. Solitary confinement and the imposition of silence on work crews (both instituted in Pennsylvania and New York in the 1820s) were meant to give prisoners opportunities to meditate on their wrongdoings and develop "penitence" (hence the name "penitentiary").

Some of the same impulses that produced asylums underlay the emergence of a new "reform" approach to the problems of Native Americans: the idea of the reservation. For several decades, the dominant thrust of the United States' policy toward the Indians had been relocation—getting the tribes out of the way of white civilization. But among some whites, there had also been another intent: to move the Indians to a place where they would be allowed to develop to a point at which assimilation might be possible.

It was a small step from the idea of relocation to the idea of the reservation. Just as prisons, asylums, and orphanages would provide society with an opportunity to train and uplift misfits and unfortunates within white society, so the reservations might provide a way to undertake what one official called "the great work of regenerating the Indian race." These optimistic goals failed to meet the expectations of the reformers.

GIRLS' EVENING SCHOOL (ca. 1840), ANONYMOUS   Schooling for women, which expanded significantly in the mid-nineteenth century, included training in domestic arts (as indicated by the sewing table at right) as well as in reading, writing, and other basic skills. (The Granger Collection, NYC)

DECLARATION OF SENTIMENTS AND RESOLUTIONS, SENECA FALLS, NEW YORK, 1848

WHEN, in the course of human events, it becomes necessary for one portion of the family of man to assume among the people of the earth a position different from that which they have hitherto occupied, but one to which the laws of nature and of nature's God entitle them, a decent respect to the opinions of mankind requires that they should declare the causes that impel them to such a course.

We hold these truths to be self-evident: that all men and women are created equal; that they are endowed by their Creator with certain inalienable rights; that among these are life, liberty, and the pursuit of happiness; that to secure these rights governments are instituted, deriving their just powers from the consent of the governed. Whenever any form of government becomes destructive of these ends, it is the right of those who suffer from it to refuse allegiance to it, and to insist upon the institution of a new government, laying its foundation on such principles, and organizing its powers in such form, as to them shall seem most likely to effect their safety and happiness. Prudence, indeed, will dictate that governments long established should not be changed for light and transient causes; and accordingly all experience hath shown that mankind are more disposed to suffer, while evils are sufferable, than to right themselves by abolishing the forms to which they are accustomed. But when a long train of abuses and usurpations, pursuing invariably the same object, evinces a design to reduce them under absolute despotism, it is their duty to throw off such government, and to provide new guards for their future security. Such has been the patient sufferance of the women under this government, and such is now the necessity which constrains them to demand the equal station to which they are entitled. The history of mankind is a history of repeated injuries and usurpations on the part of man toward woman, having in direct object the establishment of an absolute tyranny over her. To prove this, let facts be submitted to a candid world.

He has never permitted her to exercise her inalienable right to the elective franchise. He has compelled her to submit to laws, in the formation of which she had no voice. He has withheld from her rights which are given to the most ignorant and degraded men— both natives and foreigners.

Having deprived her of this first right of a citizen, the elective franchise, thereby leaving her without representation in the halls of legislation, he has oppressed her on all sides. He has made her, if married, in the eye of the law, civilly dead.

He has taken from her all right in property, even to the wages she earns.

THE RISE OF FEMINISM

Many women who became involved in reform movements in the 1820s and 1830s came to resent the social and legal restrictions that limited their participation. Out of their concerns emerged the first American feminist movement. Sarah and Angelina Grimké, sisters who became active and outspoken abolitionists, ignored claims by men that their activism was inappropriate to their gender. "Men and women were created equal," they argued. "They are both moral and accountable beings, and whatever is right for man to do, is right for women to do." Other reformers—Catharine Beecher, Harriet Beecher

He has made her, morally, an irresponsible being, as she can commit many crimes with impunity, provided they be done in the presence of her husband. In the covenant of marriage, she is compelled to promise obedience to her husband, he becoming, to all intents and purposes, her master—the law giving him power to deprive her of her liberty, and to administer chastisement.

He has so framed the laws of divorce, as to what shall be the proper causes, and in case of separation, to whom the guardianship of the children shall be given, as to be wholly regardless of the happiness of women—the law, in all cases, going upon a false supposition of the supremacy of man, and giving all power into his hands.

After depriving her of all rights as a married woman, if single, and the owner of property, he has taxed her to support a government which recognizes her only when her property can be made profitable to it.

He has monopolized nearly all the profitable employments, and from those she is permitted to follow, she receives but a scanty remuneration. He closes against her all the avenues to wealth and distinction which he considers most honorable to himself. As a teacher of theology, medicine, or law, she is not known.

He has denied her the facilities for obtaining a thorough education, all colleges being closed against her.

He allows her in church, as well as state, but a subordinate position, claiming apostolic authority for her exclusion from the ministry, and, with some exceptions, from any public participation in the affairs of the church.

He has created a false public sentiment by giving to the world a different code of morals for men and women, by which moral delinquencies which exclude women from society, are not only tolerated, but deemed of little account in man.

He has usurped the prerogative of Jehovah himself, claiming it as his right to assign for her a sphere of action, when that belongs to her conscience and to her God.

He has endeavored, in every way that he could, to destroy her confidence in her own powers, to lessen her self-respect, and to make her willing to lead a dependent and abject life.

Now, in view of this entire disfranchisement of one-half the people of this country, their social and religious degradation—in view of the unjust laws above mentioned, and because women do feel themselves aggrieved, oppressed, and fraudulently deprived of their most sacred rights, we insist that they have immediate admission to all the rights and privileges which belong to them as citizens of the United States.

UNDERSTAND, ANALYZE, & EVALUATE

1. What central claim about the relationship of men and women lies at the heart of this declaration? What evidence did the authors produce to support their claim?
2. With what demand did the authors conclude their resolution? How would you have reacted to this text?

Source: Elizabeth Cady Stanton, *A History of Woman Suffrage*, vol. 1 (Rochester, N.Y.: Fowler and Wells, 1889), pp. 70–71.

Stowe (her sister), Lucretia Mott, Elizabeth Cady Stanton, Susan B. Anthony, and Dorothea Dix—similarly pressed at the boundaries of "acceptable" female behavior.

In 1840, American female delegates arrived at a world antislavery convention in London, only to be turned away by the men who controlled the proceedings. Angered at the rejection, several of the delegates became convinced that their first duty as reformers should now be to elevate the status of women. Over the next several years, Mott, Stanton, and others began drawing pointed parallels between the plight of women and the plight of slaves; and in 1848, in Seneca Falls, New York, they organized a convention to discuss the question of women's rights. Out of the meeting came the "Declaration of Sentiments and Resolutions," which stated that "all men and women are created equal," that women no less than men are endowed with certain inalienable rights. In demanding the right to vote, they launched a movement for woman suffrage that would survive until the battle was finally won in 1920.

Many of the women involved in these feminist efforts were Quakers. Quakerism had long embraced the ideal of sexual equality and had tolerated, indeed encouraged, the emergence of women as preachers and community leaders. Of the women who drafted the Declaration of Sentiments, all but Elizabeth Cady Stanton were Quakers.

Feminists benefited greatly from their association with other reform movements, most notably abolitionism, but they also suffered as a result. The demands of women were usually assigned a secondary position to what many considered the far greater issue of the rights of slaves.

THE CRUSADE AGAINST SLAVERY

The antislavery movement was not new to the mid-nineteenth century. But not until 1830 did it begin to gather the force that would ultimately enable it to overshadow virtually all other efforts at social reform.

EARLY OPPOSITION TO SLAVERY

In the early years of the nineteenth century, those who opposed slavery were, for the most part, a calm and genteel lot, expressing moral disapproval but doing little else. To the extent that there was an organized antislavery movement, it centered on the effort to resettle American blacks in Africa or the Caribbean. In 1817, a group of prominent white Virginians organized the American Colonization Society (ACS), which proposed a gradual freeing of slaves, with masters receiving compensation. The liberated black men and women would then be transported out of the country and helped to establish a new society of their own. The ACS received some private funding, some funding from Congress, and some funding from the legislatures of Virginia and Maryland. And it arranged to have several groups of blacks transported out of the United States to the west coast of Africa, where in 1830 they established the nation of Liberia. (In 1846, Liberia became an independent black republic, with its capital, Monrovia, named for the American president who had presided over the initial settlement.)

But the ACS was in the end a negligible force. There were far too many blacks in America in the nineteenth century to be transported to Africa by any conceivable program. And the ACS met resistance, in any case, from blacks themselves, many of whom were now three or more generations removed from Africa and, despite their loathing of slavery, had no wish to emigrate.

GARRISON AND ABOLITIONISM

In 1830, with slavery spreading rapidly in the South and the antislavery movement seemingly on the verge of collapse, a new figure emerged: William Lloyd Garrison. Born in Massachusetts in 1805, Garrison was in the 1820s an assistant to the New Jersey Quaker Benjamin Lundy, who published the leading antislavery newspaper of the time. Garrison grew impatient with his employer's moderate tone, so in 1831 he returned to Boston to found his own newspaper, the *Liberator*.

Garrison's philosophy was so simple that it was genuinely revolutionary. Opponents of slavery, he said, should not talk about the evil influence of slavery on white society but rather the damage the system did to slaves. And they should, therefore, reject "gradualism" and demand the immediate abolition of slavery and the extension of all the rights of American citizenship to both slaves and free African Americans. Garrison wrote in a relentless, uncompromising tone. "I am aware," he wrote in the very first issue of the *Liberator,* "that many object to the severity of my language; but is there not cause for severity? I will be as harsh as truth, and as uncompromising as justice. . . . I am in earnest—I will not equivocate—I will not excuse—I will not retreat a single inch—and I will be heard."

Garrison soon attracted a large group of followers throughout the North, enough to enable him to found the New England Antislavery Society in 1832 and a year later, after a convention in Philadelphia, the American Antislavery Society.

Black Abolitionists

Abolitionism had a particular appeal to the free black population of the North. These free blacks lived in conditions of poverty and oppression that were at times worse than those of their slave counterparts in the South. For all their problems, however, northern blacks were fiercely proud of their freedom and sensitive to the plight of those members of their race who remained in bondage. Many in the 1830s came to support Garrison. But they also rallied to leaders of their own.

Among the earliest black abolitionists was David Walker, who preceded even Garrison in calling for an uncompromising opposition to slavery on moral grounds. In 1829, Walker, a free black man who had moved from North Carolina to Boston, published a harsh pamphlet—*An Appeal to the Coloured Citizens of the World*—that described slavery as a sin that would draw divine punishment if not abolished. "America is more our country than it is the whites'—we have enriched it with our blood and tears." He urged slaves to "kill [their masters] or be killed."

Most black critics of slavery were somewhat less violent in their rhetoric but equally uncompromising in their commitment to abolition. Sojourner Truth, a freed black, emerged as a powerful and eloquent spokeswoman for the abolition of slavery in the 1830s. The greatest African American abolitionist of all—and one of the most electrifying orators of his time, black or white—was Frederick Douglass. Born a slave in Maryland, Douglass escaped to Massachusetts in 1838, became an outspoken leader of antislavery sentiment, and spent two years lecturing in England. On his return to the United States in 1847, Douglass purchased his freedom from his Maryland owner and founded an antislavery newspaper, the *North Star,* in Rochester, New York. He achieved wide renown as well for his autobiography, *Narrative of the Life of Frederick Douglass* (1845), in which he presented a damning picture of slavery. Douglass demanded not only freedom but also full social and economic equality.

"What, to the American slave, is your 4th of July?" Douglass harshly asked in an Independence Day speech in Rochester, New York, in 1854. "I answer: a day that reveals to him, more than all other days in the year, the gross injustice and cruelty to which he is the constant victim. . . . There is not a nation on earth guilty of practices, more shocking and bloody, than are the people of these United States at this very hour."

Black abolitionists had been active for years before Douglass emerged as a leader of their cause. They held their first national convention in 1830. But with Douglass's leadership, they became a more influential force than any other African American. They began, too, to forge an alliance with white antislavery leaders such as Garrison.

THE ABOLITION OF SLAVERY

THE United States abolished slavery through the Thirteenth Amendment of the Constitution in 1865, in the aftermath of the Civil War. But the effort to abolish slavery did not begin or end in North America. Emancipation in the United States was part of a worldwide antislavery movement that began in the late eighteenth century and continued through the end of the nineteenth.

The end of slavery, like the end of monarchies and established aristocracies, was one of the ideals of the Enlightenment, which inspired new concepts of individual freedom and political equality. As Enlightenment ideas spread throughout the Western world in the seventeenth and eighteenth centuries, introducing the concept of human rights and individual liberty to the concept of civilization, people on both sides of the Atlantic began to examine slavery anew and to ask whether it was compatible with these new ideas. Some Enlightenment thinkers, including some of the founders of the American republic, believed that freedom was appropriate for white people but not for people of color. But others came to believe that all human beings had an equal claim to liberty, and their views became the basis for an escalating series of antislavery movements.

Opponents of slavery first targeted the slave trade—the vast commerce in human beings that had grown up in the seventeenth and eighteenth centuries and had come to involve large parts of Europe, Africa, the Caribbean, and North and South America. In the aftermath of the revolutions in America, France, and Haiti, the attack on the slave trade quickly gained momentum. Its central figure was the English reformer William Wilberforce, who spent years attacking Britain's connection with the slave trade on moral and religious

"AM I NOT A MAN AND A BROTHER" This bronze medallion commemorates the victory of British antislavery activists in extinguishing slavery from throughout the British Empire in 1834. It also records the close links between their movement and the American abolitionist movement led by William Lloyd Garrison. The image on this medallion of a man in chains became a popular one in American antislavery circles in the following years. (The Art Archive at Art Resource, NY)

grounds. After the Haitian Revolution, Wilberforce and other antislavery activists denounced slavery on the grounds that its continuation would create more slave revolts. In 1807, he persuaded Parliament to pass a law ending the slave trade within the entire British Empire. The British example persuaded many other nations to make the slave trade illegal as well: the United States in 1808, France in 1814, Holland in 1817, Spain in 1845. Trading in slaves continued within countries and colonies where slavery remained legal (including the United States), and some illegal slave trading continued throughout the Atlantic World. But the international sale of slaves steadily declined after 1807. The last known shipment of slaves across the Atlantic—from Africa to Cuba—occurred in 1867.

Ending the slave trade was a great deal easier than ending slavery itself, in which many people had major investments and on which much agriculture, commerce, and industry depended. But pressure to abolish slavery grew steadily throughout the nineteenth century, with Wilberforce once more helping to lead the international outcry against the institution. In Haiti, the slave revolts that began in 1791 eventually abolished not only slavery but also French rule. In some parts of South America, slavery came to an end with the overthrow of Spanish rule in the 1820s. Simón Bolívar, the great leader of Latin American independence, considered abolishing slavery an important part of his mission, freeing those who joined his armies and insisting on constitutional prohibitions of slavery in several of the constitutions he helped frame. In 1833, the British parliament passed a law abolishing slavery throughout the British Empire and compensated slaveowners for freeing their slaves. France abolished slavery in its empire, after years of agitation from abolitionists, in 1848. In the Caribbean, Spain followed Britain in slowly eliminating slavery from its colonies. Puerto Rico abolished slavery in 1873; and Cuba became the last colony in the Caribbean to end slavery, in 1886, in the face of increasing slave resistance and the declining profitability of slave-based plantations. Brazil was the last nation in the Americas, ending the system in 1888. The Brazilian military began to turn against slavery after the valiant participation of slaves in Brazil's war with Paraguay in the late 1860s; eventually, educated Brazilians began to oppose the system too, arguing that it obstructed economic and social progress.

In the United States, the power of world opinion—and the example of Wilberforce's movement in England—became an important influence on the abolitionist movement as it gained strength in the 1820s and 1830s. American abolitionism, in turn, helped reinforce the movements abroad. Frederick Douglass, the former American slave turned abolitionist, became a major figure in the international antislavery movement and was a much-admired and much-sought-after speaker in England and Europe in the 1840s and 1850s. No other nation paid such a terrible price for abolishing slavery as did the United States during its Civil War, but American emancipation was nevertheless a part of a worldwide movement toward emancipation. •

UNDERSTAND, ANALYZE, & EVALUATE

1. Why did opponents of slavery focus first on ending the slave trade, rather than abolishing slavery itself? Why was ending the slave trade easier than ending slavery?
2. How do William Wilberforce's arguments against slavery compare with those of the abolitionists in the United States?

ANTI-ABOLITIONISM

The rise of abolitionism provoked a powerful opposition. Almost all white southerners, of course, were bitterly hostile to the movement. But even in the North, abolitionists were a small, dissenting minority. Some whites feared that abolitionism would produce a destructive civil war. Others feared that it would lead to a great influx of free blacks into the North and displace white workers.

The result of such fears was an escalating wave of violence. A mob in Philadelphia attacked the abolitionist headquarters there in 1834, burned it to the ground, and began a bloody race riot. Another mob seized Garrison on the streets of Boston in 1835 and threatened to hang him. He was saved from death only by being locked in jail. Elijah Lovejoy, the editor of an abolitionist newspaper in Alton, Illinois, was victimized repeatedly and finally killed when he tried to defend his press from attack.

That so many men and women continued to embrace abolitionism in the face of such vicious opposition suggests that abolitionists were not people who made their political commitments lightly or casually. They were strong-willed, passionate crusaders who displayed not only enormous courage and moral strength but, at times, a fervency that many of their contemporaries found deeply disturbing. The mobs were only the most violent expression of a hostility to abolitionism that many, perhaps most, other white Americans shared.

FUGITIVE SLAVE LAW CONVENTION Abolitionists gathered in Cazenovia, New York, in August 1850 to consider how to respond to the law recently passed by Congress requiring northern states to return fugitive slaves to their owners. Frederick Douglass is seated just to the left of the table in this photograph of some of the participants. The gathering was unusual among abolitionist gatherings in including substantial numbers of African Americans. (Madison County Historical Society, Oneida, NY)

ABOLITIONISM DIVIDED

By the mid-1830s, the abolitionist crusade had begun to experience serious strains. One reason was the violence of the anti-abolitionists, which persuaded some members of the abolition movement that a more moderate approach was necessary. Another reason was the growing radicalism of William Lloyd Garrison, who shocked even many of his own allies (including Frederick Douglass) by attacking not only slavery but the government itself. The Constitution, he said, was "a covenant with death and an agreement with hell." In 1840, Garrison precipitated a formal division within the American Antislavery Society by insisting that women be permitted to participate in the movement on terms of full equality. He continued after 1840 to arouse controversy with new and even more radical stands: an extreme pacifism that rejected even defensive wars; opposition to all forms of coercion—not just slavery, but prisons and asylums; and finally, in 1843, a call for northern disunion from the South.

From 1840 on, therefore, abolitionism moved in many channels and spoke with many different voices. The radical and uncompromising Garrisonians remained influential. But others operated in more moderate ways, arguing that abolition could be accomplished only as the result of a long, patient, peaceful struggle. They appealed to the conscience of the slaveholders; and when that produced no results, they turned to political action, seeking to induce the northern states and the federal government to aid the cause. They joined the Garrisonians in helping runaway slaves find refuge in the North or in Canada through the underground railroad.

They also helped fund the legal battle over the Spanish slave vessel, *Amistad* (see p. 262). After the Supreme Court (in *Prigg v. Pennsylvania*, 1842) ruled that states need not aid in enforcing the 1793 law requiring the return of fugitive slaves to their owners, abolitionists won passage in several northern states of "personal liberty laws," which forbade state officials to assist in the capture and return of runaways. The antislavery societies also petitioned Congress to abolish slavery in places where the federal government had jurisdiction—in the territories and in the District of Columbia—and to prohibit the interstate slave trade.

Antislavery sentiment underlay the formation in 1840 of the Liberty Party, which ran Kentucky antislavery leader James G. Birney for president. But this party and its successors never campaigned for outright abolition. They stood instead for "Free Soil," for keeping slavery out of the territories. Some Free-Soilers were concerned about the welfare of blacks; others were people who cared nothing about slavery but simply wanted to keep the West a country for whites. But the Free-Soil position would ultimately do what abolitionism never could: attract the support of large numbers of the white population of the North.

The frustrations of political abolitionism drove some critics of slavery to embrace more drastic measures. A few began to advocate violence. A group of prominent abolitionists in New England, for example, funneled money and arms to John Brown for his bloody uprisings in Kansas and Virginia. (See pp. 305–306 and 310.) Others attempted to arouse public anger through propaganda.

The most powerful of all abolitionist propaganda was Harriet Beecher Stowe's novel *Uncle Tom's Cabin*, published as a book in 1852. It sold more than 300,000 copies within a year of publication and was reissued again and again. It succeeded in bringing the message of abolitionism to an enormous new audience—not only those who read the book but also those who watched countless theater companies reenact it across the nation. An unconfirmed statement by Lincoln to Stowe has been widely publicized: "Is this the little woman who made the great war?" Reviled throughout the South, Stowe became a hero to many in the North. And in both regions, her novel helped inflame sectional tensions to a new level of passion.

Even divided, abolitionism remained a powerful influence on the life of the nation. Only a relatively small number of people before the Civil War ever accepted the abolitionist position that slavery must be entirely eliminated in a single stroke. But the crusade that Garrison had launched, and that thousands of committed men and women kept alive for three decades, was a constant, visible reminder of how deeply the institution of slavery was dividing America.

CONCLUSION

The rapidly changing society of antebellum America encouraged interest in a wide range of reforms. Writers, artists, intellectuals, and others drew heavily from new European notions of personal liberation and fulfillment—a set of ideas often known as romanticism. But they also strove to create a truly American culture. The literary and artistic life of the nation expressed the rising interest in personal liberation—in giving individuals the freedom to explore their own souls and to find in nature a full expression of their divinity. It also called attention to some of the nation's glaring social problems.

Reformers, too, made use of the romantic belief in the divinity of the individual. They flocked to religious revivals, worked on behalf of such "moral" reforms as temperance, supported education, and articulated some of the first statements of modern feminism. And in the North, they rallied against slavery. Out of this growing antislavery movement emerged a new and powerful phenomenon: abolitionism, which insisted on immediate emancipation of slaves. The abolitionist movement galvanized much of the North and contributed greatly to the growing schism between North and South.

RECALL AND REFLECT

1. What is "romanticism" and how was it expressed in American literature and art?
2. How did religion affect reform movements, and what was the effect of these movements on religion?
3. What were the aims of the women's movement of the nineteenth century? How successful were women in the achieving these goals?
4. What arguments and strategies did the abolitionists use in their struggle to end slavery? Who opposed them and why?

13 THE IMPENDING CRISIS

LOOKING AHEAD

1. How did the annexation of western territories intensify the conflict over slavery and lead to deeper divisions between the North and the South?

2. What compromises attempted to resolve the conflicts over the expansion of slavery into new territories? To what degree were these compromises successful? Why did they eventually fail to resolve the differences between the North and the South?

3. What were the major arguments for and against slavery and its expansion into new territories?

UNTIL THE 1840s, THE TENSIONS between the North and the South remained relatively contained. Had no new sectional issues arisen, it is possible that the two sections might have resolved their differences peaceably over time. But new issues did arise. From the North came the strident and increasingly powerful abolitionist movement. From the South came a newly militant defense of slavery and the way of life it supported. And from the West, most significantly, emerged a series of controversies that would ultimately tear the fragile Union apart.

1836

Texas declares
independence from
Mexico

1844

Polk elected president

1846

Oregon boundary
dispute settled

U.S. declares war on
Mexico

Wilmot Proviso

1848

Treaty of Guadalupe
Hidalgo

Taylor elected
president

California gold rush
begins

1850

Compromise of 1850

Taylor dies; Fillmore
becomes president

1852

Pierce elected
president

1853

Gadsden Purchase

1854

Kansas–Nebraska Act

Republican Party
formed

1855–1856

"Bleeding Kansas"

1856

Buchanan elected
president

1857

Dred Scott decision

1858

Lecompton
constitution defeated

1859

John Brown raids
Harpers Ferry

1860

Lincoln elected
president

LOOKING WESTWARD

More than a million square miles of new territory came under the control of the United States during the 1840s. By the end of the decade, the nation possessed all the territory of the present-day United States except Alaska, Hawaii, and a few relatively small areas acquired later through border adjustments. Many factors accounted for this great new wave of expansion, but one of the most important was an ideology known as "Manifest Destiny."

MANIFEST DESTINY

Manifest Destiny reflected both the growing pride that characterized American nationalism in the mid-nineteenth century and the idealistic vision of social perfection that fueled so much of the reform energy of the time. It rested on the idea that America was destined—by God and by history—to expand its boundaries over a vast area.

By the 1840s, publicized by the "penny press," the idea of Manifest Destiny had spread throughout the nation. Some advocates of Manifest Destiny envisioned a vast new "empire of liberty" that would include Canada, Mexico, Caribbean and Pacific islands, and ultimately, a few dreamed, much of the rest of the world. Henry Clay and others warned that territorial expansion would reopen the painful controversy over slavery. Their voices, however, could not compete with the enthusiasm over expansion in the 1840s, which began with the issues of Texas and Oregon.

AMERICANS IN TEXAS

Twice in the 1820s, the United States had offered to purchase Texas from the Republic of Mexico, only to meet with indignant refusals. In 1824, the Mexican government enacted a colonization law offering cheap land and a four-year exemption from taxes to any American willing to move into Texas. Thousands of Americans flocked into the region, the great majority of them white southerners and their slaves, intent on establishing cotton plantations. By 1830, there were about 7,000 Americans living in Texas, more than twice the number of Mexicans there.

Most of the settlers came to Texas through the efforts of American intermediaries, who received sizable land grants from Mexico in return for bringing new residents into the region. The most successful was Stephen F. Austin, a young immigrant from Missouri who established the first legal American settlement in Texas in 1822. Austin and others created centers of power in the region that competed with the Mexican government. In 1830, the Mexican government barred any further American immigration into the region. But Americans kept flowing into Texas anyway.

Friction between the American settlers and the Mexican government was already growing in the mid-1830s when instability in Mexico itself drove General Antonio López de Santa Anna to seize power as a dictator. He increased the powers of the Mexican government at the expense of the state governments, a measure that Texans from the United States assumed was aimed specifically at them. Sporadic fighting between Americans and Mexicans in Texas began in 1835. In 1836, the American settlers defiantly proclaimed their independence from Mexico.

Santa Anna led a large army into Texas, where the American settlers were divided into several squabbling factions. Mexican forces annihilated an American garrison at the Alamo mission in San Antonio after a famous, if futile, defense by a group of Texas "patriots" that included, among others, the renowned frontiersman and former Tennessee congressman Davy Crockett. Another garrison at Goliad suffered substantially the same fate. By the end of 1836, the rebellion appeared to have collapsed.

But General Sam Houston managed to keep a small force together. And on April 21, 1836, at the Battle of San Jacinto, he defeated the Mexican army and took Santa Anna prisoner. Santa Anna, under pressure from his captors, signed a treaty giving Texas independence.

A number of Mexican residents of Texas (*Tejanos*) had fought with the Americans in the revolution. But soon after Texas won its independence, their positions grew difficult. The Americans did not trust them, feared that they were agents of the Mexican government, and in effect drove many of them out of the new republic. Most of those who stayed had to settle for a politically and economically subordinate status.

One of the first acts of the new president of Texas, Sam Houston, was to send a delegation to Washington with an offer to join the Union. But President Jackson, fearing that adding a large new slave state to the Union would increase sectional tensions, blocked annexation and even delayed recognizing the new republic until 1837.

Spurned by the United States, Texas cast out on its own. England and France, concerned about the growing power of the United States, saw Texas as a possible check on its growth and began forging ties with the new republic. At that point, President Tyler persuaded Texas to apply for statehood again in 1844. But northern senators, fearing the admission of a new slave state, defeated it.

OREGON

Control of what was known as "Oregon country," in the Pacific Northwest, was also a major political issue in the 1840s. Both Britain and the United States claimed sovereignty in the region. Unable to resolve their conflicting claims diplomatically, they agreed in an 1818 treaty to allow citizens of each country equal access to the territory. This "joint occupation" continued for twenty years.

At the time of the treaty neither Britain nor the United States had established much of a presence in Oregon country. White settlement in the region consisted largely of

WESTERN TRAILS IN 1860 As settlers began the long process of exploring and establishing farms and businesses in the West, major trails began to develop to facilitate travel and trade between the region and the more thickly settled areas to the east. Note how many of the trails led to California and how few of them led into any of the far northern regions of United States territory. Note, too, the important towns and cities that grew up along these trails. • *What forms of transportation later performed the functions that these trails performed prior to the Civil War?*

scattered American and Canadian fur trading posts. But American interest in Oregon grew substantially in the 1820s and 1830s.

By the mid-1840s, white Americans substantially outnumbered the British in Oregon. They had also devastated much of the Indian population, in part through a measles epidemic that spread through the Cayuse Indians. American settlements were spreading up and down the Pacific Coast, and the new settlers were urging the United States government to take possession of the disputed Oregon territory.

THE WESTWARD MIGRATION

The migrations into Texas and Oregon were part of a larger movement that took hundreds of thousands of white and black Americans into the far western regions of the continent between 1840 and 1860. The largest number of migrants were from the Old Northwest. Most were relatively young people who had traveled in family groups. Few were wealthy,

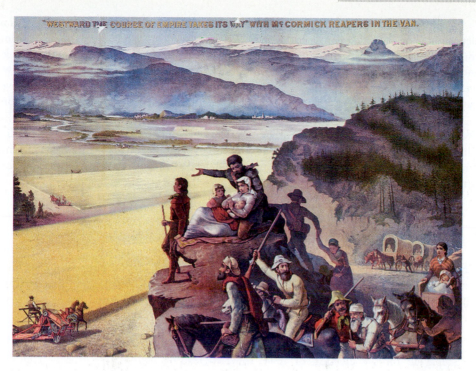

PROMOTING THE WEST   Cyrus McCormick was one of many American businessmen with an interest in the peopling of the American West. The reaper he invented was crucial to the cultivation of the new agricultural regions, and the rapid settlement of those regions was, in turn, essential to the health of his company. In this poster, the McCormick Reaper Company presents a romantic, idealized image of vast, fertile lands awaiting settlement, an image that drew many settlers westward. (Chicago History Museum, -00285)

but many were relatively prosperous. Poor people who could not afford the trip on their own usually had to join other families or groups as laborers—men as farm or ranch hands; women as domestic servants, teachers, or, in some cases, prostitutes. Groups heading for areas where mining or lumbering was the principal economic activity consisted mostly of men. Those heading for farming regions traveled mainly as families.

Migrants generally gathered in one of several major depots in Iowa and Missouri (Independence, St. Joseph, or Council Bluffs), joined a wagon train led by hired guides, and set off with their belongings piled in covered wagons, livestock trailing behind. The major route west was the 2,000-mile Oregon Trail, which stretched from Independence across the Great Plains and through the South Pass of the Rocky Mountains. From there, migrants moved north into Oregon or south (along the California Trail) to the northern California coast. Other migrations moved along the Santa Fe Trail, southwest from Independence into New Mexico.

However they traveled, overland migrants faced an arduous journey. Most passages lasted five or six months (from May to November), and there was always pressure to get through the Rockies before the snows began, often not an easy task given the very slow pace of most wagon trains. There was also the danger of disease; many groups were decimated by cholera. Almost everyone walked the great majority of the time, to lighten the load for the horses drawing the wagons. The women, who did the cooking and washing at the end of the day, generally worked harder than the men, who usually rested when the caravan halted.

Despite the traditional image of westward migrants as rugged individualists, most travelers found the journey a communal experience. That was partly because many expeditions consisted of groups of friends, neighbors, or relatives who had decided to pull up stakes and move west together. And it was also because of the intensity of the journey. It was a rare expedition in which there were not some internal conflicts before the trip was over; but those who made the journey successfully generally learned the value of cooperation.

Only a few expeditions experienced Indian attacks. In the twenty years before the Civil War, fewer than 400 migrants (slightly more than one-tenth of 1 percent) died in conflicts with the tribes. In fact, Indians were usually more helpful than dangerous to the white migrants. They often served as guides, and they traded horses, clothing, and fresh food with the travelers.

EXPANSION AND WAR

The growing number of white Americans in the lands west of the Mississippi put great pressure on the government in Washington to annex Texas, Oregon, and other territory. And in the 1840s, these expansionist pressures helped push the United States into war.

THE DEMOCRATS AND EXPANSION

In preparing for the election of 1844, the two leading candidates—Henry Clay and Martin Van Buren—both tried to avoid taking a stand on the controversial annexation of Texas. Sentiment for expansion was mild within the Whig Party, and Clay had no difficulty securing the nomination despite his noncommittal position. But many southern Democrats strongly supported annexation, and the party passed over Van Buren to nominate James K. Polk.

Polk had represented Tennessee in the House of Representatives for fourteen years, four of them as Speaker, and had subsequently served as governor. But by 1844, he had been out of public office for three years. What made his victory possible was his support for the position, expressed in the Democratic platform, "that the re-occupation of Oregon and the re-annexation of Texas at the earliest practicable period are great American measures." By combining the Oregon and Texas questions, the Democrats hoped to appeal to both northern and southern expansionists—and they did. Polk carried the election, 170 electoral votes to 105.

Polk entered office with a clear set of goals and with plans for attaining them. John Tyler accomplished the first of Polk's goals for him in the last days of his own presidency. Interpreting the election returns as a mandate for the annexation of Texas, the outgoing president won congressional approval for it in February 1845. That December, Texas became a state.

Polk himself resolved the Oregon question. The British minister in Washington brusquely rejected a compromise that would establish the United States–Canadian border at the 49th parallel. Incensed, Polk again asserted the American claim to all of Oregon. There was loose talk of war on both sides of the Atlantic—talk that in the United States often took the form of the bellicose slogan "Fifty-four forty or fight!" (a reference to where the Americans hoped to draw the northern boundary of their part of Oregon). But neither country really wanted war. Finally, the British government accepted Polk's original proposal to divide the territory at the 49th parallel. On June 15, 1846, the Senate approved a treaty that fixed the boundary there.

THE OREGON BOUNDARY, 1846   One of the last major boundary disputes between the United States and Great Britain involved the territory known as Oregon—the large region on the Pacific Coast north of California (which in 1846 was still part of Mexico). For years, America and Britain had overlapping claims on the territory. The British claimed land as far south as the present state of Oregon, while the Americans claimed land extending well into what is now Canada. Tensions over the Oregon border at times rose to the point that many Americans were demanding war, some using the slogan "54–40 or fight," referring to the latitude of the northernmost point of the American claim. • *How did President James K. Polk defuse the crisis?*

THE SOUTHWEST AND CALIFORNIA

One of the reasons the Senate and the president had agreed so readily to the British offer to settle the Oregon question was that new tensions were emerging in the Southwest. As soon as the United States admitted Texas to statehood in 1845, the Mexican government broke diplomatic relations with Washington. Mexican–American relations grew still worse when a dispute developed over the boundary between Texas and Mexico. Texans claimed the Rio Grande as their western and southern border. Mexico, although still not conceding the loss of Texas, argued nevertheless that the border had always been the Nueces River, to the north of the Rio Grande. Polk accepted the Texas claim, and in the summer of 1845 he sent a small army under General Zachary Taylor to Texas to protect the new state against a possible Mexican invasion.

Part of the area in dispute was New Mexico, whose Spanish and Indian residents lived in a multiracial society that by the 1840s had endured for nearly a century and a half. In the 1820s, the Mexican government had invited American traders into the region, hoping to speed development of the province. New Mexico, like Texas, soon became more American than Mexican, particularly after a flourishing commerce developed between Santa Fe and Independence, Missouri.

Americans were also increasing their interest in California. In this vast region lived members of several western Indian tribes and perhaps 7,000 Mexicans. Gradually, however, white Americans began to arrive: first maritime traders and captains of Pacific whaling ships, who stopped to barter goods or buy supplies; then merchants, who established stores, imported merchandise, and developed a profitable trade with the Mexicans and Indians; and finally pioneering farmers, who entered California from the east and settled in the Sacramento Valley. Some of these new settlers began to dream of bringing California into the United States.

President Polk soon came to share their dream and committed himself to acquiring both New Mexico and California for the United States. At the same time that he dispatched the troops under Taylor to Texas, he sent secret instructions to the commander of the Pacific naval squadron to seize the California ports if Mexico declared war. Representatives of the president quietly informed Americans in California that the United States would respond sympathetically to a revolt against Mexican authority there.

THE MEXICAN WAR

Having appeared to prepare for war, Polk turned to diplomacy by dispatching a special minister to try to buy off the Mexicans. But Mexican leaders rejected the American offer to purchase the disputed territories. On January 13, 1846, as soon as he heard the news, Polk ordered Taylor's army in Texas to move across the Nueces River, where it had been stationed, to the Rio Grande. For months, the Mexicans refused to fight. But finally, according to disputed American accounts, some Mexican troops crossed the Rio Grande and attacked a unit of American soldiers. On May 13, 1846, Congress declared war by votes of 40 to 2 in the Senate and 174 to 14 in the House.

Whig critics charged that Polk had deliberately maneuvered the country into the conflict and had staged the border incident that had precipitated the declaration. Many opponents also claimed that Polk had settled for less than he should have because he was preoccupied with Mexico. Opposition intensified as the war continued and as the public became aware of the casualties and expense.

Victory did not come as quickly as Polk had hoped. The president ordered Taylor to cross the Rio Grande, seize parts of northeastern Mexico, beginning with the city of Monterrey, and then march on to Mexico City itself. Taylor captured Monterrey in September 1846, but he let the Mexican garrison evacuate without pursuit. Polk now began to fear that Taylor lacked the tactical skill for the planned advance against Mexico City. He also feared that, if successful, Taylor would become a powerful political rival (as, in fact, he did).

In the meantime, Polk ordered other offensives against New Mexico and California. In the summer of 1846, a small army under Colonel Stephen W. Kearny captured Santa Fe with no opposition. He then proceeded to California, where he joined a conflict already in progress that was being staged jointly by American settlers, a well-armed exploring party led by John C. Frémont, and the American navy: the so-called Bear Flag Revolt. Kearny brought the disparate American forces together under his command, and by the autumn of 1846 he had completed the conquest of California.

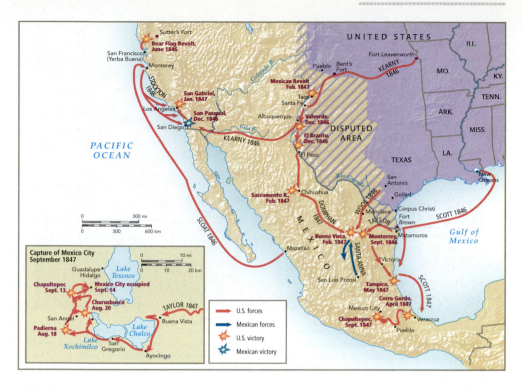

THE MEXICAN WAR, 1846-1848 Shortly after the settlement of the Oregon border dispute with Britain, the United States entered a war with Mexico over another contested border. This map shows the movement of Mexican and American troops during the fighting, which extended from the area around Santa Fe south to Mexico City and west to the coast of California. Note the American use of its naval forces to facilitate a successful assault on Mexico City, and others on the coast of California. Note, too, how unsuccessful the Mexican forces were in their battles with the United States. Mexico won only one battle—a relatively minor one at San Pasqual near San Diego—in the war. • *How did President Polk deal with the popular clamor for the United States to annex much of present-day Mexico?*

But Mexico still refused to concede defeat. At this point, Polk and General Winfield Scott, the commanding general of the army and its finest soldier, launched a bold new campaign. Scott assembled an army at Tampico, which the navy transported down the Mexican coast to Veracruz. With an army that never numbered more than 14,000, Scott advanced 260 miles along the Mexican National Highway toward Mexico City, kept American casualties low, and never lost a battle before finally seizing the Mexican capital. A new Mexican government took power and announced its willingness to negotiate a peace treaty.

President Polk continued to encourage those who demanded that the United States annex much of Mexico itself. At the same time, he was growing anxious to get the war finished quickly. Polk had sent a special presidential envoy, Nicholas Trist, to negotiate a settlement. On February 2, 1848, he reached agreement with the new Mexican government on the Treaty of Guadalupe Hidalgo, by which Mexico agreed to cede California and New Mexico to the United States and acknowledge the Rio Grande as the boundary of Texas. In return, the United States promised to assume any financial claims its new citizens had against Mexico and to pay the Mexicans $15 million. Trist had obtained most of Polk's original demands, but he had not satisfied the new, more expansive dreams of acquiring additional territory in Mexico itself. Polk angrily claimed that Trist had violated his instructions, but he soon realized that he had no choice but to accept the treaty to

AUSTIN, TEXAS, 1840 Four years after Texas declared its independence from Mexico, the new republic's capital, Austin, was still a small village, most of whose buildings were rustic cabins, as this hand-colored lithograph from the time suggests. The imposing house atop the hill at right was a notable exception. It was the residence of President Mirabeau Lamar. (Dolph Briscoe Center for American History, The University of Texas at Austin)

silence a bitter battle growing between ardent expansionists demanding the annexation of "All Mexico!" and antislavery leaders charging that the expansionists were conspiring to extend slavery to new realms. The president submitted the Trist treaty to the Senate, which approved it by a vote of 38 to 14.

THE SECTIONAL DEBATE

James Polk tried to be a president whose policies transcended sectional divisions. But conciliating the sections was becoming an ever more difficult task, and Polk gradually earned the enmity of northerners and westerners alike, who believed his policies favored the South at their expense.

SLAVERY AND THE TERRITORIES

In August 1846, while the Mexican War had been still in progress, Polk had asked Congress to appropriate $2 million for purchasing peace with Mexico. Representative David Wilmot of Pennsylvania, an antislavery Democrat, introduced an amendment to the appropriation bill prohibiting slavery in any territory acquired from Mexico. The so-called Wilmot Proviso passed the House but failed in the Senate. Southern militants contended that all Americans had equal rights in the new territories, including the right to move their slaves (which they considered property) into them.

As the sectional debate intensified, President Polk supported a proposal to extend the Missouri Compromise line through the new territories to the Pacific Coast, banning

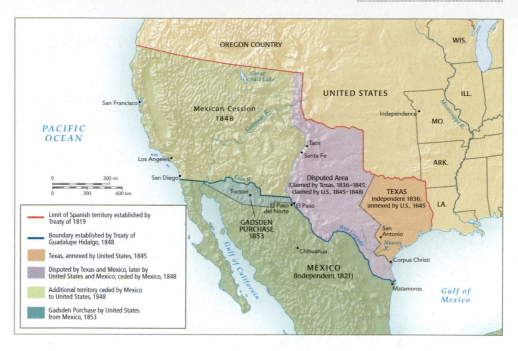

SOUTHWESTERN EXPANSION, 1845–1853 The annexation of much of what is now Texas in 1845, the much larger territorial gains won in the Mexican War in 1848, and the purchase of additional land from Mexico in 1853 completed the present continental border of the United States. • *What great event shortly after the Mexican War contributed to a rapid settlement of California by migrants from the eastern United States?*

slavery north of the line and permitting it south of the line. Others supported a plan, originally known as "squatter sovereignty" and later by the more dignified phrase "popular sovereignty," which would allow the people of each territory to decide the status of slavery there. The debate over these various proposals dragged on for many months.

The presidential campaign of 1848 dampened the controversy for a time as both Democrats and Whigs tried to avoid the slavery question. When Polk, in poor health, declined to run again, the Democrats nominated Lewis Cass of Michigan, a dull, aging party regular. The Whigs nominated General Zachary Taylor of Louisiana, hero of the Mexican War but a man with no political experience. Opponents of slavery found the choice of candidates unsatisfying, and out of their discontent emerged the new Free-Soil Party, whose candidate was former president Martin Van Buren.

Taylor won a narrow victory. But while Van Buren failed to carry a single state, he polled an impressive 291,000 votes (10 percent of the total), and the Free-Soilers elected ten members to Congress. The emergence of the Free-Soil Party as an important political force signaled the inability of the existing parties to contain the political passions slavery was creating. It was an early sign of the coming collapse of the second party system in the 1850s.

THE CALIFORNIA GOLD RUSH

By the time Taylor took office, the pressure to resolve the question of slavery in the far western territories had become more urgent as a result of dramatic events in California. In January 1848, a foreman working in a sawmill owned by John Sutter (one of California's leading ranchers) found traces of gold in the foothills of the Sierra Nevada. Within

WILMOT PROVISO TO THE NORTHWEST ORDINANCE, AUGUST 8, 1846

PROVIDED, that, as an express and fundamental condition to the acquisition of any territory from the Republic of Mexico by the United States, by virtue of any treaty which may be negotiated between them, and to the use by the Executive of the moneys herein appropriated, neither slavery nor involuntary servitude shall ever exist in any part of said territory, except for crime, whereof the party shall first be duly convicted.

UNDERSTAND, ANALYZE, & EVALUATE

1. To what territory did the Wilmot Proviso refer?
2. What condition did the proviso impose on future territory?
3. Why did this simple provision prove so controversial? What were its consequences?
4. Do you recognize the last two lines of the provision? Where do they later reappear?

months, news of the discovery had spread throughout the nation and much of the world. Almost immediately, hundreds of thousands of people began flocking to California in a frantic search for gold.

The atmosphere in California at the peak of the gold rush was one of almost crazed excitement and greed. Most migrants to the Far West prepared carefully before making the journey. But the California migrants (known as "Forty-niners") threw caution to the winds, abandoning farms, jobs, homes, and families, piling onto ships and flooding the overland trails. The overwhelming majority of the Forty-niners (perhaps 95 percent) were white men, and the society they created in California was unusually fluid and volatile because of the almost total absence of white women, children, or families.

The gold rush also attracted some of the first Chinese migrants to the western United States. News of the discoveries created great excitement in China, particularly in impoverished areas. It was, of course, extremely difficult for a poor Chinese peasant to get to America; but many young, adventurous people (mostly men) decided to go anyway—in the belief that they could quickly become rich and then return to China. Emigration brokers loaned many migrants money for passage to California, which the migrants were to pay off out of their earnings there.

The gold rush was producing a serious labor shortage in California, as many male workers left their jobs and flocked to the gold fields. That created opportunities for many people who needed work (including Chinese immigrants). It also led to a frenzied exploitation of Indians that resembled slavery in all but name. A new state law permitted the arrest of "loitering" or orphaned Indians and their assignment to a term of "indentured" labor.

The gold rush was of critical importance to the growth of California, but not for the reasons most of the migrants hoped. There was substantial gold in the hills of the Sierra Nevada, and many people got rich from it. But only a tiny fraction of the Forty-niners ever found gold. Some disappointed migrants returned home after a while. But many stayed in California and swelled both the agricultural and urban populations of the territory. By 1856, for example, San Francisco—whose population had been 1,000 before the gold rush—was the home of over 50,000 people. By the early 1850s, California, which had always had a diverse population, had become even more heterogeneous. The gold rush had attracted not just white Americans but Europeans, Chinese, South Americans, Mexicans, free blacks, and slaves who accompanied southern migrants. Conflicts over gold intersected with racial and ethnic tensions to make the territory an unusually turbulent place.

RISING SECTIONAL TENSIONS

Zachary Taylor believed statehood could become the solution to the issue of slavery in the territories. As long as the new lands remained territories, the federal government was responsible for deciding the fate of slavery within them. But once they became states, he thought, their own governments would be able to settle the slavery question. At Taylor's urging, California quickly adopted a constitution that prohibited slavery, and in December 1849 Taylor asked Congress to admit California as a free state.

Congress balked, in part because of several other controversies concerning slavery that were complicating the debate. One was the effort of antislavery forces to abolish slavery in the District of Columbia. Another was the emergence of personal liberty laws in northern states, which barred courts and police officers from returning runaway slaves to their owners. But the biggest obstacle to the president's program was the white South's fear that new free states would be added to the northern majority. The number of free and slave states was equal in 1849—fifteen each. But the admission of California would upset the balance; and New Mexico, Oregon, and Utah—all candidates for statehood— might upset it further.

Even many otherwise moderate southern leaders now began to talk about secession from the Union. In the North, every state legislature but one adopted a resolution demanding the prohibition of slavery in the territories.

THE COMPROMISE OF 1850

Faced with this mounting crisis, moderates and unionists spent the winter of 1849–1850 trying to frame a great compromise. The aging Henry Clay, who was spearheading the effort, believed that no compromise could last unless it settled all the issues in dispute. As a result, he took several measures that had been proposed separately, combined them into a single piece of legislation, and presented it to the Senate on January 29, 1850. Among the bill's provisions were the admission of California as a free state; the formation of territorial governments in the rest of the lands acquired from Mexico, without restrictions on slavery; the abolition of the slave trade, but not slavery itself, in the District of Columbia; and a new and more effective fugitive slave law. These resolutions launched a debate that raged for seven months.

In July, after six months of impassioned wrangling, a new, younger group of leaders emerged and took control of the debate from the old "triumvirate" of Webster, Clay, and Calhoun. The new leaders of the Senate were able, as the old leaders had not been, to produce a compromise. One spur to the compromise was the disappearance of the most powerful obstacle to it: the president. On July 9, 1850, Taylor suddenly died—the victim of a violent stomach disorder. He was succeeded by Millard Fillmore of New York. A dull, handsome, dignified man who understood the political importance of flexibility, Fillmore supported compromise and used his powers of persuasion to swing northern Whigs into line.

The new leaders also benefited from their own pragmatic tactics. Stephen A. Douglas, a Democratic senator from Illinois, proposed breaking up the "omnibus bill" that Clay

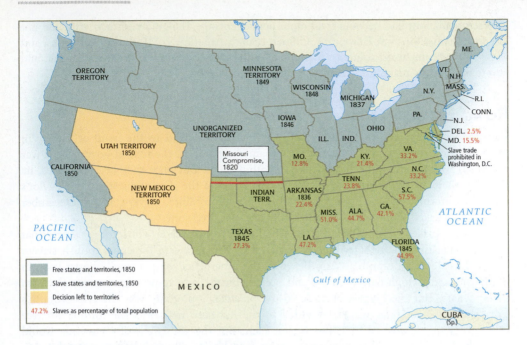

SLAVE AND FREE TERRITORIES UNDER THE COMPROMISE OF 1850   The acquisition of vast new western lands raised the question of the status of slavery in new territories organized for statehood by the United States. Tension between the North and South on this question led in 1850 to a great compromise, forged in Congress, to settle this dispute. The compromise allowed California to join the Union as a free state and introduced the concept of "popular sovereignty" for other new territories. • *How well did the compromise of 1850 work?*

had envisioned as a great, comprehensive solution to the sectional crisis and to introduce instead a series of separate measures to be voted on one by one. Thus representatives of different sections could support those elements of the compromise they liked and oppose those they did not. Douglas also gained support with complicated backroom deals linking the compromise to such nonideological matters as the sale of government bonds and the construction of railroads. As a result of his efforts, by mid-September Congress had enacted all the components of the compromise.

The Compromise of 1850 was a victory of self-interest. Still, members of Congress hailed the measure as a triumph of statesmanship; and Millard Fillmore, signing it, called it a just settlement of the sectional problem, "in its character final and irrevocable."

THE CRISES OF THE 1850s

For a few years after the Compromise of 1850, the sectional conflict seemed briefly to fade amid booming prosperity and growth. But the tensions between the North and the South did not disappear.

THE UNEASY TRUCE

Both major parties endorsed the Compromise of 1850 in 1852, and both nominated presidential candidates unidentified with sectional passions. The Democrats chose the obscure

New Hampshire politician Franklin Pierce, and the Whigs chose the military hero General Winfield Scott. The sectional question was a divisive influence in the election and the Whigs were the principal victims. They suffered massive defections from antislavery members who were angered by the party's evasiveness on the issue. Many of them flocked to the Free-Soil Party, whose antislavery presidential candidate, John P. Hale, repudiated the Compromise of 1850. The divisions among the Whigs helped produce a victory for the Democrats in 1852.

Franklin Pierce attempted to maintain harmony by avoiding divisive issues, particularly slavery. But it was an impossible task. Northern opposition to the Fugitive Slave Act intensified quickly after 1850. Mobs formed in some northern cities to prevent enforcement of the fugitive slave law, and several northern states also passed their own laws barring the deportation of fugitive slaves. White southerners watched with growing anger and alarm as the one element of the Compromise of 1850 that they had considered a victory seemed to become meaningless in the face of northern defiance.

"YOUNG AMERICA"

One of the ways Franklin Pierce hoped to dampen sectional controversy was through his support of a movement in the Democratic Party known as "Young America." Its adherents saw the expansion of American democracy throughout the world as a way to divert attention from the controversies over slavery. The great liberal and nationalist revolutions of 1848 in Europe stirred them to dream of a republican Europe with governments based on the model of the United States. They dreamed as well of acquiring new territories in the Western Hemisphere.

But efforts to extend the nation's domain could not avoid becoming entangled with the sectional crisis. Pierce had been pursuing diplomatic attempts to buy Cuba from Spain (efforts begun in 1848 by Polk). In 1854, however, a group of Polk's envoys sent him a private document from Ostend, Belgium, making a case for seizing Cuba by force. When the Ostend Manifesto, as it became known, was leaked to the public, antislavery northerners charged the administration with conspiring to bring a new slave state into the Union.

The South, for its part, opposed all efforts to acquire new territory that would not support a slave system. The kingdom of Hawaii agreed to join the United States in 1854, but the treaty died in the Senate because it contained a clause prohibiting slavery in the islands. A powerful movement to annex Canada to the United States similarly foundered, at least in part because of slavery.

SLAVERY, RAILROADS, AND THE WEST

What fully revived the sectional crisis, however, was the same issue that had produced it in the first place: slavery in the territories. By the 1850s, the line of substantial white settlement had moved beyond the boundaries of Missouri, Iowa, and what is now Minnesota into a great expanse of plains, which many white Americans had once believed was unfit for cultivation. Now it was becoming apparent that large sections of this region were, in fact, suitable for farming. In the states of the Old Northwest, prospective settlers urged the government to open the area to them, provide territorial governments, and dislodge the Indians located there so as to make room for white settlers. There was relatively little opposition from any segment of white society to this proposed violation of Indian rights. But the interest in further settlement raised two issues that did prove highly divisive and that gradually became entwined with each other: railroads and slavery.

As the nation expanded westward, broad support began to emerge for building a transcontinental railroad. The problem was where to place it—and in particular, where to locate the railroad's eastern terminus, where the line could connect with the existing rail network east of the Mississippi. Northerners favored Chicago, while southerners supported St. Louis, Memphis, or New Orleans. The transcontinental railroad had also become part of the struggle between the North and the South.

Pierce's secretary of war, Jefferson Davis of Mississippi, removed one obstacle to a southern route. Surveys indicated that a railroad with a southern terminus would have to pass through an area in Mexican territory. But in 1853, Davis sent James Gadsden, a southern railroad builder, to Mexico, where he persuaded the Mexican government to accept $10 million in exchange for a strip of land that today comprises parts of Arizona and New Mexico. The so-called Gadsden Purchase only accentuated the sectional rivalry.

THE KANSAS-NEBRASKA CONTROVERSY

As a senator from Illinois and the acknowledged leader of northwestern Democrats, Stephen A. Douglas naturally wanted the transcontinental railroad for his own section. He also realized the strength of the principal argument against the northern route: that it would run mostly through country with a substantial Indian population. As a result, he introduced a bill in January 1854 to organize (and thus open to white settlement) a huge new territory, known as Nebraska, west of Iowa and Missouri.

Douglas knew the South would oppose his bill because it would prepare the way for a new free state; the proposed territory was north of the Missouri Compromise line (36°3′) and hence closed to slavery. In an effort to make the measure acceptable to southerners, Douglas inserted a provision that the status of slavery in the territory would be determined by the territorial legislature. In theory, the region could choose to open itself to slavery. When southern Democrats demanded more, Douglas agreed to an additional clause explicitly repealing the Missouri Compromise. He also agreed to divide the area into two territories—Nebraska and Kansas—instead of one. The new, second territory (Kansas) was somewhat more likely to become a slave state. In its final form the measure was known as the Kansas-Nebraska Act. President Pierce supported the bill, and after a strenuous debate, it became law in May 1854 with the unanimous support of the South and the partial support of northern Democrats.

No piece of legislation in American history produced so many immediate, sweeping, and ominous political consequences. It divided and destroyed the Whig Party. It divided the northern Democrats (many of whom were appalled at the repeal of the Missouri Compromise) and drove many of them from the party. Most important of all, it spurred the creation of a new party that was frankly sectional in composition and creed. People in both major parties who opposed Douglas's bill began to call themselves Anti-Nebraska Democrats and Anti-Nebraska Whigs. In 1854, they formed a new organization and named it the Republican Party. It instantly became a major force in American politics. In the elections of that year, the Republicans won enough seats in Congress to permit them, in combination with allies among the Know-Nothings, to organize the House of Representatives.

"BLEEDING KANSAS"

White settlers began moving into Kansas almost immediately after the passage of the Kansas-Nebraska Act. In the spring of 1855, elections were held for a territorial legislature. There were only about 1,500 legal voters in Kansas by then, but thousands of Missourians,

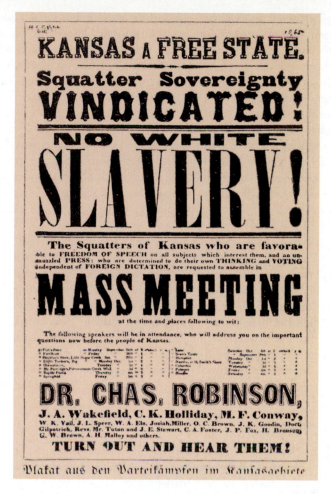

"BLEEDING KANSAS" The battle over the fate of slavery in Kansas was one of the most turbulent events of the 1850s. This 1855 poster invites antislavery forces to a meeting to protest the actions of the "bogus" pro-slavery territorial legislature, which had passed laws that, among other things, made it illegal to speak or write against slavery. "Squatter sovereignty" was another term for "popular sovereignty," the doctrine that gave residents of the prospective state the power to decide the fate of slavery there. (© Bettmann/Corbis)

some traveling in armed bands into Kansas, swelled the vote to over 6,000. As a result, pro-slavery forces elected a majority to the legislature, which immediately legalized slavery. Outraged free-staters elected their own delegates to a constitutional convention, which met at Topeka and adopted a constitution excluding slavery. They then chose their own governor and legislature and petitioned Congress for statehood. President Pierce denounced them as traitors and threw the full support of the federal government behind the pro-slavery territorial legislature. A few months later, a pro-slavery federal marshal assembled a large posse, consisting mostly of Missourians, to arrest the free-state leaders, who had set up their headquarters in Lawrence. The posse sacked the town, burned the "governor's" house, and destroyed several printing presses. Retribution came quickly.

Among the most fervent abolitionists in Kansas was John Brown, a grim, fiercely committed zealot who had moved to Kansas to fight to make it a free state. After the events in Lawrence, he gathered six followers (including four of his sons) and in one night murdered five pro-slavery settlers. This terrible episode, known as the Pottawatomie Massacre, led to more civil strife in Kansas—irregular, guerrilla warfare conducted by armed bands, some more interested in land claims or loot than in ideologies. Northerners and southerners alike came to believe that the events in Kansas illustrated (and were caused by) the aggressive designs of the rival section. "Bleeding Kansas" became a powerful symbol of the sectional controversy.

Another symbol soon appeared, in the United States Senate. In May 1856, Charles Sumner of Massachusetts, a strong antislavery leader, rose to give a speech entitled "The Crime Against Kansas." In it, he gave particular attention to Senator Andrew P. Butler of South Carolina, an outspoken defender of slavery. The South Carolinian was, Sumner claimed, the "Don Quixote" of slavery, having "chosen a mistress . . . who, though ugly to others, is always lovely to him, though polluted in the sight of the world, is chaste in his sight . . . the harlot slavery."

The pointedly sexual references and the general viciousness of the speech enraged Butler's nephew, Preston Brooks, a member of the House of Representatives from South Carolina. Several days after the speech, Brooks approached Sumner at his desk in the Senate chamber during a recess, raised a heavy cane, and began beating him repeatedly on the head and shoulders. Sumner, trapped in his chair, rose in agony with such strength that he tore the desk from the bolts holding it to the floor. Then he collapsed, bleeding and unconscious. So severe were his injuries that he was unable to return to the Senate for four years. Throughout the North, he became a hero—a martyr to the barbarism of the South. In the South, Preston Brooks became a hero, too. Censured by the House, he resigned his seat, returned to South Carolina, and stood successfully for reelection.

THE FREE-SOIL IDEOLOGY

What had happened to produce such deep hostility between the two sections? In part, the tensions were reflections of the two sections' differing economic and territorial interests. But they were also reflections of a hardening of ideas in both North and South.

In the North, assumptions about the proper structure of society came to center on the belief in "free soil" and "free labor." Most white northerners came to believe that the existence of slavery was dangerous not because of what it did to blacks but because of what it threatened to do to whites. At the heart of American democracy, they argued, was the right of all citizens to own property, to control their own labor, and to have access to opportunities for advancement.

According to this vision, the South was the antithesis of democracy—a closed, static society, in which slavery preserved an entrenched aristocracy. While the North was growing and prospering, the South was stagnating, rejecting the values of individualism and progress. The South, northern free-laborites further maintained, was engaged in a conspiracy to extend slavery throughout the nation and thus to destroy the openness of northern capitalism and replace it with the closed, aristocratic system of the South. The only solution to this "slave power conspiracy" was to fight the spread of slavery and extend the nation's democratic (i.e., free-labor) ideals to all sections of the country.

This ideology, which lay at the heart of the new Republican Party, also strengthened the commitment of Republicans to the Union. Since the idea of continued growth and progress was central to the free-labor vision, the prospect of dismemberment of the nation was to the Republicans unthinkable.

THE PRO-SLAVERY ARGUMENT

In the South, in the meantime, a very different ideology was emerging. It was a result of many things: the Nat Turner uprising in 1831, which terrified southern whites; the expansion of the cotton economy into the Deep South, which made slavery unprecedentedly lucrative; and the growth of the Garrisonian abolitionist movement, with its strident attacks on southern society. The popularity of Harriet Beecher Stowe's *Uncle Tom's Cabin* was perhaps the most glaring evidence of the power of those attacks, but other abolitionist writings had been antagonizing white southerners for years.

In response to these pressures, a number of white southerners produced a new intellectual defense of slavery. Professor Thomas R. Dew of the College of William and Mary helped begin that effort in 1832. Twenty years later, apologists for slavery summarized their views in an anthology that gave their ideology its name: *The Pro-Slavery Argument*. John C. Calhoun stated the essence of the case in 1837: Slavery was "a good—a positive good." It was good for the slaves because they enjoyed better conditions than industrial workers in the North, good for southern society because it was the only way the two races could live together in peace, and good for the entire country because the southern economy, based on slavery, was the key to the prosperity of the nation.

Above all, southern apologists argued, slavery was good because it served as the basis for the southern way of life—a way of life superior to any other in the United States, perhaps in the world. White southerners looking at the North saw a spirit of greed, debauchery, and destructiveness. "The masses of the North are venal, corrupt, covetous, mean and selfish," wrote one southerner. Others wrote with horror of the factory system and the crowded, pestilential cities filled with unruly immigrants. But the South, they believed, was a stable, orderly society, free from the feuds between capital and labor plaguing the North. It protected the welfare of its workers. And it allowed the aristocracy to enjoy a refined and accomplished cultural life. It was, in short, an ideal social order in which all elements of the population were secure and content.

The defense of slavery rested, too, on increasingly elaborate arguments about the biological inferiority of African Americans, who were, white southerners claimed, inherently unfit to take care of themselves, let alone exercise the rights of citizenship.

BUCHANAN AND DEPRESSION

In this unpromising climate, the presidential campaign of 1856 began. Democratic Party leaders wanted a candidate who, unlike President Pierce, was not closely associated with the explosive question of "Bleeding Kansas." They chose James Buchanan of Pennsylvania, who as minister to England had been safely out of the country during the recent controversies. The Republicans, participating in their first presidential contest, endorsed a Whiggish program of internal improvements, thus combining the idealism of antislavery with the economic aspirations of the North. The Democrats were eager to present a safe candidate. The Republicans nominated John C. Frémont, who had made a national reputation as an explorer of the Far West and who had no political record. The Native American, or Know-Nothing, Party was beginning to break apart, but it nominated former president Millard Fillmore, who also received the endorsement of a small remnant of the Whig Party.

After a heated, even frenzied campaign, Buchanan won a narrow victory over Frémont and Fillmore. Whether because of age and physical infirmities or because of a more fundamental weakness of character, he became a painfully timid and indecisive president at a critical moment in history. In the year Buchanan took office, a financial panic struck the country, followed by a depression that lasted several years. In the North, the depression strengthened the Republican Party because distressed manufacturers, workers, and farmers came to believe that the hard times were the result of the unsound policies of southern-controlled Democratic administrations. They expressed their frustrations by moving into an alliance with antislavery elements and thus into the Republican Party.

THE DRED SCOTT DECISION

On March 6, 1857, the Supreme Court of the United States projected itself into the sectional controversy with one of the most controversial and notorious decisions in its history—*Dred Scott v. Sandford.* Dred Scott was a Missouri slave, once owned by an army surgeon who had taken Scott with him into Illinois and Wisconsin, where slavery was forbidden. In 1846, after the surgeon died, Scott sued his master's widow for freedom on the grounds that his residence in free territory had liberated him from slavery. The claim was well grounded in Missouri law, and in 1850 the circuit court in which Scott filed the suit declared him free. By now, John Sanford, the brother of the surgeon's widow, was claiming ownership of Scott, and he appealed the circuit court ruling to the state supreme court, which reversed the earlier decision. When Scott appealed to the federal courts, Sanford's attorneys claimed that Scott had no standing to sue because he was not a citizen.

The Supreme Court (which misspelled Sanford's name in its decision) was so divided that it was unable to issue a single ruling on the case. The thrust of the various rulings, however, was a stunning defeat for the antislavery movement. Chief Justice Roger Taney, who wrote one of the majority opinions, declared that Scott could not bring a suit in the federal courts because he was not a citizen. Blacks had no claim to citizenship, Taney argued. Slaves were property, and the Fifth Amendment prohibited Congress from taking property without "due process of law." Consequently, Taney concluded, Congress possessed no authority to pass a law depriving persons of their slave property in the territories. The Missouri Compromise, therefore, had always been unconstitutional.

The ruling did nothing to challenge the right of an individual state to prohibit slavery within its borders, but the statement that the federal government was powerless to act on the issue was a drastic and startling one. Southern whites were elated: the highest tribunal in the land had sanctioned parts of the most extreme southern argument. In the North, the decision produced widespread dismay. The decision, the *New York Tribune* wrote, "is entitled to just so much moral weight as would be the judgment of a majority of those congregated in any Washington bar-room." Republicans threatened that when they won control of the national government, they would reverse the decision—by "packing" the Court with new members.

DEADLOCK OVER KANSAS

President Buchanan timidly endorsed the *Dred Scott* decision. At the same time, he tried to resolve the controversy over Kansas by supporting its admission to the Union as a slave state. In response, the pro-slavery territorial legislature called an election for delegates to a constitutional convention. The free-state residents refused to participate, claiming that the legislature had discriminated against them in drawing district lines. As a result, the pro-slavery forces won control of the convention, which met in 1857 at Lecompton, framed a constitution legalizing slavery, and refused to give voters a chance to reject it. When an election for a new territorial legislature was called, the antislavery groups turned out to vote and won a majority. The new antislavery legislature promptly submitted the Lecompton constitution to the voters, who rejected it by more than 10,000 votes.

Both sides had resorted to fraud and violence, but it was clear nevertheless that a majority of the people of Kansas opposed slavery. Buchanan, however, pressured Congress to admit Kansas under the pro-slavery Lecompton constitution. Stephen A. Douglas and other northern and western Democrats refused to support the president's proposal, which died in the House of Representatives. Finally, in April 1858, Congress approved a com- promise: The Lecompton constitution would be submitted to the voters of Kansas again. If it was approved, Kansas would be admitted to the Union; if it was rejected, statehood would be postponed. Again, Kansas voters decisively rejected the Lecompton constitution. Not until the closing months of Buchanan's administration in 1861 did Kansas enter the Union—as a free state.

THE EMERGENCE OF LINCOLN

Given the gravity of the sectional crisis, the congressional elections of 1858 took on a special importance. Of particular note was the United States Senate contest in Illinois, which pitted Stephen A. Douglas, the most prominent northern Democrat, against Abraham Lincoln, who was largely unknown outside Illinois.

Lincoln was a successful lawyer who had long been involved in state politics. He had served several terms in the Illinois legislature and one undistinguished term in Congress. But he was not a national figure like Douglas, and so he tried to increase his visibility by engaging Douglas in a series of debates. The Lincoln-Douglas debates attracted enormous crowds and received wide attention.

At the heart of the debates was a basic difference on the issue of slavery. Douglas appeared to have no moral position on the issue, Lincoln claimed. He claimed that Douglas did not care whether slavery was "voted up, or voted down." Lincoln's opposition to slavery was more fundamental. If the nation could accept that blacks were not entitled to basic human rights, he argued, then it could accept that other groups—immigrant laborers, for example—could be deprived of rights, too. And if slavery were to extend into the western territories, he argued, opportunities for poor white laborers to better their lots there would be lost. The nation's future, Lincoln argued (reflecting the central idea of the Republican Party), rested on the spread of free labor.

Lincoln believed slavery was morally wrong, but he was not an abolitionist. That was in part because he could not envision an easy alternative to slavery in the areas where it already existed. He shared the prevailing view among northern whites that the black race was not prepared to live on equal terms with whites. But even while Lincoln accepted the inferiority of black people, he continued to believe that they were entitled to basic rights. "I have no purpose to introduce political and social equality between the white and the black races . . . But I hold that . . . there is no reason in the world why the negro is not entitled to all the natural rights enumerated in the Declaration of Independence, the right to life, liberty, and the pursuit of happiness. I hold that he is as much entitled to these as the white man." Lincoln and his party would "arrest the further spread" of slavery. They would not directly challenge it where it already existed but would trust that the institution would gradually die out there of its own accord.

Douglas's position satisfied his followers sufficiently to produce a Democratic majority in the state legislature, which returned him to the Senate but aroused little enthusiasm. Lincoln, by contrast, lost the election but emerged with a growing following both in and beyond the state. And outside Illinois, the elections went heavily against the Democrats. The party retained control of the Senate but lost its majority in the House, with the result that the congressional sessions of 1858 and 1859 were bitterly deadlocked.

JOHN BROWN'S RAID

The battles in Congress, however, were almost entirely overshadowed by an event that enraged and horrified the South. In the fall of 1859, John Brown, the antislavery radical whose bloody actions in Kansas had inflamed the crisis there, staged an even more dramatic episode, this time in the South itself. With private encouragement and financial aid from some prominent abolitionists, he made elaborate plans to seize a mountain fortress in Virginia from which, he believed, he could foment a slave insurrection in the South. On October 16, he and a group of eighteen followers attacked and seized control of a United States arsenal in Harpers Ferry, Virginia. But the slave uprising Brown hoped to inspire did not occur, and he quickly found himself besieged in the arsenal by citizens, local militia companies, and, before long, United States troops under the command of Robert E. Lee. After ten of his men were killed, Brown surrendered. He was promptly tried in a Virginia court for treason and sentenced to death. He and six of his followers were hanged.

No other single event did more than the Harpers Ferry raid to convince white southerners that they could not live safely in the Union. Many southerners believed (incorrectly) that John Brown's raid had the support of the Republican Party, and it suggested to them that the North was now committed to producing a slave insurrection.

JOHN BROWN Even in this formal photographic portrait (taken in 1859, the last year of his life), John Brown conveys the fierce sense of righteousness that fueled his extraordinary activities in the fight against slavery. (Library of Congress)

THE ELECTION OF LINCOLN

As the presidential election of 1860 approached, the Democratic Party was torn apart by a battle between southerners, who demanded a strong endorsement of slavery, and westerners, who supported the idea of popular sovereignty. When the party convention met in April in Charleston, South Carolina, and endorsed popular sovereignty, delegates from eight states in the lower South walked out. The remaining delegates could not agree on a presidential candidate and finally adjourned after agreeing to meet again in Baltimore. The decimated convention at Baltimore nominated Stephen Douglas for president. In the meantime, disenchanted southern Democrats met in Richmond and nominated John C. Breckinridge of Kentucky.

The Republican leaders, in the meantime, were trying to broaden their appeal in the North. The platform endorsed such traditional Whig measures as a high tariff, internal improvements, a homestead bill, and a Pacific railroad to be built with federal financial assistance. It supported the right of each state to decide the status of slavery within its borders. But it also insisted that neither Congress nor territorial legislatures could legalize slavery in the territories. The Republican convention chose Abraham Lincoln as the party's

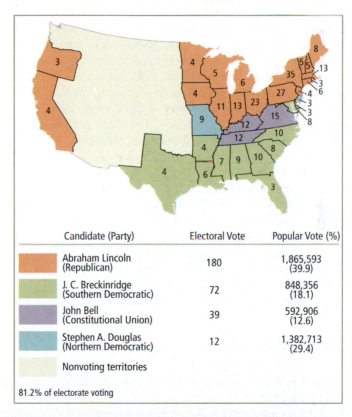

Candidate (Party)	Electoral Vote	Popular Vote (%)
Abraham Lincoln (Republican)	180	1,865,593 (39.9)
J. C. Breckinridge (Southern Democratic)	72	848,356 (18.1)
John Bell (Constitutional Union)	39	592,906 (12.6)
Stephen A. Douglas (Northern Democratic)	12	1,382,713 (29.4)
Nonvoting territories		

81.2% of electorate voting

THE ELECTION OF 1860   The stark sectional divisions that helped produce the Civil War were clearly visible in the results of the 1860 presidential election. Abraham Lincoln, the antislavery Republican candidate, won virtually all the free states. Stephen Douglas, a northern Democrat with no strong position on the issue of slavery, won two of the border states, and John Bell, a supporter of both slavery and union, won others. John Breckinridge, a strong pro-slavery southern Democrat, carried the entire Deep South. Lincoln won under 40 percent of the popular vote but, because of the four-way division in the race, managed to win a clear majority of the electoral vote. • *What impact did the election of Lincoln have on the sectional crisis?*

presidential nominee. Lincoln was appealing because of his growing reputation for elo-
quence, because of his firm but moderate position on slavery, and because his relative
obscurity ensured that he would have none of the drawbacks of other, more prominent
(and therefore more controversial) Republicans.

In the November election, Lincoln won the presidency with a majority of the electoral
votes but only about two-fifths of the fragmented popular vote. The Republicans, moreover, failed to win a majority in Congress. Even so, the election of Lincoln became the
final signal to many white southerners that their position in the Union was hopeless. And
within a few weeks of Lincoln's victory, the process of disunion began—a process that
would quickly lead to a prolonged and bloody war.

CONCLUSION

In the decades following the War of 1812, a vigorous nationalism pervaded much of
American life, helping to smooth over the growing differences among the very distinct
societies emerging in the United States. During the 1850s, however, the forces that
had worked to hold the nation together in the past fell victim to new and much more
divisive pressures.

Driving the sectional tensions of the 1850s was a battle over national policy toward the
place of slavery within the western territories. Should slavery be permitted in the new
states? And who should decide? There were strenuous efforts to craft compromises and
solutions to this dilemma: the Compromise of 1850, the Kansas-Nebraska Act of 1854,
and others. But despite these efforts, positions on slavery continued to harden in both the
North and South. Bitter battles in the territory of Kansas over whether to permit slavery
there; growing agitation by abolitionists in the North and pro-slavery advocates in the
South; the Supreme Court's controversial *Dred Scott* decision in 1857; the popularity of
Uncle Tom's Cabin throughout the decade; and the emergence of a new political party—the
Republican Party—openly and centrally opposed to slavery: all worked to destroy the
hopes for compromise and push the South toward secession.

In 1860, all pretense of common sentiment collapsed when no political party presented
a presidential candidate capable of attracting national support. The Republicans nominated
Abraham Lincoln of Illinois, a little-known politician recognized for his eloquent condem-
nations of slavery in a Senate race two years earlier. The Democratic Party split apart, with
its northern and southern wings each nominating different candidates. Lincoln won the
election easily, but with less than 40 percent of the popular vote. And almost immediately
after his victory, the states of the South began preparing to secede from the Union.

RECALL AND REFLECT

1. How were the boundary disputes over Oregon and Texas resolved? Why were the resolutions
   in the two cases so different?
2. How did Polk's decisions and actions as president intensify the sectional conflict?
3. What was the issue at stake in "Bleeding Kansas," and how did events in Kansas reflect the
   growing sectional division between the North and the South?
4. What was the *Dred Scott* decision? What was the decision's impact on the sectional crisis?
5. How did the growing sectional crisis affect the nation's major political parties?

14 | THE CIVIL WAR

LOOKING AHEAD

1. How did the annexation of western territories intensify the conflict over slavery and lead to deeper divisions between the North and the South?

2. What compromises attempted to resolve the conflicts over the expansion of slavery into new territories? To what degree were these compromises successful? Why did they eventually fail to resolve the differences between the North and the South?

3. What were the major arguments for and against slavery and its expansion into new territories?

BY THE END OF 1860, the cords that had bound the Union together had snapped. The second party system had collapsed, replaced by one that accentuated rather than muted regional controversy. The federal government was no longer a remote, unthreatening presence; the need to resolve the status of the territories had made it necessary for Washington to deal directly with sectional issues. The election of 1860 brought these tensions to a head and precipitated the most terrible war in the nation's history.

Confederate States of America formed

Davis president of Confederacy

Conflict at Fort Sumter

First Battle of Bull Run

1862

Battles of Shiloh, Antietam, Second Bull Run

Confederacy enacts military draft

1863

Emancipation Proclamation

Battle of Gettysburg

Vicksburg surrenders

Union enacts military draft

New York City antidraft riots

1864

Battle of the Wilderness

Sherman's March to the Sea

Lincoln reelected

1865

Lee surrenders to Grant

13th Amendment

THE SECESSION CRISIS

Almost as soon as news of Abraham Lincoln's election reached the South, militant leaders began to demand an end to the Union.

THE WITHDRAWAL OF THE SOUTH

South Carolina, long the hotbed of southern separatism, seceded first, on December 20, 1860. By the time Lincoln took office, six other southern states—Mississippi (January 9, 1861), Florida (January 10), Alabama (January 11), Georgia (January 19), Louisiana (January 26), and Texas (February 1)—had withdrawn from the Union. In February 1861, representatives of the seven seceded states met at Montgomery, Alabama, and formed a new nation—the Confederate States of America. Two months earlier, President James Buchanan told Congress that no state had the right to secede from the Union but that the federal government had no authority to stop a state if it did.

The seceding states immediately seized the federal property within their boundaries. But they did not at first have sufficient military power to seize two fortified offshore military installations: Fort Sumter, in the harbor of Charleston, South Carolina, garrisoned by a small force under Major Robert Anderson; and Fort Pickens, in Pensacola, Florida. Buchanan refused to yield Fort Sumter when South Carolina demanded it. Instead, in January 1861, he ordered an unarmed merchant ship to proceed to Fort Sumter with additional troops and supplies. Confederate guns turned it back. Still, neither section was yet ready to concede that war had begun. And in Washington, efforts began once more to forge a compromise.

THE FAILURE OF COMPROMISE

Gradually, the compromise efforts came together around a proposal from John J. Crittenden of Kentucky. Known as the Crittenden Compromise, it proposed reestablishing the Missouri Compromise line and extending it westward to the Pacific. Slavery would be prohibited north of the line and permitted south of it. Southerners in the Senate seemed willing to accept the plan. But the compromise would have required the Republicans to abandon their most fundamental position—that slavery not be allowed to expand—and they rejected it.

And so nothing was resolved when Abraham Lincoln arrived in Washington for his inauguration. In his inaugural address, Lincoln insisted that acts of force or violence to support secession were insurrectionary and that the government would "hold, occupy, and possess" federal property in the seceded states—a clear reference to Fort Sumter.

But Fort Sumter was running short of supplies. So Lincoln sent a relief expedition to the fort and informed the South Carolina authorities that he would send no troops or munitions unless the supply ships met with resistance. The new Confederate government ordered General P. G. T. Beauregard, commander of Confederate forces at Charleston, to take the fort. When Anderson refused to give up, the Confederates bombarded it for two days. On April 14, 1861, Anderson surrendered. The Civil War had begun.

Almost immediately, four more slave states seceded from the Union and joined the Confederacy: Virginia (April 17), Arkansas (May 6), Tennessee (May 7), and North Carolina (May 20). The four remaining slave states, Maryland, Delaware, Kentucky, and Missouri—under heavy political pressure from Washington—remained in the Union.

THE OPPOSING SIDES

All the important material advantages for waging war lay with the North, most notably an advanced industrial system able by 1862 to manufacture almost all the North's own war materials. The South had almost no industry at all.

In addition, the North had a much better transportation system, with more and better railroads than did the South. During the war, the already inferior Confederate railroad system steadily deteriorated and by early 1864 had almost collapsed.

But the South also had advantages. The Southern armies were, for the most part, fighting a defensive war on familiar land with local support. The Northern armies, on the other hand, were fighting mostly within the South amid hostile local populations; they had to maintain long lines of communication. The commitment of the white population of the South to the war was, with limited exceptions, clear and firm. In the North, opinion was more divided, and support remained shaky until very near the end. A major Southern victory at any one of several crucial moments might have proved decisive in breaking the North's will to continue the struggle. Finally, the dependence of the English and French textile industries on American cotton inclined many leaders in those countries to favor the Confederacy; and Southerners hoped, with some reason, that one or both might intervene on their behalf.

THE MOBILIZATION OF THE NORTH

In the North, the war produced considerable discord, frustration, and suffering. But it also produced prosperity and economic growth. With the South now gone from Congress, the Republican Party enjoyed almost unchallenged supremacy. During the war, it enacted an aggressively nationalistic program to promote economic development.

ECONOMIC NATIONALISM

Two 1862 acts assisted the rapid development of the West. The Homestead Act permitted any citizen or prospective citizen to purchase 160 acres of public land for a small fee after living on

THE CAUSES OF THE CIVIL WAR

ABRAHAM Lincoln, in his 1865 inaugural address, looked back at the terrible war that was now nearing its end and said, "All knew [that slavery] was somehow the cause of the war." Few historians dispute that. But disagreement has been sharp over whether slavery was the only, or even the principal, cause of the war.

The debate began even before the war itself. In 1858, Senator William H. Seward of New York took note of the two competing explanations of the sectional tensions that were then inflaming the nation. On one side, he said, stood those who believed the conflicts to be "accidental, unnecessary, the work of interested or fanatical agitators." Opposing them stood those (among them Seward himself) who believed there to be "an irrepressible conflict between opposing and enduring forces."

The "irrepressible conflict" argument dominated historical discussion of the war from the 1860s to the 1920s. War was inevitable, some historians claimed, because there was no room for compromise on the central issue of slavery. Others de-emphasized slavery and pointed to the economic differences between the agrarian South and the industrializing North. Charles and Mary Beard, for example, wrote in 1927 of the "inherent antagonisms" between the interests of planters and those of industrialists. Still others cited social and cultural differences as the source of an irrepressible conflict. Slavery, the historian Allan Nevins argued, was only one factor that was making residents of the North and South "separate peoples." Fundamental differences in "assumptions, tastes, and cultural aim" made it virtually impossible for the two societies to live together in peace.

More recent proponents of irrepressible-conflict arguments similarly emphasize culture and ideology but define the concerns of the North and the South in different terms. Eric Foner, writing in 1970, argued that the moral concerns of abolitionists and the economic concerns of industrialists were less important in explaining northern hostility to the South than was the broad-based "free-labor" ideology of the region. Northerners opposed slavery because they feared it might spread into their own region or into the West and threaten the position of free white laborers.

Other historians have argued that the war was not inevitable, beginning with a group of

it for five years. The Morrill Act transferred substantial public acreage to the state governments, which could now sell the land and use the proceeds to finance public education. This act led to the creation of many new state colleges and universities, the so-called land-grant institutions. Congress also passed a series of tariff bills that by the end of the war had raised duties to the highest level in the nation's history—a great boon to domestic industries eager for protection from foreign competition, but a hardship for many farmers and other consumers.

Congress also moved to spur completion of a transcontinental railroad. It created two new federally chartered corporations: the Union Pacific Railroad Company, which was to build westward from Omaha, and the Central Pacific, which was to build eastward from

"ON TO LIBERTY"   This painting by Theodore Kaufmann shows a group of fugitive slaves escaping from the South in the late years of the Civil War. Thousands of former slaves crossed the Union lines, where they were given their freedom. Many of them joined the Union Army. (The Granger Collection, NYC)

scholars in the 1920s known as the "revisionists." James G. Randall and Avery Craven were the two leading proponents of the view that the differences between the North and the South were not so great as to require a war, that only a "blundering generation" of leaders caused the conflict. Michael Holt revived the revisionist argument in a 1978 book, in which he, too, emphasized the partisan ambitions of politicians. Holt was, along with Paul Kleppner, Joel Silbey, and William Gienapp, one of the creators of an "ethnocultural" interpretation of the war, which emphasized the collapse of the party system and the role of temperance and nativism, which was central to the coming of the conflict.   •

UNDERSTAND, ANALYZE, & EVALUATE

1. Some arguments regarding the Civil War as inevitable focus on economic differences between the North and the South. What were these differences and how might they have led—inevitably—to war?

2. Some revisionist scholars attribute the Civil War to a "blundering generation" of political leaders. Who were these leaders and what blunders did they make? Could better decisions have avoided war?

California. The two projects were to meet in the middle and complete the link, which they did in 1869 at Promontory Point, Utah.

The National Bank Acts of 1863–1864 created a new national banking system. Existing or newly formed banks could join the system if they had enough capital and were willing to invest one-third of it in government securities. In return, they could issue United States Treasury notes as currency. This eliminated much (although not all) of the chaos and uncertainty surrounding the nation's currency.

More difficult was financing the war itself. The government tried to do so in three ways: levying taxes, issuing paper currency, and borrowing. Congress levied new taxes on almost all goods and services and in 1861 levied an income tax for the first time. But taxation raised only a small proportion of the necessary funds, and strong popular resistance prevented the government from raising the rates.

At least equally controversial was the printing of paper currency, or "greenbacks." The new currency was backed not by gold or silver but (as today) simply by the good faith and credit of the government. The value of the greenbacks fluctuated according to the fortunes of the Northern armies. Early in 1864, with the war effort bogged down, a greenback dollar was worth only 39 percent of a gold dollar. Even at the close of the war, with confidence high, it was worth only 67 percent of a gold dollar.

By far the largest source of financing for the war was loans. The Treasury persuaded ordinary citizens to buy over $400 million worth of bonds. But public bond purchases constituted only a small part of the government's borrowing, which in the end totaled $2.6 billion, most of it from banks and large financial interests.

RAISING THE UNION ARMIES

At the beginning of 1861, the regular army of the United States consisted of only 16,000 troops, many of them stationed in the West. So the Union, like the Confederacy, had to raise its army mostly from scratch. Lincoln called for an increase of 23,000 in the regular army, but the bulk of the fighting, he knew, would have to be done by volunteers in state militias. When Congress convened in July 1861, it authorized enlisting 500,000 volunteers for three-year (as opposed to the customary three-month) terms.

This voluntary system of recruitment produced adequate forces only briefly, during the first flush of enthusiasm for the war. By March 1863, Congress was forced to pass a national draft law. Virtually all young adult males were eligible to be drafted, although a man could escape service by hiring someone to go in his place or by paying the government a fee of $300.

To many who were accustomed to a remote and inactive national government, conscription was strange and threatening. Opposition to the draft law was widespread, particularly among laborers, immigrants, and Democrats opposed to the war (known as "Peace Democrats" or "Copperheads" by their opponents). Occasionally opposition to the draft erupted into violence such as when demonstrators rioted in New York City for four days in July 1863, after the first names were selected for conscription. More than 100 people died. Irish workers were at the center of violence. They were angry because black strike breakers had been used against them in a recent longshoremen's strike. They blamed African Americans generally for the war, which they thought was being fought for the benefit of slaves. The rioters lynched several African Americans and burned down black homes, businesses, and even an orphanage, leaving more than 100 dead. Only the arrival of federal troops direct from the Battle of Gettysburg halted the violence.

WARTIME POLITICS

When Abraham Lincoln arrived in Washington, many Republicans considered him a minor prairie politician who would be easily controlled by the real leaders of his party. But Lincoln was not cowed by the distinguished figures around him. The new president understood his own (and his party's) weaknesses, and he assembled a cabinet representing every faction of the Republican Party and every segment of Northern opinion. He moved boldly to use the war powers of the presidency, blithely ignoring inconvenient parts of the Constitution because, he said, it would be foolish to lose the whole by being afraid to disregard a part.

He sent troops into battle without asking Congress for a declaration of war, arguing that the conflict was a domestic insurrection. He increased the size of the regular army without receiving legislative authority to do so. He unilaterally proclaimed a naval blockade of the South.

Lincoln's greatest political problem was the widespread popular opposition to the war in the North. Lincoln ordered military arrests of civilian dissenters and suspended the right of habeas corpus (the right of an arrested person to receive a speedy trial). At first, Lincoln used these methods only in sensitive areas such as the border states; but in 1862, he proclaimed that all persons who discouraged enlistments or engaged in disloyal practices were subject to martial law.

Repression was not the only tool the North used to strengthen support for the war. In addition to arresting "disloyal" Northerners, Lincoln's administration used new tools of persuasion to build popular opinion in favor of the war. In addition to pro-war pamphlets, posters, speeches, and songs, the war mobilized a significant corps of photographers— organized by the renowned Matthew Brady, one of the first important photographers in American history—to take pictures of the war. The photographs that resulted from this effort—new to warfare—were among the grimmest ever made to that point, many of them displaying the vast numbers of dead on the Civil War battlefields. For some, the images of death contributed to a revulsion for the war. But for most Northerners, they gave evidence of the level of sacrifice that had been made for the preservation of the Union and thus spurred the nation on to victory. (Southerners used similar propaganda in the Confederacy, although less effectively.)

By the time of the 1864 election, the North was in political turmoil. The Republicans had suffered heavy losses in 1862, and in response party leaders tried to create a broad coalition of all the groups that supported the war. They called the new organization the Union Party, but it was, in reality, little more than the Republican Party and a small faction of War Democrats. They nominated Lincoln for a second term and Andrew Johnson of Tennessee, a War Democrat who had opposed his state's decision to secede, for the vice presidency.

The Democrats nominated George B. McClellan, a celebrated former Union general. The party adopted a platform denouncing the war and calling for a truce. McClellan repudiated that demand, but the Democrats were clearly the peace party in the campaign, trying to profit from growing war weariness. For a time, Lincoln's prospects for reelection seemed doubtful.

At this crucial moment, however, several Northern military victories, particularly the capture of Atlanta, Georgia, early in September, rejuvenated Northern morale and boosted Republican prospects. With the overwhelming support of Union troops, Lincoln won reelection comfortably, with 212 electoral votes to McClellan's 21.

THE POLITICS OF EMANCIPATION

Despite their surface unity in supporting the war and their general agreement on most economic matters, the Republicans disagreed sharply with one another on the issue of slavery. "Radical Republicans"—led in Congress by such men as Representative Thaddeus Stevens of Pennsylvania and Senators Charles Sumner of Massachusetts and Benjamin Wade of Ohio—wanted to use the war to abolish slavery immediately and completely.

AFRICAN AMERICAN TROOPS   Although most of the black soldiers who enlisted in the Union army performed noncombat jobs behind the lines, some black combat regiments—members of one of which are pictured here—fought with great success and valor in critical battles. (Library of Congress)

"Conservative Republicans" favored a more cautious policy—in part so as to placate the slave states that remained, precariously, within the Union.

Nevertheless, momentum began to gather behind emancipation early in the war. In 1861, Congress passed the Confiscation Act, which declared that all slaves used for "insurrectionary" purposes (that is, in support of the Confederate military effort) would be considered freed. Subsequent laws in the spring of 1862 abolished slavery in the District of Columbia and the western territories and provided for the compensation of owners. In July 1862, Radicals pushed through Congress the second Confiscation Act, which declared free the slaves of persons supporting the insurrection and authorized the president to employ African Americans as soldiers.

As the war progressed, many in the North slowly accepted emancipation as a central war aim; nothing less, they believed, would justify the enormous sacrifices the struggle had required. As a result, the Radicals gained increasing influence within the Republican Party—a development that did not go unnoticed by the president, who decided to seize the leadership of the rising antislavery sentiment himself.

On September 22, 1862, after the Union victory at the Battle of Antietam, the president announced his intention to use his war powers to issue an executive order freeing all slaves in the Confederacy. And on January 1, 1863, he formally signed the Emancipation Proclamation, which declared forever free the slaves inside the Confederacy. The proclamation did not apply to the Union slave states; nor did it affect those parts of the Confederacy already under Union control (Tennessee, western Virginia, and southern Louisiana). It applied, in short, only to slaves over whom the Union had no control. Still, the document was of great importance. It clearly and irrevocably established that the war was being fought not only to preserve the Union but also to eliminate slavery. Eventually, as federal armies occupied much of the South, the proclamation became a practical reality and led directly to the freeing of thousands of slaves.

Even in areas not directly affected by the proclamation, the antislavery impulse gained strength. The U.S. government's tentative measures against slavery were not, at first, a major factor in the liberation of slaves. Instead, the war helped African Americans to liberate themselves, and they did so in increasing numbers as the war progressed. Many slaves were taken from their plantations and put to work as workers building defenses and other chores. Once transported to the front, many of them found ways to escape across Northern lines, where they were treated as "contraband"—goods seized from people who had no right to them. They could not be returned to their masters. By 1862, the Union army often penetrated deep into the Confederacy. Almost everywhere they went, escaped slaves flocked to join them by the thousands, often whole families. Some of them joined the Union army, others simply stayed with the troops until they could find their way to free states. When the Union captured New Orleans and much of southern Louisiana, slaves refused to work for their former masters, even though the Union occupiers had not made any provisions for liberating African Americans.

By the end of the war, two Union slave states (Maryland and Missouri) and three Confederate states occupied by Union forces (Tennessee, Arkansas, and Louisiana) had abolished slavery. In 1865, Congress finally approved and the states ratified the Thirteenth Amendment, which abolished slavery in all parts of the United States. After more than two centuries, legalized slavery finally ceased to exist in the United States.

AFRICAN AMERICANS AND THE UNION CAUSE

About 186,000 emancipated blacks served as soldiers, sailors, and laborers for the Union forces. Yet in the first months of the war, African Americans were largely excluded from the military. A few black regiments eventually took shape in some of the Union-occupied areas of the Confederacy. But once Lincoln issued the Emancipation Proclamation, black enlistment increased rapidly and the Union military began actively to recruit African American soldiers and sailors in both the North and, where possible, the South.

Some of these men were organized into fighting units, of which the best known was probably the Fifty-fourth Massachusetts Infantry, which (like most black regiments) had a white commander: Robert Gould Shaw, a member of an aristocratic Boston family.

Most black soldiers, however, were assigned menial tasks behind the lines, such as digging trenches and transporting water. Even though many fewer blacks than whites died in combat, the African American mortality rate was actually higher than the rate for white soldiers because so many black soldiers died of diseases contracted while working long, arduous hours in unsanitary conditions. Conditions for blacks and whites were unequal in other ways as well. Until 1869, black soldiers were paid a third less than were white soldiers. But however dangerous, onerous, or menial the tasks that black soldiers were given, most of them felt enormous pride in their service—pride they retained throughout their lives, and often through the lives of their descendants. Many moved from the army into politics and other forms of leadership (in both the North and, after the war, the Reconstruction South). Black fighting men captured by the Confederates were sent back to their masters (if they were escaped slaves) or executed. In 1864, Confederate soldiers killed over 260 black Union soldiers after capturing them in Tennessee.

WOMEN, NURSING, AND THE WAR

Thrust into new and often unfamiliar roles by the war, women took over positions vacated by men as teachers, salesclerks, office workers, mill and factory hands, and above all nursing. The United States Sanitary Commission, an organization of civilian volunteers led by

Dorothea Dix, mobilized large numbers of female nurses to serve in field hospitals. By the end of the war, women were the dominant force in nursing.

Female nurses encountered considerable resistance from male doctors, many of whom thought it inappropriate for women to take care of male strangers. The Sanitary Commission countered such arguments by presenting nursing in domestic terms: as a profession that made use of the same maternal, nurturing roles women played as wives and mothers.

Some women came to see the war as an opportunity to win support for their own goals. Elizabeth Cady Stanton and Susan B. Anthony, who together founded the National Woman's Loyal League in 1863, worked simultaneously for the abolition of slavery and the awarding of suffrage to women.

THE MOBILIZATION OF THE SOUTH

Early in February 1861, representatives of the seven seceding states met at Montgomery, Alabama, to create a new Southern nation. When Virginia seceded several months later, the leaders of the Confederacy moved to Richmond.

There were, of course, important differences between the new Confederate nation and the nation it had left. But there were also significant similarities.

THE CONFEDERATE GOVERNMENT

The Confederate constitution was almost identical to the Constitution of the United States, with several significant exceptions. It explicitly acknowledged the sovereignty of the individual states (although not the right of secession). And it specifically sanctioned slavery and made its abolition (even by one of the states) practically impossible.

The constitutional convention at Montgomery named a provisional president and vice president: Jefferson Davis of Mississippi and Alexander H. Stephens of Georgia, who were later elected by the general public, without opposition, for six-year terms. Davis had been a moderate secessionist before the war. Stephens had argued against secession. The Confederate government, like the Union government, was dominated throughout the war by men of the political center.

Davis was a reasonably able administrator and encountered little interference from the generally tame members of his unstable cabinet. But he rarely provided genuinely national leadership, spending too much time on routine items. Unlike Lincoln, he displayed a punctiliousness about legal and constitutional requirements.

Although there were no formal political parties in the Confederacy, its politics were badly divided nevertheless. Some white Southerners opposed secession and war altogether. Most white Southerners supported the war, but as in the North, many were openly critical of the government and the military, particularly as the tide of battle turned against the South.

States' rights had become such a cult among many white Southerners that they resisted virtually all efforts to exert national authority, even those necessary to win the war. States' rights enthusiasts obstructed conscription and restricted Davis's ability to impose martial law and suspend habeas corpus. Governors such as Joseph Brown of Georgia and Zebulon M. Vance of North Carolina tried at times to keep their own troops apart from the Confederate forces.

CONFEDERATE VOLUNTEERS Smiling and apparently confident, young Southern soldiers pose for a photograph in 1861, shortly before the First Battle of Bull Run. The Civil War was one of the first military conflicts extensively chronicled by photographers. (Cook Collection, Valentine Richmond History Center)

But the national government was not impotent. It experimented, successfully for a time, with a "food draft," which permitted soldiers to feed themselves by seizing crops from farms in their path. The Confederacy also seized control of the railroads and shipping; it impressed slaves to work as laborers on military projects and imposed regulations on industry; it limited corporate profits. States' rights sentiment was a significant handicap, but the South nevertheless took important steps in the direction of centralization.

MONEY AND MANPOWER

Financing the Confederate war effort was a monumental task. The Confederate congress tried at first to requisition funds from the individual states; but the states were as reluctant to tax their citizens as the congress was. In 1863, therefore, the congress enacted an income tax. But taxation produced only about 1 percent of the government's total income. Borrowing was not much more successful. The Confederate government issued bonds in such vast amounts that the public lost faith in them, and efforts to borrow money in Europe, using cotton as collateral, fared no better.

As a result, the Confederacy had to pay for the war through the least stable, most destructive form of financing: paper currency, which it began issuing in 1861. By 1864, the Confederacy had issued the staggering total of $1.5 billion in paper money. The result was a disastrous inflation—a 9,000 percent increase in prices in the course of the war (in contrast to 80 percent in the North).

Like the United States, the Confederacy first raised armies by calling for volunteers. And as in the North, by the end of 1861 voluntary enlistments were declining. In April 1862, therefore, the congress enacted the Conscription Act, which subjected all white males between

BASEBALL AND THE CIVIL WAR

LONG before the great urban stadiums, the lights, the cameras, and the multimillion-dollar salaries, baseball was the most popular game in America. During the Civil War, it was a treasured pastime for soldiers and for thousands of men (and some women) behind the lines, in both the North and the South.

The legend that baseball was invented by Abner Doubleday—who probably never even saw the game—was created by Albert G. Spalding, a patriotic sporting-goods manufacturer eager to prove that the game had purely American origins. In fact, baseball was derived from a variety of earlier games, especially the English pastimes of cricket and rounders. American baseball took its own distinctive form beginning in the 1840s, when Alexander Cartwright, a shipping clerk, formed the New York Knickerbockers, laid out a diamond-shaped field with four bases, and declared that batters with three strikes were out and that teams with three outs were retired.

Cartwright moved west in search of gold in 1849, settling finally in Hawaii, where he introduced the game to Americans in the Pacific. But the game did not languish in his absence. Henry Chadwick, an English-born journalist, spent much of the 1850s popularizing the game and regularizing its rules. By 1860, baseball was being played by college students and Irish workers, by urban elites and provincial farmers, by people of all classes and ethnic groups from New England to Louisiana. Students at Vassar College formed "ladies" teams in the 1860s, and in Philadelphia, free black men formed the Pythians, the first of what was to become a great network of African American baseball teams. From the beginning, they were barred from playing against most white teams.

When young men marched off to war in 1861, some took their bats and balls with the ages of eighteen and thirty-five to military service for three years. As in the North, a draftee could avoid service if he furnished a substitute. But since the price of substitutes was high, the provision aroused such opposition from poorer whites that it was repealed in 1863.

Even so, conscription worked for a time, in part because enthusiasm for the war was intense and widespread among white men in most of the South. At the end of 1862, about 500,000 soldiers were in the Confederate army, not including the many slave men and women recruited by the military to perform such services as cooking, laundry, and manual labor. Small numbers of slaves and free blacks enlisted in the Confederate army, and a few participated in combat.

After 1862, however, conscription began producing fewer men, and by 1864 the Confederate government faced a critical manpower shortage. The South was suffering from intense war weariness, and many had concluded that defeat was inevitable. Nothing could attract or retain an adequate army any longer. In a frantic final attempt to raise men, the congress authorized the conscription of 300,000 slaves, but the war ended before the government could attempt this incongruous experiment.

them. Almost from the start of the fighting, soldiers in both armies took advantage of idle moments to lay out baseball diamonds and organize games. Games on battlefields were sometimes interrupted by gunfire and cannon fire. "It is astonishing how indifferent a person can become to danger," a soldier wrote home to Ohio in 1862. "The report of musketry is heard but a very little distance from us, . . . yet over there on the other side of the road is most of our company, playing Bat Ball." After a skirmish in Texas, another Union soldier lamented that, in addition to casualties, his company had lost "the only baseball in Alexandria, Texas." Far from discouraging baseball, military commanders—and the United States Sanitary Commission, the Union army's medical arm—actively encouraged the game during the war. It would, they believed, help keep up the soldiers' morale.

Away from the battlefield, baseball continued to flourish. In New York City, games between local teams drew crowds of ten thousand to twenty thousand. The National Association of Baseball Players, founded in 1859, had recruited ninety-one clubs in ten Northern states by 1865; a North Western Association of Baseball Players, organized in Chicago in 1865, indicated that the game was becoming well established in the West as well. In Brooklyn, William Cammeyer drained a skating pond on his property, built a board fence around it, and created the first enclosed baseball field in America— the Union Grounds. He charged ten cents for admission. The professionalization of the game had begun.

Despite all the commercialization and spectacle that came to be associated with baseball in the years after the Civil War, the game remained for many Americans what it was to millions of young men fighting in the most savage war in the nation's history—an American passion that at times, even if briefly, erased the barriers dividing groups from one another. "Officers and men forget, for a time, the differences in rank," a Massachusetts private wrote in 1863, "and indulge in the invigorating sport with a schoolboy's ardor." •

UNDERSTAND, ANALYZE, & EVALUATE

1. How could a competitive game of baseball erase "the barriers dividing groups from one another"?
2. Baseball during the Civil War crossed the lines of cultural differences between the North and the South. Does baseball today—professional or amateur—continue to cross lines of cultural differences?

ECONOMIC AND SOCIAL EFFECTS OF THE WAR

The war cut off Southern planters and producers from Northern markets, and a Union blockade of Confederate ports made the sale of cotton overseas much more difficult. In the North, production of all goods increased during the war; in the South, it declined by more than a third. Above all, the fighting itself wreaked havoc on the Southern landscape, destroying farmland, towns, cities, and railroads. As the war continued, the shortages, the inflation, and the carnage created increasing instability in Southern society. Resistance to conscription, food impressment, and taxation increased throughout the Confederacy, as did hoarding and black-market commerce.

The war forced many women (and some men) to perform untraditional, nondomestic tasks during the conflict. Because the war decimated the male population, women soon outnumbered men in most Southern states by significant margins. The result was a large number of unmarried or widowed women who had no choice but to find employment.

Even before emancipation, the war had far-reaching effects on the lives of slaves. Confederate leaders enforced slave codes with particular severity. Even so, many slaves—especially those near the front—escaped their masters and crossed Union lines.

STRATEGY AND DIPLOMACY

The initiative in the Civil War lay mainly with the North, since it needed to actively destroy the Confederacy. Southerners needed simply to survive. Diplomatically, however, the South needed actively to recruit support from other nations, especially Great Britain. Over time, the North succeeded in blockading the Confederacy on the sea, and that made support from other nations important to allow the South to receive important imports.

THE COMMANDERS

The most important Union military commander was Abraham Lincoln, whose previous military experience consisted only of brief service in his state militia. Despite many mistakes, Lincoln succeeded as commander in chief because he knew how to exploit the North's material advantages. He realized, too, that the proper objective of his armies was the destruction of the Confederate armies and not the occupation of Southern territory. The North was fortunate that Lincoln had a good grasp of strategy, because many of his generals did not.

From 1861 to 1864, Lincoln tried time and again to find a chief of staff capable of orchestrating the Union war effort. He turned first to General Winfield Scott, the aging hero of the Mexican War. But Scott was unprepared for the magnitude of the new conflict and soon retired. Lincoln then appointed the young George B. McClellan, who was the commander of the Union forces in the East, the Army of the Potomac; but the proud, arrogant McClellan had a wholly inadequate grasp of strategy and in any case returned to the field in March 1862. For most of the rest of the year, Lincoln had no chief of staff at all. And when he eventually appointed General Henry W. Halleck to the post, he found him an ineffectual strategist as well. Not until March 1864 did Lincoln finally find a general he trusted to command the war effort: Ulysses S. Grant, who shared Lincoln's belief in unremitting combat and in making enemy armies and resources, not enemy territory, the target of military efforts.

Lincoln's handling of the war effort faced constant scrutiny from the Committee on the Conduct of the War, a joint investigative committee of the two houses of Congress. Established in December 1861 and chaired by Senator Benjamin E. Wade of Ohio, the committee complained constantly of the inadequate ruthlessness of Northern generals, which Radicals on the committee attributed (largely inaccurately) to a secret sympathy among the officers for slavery. The committee's efforts often seriously interfered with the conduct of the war.

Southern military leadership centered on President Davis, a trained soldier who nonetheless failed to create an effective central command system. Early in 1862, Davis named General Robert E. Lee as his principal military adviser. But in fact, Davis had no intention of sharing control of strategy with anyone. After a few months, Lee left Richmond to command forces in the field, and for the next two years, Davis planned strategy alone. In February 1864, he named General Braxton Bragg as a military adviser, but Bragg never provided much more than technical advice.

ULYSSES S. GRANT One observer said of Grant (seen here posing for a photograph during the Wilderness campaign of 1864): "He habitually wears an expression as if he had determined to drive his head through a brick wall, and was about to do it." It was an apt metaphor for Grant's military philosophy, which relied on constant, unrelenting assault. As a result, Grant was willing to fight when other Northern generals held back. As such, Grant presided over some of the worst carnage of the Civil War. (Library of Congress)

At lower levels of command, men of markedly similar backgrounds controlled the war in both the North and the South. Many of the professional officers on both sides were graduates of the United States Military Academy at West Point and the United States Naval Academy at Annapolis. Amateur officers played an important role in both armies as commanders of volunteer regiments. In both the North and the South, such men were usually economic or social leaders in their communities who rounded up troops to lead. Sometimes this system produced officers of real ability; more often it did not.

THE ROLE OF SEA POWER

The Union had an overwhelming advantage in naval power. It played two important roles in the war: enforcing a blockade of the Southern coast and assisting the Union armies in field operations.

ROBERT E. LEE A moderate by the standards of Southern politics in the 1850s, Lee opposed secession and was ambivalent about slavery. But he could not bring himself to break with his region, and he left the U.S. Army to lead Confederate forces beginning in 1861. He was (and remains) the most revered of all the Confederate leaders and remained a symbol to white Southerners of the "Lost Cause" long after his surrender at Appomattox. (© Bettmann/Corbis)

The blockade, which began in the first weeks of the war, kept most oceangoing ships out of Confederate ports, but for a time small blockade runners continued to slip through. Gradually, however, federal forces tightened the blockade by seizing the Confederate ports themselves. The last important port in Confederate hands—Wilmington, North Carolina— fell to the Union early in 1865.

The Confederates made a bold attempt to break the blockade with an ironclad warship, constructed by plating with iron a former United States frigate, the *Merrimac.* On March 8, 1862, the refitted *Merrimac,* renamed the *Virginia,* left Norfolk to attack a blockading squadron of wooden ships at nearby Hampton Roads. It destroyed two of the ships and scattered the rest. But the Union government had already built ironclads of its own including the *Monitor,* which arrived only a few hours after the *Virginia*'s dramatic foray. The next day, it met the *Virginia* in battle. Neither vessel was able to sink the other, but the *Monitor* put an end to the *Virginia*'s raids and preserved the blockade.

The Union navy was particularly important in the western theater of the war, where the major rivers were navigable by large vessels. The navy transported supplies and troops and joined in attacking Confederate strong points. The South had no significant navy of its own and could defend against the Union gunboats only with ineffective fixed land fortifications.

EUROPE AND THE DISUNITED STATES

Judah P. Benjamin, the Confederate secretary of state for most of the war, was an intelligent but undynamic man who attended mostly to routine administrative tasks. William Seward, his counterpart in Washington, gradually became one of the outstanding American secretaries of state. He had invaluable assistance from Charles Francis Adams, the American minister to London. This gap between the diplomatic skills of the Union and the Confederacy was a decisive factor in the war.

At the beginning of the conflict, the sympathies of the ruling classes of England and France lay largely with the Confederacy, partly because the two nations imported much Southern cotton; but it was also because they were eager to weaken the United States, an increasingly powerful rival to them in world commerce. France was unwilling to take sides in the conflict unless England did so first. And in England, the government was reluctant to act because there was powerful popular support for the Union—particularly from the large and influential English antislavery movement. (See "America in the World," pp. 284–285.) After Lincoln issued the Emancipation Proclamation, antislavery groups worked particularly avidly for the Union. Southern leaders hoped to counter the strength of the British antislavery forces by arguing that access to Southern cotton was vital to the English and French textile industries. But English manufacturers had a surplus of both raw cotton and finished goods on hand in 1861 and could withstand a temporary loss of access to American cotton. Later, as the supply began to diminish, both England and France managed to keep at least some of their mills open by importing cotton from Egypt, India, and elsewhere. Equally important, even the 500,000 English textile workers thrown out of jobs as a result of mill closings continued to support the North. In the end, therefore, no European nation offered diplomatic recognition, financial support, or military aid to the Confederacy. No nation wanted to antagonize the United States unless the Confederacy seemed likely to win, and the South never came close enough to victory to convince its potential allies to support it. In the end, the Confederacy was on its own.

Even so, tension, and on occasion near hostilities, continued between the United States and Britain. The Union government was angry when Great Britain, France, and other nations declared themselves neutral early in the war, thus implying that the two sides to the conflict had equal stature. Washington insisted that the conflict was simply a domestic insurrection, not a war between two legitimate governments.

A more serious crisis, the so-called *Trent* affair, began in late 1861. Two Confederate diplomats, James M. Mason and John Slidell, had slipped through the then-ineffective Union blockade to Havana, Cuba, where they boarded an English steamer, the *Trent*, for England. Waiting in Cuban waters was the American frigate *San Jacinto*, commanded by the impetuous Charles Wilkes. Acting without authorization, Wilkes stopped the British vessel, arrested the diplomats, and carried them in triumph to Boston. The British government demanded the release of the prisoners, reparations, and an apology. Lincoln and Seward were aware that Wilkes had violated maritime law. They were unwilling to risk war with England, and they eventually released the diplomats with an indirect apology.

A second diplomatic crisis produced problems that lasted for years. Unable to construct large ships itself, the Confederacy bought six ships, known as commerce destroyers, from British shipyards. The United States protested that this sale of military equipment to a belligerent violated the laws of neutrality. The protests became the basis, after the war, of a prolonged battle over damage claims (known as the *Alabama* claims, a name derived from one of the ships). The controversy between the United States and Great Britain was not finally settled until 1877.

CAMPAIGNS AND BATTLES

In the absence of direct intervention by the European powers, the two contestants in North America were left to resolve the conflict between themselves. They did so in four long years of bloody combat. More than 618,000 Americans died in the course of the Civil War, far more than the 112,000 who perished in World War I or the 405,000 who died in World War II. There were nearly 2,000 deaths for every 100,000 of population during the Civil War. In World War I, the comparable figure was only 109; in World War II, 241. In some respects, it was the bloodiest war in modern times.

THE TECHNOLOGY OF WAR

Much of what happened on the battlefield in the Civil War was a result of new technologies that transformed the nature of combat.

The most obvious change was the nature of the armaments. Among the most important was the introduction of repeating weapons. Samuel Colt had patented a repeating pistol (the revolver) in 1835, but more important for military purposes was the repeating rifle, introduced in 1860 by Oliver Winchester. Also significant were greatly improved cannons and artillery, a result of earlier advances in iron and steel technology.

These new armaments made it impossibly deadly to fight battles as they had been fought for centuries, with lines of infantry soldiers standing erect in the field firing volleys at their opponents until one side withdrew. Soldiers quickly learned that the proper position for combat was staying low to the ground and behind cover. For the first time in the history of organized warfare, therefore, infantry did not fight in formation, and the battlefields became more chaotic places. Gradually, the deadliness of the new weapons encouraged armies on both sides to spend a great deal of time building elaborate fortifications and trenches to protect themselves from enemy fire. The sieges of Vicksburg and Petersburg, the defense of Richmond, and many other military events all produced the construction of vast fortifications around both cities and attacking armies. (They were the predecessors to the vast network of trenches of World War I.)

Other weapons technologies were less central to the fighting of the war, but important nevertheless. The relatively new technology of hot-air balloons was employed intermittently to provide a view of enemy formations in the field. Ironclad ships—and even torpedoes and submarine technology, which made fleeting appearances in the 1860s—suggested the dramatic changes that would soon overtake naval warfare.

Critical to the conduct of the war, however, were two other relatively new technologies: the railroad and the telegraph. The railroad was particularly important in mobilizing millions of soldiers and transferring them to the front. Transporting such enormous numbers of soldiers, and the supplies necessary to sustain them, by foot or by horse and wagon would have been almost impossible. But railroads also limited the mobility of the armies. Commanders were forced to organize their campaigns at least in part around the location of the railroads rather than on the basis of the best topography or most direct land route to a destination. The dependence on the rails—and the resulting necessity of concentrating huge numbers of men in a few places—also encouraged commanders to prefer great battles with large armies rather than smaller engagements with fewer troops.

The impact of the telegraph on the war was limited both by the scarcity of qualified telegraph operators and by the difficulty of bringing telegraph wires into the fields where battles were being fought. Things improved somewhat after the new U.S. Military Telegraph Corps, headed by Thomas Scott and Andrew Carnegie, trained and employed over 1,200 operators. Gradually, too, both the Union and Confederate armies learned to string telegraph wires along the routes of their troops, so that field commanders were able to stay in close touch with one another during battles.

THE OPENING CLASHES, 1861

The Union and the Confederacy fought their first major battle of the war in northern Virginia. A Union army of over 30,000 men under General Irvin McDowell was stationed just outside Washington. About thirty miles away, at Manassas, sat a slightly smaller Confederate army under P. G. T. Beauregard. If the Northern army could destroy the Southern one, Union leaders believed, the war might end at once. In mid-July, McDowell marched his inexperienced troops toward Manassas. Beauregard moved his troops behind Bull Run, a small stream north of Manassas, and called for reinforcements, which reached him the day before the battle.

On July 21, in the First Battle of Bull Run, or First Battle of Manassas, McDowell almost succeeded in dispersing the Confederate forces. But the Southerners managed to fight off a last strong Union assault. The Confederates then began a savage counterattack. The Union troops suddenly panicked, broke ranks, and retreated chaotically. McDowell was unable to reorganize them, and he had to order a retreat to Washington—a disorderly withdrawal complicated by the presence along the route of many civilians, who had ridden down from the capital, picnic baskets in hand, to watch the battle from nearby hills. The Confederates, as disorganized by victory as the Union forces were by defeat, did not pursue. The battle was a severe blow to Union morale and to the president's confidence in his officers.

Elsewhere, Union forces achieved some small but significant victories in 1861. A Union force under George B. McClellan moved east from Ohio into western Virginia. By the end of 1861, it had "liberated" the antisecession mountain people of the region, who created their own state government loyal to the Union; the state was admitted to the Union as West Virginia in 1863.

THE WESTERN THEATER

After the battle at Bull Run, military operations in the East settled into a long and frustrating stalemate. The first decisive operations occurred in the western theater in 1862. Here Union forces were trying to seize control of the southern part of the Mississippi River from both the north and south, moving down the river from Kentucky and up from the Gulf of Mexico toward New Orleans.

In April, a Union squadron commanded by David G. Farragut smashed past weak Confederate forts near the mouth of the Mississippi and from there sailed up to New

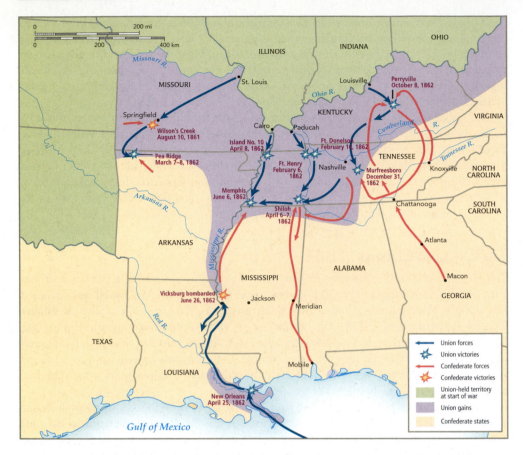

THE WAR IN THE WEST, 1861–1863 While the Union armies in Virginia were meeting with repeated frustrations, the Union armies in the West were scoring notable successes in the first two years of the war. This map shows a series of Union drives in the western Confederacy. Admiral David Farragut's ironclads led to the capture of New Orleans—a critical Confederate port—in April 1862, while forces farther north under the command of Ulysses S. Grant drove the Confederate army out of Kentucky and western Tennessee. These battles culminated in the Union victory at Shiloh, which led to Union control of the upper Mississippi River. • *Why was control of the Mississippi so important to both sides?*

Orleans. The city was virtually defenseless because the Confederate high command had expected the attack to come from the north. The surrender of New Orleans on April 25, 1862, was an important turning point in the war. From then on, the mouth of the Mississippi was closed to Confederate trade, and the South's largest city and most important banking center was in Union hands.

Farther north in the western theater, Confederate troops under Albert Sidney Johnston were stretched out in a long defensive line around two forts in Tennessee, Fort Henry and Fort Donelson. Early in 1862, Ulysses S. Grant attacked Fort Henry, whose defenders, awed by the ironclad riverboats accompanying the Union army, surrendered with almost no resistance. Grant then moved both his naval and ground forces to Fort Donelson, where the Confederates put up a stronger fight but finally, on February 16, had to surrender. Grant thus gained control of river communications and forced Confederate troops out of Kentucky and half of Tennessee.

With about 40,000 men, Grant now advanced south along the Tennessee River. At Shiloh, Tennessee, he met a force almost equal to his own, commanded by Albert Sidney

Johnston and P. G. T. Beauregard. The result was the Battle of Shiloh, April 6–7, 1862. In the first day's fighting (during which Johnston was killed), the Southerners drove Grant back to the river. But the next day, reinforced by 25,000 fresh troops, Grant recovered the lost ground and forced Beauregard to withdraw. After the narrow Union victory at Shiloh, Northern forces occupied Corinth, Mississippi, and took control of the Mississippi River as far south as Memphis.

Braxton Bragg, now in command of the Confederate army in the West, gathered his forces at Chattanooga, in eastern Tennessee, where he faced a Union army trying to capture the city. The two armies maneuvered for advantage inconclusively in northern Tennessee and southern Kentucky for several months until December 31–January 2, when they finally clashed in the Battle of Murfreesboro, or Stone's River. Bragg was forced to withdraw to the South in defeat.

By the end of 1862, Union forces had made considerable progress in the West. But the heart of the war remained in the East.

The Virginia Front, 1862

During the winter of 1861–1862, George B. McClellan, commander of the Army of the Potomac, concentrated on training his army of 150,000 men near Washington. Finally, he designed a spring campaign to capture the Confederate capital at Richmond. But instead of heading overland directly, McClellan chose a complicated route that he thought would circumvent the Confederate defenses. The navy would carry his troops down the Potomac to a peninsula east of Richmond, between the York and James rivers; the army would approach the city from there in what became known as the Peninsular campaign.

McClellan set off with 100,000 men, reluctantly leaving 30,000 members of his army behind, under General Irvin McDowell, to protect Washington. McClellan eventually persuaded Lincoln to send him the additional men. But before the president could do so, a Confederate army under Thomas J. ("Stonewall") Jackson staged a rapid march north through the Shenandoah Valley, as if preparing to cross the Potomac and attack Washington. Lincoln postponed sending reinforcements to McClellan, retaining McDowell's corps to head off Jackson. In the Valley campaign of May 4–June 9, 1862, Jackson defeated two separate Union forces and slipped away before McDowell could catch him.

Meanwhile, McClellan was fighting Confederate troops under Joseph E. Johnston outside Richmond in the two-day Battle of Fair Oaks, or Seven Pines (May 31–June 1), and holding his ground. Johnston, badly wounded, was replaced by Robert E. Lee, who then recalled Stonewall Jackson from the Shenandoah Valley. With a combined force of 85,000 to face McClellan's 100,000, Lee launched a new offensive, known as the Battle of the Seven Days (June 25–July 1), in an effort to cut McClellan off from his base on the York River. But McClellan fought his way across the peninsula and set up a new base on the James.

McClellan was now only twenty-five miles from Richmond and in a good position to renew the campaign. But despite continuing pressure from Lincoln, he did not advance. Hoping to force a new offensive against Richmond along the direct overland route he had always preferred, Lincoln finally ordered the army to move back to northern Virginia and join up with a smaller force under John Pope. As the Army of the Potomac left the peninsula by water, Lee moved north with the Army of Northern Virginia to strike Pope before McClellan could join him. Pope was as rash as McClellan

July 1861–July 1862

Confederate forces
Union forces
Confederate victories
Union victories
Inconclusive

August–December 1862

1863

THE VIRGINIA THEATER, 1861–1863   Much of the fighting during the first two years of the Civil War took place in what became known as the Virginia theater—although the campaigns in this region eventually extended north into Maryland and Pennsylvania. The Union hoped for a quick victory over the newly created Confederate army. But as these maps show, the Southern forces consistently thwarted such hopes. The map at top left shows the battles of 1861 and the first half of 1862, almost all of them won by the Confederates. The map at lower left shows the last months of 1862, during which the Southerners again defeated the Union in most of their engagements—although Northern forces drove the Confederates back from Maryland in September. The map on the right shows the troop movements that led to the climactic battle of Gettysburg in 1863. • *Why were the Union forces unable to profit more from material advantages during these first years of the war?*

was cautious, and he attacked the approaching Confederates without waiting for the arrival of all of McClellan's troops. In the Second Battle of Bull Run, or Manassas (August 29–30), Lee threw back the assault and routed Pope's army, which fled to Washington. With hopes for an overland campaign against Richmond now in disarray, Lincoln removed Pope from command and put McClellan back in charge of all the federal forces in the region.

Lee soon went on the offensive again, heading north through western Maryland, and McClellan moved out to meet him. McClellan had the good luck to get a copy of Lee's orders, which revealed that a part of the Confederate army, under Stonewall Jackson, had separated from the rest to attack Harpers Ferry. But instead of attacking quickly before the Confederates could recombine, McClellan stalled, again giving Lee time to pull most of his forces back together behind Antietam Creek, near the town of Sharpsburg. There, on September 17, McClellan's 87,000–man army repeatedly attacked Lee's force of 50,000, with staggering casualties on both sides. Late in the day, just as the Confederate line seemed ready to break, the last of Jackson's troops arrived from Harpers Ferry to reinforce it. McClellan might have broken through with one more assault. Instead, he allowed Lee to retreat into Virginia. Technically, Antietam was a Union victory; but in reality, McClellan had squandered an opportunity to destroy much of the Confederate army. In November, Lincoln finally removed McClellan from command for good.

McClellan's replacement, Ambrose E. Burnside, was a short-lived mediocrity. He tried to move toward Richmond by crossing the Rappahannock River at Fredericksburg. There, on December 13, he launched a series of attacks against Lee, all of them bloody, all of them hopeless. After losing a large part of his army, he withdrew to the north bank of the Rappahannock. He was relieved at his own request. The year 1862 ended, therefore, with a series of frustrations for the Union.

THE PROGRESS OF THE WAR

Why did the Union—with its much greater population, its much larger population, and its much better transportation and technology than the Confederacy—make so little progress in the first two years of the war? Had there been a decisive and dramatic victory by either side early in the war—for example, a major victory by the Union at the First Battle of Bull Run—the conflict might have ended quickly by destroying the Confederacy's morale. But no such decisive victory occurred in the first two years of the war.

Many Northerners blamed the military stalemate on timid or incompetent Union generals, and there was some truth to that view. But the more important reason for the drawn-out conflict was that it was not a traditional war of tactics and military strategy. It was, even if the leaders of both sides were not yet fully aware of it, a war of attrition. Winning or losing battles here and there would not determine the outcome of the war. What would bring the war to a conclusion was the steady destruction of the resources that were necessary for victory. More than two bloody years of fighting were still to come. But those last years were a testimony to the slow, steady deterioration of the Confederacy's ability to maintain the war, and the consistent growth of the resources that allowed the Union armies to grow steadily stronger.

1863: YEAR OF DECISION

At the beginning of 1863, General Joseph Hooker was commanding the still-formidable Army of the Potomac, which remained north of the Rappahannock, opposite Fredericksburg. Taking part of his army, Hooker crossed the river above Fredericksburg and moved toward the town and Lee's army. But at the last minute, he drew back to a defensive position in a desolate area of brush and scrub trees known as the Wilderness. Lee divided his forces for a dual assault on the Union army. In the Battle of Chancellorsville, May 1–5, Stonewall Jackson attacked the Union right and Lee himself

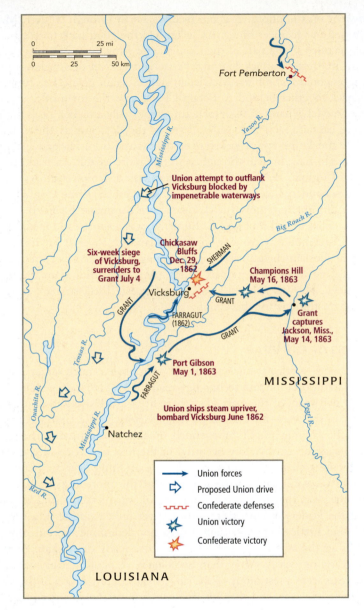

THE SIEGE OF VICKSBURG, MAY–JULY 1863 In the spring of 1863, Grant began a campaign to win control of the final piece of the Mississippi River still controlled by the Confederacy. To do that required capturing the Southern stronghold at Vicksburg—a well-defended city sitting above the river. Vicksburg's main defenses were to the north, so Grant boldly moved men and supplies around the city and attacked it from the south. Eventually, he cut off the city's access to the outside world, and after a six-week siege, its residents finally surrendered. • *What impact did the combined victories at Vicksburg and Gettysburg have on Northern commitment to the war?*

charged the front. Hooker barely managed to escape with his army. Lee had frustrated Union objectives, but he had not destroyed the Union army. And his ablest officer, Jackson, was fatally wounded in the course of the battle.

While the Union forces were suffering repeated frustrations in the East, they were winning some important victories in the West. In the spring of 1863, Ulysses S. Grant was driving at Vicksburg on the Mississippi River. Vicksburg was well protected on land and had good artillery coverage of the river itself. But in May, Grant boldly moved men and supplies—over land and by water—to an area south of the city, where the terrain was reasonably good. He then attacked Vicksburg from the rear. Six weeks later, on July 4, Vicksburg—whose residents were by then starving as a result of the prolonged siege—surrendered. At almost the same time, the other Confederate strongpoint on the river, Port Hudson, Louisiana, also surrendered to a Union force that had moved north from New Orleans. With the achievement of one of the Union's basic military aims—control of the whole length of the Mississippi—the Confederacy was split in two, with Louisiana, Arkansas, and Texas cut off from the other seceded states. The victories on the Mississippi were one of the great turning points of the war.

During the siege of Vicksburg, Lee proposed an invasion of Pennsylvania, which would, he argued, divert Union troops north. Further, he argued, if he could win a major victory on Northern soil, England and France might come to the Confederacy's aid. The war-weary North might even quit the war before Vicksburg fell.

In June 1863, Lee moved up the Shenandoah Valley into Maryland and then entered Pennsylvania. The Union Army of the Potomac, commanded first by Hooker and then (after June 28) by George C. Meade, moved north, too. The two armies finally encountered each other at the small town of Gettysburg, Pennsylvania. There, on July 1–3, 1863, they fought the most celebrated battle of the war.

Meade's army established a strong, well-protected position on the hills south of the town. Lee attacked, but his first assault on the Union forces on Cemetery Ridge failed. A day later, he ordered a second, larger effort. In what is remembered as Pickett's Charge, a force of 15,000 Confederate soldiers advanced for almost a mile across open country while being swept by Union fire. Only about 5,000 made it up the ridge, and this remnant finally had to surrender or retreat. By now, Lee had lost nearly a third of his army. On July 4, the same day as the surrender of Vicksburg, Lee withdrew from Gettysburg. The retreat was another major turning point in the war. Never again were the weakened Confederate forces able seriously to threaten Northern territory.

Before the end of the year, there was one more important turning point, this time in Tennessee. After occupying Chattanooga on September 9, Union forces under William Rosecrans began an unwise pursuit of Bragg's retreating Confederate forces. The two armies engaged in western Georgia, in the Battle of Chickamauga (September 19–20). Union forces could not break the Confederate lines and retreated back to Chattanooga.

Bragg now began a siege of Chattanooga itself, seizing the heights nearby and cutting off fresh supplies to the Union forces. Grant came to the rescue. In the Battle of Chattanooga (November 23–25), the reinforced Union army drove the Confederates back into Georgia. Union forces had now achieved a second important objective: control of the Tennessee River.

THE LAST STAGE, 1864–1865

By the beginning of 1864, Ulysses S. Grant had become general in chief of all the Union armies. Grant, like Lincoln, believed in using the North's great advantage in troops and material resources to overwhelm the South. He planned two great offensives for 1864. In Virginia, the Army of the Potomac would advance toward Richmond and force Lee into a decisive battle. In Georgia, the western army, under William T. Sherman, would advance east toward Atlanta and destroy the remaining Confederate force, now under the command of Joseph E. Johnston.

CONSIDER THE SOURCE

THE GETTYSBURG ADDRESS, NOVEMBER 19, 1863

FOUR score and seven years ago our fathers brought forth on this continent, a new nation, conceived in Liberty, and dedicated to the proposition that all men are created equal.

Now we are engaged in a great civil war, testing whether that nation, or any nation so conceived and so dedicated, can long endure. We are met on a great battlefield of that war. We have come to dedicate a portion of that field, as a final resting place for those who here gave their lives that that nation might live. It is altogether fitting and proper that we should do this.

But, in a larger sense, we can not dedicate—we can not consecrate—we can not hallow—this ground. The brave men, living and dead, who struggled here, have consecrated it, far above our poor power to add or detract. The world will little note, nor long remember what we say here, but it can never forget what they did here. It is for us the living, rather, to be dedicated here to the unfinished work which they who fought here have thus far so nobly advanced. It is rather for us to be here dedicated to the great task remaining before us—that from these honored dead we take increased devotion to that cause for which they gave the last full measure of devotion—that we here highly resolve that these dead shall not have died in vain—that this nation, under God, shall have a new birth of freedom—and that government of the people, by the people, for the people, shall not perish from the earth.

UNDERSTAND, ANALYZE, & EVALUATE

1. What purpose did Lincoln ascribe to the Civil War in the first two sentences of his speech?
2. Why did Lincoln state that he and his audience could not dedicate the battlefield?
3. What significance did Lincoln ascribe to the Battle at Gettysburg in the last sentence of this speech?
4. Why do you think this address endeared President Lincoln to many of his contemporaries and so many Americans since?

Source: Michael P. Johnson (ed.), *Abraham Lincoln, Slavery, and the Civil War: Selected Writings and Speeches* (Boston: Bedford St. Martin's, 2010), p. 263.

The northern campaign began when the Army of the Potomac, 115,000 strong, plunged into the rough, wooded Wilderness area of northwestern Virginia in pursuit of Lee's 75,000-man army. After avoiding an engagement for several weeks, Lee turned Grant back in the Battle of the Wilderness (May 5–7). Without stopping to rest or reorganize, Grant resumed his march toward Richmond and met Lee again in the bloody Battle of Spotsylvania Court House (May 8–21) in which 12,000 Union troops and a large, but unknown, number of Confederates fell. Grant kept moving, but victory continued to elude him. Lee kept his army between Grant and the Confederate capital and on June 1–3 repulsed the Union forces again, just northeast of Richmond, at Cold Harbor.

Grant now moved his army east of Richmond and headed south toward the railroad center at Petersburg. If he could seize Petersburg, he could cut off the capital's communications with the rest of the Confederacy. But Petersburg had strong defenses; and once Lee came to the city's relief, the assault became a prolonged siege.

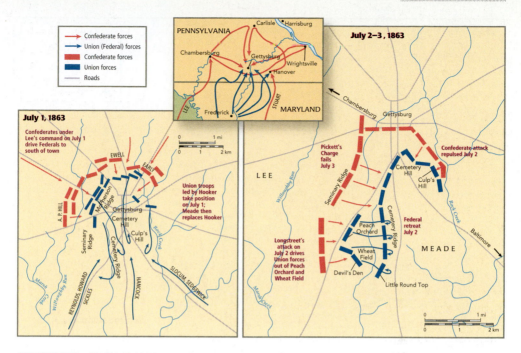

GETTYSBURG, JULY 1–3, 1863 Gettysburg was the most important single battle of the Civil War. Had Confederate forces prevailed at Gettysburg, the future course of the war might well have been very different. The map on the left shows the distribution of Union and Confederate forces at the beginning of the battle, July 1, after Lee had driven the Northern forces south of town. The map on the right reveals the pattern of the attacks on July 2 and 3. Note, in particular, Pickett's bold and costly charge, whose failure on July 3 was the turning point in the battle and, some chroniclers have argued, the war. • *Why did Robert E. Lee believe that an invasion of Pennsylvania would advance the Confederate cause?*

In Georgia, meanwhile, Sherman was facing less ferocious resistance. With 90,000 men, he confronted Confederate forces of 60,000 under Johnston. As Sherman advanced, Johnston tried to delay him by maneuvering. The two armies fought only one real battle—Kennesaw Mountain, northwest of Atlanta, on June 27—where Johnston scored an impressive victory. Even so, he was unable to stop the Union advance toward Atlanta, prompting Davis to replace him with John B. Hood. Sherman took the city on September 2 and burned it.

Hood now tried unsuccessfully to draw Sherman out of Atlanta by moving back up through Tennessee and threatening an invasion of the North. Sherman sent Union troops to reinforce Nashville. In the Battle of Nashville on December 15–16, 1864, Northern forces practically destroyed what was left of Hood's army.

Meanwhile, Sherman had left Atlanta to begin his soon-to-be-famous "March to the Sea." Living off the land, destroying supplies it could not use, his army cut a sixty-mile-wide swath of desolation across Georgia. Sherman sought not only to deprive the Confederate army of war materials and railroad communications. He was also determined to break the will of the Southern people by burning towns and plantations along his route. By December 20, he had reached Savannah, which surrendered two days later. Early in 1865, Sherman continued his destructive march, moving northward through South Carolina. He was virtually unopposed until he was well inside North Carolina, where a small force under Johnston could do no more than cause a brief delay.

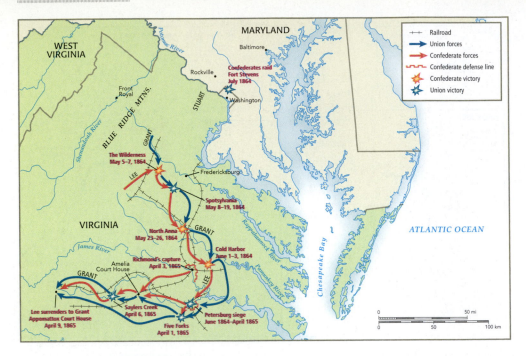

VIRGINIA CAMPAIGNS, 1864–1865 From the Confederate defeat at (and retreat from) Gettysburg until the end of the war, most of the eastern fighting took place in Virginia. By now, Ulysses S. Grant was commander of all Union forces and had taken over the Army of the Potomac. Although Confederate forces won a number of important battles during the Virginia campaign, the Union army grew steadily stronger and the Southern forces steadily weaker. Grant believed that the Union strategy should reflect the North's greatest advantage: its superiority in men and equipment. • *What effect did this decision have on the level of casualties?*

In April 1865, Grant's Army of the Potomac—still engaged in the prolonged siege at Petersburg—finally captured a vital railroad junction southwest of the town. Without rail access to the South, and plagued by heavy casualties and massive desertions, Lee informed the Confederate government that he could no longer defend Richmond. Within hours, Jefferson Davis, his cabinet, and as much of the white population as could find transportation fled. That night, mobs roamed the city, setting devastating fires. And the next morning, Northern forces entered the Confederate capital. With them was Abraham Lincoln, who walked through the streets of the burned-out city surrounded by black men and women cheering him as the "Messiah" and "Father Abraham." In one particularly stirring moment, the president turned to a former slave kneeling on the street before him and said: "Don't kneel to me. . . . You must kneel to God only, and thank Him for the liberty you will enjoy hereafter."

With the remnant of his army, now about 25,000 men, Lee began moving west in the forlorn hope of finding a way around the Union forces so that he could move south and link up with Johnston in North Carolina. But the Union army pursued him and blocked his escape route. Lee finally recognized that further bloodshed was futile. He arranged to meet Grant at a private home in the small town of Appomattox Court House, Virginia, where on April 9 he surrendered what was left of his forces. Nine days later, near Durham, North Carolina, Johnston surrendered to Sherman. The long war was now effectively over. Jefferson Davis was finally captured in Georgia. A few Southern

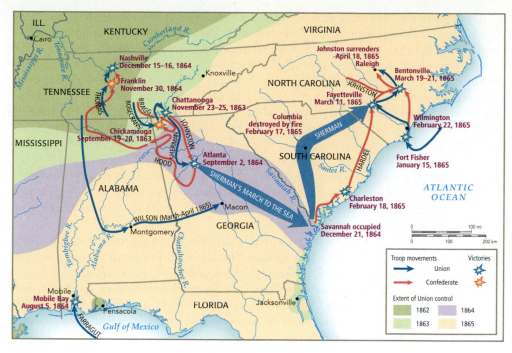

SHERMAN'S MARCH TO THE SEA, 1864-1865 While Grant was wearing Lee down in Virginia, General William Tecumseh Sherman was moving east across Georgia. After a series of battles in Tennessee and northwest Georgia, Sherman captured Atlanta and then marched unimpeded to Savannah, on the Georgia coast—deliberately devastating the towns and plantations through which his troops marched. Note that after capturing Savannah by Christmas 1864, Sherman began moving north through the Carolinas. A few days after Lee surrendered to Grant at Appomattox, Confederate forces farther south surrendered to Sherman. • *What did Sherman believe his devastating March to the Sea would accomplish?*

diehards continued to fight, but even their resistance collapsed before long. General George Meade's shout, "It's all over," described in simple terms one of the most momentous events in the nation's history.

The war ensured the permanence of the Union, but many other issues remained far from settled. What would happen to the freedmen (the term used for slaves who were now liberated)? Could the South and the North reconcile? Would the massive industrial growth in the North during the Civil War spread to the South, or would the South remain an agrarian region with much less wealth than in the North? The end of the war was the beginning of more than a generation of struggle to determine the legacy of the Civil War.

CONCLUSION

The American Civil War began with high hopes and high ideals on both sides. In the North and the South alike, thousands of men enthusiastically enlisted in local regiments and went off to war. Four years later, over 600,000 of them were dead and many more maimed and traumatized for life. A fight for "principles" and "ideals"—a fight few people had thought would last more than a few months—had become one of the longest wars, and by far the bloodiest war, in American history, before or since.

During the first two years of fighting, the Confederate forces seemed to have all the advantages. They were fighting on their own soil. Their troops seemed more committed to the cause than those of the North. Their commanders were exceptionally talented, while Union forces were, for a time, erratically led. Gradually, however, the Union's advantages began to assert themselves. The North had a stabler political system led by one of the greatest leaders in the nation's history. It had a much larger population, a far more developed industrial economy, superior financial institutions, and a better railroad system. By the middle of 1863, the tide of the war had shifted; over the next two years, Union forces gradually wore down the Confederate armies before finally triumphing in 1865.

The war strengthened the North's economy, giving a spur to industry and railroad development. It greatly weakened the South's by destroying millions of dollars of property and depleting the region's young male population. Southerners had gone to war in part because of their fears of growing Northern dominance. The war itself, ironically, confirmed and strengthened that dominance.

But most of all, the Civil War was a victory for millions of African American slaves. The war produced Abraham Lincoln's epochal Emancipation Proclamation and, later, the Thirteenth Amendment to the Constitution, which abolished slavery altogether. It also encouraged hundreds of thousands of slaves literally to free themselves, to desert their masters and seek refuge behind Union lines—at times to fight in the Union armies. The future of the freed slaves was not to be an easy one, but three and a half million people who had once lived in bondage emerged from the war as free men and women.

RECALL AND REFLECT

1. Assess the advantages of the North and those of the South at the beginning of the Civil War. How did the advantages of each side change over the course of the war?
2. How did the Confederate government differ from the federal government of the United States?
3. How did the war affect the lives of women in the North and in the South?
4. Compare Lincoln and Davis as heads of government and commanders in chief.
5. Why did Lincoln issue the Emancipation Proclamation, and what were its effects?

15 RECONSTRUCTION AND THE NEW SOUTH

THE PROBLEMS OF PEACEMAKING

RADICAL RECONSTRUCTION

THE SOUTH IN RECONSTRUCTION

THE GRANT ADMINISTRATION

THE ABANDONMENT OF RECONSTRUCTION

THE NEW SOUTH

LOOKING AHEAD

1. What were the various plans for Reconstruction proposed by Lincoln, Johnson, and Congress? Which plan was enacted and why?
2. What were the effects of Reconstruction for blacks and whites in the South?
3. What were the political achievements and failures of the Grant administration?

FEW PERIODS IN THE HISTORY of the United States have produced as much bitterness or created such enduring controversy as the era of Reconstruction—the years following the Civil War during which Americans attempted to reunite their shattered nation. To many white Southerners, Reconstruction was a vicious and destructive experience—a period when vindictive Northerners inflicted humiliation and revenge on the defeated South. Northern defenders of Reconstruction, in contrast, argued that their policies were the only way to prevent unrepentant Confederates from restoring Southern society to what it had been before the war.

To most African Americans at the time, and to many people of all races since, Reconstruction was notable for other reasons. Neither a vicious tyranny, as white Southerners charged, nor a thoroughgoing reform, as many Northerners hoped, it was, rather, a small but important first step in the effort to secure civil rights and economic power for the former slaves. Reconstruction did not provide African Americans with either the legal protections or the material resources to ensure anything like real equality. Most black men and women had little power to resist their oppression for many decades.

And yet for all its shortcomings, Reconstruction did help African Americans create new institutions and some important legal precedents that helped them survive and that ultimately, well into the twentieth century, became the basis of later efforts to win greater freedom and equality.

TIME LINE

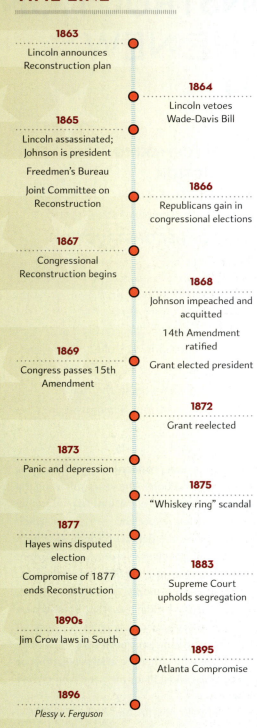

1863
Lincoln announces Reconstruction plan

1864
Lincoln vetoes Wade-Davis Bill

1865
Lincoln assassinated; Johnson is president

Freedmen's Bureau

Joint Committee on Reconstruction

1866
Republicans gain in congressional elections

1867
Congressional Reconstruction begins

1868
Johnson impeached and acquitted

14th Amendment ratified

Grant elected president

1869
Congress passes 15th Amendment

1872
Grant reelected

1873
Panic and depression

1875
"Whiskey ring" scandal

1877
Hayes wins disputed election

Compromise of 1877 ends Reconstruction

1883
Supreme Court upholds segregation

1890s
Jim Crow laws in South

1895
Atlanta Compromise

1896
Plessy v. Ferguson

THE PROBLEMS OF PEACEMAKING

Although it was clear in 1865 that the war was almost over, the path to actual peace was not yet clear. Abraham Lincoln could not negotiate a treaty with the defeated government; he continued to insist that the Confederacy had no legal right to exist. Yet neither could he simply readmit the Southern states into the Union.

THE AFTERMATH OF WAR AND EMANCIPATION

The South after the Civil War was a desolate place. Towns had been gutted, plantations burned, fields neglected, bridges and railroads destroyed. Many white Southerners—stripped of their slaves through emancipation and of capital invested in now worthless Confederate bonds and currency—had almost no personal property. More than 258,000 Confederate soldiers had died in the war, and thousands more returned home wounded or sick. Some white Southerners faced starvation and homelessness.

If conditions were bad for Southern whites, they were far worse for Southern blacks—the three and a half million men and women now emerging from bondage. As soon as the war ended, hundreds of thousands of them left their plantations in search of a new life in freedom. But most had nowhere to go, and few had any possessions except the clothes they wore.

COMPETING NOTIONS OF FREEDOM

For blacks and whites alike, Reconstruction became a struggle to define the meaning of the war and, above all, the meaning of freedom. But the former slaves and the defeated whites had very different conceptions of what freedom meant.

Some African Americans believed the only way to secure freedom was land reform—to have the government take land away from whites, who owned virtually all of it, and give it to black people, who owned virtually none. Others asked only for legal equality, confident that they could advance successfully in American society once the formal obstacles to their advancement disappeared. But whatever their demands, virtually all former slaves were united in their desire for independence from white control. Throughout the South, African Americans separated themselves from white institutions—pulling out of white-controlled churches and establishing their own, creating their own clubs and societies, and in some cases starting their own schools.

For most white Southerners, freedom meant something very different. It meant the ability to control their own destinies without interference from the North or the federal government. And in the immediate aftermath of the war, this meant trying to restore their society to its antebellum form. When these white Southerners fought for what they considered freedom, they were fighting above all to preserve local and regional autonomy and white supremacy.

In the war's immediate aftermath, the federal government's contribution to solving the question of the South's future was modest. Federal troops remained to preserve order and protect the freedmen. And in March 1865, Congress established the Freedmen's Bureau, an agency of the army directed by General Oliver O. Howard. The Freedmen's Bureau distributed food to millions of former slaves. It established schools, staffed by missionaries and teachers sent by Freedmen's Aid Societies and other private and church groups in the North. It even made a modest effort to settle blacks on lands of their own. But the Freedmen's Bureau was not a permanent solution. With authority to operate for only

RICHMOND, 1865   By the time Union forces captured Richmond in early 1865, the Confederate capital had been under siege for months and much of the city lay in ruins, as this photograph reveals. On April 4, President Lincoln, accompanied by his son Tad, visited Richmond. As he walked through the streets of the shattered city, hundreds of former slaves emerged from the rubble to watch him pass. "No triumphal march of a conqueror could have equalled in moral sublimity the humble manner in which he entered Richmond," a black soldier serving with the Union army wrote. "It was a great deliverer among the delivered. No wonder tears came to his eyes." (Library of Congress)

one year, it was, in any case, far too small to deal effectively with the enormous problems facing Southern society. In the meantime, other proposals for reconstructing the defeated South were emerging.

PLANS FOR RECONSTRUCTION

Control of Reconstruction rested in the hands of the Republicans, who were divided in their approach to the issue. Conservatives within the party insisted that the South accept abolition, but they proposed few other conditions for the readmission of the seceded states. The Radicals, led by Representative Thaddeus Stevens of Pennsylvania and Senator Charles Sumner of Massachusetts, urged a much harsher course, including

A MONUMENT TO THE CONFEDERATE DEAD This monument in the town square of Greenwood, South Carolina, was typical of many such memorials erected all across the South. They served to commemorate the soldiers who had died in the struggle, but also to remind white Southerners of what was by the 1870s already widely known and romanticized as the "Lost Cause." (Museum of the Confederacy, Richmond, Virginia)

disenfranchising large numbers of Southern whites, protecting black civil rights, confiscating the property of wealthy whites who had aided the Confederacy, and distributing the land among the freedmen. Republican Moderates rejected the most stringent demands of the Radicals but supported extracting at least some concessions from the South on black rights.

President Lincoln favored a lenient Reconstruction policy, believing that Southern Unionists (mostly former Whigs) could become the nucleus of new, loyal state governments in the South. Lincoln announced his Reconstruction plan in December 1863, more than a year before the war ended. It offered a general amnesty to white Southerners—other than high officials of the Confederacy—who would pledge an oath of loyalty to the government and accept the abolition of slavery. When 10 percent of a state's total number of voters in 1860 took the oath, those loyal voters could set up a state government. Lincoln also proposed extending suffrage to African Americans who were educated, owned property, or had served in the Union army. Three Southern states—Louisiana, Arkansas, and Tennessee, all under Union occupation—reestablished loyal governments under the Lincoln formula in 1864.

Outraged at the mildness of Lincoln's program, the Radical Republicans refused to admit representatives from the three "reconstructed" states to Congress. In July 1864, they pushed their own plan through Congress: the Wade-Davis Bill. It called for the president to appoint a provisional governor for each conquered state. When a majority of the white males of a state pledged their allegiance to the Union, the governor could summon a state constitutional convention, whose delegates were to be elected by voters who had never borne arms against the United States. The new state constitutions would be required to abolish slavery, disenfranchise Confederate civil and military leaders, and repudiate debts accumulated by the state governments during the war. Only then would Congress readmit the states to the Union. Like the president's proposal, the Wade-Davis Bill left the question of political rights for blacks up to the states.

Congress passed the bill a few days before it adjourned in 1864, but Lincoln disposed of it with a pocket veto that enraged the Radical leaders, forcing the pragmatic Lincoln to recognize he would have to accept at least some of the Radical demands.

THE DEATH OF LINCOLN

What plan the president might have produced no one can say. On the night of April 14, 1865, Lincoln and his wife attended a play at Ford's Theater in Washington. John Wilkes Booth, an actor fervently committed to the Southern cause, entered the presidential box from the rear and shot Lincoln in the head. Early the next morning, the president died.

The circumstances of Lincoln's death earned him immediate martyrdom. They also produced something close to hysteria throughout the North, especially because it quickly became clear that Booth had been the leader of a conspiracy. One of his associates shot and wounded Secretary of State William Seward on the night of the assassination, and another abandoned at the last moment a plan to murder Vice President Andrew Johnson. Booth himself escaped on horseback into the Maryland countryside, where, on April 26, he was cornered by Union troops and shot to death in a blazing barn. Eight other people were convicted by a military tribunal of participating in the conspiracy. Four were hanged.

RECONSTRUCTION

DEBATE over the nature of Reconstruction has been unusually intense. Indeed, few issues in American history have raised such deep and enduring passions.

Beginning in the late nineteenth century and continuing well into the twentieth, a relatively uniform and highly critical view of Reconstruction prevailed among historians. William A. Dunning's *Reconstruction, Political* *and Economic* (1907) was the principal scholarly expression of this view. Dunning portrayed Reconstruction as a corrupt and oppressive outrage imposed on a prostrate South by a vindictive group of Northern Republican Radicals. Unscrupulous carpetbaggers flooded the South and plundered the region. Ignorant and unfit African Americans were thrust into political offices. Reconstruction governments were awash in

THE FREEDMEN'S BUREAU For four years after the Civil War, the Freedmen's Bureau served newly freed slaves, helping them to get housing, food, education, and other services. This image shows African American men and women waiting for rations, most of them old and sick. (The New York Public Library/Art Resource, NY)

corruption and compiled enormous levels of debt. The Dunning interpretation dominated several generations of historical scholarship and helped shape such popular images of Reconstruction as those in the novel and film *Gone with the Wind*.

W. E. B. Du Bois, the great African American scholar, offered one of the first alternative views in *Black Reconstruction* (1935). To Du Bois, Reconstruction was an effort by freed blacks (and their white allies) to create a more democratic society in the South, and it was responsible for many valuable social innovations. In the early 1960s, John Hope Franklin and Kenneth Stampp, building on a generation of work by other scholars, published new histories of Reconstruction that also radically revised the Dunning interpretation. Reconstruction, they argued, was a genuine, if inadequate, effort to solve the problem of race in the South. Congressional Radicals were not saints, but they were genuinely concerned with protecting the rights of former slaves. Reconstruction had brought important, if temporary, progress to the South and had created no more corruption there than was evident in the North at the same time. What was tragic about Reconstruction, the revisionists claimed, was not what it did to Southern whites but what it failed to do for Southern blacks. It was, in the end, too weak and too short-lived to guarantee African Americans genuine equality.

In more recent years, some historians have begun to question the assessment of the first revisionists that, in the end, Reconstruction accomplished relatively little. Leon Litwack argued in *Been in the Storm So Long* (1979) that former slaves used the protections Reconstruction offered them to carve out a certain level of independence for themselves within Southern society: strengthening churches, reuniting families, and resisting the efforts of white planters to revive the gang labor system.

Eric Foner's *Reconstruction: America's Unfinished Revolution* (1988) and *Forever Free* (2005) also emphasized how far African Americans moved toward freedom and independence in a short time and how important they were in shaping the execution of Reconstruction policies. Reconstruction, he argues, "can only be judged a failure" as an effort to secure "blacks' rights as citizens and free laborers." But it "closed off even more oppressive alternatives. . . . The post-Reconstruction labor system embodied neither a return to the closely supervised gang labor of antebellum days, nor the complete dispossession and immobilization of the black labor force and coercive apprenticeship systems envisioned by white Southerners in 1865 and 1866. . . . The doors of economic opportunity that had opened could never be completely closed." •

UNDERSTAND, ANALYZE, & EVALUATE

1. According to the essay, *The Birth of a Nation* and *Gone with the Wind* are popular depictions of Reconstruction that reflect Dunning's interpretation of the era. Can you find other popular depictions that reflect other interpretations of Reconstruction?

2. A new view of Reconstruction began to emerge in the 1960s, the end of the civil rights movement. Why do you think the civil rights movement might have encouraged historians and others to reexamine Reconstruction?

ABRAHAM LINCOLN This haunting photograph of Abraham Lincoln, showing clearly the weariness and aging that four years as a war president had created, was taken in Washington only four days before his assassination in 1865. (Library of Congress)

To many Northerners, however, the murder of the president seemed evidence of an even greater conspiracy—masterminded and directed by the unrepentant leaders of the defeated South. Militant Republicans exploited such suspicions relentlessly in the ensuing months.

JOHNSON AND "RESTORATION"

Leadership of the Moderates and Conservatives fell to Lincoln's successor, Andrew Johnson of Tennessee. A Democrat until he had joined the Union ticket in 1864, he became president at a time of growing partisan passions.

Johnson revealed his plan for Reconstruction—or "Restoration," as he preferred to call it—soon after he took office and implemented it during the summer of 1865 when Congress was in recess. Like Lincoln, he offered some form of amnesty to Southerners who would take an oath of allegiance. In most other respects, however, his plan resembled the Wade-Davis Bill. The new president appointed a provisional governor in each state and charged him with inviting qualified voters to elect delegates to a constitutional convention. To win readmission to Congress, a state had to revoke its ordinance of secession, abolish slavery and ratify the Thirteenth Amendment, and repudiate Confederate and state war debts.

By the end of 1865, all the seceded states had formed new governments—some under Lincoln's plan, others under Johnson's—and awaited congressional approval of them. But Radicals in Congress vowed not to recognize the Johnson governments, for, by now, Northern opinion had become more hostile toward the South. Delegates to the Southern conventions had angered much of the North by their apparent reluctance to abolish slavery and by their refusal to grant suffrage to any blacks. Southern states had also seemed to defy the North by electing prominent Confederate leaders to represent them in Congress, such as Alexander Stephens of Georgia, who had been vice president of the Confederacy.

RADICAL RECONSTRUCTION

Reconstruction under Johnson's plan—often known as "presidential Reconstruction"—continued only until Congress reconvened in December 1865. At that point, Congress refused to seat the representatives of the "restored" states and created a new Joint Committee on Reconstruction to frame a policy of its own. The period of "congressional," or "Radical," Reconstruction had begun.

THE BLACK CODES

Meanwhile, events in the South were driving Northern opinion in still more radical directions. Throughout the South in 1865 and early 1866, state legislatures enacted sets of laws known as the Black Codes, which authorized local officials to apprehend unemployed blacks, fine them for vagrancy, and hire them out to private employers to satisfy the fines. Some codes forbade blacks to own or lease farms or to take any jobs other than as plantation workers or domestic servants, jobs formerly held by slaves.

Congress first responded to the Black Codes by passing an act extending the life and expanding the powers of the Freedmen's Bureau so that it could nullify work agreements forced on freedmen under the Black Codes. Then, in April 1866, Congress passed the first Civil Rights Act, which declared blacks to be citizens of the United States and gave the federal government power to intervene in state affairs to protect the rights of citizens. Johnson vetoed both bills, but Congress overrode him on each of them.

THE FOURTEENTH AMENDMENT

In April 1866, the Joint Committee on Reconstruction proposed the Fourteenth Amendment to the Constitution. Congress approved it in early summer and sent it to the states for ratification. It offered the first constitutional definition of American citizenship. Everyone born in the United States, and everyone naturalized, was automatically a citizen and entitled to all the "privileges and immunities" guaranteed by the Constitution, including equal protection of the laws by both the state and national governments. There could be no other requirements for citizenship. The amendment also imposed penalties on states that denied suffrage to any adult male inhabitants. (Supporters of woman suffrage were dismayed by the addition of the word "male" to the amendment.) Finally, it prohibited former members of Congress or other former federal officials who had aided the Confederacy from holding any state or federal office unless two-thirds of Congress voted to pardon them.

Congressional Radicals offered to readmit to the Union any state whose legislature ratified the Fourteenth Amendment. Only Tennessee did so. All the other former

Confederate states, along with Delaware and Kentucky, refused, leaving the amendment temporarily without the necessary approval of three-fourths of the states.

But by now, the Radicals were growing more confident and determined. Bloody race riots in New Orleans and other Southern cities were among the events that strengthened their hand. In the 1866 congressional elections, Johnson actively campaigned for Conservative candidates, but he did his own cause more harm than good with his intemperate speeches. The voters returned an overwhelming majority of Republicans, most of them Radicals, to Congress. In the Senate, there were now 42 Republicans to 11 Democrats; in the House, 143 Republicans to 49 Democrats. Congressional Republicans were now strong enough to enact a plan of their own even over the president's objections.

THE CONGRESSIONAL PLAN

The Radicals passed three Reconstruction bills early in 1867 and overrode Johnson's vetoes of all of them. These bills finally established, nearly two years after the end of the war, a coherent plan for Reconstruction.

Under the congressional plan, Tennessee, which had ratified the Fourteenth Amendment, was promptly readmitted. But Congress rejected the Lincoln-Johnson governments of the other ten Confederate states and, instead, combined those states into five military districts. A military commander governed each district and had orders to register qualified voters (defined as all adult black males and those white males who had not participated in the rebellion). Once registered, voters would elect conventions to prepare new state constitutions, which had to include provisions for black suffrage. Once voters ratified the new constitutions, they could elect state governments. Congress had to approve a state's constitution, and the state legislature had to ratify the Fourteenth Amendment. Once enough states ratified the amendment to make it part of the Constitution, the former Confederate states could be restored to the Union.

By 1868, seven of the ten remaining former Confederate states had fulfilled these conditions and were readmitted to the Union. Conservative whites held up the return of Virginia and Texas until 1869 and Mississippi until 1870. By then, Congress had added an additional requirement for readmission—ratification of another constitutional amendment, the Fifteenth, which forbade the states and the federal government to deny suffrage to any citizen on account of "race, color, or previous condition of servitude." Ratification by the states was completed in 1870.

To stop Johnson from interfering with their plans, the congressional Radicals passed two remarkable laws of dubious constitutionality in 1867. One, the Tenure of Office Act, forbade the president to remove civil officials, including members of his own cabinet, without the consent of the Senate. The principal purpose of the law was to protect the job of Secretary of War Edwin M. Stanton, who was cooperating with the Radicals. The other law, the Command of the Army Act, prohibited the president from issuing military orders except through the commanding general of the army (General Grant), who could not be relieved or assigned elsewhere without the consent of the Senate.

The congressional Radicals also took action to stop the Supreme Court from interfering with their plans. In 1866, the Court had declared in the case of *Ex parte Milligan* that

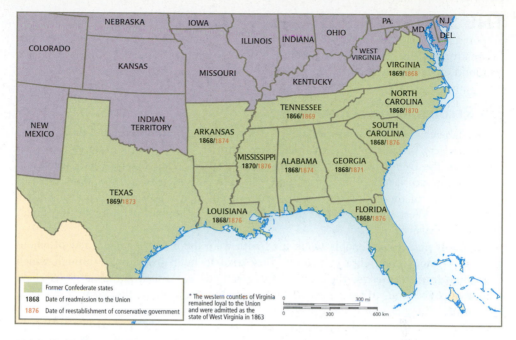

RECONSTRUCTION, 1866–1877 This map shows the former Confederate states and provides the date when each was readmitted to the Union as well as a subsequent date when each state managed to return political power to traditional white, conservative elites—a process white Southerners liked to call "redemption." • *What had to happen for a state to be readmitted to the Union? What had to happen before a state could experience "redemption"?*

military tribunals were unconstitutional in places where civil courts were functioning. Radicals in Congress immediately proposed several bills that would require two-thirds of the justices to support any decision overruling a law of Congress, would deny the Court jurisdiction in Reconstruction cases, would reduce its membership to three, and would even abolish it. The justices apparently took notice. Over the next two years, the Court refused to accept jurisdiction in any cases involving Reconstruction.

THE IMPEACHMENT OF ANDREW JOHNSON

President Johnson had long since ceased to be a serious obstacle to the passage of Radical legislation, but he was still the official charged with administering the Reconstruction programs. As such, the Radicals believed, he remained a major impediment to their plans. Early in 1867, they began looking for a way to remove him from office, and a search for grounds for impeachment began. Republicans found them, they believed, when Johnson dismissed Secretary of War Stanton despite Congress's refusal to agree. Elated Radicals in the House quickly impeached the president and sent the case to the Senate for trial.

The trial lasted throughout April and May 1868. The Radicals put heavy pressure on all the Republican senators, but the Moderates vacillated. On the first three charges to come to a vote, seven Republicans joined the Democrats and independents to support acquittal. The vote was 35 to 19, one vote short of the constitutionally required two-thirds majority. After that, the Radicals dropped the impeachment effort.

THE SOUTH IN RECONSTRUCTION

Reconstruction may not have accomplished what its framers intended, but it did have profound effects on the South.

THE RECONSTRUCTION GOVERNMENTS

Critics labeled Southern white Republicans with the derogatory terms "scalawags" and "carpetbaggers." Many of the "scalawags" were former Whigs who had never felt comfortable in the Democratic Party or farmers who lived in remote areas where there had been little or no slavery. The "carpetbaggers" were white men from the North, most of them veterans of the Union army who looked on the South as a more promising frontier than the West and had settled there at war's end as hopeful planters, businessmen, or professionals.

The most numerous Republicans in the South were the black freedmen, few of whom had any previous experience in politics. They tried to build institutions through which they could learn to exercise their power. In several states, African American voters held their own conventions to chart their future course. Their newfound religious independence from white churches also helped give them unity and self-confidence.

African Americans played significant roles in the politics of the Reconstruction South. They served as delegates to the constitutional conventions and held public offices of practically every kind. Between 1869 and 1901, twenty blacks served in the United States House of Representatives, two in the Senate. They served, too, in state legislatures and in various other state offices. Southern whites complained loudly about "Negro rule," but in the South as a whole, the percentage of black officeholders was small—and always far lower than the percentage of blacks in the population.

The record of the Reconstruction governments is mixed. Critics at the time and later denounced them for corruption and financial extravagance, and there is some truth to both charges. But the corruption in the South, real as it was, was hardly unique to the Reconstruction governments. Corruption had been rife in some antebellum and Confederate governments, and it was at least as rampant in the Northern states. And the large state expenditures of the Reconstruction years were huge only in comparison with the meager budgets of the antebellum era. They represented an effort to provide the South with desperately needed services that antebellum governments had never provided.

EDUCATION

Perhaps the most important accomplishment of the Reconstruction governments was a dramatic improvement in Southern education. Much of the impetus for educational reform in the South came from outside groups—the Freedmen's Bureau, Northern private philanthropic organizations, the many Northern white women who traveled to the South to teach in freedmen's schools—and from African Americans themselves. Over the opposition of many Southern whites, who feared that education would give blacks "false notions of equality," these reformers established a large network of schools for former slaves—4,000 schools by 1870, staffed by 9,000 teachers (half of them black), teaching 200,000 students. In the 1870s, Reconstruction governments began to build a comprehensive public school system. By 1876, more than half of all white children and about 40 percent of all black children were attending schools in the South (although almost all such schools were racially segregated). Several black "academies," offering more advanced education, also began operating. Gradually, these academies grew into an important network of black colleges and universities.

LANDOWNERSHIP AND TENANCY

The most ambitious goal of the Freedmen's Bureau, and of some Republican Radicals in Congress, was to reform landownership in the South. The effort failed. By June 1865, the bureau had settled nearly 10,000 black families on their own land—most of it drawn from abandoned plantations in areas occupied by the Union armies. By the end of that year, however, Southern plantation owners were returning and demanding the restoration of their property. President Johnson supported their demands, and the government eventually returned most of the confiscated lands to their original white owners.

Even so, the distribution of landownership in the South changed considerably in the postwar years. Among whites, there was a striking decline in landownership, from 80 percent before the war to 67 percent by the end of Reconstruction. Some whites lost their land because of unpaid debt or increased taxes; others left the marginal lands they had owned to move to more fertile areas, where they rented. Among blacks, during the same period, the proportion of landowners rose from virtually none to more than 20 percent.

Still, most blacks, and a growing minority of whites, did not own their own land during Reconstruction and, instead, worked for others in one form or another. Many black agricultural laborers—perhaps 25 percent of the total—simply worked for wages. Most, however, became tenants of white landowners—that is, they worked their own plots of land and paid their landlords either a fixed rent or a share of their crops (hence the term "sharecropping"). As tenants and sharecroppers, blacks enjoyed at least a physical independence from their landlords and had the sense of working their own land, even if in most cases they could never hope to buy it. But tenantry also benefited landlords in some ways, relieving them of the cost of purchasing slaves and of responsibility for the physical well-being of their workers.

INCOMES AND CREDIT

In some respects, the postwar years were a period of remarkable economic progress for African Americans in the South. The per capita income of blacks (when the material benefits of slavery are counted as income) rose 46 percent between 1857 and 1879, while the per capita income of whites declined 35 percent. African Americans were also able to work less than they had under slavery. Women and children were less likely to labor in the fields, and adult men tended to work shorter days. In all, the black labor force worked about one-third fewer hours during Reconstruction than it had been compelled to work under slavery—a reduction that brought the working schedule of blacks roughly into accord with that of white farm laborers.

But other developments limited these gains. While the black share of profits was increasing, the total profits of Southern agriculture were declining. Nor did the income redistribution of the postwar years lift many blacks out of poverty. Black per capita income rose from about one-quarter of white per capita income (which was itself low) to about one-half in the first few years after the war. After this initial increase, however, it rose hardly at all.

Blacks and poor whites alike found themselves virtually imprisoned by the crop-lien system. Few of the traditional institutions of credit in the South—the "factors" and

SOUTHERN BLACKS ASK FOR HELP, 1865

WE, the undersigned members of a Convention of colored citizens of the State of Virginia, would respectfully represent that, although we have been held as slaves, and denied all recognition as a constituent of your nationality for almost the entire period of the duration of your Government, and that by your *permission* we have been denied either home or country, and deprived of the dearest rights of human nature; yet when you and our immediate oppressors met in deadly conflict upon the field of battle—the one to destroy and the other to save your Government and nationality, we, with scarce an exception, in our inmost souls espoused your cause, and watched, and prayed, and waited, and labored for your success. . . .

When the contest waxed long, and the result hung doubtfully, you appealed to us for help, and how well we answered is written in the rosters of the two hundred thousand colored troops now enrolled in your Service;

and as to our undying devotion to your cause, let the uniform acclamation of escaped prisoners, "whenever we saw a black face we felt sure of a friend," answer.

Well, the war is over, the rebellion is "put down," and we are *declared* free! Four fifths of our enemies are paroled or amnestied, and the other fifth are being pardoned, and the President has, in his efforts at the reconstruction of the civil government of the States, late in rebellion, left us entirely at the mercy of these subjugated but unconverted rebels, in *everything* save the privilege of bringing us, our wives and little ones, to the auction block. *We know* these men—know them well—and we assure you that, with the majority of them, loyalty is only "lip deep," and that their professions of loyalty are used as a cover to the cherished design of getting restored to their former relations with the Federal Government, and then, by all sorts of "unfriendly legislation," to render the freedom you have given us

banks—returned after the war. In their stead emerged a new credit system, centered in large part on local country stores—some of them owned by planters, others owned by independent merchants. Blacks and whites, landowners and tenants—all depended on these stores. And since farmers did not have the same steady cash flow as other workers, customers usually had to rely on credit from these merchants to purchase what they needed. Most local stores had no competition and thus could set interest rates as high as 50 or 60 percent. Farmers had to give the merchants a lien (or claim) on their crops as collateral for the loans (thus the term "crop-lien system," generally used to describe Southern farming in this period). Farmers who suffered a few bad years in a row, as many did, could become trapped in a cycle of debt from which they could never escape.

As a result of this burdensome credit system, some blacks who had acquired land during the early years of Reconstruction, and many poor whites who had owned land for years, gradually lost it as they fell into debt. Southern farmers also became almost wholly dependent on cash crops—and most of all on cotton—because only such marketable commodities seemed to offer any possibility of escape from debt. The relentless planting of more Intolerable than the slavery they intended for us.

We warn you in time that our only safety is in keeping them under Governors of the *military persuasion* until you have so amended the Federal Constitution that it will prohibit the States from making any distinction between citizens on account of race or color. In one word, the only salvation for us besides the power of the Government, is in the *possession of the ballot.* Give us this, and we will protect ourselves. . . . But, 'tis said we are ignorant. Admit it. Yet who denies we *know* a traitor from a loyal man, a gentleman from a rowdy, a friend from an enemy? . . . All we ask is an *equal chance* with the white *traitors* varnished and japanned with the oath of amnesty. Can you deny us this and still keep faith with us? . . .

We are "sheep in the midst of wolves," and nothing but the military arm of the Government prevents us and all the *truly* loyal white men from being driven from the land of our birth. Do not then, we beseech you, give to one of these "wayward sisters" the rights they abandoned and forfeited when they rebelled until you have secured our rights by the aforementioned amendment to the Constitution.

UNDERSTAND, ANALYZE, & EVALUATE

1. What did the authors of this petition emphasize in the first two paragraphs, and why did they feel this was important?
2. Why did the authors emphasize that they had been "declared" free? What dangers to their prospect of freedom did they observe?
3. What federal legal responses did they propose? Can you recognize these suggestions in the constitutional changes that came with Reconstruction?

Source: "Proceedings of the Convention of the Colored People of Virginia, Held in the City of Alexandria, August 2, 3, 4, 5, 1865" (Alexandria, Va., 1865), in W. L. Fleming (ed.), *Documentary History of Reconstruction* (Cleveland, Ohio, 1906), vol. 1, pp. 195–196; located in "Southern Blacks Ask for Help (1865)," in Thomas A. Bailey and David M. Kennedy (eds.), *The American Spirit,* vol. 1, 7th ed. (Lexington, Mass., 1991), pp. 466–467.

cotton contributed to soil exhaustion, which undermined the Southern agricultural economy over time.

THE AFRICAN AMERICAN FAMILY IN FREEDOM

A major reason for the rapid departure of so many blacks from plantations was the desire to find lost relatives and reunite families. Thousands of African Americans wandered through the South looking for husbands, wives, children, or other relatives from whom they had been separated. Former slaves rushed to have their marriages, previously without legal standing, sanctified by church and law.

Within the black family, the definition of male and female roles quickly came to resemble that within white families. Many women and children ceased working in the fields. Such work, they believed, was a badge of slavery. Instead, many women restricted themselves largely to domestic tasks. Still, economic necessity often compelled black women to engage in income-producing activities: working as domestic servants, taking in laundry, or helping their husbands in the fields. By the end of Reconstruction, half of all black women over the age of sixteen were working for wages.

A VISIT FROM THE OLD MISTRESS Winslow Homer's 1876 painting of an imagined visit by a Southern white woman to a group of her former slaves was an effort to convey something of the tension in relations between the races in the South during Reconstruction. The women, once intimately involved in one another's lives, look at one another guardedly, carefully maintaining the space between them. White Southerners attacked the painting for portraying white and black women on a relatively equal footing. Some black Southerners criticized it for depicting poor rural African Americans instead of the more prosperous professional blacks who were emerging in Southern cities. "There were plenty of well-dressed negroes if he would but look for them," one wrote. (Smithsonian American Art Museum, Washington, DC/Art Resource, NY)

THE GRANT ADMINISTRATION

American voters in 1868 yearned for a strong, stable figure to guide them through the troubled years of Reconstruction. They turned trustingly to General Ulysses S. Grant.

THE SOLDIER PRESIDENT

Grant could have had the nomination of either party in 1868. But believing that Republican Reconstruction policies were more popular in the North, he accepted the Republican nomination. The Democrats nominated former governor Horatio Seymour of New York. The campaign was a bitter one, and Grant's triumph was surprisingly narrow. Without the 500,000 new black Republican voters in the South, he would have had a minority of the popular vote.

Grant entered the White House with no political experience, and his performance was clumsy and ineffectual from the start. Except for Hamilton Fish, whom Grant appointed secretary of state, most members of the cabinet were ill-equipped for their tasks. Grant relied chiefly on established party leaders—the group most ardently devoted to patronage, and his administration used the spoils system even more blatantly than most of its predecessors. Grant also alienated the many Northerners who were growing disillusioned with the Radical Reconstruction policies, which the president continued to support. Some Republicans suspected, correctly, that there was also corruption in the Grant administration itself.

By the end of Grant's first term, therefore, members of a substantial faction of the party—who referred to themselves as Liberal Republicans—had come to oppose what they called "Grantism." In 1872, hoping to prevent Grant's reelection, they bolted the party and nominated their own presidential candidate: Horace Greeley, veteran editor and publisher of the *New York Tribune*. The Democrats, somewhat reluctantly, named Greeley their candidate as well, hoping that the alliance with the Liberals would enable them to defeat Grant. But the effort was in vain. Grant won a substantial victory, polling 286 electoral votes to Greeley's 66.

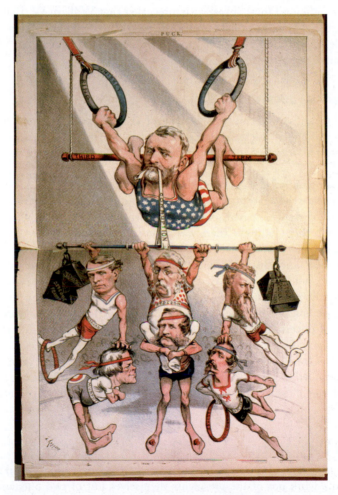

GRANT THE TRAPEZE ARTIST   This cartoon by eminent cartoonist Joseph Keppler shows President Ulysses S. Grant swinging on a trapeze holding on to the "whiskey ring" and the "navy ring" (references to two of the many scandals that plagued his presidency). Using a strap labeled "corruption," he holds aloft some of the most notorious figures in those scandals. The cartoon was published in 1880, when Grant was attempting to win the Republican nomination to run for another term as president. (Library of Congress)

THE GRANT SCANDALS

During the 1872 campaign, the first of a series of political scandals came to light that would plague Grant and the Republicans for the next four years. It involved the French-owned Crédit Mobilier construction company, which had helped build the Union Pacific Railroad. The heads of Crédit Mobilier had used their positions as Union Pacific stock-holders to steer large fraudulent contracts to their construction company, thus bilking the Union Pacific of millions. To prevent investigations, the directors had given Crédit Mobilier stock to key members of Congress. But in 1872, Congress did conduct an investigation, which revealed that some highly placed Republicans—including Schuyler Colfax, now Grant's vice president—had accepted stock.

One dreary episode followed another in Grant's second term. Benjamin H. Bristow, Grant's third Treasury secretary, discovered that some of his officials and a group of distillers operating as a "whiskey ring" were cheating the government out of taxes by filing false reports. Then a House investigation revealed that William W. Belknap, secretary of war, had accepted bribes to retain an Indian-post trader in office (the so-called Indian ring). Other, lesser scandals also added to the growing impression that "Grantism" had brought rampant corruption to government.

THE GREENBACK QUESTION

Compounding Grant's problems was a financial crisis, known as the Panic of 1873. It began with the failure of a leading investment banking firm, Jay Cooke and Company, which had invested too heavily in postwar railroad building. There had been panics before—in 1819, 1837, and 1857—but this was the worst one yet.

Debtors now pressured the government to redeem federal war bonds with greenbacks, which would increase the amount of money in circulation. But Grant and most Republicans wanted a "sound" currency—based solidly on gold reserves—which would favor the interests of banks and other creditors. There was approximately $356 million in paper currency issued during the Civil War that was still in circulation. In 1873, the Treasury issued more in response to the panic. But in 1875, Republican leaders in Congress passed the Specie Resumption Act, which provided that after January 1, 1879, greenback dollars would be redeemed by the government and replaced with new certificates, firmly pegged to the price of gold. The law satisfied creditors, who had worried that debts would be repaid in paper currency of uncertain value. But "resumption" made things more difficult for debtors, because the gold-based money supply could not easily expand.

In 1875, the "Greenbackers" formed their own political organization: the National Greenback Party. It failed to gain widespread support, but the money issue was to remain one of the most controversial and enduring issues in late-nineteenth-century American politics.

REPUBLICAN DIPLOMACY

The Johnson and Grant administrations achieved their greatest successes in foreign affairs as a result of the work not of the presidents themselves but of two outstanding secretaries of state: William H. Seward and Hamilton Fish.

An ardent expansionist, Seward acted with as much daring as the demands of Reconstruction politics and the Republican hatred of President Johnson would permit. He accepted a Russian offer to buy Alaska for $7.2 million, despite criticism from many who derided the purchase as "Seward's Folly." In 1867, Seward also engineered the American annexation of the tiny Midway Islands, west of Hawaii.

Hamilton Fish's first major challenge was resolving the long-standing controversy over the American claims that Britain had violated neutrality laws during the Civil War by permitting English shipyards to build ships (among them the *Alabama*) for the Confederacy. American demands that England pay for the damage these vessels had caused became known as the "*Alabama* claims." In 1871, after a number of failed efforts, Fish forged an agreement, the Treaty of Washington, which provided for international arbitration.

THE ABANDONMENT OF RECONSTRUCTION

As the North grew increasingly preoccupied with its own political and economic problems, interest in Reconstruction began to wane. By the time Grant left office, Democrats had taken back seven of the governments of the former Confederate states. For three other states—South Carolina, Louisiana, and Florida—the end of Reconstruction had to wait for the withdrawal of the last federal troops in 1877.

THE SOUTHERN STATES "REDEEMED"

In the states where whites constituted a majority—the states of the upper South—overthrowing Republican control was relatively simple. By 1872, all but a handful of Southern whites had regained suffrage. Now a clear majority, they needed only to organize and elect their candidates.

In other states, where blacks were a majority or where the populations of the two races were almost equal, whites used intimidation and violence to undermine the Reconstruction regimes. Secret societies—the Ku Klux Klan, the Knights of the White Camellia, and others—used terrorism to frighten or physically bar blacks from voting. Paramilitary organizations—the Red Shirts and White Leagues—armed themselves to "police" elections and worked to force all white males to join the Democratic Party. Strongest of all, however, was the simple weapon of economic pressure. Some planters refused to rent land to Republican blacks; storekeepers refused to extend them credit; employers refused to give them work.

The Republican Congress responded to this wave of repression with the Enforcement Acts of 1870 and 1871 (better known as the Ku Klux Klan Acts), which prohibited states from discriminating against voters on the basis of race and gave the national government the authority to prosecute crimes by individuals under federal law. The laws also authorized the president to use federal troops to protect civil rights—a provision President Grant used in 1871 in nine counties of South Carolina. The Enforcement Acts, although seldom enforced, discouraged Klan violence, which declined by 1872.

WANING NORTHERN COMMITMENT

But this Northern commitment to civil rights did not last long. After the adoption of the Fifteenth Amendment in 1870, some reformers convinced themselves that their long campaign on behalf of black people was now over, that with the vote blacks ought to be able to take care of themselves. Former Radical leaders such as Charles Sumner and Horace

Greeley now began calling themselves Liberals, cooperating with the Democrats, and denouncing what they viewed as black-and-carpetbag misgovernment. Within the South itself, many white Republicans now moved into the Democratic Party.

The Panic of 1873 further undermined support for Reconstruction. In the congressional elections of 1874, the Democrats won control of the House of Representatives for the first time since 1861. Grant reduced the use of military force to prop up the Republican regimes in the South.

THE COMPROMISE OF 1877

Grant had hoped to run for another term in 1876, but most Republican leaders—shaken by recent Democratic successes and scandals by the White House—resisted. Instead, they settled on Rutherford B. Hayes, three-time governor of Ohio and a champion of civil service reform. The Democrats united behind Samuel J. Tilden, the reform governor of New York, who had been instrumental in overthrowing the corrupt Tweed Ring of New York City's Tammany Hall.

Although the campaign was a bitter one, few differences of principle distinguished the candidates from one another. The election produced an apparent Democratic victory. Tilden carried the South and several large Northern states, and his popular margin over Hayes was nearly 300,000 votes. But disputed returns from Louisiana, South Carolina, Florida, and Oregon, whose electoral votes totaled 20, threw the election in doubt. Hayes could still win if he managed to receive all 20 disputed votes.

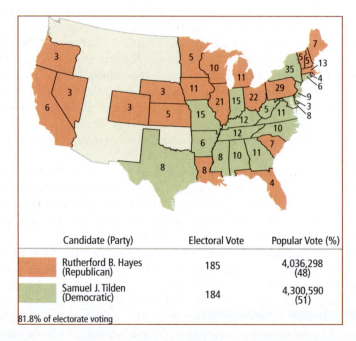

Candidate (Party)	Electoral Vote	Popular Vote (%)
Rutherford B. Hayes (Republican)	185	4,036,298 (48)
Samuel J. Tilden (Democratic)	184	4,300,590 (51)

81.8% of electorate voting

THE ELECTION OF 1876   The election of 1876 was one of the most controversial in American history. As in the elections of 1824, 1888, and 2000, the winner of the popular vote—Samuel J. Tilden—was not the winner of the electoral college, which he lost by one vote. The final decision as to who would be president was not made until the day before the official inauguration in March. • *How did the Republicans turn this apparent defeat into a victory?*

The Constitution had established no method to determine the validity of disputed returns. The decision clearly lay with Congress, but it was not clear with which house or through what method. (The Senate was Republican, and the House was Democratic.) Members of each party naturally supported a solution that would yield them the victory. Finally, late in January 1877, Congress tried to break the deadlock by creating a special electoral commission composed of five senators, five representatives, and five justices of the Supreme Court. The congressional delegation consisted of five Republicans and five Democrats. The Court delegation would include two Republicans, two Democrats, and the only independent, Justice David Davis. But when the Illinois legislature elected Davis to the United States Senate, the justice resigned from the commission. His seat went instead to a Republican justice. The commission voted along straight party lines, 8 to 7, awarding every disputed vote to Hayes.

Behind this seemingly partisan victory, however, lay a series of elaborate compromises among leaders of both parties. When a Democratic filibuster threatened to derail the commission's report, Republican Senate leaders met secretly with Southern Democratic leaders. As the price of their cooperation, the Southern Democrats exacted several pledges from the Republicans: the appointment of at least one Southerner to the Hayes cabinet, control of federal patronage in their areas, generous internal improvements, federal aid for the Texas and Pacific Railroad, and most important, withdrawal of the remaining federal troops from the South.

In his inaugural address, Hayes announced that the South's most pressing need was the restoration of "wise, honest, and peaceful local self-government," and he soon withdrew the troops and let white Democrats take over the remaining Southern state governments. That produced charges that he was paying off the South for acquiescing in his election. But the election had already created such bitterness that not even Hayes's promise to serve only one term could mollify his critics.

The president and his party hoped to build up a "new Republican" organization in the South committed to modest support for black rights. But although many white Southern leaders sympathized with Republican economic policies, resentment of Reconstruction was so deep that supporting the party became politically impossible. The "solid" Democratic South, which would survive until the mid-twentieth century, was taking shape.

THE LEGACY OF RECONSTRUCTION

Reconstruction made important contributions to the efforts of former slaves to achieve dignity and equality in American life. There was a significant redistribution of income and a more limited but not unimportant redistribution of landownership. Perhaps most important, African Americans themselves managed to carve out a society and culture of their own and to create or strengthen their own institutions.

Reconstruction was not as disastrous for Southern white elites as most believed at the time. Within little more than a decade after a devastating war, the white South had regained control of its own institutions and, to a great extent, restored its traditional ruling class to power. The federal government imposed no drastic economic reforms on the region and, indeed, few lasting political changes of any kind other than the abolition of slavery.

Reconstruction was notable, finally, for its limitations. For in those years, the United States failed in its first serious effort to resolve its oldest and deepest social problem—the problem of race. The experience so disillusioned white Americans that it would be nearly a century before they would try again to combat racial injustice.

Given the odds confronting them, however, African Americans had reason for considerable pride in the gains they were able to make during Reconstruction. And future generations could be grateful for two great charters of freedom—the Fourteenth and Fifteenth Amendments to the Constitution—which, although widely ignored at the time, would one day serve as the basis for a "Second Reconstruction" that would renew the drive to bring freedom to all Americans.

THE NEW SOUTH

The Compromise of 1877 was supposed to be the first step toward developing a stable, permanent Republican Party in the South. In that respect at least, it failed. In the years following the end of Reconstruction, white southerners established the Democratic Party as the only viable political organization for the region's whites. Even so, the South did change in some of the ways the framers of the Compromise had hoped.

THE "REDEEMERS"

Many white southerners rejoiced at the restoration of what they liked to call "home rule." But in reality, political power in the region was soon more restricted than at any time since the Civil War. Once again, most of the South fell under the control of a powerful, conservative oligarchy, whose members were known variously as the "Redeemers" or the "Bourbons."

In some places, this post-Reconstruction ruling class was much the same as the ruling class of the antebellum period. In Alabama, for example, the old planter elite retained much of its former power. In other areas, however, the Redeemers constituted a genuinely new ruling class of merchants, industrialists, railroad developers, and financiers. Some of them were former planters, some of them northern immigrants, some of them ambitious, upwardly mobile white southerners from the region's lower social tiers. They combined a defense of "home rule" and social conservatism with a commitment to economic development.

The various Bourbon governments of the New South behaved in many respects quite similarly. Virtually all the new Democratic regimes lowered taxes, reduced spending, and drastically diminished state services. One state after another eliminated or reduced its support for public school systems.

INDUSTRIALIZATION AND THE NEW SOUTH

Many white southern leaders in the post-Reconstruction era hoped to see their region develop a vigorous industrial economy, a "New South." Henry Grady, editor of the *Atlanta Constitution*, and other New South advocates seldom challenged white supremacy, but they did promote the virtues of thrift, industry, and progress—qualities that prewar southerners had often denounced in northern society.

Southern industry did expand dramatically in the years after Reconstruction, most visibly in textile manufacturing. In the past, southern planters had usually shipped their cotton to manufacturers in the North or in Europe. Now textile factories appeared in the South itself—many of them drawn to the region from New England by the abundance of water power, the ready supply of cheap labor, the low taxes, and the accommodating conservative governments. The tobacco processing industry similarly established an important foothold in the region. In the lower South, and particularly in Birmingham, Alabama, the iron (and, later, steel) industry grew rapidly.

Railroad development also increased substantially in the post-Reconstruction years. Between 1880 and 1890, trackage in the South more than doubled. And in 1886, the South changed the gauge (width) of its trackage to correspond with the standards of the North. No longer would it be necessary for cargoes heading into the South to be transferred from one train to another at the borders of the region.

Yet southern industry developed within strict limits, and its effects on the region were never even remotely comparable to the effects of industrialization on the North. The southern share of national manufacturing doubled in the last twenty years of the century, but it was still only 10 percent of the total. Similarly, the region's per capita income increased 21 percent in the same period, but average income in the South was still only 40 percent of that in the North; in 1860 it had been more than 60 percent. And even in those industries where development had been most rapid—textiles, iron, railroads—much of the capital had come from, and many of the profits thus flowed to, the North.

The growth of southern industry required the region to recruit a substantial industrial workforce for the first time. From the beginning, a high percentage of the factory workers were women. Heavy male casualties in the Civil War had helped create a large population of unmarried women who desperately needed employment. Hours were long (often as much as twelve hours a day), and wages were far below the northern equivalent; indeed, one of the greatest attractions of the South to industrialists was that employers were able to pay workers there as little as one-half of what northern workers received. Life in most mill towns was rigidly controlled by the owners and managers of the factories, who rigorously suppressed attempts at protest or union organization. Company stores sold goods to workers at inflated prices and issued credit at exorbitant rates (much as country stores did in agrarian areas), and mill owners ensured that no competing merchants were able to establish themselves in the community.

Some industries, such as textiles, offered virtually no opportunities to African American workers. Others—tobacco, iron, and lumber, for example—did provide some employment for blacks. Some mill towns, therefore, were places where the black and white cultures came into close contact, increasing the determination of white leaders to take additional measures to protect white supremacy.

TENANTS AND SHARECROPPERS

The most important economic problem in the post-Reconstruction South was the impoverished state of agriculture. The 1870s and 1880s saw an acceleration of the process that had begun in the immediate postwar years: the imposition of systems of tenantry and debt peonage on much of the region; the reliance on a few cash crops rather than on a diversified agricultural system; and increasing absentee ownership of valuable farmlands. During Reconstruction, perhaps a third or more of the farmers in the South were tenants; by 1900, the figure had increased to 70 percent.

AFRICAN AMERICANS AND THE NEW SOUTH

The "New South creed" was not the property of whites alone. Many African Americans were attracted to the vision of progress and self-improvement as well. Some former slaves (and, as the decades passed, their offspring) succeeded in elevating themselves into the

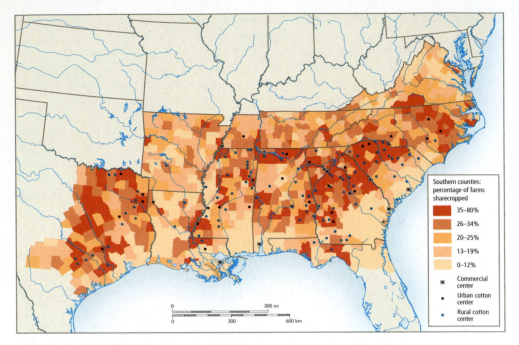

THE CROP-LIEN SYSTEM IN 1880   In the years after the Civil War, more and more southern farmers—white and black—became tenants or sharecroppers on land owned by others. This map shows the percentage of farms that were within the so-called crop-lien system, the system by which people worked their lands for someone else, who had a claim (or "lien") on a part of the farmers' crops. Note the high density of sharecropping and tenant farming in the most fertile areas of the Deep South, the same areas where slaveholding had been most dominant before the Civil War.   • *How did the crop-lien system contribute to the shift in southern agriculture toward one-crop farming?*

middle class, acquired property, established small businesses, or entered professions. Believing strongly that education was vital to the future of their people, they expanded the network of black colleges and institutes that had taken root during Reconstruction into an important educational system.

The chief spokesman for this commitment to education was Booker T. Washington, founder and president of the Tuskegee Institute in Alabama. Born into slavery, Washington had worked his way out of poverty after acquiring an education (at Virginia's Hampton Institute). He urged other blacks to follow the same road to self-improvement.

Washington's message was both cautious and hopeful. African Americans should attend school, learn skills, and establish a solid footing in agriculture and the trades. Industrial, not classical, education should be their goal. Blacks should, moreover, refine their speech, improve their dress, and adopt habits of thrift and personal cleanliness; they should, in short, adopt the standards of the white middle class. Only thus, he claimed, could they win the respect of the white population.

In a famous speech in Georgia in 1895, Washington outlined a controversial philosophy of race relations that became widely known as the Atlanta Compromise. Blacks, he said, should forgo agitation for political rights and concentrate on self-improvement and preparation for equality. Washington offered a powerful challenge to those whites who wanted to discourage African Americans from acquiring an education or winning any economic gains. But his message was also intended to assure whites that blacks would not challenge the emerging system of segregation.

THE BIRTH OF JIM CROW

Few white southerners had ever accepted the idea of racial equality. That the former slaves acquired any legal and political rights at all after emancipation was in large part the result of their own efforts and critical federal support. That outside support all but vanished after 1877, when federal troops withdrew and the Supreme Court stripped the Fourteenth and Fifteenth Amendments of much of their significance. In the so-called civil rights cases of 1883, the Court ruled that the Fourteenth Amendment prohibited state governments from discriminating against people because of race but did not restrict private organizations or individuals from doing so.

Eventually, the Court also validated state legislation that institutionalized the separation of the races. In *Plessy v. Ferguson* (1896), a case involving a Louisiana law that required segregated seating on railroads, the Court held that separate accommodations did not deprive blacks of equal rights if the accommodations were equal. In *Cumming v. County Board of Education* (1899), the Court ruled that communities could establish schools for whites only, even if there were no comparable schools for blacks.

Even before these dubious decisions, white southerners were working to separate the races to the greatest extent possible, and were particularly determined to strip African Americans of the right to vote. In some states, disenfranchisement had begun almost as soon as Reconstruction ended. But in other areas, black voting continued for some time after Reconstruction—largely because conservative whites believed they could control the black electorate and use it to beat back the attempts of poor white farmers to take control of the Democratic Party.

TUSKEGEE INSTITUTE, 1881 From these modest beginnings, Booker T. Washington's Tuskegee Institute in Alabama became the preeminent academy offering technical and industrial training to black men. It deliberately de-emphasized the traditional liberal arts curricula of most colleges. Washington considered such training less important than developing practical skills. (© Bettmann/Corbis)

In the 1890s, however, franchise restrictions became much more rigid. During those years, some small white farmers began to demand complete black disenfranchisement—because they objected to the black vote being used against them by the Bourbons. At the same time, many members of the conservative elite began to fear that poor whites might unite politically with poor blacks to challenge them.

In devising laws to disenfranchise black males, the southern states had to find ways to evade the Fifteenth Amendment, which prohibited states from denying anyone the right to vote because of race. Two devices emerged before 1900 to accomplish this goal: the poll tax or some form of property qualification (few blacks were prosperous enough to meet such requirements) or the "literacy" or "understanding" test, which required voters to demonstrate an ability to read and to interpret the Constitution. Even those African Americans who could read had a hard time passing the difficult test white officials gave them. (The laws affected poor white voters as well as blacks.) By the late 1890s, the black vote had decreased by 62 percent, the white vote by 26 percent.

Laws restricting the franchise and segregating schools were only part of a network of state and local statutes—known as the Jim Crow laws—that by the first years of the twentieth century had institutionalized an elaborate system of segregation reaching into almost every area of southern life. Blacks and whites could not ride together in the same railroad cars, sit in the same waiting rooms, use the same washrooms, eat in the same restaurants, or sit in the same theaters. Blacks had no access to many public parks, beaches, or picnic areas; they could not be patients in many hospitals. Much of the new legal structure did no more than confirm what had already been widespread social practice in the South. But the Jim Crow laws also stripped blacks of many of the modest social, economic, and political gains they had made in the late nineteenth century.

More than legal efforts were involved in this process. The 1890s witnessed a dramatic increase in white violence against blacks, which, along with the Jim Crow laws, served to inhibit black agitation for equal rights. The worst such violence—lynching of blacks by white mobs—reached appalling levels. In the nation as a whole in the 1890s, there was an average of 187 lynchings each year, more than 80 percent of them in the South. The vast majority of victims were black. Those who participated in lynchings often saw their actions as a legitimate form of law enforcement, and some victims of lynchings had in fact committed crimes. But lynchings were also a means by which whites controlled the black population through terror and intimidation.

The rise of lynchings shocked the conscience of many white Americans in a way that other forms of racial injustice did not. In 1892, Ida B. Wells, a committed black journalist, published a series of impassioned articles after the lynching of three of her hometown friends in Memphis, Tennessee; her articles launched what became an international antilynching movement. The movement gradually attracted substantial support from whites in both the North and South (particularly from white women). Its goal was a federal antilynching law, which would allow the national government to do what state and local governments in the South were generally unwilling to do: punish those responsible for lynchings.

But the substantial southern white opposition to lynchings stood as an exception to the general white support for suppression of African Americans. Indeed, just as in the antebellum period, the shared commitment to white supremacy helped dilute class animosities between poorer whites and the Bourbon oligarchies. Economic issues tended to play a secondary role to race in southern politics, distracting people from the glaring social inequalities that afflicted blacks and whites alike.

A LYNCH MOB, 1893   A large, almost festive crowd gathers to watch the lynching of a black man accused of the murder of a three-year-old white girl. Lynchings remained frequent in the South until as late as the 1930s, but they reached their peak in the 1890s and the first years of the twentieth century. Lynchings such as this one—publicized well in advance and attracting whole families who traveled great distances to see them—were relatively infrequent. Most lynchings were the work of smaller groups, operating with less visibility. (Library of Congress)

CONCLUSION

Reconstruction was a profoundly important moment in American history. Despite the bitter political battles in Washington and throughout the South, culminating in the unsuccessful effort to remove President Andrew Johnson from office, the most important result of the effort to reunite the nation after its long and bloody war was a reshaping of the lives of ordinary people in all regions.

In the North, Reconstruction solidified the power of the Republican Party. The rapid expansion of the northern economy continued and accelerated, drawing more and more of its residents into a burgeoning commercial world.

In the South, Reconstruction fundamentally rearranged the relationship between the region's white and black citizens. Only for a while did Reconstruction permit African Americans to participate actively and effectively in southern politics. After a few years of widespread black voting and significant black officeholding, the forces of white supremacy ushered most African Americans to the margins of the southern political world, where they would mostly remain until the 1960s.

In other ways, however, the lives of southern blacks changed dramatically and permanently. Overwhelmingly, they left the plantations. Some sought work in towns and cities. Others left the region altogether. But the great majority began farming on small farms of their own—not as landowners, except in rare cases, but as tenants and sharecroppers on land owned by whites. The result was a form of economic bondage, driven by debt, only scarcely less oppressive than the legal bondage of slavery. Within this system, however, African Americans managed to carve out a much larger sphere of social and cultural activity than they had ever been able to create under slavery. Black churches proliferated in great numbers. African American schools emerged in some communities, and black colleges began to operate in the region. Some former slaves owned businesses and flourished.

Strenuous efforts by "New South" advocates to advance industry and commerce in the region produced significant results in a few areas. But the South on the whole remained what it had always been: a largely rural society with a sharply defined class structure. It also maintained a deep commitment among its white citizens to the subordination of African Americans—a commitment solidified in the 1890s and the early twentieth century when white southerners erected an elaborate legal system of segregation (the Jim Crow laws). The promise of the great Reconstruction amendments to the Constitution—the Fourteenth and Fifteenth—remained largely unfulfilled in the South as the century drew to its close.

RECALL AND REFLECT

1. What were the principal questions facing the nation at the end of the Civil War?
2. What were the achievements of Reconstruction? Where did it fail and why?
3. What new problems arose in the South as the North's interest in Reconstruction waned?
4. What was the Compromise of 1877, and how did it affect Reconstruction?
5. How did the New South differ from the South before the Civil War?

APPENDICES

Documents & Tables

THE DECLARATION OF INDEPENDENCE

In Congress, July 4, 1776,

THE UNANIMOUS DECLARATION OF THE THIRTEEN UNITED STATES OF AMERICA

When, in the course of human events, it becomes necessary for one people to dissolve the political bands which have connected them with another, and to assume, among the powers of the earth, the separate and equal station to which the laws of nature and of nature's God entitle them, a decent respect to the opinions of mankind requires that they should declare the causes which impel them to the separation.

We hold these truths to be self-evident, that all men are created equal; that they are endowed by their Creator with certain unalienable rights; that among these, are life, liberty, and the pursuit of happiness. That, to secure these rights, governments are instituted among men, deriving their just powers from the consent of the governed; that, whenever any form of government becomes destructive of these ends, it is the right of the people to alter or to abolish it, and to institute a new government, laying its foundation on such principles, and organizing its powers in such form, as to them shall seem most likely to effect their safety and happiness. Prudence, indeed, will dictate that governments long established, should not be changed for light and transient causes; and, accordingly, all experience hath shown, that mankind are more disposed to suffer, while evils are sufferable, than to right themselves by abolishing the forms to which they are accustomed. But, when a long train of abuses and usurpations, pursuing invariably the same object, evinces a design to reduce them under absolute despotism, it is their right, it is their duty, to throw off such government and to provide new guards for their future security. Such has been the patient sufferance of these colonies, and such is now the necessity which constrains them to alter their former systems of government. The history of the present King of Great Britain is a history of repeated injuries and usurpations, all having, in direct object, the establishment of an absolute tyranny over these States. To prove this, let facts be submitted to a candid world:

He has refused his assent to laws the most wholesome and necessary for the public good.

He has forbidden his governors to pass laws of immediate and pressing importance, unless suspended in their operation till his assent should be obtained; and, when so suspended, he has utterly neglected to attend to them.

He has refused to pass other laws for the accommodation of large districts of people, unless those people would relinquish the right of representation in the legislature; a right inestimable to them, and formidable to tyrants only.

He has called together legislative bodies at places unusual, uncomfortable, and distant from the depository of their public records, for the sole purpose of fatiguing them into compliance with his measures.

He has dissolved representative houses repeatedly for opposing, with manly firmness, his invasions on the rights of the people.

He has refused, for a long time after such dissolutions, to cause others to be elected; whereby the legislative powers, incapable of annihilation, have returned to the people at large for their exercise; the state remaining, in the meantime, exposed to all the danger of invasion from without, and compulsions within.

He has endeavored to prevent the population of these States; for that purpose, obstructing the laws for naturalization of foreigners, refusing to pass others to encourage their migration hither, and raising the conditions of new appropriations of lands.

He has obstructed the administration of justice, by refusing his assent to laws for establishing judiciary powers.

He has made judges dependent on his will alone, for the tenure of their offices, and the amount and payment of their salaries.

He has erected a multitude of new offices, and sent hither swarms of officers to harass our people, and eat out their substance.

He has kept among us, in time of peace, standing armies, without the consent of our legislatures.

He has affected to render the military independent of, and superior to, the civil power.

He has combined, with others, to subject us to a jurisdiction foreign to our Constitution, and unacknowledged by our laws; giving his assent to their acts of pretended legislation:

For quartering large bodies of armed troops among us:

For protecting them by a mock trial, from punishment, for any murders which they should commit on the inhabitants of these States:

For cutting off our trade with all parts of the world:

For imposing taxes on us without our consent:

For depriving us, in many cases, of the benefit of trial by jury:

For transporting us beyond seas to be tried for pretended offences:

For abolishing the free system of English laws in a neighboring province, establishing therein an arbitrary government, and enlarging its boundaries, so as to render it at once an example and fit instrument for introducing the same absolute rule into these colonies:

For taking away our charters, abolishing our most valuable laws, and altering, fundamentally, the powers of our governments:

For suspending our own legislatures, and declaring themselves invested with power to legislate for us in all cases whatsoever.

He has abdicated government here, by declaring us out of his protection, and waging war against us.

He has plundered our seas, ravaged our coasts, burnt our towns, and destroyed the lives of our people.

He is, at this time, transporting large armies of foreign mercenaries to complete the works of death, desolation, and tyranny, already begun, with circumstances of cruelty and perfidy scarcely paralleled in the most barbarous ages, and totally unworthy the head of a civilized nation.

He has constrained our fellow citizens, taken captive on the high seas, to bear arms against their country, to become the executioners of their friends, and brethren, or to fall themselves by their hands.

He has excited domestic insurrections amongst us, and has endeavored to bring on the inhabitants of our frontiers, the merciless Indian savages, whose known rule of warfare is an undistinguished destruction of all ages, sexes, and conditions.

In every stage of these oppressions, we have petitioned for redress, in the most humble terms; our repeated petitions have been answered only by repeated injury. A prince, whose character is thus marked by every act which may define a tyrant, is unfit to be the ruler of a free people.

Nor have we been wanting in attention to our British brethren. We have warned them, from time to time, of attempts made by their legislature to extend an unwarrantable jurisdiction over us. We have reminded them of the circumstances of our emigration and settlement here. We have appealed to their native justice and magnanimity, and we have conjured them, by the ties of our common kindred, to disavow these usurpations, which would inevitably interrupt our connections and correspondence. They, too, have been deaf to the voice of justice and consanguinity. We must, therefore, acquiesce in the necessity which denounces our separation, and hold them as we hold the rest of mankind, enemies in war, in peace, friends.

We, therefore, the representatives of the United States of America, in general Congress assembled, appealing to the Supreme Judge of the world for the rectitude of our intentions, do, in the name, and by the authority of the good people of these colonies, solemnly publish and declare, that these united colonies are, and of right ought to be, free and independent states: that they are absolved from all allegiance to the British Crown, and that all political connection between them and the state of Great Britain is, and ought to be, totally dissolved; and that, as free and independent states, they have full power to levy war, conclude peace, contract alliances, establish commerce, and to do all other acts and things which independent states may of right do. And, for the support of this declaration, with a firm reliance on the protection of Divine Providence, we mutually pledge to each other our lives, our fortunes, and our sacred honor.

The foregoing Declaration was, by order of Congress, engrossed, and signed by the following members:

John Hancock

NEW HAMPSHIRE
Josiah Bartlett
William Whipple
Matthew Thornton

CONNECTICUT
Roger Sherman
Samuel Huntington
William Williams
Oliver Wolcott

NEW YORK
William Floyd
Philip Livingston
Francis Lewis
Lewis Morris

NEW JERSEY
Richard Stockton
John Witherspoon
Francis Hopkinson
John Hart
Abraham Clark

MASSACHUSETTS BAY
Samuel Adams
John Adams
Robert Treat Paine
Elbridge Gerry

PENNSYLVANIA
Robert Morris
Benjamin Rush
Benjamin Franklin
John Morton
George Clymer
James Smith
George Taylor
James Wilson
George Ross

DELAWARE
Caesar Rodney
George Read
Thomas M'Kean

MARYLAND
Samuel Chase
William Paca
Thomas Stone
Charles Carroll, of
  Carrollton

RHODE ISLAND
Stephen Hopkins
William Ellery

VIRGINIA
George Wythe
Richard Henry Lee
Thomas Jefferson
Benjamin Harrison
Thomas Nelson Jr.
Francis Lightfoot Lee
Carter Braxton

NORTH CAROLINA
William Hooper
Joseph Hewes
John Penn

SOUTH CAROLINA
Edward Rutledge
Thomas Heyward Jr.
Thomas Lynch Jr.
Arthur Middleton

GEORGIA
Button Gwinnett
Lyman Hall
George Walton

Resolved, That copies of the Declaration be sent to the several assemblies, conventions, and committees, or councils of safety, and to the several commanding officers of the continental troops; that it be proclaimed in each of the United States, at the head of the army.

THE CONSTITUTION OF THE UNITED STATES[1]

We the People of the United States, in Order to form a more perfect Union, establish Justice, insure domestic Tranquility, provide for the common defence, promote the general Welfare, and secure the Blessings of Liberty to ourselves and our Posterity, do ordain and establish this CONSTITUTION for the United States of America.

Article I

Section 1.
All legislative Powers herein granted shall be vested in a Congress of the United States, which shall consist of a Senate and House of Representatives.

Section 2.
The House of Representatives shall be composed of Members chosen every second Year by the People of the several States, and the Electors in each State shall have the Qualifications requisite for Electors of the most numerous Branch of the State Legislature.

No Person shall be a Representative who shall not have attained to the Age of twenty-five Years, and been seven Years a Citizen of the United States, and who shall not, when elected, be an Inhabitant of that State in which he shall be chosen.

[Representatives and direct Taxes[2] shall be apportioned among the several States which may be included within this Union, according to their respective Numbers, which shall be determined by adding to the whole Number of free Persons, including those bound to Service for a Term of Years, and excluding Indians not taxed, three fifths of all other Persons.][3] The actual Enumeration shall be made within three Years after the first Meeting of the Congress of the United States, and within every subsequent Term of ten Years, in such Manner as they shall by Law direct. The Number of Representatives shall not exceed one for every thirty Thousand, but each State shall have at Least one Representative; and until such enumeration shall be made, the State of New Hampshire shall be entitled to chuse three, Massachusetts eight, Rhode-Island and Providence Plantations one, Connecticut five, New York six, New Jersey four, Pennsylvania eight, Delaware one, Maryland six, Virginia ten, North Carolina five, South Carolina five, and Georgia three.

When vacancies happen in the Representation from any State, the Executive Authority thereof shall issue Writs of Election to fill such Vacancies.

The House of Representatives shall chuse their Speaker and other Officers; and shall have the sole Power of Impeachment.

Section 3.
The Senate of the United States shall be composed of two Senators from each State, chosen by the Legislature thereof, for six Years; and each Senator shall have one Vote.

Immediately after they shall be assembled in Consequence of the first Election, they shall be divided as equally as may be into three Classes. The Seats of the Senators of the first Class shall be vacated at the Expiration of the second Year, of the second Class at the Expiration of the fourth Year, and of the third Class at the Expiration of the sixth

---

[1]This version, which follows the original Constitution in capitalization and spelling, was published by the United States Department of the Interior, Office of Education, in 1935.
[2]Altered by the Sixteenth Amendment.
[3]Negated by the Fourteenth Amendment.

Year, so that one-third may be chosen every second Year; and if Vacancies happen by Resignation, or otherwise, during the Recess of the Legislature of any State, the Executive thereof may make temporary Appointments until the next Meeting of the Legislature, which shall then fill such Vacancies.

No Person shall be a Senator who shall not have attained to the Age of thirty Years, and been nine Years a Citizen of the United States, and who shall not, when elected, be an Inhabitant of that State for which he shall be chosen.

The Vice President of the United States shall be President of the Senate, but shall have no vote, unless they be equally divided.

The Senate shall chuse their other Officers, and also a President pro tempore, in the absence of the Vice President, or when he shall exercise the Office of President of the United States.

The Senate shall have the sole Power to try all Impeachments. When sitting for that purpose they shall be on Oath or Affirmation. When the President of the United States is tried, the Chief Justice shall preside: And no person shall be convicted without the Concurrence of two thirds of the Members present.

Judgment in Cases of Impeachment shall not extend further than to removal from Office, and disqualification to hold and enjoy any Office of honor, Trust, or Profit under the United States: but the Party convicted shall nevertheless be liable and subject to Indictment, Trial, Judgment, and Punishment, according to Law.

Section 4.

The Times, Places and Manner of holding Elections for Senators and Representatives, shall be prescribed in each State by the Legislature thereof; but the Congress may at any time by Law make or alter such Regulations, except as to the Places of Chusing Senators.

The Congress shall assemble at least once in every Year, and such Meeting shall be on the first Monday in December, unless they shall by Law appoint a different Day.

Section 5.

Each House shall be the Judge of the Elections, Returns and Qualifications of its own Members, and a Majority of each shall constitute a Quorum to do Business; but a smaller number may adjourn from day to day, and may be authorized to compel the Attendance of absent Members, in such Manner, and under such Penalties, as each House may provide.

Each House may determine the Rules of its Proceedings, punish its Members for disorderly Behaviour, and, with the Concurrence of two thirds, expel a Member.

Each House shall keep a Journal of its Proceedings, and from time to time publish the same, excepting such Parts as may in their Judgment require Secrecy; and the Yeas and Nays of the Members of either House on any question shall, at the Desire of one fifth of those Present, be entered on the Journal.

Neither House, during the Session of Congress, shall, without the Consent of the other, adjourn for more than three days, nor to any other Place than that in which the two Houses shall be sitting.

Section 6.

The Senators and Representatives shall receive a Compensation for their Services, to be ascertained by Law, and paid out of the Treasury of the United States. They shall in all Cases, except Treason, Felony, and Breach of the Peace, be privileged from Arrest during their Attendance at the Session of their respective Houses, and in going to and returning from the same; and for any Speech or Debate in either House, they shall not be questioned in any other Place.

No Senator or Representative shall, during the Time for which he was elected, be appointed to any civil Office under the Authority of the United States, which shall have been created, or the Emoluments whereof shall have been increased, during such time; and no Person holding any Office under the United States shall be a Member of either House during his continuance in Office.

Section 7.

All Bills for raising Revenue shall originate in the House of Representatives; but the Senate may propose or concur with Amendments as on other bills.

Every Bill which shall have passed the House of Representatives and the Senate, shall, before it become a Law, be presented to the President of the United States; If he approve he shall sign it, but if not he shall return it, with his Objections, to that House in which it shall have originated, who shall enter the Objections at large on their Journal, and proceed to reconsider it. If after such Reconsideration two thirds of that House shall agree to pass the bill, it shall be sent, together with the objections, to the other House, by which it shall likewise be reconsidered, and if approved by two thirds of that House, it shall become a Law. But in all such Cases the Votes of both Houses shall be determined by Yeas and Nays, and the Names of the Persons voting for and against the Bill shall be entered on the Journal of each House respectively. If any Bill shall not be returned by the President within ten Days (Sundays excepted) after it shall have been presented to him, the Same shall be a Law, in like Manner as if he had signed it, unless the Congress by their Adjournment prevent its Return, in which Case it shall not be a Law.

Every Order, Resolution, or Vote to which the Concurrence of the Senate and House of Representatives may be necessary (except on a question of Adjournment) shall be presented to the President of the United States; and before the Same shall take Effect, shall be approved by him, or being disapproved by him, shall be repassed by two thirds of the Senate and House of Representatives, according to the Rules and Limitations prescribed in the Case of a Bill.

Section 8.

The Congress shall have Power To lay and collect Taxes, Duties, Imposts and Excises, to pay the Debts and provide for the common Defence and general Welfare of the United States; but all Duties, Imposts and Excises shall be uniform throughout the United States;

To borrow money on the credit of the United States;

To regulate Commerce with foreign Nations, and among the several States, and with the Indian Tribes;

To establish an uniform rule of Naturalization, and uniform Laws on the subject of Bankruptcies throughout the United States;

To coin Money, regulate the Value thereof, and of foreign Coin, and fix the Standard of Weights and Measures;

To provide for the Punishment of counterfeiting the Securities and current Coin of the United States;

To establish Post Offices and post Roads;

To promote the Progress of Science and useful Arts, by securing for limited Times to Authors and Inventors the exclusive Right to their respective Writings and Discoveries;

To constitute Tribunals inferior to the Supreme Court;

To define and punish Piracies and Felonies committed on the high Seas, and Offenses against the Law of Nations;

To declare War, grant Letters of Marque and Reprisal, and make Rules concerning Captures on Land and Water;

To raise and support Armies, but no Appropriation of Money to that Use shall be for a longer Term than two Years;

To provide and maintain a Navy;

To make Rules for the Government and Regulation of the land and naval forces;

To provide for calling forth the Militia to execute the Laws of the Union, suppress Insurrections and repel Invasions;

To provide for organizing, arming, and disciplining the Militia, and for governing such Part of them as may be employed in the Service of the United States, reserving to the States respectively, the Appointment of the Officers, and the Authority of training the Militia according to the discipline prescribed by Congress;

To exercise exclusive Legislation in all Cases whatsoever, over such District (not exceeding ten Miles square) as may, by Cession of particular States, and the acceptance of Congress, become the Seat of the Government of the United States, and to exercise like Authority over all Places purchased by the Consent of the Legislature of the State in which the Same shall be, for the Erection of Forts, Magazines, Arsenals, Dock-yards, and other needful Buildings;—And

To make all Laws which shall be necessary and proper for carrying into Execution the foregoing Powers, and all other Powers vested by this Constitution in the Government of the United States, or in any Department or Officer thereof.

Section 9.

The Migration or Importation of such Persons as any of the States now existing shall think proper to admit, shall not be prohibited by the Congress prior to the Year one thousand eight hundred and eight, but a tax or duty may be imposed on such Importation, not exceeding ten dollars for each Person.

The privilege of the Writ of Habeas Corpus shall not be suspended, unless when in Cases of Rebellion or Invasion the public Safety may require it.

No bill of Attainder or ex post facto Law shall be passed.

No capitation, or other direct, Tax shall be laid unless in Proportion to the Census or Enumeration herein before directed to be taken.

No Tax or Duty shall be laid on Articles exported from any State.

No Preference shall be given by any Regulation of Commerce or Revenue to the Ports of one State over those of another: nor shall Vessels bound to, or from, one State, be obliged to enter, clear, or pay Duties in another.

No Money shall be drawn from the Treasury, but in Consequence of Appropriations made by Law; and a regular Statement and Account of the Receipts and Expenditures of all public Money shall be published from time to time.

No Title of Nobility shall be granted by the United States: And no Person holding any Office of Profit or Trust under them, shall, without the Consent of the Congress, accept of any present, Emolument, Office, or Title, of any kind whatever, from any King, Prince, or foreign State.

Section 10.

No State shall enter into any Treaty, Alliance, or Confederation; grant Letters of Marque and Reprisal; coin Money; emit Bills of Credit; make any Thing but gold and silver Coin a Tender in Payment of Debts; pass any Bill of Attainder, ex post facto Law, or Law impairing the Obligation of Contracts, or grant any Title of Nobility.

No State shall, without the Consent of the Congress, lay any Imposts or Duties on Imports or Exports, except what may be absolutely necessary for executing its inspection Laws; and the net Produce of all Duties and Imposts, laid by any State on Imports or Exports, shall be for the use of the Treasury of the United States; and all such Laws shall be subject to the Revision and Control of the Congress.

No state shall, without the Consent of Congress, lay any duty of Tonnage, keep Troops, or Ships of War in time of Peace, enter into any Agreement or Compact with another State, or with a foreign Power, or engage in War, unless actually invaded, or in such imminent Danger as will not admit of delay.

Article II

Section 1.

The executive Power shall be vested in a President of the United States of America. He shall hold his Office during the Term of four years, and, together with the Vice President, chosen for the same Term, be elected, as follows:

Each State shall appoint, in such Manner as the Legislature thereof may direct, a Number of Electors, equal to the whole Number of Senators and Representatives to which the State may be entitled in the Congress: but no Senator or Representative, or Person holding an Office of Trust or Profit under the United States, shall be appointed an Elector.

[The Electors shall meet in their respective States, and vote by Ballot for two persons, of whom one at least shall not be an Inhabitant of the same State with themselves. And they shall make a List of all the Persons voted for, and of the Number of Votes for each; which List they shall sign and certify, and transmit sealed to the Seat of the Government of the United States, directed to the President of the Senate. The President of the Senate shall, in the Presence of the Senate and House of Representatives, open all the Certificates, and the Votes shall then be counted. The Person having the greatest Number of Votes shall be the President, if such Number be a Majority of the whole Number of Electors appointed; and if there be more than one who have such Majority, and have an equal Number of Votes, then the House of Representatives shall immediately chuse by Ballot one of them for President; and if no Person have a Majority, then from the five highest on the List the said House shall in like Manner chuse the President. But in chusing the President, the Votes shall be taken by States, the Representation from each State having one Vote; a quorum for this Purpose shall consist of a Member or Members from two-thirds of the States, and a Majority of all the States shall be necessary to a Choice. In every Case, after the Choice of the President, the Person having the greatest Number of Votes of the Electors shall be the Vice President. But if there should remain two or more who have equal votes, the Senate shall chuse from them by Ballot the Vice President.][4]

The Congress may determine the Time of chusing the Electors, and the Day on which they shall give their Votes; which Day shall be the same throughout the United States.

No person except a natural-born Citizen, or a Citizen of the United States, at the time of the Adoption of this Constitution, shall be eligible to the Office of President; neither shall any Person be eligible to that Office who shall not have attained to the Age of thirty-five years, and been fourteen Years a Resident within the United States.

In Case of the Removal of the President from Office, or of his Death, Resignation, or Inability to discharge the Powers and Duties of the said Office, the same shall devolve

[4]Revised by the Twelfth Amendment.

on the Vice President, and the Congress may by Law provide for the Case of Removal, Death, Resignation, or Inability, both of the President and Vice President, declaring what Officer shall then act as President, and such Officer shall act accordingly, until the disability be removed, or a President shall be elected.

The President shall, at stated Times, receive for his Services a Compensation, which shall neither be increased nor diminished during the Period for which he shall have been elected, and he shall not receive within that Period any other Emolument from the United States, or any of them.

Before he enter on the execution of his Office, he shall take the following Oath or Affirmation:—"I do solemnly swear (or affirm) that I will faithfully execute the Office of President of the United States, and will, to the best of my Ability, preserve, protect, and defend the Constitution of the United States."

Section 2.

The President shall be Commander in Chief of the Army and Navy of the United States, and of the Militia of the several States, when called into the actual Service of the United States; he may require the Opinion, in writing, of the principal Officer in each of the executive Departments, upon any subject relating to the Duties of their respective Offices, and he shall have Power to Grant Reprieves and Pardons for Offenses against the United States, except in Cases of Impeachment.

He shall have Power, by and with the Advice and Consent of the Senate, to make Treaties, provided two-thirds of the Senators present concur; and he shall nominate, and by and with the Advice and Consent of the Senate, shall appoint Ambassadors, other public Ministers and Consuls, Judges of the supreme Court, and all other Officers of the United States, whose Appointments are not herein otherwise provided for, and which shall be established by Law: but the Congress may by Law vest the Appointment of such inferior Officers, as they think proper, in the President alone, in the Courts of Law, or in the Heads of Departments.

The President shall have Power to fill up all Vacancies that may happen during the Recess of the Senate, by granting Commissions which shall expire at the End of their next Session.

Section 3.

He shall from time to time give to the Congress Information of the State of the Union, and recommend to their Consideration such Measures as he shall judge necessary and expedient; he may, on extraordinary occasions, convene both Houses, or either of them, and in Case of Disagreement between them, with respect to the Time of Adjournment, he may adjourn them to such Time as he shall think proper; he shall receive Ambassadors and other public Ministers; he shall take care that the Laws be faithfully executed, and shall Commission all the Officers of the United States.

Section 4.

The President, Vice President and all civil Officers of the United States, shall be removed from Office on Impeachment for, and Conviction of, Treason, Bribery, or other high Crimes and Misdemeanors.

Article III

Section 1.

The judicial Power of the United States, shall be vested in one supreme Court, and in such inferior Courts as the Congress may from time to time ordain and establish. The Judges, both of the supreme and inferior Courts, shall hold their Offices during good

Behaviour, and shall, at stated Times, receive for their Services, a Compensation, which shall not be diminished during their Continuance in Office.

Section 2.
The judicial Power shall extend to all Cases, in Law and Equity, arising under this Constitution, the Laws of the United States, and Treaties made, or which shall be made, under their Authority;—to all Cases affecting ambassadors, other public ministers and consuls;—to all cases of admiralty and maritime Jurisdiction;—to Controversies to which the United States shall be a Party;—to Controversies between two or more States;—between a State and Citizens of another State;[5]—between Citizens of different States—between Citizens of the same State claiming Lands under Grants of different States, and between a State, or the Citizens thereof, and foreign States, Citizens, or Subjects.

In all Cases affecting Ambassadors, other public Ministers and Consuls, and those in which a State shall be Party, the supreme Court shall have original Jurisdiction. In all the other Cases before mentioned, the supreme Court shall have appellate Jurisdiction, both as to Law and Fact, with such Exceptions, and under such Regulations as the Congress shall make.

The trial of all Crimes, except in Cases of Impeachment, shall be by Jury; and such Trial shall be held in the State where the said Crimes shall have been committed; but when not committed within any State, the Trial shall be at such Place or Places as the Congress may by Law have directed.

Section 3.
Treason against the United States, shall consist only in levying War against them, or in adhering to their Enemies, giving them Aid and Comfort. No Person shall be convicted of Treason unless on the Testimony of two Witnesses to the same overt Act, or on Confession in open Court.

The Congress shall have power to declare the Punishment of Treason, but no Attainder of Treason shall work Corruption of Blood, or Forfeiture except during the Life of the Person attained.

Article IV

Section 1.
Full Faith and Credit shall be given in each State to the public Acts, Records, and judicial Proceedings of every other State. And the Congress may by general Laws prescribe the Manner in which such Acts, Records and Proceedings shall be proved, and the Effect thereof.

Section 2.
The Citizens of each State shall be entitled to all Privileges and Immunities of Citizens in the several States.

A Person charged in any State with Treason, Felony, or other Crime, who shall flee from Justice, and be found in another State, shall on demand of the executive Authority of the State from which he fled, be delivered up, to be removed to the State having Jurisdiction of the crime.

[5]Qualified by the Eleventh Amendment.

No Person held to Service or Labour in one State, under the Laws thereof, escaping into another, shall, in Consequence of any Law or Regulation therein, be discharged from such Service or Labour, but shall be delivered up on Claim of the Party to whom such Service or Labour may be due.

Section 3.
New States may be admitted by the Congress into this Union; but no new State shall be formed or erected within the Jurisdiction of any other State; nor any State be formed by the Junction of two or more States, or parts of States, without the Consent of the Legislatures of the States concerned as well as of the Congress.

The Congress shall have Power to dispose of and make all needful Rules and Regulations respecting the Territory or other Property belonging to the United States; and nothing in this Constitution shall be so construed as to Prejudice any Claims of the United States, or of any particular State.

Section 4.
The United States shall guarantee to every State in this Union a Republican Form of Government, and shall protect each of them against Invasion; and on Application of the Legislature, or of the Executive (when the Legislature cannot be convened) against domestic Violence.

Article V

The Congress, whenever two-thirds of both Houses shall deem it necessary, shall propose Amendments to this Constitution, or, on the Application of the Legislatures of two-thirds of the several States, shall call a Convention for proposing Amendments, which, in either Case, shall be valid to all Intents and Purposes, as part of this Constitution, when ratified by the Legislatures of three-fourths of the several States, or by Conventions in three-fourths thereof, as the one or the other Mode of Ratification may be proposed by the Congress; Provided that no Amendment which may be made prior to the Year One thousand eight hundred and eight shall in any Manner affect the first and fourth Clauses in the Ninth Section of the first Article; and that no State, without its Consent, shall be deprived of its equal Suffrage in the Senate.

Article VI

All Debts contracted and Engagements entered into, before the Adoption of this Constitution, shall be as valid against the United States under this Constitution, as under the Confederation.

This Constitution, and the Laws of the United States which shall be made in Pursuance thereof; and all Treaties made, or which shall be made, under the Authority of the United States, shall be the supreme Law of the Land; and the Judges in every State shall be bound thereby, any Thing in the Constitution or Laws of any State to the Contrary notwithstanding.

The Senators and Representatives before mentioned, and the Members of the several State Legislatures, and all executive and judicial Officers, both of the United States and of the several States, shall be bound by Oath or Affirmation to support this Constitution; but no religious Tests shall ever be required as a qualification to any Office or public Trust under the United States.

Article VII

The Ratification of the Conventions of nine States shall be sufficient for the Establishment of this Constitution between the States so ratifying the same.

Done in Convention by the Unanimous Consent of the States present the Seventeenth Day of September in the Year of our Lord one thousand seven hundred and Eighty seven, and of the Independence of the United States of America the Twelfth. In Witness whereof We have hereunto subscribed our Names.[6]

George Washington
President and deputy from Virginia

NEW HAMPSHIRE
John Langdon
Nicholas Gilman

MASSACHUSETTS
Nathaniel Gorham
Rufus King

CONNECTICUT
William Samuel Johnson
Roger Sherman

NEW YORK
Alexander Hamilton

NEW JERSEY
William Livingston
David Brearley
William Paterson
Jonathan Dayton

PENNSYLVANIA
Benjamin Franklin
Thomas Mifflin
Robert Morris
George Clymer
Thomas FitzSimons
Jared Ingersoll
James Wilson
Gouverneur Morris

DELAWARE
George Read
Gunning Bedford Jr.
John Dickinson
Richard Bassett
Jacob Broom

MARYLAND
James McHenry
Daniel of St. Thomas Jenifer
Daniel Carroll

VIRGINIA
John Blair
James Madison Jr.

NORTH CAROLINA
William Blount
Richard Dobbs Spaight
Hugh Williamson

SOUTH CAROLINA
John Rutledge
Charles Coteswort
  Pinckney
Charles Pinckney
Pierce Butler

GEORGIA
William Few
Abraham Baldwin

Articles in Addition to, and Amendment of, the Constitution of the United States of America, Proposed by Congress, and Ratified by the Legislatures of the Several States, Pursuant to the Fifth Article of the Original Constitution.[7]

[Article I]

Congress shall make no law respecting an establishment of religion, or prohibiting the free exercise thereof; or abridging the freedom of speech, or of the press; or the right of the people peaceably to assemble, and to petition the Government for a redress of grievances.

[Article II]

A well regulated Militia, being necessary to the security of a free State, the right of the people to keep and bear Arms shall not be infringed.

---

[6]These are the full names of the signers, which in some cases are not the signatures on the document.
[7]This heading appears only in the joint resolution submitting the first ten amendments.

[Article III]

No Soldier shall, in time of peace, be quartered in any house, without the consent of the Owner, nor in time of war, but in a manner to be prescribed by law.

[Article IV]

The right of the people to be secure in their persons, houses, papers, and effects, against unreasonable searches and seizures, shall not be violated, and no Warrants shall issue, but upon probable cause, supported by Oath or affirmation, and particularly describing the place to be searched, and the persons or things to be seized.

[Article V]

No person shall be held to answer for a capital or otherwise infamous crime, unless on a presentment or indictment of a Grand Jury, except in cases arising in the land or naval forces, or in the Militia, when in actual service in time of War or public danger; nor shall any person be subject for the same offence to be twice put in jeopardy of life or limb; nor shall be compelled in any criminal case to be a witness against himself, nor be deprived of life, liberty, or property, without due process of law; nor shall private property be taken for public use, without just compensation.

[Article VI]

In all criminal prosecutions, the accused shall enjoy the right to a speedy and public trial, by an impartial jury of the State and district wherein the crime shall have been committed, which district shall have been previously ascertained by law, and to be informed of the nature and cause of the accusation; to be confronted with the witnesses against him; to have compulsory process for obtaining witnesses in his favour, and to have the Assistance of Counsel for his defense.

[Article VII]

In suits at common law, where the value in controversy shall exceed twenty dollars, the right of trial by jury shall be preserved, and no fact tried by a jury, shall be otherwise reexamined in any Court of the United States, than according to the rules of the common law.

[Article VIII]

Excessive bail shall not be required, nor excessive fines imposed, nor cruel and unusual punishments inflicted.

[Article IX]

The enumeration of the Constitution, of certain rights, shall not be construed to deny or disparage others retained by the people.

[Article X]

The powers not delegated to the United States by the Constitution, nor prohibited by it to the States, are reserved to the States respectively, or to the people.
  [Amendments I–X, in force 1791.]

[Article XI][8]

The Judicial power of the United States shall not be construed to extend to any suit in law or equity, commenced or prosecuted against one of the United States by Citizens of another State, or by Citizens or Subjects of any Foreign State.

[Article XII][9]

The Electors shall meet in their respective States and vote by ballot for President and Vice-President, one of whom, at least, shall not be an inhabitant of the same State with themselves; they shall name in their ballots the person voted for as President, and in distinct ballots the person voted for as Vice-President, and they shall make distinct lists of all persons voted for as President, and of all persons voted for as Vice-President, and of the number of votes for each, which lists they shall sign and certify, and trans-mit sealed to the seat of the government of the United States, directed to the President of the Senate;—The President of the Senate shall, in the presence of the Senate and House of Representatives, open all the certificates and the votes shall then be counted;—The person having the greatest number of votes for President, shall be the President, if such number be a majority of the whole number of Electors appointed; and if no person have such majority, then from the persons having the highest numbers not exceeding three on the list of those voted for as President, the House of Representatives shall choose immediately, by ballot, the President. But in choosing the President, the votes shall be taken by states, the representation from each state having one vote; a quorum for this purpose shall consist of a member or members from two-thirds of the states, and a majority of all the states shall be necessary to a choice. And if the House of Representatives shall not choose a President whenever the right of choice shall devolve upon them, before the fourth day of March next following, then the Vice-President shall act as President, as in the case of the death or other constitutional disability of the President.—The person having the greatest number of votes as Vice-President, shall be the Vice-President, if such number be a majority of the whole number of Electors appointed, and if no person have a majority, then from the two highest numbers on the list, the Senate shall choose the Vice-President; a quorum for the purpose shall consist of two-thirds of the whole number of Senators, and a major-ity of the whole number shall be necessary to a choice. But no person constitutionally ineligible to the office of President shall be eligible to that of Vice-President of the United States.

[Article XIII][10]

Section 1.
Neither slavery nor involuntary servitude, except as a punishment for crime whereof the party shall have been duly convicted, shall exist within the United States, or any place subject to their jurisdiction.

Section 2.
Congress shall have power to enforce this article by appropriate legislation.

[8]Adopted in 1798.
[9]Adopted in 1804.
[10]Adopted in 1865.

[Article XIV][11]

Section 1.

All persons born or naturalized in the United States, and subject to the jurisdiction thereof, are citizens of the United States and of the State wherein they reside. No State shall make or enforce any law which shall abridge the privileges or immunities of citizens of the United States; nor shall any State deprive any person of life, liberty, or property, without due process of law; nor deny to any person within its jurisdiction the equal protection of the laws.

Section 2.

Representatives shall be apportioned among the several States according to their respective numbers, counting the whole number of persons in each State, excluding Indians not taxed. But when the right to vote at any election for the choice of electors for President and Vice-President of the United States, Representatives in Congress, the Executive and Judicial officers of a State, or the members of the Legislature thereof, is denied to any of the male inhabitants of such State, being twenty-one years of age, and citizens of the United States, or in any way abridged, except for participation in rebellion, or other crime, the basis of representation therein shall be reduced in the proportion which the number of such male citizens shall bear to the whole number of male citizens twenty-one years of age in such State.

Section 3.

No person shall be a Senator or Representative in Congress, or elector of President and Vice-President, or hold any office, civil or military, under the United States, or under any State, who, having previously taken an oath, as a member of Congress, or as an officer of the United States, or as a member of any State legislature, or as an executive or judicial officer of any State, to support the Constitution of the United States, shall have engaged in insurrection or rebellion against the same, or given aid or comfort to the enemies thereof. But Congress may by a vote of two-thirds of each House, remove such disability.

Section 4.

The validity of the public debt of the United States, authorized by law, including debts incurred for payment of pensions and bounties for services in suppressing insurrection or rebellion, shall not be questioned. But neither the United States nor any State shall assume or pay any debts or obligation incurred in aid of insurrection or rebellion against the United States, or any claim for the loss or emancipation of any slave; but all such debts, obligations, and claims shall be held illegal and void.

Section 5.

The Congress shall have the power to enforce, by appropriate legislation, the provisions of this article.

[Article XV][12]

Section 1.

The right of citizens of the United States to vote shall not be denied or abridged by the United States or by any State on account of race, color, or previous condition of servitude—

Section 2.

The Congress shall have power to enforce this article by appropriate legislation.

[11]Adopted in 1868.
[12]Adopted in 1870.

[Article XVI][13]

The Congress shall have power to lay and collect taxes on incomes, from whatever source derived, without apportionment among the several States, and without regard to any census or enumeration.

[Article XVII][14]

The Senate of the United States shall be composed of two Senators from each State, elected by the people thereof, for six years; and each Senator shall have one vote. The electors in each State shall have the qualifications requisite for electors of the most numerous branch of the State legislatures.

When vacancies happen in the representation of any State in the Senate, the executive authority of such State shall issue writs of election to fill such vacancies: *Provided*, That the legislature of any State may empower the executive thereof to make temporary appointments until the people fill the vacancies by election as the legislature may direct.

This amendment shall not be so construed as to affect the election or term of any Senator chosen before it becomes valid as part of the Constitution.

[Article XVIII][15]

Section 1.
After one year from the ratification of this article the manufacture, sale, or transportation of intoxicating liquors within, the importation thereof into, or the exportation thereof from the United States and all territory subject to the jurisdiction thereof for beverage purposes is hereby prohibited.

Section 2.
The Congress and the several States shall have concurrent power to enforce this article by appropriate legislation.

Section 3.
This article shall be inoperative unless it shall have been ratified as an amendment to the Constitution by the legislatures of the several States, as provided in the Constitution, within seven years from the date of the submission hereof to the States by the Congress.

[Article XIX][16]

The right of citizens of the United States to vote shall not be denied or abridged by the United States or by any State on account of sex.

Congress shall have power to enforce this article by appropriate legislation.

[Article XX][17]

Section 1.
The terms of the President and Vice-President shall end at noon on the 20th day of January, and the terms of Senators and Representatives at noon on the 3d day of January,

[13] Adopted in 1913.
[14] Adopted in 1913.
[15] Adopted in 1918.
[16] Adopted in 1920.
[17] Adopted in 1933.

of the years in which such terms would have ended if this article had not been ratified; and the terms of their successors shall then begin.

Section 2.
The Congress shall assemble at least once in every year, and such meeting shall begin at noon on the 3d day of January, unless they shall by law appoint a different day.

Section 3.
If, at the time fixed for the beginning of the term of the President, the President elect shall have died, the Vice-President elect shall become President. If a President shall not have been chosen before the time fixed for the beginning of his term or if the President elect shall have failed to qualify, then the Vice-President elect shall act as President until a President shall have qualified; and the Congress may by law provide for the case wherein neither a President elect nor a Vice-President elect shall have qualified, declaring who shall then act as President, or the manner in which one who is to act shall be selected, and such person shall act accordingly until a President or Vice-President shall have qualified.

Section 4.
The Congress may by law provide for the case of the death of any of the persons from whom the House of Representatives may choose a President whenever the right of choice shall have devolved upon them, and for the case of the death of any of the persons from whom the Senate may choose a Vice-President whenever the right of choice shall have devolved upon them.

Section 5.
Sections 1 and 2 shall take effect on the 15th day of October following the ratification of this article.

Section 6.
This article shall be inoperative unless it shall have been ratified as an amendment to the Constitution by the legislatures of three-fourths of the several States within seven years from the date of its submission.

[Article XXI][18]

Section 1.
The eighteenth article of amendment to the Constitution of the United States is hereby repealed.

Section 2.
The transportation or importation into any State, Territory, or possession of the United States for delivery or use therein of intoxicating liquors, in violation of the laws thereof, is hereby prohibited.

Section 3.
This article shall be inoperative unless it shall have been ratified as an amendment to the Constitution by conventions in the several States, as provided in the Constitution, within seven years from the date of the submission hereof to the States by the Congress.

[18]Adopted in 1933.

[Article XXII][19]

No person shall be elected to the office of the President more than twice, and no person who has held the office of President, or acted as President, for more than two years of a term to which some other person was elected President shall be elected to the office of the President more than once.

But this Article shall not apply to any person holding the office of President when this Article was proposed by the Congress, and shall not prevent any person who may be holding the office of President, or acting as President, during the term within which this Article becomes operative from holding the office of President or acting as President during the remainder of such term.

This article shall be inoperative unless it shall have been ratified as an amendment to the Constitution by the legislatures of three-fourths of the several states within seven years from the date of its submission to the states by the Congress.

[Article XXIII][20]

Section 1.
The District constituting the seat of Government of the United States shall appoint in such manner as the Congress may direct:

A number of electors of President and Vice-President equal to the whole number of Senators and Representatives in Congress to which the District would be entitled if it were a State, but in no event more than the least populous State; they shall be in addition to those appointed by the States, but they shall be considered, for the purposes of the election of President and Vice-President, to be electors appointed by a State; and they shall meet in the District and perform such duties as provided by the twelfth article of amendment.

Section 2.
The Congress shall have power to enforce this article by appropriate legislation.

[Article XXIV][21]

Section 1.
The right of citizens of the United States to vote in any primary or other election for President or Vice President, for electors for President or Vice President, or for Senator or Representative in Congress, shall not be denied or abridged by the United States or any state by reason of failure to pay any poll tax or other tax.

Section 2.
The Congress shall have the power to enforce this article by appropriate legislation.

[Article XXV][22]

Section 1.
In case of the removal of the President from office or of his death or resignation, the Vice President shall become President.

---

[19] Adopted in 1951.
[20] Adopted in 1961.
[21] Adopted in 1964.
[22] Adopted in 1967.

Section 2.

Whenever there is a vacancy in the office of the Vice President, the President shall nominate a Vice President who shall take office upon confirmation by a majority vote of both Houses of Congress.

Section 3.

Whenever the President transmits to the President Pro Tempore of the Senate and the Speaker of the House of Representatives his written declaration that he is unable to discharge the powers and duties of his office, and until he transmits to them a written declaration to the contrary, such powers and duties shall be discharged by the Vice President as Acting President.

Section 4.

Whenever the Vice President and a majority of either the principal officers of the executive departments or of such other body as Congress may by law provide, transmit to the President Pro Tempore of the Senate and the Speaker of the House of Representatives their written declaration that the President is unable to discharge the powers and duties of his office, the Vice President shall immediately assume the powers and duties of the office as Acting President.

Thereafter, when the President transmits to the President Pro Tempore of the Senate and the Speaker of the House of Representatives his written declaration that no inability exists, he shall resume the powers and duties of his office unless the Vice President and a majority of either the principal officers of the executive departments or of such other body as Congress may by law provide, transmit within four days to the President Pro Tempore of the Senate and the Speaker of the House of Representatives their written declaration that the President is unable to discharge the powers and duties of his office. Thereupon Congress shall decide the issue, assembling within forty-eight hours for that purpose if not in session. If the Congress, within twenty-one days after receipt of the latter written declaration, or, if Congress is not in session, within twenty-one days after Congress is required to assemble, determines by two-thirds vote of both Houses that the President is unable to discharge the powers and duties of his office, the Vice President shall continue to discharge the same as Acting President; otherwise, the President shall resume the powers and duties of his office.

[Article XXVI][23]

Section 1.

The right of citizens of the United States, who are eighteen years of age or older, to vote shall not be denied or abridged by the United States or by any State on account of age.

Section 2.

The Congress shall have power to enforce this article by appropriate legislation.

[Article XXVII][24]

No law varying the compensation for the services of the Senators and Representatives shall take effect until an election of Representatives shall have intervened.

[23]Adopted in 1971.
[24]Adopted in 1992.

PRESIDENTIAL ELECTIONS

Year	Candidates	Parties	Popular Vote	Percentage of Popular Vote	Electoral Vote	Percentage of Voter Participation
1789	George Washington (Va.)*				69	
	John Adams				34	
	Others				35	
1792	George Washington (Va.)				132	
	John Adams				77	
	George Clinton				50	
	Others				5	
1796	John Adams (Mass.)	Federalist			71	
	Thomas Jefferson	Democratic-Republican			68	
	Thomas Pinckeny	Fedearalist			59	
	Aaron Burr	Dem.-Rep.			30	
	Others				48	
1800	Thomas Jefferson (Va.)	Dem.-Rep.			73	
	Aaron Burr	Dem.-Rep.			73	
	John Adams	Federalist			65	
	C. C. Pinckney	Federalist			64	
	John Jay	Federalist			1	
1804	Thomas Jefferson (Va.)	Dem.-Rep.			162	
	C. C. Pinckney	Federalist			14	
1808	James Madison (Va.)	Dem.-Rep.			122	
	C.C. Pickney	Federalist			47	
	George Clinton	Dem.-Rep.			6	

*State of residence at time of election.

Year	Candidates	Party	Popular Vote	% Popular Vote	Electoral Vote	% Voter Participation
1812	**James Madison (Va.)**	DemRep.			128	
	De Witt Clinton	Federalist			89	
1816	**James Monroe (Va.)**	DemRep.			183	
	Rufus King	Federalist			34	
1820	**James Monroe (Va.)**	DemRep.			231	
	John Quincy Adams	DemRep.			1	
1824	**John Q. Adams (Mass.)**	DemRep.	108,740	30.5	84	26.9
	Andrew Jackson	DemRep.	153,544	43.1	99	
	William H. Crawford	DemRep.	46,618	13.1	41	
	Henry Clay	DemRep.	47,136	13.2	37	
1828	**Andrew Jackson (Tenn.)**	Democratic	647,286	56.0	178	57.6
	John Quincy Adams	National Republican	508,064	44.0	83	
1832	**Andrew Jackson (Tenn.)**	Democratic	687,502	55.0	219	55.4
	Henry Clay	National Republican	530,189	42.4	49	
	John Floyd	Independent			11	
	William Wirt	Anti-Mason	33,108	2.6	7	
1836	**Martin Van Buren (N.Y.)**	Democratic	765,483	50.9	170	57.8
	W. H. Harrison	Whig			73	
	Hugh L. White	Whig	739,765	49.1	26	
	Daniel Webster	Whig			14	
	W. P. Magnum	Independent			11	
1840	**William H. Harrison (Ohio)**	Whig	1,274,624	53.1	234	80.2
	Martin Van Buren	Democratic	1,127,781	46.9	60	
	J. G. Birney	Liberty	7,069		—	

(continued)

Year	Candidates	Parties	Popular Vote	Percentage of Popular Vote	Electoral Vote	Percentage of Voter Participation
1844	James K. Polk (Tenn.)	Democratic	1,338,464	49.6	170	78.9
	Henry Clay	Whig	1,300,097	48.1	105	
	J. G. Birney	Liberty	62,300	2.3	—	
1848	Zachary Taylor (La.)	Whig	1,360,967	47.4	163	72.7
	Lewis Cass	Democratic	1,222,342	42.5	127	
	Martin Van Buren	Free-Soil	291,263	10.1	—	
1852	Franklin Pierce (N.H.)	Democratic	1,601,117	50.9	254	69.6
	Winfield Scott	Whig	1,385,453	44.1	42	
	John P. Hale	Free-Soil	155,825	5.0	—	
1856	James Buchanan (Pa.)	Democratic	1,832,955	45.3	174	78.9
	John C. Frémont	Republican	1,339,932	33.1	114	
	Millard Fillmore	American	871,731	21.6	8	
1860	Abraham Lincoln (Ill.)	Republican	1,865,593	39.9	180	81.2
	Stephen A. Douglas	Democratic	1,382,713	29.4	12	
	John C. Breckinridge	Democratic	848,356	18.1	72	
	John Bell	Union	592,906	12.6	39	
1864	Abraham Lincoln (Ill.)	Republican	2,213,655	55.0	212	73.8
	George B. McClellan	Democratic	1,805,237	45.0	21	
1868	Ulysses S. Grant (Ill.)	Republican	3,012,833	52.7	214	78.1
	Horatio Seymour	Democratic	2,703,249	47.3	80	
1872	Ulysses S. Grant (Ill.)	Republican	3,597,132	55.6	286	71.3
	Horace Greeley	Democratic; Liberal Republican	2,834,125	43.9	66	
1876	Rutherford B. Hayes (Ohio)	Republican	4,036,298	48.0	185	81.8
	Samuel J. Tilden	Democratic	4,300,590	51.0	184	
1880	James A. Garfield (Ohio)	Republican	4,454,416	48.5	214	79.4
	Winfield S. Hancock	Democratic	4,444,952	48.1	155	

Year	Candidate	Party	Popular Vote	%	Electoral Vote	% Participation
1884	Grover Cleveland (N.Y.)	Democratic	4,874,986	48.5	219	77.5
	James G. Blaine	Republican	4,851,981	48.2	182	
1888	Benjamin Harrison (Ind.)	Republican	5,439,853	47.9	233	79.3
	Grover Cleveland	Democratic	5,540,309	48.6	168	
1892	Grover Cleveland (N.Y.)	Democratic	5,556,918	46.1	277	74.7
	Benjamin Harrison	Republican	5,176,108	43.0	145	
	James B. Weaver	People's	1,041,028	8.5	22	
1896	William McKinley (Ohio)	Republican	7,104,779	51.1	271	79.3
	William J. Bryan	Democratic People's	6,502,925	47.7	176	
1900	William McKinley (Ohio)	Republican	7,207,923	51.7	292	73.2
	William J. Bryan	Dem.-Populis	6,358,133	45.5	155	
1904	Theodore Roosevelt (N.Y.)	Republican	7,623,486	57.9	336	65.2
	Alton B. Parker	Democratic	5,077,911	37.6	140	
	Eugene V. Debs	Socialist	402,283	3.0	—	
1908	William H. Taft (Ohio)	Republican	7,678,908	51.6	321	65.4
	William J. Bryan	Democratic	6,409,104	43.1	162	
	Eugene V. Debs	Socialist	420,793	2.8	—	
1912	Woodrow Wilson (N.J.)	Democratic	6,293,454	41.9	435	58.8
	Theodore Roosevelt	Progressive	4,119,538	27.4	88	
	William H. Taft	Republican	3,484,980	23.2	8	
	Eugene V. Debs	Socialist	900,672	6.0	—	
1916	Woodrow Wilson (N.J.)	Democratic	9,129,606	49.4	277	61.6
	Charles E. Hughes	Republican	8,538,221	46.2	254	
	A. L. Benson	Socialist	585,113	3.2	—	

(continued)

Year	Candidates	Parties	Popular Vote	Percentage of Popular Vote	Electoral Vote	Percentage of Voter Participation
1920	Warren G. Harding (Ohio)	Republican	16,152,200	60.4	404	49.2
	James M. Cox	Democratic	9,147,353	34.2	127	
	Eugene V. Debs	Socialist	919,799	3.4	—	
1924	Calvin Coolidge (Mass.)	Republican	15,725,016	54.0	382	48.9
	John W. Davis	Democratic	8,386,503	28.8	136	
	Robert M. La Follette	Progressive	4,822,856	16.6	13	
1928	Herbert Hoover (Calif.)	Republican	21,391,381	58.2	444	56.9
	Alfred E. Smith	Democratic	15,016,443	40.9	87	
	Norman Thomas	Socialist	267,835	0.7	—	
1932	Franklin D. Roosevelt (N.Y.)	Democratic	22,821,857	57.4	472	56.9
	Herbert Hoover	Republican	15,761,841	39.7	59	
	Norman Thomas	Socialist	881,951	2.2	—	
1936	Franklin D. Roosevelt (N.Y.)	Democratic	27,751,597	60.8	523	61.0
	Alfred M. Landon	Republican	16,679,583	36.5	8	
	William Lemke	Union	882,479	1.9	—	
1940	Franklin D. Roosevelt (N.Y.)	Democratic	27,244,160	54.8	449	62.5
	Wendell L. Willkie	Republican	22,305,198	44.8	82	
1944	Franklin D. Roosevelt (N.Y.)	Democratic	25,602,504	53.5	432	55.9
	Thomas E. Dewey	Republican	22,006,285	46.0	99	
1948	Harry S. Truman (Mo.)	Democratic	24,105,695	49.5	303	53.0
	Thomas E. Dewey	Republican	21,969,170	45.1	189	
	J. Strom Thurmond	States' Rights Democratic	1,169,021	2.4	39	
	Henry A. Wallace	Progressive	1,156,103	2.4	—	
1952	Dwight D. Eisenhower (N.Y.)	Republican	33,936,252	55.1	442	63.3
	Adlai E. Stevenson	Democratic	27,314,992	44.4	89	

Year	Candidates	Parties	Popular Vote	% of Popular Vote	Electoral Vote	% Voter Participation
1956	**Dwight D. Eisenhower (N.Y.)**	Republican	35,575,420	57.6	457	60.6
	Adlai E. Stevenson	Democratic	26,033,066	42.1	73	
	Other	—	—		1	
1960	**John F. Kennedy (Mass.)**	Democratic	34,227,096	49.7	303	64.0
	Richard M. Nixon	Republican	34,108,546	49.6	219	
	Other	—	—		15	
1964	**Lyndon B. Johnson (Tex.)**	Democratic	43,126,506	61.1	486	61.7
	Barry M. Goldwater	Republican	27,176,799	38.5	52	
1968	**Richard M. Nixon (N.Y.)**	Republican	31,770,237	43.4	301	60.6
	Hubert H. Humphrey	Democratic	31,270,533	42.3	191	
	George Wallace	American Independent	9,906,141	12.9	46	
1972	**Richard M. Nixon (N.Y.)**	Republican	47,169,911	60.7	520	55.2
	George S. McGovern	Democratic	29,170,383	37.5	17	
	Other	—	—		1	
1976	**Jimmy Carter (Ga.)**	Democratic	40,828,587	50.0	297	53.5
	Gerald R. Ford	Republican	39,147,613	47.9	240	
	Other	—	1,575,459	2.1	1	
1980	**Ronald Reagan (Calif.)**	Republican	43,901,812	50.7	489	52.6
	Jimmy Carter	Democratic	35,483,820	41.0	49	
	John B. Anderson	Independent	5,719,722	6.6	—	
	Ed Clark	Libertarian	921,188	1.1	—	
1984	**Ronald Reagan (Calif.)**	Republican	54,455,075	59.0	525	53.3
	Walter Mondale	Democratic	37,577,185	41.0	13	
1988	**George Bush (Tex.)**	Republican	47,946,422	54.0	426	50.0
	Michael S. Dukakis	Democratic	41,016,429	46.0	112	
1992	**William J. Clinton (Ark.)**	Democratic	44,909,889	43.0	370	55.2
	George Bush	Republican	39,104,545	38.0	168	
	Ross Perot	Independent	19,742,267	19.0	0	

(continued)

Year	Candidates	Parties	Popular Vote	Percentage of Popular Vote	Electoral Vote	Percentage of Voter Participation
1996	William J. Clinton (Ark.)	Democratic	47,401,185	49.3	379	49.0
	Robert Dole	Republican	39,197,469	40.7	159	
	Ross Perot	Reform	8,085,294	8.4	—	
2000	George W. Bush (Tex.)	Republican	50,459,211	47.89	271	51.0
	Albert Gore Jr.	Democratic	51,003,894	48.41	266	
	Ralph Nader	Green	2,834,410	2.69	—	
2004	George W. Bush (Tex.)	Republican	62,028,285	50.73	286	60.0
	John Kerry	Democratic	59,028,109	48.27	251	
	Ralph Nader	Independent	463,647	0.38	0	
2008	Barack Obama (Ill.)	Democratic	65,070,489	53	364	61.7
	John McCain	Republican	57,154,810	46	174	

INDEX